SHELLEY'S PROSE

SHELLEY'S PROSE

OR

THE TRUMPET OF A PROPHECY

EDITED
WITH AN INTRODUCTION AND NOTES BY
DAVID LEE CLARK

A man will turn over half a library
*to make one book.—*SAMUEL JOHNSON.

NEW PREFACE
BY
HAROLD BLOOM
Sterling Professor of Humanities
Yale University

NEW AMSTERDAM · NEW YORK

ISBN 0-941533-29-8

Printed and bound in Great Britain.

NEW PREFACE

Everything gathered in David Lee Clark's admirable *Shelley's Prose: or the Trumpet of a Prophecy* is of lasting literary and spiritual value, and *A Defence of Poetry* is the crown. It is hardly considered an indisputable classic of literary theory by the assorted formalists and historicists who proliferate among us. But then Shelley's *Defence*, as Paul H. Fry observes, is thoroughly Longinian in spirit, as Shelley perhaps did not know. Yeats proclaimed the *Defence* to be "the profoundest essay on the foundations of poetry in English", a judgment echoed by Croce and by Wilson Knight. I would go further, and place it with Longinus himself as the two central discourses upon poetry in Western critical tradition. It is from Longinus and from Shelley that sensitive readers, poets and critics, have learned the precise *use of inspiration* which, as Fry says, is to reproduce itself, to create by contagion.

Shelley's *Defence* was inspired, in this Longinian sense, by his close friend Thomas Love Peacock's splendidly ambivalent attack in *The Four Ages of Poetry* (1820). Peacock, a superb parodist, chose Wordsworth as target, but the exuberances of parody and the comprehensiveness of Wordsworth combined so as to make poetry itself appear the object of the Peacockian scorn. *The Four Ages of Poetry* has many delights, of which its most famous paragraph is perhaps the grandest:

In the origin and perfection of poetry, all the associations of life were composed of poetical materials. With us it is decidedly the reverse. We know too that there are no Dryads in Hyde-park nor Naiads in the Regent's-canal. But barbaric manners and supernatural interventions are essential to poetry. Either in the scene, or in the time, or in both, it must be remote from our ordinary perceptions. While the historian and the philosopher are advancing in, and accelerating, the progress of knowledge, the poet is wallowing in the rubbish of departed ignorance, and raking up the ashes of dead savages to find gewgaws and rattles for the grown babies of the age. Mr Scott digs up the poachers and cattle-stealers of the ancient border. Lord Byron cruises for thieves and pirates on the shores of Morea and among the Greek Islands. Mr Southey wades through ponderous volumes of travels and old chronicles, from which he carefully selects all that is false, useless, and absurd, as being essentially poetical; and when he has a commonplace book full of monstrosities, strings them into an epic. Mr Wordsworth picks up village legends from old women and sextons; and Mr Coleridge, to the valuable information acquired from similar sources, superadds the dreams of crazy theologians and the mysticisms of German metaphysics, and favours the world with visions in verse, in which the quadruple elements of sexton, old woman, Jeremy Taylor, and Emanuel Kant, are harmonized into a delicious poetical compound. Mr Moore presents us with a Persian, and Mr Campbell with a Pennsylvanian tale, both formed on the same principle as Mr Southey's epics, by extracting from a perfunctory and desultory perusal of a collection of voyages and travels, all that useful investigation would not seek for and that common sense would reject.

One is charmed to think of the grim and pompous Wordsworth having the patience to pick up village legends from old women and sextons, particularly when one remembers how the aged leech-gatherer has to repeat himself in 'Resolution and Independence'. Peacock anticipates the two marvellous parodies of Wordsworth's habit of listening only to himself in Lewis Carroll's 'The White Knight's Song' and Edward Lear's 'Incidents in the Life of my Uncle Arly'. "Frippery and barbarism", Peacock goes on to cry aloud, rejecting the Wordsworthian project for bringing the past alive into the present. This is hardly Peacock at his best, but this is: "Poetry is the mental rattle that awakened the attention of intellect in the infancy of society". It is the presence of apothegms of such quality that provoked Shelley to the sublimity of his reply.

M.H. Abrams reads the *Defence* as a Platonic aesthetic, but I cannot agree, except that shelley's Plato, like Montaigne's, is a sceptic. Ironically, Peacock's *Four Ages* adopts something of *The Republic*'s stance towards poetry, whereas Shelley takes up the Homeric position that Plato attacked. This, to me, calls into question Abrams' contention that *Defence* is not useful for the practical criticism of poems. Abrams asks: "For all its planetary music, has any critical essay of comparable scope and reputation ever contained less of specifically *literary* criticism?" The question is meant to be rhetorical, but is asked from a position partly historicist, partly formalist. Earl Wasserman, meeting Abrams' challenge, converted the *Defence* into historicism and formalism. Longinus and Shelley are Sublime theorists, and I myself find their essays supremely useful for a Sublime or antithetical practical criticism.

The cosmos, to Shelley as to Nietzsche after him, is the primordial poem of mankind. It is not accidental that Wallace Stevens' *Notes Toward a Supreme Fiction* so agilely assimilates the Shelley of the *Defence* to Nietzsche as contemplating this invented world, the supreme fiction in which we dwell. Stevens' "inconceivable idea of the sun" follows Shelley's appropriation of the sun as the image of images, not so much Platonic as Shakespearean. Indeed, the sun in the *Defence* is at once a metaphor for the imagination and for poetic language as such. But this is the sun of each fresh day's creation of that particular day; it is not a Platonic sun beyond the sun. The imagination in Shelley's *Defence*, like the colours (tropes) of poetic language, is revising itself endlessly, revolving even as reality moves.

Innovation – in the heavens, in our institutions, in the new poem – is a Shelleyan synonym for imagination. The Shelleyan imagination, like the Longinian or the Nietzschean, is agonistic in the extreme, a crucial truth that only Paul Fry among the exegetes of the *Defence* seems to have recovered. Poetry, Shelley knows, is always a response to prior poetry, a response that wavers dialectically between partial receptivity and partial opposition. Shelley, a superb critic of his own work, was telling a story of his relation to Dante, Shakespeare, and Milton, but above all the vexed tale of his immensely complex relations to Wordsworth. In some instances, poets write crucial essays on their precursors, as Browning and Yeats did on Shelley. But Shelley, subtly sceptical as an intellect, partly concealed, even from himself, that his *Defence of Poetry* was also a defence against Wordsworth.

There are paragraphs in the *Defence* that can be regarded as immensely eloquent prose reductions of Wordsworth, prophetic of moments to come in John Stuart Mill and George Eliot:

> We have more moral, political, and historical wisdom (see than we know how to reduce into practice; we have more scientific and economic knowledge than can be accommodated to the just distribution of the produce which it multiplies. The poetry in these systems of thought is concealed by the accumulation of facts and calculating processes. There is no want of knowledge respecting what is wisest and best in morals, government, and political economy, or at least, what is wiser and better than what men now practise and endure. But we let *"I dare not* wait upon *I would*, like the poor cat i' the adage"*. We want the creative faculty to imagine that which we know; we want the generous impulse to act that which we imagine; we want the poetry of life; our calculations have outrun our conception; we have eaten more than we can digest. The cultivation of those sciences which have enlarged the limits of the empire of man over the external world has for want of the poetical faculty proportionally circumscribed those of the internal world; and man, having enslaved the elements, remains himself a slave. To what but a cultivation of the mechanical arts in a degree disproportioned to the presence of the creative faculty, which is the basis of all knowledge, is to be attributed the abuse of all invention for abridging and combining labour to the exasperation of the inequality of mankind? From what other cause has it arisen that the discoveries which should have lightened, have added a weight to the curse imposed on Adam? Thus poetry and the principle of self, of which money is the visible incarnation, are the God and Mammon of the world.

The Wordsworth of 1821 would not have endorsed the economic, social, and political radicalism of this passage, but it is pure Wordsworth of 1798. Shrewdly evading any mention of Wordsworth by name, Shelley has him in mind in the profound absolution granted to the great poets: "they have been washed in the blood of the mediator and redeemer, time". The great closing passage of the *Defence* centres itself upon Wordsworth, and to a lesser degree Coleridge, defining both their glory and their fall into the quotidian, while also stating the credo for Shelley's life and work:

> For the literature of England, an energetic development of which has ever preceded or accompanied a great and free development of the national will, has arisen as it were from a new birth. In spite of the low-thoughted envy which would undervalue contemporary merit, our own will be a memorable age in intellectual achievements, and we live among such philosophers and poets as surpass beyond comparison any who have appeared since the last national struggle for civil and religious liberty. The most unfailing herald, companion, and follower of the awakening of a great people to work a beneficial change in opinion or institution is poetry. At such periods there is an accumulation of the power of communicating and receiving intense and impassioned conceptions respecting man and nature. The persons in whom this power resides may often, as far as regards many portions of their nature, have little apparent correspondence with that spirit of good of which they are the ministers. But even while they deny and abjure, they are yet compelled to serve the power which is seated on the throne of their own soul. It is impossible to read the compositions of the most celebrated writers of the present day without being startled with the electric life which burns within their words. They measure the circumference and sound the depths of human nature with a comprehensive and all-penetrating spirit, and they are themselves perhaps the most sincerely astonished at its manifestations; for it is less their spirit than the spirit of the age. Poets are the hierophants of an unapprehended inspiration; the mirrors of the gigantic shadows which futurity casts upon the present; the words which express what they understand not; the trumpets which sing to battle and feel not what they inspire; the influence which is moved not, but moves. Poets are the unacknowledged legislators of the world.

Unquestionably, the poets of whom Shelley is speaking here are not himself, Byron, and Keats, but primarily Wordsworth and secondarily Coleridge. It does not matter, Shelley says, that as men Wordsworth and Coleridge have become Tories in politics, pillars of the established Church in religion, and mere time-servers in literature. "Even while they deny and abjure" the imagination, Wordsworth and Coleridge serve its power. Wordsworth is a hierophant or expounder of the mysterious, even though he himself cannot apprehend what he expounds. Wordsworth is a transumptive mirror of futurity, and sings Shelley on to the battle of poetry long after Wordsworth himself is uninspired. And then comes the beautifully summarising formula: Wordsworth is the unmoved mover, as an *influence*. The famous, much misinterpreted last sentence, "Poets are the unacknowledged legislators of the world", clearly needs to be interpreted in the context of the paradox that Shelley himself calls poetic "influence". The late W.H. Auden had a passionate dislike of Shelley, and once went so far as to interpret the last sentence of *A Defence of Poetry* as meaning that Shelley thought that poets were in league with the secret police. An unacknowledged legislator is simply an unacknowledged influence, and since Shelley equates Wordsworth with the *Zeitgeist*, it is hardly an overestimate to say that Wordsworth's influence created a series of laws for a world of feeling and thinking that went beyond the domain of poetry. Very strong poet that he was, Shelley nevertheless had the wisdom and the sadness of knowing overtly what other poets since have evaded knowing, except in the involuntary patterns of their work. Wordsworth will legislate and go on legislating for your poem, no matter how you resist or evade or even unconsciously ignore him.

I do not want to end these remarks on the *Defence* on such a tone of realistic sorrow and wisdom, even though the superbly intelligent Shelley is not ill-represented by such a tone. He knew that he could not escape the shadow of Wordsworth, and of and in that knowing he made his own poetry. I end by applying to him the last stanza of his own 'Hymn of Apollo'. He would not have wanted us to think of him as the speaker of these lines, but he came as close, I think, as any poet since Wordsworth, down to our present day, to justifying our going beyond his intentions, and hearing the poet himself in this great declaration:

> I am the eye with which the Universe
> Beholds itself and knows itself divine;
> All harmony of instrument or verse,
> All prophecy, all medicine is mine,
> All light of art or nature; – to my song
> Victory and praise in its own right belong.

A Defence of Poetry is not unique in intellectual power or eloquence in Shelley's prose-writings. I myself favour 'On Love' and 'On a Future State' among these essays and meditations, but all of them bear the intense sign of Shelley's genius, of his remorseless spirit. Their motto might well be what Shelley said of himself in a letter: "I always go on until I am stopped, and I never am stopped". His prose, like his poetry, has the capacity always of quickening a new birth in us, of reanimating the sparks amid the ashes of our psyches.

Harold Bloom
Sterling Professor of Humanities
Yale University
1988

PREFACE

There is no complete edition of Shelley's prose. In only the rare Forman and Julian Editions may the Shelley student find anything like all of the prose. This volume, then, should fill a long-felt need in making available to the general public, to college classes, to Shelley specialists, and to libraries a complete edition. Except for the letters and two romances, this volume contains all the known original prose of Shelley. His translations have been excluded because in thought, organization, and often in phrase and imagery, they are not Shelley's.

The text of the present edition has been collated with all available manuscripts and first editions. The text has been checked against the Julian Editions and others, and in the case of variants, I have adopted the readings which to me seem to convey most clearly Shelley's meaning. To former editors—especially to Mary Shelley, Lady Jane Shelley, Richard Garnett, H. Buxton Forman, Richard Herne Shepherd, and others—I wish to acknowledge my appreciation for innumerable helpful suggestions. For the interpretation of Shelley's life and thought, I have relied mainly on Shelley's own words, but my debt to a host of Shelley scholars is as obvious as it is deeply felt. Yet for whatever errors of transcription or of interpretation which the present edition may contain, I am solely responsible. It should be noted, however, that this edition is not a study in textual criticism. The spelling and punctuation have been modernized and Americanized in the interest of consistency and intelligibility.

The Introduction, the headnotes, and the footnotes are original, and are designed to interpret Shelley's philosophy to the reader. The editor is convinced that one who would understand Shelley's poetry must study his prose essays, preferably *before* he reads the poetry. The varied and complex ideas of the poetry are the same ideas encountered in the prose, but more difficult to understand because they have been translated into highly figurative language and colorful imagery. The advisability—indeed the necessity—of approaching Shelley first through his prose essays is even to the casual reader at once evident.

I gratefully acknowledge the kind permission of the Duke University Press to reprint pages 409-413 of James A. Notopoulos's *The Platonism of Shelley;* and my thanks are due to the Library of Congress for permission to reprint two fragments, without title, one on the Game Laws and the other on the Christian Religion, both contained in a Mary Shelley Notebook.

SHELLEY'S PROSE

I wish to express my gratitude to the Research Council of the University of Texas for research leave from teaching duties during the fall semester of 1949 for the purpose of prosecuting this study; my thanks are also due to two of my colleagues of the Department of English, Professor Truman Guy Steffan and the late Mr. E. F. Bennett, for reading large portions of the manuscript and making constructive suggestions—and particularly to the latter for his translation of the quotation from Holbach's *Système de la Nature*. To others of my colleagues, Professors H. J. Leon, T. S. Duncan, W. J. Battle, H. L. Russell, and Mrs. Minnie Lee Shepard, of the Classical Languages department, I am indebted for translations of Greek and Latin passages. To the staff of the Library of the University of Texas, particularly to Miss Julia Harris and Miss Kathleen Blow, I am grateful for innumerable courtesies. To the staff of the University of New Mexico Press, and especially to Mr. Roland F. Dickey, Associate Editor, I wish to express my appreciation for their devotion to every detail of designing and producing this volume. But my greatest debt is to my wife, whose wise counsel and unfailing devotion to all phases of the work made this study more trustworthy in content and more pleasant in pursuit.

D. L. C.

University of Texas
Austin, Texas
September 18, 1953

CONTENTS

APPENDIXES

BIBLIOGRAPHY

INTRODUCTION

3

THE GROWTH OF SHELLEY'S MIND

It is my purpose to trace the growth of Shelley's mind as seen in his reading and his recorded utterances. I begin with no preconceived thesis, and I shall make no apology or defence for what Shelley thought or said. My primary purpose is to state the facts as objectively as the existing data will permit. I intend to quote directly from his recorded statements for corroboration of my interpretation. I shall trace more or less chronologically Shelley's ideas of God, his conception of the place of religion in the life of man, the principles upon which his ethics were based, and his attitude to the great social problems of his day. Recent Shelley scholarship, particularly the work of Professors Carl Grabo, Carlos Baker, Kenneth Cameron, and N. I. White will be weighed, but in matters of opinion I shall draw, when possible, upon Shelley's own works for final authority.

During the last century and a half, two Shelleys have emerged from the vast sea of criticism: one, "The beautiful and ineffectual angel," who could do no wrong; the other, the radical reformer, the starry-eyed dreamer, the enemy of God and religion and marriage, who could do nothing noble. With these I shall have no commerce.

Born in 1792 as the dawn of the French Revolution brought to millions of hearts the promise of glad confident morning, Shelley became the epitome of the hopes and fears thus awakened. Son of a conservative, provincial country squire, Shelley was soon to clash with the established, but crumbling, order which his father represented.

At the age of ten Shelley, on entering Sion House Academy, first encountered cruelty and tyranny in the system of fagging and other indignities imposed upon the younger by the older boys. Shelley rebelled, just as he was ever to rebel, against oppression. Sympathy for the underdog, here first evinced, became a principle in his life. In 1804 he was sent to Eton where, even more than at Sion House, bullying by the older boys and flogging by the Headmaster prevailed. Shelley defied both. More than once he was rusticated for reading forbidden books, particularly those on chemistry. To be found with a chemistry book under one's arm then was much like being caught now by the Un-American Activities Committee with *Das Kapital*. In the library of Dr. Lind he read that most heretical of books in his day, Godwin's *Political Justice*. Here too he studied Franklin, who convinced him of the eventual triumph of mind over matter; Pliny's *Natural History,* whose chapter *De Deo* destroyed any rational belief in an anthropomorphic God; Lucretius, whose *De Rerum Natura* helped to free Shelley's mind from the trammels of superstition and to give him respect for a realistic, scientific approach to the problems of life. While at Eton, be it noted, Shelley was an enthusiastic auditor of Adam Walker's quasi-scientific lectures on the nature of electricity, light, water, and indeed the universe itself. These lectures aroused his scientific curiosity and had a significant influence on his later thought.

Here too the future poet read the forbidden lore of Albertus Magnus and Paracelsus. Albertus (1206?-1280), the great interpreter of Aristotle, insisted that philosophy's wings should never be clipped by theology. He proved the existence of God by inferences from the nature of the universe. So what Shelley learned from Albertus—an Aristotelian, not a Platonist or a Neo-Platonist as commonly asserted—was respect for his profound knowledge and the scientific bent of his mind. Paracelsus (1493-1541) was a distinguished Swiss doctor, who held new and radical ideas of medicine; who broke with the past, but was unable to free himself from the contaminating influences of alchemy. Mysticism and magic, in unhappy alliance with Neo-Platonism, infested his philosophy. With him God was the First Cause and the essence of all things; the smallest atom of matter was animated; man was a miniature (microcosm) of the universe, and his mind was part of its soul. This mystical strain in Paracelsus came in time to overshadow his more solid ideas. It is probable that the Neo-Platonism of his philosophy was attractive to the youthful, plastic mind of the oppidan at Eton. But whatever that influence, it made no deep impression and was offset by his reading of the more respectable Albertus and Lucretius.

It is not unlikely that Dr. Lind's library at Eton also contained Locke, Spinoza, Hume, and the French philosophers of the Enlightenment. In all of these, no doubt, the aspiring metaphysician browsed at will and acquired a store of ideas from which he was later to draw so heavily.

Because he mastered the curriculum at Eton in half the time of the average boy, Shelley had the opportunity not only for reading great books but also for writing books of his own. It was here, perhaps in the library of Dr. Lind, that Shelley conceived and wrote his two romances: *Zastrozzi* (1809) and *St. Irvyne* (1810). In the closing chapters of *Zastrozzi* we find suggestions that Shelley's mind was even then busy with "dangerous" speculations on a future state and the non-existence of a deity. In *St. Irvyne* also Shelley showed his early contempt for the Christian deity and the canting monks of Christianity. In Chapter Ten of this romance Shelley put radical speculations, probably his own, into the mouth of Ginotti, when he had him say:

> I was now about seventeen: I had dived into the depths of metaphysical calculations. With sophistical arguments had I convinced myself of the non-existence of a First Cause, and by every combined modification of the essences of matter had I apparently proved that no existences could possibly be, unseen by human vision . . . . I have no right to suppose otherwise than that at the end of the time allotted by nature for the existence of the atoms which compose my being, I must like all other men perish, perhaps everlastingly . . . .[1]

Such then were Shelley's ideas and his reading at the time he left Eton in 1810, and matriculated at Oxford in the fall of that year. His metaphysical speculations continued at the University, bringing upon him much annoying

1. By now Shelley was suspected by his father and others of holding deistical ideas and thus doubting certain fundamental tenets of Christianity. The suspicion was probably well founded, for on November 11, 1810, Shelley wrote to his London publisher, J. J. Stockdale, for a book, "an Hebrew essay, demonstrating that the Christian religion is false." This work has not been definitely identified.

notoriety. Shelley was soon to learn that even at Oxford religion and morals were not to be approached with reason, as one would essay a proposition in Euclid. He was already beginning to feel the strong arm of religion and morality. Had not superstition and intolerance alienated his father and his fiancée? Then toward the end of 1810 Shelley dedicated himself to the eradication of religious and moral prejudices, declaring that nothing would be sacred to him but Truth.[2] So after only a few months in the University, with Locke and Hume as bodyguard, Shelley sallied forth to break his lance with the Fathers of the Church.

Since his ideas on the fundamental principles of metaphysics, morals, religion, science, and politics were not matured, Shelley continued with happy disregard of the Oxford curriculum to pursue vigorously his reading of the outstanding books in all areas of learning, taking nothing on faith and bringing all theories and opinions to the test of reason—à la Godwin. He was clearly impatient with the medieval curriculum at the University and in open rebellion against the narrow-minded antagonism to new ideas, particularly in science, which characterized the dons. Shelley had little interest in abstract learning of any kind; with him as with Bacon whom he so greatly admired, the vital question was always, What will this new idea or discovery contribute to the happiness of man? There must be fearless investigation and unfettered thought in the examination of the established order to the end that the outmoded and worthless, however sacred or well entrenched, might be discarded, giving place to the new and promising.

Shelley's Idea of God

Shelley was born into a smug, conventionally Christian home, and was no doubt exposed to the doctrines of the Anglican Church. But we can be certain that he early questioned the validity of some of the fundamental tenets of the Christian religion as represented by that church. "The first doubts," he wrote to Godwin on June 11, 1812, "which arose in my boyish mind concerning the genuineness of the Christian religion as a revelation from the divinity were excited by a contemplation of the virtues and genius of Greece and Rome. Shall Socrates and Cicero perish whilst the meanest hind of modern England inherits eternal life?"

It is a fact that sometime between 1805 and 1810 Shelley definitely rejected the idea of the Christian God and had become a believer in deism—the widely accepted philosophical, religious creed of the seventeenth and eighteenth centuries.[3] No matter what was their church membership, or organized Christian sect, the leading men of that period were confirmed deists. It was an intellectual system of beliefs, based for the most part upon scientific facts and commonsense. The fundamental tenets of this philosophy therefore appealed

---

2. Letter to Hogg, December 20, 1810. Unless otherwise noted, dates of Shelley's separate works in this Introduction are dates of composition.
3. For a discussion of this idea see pp. 31-40 of Carlos Baker's *Shelley's Major Poetry: The Fabric of a Vision* (Princeton University Press, 1948). Compare Professor Carl Grabo's *The Magic Plant*, pp. 24-43, for slightly divergent interpretations.

to the intellectual and the educated. To them it offered a satisfactory basis of religion and sound principles of morals. To the deist God was some superhuman Being who created the universe and all that it contains and set it to work by the inviolable laws of Nature. To the deist the universe is a perfect machine, with God as its designer and helpless observer, and man as an integral part of that machine. To the deist God reveals himself and proves his goodness, benevolence, and perfection in the design which man's mind everywhere discovers in the natural universe. Therefore, to know Nature is to know God. The deist, then, needed no supernatural revelation such as the Christian found in his Bible. To the deist the Bible was but another historical record of a primitive people, in many instances an incredible, unreliable, and self-contradictory account.

Because it satisfied his scientific spirit, his sense of a reasonable ethics and commonsense morality, deism made a strong, but short-lived, appeal to Shelley, yet he could not go the whole way with the deists. Their notion of a deity who created this vast universe and who then retired helpless and impotent on the completion of his work did not make *sense* to him. And, too, he came gradually to doubt the absolutes upon which the deist built his system of morals. Early, as the letter to Janetta Phillips, May, 1811, will testify, Shelley rejected both the god of Christianity and of deism: "As you mention Religion, I will say that my rejection of *revealed* [Christianity] proceeds from my perfect conviction of its insufficiency to the happiness of man—to this course *I* can trace murder, war, intolerance. My rejection of *Natural* [Deism] arises wholly from *reason*. I once was an enthusiastic Deist, but never a Christian."

On January 3, 1811 (?) in a letter to Hogg, Shelley maintained, "Before we doubt or believe the existence of anything, it is necessary that we should have a *tolerably* clear idea of what it is. The word *God* has been, will continue to be the source of numberless errors . . . . It does not imply 'the Soul of the universe, the intelligent and necessarily beneficent, actuating principle.'[4] This I believe in . . . . I think that the leaf of a tree, the meanest insect on which we trample, are in themselves arguments more conclusive than any which can be adduced that some vast intellect animates Infinity." Paracelsus asserted as much, and Spinoza had confirmed it, with both of whom Shelley was familiar. So, at this period of his life, he cannot be, except in the most provincial use of the word, called an atheist. He merely rejected the idea of an anthropomorphic, personal, creative deity.[5]

On January 6, in a letter—not in *New Shelley Letters*—to the cynical and worldly Hogg, Shelley wrote, "I will consider your argument against the non-existence of a Deity. Do you allow that some supernatural power actuates

---

4. In *New Shelley Letters*, edited by W. S. Scott (London, 1948), where the date of this letter is Dec. 8, 181(?), this sentence begins, "It does not," instead of "Does it not," in Hogg's *Life*, thus making nonsense of what follows.

5. Professor Ellsworth Barnard in *Shelley's Religion* (1937), pp. 17-97, arrives at the untenable conclusion that Shelley came to believe in a *personal* God. Note, however, that in the Introduction to his *Shelley, Selected Poems, Essays, and Letters* (1944), p. xxxviii, he takes a somewhat different position: "Any assertion that Shelley believed in a 'personal' Deity must be definitely qualified."

the organization of physical causes? It is evident so far as this, that if *power* and *wisdom* are employed in the continual arrangement of these affairs, that this power, etc., is something out of the comprehension of man as he now exists; at least if we allow that the soul is *not* matter." He then defined God as the soul of the universe as gravitation is the soul of a clock, as animation is the soul of an oyster. Finally he observed, "I think we may not inaptly define *Soul* as the most supreme, superior, and distinguished abstract appendage to the nature of things."[6]

What, then, was Shelley's own mature conception of the deity at the time he first expressed himself publicly on the subject, in *The Necessity of Atheism?* What of this provocative document with its inflammatory title? Shelley insisted in the first paragraph that the subject of existence or the nonexistence of a deity is of such outstanding importance as to demand the closest examination of the evidence; then, with Locke, Shelley maintained that *belief* is *involuntary,* and that when a proposition is presented, the mind perceives the agreement or disagreement. The perception of the agreement is called *belief*. With Locke Shelley maintained that as the senses are the source of all knowledge to the mind, they claim the strongest evidence to assent; the decision of the mind based on experience gives the next best proof; and finally the weakest evidence is the testimony of others. Consequently no testimony contrary to fact or reason can be admitted. To these three all evidence for the existence of a deity must be referred.[7]

On May 8, 1811, Shelley wrote to Hogg: "A few days ago I had a polite note from Mr. Hunt[8] . . . . [in which it is maintained that the Deity] is neither omnipotent, omnipresent, nor identical. . . . He says that God is comprehensible, not doubting but an adequate exertion of reason . . . would lead us from a contemplation of his works to a definite knowledge of his attributes, which are by no means limited. Now, here is a new god for you! . . . He believes that this creator is by no means perfect, but composed of good and evil, like man, producing that mixture of these principles which is evident."

This statement from Hunt seems to have made a deep impression on Shelley, perhaps leading him to make a definite break with deism. That his repudiation of deism came at this time can be seen from the letter to Janetta Phillips, May, 1811, quoted on page 6.

On June 11, 1811, to Elizabeth Hitchener, Shelley, taking Locke as his authority, declared that there are no innate ideas, and thus no innate speculative or practical principles. This fact overturns all appeal to *feeling* in favor of a deity. Shelley went on to explain his idea of God, essentially pantheistic:

6. In the Letters of January 11, 12, and of February 6, 1811, Shelley seems to be wavering between a pantheistic and a deistic conception of God.

7. See *New Shelley Letters*, pp. 36-37, for Locke's influence. See also Shelley's letter to his father on February 6, 1811, for similar ideas. On March 29 to his father: Shelley, insisting that his expulsion from the University was a demonstration of weakness on the part of the authorities, submitted proposals to his father, one clause of which promised never again "to obtrude atheistical opinions upon any one whatever." This gesture of repentance meeting rebuff from an intransigent father ended Shelley's effort at reconciliation.

8. James Henry Leigh Hunt, the liberal editor of *The Examiner*.

[God] is a name which expresses the unknown cause, the supposititious origin of all existence. When we speak of the soul of man, we mean that unknown cause which produces the observable effect evinced by his intelligence and bodily animation which are in their nature conjoined . . . and inseparable. The word *God,* then, in the sense in which you take it analogizes with the *universe* as the soul of man to his body, as the vegetative power to vegetables . . . . In this sense I acknowledge a god, but merely as a synonym for *the existing power of existence* . . . . I do not in this . . . recognize a Being which has created that to which it is confessedly annexed as an essence, as that without which the universe would not be what it is. It is therefore the *essence* of the universe, the universe the essence of it.[9]

The statement of this pantheistic idea seems to come directly from Spinoza; but it should be remembered that this conception is discussed at length in Hume's *Dialogues,* which Shelley had only recently read.[10]

Shelley began the year 1812 with a very definite statement of his religious views; on January 2, to Elizabeth Hitchener he wrote, "I have lately had some conversation with Southey which has elicited my true opinions of God. He says I ought not to call myself an atheist since in reality I believe that the universe is God. I tell him I believe that God is another signification of the universe . . . that everything is animation . . . . Southey agrees in my idea of deity, the mass of infinite *intelligence.*" It will be seen that this pantheistic conception has not undergone any significant change since its adoption more than a year earlier.[11]

In *A Refutation of Deism* (1813), which is a dialogue, after the manner of Hume's *Dialogues Concerning Natural Religion,* between a Christian and a deist, Shelley maintained that neither deism nor Christianity is tenable. He represented in this dialogue the God of the deist as being at least respectable, but that of the Christian as primitive, cruel, revengeful, obscene, having created man weak and sinful and then damned him for being so. The standard deistic argument from design and Final Cause for the existence of God Shelley here demolished with withering logic. Following reason as his guide, he stated cogently and persuasively that the God of the deist like that of the Christian is an absurd and unrealistic God. In conclusion he repeated his former pantheistic belief that the Universe is animated, and *is God.*[12]

In the Note to *Queen Mab* (1813) to the line, "Necessity, Thou Mother of the world," Shelley maintained, to paraphrase and condense his argument, that religion is the perception of the relation in which one stands to the principle of the universe. But if the principle of the universe is not an organic being, the model and prototype of man, the relation between it and human

---

9. A reiteration of this opinion was expressed in a letter to Elizabeth Hitchener on June 25, 1811. For further discussion see Baker, *op. cit.,* pp. 31-32. See also Kenneth Cameron's *The Young Shelley,* pp. 113 ff. Compare with Grabo, *op. cit.,* pp. 24-43.

10. Shelley stated in his letter to Elizabeth Hitchener, October 27, 1811, that he refused to follow Hume in believing that "those who *really feel* the

being of a God have the best right to believe it."

11. It is a curious fact that, with one notable exception—to be considered later—there are no significant references to a deity in the letters after 1812.

12. For a more detailed discussion of this work see Cameron, *op. cit.,* pp. 274-287, and Baker, *op. cit.,* pp. 30-38.

beings is absolutely none. And then he observed, "It is probable that the word *God* was originally only an expression denoting the unknown cause of the known events which men perceive in the universe . . . . Necessity teaches us that . . . if God is the author of good, He is also the author of evil . . . . He is also subject to the dominion of an immutable Necessity . . . . God made man such as he is and then damned him for being so."[13]

In another Note in *Queen Mab,* to the line, "There is no God," Shelley repeated the argument of *The Necessity of Atheism,* with slight expansion and with one significant word added and underscored—that word was *creative.* The opening paragraph reads, "There is no *creative* god. This negation must be understood solely to affect a creative deity. The hypothesis of a pervading Spirit, co-eternal with the universe remains unshaken." In other words Shelley is here reasserting his former denial that this spirit or soul created the universe.

So our knowledge of Shelley's idea of God grows. Although his God is still the soul of the universe, that animating force in all nature, Shelley considers that this God is subject to the Principle of Necessity—a mysterious and omnipotent Power that sustains and governs all life. Such a system of thought might be called pantheistic naturalism.[14]

In the *Essay on the Punishment of Death* (1813-14?) Shelley stated that the vital principle within us must lose that consciousness of definite and individual being and become a unit in the vast sum of action and of thought which disposes and animates the universe, and is called God. Shelley had probably found this idea of a world-soul in ancient literature, particularly in Plato, but at the time he first used this term Shelley had only a school-boy acquaintance with Greek philosophy. True, this notion of a world-soul is in Paracelsus, but it is far more likely that Shelley had been impressed by this idea from his reading of Hume's *Dialogues Concerning Natural Religion,* and Holbach's *Système de la Nature.*

In the *Essay on Christianity* (1812-15?) Shelley pointed out that the word *God* has various connotations, and no two individuals hold the same idea, but most agree that it is a term devised by man to express the sum of mystery, or

13. Compare this with his Manichaean philosophy in the *Essay on Christianity*. The substance of this paragraph comes directly from Chapter 4 of Holbach's *Système de la Nature* (Translated by H. D. Robinson, two volumes, Boston, 1877), where the editor, probably Diderot, attributes the phrase "Necessity, thou Mother of the world" to Plato. A. E. Hancock in *The French Revolution and the English Poets,* pp. 63-64, was the first, I believe, to point out this indebtedness of Shelley to Holbach. See also Cameron, *op. cit.,* p. 254 and p. 396. The present writer has an extended study of Shelley's debt to Holbach in preparation.

14. For a different view of Shelley's pantheism, see Barnard's *Shelley's Religion,* pp. 18, 56, 62, 66, 93, 217. In his *Essay on Life* (1815?), largely metaphysical in nature, Shelley said that he agreed with those philosophers who assert that nothing exists but as it is perceived, and that his reading in the popular philosophy of mind and matter had early conducted him to materialism. Then following Hume and denying Berkeley, he said, "Yet, that the basis of all things cannot be, as the popular philosophy alleges, mind, is sufficiently evident. Mind as far as we have any experience of its properties—and beyond that experience how vain is argument—cannot create, it can only perceive . . . . It is infinitely improbable that the cause of mind, that is, of existence, is similar to mind." So, Shelley would seem here to say that God is *not* mind or soul, literally defined. Has his previous use of these terms been strictly figurative? Compare this philosophy with the definitely materialistic position in the *Essay on a Future State* (1812-13?). Holbach is probably the source of this idea. See *Système de la Nature,* 1.15-16.

majesty, or power which the invisible world contains. Then he explored the
idea of God held by Jesus, with whose opinion he seems in perfect accord.

> We can distinctly trace in the tissue of his doctrines the persuasion that God
> is some universal Being differing from man and the mind of man . . . the
> overruling Spirit of all the energy and wisdom included within the circle of
> existing things . . . something mysteriously and illimitably pervading the
> frame of things . . . the overruling Spirit of the collective energy of the moral
> and material world. . . . The doctrine of a peculiar Providence; that is, of
> some Power beyond and superior to that which ordinarily guides the operations
> of the universe . . . is explicitly denied by Jesus Christ . . . . This much is
> certain that Jesus Christ represents God as the fountain of all goodness, the
> eternal enemy of pain and evil, the uniform and unchanging motive of the
> salutary operations of the material world. According to Jesus Christ, and
> according to the indisputable facts of the case, some evil spirit has dominion
> in this imperfect world. But there will come a time when the human mind
> shall be visited exclusively by the influence of the benignant Power.[15]

In the notes to his last long poem—*Hellas,* composed a few months before
his death—Shelley asserted that the received hypothesis of a Being resembling
men in the moral attributes of his nature would remain inexplicable and
incredible. The reader will observe that in this remark Shelley had definitely
in mind the God of Christianity, and not the spirit or soul of the universe
which he had come to accept as the real God.

What, then, are we to conclude from all these citations was Shelley's mature
idea of God? First, he definitely and positively rejected the Christian God;
secondly, he early announced his belief in a soul or mind of the universe, such
as that postulated by Spinoza, and later by Hume in his *Dialogues Concerning
Natural Religion,* a God having many parallels with that set forth by Berkeley,
and in some particulars, by Plato. Shelley's God as the soul of the universe
must not be confounded with Plato's world-soul, nor has he any of the attributes
given to him by Christians. Shelley's God is the soul of goodness pervading
life; he is the charity men feel in their hearts; he is the principle of harmony
throughout nature; he is the music heard in the heart of man; he is Intellectual
Beauty. And finally he is *not* a person or a thing, nor has he a local habitation
or a name.

After his early rejection of what he considered was the incredible deity of
both Christianity and deism, Shelley cannot be said to have changed his conception of God. There was perhaps a certain degree of refinement, but his
God of 1822 was by and large the same God he described in 1812.

Closely allied to his idea of God are several essentially metaphysical concepts—such as the origin of life, immortality, the nature of reality, and constitution of the mind. Let us dispose of these as rapidly as their complex nature
and Shelley's inconclusive and random remarks will permit.

15. This idea of an eternal warfare between the
spirit of evil and the spirit of good is the heart of
Zoroaster's philosophy. The thought of this Persian
religious leader exerted considerable influence on the
religion of the West, entering probably through
Judaism and Christianity. See Shelley's *Essay on the
Devil and Devils* for his Manichaean philosophy.
For Barnard's view, see *Shelley's Religion,* pp. 17-97
and 152. Compare Cameron, *op. cit.,* pp. 285-287,
for slightly divergent ideas.

As to the origin of life—that is, consciousness, Shelley was in doubt, calling that the great miracle. In his *Essay on Life* and *Essay on a Future State,* stating the views of two opposing groups of philosophers and natural scientists, he concluded, I believe, in the latter essay that thought or mind— that is, life—is no more than the combination of particles of matter—that matter and motion are sufficient to account for all life. But life was not created, nor did the mind or soul antedate birth nor will it survive death. Shelley, in agreement with Locke and Hume, insisted that since there are no innate ideas—thus denying Plato and all his followers—then the mind simply grows with the body and inevitably decays and perishes with the body. This is the sheerest materialism, and is in perfect accord with the philosophy of the French Enlightenment. But in the *Essay on Life* and *Essay on Christianity* Shelley somewhat modified this position. He said in the *Essay on Life:* "This materialism is a seducing system to young and superficial minds . . . . I was discontented with such a view of things as it afforded; man is a being of high aspirations . . . disclaiming alliance with transcience and decay, incapable of imaging to himself annihilation . . . . Whatever may be his true and final destination, there is a spirit within him at enmity with nothingness and dissolution." But he concluded the *Essay on Life* and the *Essay on a Future State* with a thorough-going Humean scepticism. Indeed Shelley had not arrived at a satisfying answer to this metaphysical problem. He had too much respect for reason to accept anything merely on faith. He sincerely wished that the grave is not the goal of life, but he could not assure himself that it is not.[16]

As to the nature of reality, Shelley was even more at sea. With Locke and Hume as his inspiration he finally arrived at the notion that reality *exists in the mind* when apprehending an objective world of things which exist, to be sure, outside the mind, but which indeed have no meaning unperceived by mind. His speculations on metaphysics and on the mind were fragmentary and inconclusive. Shelley never, I believe, came to the extreme position of Plato or Berkeley that all reality lies in thought or soul or mind. He was never able to divorce the subjective from the objective apprehension of that reality. Above all, Shelley was disgusted with the way philosophers, entangled in their own web of meaningless words, raised a dust and then complained that they could not see. He tried to cut through the dense thicket of words, but without satisfaction. Understood in their present-day connotations, the words *atheist, Platonist, materialist,* or *immaterialist,* cannot without considerable discrimination, it seems to me, be at any time applied to Shelley.[17]

Shelley's Conception of Jesus

Throughout his life, so far as his recorded statements show, Shelley had a profound admiration for the character and social teachings of Jesus. He con-

16. For further discussion of this problem see his letters to Elizabeth Hitchener, October 15 (?) and November 24, 1811. For a slightly different opinion concerning his ideas of life and a future state, see Cameron, *op. cit.,* pp. 285-287, and Grabo, *op. cit.,* pp. 24-43.

17. For differing views in this matter see White, Cameron, Barnard, Baker, Grabo, and Notopoulos.

sidered him, along with Plato and Socrates, a great, perhaps the greatest, moral teacher the world has known. There are, however, three instances of Shelley's apparent condemnation of the character of Jesus. In a letter to Hogg on April 24, 1811 (?) Shelley wrote:

> The Galilean is not a favorite of mine. So far from owing him any thanks for his favor, I cannot avoid confessing that I owe a secret grudge to his carpentership. The reflecting part of the community, that part in whose happiness we have so strong an interest, certainly do not require the morality which, when there is not *vice,* fetters *virtue.* There we agree. Let this horrid Galilean rule the canaille then. I give them up; I will no more mix politics and virtue, they are incompatible.[18]

Again in the letter to Hogg, April 26, 1811, desperate over the loss of his fiancée and his expulsion from the University, Shelley cried out, "I could once *tolerate* Christ; he then merely injured me; he merely deprived *me* of all that I cared for, touching myself, on earth; but now he has done more, and I cannot forgive." Shelley, it appears, is here using the term *Christ* as symbolic of Christianity, and not for the character of Jesus. The third instance was plainly casual, and not the result of conviction. After he had carefully discriminated in the poem *Queen Mab* the two conceptions of Jesus—one the distorted and unbelievable character created by Christianity; the other, the *real* Jesus— Shelley recorded in a brief footnote to the passage that perhaps Jesus was an ambitious man aspiring to the throne of Judea.[19]

Critics have seized upon these three apparently incidental remarks as Shelley's real opinion of Jesus in total disregard of the scores of times that he extolled the character of the great Nazarene.

Since Jesus is usually considered to be the founder of Christianity, we shall examine the two together.

Shelley's objection to institutionalized Christianity were many; chief among them were its doctrine of reward and punishment and the consideration of *belief* as a voluntary act of the mind. The first, he felt, militated against the pursuit of virtue. In the letter to Hogg on April 2, 1811, Shelley said, "How can the hope of a higher reward stimulating an action make it virtuous?" And in the long letter to Hogg two days later, he deplored the idea that the Christian moral virtues are based on *belief* and *faith,* and *duty* rather than upon reason, etc. To Elizabeth Hitchener on June 20, 1811, in a long passage on virtue, vice, belief, etc., Shelley stated that "Where the doctrines of Christ do not

18. The letter is thus printed in the *New Shelley Letters,* but in Hogg's *Life of Shelley* the letter reads, " 'The Galilean is not a favorite of mine,' a French author writes. 'The French write audaciously— rashly,' " thus making a French writer, and not Shelley, condemn Jesus. If the manuscript letter is genuine and shows no tampering with by Hogg or others, it will be difficult to harmonize this unfavorable opinion with the very laudatory remarks on Jesus immediately before and after.

19. Professor N. I. White's *Shelley* (1940), I:293, says that Shelley, in *Queen Mab* "presents Christ as a vengeful, hypocritical demagogue." In II:125, writing of Shelley's changing ideas, Professor White remarks: "Christ, who had been sneered at as an imposter in *Queen Mab,* is treated sympathetically in *Prometheus Unbound.*" See also II:112-113. Baker (p. 29) and Cameron (p. 402) fail to distinguish between the mythical and the real character of Jesus, which Shelley clearly and painstakingly makes in the Note to the line, "I will beget a son."

differ from virtue, *there* I follow *them* . . . ." In the famous letter to his father September 27, 1811, in a sarcastic vein Shelley asked his father to put to the test his vaunted Christian virtue and *forgive* his son. Maintaining that the typical Christian is a hypocrite, Shelley again appealed to his father on October 12 to forgive him, and judge not. To Elizabeth Hitchener on January 2, 1812, he wrote:

> If what I have urged against Christianity be insufficient, read its very books. . . . Considering that *belief* is not a voluntary operation of the mind, any system which makes it a subject of reward or punishment cannot be supposed to emanate from one who has a master's knowledge of the human mind. All the investigations of the era of the world's existence are incongruous with that of Moses . . . . Besides, Moses writes the history of his own death . . . . Southey [is] no believer in original sin; he thinks that which appears to be a taint of our nature is in effect the result of unnatural political institutions; there we agree.

To Elizabeth Hitchener on February 27, 1812, he wrote from Ireland: "I have met with some waverers between Christianity and Deism. I shall attempt to make them reject all the bad and take all the good of the Jewish books." Then he stated that he planned to make a collection of the moral sayings of Jesus stripped of the mystery and immorality that surround them, for a little Easter present.[20] And on June 2, to Miss Hitchener, he emphatically said: "If every day takes from the fervor of my opposition to Christianity . . . it adds to the perfect conviction I feel of its falsehood and mischief." In *An Address to the Irish People* (1812) are several important statements about Jesus and Christianity. Shelley, saying that "all religions are good which make men good," pointed to the bloody wars fostered by Christianity and to the priestcraft's unholy alliance with kings and dictators to keep the people in ignorance and subjection. But "anything short of unlimited toleration and complete charity with all men, on which you will recollect Jesus Christ principally insisted, is wrong."

Shelley went on: "A camel shall as soon pass through the eye of a needle as a rich man enter the kingdom of heaven. This is not to be understood literally. Jesus Christ appears to me only to have meant that riches have generally the effect of hardening and vitiating the heart—so has poverty." Then speaking particularly, he said, "Protestants, hath your religion always been characterized by the mildness of benevolence which Jesus Christ recommended?"[21]

In his *Proposals for an Association of Philanthropists* (1812) Shelley maintained that a union of church and state is "contrary to the principles and practice of Jesus, contrary to that equality which he fruitlessly endeavored to teach mankind."

In *A Letter to Lord Ellenborough* (1812) Shelley, making a plea for an understanding of the deist by the Christian, said that Jesus was crucified

---

20. See David Lee Clark's "Shelley's *Biblical Extracts*," *Modern Language Notes*, Vol. LXVI, November 1951, pp. 435-441.

21. From *An Address to the Irish People* (1812). Observe that Shelley always insisted upon a return to the simple social teachings of Jesus.

"because he attempted to supersede the ritual of Moses with regulations more moral and humane."

Then deploring the bloody method of Christianity's defence of itself through its long history, Shelley—quoting Holbach's *Système de la Nature*—asked, "If God has spoken, why is not the universe convinced?" And he finally concluded, "The thinking part of the community has not received as indisputable the truth of Christianity, as they have that of the Newtonian system."

In an important Note to the line, "I will beget a Son," in *Queen Mab* (1813) Shelley, after giving a brief account of creation according to the Bible, said that "at length men arose who suspected that [this story of Creation] was a fable and imposture, and that Jesus Christ, so far from being a God was only a man like themselves . . . . He was a man of pure life, who desired to rescue his countrymen from the tyranny of their barbarous and degrading superstitions . . . . It is of importance, therefore, to distinguish between the *pretended character* of this being as the son of God and the Saviour of the world, and his *real character* as a man who, for a vain attempt to reform the world, paid the forfeit of his life to that overbearing tyranny which has since so long desolated the universe in his name." Shelley went on to say that the real Jesus "stands in the foremost list of those true heroes who have died in the glorious martyrdom of liberty and have braved torture, contempt, and poverty in the cause of suffering humanity."

A Refutation of Deism (1813) is a long dialogue between a deist and a Christian, in which the leading doctrines of each are set forth and argued. Theosophus, the deist, ridicules all the tenets of Christianity, including its mysteries and miracles, its irrational and contradictory doctrines, and all else that is contrary to reason and commonsense. He insists that Christianity can be judged only by its fruits, which have been bitter. The Christian morality, he maintains, inculcates abjectness, deception, cruelty, war, just as it frowns on love and happy living. It stresses blind faith and considers belief the test of salvation. Its miracles and prophecies, Shelley insists, are insults to commonsense and reason.

On his first visit to the continent (1814) Shelley began *The Assassins*, a story based upon the moral teachings of Jesus. It is the fragmentary account of a small band of real Christians who had fled Jerusalem when the Roman army attacked the city. Taking reason or the human understanding to be their guide and assuming "the doctrine of the Messiah concerning benevolence and justice for the regulations of their action," they sought peace in a secluded vale in the Lebanon mountains, and there they endeavored to live the good life as outlined by Jesus.

The Devil and Devils (1819) is a remarkably clever revelation of Shelley's ideas of God, Jesus, religion, and Christianity, but as it is couched in humorous, witty, and frequently sarcastic language, it would be perhaps unsafe, or at least misleading, to trust to excerpts from it. Only a careful reading of the whole will suffice. There is nothing in it, however, to alter the impression we already have of Shelley's idea of Jesus and Christianity.

Then there is the famous letter to Southey on August 17, 1820, in which Shelley denounced Christianity and its bad effects on the morals of men:

> I confess your recommendation to adopt the system of ideas you call Christianity has little weight with me, whether you mean the popular superstition in all its articles, or some other more refined theory with respect to those events and opinions which put an end to the graceful religion of the Greeks. To judge of the doctrines by their effects, one would think that this religion were called the religion of Christ and Charity *ut lucus a non lucendo*,[22] when I considered the manner in which they seem to have transformed the disposition and understanding of you and men of the most amiable manners and the highest accomplishments, so that even when recommending Christianity you cannot forbear breathing out defiance against the express words of Christ.

In the notes to his poem *Hellas* (1821), Shelley, not wishing to be misunderstood as defending Christianity, asserted that "the popular notions of Christianity are represented in this chorus as true in their relation to the worship they superseded . . . without considering their merits in a relation more universal." Shelley went on to say that "the sublime character of Jesus Christ was deformed by an imputed identification with a Power who tempted, betrayed, and punished the innocent beings and for the period of a thousand years, the spirit of this most just, wise, and benevolent of men has been propitiated with myriads of hecatombs of those who approached the nearest to his innocence and wisdom sacrificed under every aggravation of atrocity and variety of torture."

In *A Philosophical View of Reform* (1819-1820—not published until 1920), Shelley made several striking remarks about Jesus and Christianity. At the outset in reference to the schemes employed to enslave mankind he said that names have been borrowed from the life and opinions of Jesus and employed as symbols of domination and imposture.

Shelley went on to defend Jesus from the distortions put upon his simple social teachings by his pretended followers:

> How distinct from the opinions of any of those professing themselves establishers were the doctrines and actions of Jesus Christ . . . . Berkeley and Hume, [and] Hartley [at a] later age . . . have clearly established the certainty of our ignorance with respect to those obscure questions which under the name of religious truths have been watchwords of contention and the symbols of unjust power ever since they were distorted by the narrow passions of the immediate followers of Jesus from that meaning to which philosophers are even now restoring them.

Finally in a letter to Horace Smith, April 11, 1822, concerning his regret that Thomas Moore the poet should hold an adverse opinion of him, Shelley wrote with a definiteness and a finality not easily misinterpreted:

22. Literally, "a grove from not being light,"—meaning anything inconsequential or illogical.

> I differ with Moore in thinking Christianity useful to the world; no man of sense can think it true; and the alliance of the monstrous superstitions of the popular worship with the pure doctrines of Theism of such a man as Moore, turns to the profit of the former and makes the latter the fountain of its own pollution. I agree with him that the doctrines of the French and material philosophy are as false as they are pernicious, but still they are better than Christianity inasmuch as anarchy is better than despotism—for this reason, that the former is for a season, and the latter is eternal.

This letter alone—near the end of his life—precludes any idea entertained by Browning and other Shelley apologists that had Shelley lived longer he would have become a Christian. Let it not be thought, however, that Shelley considered Christianity utterly worthless, for in *A Defence of Poetry* (1820) he pointed out its good effects, particularly as a civilizing influence during the Dark Ages, primarily through the poetry it inspired. "It is probable that the poetry of Moses, Job, David, Solomon, and Isaiah had produced a great effect upon the mind of Jesus and his disciples . . . . But his [Jesus] doctrines seem to have been quickly distorted . . . . The poetry in the doctrines of Jesus Christ . . . outlived the darkness and convulsions connected with their growth . . . . Jesus Christ divulged the sacred and eternal truths contained in these views [views held by Plato and Pythagoras] to mankind, and Christianity in its abstract purity became the exoteric expression of the esoteric doctrines of the poetry and wisdom of antiquity."

Shelley never was a Christian. But he was for a brief time a deist. But the God of deism did not satisfy his logical mind. Shelley's God, then, was the soul or mind or spirit of the universe, the animating principle of all life, in no wise personal, and incapable of meddling in the affairs of men.

In Shelley's mind Jesus was a man, a great moral reformer like Socrates, and not divine or supernatural, and not superhuman; consequently Shelley did not believe in the miraculous birth or death or mission of Jesus.

Christianity in its infancy was based upon the teachings of Jesus, which were primarily socialistic and humanitarian. But his disciples soon distorted his doctrines to their own ignorant or selfish or evil purposes, and thus made Jesus out to be a thoroughly impossible creature, neither man nor god. Christianity became not the pure and refined ethical religion of its founder, but a system embodying the whims and fancies of its leaders—the Pope, Luther, Calvin, Wesley, and a thousand lesser lights. Among them they succeeded in completely falsifying the teachings of Jesus.

Shelley's System of Morals

Shelley defined certain general principles of morals and then applied them to specific laws and institutions, giving especial attention to the ethical basis of the state, the church, and social customs such as matrimony.

Shelley believed that the inculcation of sound moral principles to be the highest good to which any man could aspire. More than once did he assert that he planned to write a treatise on morals—indeed he left a fragment on this theme. To Peacock on January 24, 1819, he wrote "I consider poetry very subordinate to moral and political science, and if I were well, certainly I should aspire to the latter." He also emphasized his conviction that under no circumstance should politics and morals be divorced.[23]

Shelley's system of morals was based upon these fundamental ideas: the supremacy of love and sympathy in all human relations; the civilizing influence of the imagination; and the necessity of the essential disinterestedness of one's motives. His ethics in their practical aspects grew out of the empirical, utilitarian philosophy of Mill and Bentham, and not out of the abstractions of Godwin.

Shelley's earliest *recorded* idea of love and marriage was expressed in *St. Irvyne* (1810). Near the end of the novel the villain, Nempere, endeavoring to seduce the heroine by sophistical arguments, said, "Why are we taught to believe that the union of two who love each other is wicked, unless authorized by certain rites and ceremonials, which certainly cannot change the tenor of sentiments which it is destined that these two people should entertain of each other?" To which Eloise replied: "It is, I suppose . . . because God has willed it so." Then, in the end the hero, Fitzeustace, who probably represents Shelley, insisted that "before we go to England, before my father will see us, it is necessary that we should be married . . . . I view it [matrimony] in the light that you do; I consider it an inhuman institution and incapable of furnishing that bond of union by which alone can intellect be conjoined; I regard it but as a chain, which, although it keeps the body bound, still leaves the soul unfettered; it is not so with love. But still, Eloise, to those who think like us, it is at all events harmless; it is but yielding to the prejudices of the world wherein we live and procuring moral expediency at a slight sacrifice of what we conceive to be right."

Shortly after he wrote this, Shelley's fiancée, Harriet Grove, deserted him because of his radical ideas on this and other subjects. He then swore eternal war upon the narrow and tyrannizing morality of the Christian Church—and he kept his vow.

To Hogg in a letter postmarked May 2, 1811, Shelley wrote: "Yes, *marriage* is hateful, detestable. A kind of ineffable, sickening disgust seizes my mind when I think of this most despotic, most unrequited fetter which prejudice has forged to confine its energies."

On June 21, 1811, to Hogg, Shelley wrote: "Matrimony . . . is it not the most horrible of all the means which the world has had recourse to to bind the noble to itself?" To the same correspondent on October 8, Shelley justified his submission to the marriage rites, insisting that until considerable improvement in morals has been brought about it would be advisable to maintain the institution of matrimony. That Shelley fully believed in this idea may be seen from his

23. This idea was the core of Godwin's moral system, but it was not original with him, for Spinoza, Hume, Bentham, and Paine had each in his individual way taken the same position. It should be noted that Shelley had read these authors, some of them before and others after, he had studied Godwin. I am convinced that Godwin's influence on Shelley has been overstressed. It was rather Godwin's persuasive way of expressing already well-known ideas that appealed to Shelley.

marriage to Harriet Westbrook on August 29, 1811. Three months later to Elizabeth Hitchener he wrote: "Marriage is monopolizing, exclusive, jealous; the tie which binds it bears the same relation to 'friendship in *which excess is lovely*' that the body does to the soul. Everything which relates simply to this clay-formed dungeon is comparatively despicable, and, in a state of perfectible society, could not be made the subjects of either virtue or vice." On July 7, 1812, to his mentor William Godwin, Shelley made it clear that he did not believe in promiscuous sexual relations. "Probably, in a regenerated state of society," he asserted, "agriculture and manufacture would be compatible with the most powerful intellect and most polished manners; probably delicacy, as it relates to sexual distinction, would disappear. Yet now, a plowboy can with difficulty acquire refinement of intellect; and promiscuous sexual intercourse under the present system of thinking would inevitably lead to consequences the most injurious to the happiness of mankind." Despite Shelley's own statements some critics continue to say that he believed in and practiced free love—in the ordinary sense of that term.[24]

It was August 17, 1812, that Shelley wrote to Sir James Henry Lawrence, author of *The Empire of the Nairs* (1800), concerning the principles of marriage and morals:

> Your *Empire of the Nairs,* which I read this spring, succeeded in making me a perfect convert to its doctrines. I then retained no doubts of the evils of marriage—Mrs. Wollstonecraft reasons too well for that; but I had been dull enough not to perceive the greatest argument against it, until developed in the Nairs, viz., prostitution both *legal* and *illegal.*
>
> I am a young man, not yet of age, and have been married a year to a woman younger than myself. Love seems inclined to stay in the prison, and my only reason for putting him in chains, while convinced of the unholiness of the act, was a knowledge that in the present state of society, if love is not thus villainously treated, she who is most loved will be treated worse by a mis-judging world. In short, seduction, which term could have no meaning in a rational society, has now a most tremendous one; the fictitious merit attached to chastity has made that a forerunner of the most terrible of ruins, which in Malabar would be a pledge of honor and homage. If there is any enormous and desolating crime of which I should shudder to be accused, it is seduction.

After nearly two years of warring against the shackles the church puts upon the minds and actions of men, Shelley again went on record about marriage and morals. This time it was more pronounced and more vindictive because he had been injured. In commenting on the line in *Queen Mab,* "Even love is sold," Shelley deplored the curtailment of love by positive institutions. Insisting that love cannot be so limited, and maintaining that marriage is the concern only of the interested parties, Shelley asserted that love withers under con-

24. See Peck's *Life of Shelley,* II:190. See White's *Shelley* on this subject. See Cameron, pp. 78-79, 120-121, 266-270, for a full discussion of this important topic. Compare letters in regard to Hogg's attempted seduction of Harriet in *New Shelley Letters,* pp. 54-69. See Shelley's letter to Hogg, August 15, 1811, in which he says that "I am become a perfect convert to matrimony"—primarily because of the sacrifice made by the woman.

straints, and that it is "most pure, perfect, and unlimited where its votaries live in confidence, equality, and unreserve . . . . A husband and wife ought to continue so long united as they love each other, and any law which should bind them to co-habitation for one moment after the decay of their affection would be a most intolerable tyranny." He went on to say that the unenlightened morality of the Christian religion greatly aggravated the evils of marriage. It was not even until lately, Shelley said, that mankind has admitted "that happiness is the sole end of the science of ethics, as of all other sciences . . . ."[25] The substance of this passage could derive from Mary Wollstonecraft, Godwin, Gibbon, Paine, or Hume. Indeed, it should be remembered that it was during this revolutionary period that the system of marriage like many other social institutions was subjected to severe criticism by many respectable people—and particularly by the liberals of the day.

In the review (1814) of *Prince Alexy Haimatoff,* a novel by his friend Hogg, Shelley openly condemned the loose morals advocated therein, saying, "The author appears to deem the loveless intercourse of brutal appetite a venial offence against delicacy and virtue . . . . It is our duty to protest against so pernicious and disgusting an opinion. No man can rise pure from the poisonous embraces of a prostitute, or sinless from the desolated hopes of a confiding heart. Whatever may be the claims of chastity, whatever the advantage of simple and pure affection, these ties, these benefits are of equal obligation to either sex. Domestic relations depend for their integrity upon a complete reciprocity of duties."

Bearing directly on this subject is the Fragment on marriage, perhaps a portion of the *Essay on Christianity.* The material is drawn probably from Hume's *Essay on Polygamy and Divorce,* and from Godwin's *Political Justice* (2: 499-514). Shelley stated that probably in prehistoric times men practised promiscuous concubinage and that there was no moral affection arising from such relations. The practice of considering women mere property in time became sanctioned and hallowed by law and custom, which to trespass upon was a crime. Such was Shelley's conception of the origin of the institution of matrimony.

Shelley and Harriet became estranged in the spring of 1814. Since he was convinced of her infidelity, and since there was small chance for a divorce in England, he deserted her; and on July 28, 1814, he and Mary Godwin fled to the Continent. On Harriet's death on December 15, 1816, Shelley and Mary, being free to marry, hastened to London and were united in matrimony on December 30. That day Shelley wrote to Clara Jane Clairmont that the ceremony was very "magical in its effect," and the Great Godwin smiled his approval!

It is clear from Shelley's recorded statements that he did not believe in free or promiscuous love, that he considered the marriage tie superfluous where there is genuine love, and that where love has flown, to compel two people to remain

25. This conception of love, although usually designated Platonic, would be more accurately called imaginative sympathy—an idea which dominated large sections of eighteenth century moral philosophy in England. For further light on this see Cameron, *op. cit.,* pp. 266, 404.

united, would be the vilest tyranny. Shelley advocated liberal divorce laws as a correction of the intolerable system of matrimony then prevailing in England. He maintained that the existing system, bad as it was, should be followed until the general moral tone of the nation had been improved. With all these facts known, it is difficult to see how the very damaging criticism of Shelley's sexual immorality can continue to be broadcast.[26]

So much for this aspect of the subject. What of his more general notions of morality?

Shelley asserted in *Proposals for an Association of Philanthropists* (1812) that man has a heart to feel, a brain to think, and a tongue to utter. The laws of his moral as of his physical nature are immutable, as is everything of nature. "A man must have a right to do a thing before he can have a *duty*, [and] conscience is a government before which all others sink into nothingness."

In *An Address to the Irish People* (1812) are several moral axioms which Shelley lived by—among them are: "Never do evil that good may come"; "Be free and be happy, but first be wise and good"; "Liberty and happiness are founded upon virtue and justice"; "Temperance, sobriety, charity, and independence will give you virtue"; "It is vain to hope for any liberty and happiness without reason and virtue."

In *The Letter to Lord Ellenborough* (1812), defending Daniel I. Eaton, publisher of part of Paine's *The Age of Reason,* Shelley's moral principles are clearly and vigorously set forth. He maintained that there are (in the Platonic sense) no absolute and immutable principles of conduct, and with Locke, Godwin, and Hume that moral standards are derived *solely from experience*. Moral laws like civil laws originate in the customs and manners of the age. Since the basic concepts of morality inhere in our ideas of pain and pleasure, it is possible to establish the principles of morals through sound reasoning. This is, of course, pure Locke. Shelley was here plainly refuting the Platonists and the eighteenth century moralists who maintain that the principles of morals are self-evident and are archetypal in their nature. Like Adam Smith, Shelley rejected the notion that "the moral sense" was divinely established and also like Smith he grounded his principles of morals in sympathy and love. In this respect Locke, Smith, and Shelley are at variance with Hume, who flatly denied that moral principles can be derived from reason, or as Locke says, mathematically demonstrated. Shelley wrote in the *Letter:*

> What moral truth is spoken of with irreverence or ridicule in the book which he [Eaton] published? Morality, or the duty of a man and a citizen, is founded on the relations which arise from the association of human beings, and which vary with the circumstances produced by the different states of this association. This duty in similar situations must be precisely the same in all ages and nations. The opinion contrary to this has arisen from a supposition that the will of God is the source or criterion of morality; it is plain that the utmost exertion of Omnipotence could not cause that to be virtuous which actually is vicious.

26. See especially Cameron, *The Young Shelley,* pp. 78-79, 120-121, 266-270, 331-332, 350.

Shortly after writing this *Letter,* Shelley, then only twenty years old, in a Note on Necessity in *Queen Mab* (1813) even more daringly set forth his ideas concerning morality. Following the argument of Holbach in *Système de la Nature*,[27] he declared that the doctrine of Necessity is as applicable to the moral as it is to the physical universe, for "Motive is to voluntary action in the human mind what cause is to effect in the material universe." He went on: "The precise character and motives of any man on any occasion being given, the moral philosopher could predict his action with as much certainty as the natural philosopher could predict the effects of the mixture of any particular chemical substances."

Wishing to make it clear that morals are subject to the principle of Necessity, Shelley said that "history, politics, morals, criticism, all grounds of reasonings, all principles of science alike assume the truth of the doctrine of Necessity; . . . the doctrine of Necessity tends to introduce a great change in the established notions of morality, and utterly to destroy religion . . . . But utility is morality; that which is incapable of producing happiness is useless . . . . At the same time, the doctrine of Necessity does not in the least diminish our disapprobation of vice.[28]

It is evident that this idea of Necessity introduces a new conception of the absolutes—one based upon the immutable laws of nature, and discoverable by reason. But we must beware of identifying this conception with the Platonic Ideas, much less with the Platonic World-Soul, revived by the Cambridge Platonists, particularly Cudworth, under the mystical concept of the Plastic Medium in which all modifications of the physical world move and have meaning. At the same time there was one current of English thought in respect to morality which linked directly with the idea of Necessity as propounded by Shelley and other adherents of that system. It sprang directly from Locke and culminated in Hume. It seems to me that Shelley under the withering blows of Hume's logic somewhat modified his early view of Necessity and accepted the notion that moral standards are grounded in ethics. But Shelley never fully repudiated his belief in the principle of Necessity; he merely shifted his position and substituted sympathy or "Platonic love" for the more physical force which dominated his earlier thinking. Indeed there was no radical change in his early philosophy: his ethics, his principles of morals, his religion remained essentially what they were in 1811.

Shelley declared in *A Refutation of Deism* (1813) that the morality set up by the Christian religion was narrow and unenlightened, that only those axioms of morals it borrowed from Greece and India were worthy of our regard. "But the purest and most elevated lessons of morality must remain nugatory, the most probable inducements to virtue must fail of their effect, so long as the

27. See Chapters IV, VI and IX. For a similar position see Godwin's *Political Justice* 1.361-383 (edited by F. E. L. Priestley, 1946), and Spinoza (*The Philosophy of Spinoza,* Modern Library, edited by Joseph Ratner, 1927), pp. 191-210.

28. Shelley is here following in a general way the philosophy of Bentham, Godwin, Spinoza, Mill, and Adam Smith. But his chief source is Holbach: see *Système,* 1.11-47, especially.

slightest weight is attached to that dogma which is the vital essence of revealed religion"—the doctrine of reward and punishment.[29]

In *A Defence of Poetry* (1820) Shelley stated his belief in the importance of high moral principles for the welfare of the individual as of the nation. He asserted in regard to the moral improvement exerted by poetry that ethical science arranges the elements which poetry has created and propounds schemes for the improvement of civil and domestic life. It is not for want of admirable moral precepts that men hate and deceive and war against one another, but it is to the dearth of *sympathy* and of *love* in human affairs. We have forgotten or have never known that the great secret of morals is *love*. "A man to be greatly good," said Shelley, "must imagine intensely and comprehensively; he must put himself in the place of another and of many others; the pains and pleasures of his species must become his own. The great instrument of morals is the imagination."

Then follows that notable passage on the moral and spiritual value of the great poets and artists:

> The exertions of Locke, Hume, Gibbon, Voltaire, Rousseau, and their disciples in favor of oppressed and deluded humanity are entitled to the gratitude of mankind. Yet it is easy to calculate the degree of moral and intellectual improvement which the world would have exhibited had they never lived . . . . But it exceeds all imagination to conceive what would have been the moral condition of the world if neither Dante, Petrarch, Boccaccio, Chaucer, Shakespeare, Calderon, Bacon, nor Milton had ever existed; if Raphael and Michael Angelo had never been born; if the Hebrew poetry had never been translated; if a revival of the study of Greek literature had never taken place; if no monument of ancient sculpture had been handed down to us; and if the poetry of the religion of the ancient world had been extinguished together with its belief.

But it was in his *A Treatise on Morals* that Shelley stated accurately and explicitly his practical principles of morals. Following Hume, Bentham, Godwin, and Smith, Shelley asserted that the greatest happiness for the greatest number of individuals is the ideal of moral science. He then defined moral science as "the doctrine of the *voluntary* action of man as a sentient and social being." Love, he insisted, is the basis of any high moral system; sympathy aroused by a vivid imagination is the mainspring to action. Shelley went on in the language of Spinoza, Locke, and Hume to define good and evil: "That is called good which produces pleasure; that is called evil which produces pain." In his moral system benevolence and justice are the constituent parts of virtue, which is the ultimate goal of all living. With Shaftesbury, Butler, and others Shelley held that benevolent propensities are inherent in the human mind, and that thus we are *impelled* to seek the happiness of others. Shelley then gave a detailed statement of the application of benevolence and justice in his system of morals. It will be noted that he again denounced the Christian idea of morals as narrow and selfish, based as it is, on fear and obedience and duty—words which should

29. For a similar position see the *Essay on the Revival of Literature* (c. 1815). Compare Gibbon's position in the famous fifteenth chapter of the *Decline and Fall* on this idea of the Christian religion. See also Spinoza's *Tractatus* and Paine's *Age of Reason*, Part Two.

never occur in a system of morals. What, then, are the words which give meaning to morality? They are love, sympathy, justice, benevolence, virtue, and disinterested motives. They are the keystones of all righteous living, and together they constitute the solid rock upon which the moral reformer must build.

Shelley's Political Ideas

Throughout his life Shelley had an intense interest in government, his primary concern being how the state could best contribute to the happiness of the people as a whole; consequently, he was in the van of every movement for reform. He maintained that politics and morals should be integrated, for a government can rise no higher than the morals of the nation. With Rousseau and others Shelley believed that all men are created equal—before the law—and like Rousseau he contended that designing men had destroyed that equality.[30]

In a letter to Elizabeth Hitchener, July 25, 1811, after stating as an incontrovertible fact that men were created equal, Shelley went on to advocate equal, or at least a more equable, distribution of wealth. He did not expect immediate reform or redress of grievances; but he was content with laying the foundations for a gradual, progressive amelioration of society. To Godwin, on June 3, 1812, Shelley stated that "before I was a republican [democrat], Athens appeared to me the model of governments; but afterwards, Athens bore in my mind the same relation to perfection that Great Britain did to Athens." And to the same correspondent on July 29, he expressed his deep abhorrence of oppressive government. Now a determined republican, in its full French significance, he was even more impatient with the corruption everywhere evident in the existing English government.

In *An Address to the Irish People* (1812) Shelley maintained, to paraphrase his words, that no act of a national assembly can make anything wrong which was not wrong before; that "it cannot change virtue and truth, and for a very plain reason: they are unchangeable." He went on to say that "an Act passed in the British Parliament to take away the rights of Catholics to act in the National Assembly does not really take them away. It merely prevents them from doing it by force . . . . But force is not the test of truth; they will never have recourse to violence who acknowledge no other rule of behavior but virtue and justice . . . ."

Then borrowing directly from Paine's *Common Sense,* and not from Godwin as is usually stated, Shelley continued: "The benefit of the governed is the origin and meaning of government . . . . The goodness of government consists in the happiness of the governed . . . . Government is an evil; it is only the thoughtlessness and vices of men that make it a necessary evil. When all men are good and wise, government will of itself decay . . . . Society is produced by the wants, government by the wickedness, and a state of just and happy equality by the improvement and reason of man. It is vain to hope for any liberty and

30. For a detailed analysis of Shelley's political   philosophy, see Cameron, *op. cit.,* pp. 51-53, 69-70, 117-118, 149-150, 153-155, 262-263.

happiness without reason and virtue, for where there is no virtue there will be crime, and where there is crime, there must be government. . . . But I do not consider that they will or can immediately happen; their arrival will be gradual, and it all depends upon yourselves how soon or how late these great changes will happen. . . . I conclude with the words of Lafayette. . . : 'For a nation to love liberty it is sufficient that she knows it; to be free it is sufficient that she wills it.' " This is a complete refutation of those critics who see Shelley as radical reformer and bent upon bringing about reform by force or by revolution.[31]

In the same year (1812) Shelley published *Proposals for an Association of Philanthropists,* the primary purpose of which was to enlighten the people and to correct abuses of power. In this pamphlet Shelley reiterated his belief in the fundamental principles of government:

> Government can have no rights; it is a delegation for the purpose of securing them to others. Man becomes a subject of government, not that he may be in a worse but that he may be in a better state than that of unorganized society. The strength of government is the happiness of the governed. All government existing for the happiness of others is just only so far as it exists by their consent, and useful only so far as it operates to their well-being. Constitution is to government what government is to law.

And how true are his words for us today when he continued: "A political or religious system may burn and imprison those who investigate its principles; but it is an invariable proof of their falsehood and hollowness." Then Shelley made a plea for freedom of speech and of press, insisting that in reality no government has the right to limit freedom:

> Man has a right to feel, to think, and to speak, nor can any act of legislature destroy that right. He will feel, he must think, and he ought to give utterance to those thoughts and feelings with the readiest sincerity and the strictest candor. A man must have a right to do a thing before he can have a duty; this right must permit before his duty can enjoin him to any act. Any law is bad which attempts to make it criminal to do what the plain dictates within the breast of every man tell him he ought to do.[32]

By 1816 Shelley was definitely convinced that a great political change was imminent in England. The popular party had gained strength, and it appeared, to his great satisfaction, that reform might be brought about peacefully.

In 1817 in a pamphlet entitled *A Proposal for Putting Reform to the Vote throughout the Kingdom,* Shelley was very specific as to what ought to be done in a sane and peaceful way to reform the government before a revolution overthrew the whole structure. He said that since the Commons does not represent the people, the only question to be settled at once was whether the people ought either to take matters into their own hands and legislate for themselves or to be governed by laws and impoverished by taxes imposed by an unrepresenta-

31. On November 20, 1816, in a letter to Lord Byron, Shelley reiterated his hope that if reform came, it would be gradual and without bloodshed.

32. The substance of this as of the preceding quotation Shelley could have found in Paine's *Common Sense* and *The Rights of Man.*

tive assembly.[33] Shelley was for *direct* action here, and called for the restoration to the people of their rightful sovereignty. But he asked, Do the people really wish those rights restored? The only way to ascertain the people's will in this matter is to put it to the vote. He then outlined a plan by which this desired end might be achieved.

As every one knows, Shelley had an exalted notion of the legislator, in his abstract purity. This idea he emphasized in *A Philosophical View of Reform* (1819-20) and later repeated in the last sentence in *A Defence of Poetry* (1820) where he called the poets "the unacknowledged *legislators* of the world."

Shelley's strong social sense was everywhere evident whenever he contemplated the political condition of man. He insisted that the laws of a nation should be mild and humane, aiming not at punishment for its own sake but at the education of the offender. Prevention of crime, in his opinion, was more important than punishment of the criminal. In the *Essay on the Punishment of Death* Shelley advocated the abolition of capital punishment as cruel and ineffectual. He called for the re-education of the criminal as well as of society; in this conception Shelley was ultra-modern, a forerunner of Lewis Edward Lawes, Warden of Sing-Sing. "It is almost a proverbial remark," he wrote, "that those nations in which the penal code has been particularly mild have been distinguished from all others by the rarity of crime."

It is not surprising that Shelley, admirer of Jesus that he was, advocated a communistic scheme for the distribution of wealth and power. He wrote in the *Essay on Christianity:*

> In proportion to the love existing among men, so will be the community of property and power. Among true and real friends, all is common; and were ignorance and envy and superstition banished from the world, all mankind would be friends. The only perfect and genuine republic is that which comprehends every living being.

The wedding of morals and social (political) ideals was characteristic of Shelley's thinking as it was that of Jesus. But to the so-called realist such thinking is absurdly romantic—to which Shelley might retort, "See to what an unbearable condition the realist, who has prevailed in politics and in business, has brought the world." Shelley insisted that before man can be free, and equal, and truly wise, he must cast aside the chains of habit and superstition; he must strip sensuality of its pomp, and selfishness of its excuses, and contemplate actions and objects as they really are. He will discover the wisdom of universal love. Like Jesus, too, Shelley had a profound sense of social justice. Paraphrasing Jesus, he said: "Clothing and food and shelter are not, as they suppose, the true end of human life, but only certain means, to be valued in proportion to their subserviency to that end. These means it is right of every human being to possess, and that in the same degree." He went on to say: "The system of equality was attempted, after Jesus Christ's death, to be carried into effect

---

33. See the fragment *On The Game Laws*, Appendix C, for a similar charge against the government, as well as *A Philosophical View of Reform* and the *Two Fragments on Reform*.

by his followers. 'They that believed had all things common; they sold their possessions and goods and parted them to all men, as every man had need.' " [Acts 2.44-45.]

Shelley closed his *Essay on Christianity* by pointing out that the moral improvement of man must precede political advancement. And again he reverted to the doctrine of the benevolent stewardship over property:

> It was a circumstance of no moment that the first adherents of the system of Jesus Christ cast their property into a common stock . . . . Every man in proportion to his virtue considers himself with respect to the great community of mankind as the steward and guardian of the interests in the property which he chances to possess. Every man in proportion to his wisdom sees the manner in which it is his duty to employ the resources which the consent of mankind has entrusted to his discretion . . . . So gradually and inevitably is the progress of equality accommodated to the progress of wisdom and of virtue among mankind.
>
> Meanwhile, some benefit has not failed to flow from the imperfect attempts which have been made to erect a system of equal rights to property and power upon the basis of arbitrary institutions. They have undoubtedly, in every case, from the instability of their formation, failed.

So much for the general remarks about the political and social thought of Shelley. It was in 1819 that he made a serious and formal attempt to state more specifically his views on reform in his essay *A Philosophical View of Reform*. After a cursory sketch of ancient governments, as well as those of the Middle Ages, and after paying glowing tribute to the government of the United States of America, he concentrated on the necessity of reform of the contemporary English government. Shelley saw as all the friends of freedom saw that the condition of the people following the Napoleonic wars was intolerable. There was untold suffering among the laboring groups, and even the majority of the middle class felt the pinch of hunger. Bread lines were common; unrest was general. Speculation on the markets by the rich and the privileged was rife, resulting in ruinous inflation for the nation. The public debt, incurred largely to finance the war and to maintain in luxury the old landed gentry as well as the new mercantile aristocracy which the war had created, had reached unheard of heights, and taxes to pay interest on this huge debt were imposed on the poorer classes. These conditions occasioned widespread discontent among the masses, and bloody riots in the mill districts were not uncommon.

Shelley from far away Italy, but always in close touch with developments in his own country, was not alone in thinking that rebellion was near. It was rebellion that Shelley sincerely wished to forestall, for as we have seen, he distrusted the use of force in effectuating reform. So, he advised first of all the method of peaceful resistance and of slow, gradual reform. This failing, he would range himself with those who advocated open rebellion against the oppressors of mankind. Shelley steadfastly maintained his faith in the people to accept gradual amelioration. But as people for the most part are ignorant of the cause and therefore of the cure of their unhappy state, they must first be educated in the ways of political action. To this end, Shelley believed that societies similar to those that existed in America and in France during and immediately following the revolutions ought to be formed to enlighten the people as to their rights and duties as citizens of a free country.

What, then, are some of the principal specific reforms, expressed or implied, which Shelley advocated for the immediate improvement of the existing conditions as well as for the betterment of remote ages? He would abolish the unholy alliance of church and state; he would *humanize* punishment for all sorts of crimes, doing away completely with capital punishment and setting about a revision of the criminal code and a re-education of those who show criminal inclination; he "would make justice cheap, certain and speedy, and extend the institution of juries to every possible occasion of jurisprudence"; Shelley would abolish the national debt, because it was contracted by the rich and privileged classes for their own advancement; he would disband the standing army since it was a tool for tyranny in the hands of the oppressors; he would, with every possible regard to the existing interests of the holder, abolish sinecures of all descriptions; he "would abolish tithes and make all religions, all forms of opinion respecting the origin and government of the universe, equal in the eyes of the law."

Strange as it may seem, Shelley would limit suffrage until the electorate are better educated politically. Thus for the present, he would exclude women from the suffrage and all men not possessing a nominal amount of property. But these limitations on suffrage would be temporary and for expediency only.

The immediate concern of the friends of reform should be the reformation of the House of Commons to make it truly representative of the people. It should be elected by direct ballot by the people and for the people. Shelley said, "For if the House of Peers be a permanent representation of the privileged classes . . . while the House of Commons be not chosen by the mass of the population, what becomes of that democratic element upon the presence of which it has been supposed that the waning superiority of England over the surrounding nations has depended?" Shelley went on to predict that if the existing government should compel the nation to take the task of reform into its own hands, one of the obvious consequences of such a circumstance would be the abolition of monarchy and aristocracy. In case the government should compel the people to revolt to establish a representative assembly in defiance of the existing government a bloody revolution might follow. "No friend of mankind and of his country can desire that such a crisis should suddenly arrive."

Believing as he did in the unlimited freedom of the individual, it is surprising to find Shelley advocating cautious, conservative procedure in extending freedom to the masses. Not until the people were educated to govern themselves would he relax the power of the state. While he considered political government a necessary evil, he believed that chaos or anarchy would follow its abolition. Shelley's primary concern was the happiness of the greatest number of people, and any government which promoted this ideal was to that extent a good government. He held with Locke that government should exist only by the consent of the governed; with Rousseau that the least government is the best government; and with Paine that government is necessary so long as there are wicked men. Perhaps the most notable fact about the politics of this "radical" reformer is its utter practicality. Many, if not most of his ideals, have been realized in fact. That the reforms which he advocated have been long in coming is perfectly consonant with his political philosophy. Where then is the impractical dreamer about whom we have heard so much? The answer is short and simple: he never really existed.

Shelley's Theory of Poetry

Even as early as 1811 Shelley had come to the conclusion that art, particularly poetry, should have a moral foundation. But *mere didacticism was his abhorrence*.

Shelley left one essay on the philosophy and nature of poetry, but that is not a formal treatise. There are, in addition, scattered through his letters, essays, and prefaces to his poems several statements on the subject. These we shall now examine with no effort to distinguish between his theory and his practice. Shelley was in his youth fascinated by the Gothic romance, and his early verse shows unmistakable influences of the ballad of the Lewis-Scott school and of the sentimentality of the Gray-Goldsmith group. But these influences soon gave way to those of the more liberal and thoughtful group of writers. The Gothic romance was succeeded by the Novel of Purpose of Bage, Holcroft, and Godwin, and the moralizing poetry by the didacticism of Southey. *The Curse of Kehama* became his favorite poem, and Miss Owenson's *The Missionary* his favorite novel.

To Elizabeth Hitchener on June 5, 1811, Shelley wrote: "My opinion is that all poetical beauty ought to be subordinate to the inculcated moral . . . that metaphorical language ought to be a pleasing vehicle for useful and momentous instruction." Thereafter both his poetry and his prose were largely metaphysical and moral, though not didactic. Again in a letter to Byron, September 29, 1816, he asked, "What would the human race have been if Homer, or Shakespeare had never written? Or if any false modesty or mistake of their powers had withheld them from consummating those unequalled achievements of mind by which we are so deeply benefited?"

An examination of Shelley's literary development will show that the consideration of *form* was to him of secondary importance while *substance* or *idea* was the prime essential. Thus in Shelley's mind Plato and Bacon were, by virtue of the poetry of their ideas, by the power of their language, by their clear-cut imagery, and by the moral insight of their writings, poets of the first order.

Important aids to the understanding of Shelley's philosophy of composition are his literary judgments. We learn much, for instance, about his conception of the place of form in poetry from his letter to Hunt, December 8, 1816, in which he showed his independence of rules for composing poetry. "The *story* of the poem [*Rimini*] has an interest of a very common and irresistible character, though it appears to me that you have subjected yourself to the same rules in the composition which fetter your genius and diminish the effect of the conception." Again we see his minimizing the importance of rules, in his letter to Lord Byron on July 9, 1817: "I have read *Manfred* with the greatest admiration. The same freedom from common rules that marked the 3rd canto and *Chillon* is visible here; and it was that which all your earlier productions, except *Lara,* wanted."

That Shelley was not, however, indifferent to form and style in his poetry may be seen from a remark about *Laon and Cythna* in his letter to Byron, September 24, 1817: "It is in the style and for the same object as *Queen Mab,* but interwoven with a story of human passion, and composed with more attention to the refinement and accuracy of language, and the connection of its parts." Again concerning the same poem, Shelley wrote to a publisher on October 13, 1817: "I am conscious, indeed, that some of the concluding cantos, when 'the plot thickens' and human passions are brought into more critical situations or development are written with more energy and clearness; and that to see a work of which unity is one of the qualifications aimed at by the author in a disjoined state is in a certain degree unfavorable to the general impression."

In the Preface to *Laon and Cythna* (1817) are several pertinent remarks on the nature and content of great poetry. Shelley insists that metrical language, the ethereal combinations of the fancy, the rapid and subtle transition of human passion should be employed in poetry. He "would only awaken the feelings, so that the reader should see the beauty of true virtue . . . . It is the business of the Poet," he said, "to communicate to others the pleasure and the enthusiasm arising out of those images and feelings in the vivid presence of which within his own mind consists at once his inspiration and his reward."

On December 11, 1817, in a letter to Godwin, Shelley deplored Godwin's misinterpretation of his literary powers in *Laon and Cythna*. "I feel that the sentiments were true, not assumed. And in this have I long believed that my power consists in sympathy and that part of the imagination which relates to sentiment and contemplation. I am formed, if for anything not in common with the herd of mankind, to apprehend minute and remote distinctions of feelings whether relative to external nature, or the living beings which surround us, and to communicate the conceptions which result from considering either the moral or the material universe as a whole."

Shelley found it difficult to express to Hunt his disgust with his friend's banalities. Of Hunt's *The Nymphs* Shelley wrote on March 22, 1818: "It is truly *poetical,* in the intense and emphatic sense of the word. If six hundred miles were not between us, I should say what a pity that [the word] *glib* was not omitted, and that the poem is not as faultless as it is beautiful."

When the Shelleys reached Italy in April, 1818, they set about learning the language by reading the great Italian writers. In a letter to the Gisbornes,

July 16, 1818, we gain considerable insight into Shelley's literary ideas. In regard to the poetic ability of Ariosto, he remarked:

> Where is the gentle seriousness, the delicate sensibility, the calm and sustained energy without which true greatness cannot be? He is so cruel, too, in his descriptions; his most prized virtues are vices almost without disguise. He constantly vindicates and embellishes revenge in its grossest form—the most deadly superstition that ever infested the world. How different from the tender and solemn enthusiasm of Petrarch—or even the delicate moral sensibility of Tasso, though somewhat obscured by an assumed and artificial style.

We have seen so far that Shelley was primarily interested in the substance, the thought, of a poem, but the following letter to Peacock, August 16, 1818, shows again his concern with form: "Its structure [*Rosalind and Helen*] is slight and aery; its subject ideal. The meter corresponds with the spirit of the poem and varies with the flow of feeling." There is a passage in the same letter, however, which stresses the supreme importance of the thought and spirit of a work of art:

> What a wonderful passage there is in *Phaedrus* the beginning, I think, of one of the speeches of Socrates—in praise of poetic madness, and in definition of what poetry is, and how a man becomes a poet. Every man who lives in this age and desires to write poetry ought, as a preservative against the false and narrow systems of criticism which every poetical empiric vents, to impress himself with this sentence, if he would be numbered among those to whom may apply this proud, though sublime, expression of Tasso: "non c'è in mondo chi merita nome di creatore, che Dio ed il Poeta." [There is no other in the world worthy the name of Creator but God and the Poet. See Footnote 1 in the *Essay on Life*.]

In the preface to *Prometheus Unbound* (1819) Shelley gave the reader an accurate and revealing conception of the poet and his art. Here he emphasized the form, the spirit, and the substance of poetry: "[Poetry] creates, but it creates by combination and representation . . . . A poet is the combined product of such internal powers as modify the nature of others, and of such external influences as excite and sustain these powers; he is not one, but both . . . .

"Didactic poetry is my abhorrence; nothing can be equally well expressed in prose that is not tedious and supererogatory in verse. My purpose has hitherto been simply to familiarize the highly refined imagination of the more select classes of moral excellence, aware that until the mind can love, and admire, and trust, and hope, and endure, reasoned principles of moral conduct are seeds cast upon the highway of life which the unconscious passenger tramples into dust, although they would bear the harvest of his happiness."

And finally in the preface to *The Cenci* (1819) Shelley gave a detailed analysis of his method of dramatic composition:

In a dramatic composition the imagery and the passion should interpenetrate one another, the former being reserved simply for the full development and illustration of the latter. Imagination is as the immortal God which should assume flesh for the redemption of mortal passion. It is thus that the most remote and the most familiar imagery may alike be fit for dramatic purposes when employed in the illustration of strong feeling, which raises what is low and levels to the apprehension that which is lofty, casting over all the shadow of its own greatness.

He added that he was in perfect agreement with Wordsworth and others who insisted that the language of poetry should be the familiar language of men. "But it must be the real language of men in general and not of any particular class to whose society the writer happens to belong."[34]

In November, 1819, Shelley in a letter to Hunt, although appreciative of the form, again emphasized the substance and the spirit as the essence of all great poetry:

I speak rather of the *Nymphs* than the *Story of Rimini,* because the former is in my judgment more intensely and perfectly a poem in the sense in which Tasso speaks of poetry: "Non c'e creatore fourche Iddio ed il Poeta." The latter affects the passions and searches the understanding more completely, but the former appeals to the imagination, who is the master of them both, their God, and the Spirit by which they live and are.

While Shelley considered Wordsworth a great, and Byron the greatest, poet of the age, he looked upon Keats as essentially a poet of one poem—*Hyperion,* but that poem he ranked among the finest of all times. In his letter to Keats, July 27, 1820, are several clues to Shelley's ideas of what constitutes great poetry: "I have lately read your *Endymion* again and ever with a new sense of the treasures of poetry it contains, though treasures poured forth with indistinct profusion . . . . In poetry I have sought to avoid system and mannerism; I wish those who excel me in genius would pursue the same plan." To Marianne Hunt, late in 1820, Shelley wrote in praise of Keats's *Hyperion,* but of his other poetry, he said:

His other things are imperfect enough and, what is worse, written in the bad sort of style which is becoming fashionable among those who fancy that they are imitating Hunt and Wordsworth . . . . His indecencies too, both against sexual nature and against human nature in general, sit very awkwardly upon him . . . . In Lord Byron all this has an analogy with the general system of his character, and the wit and poetry which surround, hide with their light the darkness of the thing itself. They contradict it even; they prove that the strength and beauty of human nature can survive and conquer all that appears most inconsistent with it. But for a writer to be at once filthy and dull is a crime against gods, men, and columns.

34. The idea in this sentence is a direct reflection of Coleridge's strictures on Wordsworth's poetic theories.

In November he wrote to Gifford in behalf of Keats and in highest commendation of *Hyperion:* "This piece is surely in the very highest style of poetry. I speak impartially, for the canons of taste to which Keats has conformed in his other compositions are the very reverse of my own."

Although Shelley considered Lord Byron's the greatest poetry of his time, he could see its flaws. To Mary he wrote August 7, 1821: "We [Byron and Shelley] talked a great deal of poetry and such matters last night; and as usual differed and, I think, more than ever. He affects to patronize a system of criticism for the production of mediocrity, and although all his fine poems and passages have been produced in defiance of this system, yet I recognize the pernicious effects of it in the *Doge of Venice."*

There remains to be considered his one essay on the subject of poetry. Shelley began *A Defence of Poetry* (1820) by distinguishing between reason and imagination, concluding that while they are equal partners in the mental life, "reason is to imagination as the instrument to the agent, as the body to the spirit, as the shadow to the substance." He defined poetry as "the expression of the imagination." Thus poetry is the *agent,* the *spirit,* the *substance* of reality. The poet is he who through the activity of the imagination discovers the indestructible order in the universe, finds harmony in the chaos of the heterogeneous around us.[35] Possessing this insight and moved by this sense of harmony, he clothes his thoughts in imperishable *form* be it music, sculpture, painting, or poetry; by giving concrete expression to this order the poet becomes a *creator.*

It will be noted that Shelley is primarily concerned with the *spirit* and the substance of the poet's creation, and not its *form.* Thus any work of art, or of thought, is great in so far as it embodies the harmony, the order, the beauty, which the happiest and best minds discover in the best and happiest moments. In such a conception of poetry, the language, the color, the forms are but the materials, the instruments of poetry. In this respect exalted passages of "prose" are really poetry. It must be understood by this, however, that Shelley was not careless as to the form of his poetry. Perhaps no one took more pains with his periods, or with the order and the rhythm and the imagery in his verse. His great lyrics as well as the longer poems, in the main, show his consummate craftsmanship. Sensing the nature of rhythm and order in the universe, indeed in all forms of life, Shelley was able to communicate that rhythm and harmony to his poetry. He maintained that in order to be a poet, one must "apprehend the true and beautiful—in a word, the good which exists in the relations subsisting" between existence and perception, and between perception and expression. Since poetry awakens our sense of love and beauty, and since "the great secret of morals is love . . . and since the great instrument of moral good is the imagination," the poets become the great moral leaders, "the unacknowledged legislators of the world."

35. For an informative discussion of the function of the imagination in English Romantic poetry, see *The Romantic Imagination* by C. M. Bowra, (Harvard University Press, 1949). However, I cannot agree with the author that Shelley endeavored through the imagination to find "some transcendental order which explains the world of appearances."

Conclusion

As we look over this brief sketch of the growth of Shelley's mind, the thing that strikes us most forcefully is the remarkable consistency of his ideas from his youthful to his mature thought. There was development, but there was no significant change. What development there was lay in the gradual and careful pruning and logical modification. Shelley was often tentative in expressing his ideas, and when convinced of his error, he was courageous in admitting mistakes and in changing his point of view. His was the mind of a scientist in search for truth.

What is perhaps the most pronounced fact in Shelley's mental growth was the solid strength of his early ideas. His youthful conceptions of God, Jesus, Christianity, morals, politics, and poetry were so grounded in the then-known scientific and historical facts that Shelley found small occasion to modify those ideas significantly. To picture Shelley as turning away from his early scientific and humanitarian point of view, with its clear-cut emphasis on the reality of the world around us, to a vague and elusive Platonism with its stress on the unreality of this life, is, I believe, to misinterpret Shelley's ideas and bring confusion worse confounded.

Shelley's mind grew, but it grew in breadth and in depth, and not by radical change from one position to another. In early youth, for instance, he examined the tenets of institutional Christianity and found them wanting; he then accepted the current eighteenth century religious philosophy of deism, and after a careful study of its principles, he rejected it in June, 1811, when he was not yet nineteen years old. Shortly thereafter he found a comfortable berth within the elusive bounds of naturalistic pantheism, where he remained the rest of his life. In other aspects of his thought—in morals, in politics, and in metaphysics—Shelley modified his ideas, but only imperceptibly. Perhaps the most radical change was in his ethical principles. Here he gradually moved from the prevailing eighteenth century conception of the absolute, fixed, and discoverable principles of morals to the nineteenth, or even the twentieth century, conception of morals as purely relative in value and as based in utility. Love, or sympathy for one's fellows, was for him the basis of the moral life, and the imagination was the civilizing force in society. Given knowledge of the facts of nature and good will toward all men, Shelley believed that love, made active by a sympathetic imagination, would usher in the Good Life. Shelley has frequently been referred to as a modern Prometheus or a latter-day prophet—with what justification the prose in this volume will bear witness. Certainly, the dominant theme in his prose as in his poetry is the prophetic assurance that mankind can achieve the Good Life only by the wedding of knowledge and love or human sympathy. This thought he powerfully expressed in the closing lines of *Prometheus Unbound*:

> To suffer woes which Hope thinks infinite;
> To forgive wrongs darker than death or night;
> To defy Power, which seems omnipotent;

> To love, and bear; to hope till Hope creates
> From its own wreck the thing it contemplates;
>   Neither to change, nor falter, nor repent;
> This, like thy glory, Titan, is to be
> Good, great and joyous, beautiful and free;
> This is alone Life, Joy, Empire, and Victory.

This is the key to Shelley's every thought and deed. This is the ethical message of his greatest prose and poetry. Shelley at all times emphasized the fact that, in his own words, "We have more moral, political, and historical wisdom than we know how to reduce into practice; we have more scientific and economic knowledge than can be accommodated to the just distribution of the produce which it multiplies." After a careful study and an understanding of Shelley's prose, the student will find in the beautiful imagery of his poetry the same ideas; Shelley has merely changed the vehicle of expression from a matter-of-fact prose to that of highly figurative poetry. Indeed Shelley's prose is *the trumpet of a prophecy* heard in the soul-animating strains of his poetry.

ESSAYS

THE NECESSITY OF ATHEISM

[On the title-page of the pamphlet is a quotation from Bacon's *De Augmentis Scientiarum* which reads: "Quod clara et perspicua demonstratione careat pro vero habere mens omnino nequit humana."[1] This is followed by an "advertisement," stating the author's purpose and asking for a rebuttal: "*As a love of truth is the only motive which actuates the Author of this little tract, he earnestly entreats that those of his readers who may discover any deficiency in his reasoning, or may be in possession of proofs which his mind could never obtain, would offer them, together with their objections to the Public, as briefly, as methodically, as plainly as he has taken the liberty of doing. Thro' deficiency of proof,* AN ATHEIST."

The Necessity of Atheism was written sometime between the Christmas holidays, 1810, and February 9, 1811, when it was advertised as "speedily" to be published. It appeared on February 13.

This temperate and calmly reasoned pamphlet at once aroused a storm of protest which in the end resulted in the burning of all undistributed copies and the expulsion of Shelley and his friend Hogg from the University. Some Shelley scholars maintain—unsuccessfully, I believe—that this work is the result of joint authorship of Hogg and Shelley.[2]

In the essay Shelley does little more than restate the well-known arguments of England's two great philosophers, John Locke and David Hume. He does not here, nor did he ever, flatly deny the existence of God. He merely asserts that with existing data and the known laws of logic, the existence of God cannot be proved. An examination of the letters of this period will convince the most skeptical of Shelley's sincerity in asking for a straightforward rebuttal of his arguments. There is no evidence that he was merely bear-baiting the bishops.]

A close examination of the validity of the proofs adduced to support any proposition has ever been allowed to be the only sure way of attaining truth, upon the advantages of which it is unnecessary to descant; our knowledge of the existence of a Deity is a subject of such importance that it cannot be too minutely investigated; in consequence of this conviction, we proceed briefly and impartially to examine the proofs which have been adduced. It is necessary first to consider the nature of Belief.

When a proposition is offered to the mind, it perceives the agreement or disagreement of the ideas of which it is composed. A perception of their agreement is termed belief; many obstacles frequently prevent this perception from being immediate; these the mind attempts to remove in order that the perception may be distinct. The mind is active in the investigation, in order to perfect the state of perception, which is passive; the investigation being confused with the perception has induced many falsely to imagine that the mind is active in belief, that belief is an act of volition, in consequence of which

1. "The human mind cannot in any way accept as true that which lacks a clear and obvious demonstration."

2. See F. L. Jones's article in *PMLA*, 52: 423-426, for argument for joint authorship, and for a summary of the pros and cons of this claim consult Cameron, *The Young Shelley*, pp. 328-330. See also Shelley's draft of a letter to a friend, *New Shelley Letters*, pp. 36-39.

it may be regulated by the mind; pursuing, continuing this mistake they have attached a degree of criminality to disbelief, of which in its nature it is incapable; it is equally so of merit.[3]

The strength of belief like that of every other passion is in proportion to the degrees of excitement.

The degrees of excitement are three.

The senses are the sources of all knowledge to the mind; consequently their evidence claims the strongest assent.

The decision of the mind founded upon our own experience derived from these sources claims the next degree.

The experience of others, which addresses itself to the former one, occupies the lowest degree.

Consequently, no testimony can be admitted which is contrary to reason; reason is founded on the evidence of our senses.

Every proof may be referred to one of these three divisions; we are naturally led to consider what arguments we receive from each of them to convince us of the existence of a Deity.

1st. The evidence of the senses. If the Deity should appear to us, if he should convince our senses of his existence, this revelation would necessarily command belief. Those to whom the Deity has thus appeared have the strongest possible conviction of his existence.

Reason claims the 2nd. place. It is urged that man knows that whatever is must either have had a beginning or existed from all eternity; he also knows that whatever is not eternal must have had a cause. Where this is applied to the existence of the universe, it is necessary to prove that it was created.

Until that is clearly demonstrated, we may reasonably suppose that it has endured from all eternity.[4] In a case where two propositions are diametrically opposite, the mind believes that which is less incomprehensible. It is easier to suppose that the universe has existed from all eternity than to conceive a being capable of creating it; if the mind sinks beneath the weight of one, is it an alleviation to increase the intolerability of the burden?[5] The other argument, which is founded upon a man's knowledge of his own existence, stands thus: A man knows not only he now is, but that there was a time when he did not exist; consequently, there must have been a cause. But what does this prove? We can only infer from effects causes exactly adequate to those effects. But there certainly is a generative power which is effected by particular instruments; we cannot prove that it is inherent in these instruments, nor is the contrary hypothesis capable of demonstration; we admit that the generative power is incomprehensible, but to suppose that the same effect is produced by an eternal, omniscient, Almighty Being, leaves the cause in the obscurity, but renders it more incomprehensible.

The 3rd. and last degree of assent is claimed by Testimony. It is required that it should not be contrary to reason. The testimony that the Deity convinces the senses of men of his existence can only be admitted by us if our mind considers it less probable that these men should have been deceived than that the Deity should have appeared to them. Our reason can never admit the testimony of men who not only declare that they were eye-witnesses of miracles but that the Deity was irrational, for he commanded that

3. Shelley is here restating Locke's ideas as found in *The Essay on the Human Understanding*, 12th Edition, II.4.1,15,16, London, 1741. See the draft of letters in *New Shelley Letters*, pp. 36-39, for acknowledgment of debt to Locke.

4. "We must prove design before we can infer a designer. The only idea we can form of causation is derivable from the constant conjunction of objects, and the consequent inference of one from the other," from the Note to *Queen Mab* to the line

"There is no God." This statement is derived directly from Hume's *Dialogues Concerning Natural Religion. Selections*, edited by C. W. Hendel, pp. 302-339. Compare Holbach, *Système de la Nature*, pp. 16-23, for a similar statement.

5. For this idea and those that follow, touching the nature of evidence, see the reference above to Locke. Compare Hume's *A Treatise of Human Nature*, Bk. I, Part 3, Sec. 7.

he should be believed; he proposed the highest rewards for faith, eternal punishments for disbelief. We can only command voluntary actions; belief is not an act of volition— the mind is even passive; from this it is evident that we have not sufficient testimony, or rather that testimony is insufficient to prove the being of a God; we have before shown that it cannot be deduced from reason. They who have been convinced by the evidence of the senses, they only can believe it.

From this it is evident that having no proofs from any of the three sources of conviction, the mind *cannot* believe the existence of a God; it is also evident that as belief is a passion of the mind, no degree of criminality can be attached to disbelief; they only are reprehensible who willingly neglect to remove the false medium thro' which their mind views the subject.

It is almost unnecessary to observe that the general knowledge of the deficiency of such proof cannot be prejudicial to society: Truth has always been found to promote the best interests of mankind. Every reflecting mind must allow that there is no proof of the existence of a Deity. Q.E.D.

AN ADDRESS TO THE IRISH PEOPLE[1]

[The American and French Revolutions re-awakened in the Irish a desire for freedom from British oppression. In the two decades from 1790 to 1810 occurred several minor abortive uprisings. A reign of terror followed the unsuccessful rebellion in 1798 under the Society of United Irishmen. William Pitt, the British Prime Minister, maintained that a union of the two countries was the only remedy for these chaotic conditions. After some underhand policies, Pitt succeeded in persuading the Irish Parliament—wholly Protestant— on January 1, 1801, to pass the Act of Union. But this did not bring peace. For the next hundred and twenty-five years the history of Ireland was a record of oppression and a consequent struggle for political and religious freedom, and for separation from England.

It is in this struggle that Shelley joined enthusiastically. Shortly after his marriage, in Scotland, to Harriet Westbrook, they settled in York and in Keswick in the English Lake country. There his ardor for reform led him to cast his lot temporarily with the Irish. Immediately he set about writing his first pamphlet, whose ostensible aim was to forward Catholic Emancipation and the repeal of the Act of Union. We first learn of the *Address to the Irish People* from a letter to Godwin, January 16, 1812, in which Shelley said, "We

1. The title page carried the following Advertisement: *The lowest possible price is set on this publication, because it is the intention of the Author to awaken in the minds of the Irish poor, a knowledge of their real state, summarily pointing out the evils of that state, and suggesting rational means of remedy. Catholic Emancipation, and a Repeal of the Union Act, (the latter, the most successful engine that England ever wielded over the misery of fallen Ireland,) being treated of in the following address, as grievances which unanimity and resolution may remove, and associations conducted with peaceable firmness, being earnestly recommended, as means for embodying that unanimity and firmness, which must finally be successful.*

go principally to forward as much as we can Catholic Emancipation." Four days later he wrote to Elizabeth Hitchener, "I am now writing an address to the poor Irish Catholics," and quotes a long paragraph from the *Address*. And again on January 26, he wrote to Miss Hitchener, "It is intended to familiarize to uneducated apprehensions ideas of liberty, benevolence, peace, and toleration." But his real purpose is discovered in the next sentence, "It is secretly intended also as a preliminary to other pamphlets to shake Catholicism at its basis, and induce Quakerish and Socinian principles of politics, without objecting to the Christian religion."

The Shelleys left Keswick, February 2 and arrived in Dublin ten days later. The *Address* was ready for distribution by February 24, and by March 18 almost the whole of the 1500 copies printed had been distributed to the unsuspecting vulgar.

Before leaving England Shelley had made it clear to his anxious friends that he would not do anything rash or publish any libelous matter. This promise he kept religiously, for his approach to the subject was calm and mild and reasonable. Admitting the grievous wrongs the Irish had suffered from the Act of Union and the disqualification of all Catholics, Shelley none the less urged that the most pacific means be used to rectify these wrongs. Let your actions, he pleaded, be characterized by sobriety, moderation, tolerance, and wisdom. You must not join secret societies, Shelley insisted, but always act in the open. Temperance, charity, and independence of thought will give you virtue; reading, talking, and thinking will give you wisdom, and having these you can defy the tyrant.

Not content with merely publishing his views, Shelley appeared at a meeting on February 28 in the Fishamble Street Theatre to speak in behalf of Catholic Emancipation. Speaking for more than an hour, repeating and re-emphasizing the main points of the *Address,* he was enthusiastically received until he came to the subject of religion—when he was roundly hissed. Nothing daunted, however, he began the writing of two additional pamphlets in the cause. Both Holbach and Godwin are Shelley's sources in this pamphlet. See *Système de la Nature,* pp. 139-163.]

Fellowmen, I am not an Irishman, yet I can feel for you. I hope there are none among you who will read this address with prejudice or levity, because it is made by an Englishman; indeed, I believe there are not. The Irish are a brave nation. They have a heart of liberty in their breasts, but they are much mistaken if they fancy that a stranger cannot have as warm a one. Those are my brothers and my countrymen who are unfortunate. I should like to know what there is in a man being an Englishman, a Spaniard, or a Frenchman that makes him worse or better than he really is. He was born in one town, you in another, but that is no reason why he should not feel for you, desire your benefit, or be willing to give you some advice which may make you more capable of knowing your own interest, or acting so as to secure it. There are many Englishmen who cry down the Irish and think it answers their ends to revile all that belongs to Ireland; but it is not because these men are Englishmen that they maintain such opinions, but because they wish to get money, and titles, and power. They would act in this manner to whatever country they might belong, until mankind is much altered for the better, which reform, I hope, will one day be effected.[2] I address you, then, as my brothers and my fellowmen, for I should wish to see the Irishman who, if England was persecuted as Ireland is; who, if France was persecuted as Ireland is; who if any set of men that helped to do a public service were prevented from enjoying its benefits as Irishmen are—I should like to see the man, I say, who would see these misfortunes and not attempt to succor the sufferers when he could, just that I might tell him that he was no Irishman, but some bastard mongrel bred up in a court, or some coward fool who was a democrat to all above him, and an aristocrat to all below him. I think there are few true Irishmen who would not be ashamed of such a character, still fewer who possess it. I know that there are some—not among you, my friends, but among your enemies—who seeing the title of this piece will take it up with a sort of hope that it may recommend violent measures and thereby disgrace the cause of freedom, that the warmth of an heart desirous that liberty should be possessed equally by all will vent itself in abuse on the enemies of liberty, bad men who deserve the contempt of the good, and ought not to excite their indignation to the harm of their cause. But these men will be disappointed—I know the warm feelings of an Irishman sometimes carries him beyond the point of prudence. I do not desire to root out, but to moderate this honorable warmth. This will disappoint the pioneers of oppression, and they will be sorry that through this address nothing will occur which can be twisted into any other meaning but what is calculated to fill you with that moderation which they have not, and make you give them that toleration which they refuse to grant to you. You profess the Roman Catholic religion, which your fathers

professed before you. Whether it is the best religion or not, I will not here inquire; all religions are good which make men good;[3] and the way that a person ought to prove that his method of worshipping God is best is for himself to be better than all other men. But we will consider what your religion was in old times and what it is now; you may say it is not a fair way for me to proceed as a Protestant, but I am not a Protestant nor am I a Catholic, and therefore not being a follower of either of these religions, I am better able to judge between them. A Protestant is my brother, and a Catholic is my brother. I am happy when I can do either of them a service, and no pleasure is so great to me than that which I should feel if my advice could make men of any professions of faith, wiser, better, and happier.

The Roman Catholics once persecuted the Protestants; the Protestants now persecute the Roman Catholics. Should we think that one is as bad as the other? No, you are not answerable for the faults of your fathers any more than the Protestants are good for the goodness of their fathers. I must judge of people as I see them; the Irish Catholics are badly used. I will not endeavor to hide from them their wretchedness; they would think that I mocked at them if I should make the attempt. The Irish Catholics now demand for themselves and profess for others unlimited toleration, and the sensible part among them, which I am willing to think constitutes a very large portion of their body, know that the gates of Heaven are open to people of every religion, provided they are good. But the Protestants, although they may think so in their hearts, which certainly, if they think at all, they must seem to act as if they thought that God was better pleased with them than with you; they trust the reins of earthly government only to the hands of their own sect. In spite of this I never found one of them impudent enough

---

2. This is a profound truth which, if rightly appreciated, would greatly ease the tension among men and nations.

3. Compare the statement in Paine's *The Rights of Man* (Everyman's edition), p. 269: "Every religion is good that teaches man to be good."

to say that a Roman Catholic, or a Quaker, or a Jew, or a Mahometan, if he was a virtuous man and did all the good in his power, would go to Heaven a bit the slower for not subscribing to the thirty-nine articles[4]—and if he should say so, how ridiculous in a foppish courtier not six feet high to direct the spirit of universal harmony[5] in what manner to conduct the affairs of the universe!

The Protestants say that there was a time when the Roman Catholics burned and murdered people of different sentiments, and that their religious tenets are now as they were then. This is all very true. You certainly worship God in the same way that you did when these barbarities took place, but is that any reason that you should now be barbarous? There is as much reason to suppose it as to suppose that because a man's great-grandfather, who was a Jew, had been hung for sheep-stealing, that I, by believing the same religion as he did, must certainly commit the same crime. Let us then see what the Roman Catholic religion has been. No one knows much of the early times of the Christian religion until about three-hundred years after its beginning; two great Churches, called the Roman and the Greek Churches, divided the opinions of men. They fought for a very long time, a great many words were wasted, and a great deal of blood shed.

This, as you may suppose, did no good. Each party, however, thought they were doing God a service and that he would reward them. If they had looked an inch before their noses, they might have found that fighting and killing men and cursing them and hating them was the very worst way for getting into favor with a Being who is allowed by all to be best pleased with deeds of love and charity. At last, however, these

two religions entirely separated, and the popes reigned like kings and bishops at Rome, in Italy. The Inquisition was set up, and in the course of one year 30,000 people were burned in Italy and Spain for entertaining different opinions from those of the Pope and the Priest. There was an instance of shocking barbarity which the Roman Catholic clergy committed in France by order of the Pope. The bigoted monks of that country, in cold blood, in one night massacred 80,000 Protestants;[6] this was done under the authority of the Pope, and there was only one Roman Catholic bishop who had virtue enough to refuse to help. The vices of monks and nuns in their convents were in those times shameful. People thought that they might commit any sin, however monstrous, if they had money enough to prevail upon the priests to absolve them. In truth, at that time the priests shamefully imposed upon the people; they got all the power into their own hands; they persuaded them that a man could not be entrusted with the care of his own soul, and by cunningly obtaining possession of their secrets, they became more powerful than kings, princes, dukes, lords, or ministers. This power made them bad men; for although rational people are very good in their natural state, there are now, and ever have been, very few whose good dispositions despotic power does not destroy. I have now given a fair description of what your religion was; and, Irishmen, my brothers, will you make your friend appear a liar, when he takes upon himself to say for you that you are not now what the professors of the same faith were in times of yore? Do I speak false when I say that the Inquisition is the object of your hatred? Am I a liar if I assert that an Irishman prizes liberty dearly, that he will preserve that

4. Articles of faith of the Church of England, adopted in 1562.

5. The concept of God as a universal spirit—soul of the Universe—Shelley early held, and in fact never relinquished. For a discussion of Shelley as an atheist see Professor Cameron, *op. cit.*, pp. 70-82, and for his idea of God see Holbach, *op. cit.*, pp. 163-187, large sections of which Shelley quotes

in a Note on *Queen Mab*. See also Hume's *Dialogues Concerning Natural Religion, Selections*, pp. 320-352.

6. The Massacre of Saint Bartholomew, August 24-September 17, 1572, in which unknown thousands of French Huguenots (Protestants) were massacred by the Catholics. The Pope solemnly celebrated the event.

right, and if it be wrong, does not dream that money can give to a priest, or the talking of another man erring like himself, can in the least influence the judgment of the eternal God? I am not a liar if I affirm in your name that you believe a Protestant equally with yourself to be worthy of the kingdom of Heaven, if he be equally virtuous; that you will treat men as brethren wherever you may find them, and that difference of opinion in religious matters shall not, does not, in the least on your part obstruct the most perfect harmony on every other subject. Ah! no, Irishmen, I am not a liar. I seek your confidence, not that I may betray it, but that I may teach you to be happy, and wise, and good. If you will not repose any trust in me, I shall lament; but I will do everything in my power that is honorable, fair, and open to gain it. Some teach you that others are heretics, that you alone are right; some teach that rectitude consists in religious opinions, without which no morality is good. Some will tell you that you ought to divulge your secrets to one particular set of men. Beware, my friends, how you trust those who speak in this way. They will, I doubt not, attempt to rescue you from your present miserable state, but they will prepare a worse. It will be out of the frying-pan into the fire. Your present oppressors, it is true, will then oppress you no longer, but you will feel the lash of a master a thousand times more blood-thirsty and cruel. Evil designing men will spring up who will prevent your thinking as you please—will burn you if you do not think as they do. There are always bad men who take advantage of hard times. The monks and priests of old were very bad men; take care no such abuse your confidence again. You are not blind to your present situation; you are villainously treated; you are badly used. That this slavery shall cease, I will venture to prophesy. Your enemies dare not to persecute you longer, the spirit of Ireland is bent, but it is not broken, and that they very well know. But I wish your views to embrace a wider scene—I wish you to think for

your children and your children's children; to take great care (for it all rests with you) that while one tyranny is destroyed, another more fierce and terrible does not spring up. Take care then of smooth-faced imposters, who talk indeed of freedom, but who will cheat you into slavery. Can there be worse slavery than the depending for the safety of your soul on the will of another man? Is one man more favored than another by God? No, certainly, they are all favored according to the good they do, and not according to the rank and profession they hold. God values a poor man as much as a priest, and has given him a soul as much to himself. The worship that a kind Being must love is that of a simple affectionate heart that shows its piety in good works, and not in ceremonies, or confessions, or burials, or processions, or wonders. Take care then that you are not led away. Doubt everything that leads you not to charity and think of the word "heretic" as a word which some selfish knave invented for the ruin and misery of the world to answer his own paltry and narrow ambition. Do not inquire if a man be a heretic, if he be a Quaker, or a Jew, or a heathen; but if he be a virtuous man, if he loves [love?] liberty and truth, if he wish the happiness and peace of human kind. If a man be ever so much a believer, and love not these things, he is a heartless hypocrite, a rascal, and a knave. Despise and hate him as ye despise a tyrant and a villain. Oh! Ireland! thou emerald of the ocean, whose sons are generous and brave, whose daughters are honorable and frank and fair, thou art the isle on whose green shores I have desired to see the standard of liberty erected—a flag of fire—a beacon at which the world shall light the torch of Freedom!

We will now examine the Protestant religion. Its origin is called the Reformation. It was undertaken by some bigoted men who showed how little they understood the spirit of reform by burning each other. You will observe that these men burned each other—indeed they universally betrayed a taste for destroying—and vied with the chiefs of the

Roman Catholic religion in not only hating their enemies but those men who least of all were their enemies, or anybody's enemies. Now do the Protestants or do they not hold the same tenets as they did when Calvin burned Servetus? They swear that they do. We can have no better proof. Then, with what face can the Protestants object to Catholic Emancipation on the plea that Catholics once were barbarous, when their own establishment is liable to the very same objections, on the very same grounds? I think this is a specimen of barefaced intoleration which I had hoped would not have disgraced this age; this age, which is called the age of reason, of thought diffused, of virtue acknowledged, and its principles fixed. Oh! that it may be so. I have mentioned the Catholic and Protestant religions more to show that any objection to the toleration of the one forcibly applies to the non-permission of the other, or rather to show that there is no reason why both might not be tolerated; why every religion, every form of thinking might not be tolerated. But why do I speak of *toleration?* This word seems to mean that there is some merit in the person who tolerates: he has this merit, if it be one, of refraining to do an evil act, but he will share the merit with every other peaceable person who pursues his own business and does not hinder another of his rights. It is not a merit to tolerate, but it is a crime to be intolerant; it is not a merit in me that I sat [sit?] quietly at home without murdering any one, but it is a crime if I do so. Besides, no act of a national representation can make anything wrong which was not wrong before; it cannot change virtue and truth, and for a very plain reason: because they are unchangeable. An Act passed in the British Parliament to take away the rights of Catholics to act in that assembly does not really take them away. It prevents them from doing it by force. This is in such cases the last and only efficacious way. But force is not the

test of truth: they will never have recourse to violence who acknowledge no other rule of behavior but virtue and justice.

The folly of persecuting men for their religion will appear if we examine it. Why do we persecute them? To make them believe as we do. Can anything be more barbarous or foolish. For, although we may make them say they believe as we do, they will not in their hearts do any such thing—indeed they cannot; this devilish method can only make them false hypocrites. For what is belief? We cannot believe just what we like,[7] but only what we think to be true; for you cannot alter a man's opinion by beating or burning, but by persuading him that what you think is right, and this can only be done by fair words and reason. It is ridiculous to call a man a heretic because he thinks differently from you; he might as well call you one. In the same sense the word orthodox is used; it signifies "to think rightly," and what can be more vain and presumptuous in any man or any set of men, to put themselves so out of the ordinary course of things as to say, "What we think is right; no other people throughout the world have opinions anything like equal to ours." Anything short of unlimited toleration and complete charity with all men, on which you will recollect that Jesus Christ principally insisted, is wrong, and for this reason, What makes a man to be a good man? Not his religion, or else there could be no good men in any religion but one, when yet we find that all ages, countries, and opinions have produced them. Virtue and wisdom always so far as they went produced liberty or happiness long before any of the religions now in the world had ever [been] heard of. The only use of a religion that ever I could see is to make men wiser and better; so far as it does this, it is a good one. Now, if people are good, and yet have sentiments differing from you, then all the purposes are answered which any reasonable

7. This idea is fundamental in Shelley's philosophy and appears in many of his writings. For its probable sources see Spinoza's *Tractatus* and Hume's *Essays.*

man could want, and whether he thinks like you or not is of too little consequence to employ means which must be disgusting and hateful to candid minds; nay, they cannot approve of such means. For, as I have before said, you cannot believe or disbelieve what you like—perhaps some of you may doubt this, but just try. I will take a common and familiar instance. Suppose you have a friend of whom you wish to think well; he commits a crime, which proves to you that he is a bad man. It is very painful to you to think ill of him, and you would still think well of him if you could. But, mark the word, you *cannot* think well of him; not even to secure your own peace of mind can you do so. You try, but your attempts are vain. This shows how little power a man has over his belief, or rather, that he cannot believe what he does not think true. And what shall we think now? What fools and tyrants must not those men be who set up a particular religion, say that this religion alone is right, and that everyone who disbelieves it ought to be deprived of certain rights which are really his and which would be allowed him if he believed. Certainly, if you cannot help disbelief, it is not any fault in you. To take away a man's rights and privileges, to call him a heretic, or to think worse of him, when at the same time you cannot help owning that he has committed no fault is the grossest tyranny and intoleration. From what has been said I think we may be justified in concluding that people of all religions ought to have an equal share in the state, that the words heretic and orthodox were invented by a vain villain, and have done a great deal of harm in the world, and that no person is answerable for his belief whose actions are virtuous and moral, that the religion is best whose members are the best men, and that no person can help either his belief or disbelief. Be in charity with all men. It does not therefore signify what your religion *was,* or what the Protestant religion *was*; we must consider them as we find them. What are they *now?* Yours is not intolerant; indeed, my friends, I have ventured

to pledge myself for you that it is not. You merely desire to go to Heaven in your own way, nor will you interrupt fellow travellers, although the road which you take may not be that which they take. Believe me that goodness of heart and purity of life are things of more value in the eye of the Spirit of Goodness than idle earthly ceremonies and things which have anything but charity for their object. And is it for the first or the last of these things that you or the Protestants contend? It is for the last. Prejudiced people indeed are they who grudge to the happiness and comfort of your souls things which can do harm to no one. They are not compelled to share in these rites. Irishmen! knowledge is more extended than in the early period of your religion, people have learned to think, and the more thought there is in the world, the more happiness and liberty will there be; men begin now to think less of idle ceremonies and more of realities. From a long night have they risen, and they can perceive its darkness. I know no men of thought and learning who do not consider the Catholic idea of purgatory much nearer the truth than the Protestant one of eternal damnation. Can you think that the Mahometans and the Indians, who have done good deeds in this life, will not be rewarded in the next? The Protestants believe that they will be eternally damned, at least they swear that they do. I think they appear in a better light as perjurers than believers in a falsehood so hurtful and uncharitable as this. I propose unlimited toleration, or rather the destruction both of toleration and intoleration. The act permits certain people to worship God after such a manner, which, in fact, if not done, would as far as in it lay prevent God from hearing their address. Can we conceive anything more presumptuous, and at the same time more ridiculous, than a set of men granting a license to God to receive the prayers of certain of his creatures? Oh, Irishmen! I am interested in your cause; and it is not because you are Irishmen or Roman Catholics that I feel with you and feel for you; but because you are men and sufferers.

Were Ireland at this moment peopled with Brahmins, this very same Address would have been suggested by the same state of mind. You have suffered not merely for your religion, but some other causes which I am equally desirous of remedying. The Union of England with Ireland has withdrawn the Protestant aristocracy and gentry from their native country, and with these their friends and connections. Their resources are taken from this country, although they are dissipated in another; the very poor people are most infamously oppressed by the weight of burden which the superior ranks lay upon their shoulders. I am no less desirous of the reform of these evils (with many others) than for the Catholic Emancipation.

Perhaps you all agree with me on both these subjects; we now come to the method of doing these things. I agree with the Quakers so far as they disclaim violence and trust their cause wholly and solely to its own truth. If you are convinced of the truth of your cause, trust wholly to its truth; if you are not convinced, give it up. In no case employ violence; the way to liberty and happiness is never to transgress the rules of virtue and justice. Liberty and happiness are founded upon virtue and justice; if you destroy the one you destroy the other. However ill others may act, this will be no excuse for you if you follow their example; it ought rather to warn you from pursuing so bad a method. Depend upon it, Irishmen, your cause shall not be neglected. I will fondly hope that the schemes for your happiness and liberty, as well as those for the happiness and liberty of the world, will not be wholly fruitless. One secure method of defeating them is violence on the side of the injured party. If you can descend to use the same weapons as your enemy, you put yourself on a level with him on this score; you must be convinced that he is on these grounds your superior. But appeal to the sacred principles of virtue and justice, then how is he awed into nothing! How does truth show him in his real colors and place the cause of toleration and reform in the clearest light! I extend my view not only to you as Irishmen but to all of every persuasion, of every country. Be calm, mild, deliberate, patient; recollect that you can in no measure more effectually forward the cause of reform than by employing your leisure time in reasoning or the cultivation of your minds. Think and talk and discuss; the only subjects you ought to propose are those of happiness and liberty. Be free and be happy, but first be wise and good. For you are not all wise or good. You are a great and a brave nation, but you cannot yet be all wise or good. You may be at some time, and then Ireland will be an earthly paradise. You know what is meant by a mob. It is an assembly of people who, without foresight or thought, collect themselves to disapprove of by force any measure which they dislike. An assembly like this can never do anything but harm; tumultuous proceedings must retard the period when thought and coolness will produce freedom and happiness, and that to the very people who make the mob. But if a number of human beings, after thinking of their own interests, meet together for any conversation on them and employ resistance of the mind, not resistance of the body, these people are going the right way to work. But let no fiery passions carry them beyond this point. Let them consider that in some sense the whole welfare of their countrymen depends on their prudence, and that it becomes them to guard the welfare of others as their own. Associations for purposes of violence are entitled to the strongest disapprobation of the real reformist. Always suspect that some knavish rascal is at the bottom of things of this kind, waiting to profit by the confusion. All secret associations are also bad. Are you men of deep designs, whose deeds love darkness better than light? Dare you not say what you think before any man? Can you not meet in the open face of day in conscious innocence? Oh, Irishmen, ye can! Hidden arms, secret meetings, and designs violently to separate England from Ireland are all very bad. I do not mean to say the very end of them is bad; the object you have in view may be just enough, while the way you go about it is wrong, may be calculated to produce an opposite effect. Never do evil that good may come; always think of others as well as yourself, and cautiously look how your conduct may do good or evil, when you yourself shall be mouldering in the grave. Be fair, open, and you will be terrible to your enemies. A friend cannot defend you, much as he may feel for your sufferings, if you have recourse to methods of which virtue and justice disapprove. No cause is in itself so dear to liberty as yours. Much depends on you; far may your efforts spread either hope or despair; do not then cover in darkness wrongs at which the face of day and the tyrants who bask in its warmth ought to blush. Wherever has violence succeeded? The French Revolution, although undertaken with the best intentions, ended ill for the people, because violence was employed. The cause which they vindicated was that of truth, but they gave it the appearance of a lie by using methods which will suit the purposes of liars as well as their own. Speak boldly and daringly what you think; an Irishman was never accused of cowardice, do not let it be thought possible that he is a coward. Let him say what he thinks; a lie is the basest and meanest employment of men; leave lies and secrets to courtiers and lordlings. Be open, sincere, and single-hearted. Let it be seen that the Irish votaries of Freedom dare to speak what they think; let them resist oppression, not by force of arms, but by power of mind and reliance on truth and justice. Will any be arraigned for libel—will imprisonment or death be the consequences of this mode of proceeding? Probably not. But if it were so? Is danger frightful to an Irishman who speaks for his own liberty and the liberty of his wife and children? No, he will steadily persevere, and sooner shall pensioners cease to vote with their benefactors than an Irishman swerve from the path of duty. But steadily persevere in the system above laid

8. George the Third died on January 29, 1820.

down, its benefits will speedily be manifested. Persecution may destroy some, but cannot destroy all, or nearly all; let it do its will. Ye have appealed to truth and justice, show the goodness of your religion by persisting in a reliance on these things, which must be the rules even of the Almighty's conduct. But before this can be done with any effect, habits of Sobriety, Regularity, and Thought must be entered into, and firmly resolved upon.

My warm-hearted friends who meet together to talk of the distresses of your countrymen until social chat induces you to drink rather freely; as ye have felt passionately, so reason coolly. Nothing hasty can be lasting; lay up the money with which you usually purchase drunkenness and ill-health to relieve the pains of your fellow sufferers. Let your children lisp of freedom in the cradle—let your deathbed be the school for fresh exertions—let every street of the city and field of country be connected with thoughts which liberty has made holy. Be warm in your cause, yet rational, and charitable, and tolerant—never let the oppressor grind you into justifying his conduct by imitating his meanness.

Many circumstances, I will own, may excuse what is called rebellion, but no circumstances can ever make it good for your cause, and however honorable to your feelings, it will reflect no credit on your judgments. It will bind you more closely to the block of the oppressor, and your children's children, while they talk of your exploits, will feel that you have done them injury instead of benefit.

A crisis is now arriving which shall decide your fate. The King of Great Britain has arrived at the evening of his days. He has objected to your emancipation; he has been inimical to you; but he will in a certain time be no more.[8] The present Prince of Wales will then be king. It is said that he has promised to restore you to freedom; your real and natural right will, in that case, be no longer kept from you. I hope he has pledged himself to this act of justice, because there will then exist some obligation to bind him to do right. Kings are but too apt to think little, as they should do: they think everything in the world is made for them—when the truth is, that it is only the vices of men that make such people necessary, and they have no other right of being kings but in virtue of the good they do.

The benefit of the governed is the origin and meaning of government.[9] The Prince of Wales has had every opportunity of knowing how he ought to act about Ireland and liberty. That great and good man Charles Fox, who was your friend and the friend of freedom, was the friend of the Prince of Wales. He never flattered nor disguised his sentiments, but spoke them *openly* on every occasion, and the Prince was the better for his instructive conversation. He saw the truth, and he believed it. Now I know not what to say; his staff is gone,[10] and he leans upon a broken reed; his present advisers are not like Charles Fox; they do not plan for liberty and safety, not for the happiness, but for the glory of their country; and what, Irishmen, is the glory of a country divided from their happiness? It is a false light hung out by the enemies of freedom to lure the unthinking into their net. Men like these surround the Prince, and whether or no he has really promised to emancipate you— whether or no he will consider the promise of a Prince of Wales binding to a King of England—is yet a matter of doubt. We cannot at least be quite certain of it; on this you cannot certainly rely. But there are men who, wherever they find a tendency to freedom, go there to increase, support, and regulate that tendency. These men, who join to a rational disdain of danger a practice of speaking the truth and defending the cause of the oppressed against the oppressor—these men see what is right and will pursue it. On such as these you may safely rely; they love

you as they love their brothers; they feel for the unfortunate and never ask whether a man is an Englishman or an Irishman, a Catholic, a heretic, a Christian, or a heathen, before their hearts and their purses are opened to feel with their misfortunes and relieve their necessities; such are the men who will stand by you forever. Depend then not upon the promises of princes, but upon those of virtuous and disinterested men; depend not upon force of arms or violence, but upon the force of the truth of the rights which you have to share equally with others, the benefits and the evils of government.

The crisis to which I allude as the period of your emancipation is not the death of the present King, or any circumstance that has to do with kings, but something that is much more likely to do you good: it is the increase of virtue and wisdom which will lead people to find out that force and oppression are wrong and false; and this opinion, when it once gains ground, will prevent government from severity. It will restore those rights which government has taken away. Have nothing to do with force or violence, and things will safely and surely make their way to the right point. The Ministers have now in Parliament a very great majority, and the Ministers are against you. They maintain the falsehood that, were you in power, you would prosecute [persecute] and burn, on the plea that you once did so. They maintain many other things of the same nature. They command the majority of the House of Commons, or rather the part of that assembly who receive pensions from government or whose relatives receive them. These men of course are against you, because their employers are. But the sense of the country is not against you; the people of England are not against you—they feel warmly for you—in some respects they feel with you. The sense of the English and of their governors is opposite—there must be an end of this; the goodness of a govern-

9. See Paine's *Common Sense*, Sec. I.

10. Fox had died in 1806.

ment consists in the happiness of the governed.[11] If the governed are wretched and dissatisfied, the government has failed in its end. It wants altering and mending. It will be mended, and a reform of English government will produce good to the Irish—good to all human kind, excepting those whose happiness consists in others' sorrows, and it will be a fit punishment for these to be deprived of their devilish joy. This I consider as an event which is approaching, and which will make the beginning of our hopes for that period which may spread wisdom and virtue so wide as to leave no hole in which folly or villainy may hide themselves. I wish you, O Irishmen, to be as careful and thoughtful of your interests as are your real friends. Do not drink, do not play, do not spend any idle time, do not take everything that other people say for granted—there are numbers who will tell you lies to make their own fortunes; you cannot more certainly do good to your own cause than by defeating the intentions of these men. Think, read, and talk; let your own condition and that of your wives and children fill your minds; disclaim all manner of alliance with violence; meet together if you will, but do not meet in a mob. If you think and read and talk with a real wish of benefiting the cause of truth and liberty, it will soon be seen how true a service you are rendering, and how sincere you are in your professions; but mobs and violence must be discarded. The certain degree of civil and religious liberty which the usage of the English Constitution allows is such as the worst of men are entitled to, although you have it not; but that liberty which we may one day hope for, wisdom and virtue can alone give you a right to enjoy. This wisdom and this virtue I recommend on every account that you should *instantly begin* to practice. Lose not a day, not an hour, not a moment. Temperance, sobriety, charity, and independence will give you virtue; and reading, talking, thinking, and searching will give you wisdom; when

you have those things you may defy the tyrant. It is not going often to chapel, crossing yourselves, or confessing that will make you virtuous; many a rascal has attended regularly at mass, and many a good man has never gone at all. It is not paying priests or believing in what they say that makes a good man, but it is doing good actions or benefiting other people; this is the true way to be good, and the prayers and confessions and masses of him who does not these things are good for nothing at all. Do your work regularly and quickly; when you have done, think, read, and talk; do not spend your money in idleness and drinking, which, so far from doing good to your cause, will do it harm. If you have anything to spare from your wife and children, let it do some good to other people, and put them in a way of getting wisdom and virtue, as the pleasure that will come from these good acts will be much better than the headache that comes from a drinking bout. And never quarrel between each other; be all of one mind as nearly as you can; do these things, and I will promise you liberty and happiness. But if, on the contrary of these things, you neglect to improve yourselves, continue to use the word heretic, and demand from others the toleration which you are unwilling to give, your friends and the friends of liberty will have reason to lament the death-blow of their hopes. I expect better things from you; it is for yourselves that I fear and hope. Many Englishmen are prejudiced against you; they sit by their own firesides, and certain rumors artfully spread are ever on the wing against you. But these people who think ill of you and of your nation are often the very men who, if they had better information, would feel for you most keenly. Wherefore are these reports spread? How do they begin? They originate from the warmth of the Irish character, which the friends of the Irish nation have hitherto encouraged rather than repressed; this leads them in those moments, when their wrongs

11. In Paine's *Common Sense*, Sec. I.

appear so clearly, to commit acts which justly excite displeasure. They begin therefore from yourselves, although falsehood and tyranny artfully magnify and multiply the cause of offence. Give no offence.

I will for the present dismiss the subject of the Catholic Emancipation; a little reflection will convince you that my remarks are just. Be true to yourselves, and your enemies shall not triumph. I fear nothing, if charity and sobriety mark your proceedings. Everything is to be dreaded—you yourselves will be unworthy of even a restoration to your rights—if you disgrace the cause which, I hope, is that of truth and liberty, by violence; if you refuse to others the toleration which you claim for yourselves. But this you will not do. I rely upon it, Irishmen, that the warmth of your character will be shown as much in union with Englishmen and what are called heretics, who feel for you and love you, as in avenging your wrongs, or forwarding their annihilation. It is the heart that glows and not the cheek. The firmness, sobriety, and consistence of your outward behavior will not at all show any hardness of heart, but will prove that you are determined in your cause, and are going the right way to work. I will repeat that virtue and wisdom are necessary to true happiness and liberty. The Catholic Emancipation, I consider, is certain.[12] I do not see that anything but violence and intolerance among yourselves can leave an excuse to your enemies for continuing your slavery. The other wrongs under which you labor will probably also soon be done away. You will be rendered equal to the people of England in their rights and privileges, and will be in all respects, so far as concern the state, as happy. And now, Irishmen, another and a more wide prospect opens to my view. I cannot avoid, little as it may appear to have anything to do with your present situation, to talk to you on the subject. It intimately concerns the well-being of your children and

your children's children, and will perhaps more than anything prove to you the advantage and necessity of being thoughtful, sober, and regular; of avoiding foolish and idle talk, and thinking of yourselves as of men who are able to be much wiser and happier than you now are; for habits like these will not only conduce to the successful putting aside your present and immediate grievances but will contain a seed which in future times will spring up into the tree of liberty and bear the fruit of happiness.

There is no doubt but [that] the world is going wrong, or rather that it is very capable of being much improved. What I mean by this improvement is the inducement of a more equal and general diffusion of happiness and liberty. Many people are very rich and many are very poor. Which do you think are happiest? I can tell you that neither are happy so far as their station is concerned. Nature never intended that there should be such a thing as a poor man or a rich one. Being put in an unnatural situation, they can neither of them be happy, so far as their situation is concerned. The poor man is born to obey the rich man, though they both come into the world equally helpless and equally naked. But the poor man does the rich no service by obeying him—the rich man does the poor no good by commanding him. It would be much better if they could be prevailed upon to live equally like brothers—they would ultimately both be happier. But this can be done neither today nor tomorrow; much as such a change is to be desired, it is quite impossible. Violence and folly in this, as in the other case, would only put off the period of its event. Mildness, sobriety, and reason are the effectual methods of forwarding the ends of liberty and happiness.

Although we may see many things put in train during our life-time, we cannot hope to see the work of virtue and reason finished now; we can only lay the foundation

12. Shelley did not live to see this realized. The bill for Catholic Emancipation passed the English Parliament in April, 1829.

for our posterity. Government is an evil; it is only the thoughtlessness and vices of men that make it a necessary evil.[13] When all men are good and wise, government will of itself decay. So long as men continue foolish and vicious, so long will government, even such a government as that of England, continue necessary in order to prevent the crimes of bad men. Society is produced by the wants, government by the wickedness, and a state of just and happy equality by the improvement and reason of man. It is in vain to hope for any liberty and happiness without reason and virtue, for where there is no virtue there will be crime, and where there is crime there must be government. Before the restraints of government are lessened, it is fit that we should lessen the necessity for them. Before government is done away with, we must reform ourselves. It is this work which I would earnestly recommend to you. O Irishmen, *Reform Yourselves,* and I do not recommend it to you particularly because I think that you most need it but because I think that your hearts are warm and your feelings high, and you will perceive the necessity of doing it more than those of a colder and more distant nature.

I look with an eye of hope and pleasure on the present state of things, gloomy and incapable of improvement as they may appear to others. It delights me to see that men begin to think and to act for the good of others. Extensively as folly and selfishness have predominated in this age, it gives me hope and pleasure at least to see that many know what is right. Ignorance and vice commonly go together; he that would do good must be wise. A man cannot be truly wise who is not truly virtuous. Prudence and wisdom are very different things. The prudent man is he who carefully consults for his own good; the wise man is he who carefully consults for the good of others.

I look upon Catholic Emancipation and the restoration of the liberties and happiness of Ireland, so far as they are compatible with the English Constitution, as great and important events. I hope to see them soon. But if all ended here, it would give me little pleasure. I should still see thousands miserable and wicked; things would still be wrong. I regard then the accomplishment of these things as the road to a greater reform, that reform after which virtue and wisdom shall have conquered pain and vice —when no government will be wanted but that of your neighbor's opinion. I look to these things with hope and pleasure, because I consider that they will certainly happen, and because men will not then be wicked and miserable. But I do not consider that they will or can immediately happen; their arrival will be gradual, and it all depends upon yourselves how soon or how late these great changes will happen. If all of you tomorrow were virtuous and wise, government which today is a safeguard would then become a tyranny. But I cannot expect a rapid change. Many are obstinate and determined in their vice, whose selfishness makes them think only of their own good, when in fact the best way even to bring that about is to make others happy. I do not wish to see things changed now, because it cannot be done without violence, and we may assure ourselves that none of us are fit for any change, however good, if we condescend to employ force in a cause which we think right. Force makes the side that employs it directly wrong, and as much as we may pity we cannot approve the headstrong and intolerant zeal of [its] adherents.[14]

Can you conceive, O Irishmen! a happy state of society, conceive men of every way of thinking living together like brothers? The descendant of the greatest prince would then be entitled to no more respect than

13. In Paine's *Common Sense,* Sec. I, from which Shelley took both the idea and the phrasing.

14. This socialistic conception of the state was soon to be repeated in the *Essay on Christianity* and *A Philosophical View of Reform.*

the son of a peasant. There would be no pomp and no parade; but that which the rich now keep to themselves would then be distributed among the people. None would be in magnificence, but the superfluities then taken from the rich would be sufficient when spread abroad to make every one comfortable.[15] No lover would then be false to his mistress, no mistress could desert her lover. No friend would play false; no rents, no debts, no taxes, no frauds of any kind would disturb the general happiness; good as they would be, wise as they would be, they would be daily getting better and wiser. No beggars would exist, nor any of those wretched women who are now reduced to a state of the most horrible misery and vice by men whose wealth makes them villainous and hardened; no thieves or murderers, because poverty would never drive men to take away comforts from another when he had enough for himself. Vice and misery, pomp and poverty, power and obedience would then be banished altogether. It is for such a state as this, Irishmen, that I exhort you to prepare. "A camel shall as soon pass through the eye of a needle, as a rich man enter the kingdom of heaven."[16] This is not to be understood literally. Jesus Christ appears to me only to have meant that riches have generally the effect of hardening and vitiating the heart; so has poverty. I think those people then are very silly, and cannot see one inch beyond their noses, who say that human nature is depraved; when at the same time wealth and poverty, those two great sources of crime, fall to the lot of a great majority of people; and when they see that people in moderate circumstances are always most wise and good. People say that poverty is no evil; they have never felt it, or they would not think so; that wealth is necessary to encourage the arts—but are not the arts

very inferior things to virtue and happiness?—the man would be very dead to all generous feelings who would rather see pretty pictures and statues than a million free and happy men.[17]

It will be said that my design is to make you dissatisfied with your present condition and that I wish to raise a rebellion. But how stupid and sottish must those men be who think that violence and uneasiness of mind have anything to do with forwarding the views of peace, harmony, and happiness. They should know that nothing was so well fitted to produce slavery, tyranny, and vice as the violence which is attributed to the friends of liberty, and which the real friends of liberty are the only persons who disdain. As to your being dissatisfied with your present condition, anything that I may say is certainly not likely to increase that dissatisfaction. I have advanced nothing concerning your situation but its real case, but what may be proved to be true. I defy any one to point out a falsehood that I have uttered in the course of the Address. It is impossible, but the blindest among you must see that everything is not right. This sight has often pressed some of the poorest among you to take something from the rich man's store by violence to relieve his own necessities. I cannot justify, but I can pity him. I cannot pity the fruits of the rich man's intemperance. I suppose some are to be found who will justify him. This sight has often brought home to a day-laborer the truth which I wish to impress upon you that all is not right. But I do not merely wish to convince you that our present state is bad, but that its alteration for the better depends on your own exertions and resolutions.

But he has never found out the method of mending it who does not first mend his own conduct, and then prevail upon others

15. Shelley was genuinely socialistic in the conception of government. Compare this sentence of his with similar remarks of Jesus. See *Essay on Christianity* and *A Philosophical View of Reform.*

16. Shelley here misquotes. See Matt. 19.23-24.
17. For a similar discussion of the deadening effect of either riches or poverty, see the *Essay on Christianity.*

to refrain from any vicious habits which they may have contracted, much less does the poor man suppose that wisdom as well as virtue is necesssary, and that the employing his little time in reading and thinking is really doing all that he has in his power to do towards the state, when pain and vice shall perish altogether.

I wish to impress upon your minds that without virtue or wisdom there can be no liberty or happiness; and that temperance, sobriety, charity, and independence of soul will give you virtue, as thinking, inquiring, reading, and talking will give you wisdom. Without the first the last is of little use, and without the last the first is a dreadful curse to yourselves and others.[18]

I have told you what I think upon this subject, because I wish to produce in your minds an awe and caution necessary, before the happy state of which I have spoken can be introduced. This cautious awe is very different from the prudential fear which leads you to consider yourself as the first object, as, on the contrary, it is full of that warm and ardent love for others that burns in your hearts, O Irishmen! and from which I have fondly hoped to light a flame that may illumine and invigorate the world.

I have said that the rich command and the poor obey, and that money is only a kind of sign which shows that according to government the rich man has a right to command the poor man, or rather that the poor man, being urged by having no money to get bread, is forced to work for the rich man, which amounts to the same thing. I have said that I think all this very wrong, and that I wish the whole business was altered. I have also said that we can expect little amendment in our own time, and that we must be contented to lay the foundation of liberty and happiness by virtue and wisdom. This, then, shall be my work; let this be yours, Irishmen. Never shall that glory fail which I am anxious that you shall

deserve: the glory of teaching to a world the first lessons of virtue and wisdom.

Let poor men still continue to work. I do not wish to hide from them a knowledge of their relative condition in society, I esteem it next [to] impossible to do so. Let the work of the laborer, of the artificer—let the work of every one, however employed, still be exerted in the accustomed way. The public communication of this truth ought in no manner to impede the established usages of society; however, it is fitted in the end to do them away. For this reason it ought not to impede them, because if it did, a violent and unaccustomed and sudden sensation [cessation?] would take place in all ranks of men, which would bring on violence and destroy the possibility of the event of that which in its own nature must be gradual, however rapid, and rational, however warm. It is founded on the reform of private men, and without individual amendment it is vain and foolish to expect the amendment of a state or government. I would advise them, therefore, whose feelings this Address may have succeeded in affecting (and surely those feelings which charitable and temperate remarks excite can never be violent and intolerant), if they be, as I hope, those whom poverty has compelled to class themselves in the lower orders of society, that they will as usual attend to their business and the discharge of those public or private duties which custom has ordained. Nothing can be more rash and thoughtless than to show in ourselves singular instances of any particular doctrine before the general mass of the people are so convinced by the reasons of the doctrine that it will be no longer singular. That reasons as well as feelings may help the establishment of happiness and liberty on the basis of wisdom and virtue, is our aim and intention. Let us not be led into any means which are unworthy of this end, nor, as so much depends upon

18. This same idea is in *A Treatise on Morals*.

yourselves, let us [not] cease carefully to watch over our conduct, that when we talk of reform it be not objected to us that reform ought to begin at home. In the interval that public or private duties and necessary labors allow, husband your time so that you may do to others and yourselves the most real good. To improve your own minds is to join these two views; conversation and reading are the principal and chief methods of awaking the mind to knowledge and goodness. Reading or thought will principally bestow the former of these—the benevolent exercise of the powers of the mind in communicating useful knowledge will bestow an habit of the latter; both united will contribute so far as lies in your individual power to that great reform which will be perfect and finished the moment every one is virtuous and wise. Every folly refuted, every bad habit conquered, every good one confirmed, is so much gained in this great and excellent cause.

To begin to reform the government is immediately necessary, however good or bad individuals may be; it is the more necessary if they are eminently the latter in some degree to palliate or do away the cause as political institution has even [ever] the greatest influence on the human character, and is that alone which differences the Turk from the Irishman.

I write now not only with a view for Catholic Emancipation but for universal emancipation; and this emancipation complete and unconditional, that shall comprehend every individual of whatever nation or principles, that shall fold in its embrace all that think and all that feel; the Catholic cause is subordinate, and its success preparatory to this great cause which adheres to no sect but society, to no cause but that of universal happiness, to no party but the people. I desire Catholic Emancipation, but I desire not to stop here; and I hope there are few who having perused the preceding arguments will not concur with me in desiring a complete, a lasting, ·and a happy amendment. That all steps, however good and salutary, which may be taken, all reforms consistent with the English constitution that may be effectuated can only be subordinate and preparatory to the great and lasting one which shall bring about the peace, the harmony, and the happiness of Ireland, England, Europe, the World. I offer merely an outline of that picture which your own hopes may gift with the colors of reality.

Government will not allow a peaceable and reasonable discussion of its principles by any association of men who assemble for that express purpose. But have not human beings a right to assemble to talk upon what subject they please? Can anything be more evident than that as government is only of use as it conduces to the happiness of the governed those who are governed have a right to talk on the efficacy of the safeguard employed for their benefit? Can any topic be more interesting or useful than on discussing how far the means of government is or could be made in a higher degree effectual to producing the end? Although I deprecate violence and the cause which depends for its influence on force, yet I can by no means think that assembling together merely to talk of how things go on, I can by no means think that societies formed for talking on any subject, however Government may dislike them, come in any way under the head of force or violence. I think that associations conducted in the spirit of sobriety, regularity, and thought are one of the best and most efficient of those means which I would recommend for the production of happiness, liberty, and virtue.

Are you slaves, or are you men? If slaves, then crouch to the rod and lick the feet of your oppressors; glory [in] your shame; it will become you, if brutes, to act according to your nature. But you are men; a real man is free, so far ·as circumstances will permit him. Then firmly, yet quietly, resist. When one cheek is struck, turn the other to the insulting coward. You will be truly brave; you will resist and conquer. The discussion of any subject is a right that you have brought into the world with your heart and tongue. Resign your heart's blood before you part with this inestimable privilege of man. For it is fit that the governed should inquire into the proceedings of government, which is of no use the moment it is conducted on any other principle but that of safety. You have much to think of. Is war necessary to your happiness and safety? The interests of the poor gain nothing from the wealth or extension of a nation's boundaries; they gain nothing from glory, a word that has often served as a cloak to the ambition or avarice of statesmen. The barren victories of Spain, gained in behalf of a bigoted and tyrannical government, are nothing to them. The conquests in India, by which England has gained glory indeed, but a glory which is not more honorable than that of Buonaparte, are nothing to them. The poor purchase this glory and this wealth at the expense of their blood and labor and happiness and virtue. They die in battle for this infernal cause. Their labor supplies money and food for carrying it into effect; their happiness is destroyed by the oppression they undergo; their virtue is rooted out by the depravity and vice that prevail throughout the army, and which under the present system are perfectly unavoidable. Who does not know that the quartering of a regiment on any town will soon destroy the innocence and happiness of its inhabitants? The advocates for the happiness and liberty of the great mass of the people, who pay for war with their lives and labor, ought never to cease writing and speaking until nations see, as they must feel, the folly of fighting and killing each other in uniform for nothing at all. You have much to think of. The state of your representation in the House, which is called the collective representation of the country, demands your attention.

It is horrible that the lower classes must waste their lives and liberty to furnish means for their oppressors to oppress them yet more terribly. It is horrible that the poor must give in taxes what would save them and their families from hunger and cold; it is still more horrible that they should do this to furnish further means of their own abjectedness and misery. But what words can express the enormity of the abuse that prevents them from choosing representatives with authority to inquire into the manner in which their lives and labor, their happiness and innocence, are expended, and what advantages result from the expenditure which may counterbalance so horrible and monstrous an evil? There is an outcry raised against amendment; it is called innovation and condemned by many unthinking people who have a good fire and plenty to eat and drink. Hard-hearted or thoughtless beings, how many are famishing while you deliberate, how many perish to contribute to your pleasures? I hope that there are none such as these native Irishmen; indeed I scarcely believe that there are.

Let the object of your associations (for I conceal not my approval of assemblies conducted with regularity, *peaceableness,* and thought for any purpose) be the amendment of these abuses; it will have for its object universal emancipation, liberty, happiness, and virtue. There is yet another subject, "the Liberty of the Press." The liberty of the press consists in a right to publish any opinion on any subject which the writer may entertain. The Attorney-General in 1793, on the trial of Mr. Percy [or Perry], said, "I never will dispute the right of any man fully to discuss topics respecting Government and honestly to point out what he may consider a proper remedy of grievances." The liberty of the press is placed as a sentinel to alarm us when any attempt is made on our liberties. It is this sentinel, Oh Irishmen, whom I now awaken! I create to myself a freedom which exists not. There is no liberty of the press for the subjects of British government.

It is really ridiculous to hear people yet boasting of this inestimable blessing when they daily see it successfully muzzled and outraged by the lawyers of the Crown, and by virtue of what are called *ex officio* informations. Blackstone says that "if a person publishes what is improper, mischievous, or illegal, he must take the consequences of his own temerity." And Lord Chief Baron Comyns defines libel as "a contumely, or reproach, published to the defamation of the Government, of a magistrate, or of a private person." Now, I beseech you to consider the words mischievous, improper, illegal, contumely, reproach, or defamation. May they not make that mischievous or improper which they please? Is not law with them as clay in the potter's hand? Do not the words contumely, reproach, or defamation express all degrees and forces of disapprobation? It is impossible to express yourself displeased at certain proceedings of Government, or the individuals who conduct it, without uttering a reproach. We cannot honestly point out a proper remedy of grievances with safety, because the very mention of these grievances will be reproachful to the personages who countenance them and therefore will come under a definition of libel. For the persons who thus directly or indirectly undergo reproach will say for their own sakes that the exposure of their corruption is mischievous and improper; therefore, the utterer of the reproach is a fit subject for three years' imprisonment. Is there anything like the liberty of the press in restrictions so positive, yet pliant, as these? The little freedom which we enjoy in this most important point comes from the clemency of our rulers, or their fear lest public opinion, alarmed at the discovery of its enslaved state, should violently assert a right to extension and diffusion. Yet public opinion may not always be so formidable; rulers may not always be so merciful or so timid; at any rate, evils, and great evils, do result from the present system of intellectual slavery, and you have enough to think of if this grievance alone remained

in the constitution of society. I will give but one instance of the present state of our press.

A countryman of yours is now confined in an English gaol.[19] His health, his fortune, his spirits suffer from close confinement. The air which comes through the bars of a prison-grate does not invigorate the frame nor cheer the spirits. But Mr. Finnerty, much as he has lost, yet retains the fair name of truth and honor. He was imprisoned for persisting in the truth. His judge told him on his trial that truth and falsehood were indifferent to the law, and that if he owned the publication, any consideration whether the facts that it related were well or ill-founded was totally irrelevant. Such is the libel law; such the liberty of the press—there is enough to think of. The right of withholding your individual assent to war, the right of choosing delegates to represent you in the assembly of the nation, and that of freely opposing intellectual power to any measures of Government of which you may disapprove are, in addition to the indifference with which the Legislative and the Executive power ought to rule their conduct towards professors of every religion, enough to think of.

I earnestly desire peace and harmony: peace, that whatever wrongs you may have suffered, benevolence, and a spirit of forgiveness should mark your conduct towards those who have persecuted you; harmony, that among yourselves may be no divisions, that Protestants and Catholics unite in a common interest, and that whatever be the belief and principles of your countryman and fellow-sufferer, you desire to benefit his cause at the same time that you vindicate your own. Be strong, and unbiassed by selfishness and prejudice—for, Catholics, your religion has not been spotless; crime in past ages have sullied it with a stain which let it be your glory to remove. Nor, Protestants, hath your religion always been

19. Peter Finnerty, an Irish journalist, had more than a year before been sentenced to eighteen months in prison for publishing a letter in the London *Morning Chronicle* for opposing the ill-fated Walcheren expedition. The letter was pronounced libelous by the Government, and Finnerty was not allowed to defend himself in Court. Shelley contributed to a fund for the victim's relief.

characterized by the mildness of benevolence which Jesus Christ recommended. Had it anything to do with the present subject I could account for the spirit of intolerance which marked both religions; I will, however, only adduce the fact, and earnestly exhort you to root out from your own minds everything which may lead to uncharitableness, and to reflect that yourselves as well as your brethren may be deceived. Nothing on earth is infallible. The priests that pretend to it are wicked and mischievous imposters; but it is an imposture which every one more or less assumes who encourages prejudice in his breast against those who differ from him in opinion, or who sets up his own religion as the only right and true one, when no one is so blind as [not] to see that every religion is right and true which makes men beneficent and sincere. I therefore earnestly exhort both Protestants and Catholics to act in brotherhood and harmony, never forgetting because the Catholics alone are heinously deprived of religious rights that the Protestants and a certain rank of people of every persuasion share with them all else that is terrible, galling, and intolerable in the mass of political grievance.

In no case employ violence or falsehood. I cannot too often or too vividly endeavor to impress upon your minds that these methods will produce nothing but wretchedness and slavery—that they will at the same time rivet the fetters with which ignorance and oppression bind you to abjectness, and deliver you over to a tyranny which shall render you incapable of renewed efforts. Violence will immediately render your cause a bad one. If you believe in a providential God, you must also believe that he is a good one. And it is not likely a merciful God would befriend a bad cause. Insincerity is no less hurtful than violence; those who are in the habit of either would do well to reform themselves. A lying bravo will never promote the good of his country—he cannot be a good man. The courageous and sincere may, at the same time, successfully oppose corruption by uniting their voice with that of others, or individually raise up intellectual opposition to counteract the abuses of Government and society. In order to benefit yourselves and your country to any extent, habits of sobriety, regularity, and thought are previously so necessary that, without these preliminaries, all that you have done falls to the ground. You have built on sand; secure a good foundation, and you may erect a fabric to stand for ever—the glory and the envy of the world!

I have purposely avoided any lengthened discussion on these grievances to which your hearts are, from custom and the immediate interest of the circumstances, probably most alive at present. I have not, however, wholly neglected them. Most of all have I insisted on their instant palliation and ultimate removal; nor have I omitted a consideration of the means which I deem most effectual for the accomplishment of this great end. How far you will consider the former worthy of your adoption, so far shall I deem the latter probable and interesting to the lovers of human kind. And I have opened to your view a new scene —does not your heart bound at the bare possibility of your posterity possessing that liberty and happiness of which, during our lives, powerful exertions and habitual abstinence may give us a foretaste? Oh! if your hearts do not vibrate at such as this, then ye are dead and cold—ye are not men.

I now come to the application of my principles, the conclusion of my Address; and, O Irishmen, whatever conduct ye may feel yourselves bound to pursue, the path which duty points to lies before me clear and unobscured. Dangers may lurk around it, but they are not the dangers which lie beneath the footsteps of the hyprocrite or temporizer.

For I have not presented to you the picture of happiness on which my fancy doats as an uncertain meteor to mislead honorable enthusiasm, or blindfold the judgment which makes virtue useful. I have not pro-

SHELLEY'S PROSE

posed crude schemes, which I should be incompetent to mature, or desired to excite in you any virulence against the abuses of political institution; where I have had occasion to point them out, I have recommended moderation while yet I have earnestly insisted upon energy and perseverance; I have spoken of peace, yet declared that resistance is laudable; but the intellectual resistance which I recommend, I deem essential to the introduction of the millennium of virtue, whose period every one can, so far as he is concerned, forward by his own proper power. I have not attempted to show that the Catholic claims, or the claims of the people to a full representation in Parliament, or any of these claims to real rights which I have insisted upon as introductory to the ultimate claim of *all*, to universal happiness, freedom, and equality; I have not attempted, I say, to show that these can be granted consistently with the spirit of the English Constitution;[20] this is a point which I do not feel myself inclined to discuss, and which I consider foreign to my subject. But I have shown that these claims have for their basis truth and justice, which are immutable, and which in the ruin of governments shall rise like a phoenix from their ashes.

Is any one inclined to dispute the possibility of a happy change in society? Do they say that the nature of man is corrupt, and that he was made for misery and wickedness? Be it so. Certain as are opposite conclusions, I will concede the truth of this for a moment. What are the means which I take for melioration? Violence, corruption, rapine, crime? Do I do evil that good may come? I have recommended peace, philanthropy, wisdom. So far as my arguments influence, they will influence to these; and if there is any one *now* inclined to say that "private vices are public benefits,"[21] and that peace, philanthropy, and wisdom will, if once they gain ground, ruin the human

race, he may revel in his happy dreams; though were *I* this man I should envy Satan's hell. The wisdom and charity of which I speak are the *only* means which I will countenance for the redress of your grievances and the grievances of the world. So far as they operate, I am willing to stand responsible for their *evil* effects. I expect to be accused of a desire for renewing in Ireland the scenes of revolutionary horror which marked the struggles of France twenty years ago. But it is the renewal of that unfortunate era which I strongly deprecate, and which the tendency of this Address is calculated to obviate. For can burthens be borne forever, and the slave crouch and cringe the while? Is misery and vice so consonant to man's nature that he will hug it to his heart? But when the wretched one in bondage beholds the emancipation near, will he not endure his misery awhile with hope and patience, then spring to his preserver's arms and start into a man?

It is my intention to observe the effect on your minds, O Irishmen, which this Address, dictated by the fervency of my love and hope, will produce. I have come to this country to spare no pains where expenditure may purchase you real benefit. The present is a crisis which of all others is the most valuable for fixing the fluctuation of public feeling; as far as my poor efforts may have succeeded in fixing it to virtue, Irishmen, so far shall I esteem myself happy. I intend this Address as introductory to another. The organization of a society whose institution shall serve as a bond to its members for the purposes of virtue, happiness, liberty, and wisdom, by the means of intellectual opposition to grievances, would probably be useful. For the formation of such society I avow myself anxious.

Adieu, my friends! May every sun that shines on your green island see the annihilation of an abuse and the birth of an embryon of melioration! Your own hearts may

---

20. The excellence of the Constitution of Great Britain appears to me to be its indefiniteness and versatility, whereby it may be unresistingly accommodated to the progression of wisdom and virtue.

Such accommodation I desire; but I wish for the cause before the effect. [Shelley's Note.]

21. This quotation is the subtitle of Mandeville's *The Fable of the Bees* (1714).

they become the shrines of purity and freedom, and never may smoke to the Mammon of unrighteousness ascend from the unpolluted altar of their devotion!

POSTSCRIPT

I have now been a week in Dublin, during which time I have endeavored to make myself more accurately acquainted with the state of the public mind on those great topics of grievances which induced me to select Ireland as a theatre, the widest and fairest, for the operations of the determined friend of religious and political freedom.

The result of my observations has determined me to propose an association for the purposes of restoring Ireland to the prosperity which she possessed before the Union Act, and the religious freedom which the involuntariness of faith ought to have taught all monopolists of Heaven long, long ago, that every one had a right to possess.

For the purpose of obtaining the emancipation of the Catholics from the penal laws that aggrieve them, and a repeal of the Legislative Union Act, and grounding upon the remission of the church-craft and oppression which caused these grievances: *a plan of amendment and regeneration in the moral and political state of society, on a comprehensive and systematic philanthropy which shall be sure though slow in its projects; and as it is without the rapidity and danger of revolution, so will it be devoid of the time-servingness of temporizing reform*—which in its deliberate capacity, having investigated the state of the government of England, shall oppose those parts of it by intellectual force which will not bear the touch-stone of reason.

For information respecting the principles which I possess, and the nature and spirit of the association which I propose, I refer the reader to a small pamphlet, which I shall publish on the subject in the course of a few days.

I have published the above Address (written in England) in the cheapest possible form, and have taken pains that the remarks which it contains should be intelligible to the most uneducated minds. Men are not slaves and brutes because they are poor; it has been the policy of the thoughtless or wicked of the higher ranks (as a proof of the decay of which policy I am happy to see the rapid success of a comparatively enlightened system of education) to conceal from the poor the truths which I have endeavored to teach them. In doing so I have but translated my thoughts into another language; and, as language is only useful as it communicates ideas, I shall think my style so far good as it is successful as a means to bring about the end which I desire on any occasion to accomplish.

A Limerick paper, which I suppose professes to support certain *loyal* and *John Bullish* principles of freedom, has in an essay for advocating the Liberty of the Press, the following clause: "For lawless license of discussion never did we advocate, nor do we now." What is lawless license of discussion? Is it not as indefinite as the words *contumely, reproach, defamation*, that allow at present such latitude to the outrages that are committed on the free expression of individual sentiment? Can they not see that what is rational will stand by its reason, and what is true stand by its truth, as all that is foolish will fall by its folly, and all that is false be controverted by its own falsehood? Liberty gains nothing by the reform of politicians of this stamp, any more than it gains from a change of Ministers in London. What at present is contumely and defamation would at the period of this Limerick amendment be "lawless license of discussion," and such would be the mighty advantage which this doughty champion of liberty proposes to effect.

I conclude with the words of Lafayette, a name endeared by its peerless bearer to every lover of the human race, "For a nation to love Liberty it is sufficient that she knows it; to be free, it is sufficient that she wills it."[22]

22. From Paine's *The Rights of Man*, p. 17.

PROPOSALS FOR AN ASSOCIATION
OF PHILANTHROPISTS[1]

[This essay appeared on March 2, 1812, and was intended for a more select group of readers than was *An Address*. For the most part it is a condensed restatement of the substance of *An Address*, with emphasis on the advisability and the method of founding societies to lay the foundations for the achievement of Catholic Emancipation and the revocation of the Act of Union. As in *An Address*, Shelley cautioned patience and mildness, toleration and wisdom, in the societies.

Shelley's advice is a counsel of perfection, and under the tense conditions, with the widespread poverty and wholesale illiteracy of the Irish people, it was highly impractical. But under more favorable circumstances his philosophy would be considered as full of wisdom and practicality. While his attempt at reform in Ireland may have seemed rash and Utopian to some, to men of goodwill the conditions laid down by Shelley were the only sound basis for social regeneration, then as now. As in *An Address*, Shelley's main source is Godwin's *Political Justice*. In the light of its importance in Shelley's philosophy the author's explanation of the failure of the French Revolution holds especial interest for the Shelley student.

In his letter to Godwin, March 18, 1812, Shelley states that "My association scheme undoubtedly grew out of my notions of political justice, first generated by your book on that subject." While this is doubtless true, Shelley did not hesitate openly to disagree with Godwin's ideas in social and political matters. For an extended analysis of the *Proposals*, see Cameron, *op. cit.*, pp. 147-153.]

I propose an association which shall have for its immediate objects Catholic Emancipation and the Repeal of the Act of Union between Great Britain and Ireland; and grounding on the removal of these grievances an annihilation or palliation of whatever moral or political evil it may be within the compass of human power to assuage or eradicate.

Man cannot make occasions, but he may seize those that offer. None are more interesting to philanthropy than those which excite the benevolent passions, that generalize and expand private into public feelings, and make the hearts of individuals vibrate not merely for themselves, their families, and their friends, but for posterity, *for a people*, till their country becomes the world and their family the sensitive creation.[2]

A recollection of the absent and a taking into consideration the interests of those unconnected with ourselves is a principal source of that feeling which generates occasions wherein a love for humankind may become eminently useful and active. Public topics of fear and hope, such as sympathize with general grievance, or hold out hopes of general amendment, are those on which the philanthropist would dilate with the warmest feeling; because these are accustomed to

1. The remainder of the title is: WHO CONVINCED OF THE INADEQUACY OF THE MORAL AND POLITICAL STATE OF IRELAND TO PRODUCE BENEFITS WHICH ARE NEVERTHELESS ATTAINABLE ARE WILLING TO UNITE TO ACCOMPLISH ITS REGENERATION.

2. Like Paine, Shelley was a true internationalist, seeing in nationalism a source of war and other evils. The phrase "their country becomes the world" is an echo of Paine's "My country is the World." *The Rights of Man* (Everyman edition), p. 233.

place individuals at a distance from self; for in proportion as he is absorbed in public feeling, so will a consideration of his proper benefit be generalized. In proportion as he feels with or for a nation or a world, so will man consider himself less as that center to which we are but too prone to believe that every line of human concern does or ought to converge.

I should not here make the trite remark that selfish motive biasses, brutalizes, and degrades the human mind, did it not thence follow that to seize those occasions wherein the opposite spirit predominates is a duty which philanthropy imperiously exacts of her votaries, that occasions like these are the proper ones for leading mankind to their own interest by awakening in their minds a love for the interest of their fellows—a plant that grows in every soil, though too often it is choked by tares before its lovely blossoms are expanded. Virtue produces pleasure; it is as the cause to the effect; I feel pleasure in doing good to my friend, because I love him. I do not love him for the sake of that pleasure.

I regard the present state of the public mind in Ireland to be one of those occasions which the ardent votary of the religion of philanthropy dare not leave unseized. I perceive that the public interest is excited; I perceive that individual interest has, in a certain degree, quitted individual concern to generalize itself with universal feeling. Be the Catholic Emancipation a thing of great or of small misfortune,[3] be it a means of adding happiness to four millions of people, or a reform which will only give honor to a few of the higher ranks, yet a benevolent and disinterested feeling has gone abroad and I am willing that it should never subside. I desire that means should be taken with energy and expedition, in this important yet fleeting crisis, to feed the unpolluted

flame at which nations and ages may light the torch of Liberty and Virtue!

It is my opinion that the claims of the Catholic inhabitants of Ireland, if gained tomorrow, would in a very small degree aggrandize their liberty and happiness. The disqualifications principally affect the higher orders of the Catholic persuasion; these would principally be benefited by their removal. Power and wealth do not benefit, but injure the cause of virtue and freedom. I am happy, however, at the near approach of this emancipation, because I am inimical to all disqualifications for opinion. It gives me pleasure to see the approach of this enfranchisement, not for the good which it will bring with it, but because it is a sign of benefits approaching, a prophet of good about to come; and therefore, do I sympathize with the inhabitants of Ireland in this great cause; a cause which though in its own accomplishment will add not one comfort to the cottager, will snatch not one from the dark dungeon, will root not out one vice, alleviate not one pang, yet it is the foreground of a picture in the dimness of whose distance I behold the lion lay down with the lamb and the infant play with the basilisk.[4] For it supposes the extermination of the eyeless monster Bigotry, whose throne has tottered for two hundred years. I hear the teeth of the palsied beldame Superstition chatter, and I see her descending to the grave! Reason points to the open gates of the Temple of Religious Freedom, Philanthropy kneels at the altar of the common God! There, wealth and poverty, rank and abjectness are names known but as memorials of past time—meteors[5] which play over the loathsome pool of vice and misery to warn the wanderer where dangers lie. Does a God rule this illimitable universe; are you thankful for his beneficence—do you adore his wisdom—do you hang upon his altar the

3. The word *misfortune* is perhaps an error for *importance*.
4. Compare this idea with a similar one in

Queen Mab, VIII, 85-130.
5. *Meteor* here means any phenomenon, as hail, halos, rainbow.

garland of your devotion? Curse not your brother, though he hath enwreathed with his flowers of a different hue; the purest religion is that of Charity; its loveliness begins to proselyte the hearts of men. The tree is to be judged of by its fruit. I regard the admission of the Catholic claims and the Repeal of the Union Act as blossoms of that fruit which the Summer Sun of improved intellect and progressive virtue is destined to mature.

I will not pass unreflected on the legislative Union of Great Britain and Ireland, nor will I speak of it as a grievance so tolerable or unimportant in its own nature as that of Catholic disqualification. The latter affects few; the former affects thousands. The one disqualifies the rich from power; the other impoverishes the peasant, adds beggary to the city, famine to the country, multiplies abjectedness, while misery and crime play into each other's hands under its withering auspices. I esteem, then, the annihilation of this second grievance to be something more than a mere sign of coming good. I esteem it to be in itself a substantial benefit. The aristocracy of Ireland (for much as I may disapprove other distinctions than those of virtue and talent, I consider it useless, hasty, and violent, not for the present to acquiesce in their continuance). The aristocracy of Ireland suck the veins of its inhabitants and consume the blood in England. I mean not to deny the unhappy truth that there is much misery and vice in the world. I mean to say that Ireland shares largely of both. England has made her poor, and the poverty of a rich nation will make its people very desperate and wicked.

I look forward, then, to the redress of both these grievances, or rather, I perceive the state of the public mind that precedes them as the crisis of beneficial innovation. The latter I consider to be the cause of the former, as I hope it will be the cause of more comprehensively beneficial amendments. It forms that occasion which should energetically and quickly be occupied. The voice of the whole human race, their crimes, their miseries, and their ignorance invoke us to the task. For the miseries of the Irish poor, exacerbated by the union of their country with England, are not peculiar to themselves. England, the whole civilized world, with few exceptions, is either sunk in disproportioned abjectness, or raised to unnatural elevation. The Repeal of the Union Act will place Ireland on a level, so far as concerns the well-being of its poor, with her sister nation. Benevolent feeling has gone out in this country in favor of the happiness of its inhabitants—may this feeling be corroborated, methodized, and continued! May it never fail! But it will not be kept alive by each citizen sitting quietly by his own fireside and saying that things are going on well, because the rain does not beat on *him,* because *he* has books and leisure to read them, because *he* has money and is at liberty to accumulate luxuries to *himself.* Generous feeling dictates no such sayings. When the heart recurs to the thousands who have no liberty and no leisure, it must be rendered callous by long contemplation of wretchedness, if after such recurrence it can beat with contented evenness. Why do I talk thus? Is there anyone who doubts that the present state of politics and morals is wrong? They say, Show us a safe method of improvement. There is no safer than the corroboration and propagation of generous and philanthropic feeling, than the keeping continually alive a love for the human race, than the putting in train causes which shall have for their consequences virtue and freedom; and because I think that individuals acting singly with whatever energy can never effect so much as a society; I propose that all those whose views coincide with those that I have avowed, who perceive the state of the public mind in Ireland, who think the present a fit opportunity for attempting to fix its fluctuations at philanthropy, who love all mankind, and are willing actively to engage in its cause, or passively to endure the persecutions of those who are inimical to its success; I propose to these to form an association for the purposes, first, of debating on the propriety of whatever measures may be agitated, and secondly, for carrying, by united or individual exertion, such measures into effect when determined on. That it should be an association for discussing[6] knowledge and virtue throughout the poorer classes of society in Ireland, for co-operating with any enlightened system of education, for discussing topics calculated to throw light on any methods of alleviation of moral and political evil, and as far as lays in its power, actively interesting itself in whatever occasions may arise for benefiting mankind.

When I mention Ireland, I do not mean to confine the influence of the association to this, or to any other country, but for the time being. Moreover, I would recommend that this association should attempt to form others and to actuate them with a similar spirit; and I am thus indeterminate in my description of the association which I propose, because I conceive that an assembly of men meeting to do all the good that opportunity will permit them to do must be in its nature as indefinite and varying as the instances of human vice and misery that precede, occasion, and call for its institution.

As political institution and its attendant evils constitute the majority of those grievances which philanthropists desire to remedy, it is probable that existing Governments will frequently become the topic of their discussion, the results of which may little coincide with the opinions which those who profit by the supineness of human belief desire to impress upon the world. It is probable that this freedom may excite the odium of certain well-meaning people who pin their faith upon their grandmother's apron-string. The minority in number are the majority in intellect and power. The former govern the latter, though it is by the sufferance of the latter that this originally delegated power is exercised. This power is become hereditary and has ceased to be necessarily united with intellect.

6. Perhaps an error for *diffusing*.

It is certain, therefore, that any questioning of established principles would excite the abhorrence and opposition of those who derived power and honor (such as it is) from their continuance.

As the association which I recommend would question those principles (however they may be hedged in with antiquity and precedent) which appeared ill adapted for the benefit of the human kind; it would probably excite the odium of those in power. It would be obnoxious to the government, though nothing would be further from the views of associated philanthropists than attempting to subvert establishments forcibly, or even hastily. Aristocracy would oppose it, whether oppositionists or ministerialists, (for philanthropy is of no party) because its ultimate views look to a subversion of all factitious distinctions, although from its immediate intentions I fear that aristocracy can have nothing to dread. The priesthood would oppose it, because a union of church and state—contrary to the principles and practice of Jesus, contrary to that equality which he fruitlessly endeavored to teach mankind—is of all institutions that from the rust of antiquity are called venerable the least qualified to stand free and cool reasoning, because it least conduces to the happiness of human kind; yet did either the minister, the peer, or the bishop, know their true interest, instead of that virulent opposition which some among them have made to freedom and philanthropy, they would rejoice and co-operate with the diffusion and corroboration of those principles that would remove a load of paltry equivocation, paltrier grandeur, and of wigs that crush into emptiness the brains below them from their shoulders; and by permitting them to reassume the degraded and vilified title of man would preclude the necessity of mystery and deception, would bestow on them a title more ennobling and a dignity which, though it would be without the gravity of an ape, would possess the ease and consistency of a man.

For the reasons above alleged, falsely, prejudicedly, and narrowly, will those very persons whose ultimate benefit is included in the general good, whose promotion is the essence of a philanthropic association, will they persecute those who have the best intentions towards them, malevolence towards none.

I do not, therefore, conceal that those who make the favor of Government the sunshine of their moral day [and] confide in the political creed makers of the hour are willing to think things that are rusty and decayed venerable and are uninquiringly satisfied with evils as these are, because they find them established and unquestioned as they do sunlight and air when they come into existence; that they had better not even think of philanthropy. I conceal not from them that the discountenance which Government will show to such an association as I am desirous to establish will come under their comprehensive definition of danger: that virtue and any assembly instituted under its auspices demands a voluntariness on the part of its devoted individuals to sacrifice personal to public benefit, and that it is possible that a party of beings associated for the purpose of disseminating virtuous principles, may, considering the ascendency which long custom has conferred on opposite motives to action, meet with inconveniences that may amount to personal danger. These considerations are, however, to the mind of the philanthropist as is a drop to an ocean; they serve by their possible existence as tests whereby to discover the really virtuous man from him who calls himself a patriot for dishonorable and selfish purposes. I propose, then, to such as think with me a philanthropic association, in spite of the danger that may attend the attempt. I do not this

beneath the shroud of mystery and darkness. I propose not an Association of Secrecy. Let it open as the beam of day. Let it rival the sunbeam in its stainless purity, as in the extensiveness of its effulgence.

I disclaim all connection with insincerity and concealment. The latter implies the former, as much as the former stands in need of the latter. It is a very latitudinarian system of morality that permits its professor to employ bad means for any end whatever. Weapons which vice *can* use are unfit for the hands of virtue. Concealment implies falsehood; it is bad, and can therefore never be serviceable to the cause of philanthropy.

I propose, therefore, that the association shall be established and conducted in the open face of day, with the utmost possible publicity. It is only vice that hides itself in holes and corners,[7] whose effrontery shrinks from scrutiny, whose cowardice lets "*I dare not* wait upon *I would,* like the poor cat i' the adage."[8] But the eye of virtue, eagle-like, darts through the undazzling beam of eternal truth, and from the undiminished fountain of its purity gathers wherewith to vivify and illuminate a universe.[9]

I have hitherto abstained from inquiring whether the association which I recommend be or be not consistent with the English constitution. And here it is fit briefly to consider what a constitution is.

Government can have no rights: it is a delegation for the purpose of securing them to others. Man becomes a subject of government, not that he may be in a worse, but that he may be in a better state than that of unorganized society. The strength of government is the happiness of the governed.[10] All government existing for the happiness of others is just only so far as it exists by their consent, and useful only so far as it operates to their well-being. Constitution is to government what government is to law.

---

7. Shakespeare's *Winter's Tale,* 1.2.289, is the probable source of this idea. Compare this with a similar thought in *Letter to Lord Ellenborough.*
8. Shakespeare's *Macbeth,* 1.7.44-45.

9. The thought and imagery of this sentence anticipate the poetry of Shelley's maturity.
10. Compare this with a passage in Paine's *Common Sense:* "upon cooperation depends the strength of government and the happiness of the governed."

Constitution may, in this view of the subject, be defined to be not merely something constituted for the benefit of any nation or class of people, but something constituted by themselves for their own benefit.[11] The nations of England and Ireland have no constitution, because at no one time did the individuals that compose them constitute a system for the general benefit. If a system determined on by a very few, at a great length of time; if Magna Charta, the Bill of Rights, and other usages for whose influence the improved state of human knowledge is rather to be looked to than any system which courtiers pretend to exist and perhaps believe to exist, a system whose spring of agency they represent as something secret, undiscoverable, and awful as the law of nature; if these make a constitution, then England has one. But if (as I have endeavored to show they do not) a constitution is something else, then the speeches of Kings or commissioners, the writings of courtiers, and the journals of Parliament, which teem with its glory, are full of political cant, exhibit the skeleton of national freedom, and are fruitless attempts to hide evils in whose favor they cannot prove an alibi. As, therefore, in the true sense of the expression, the spot of earth on which we live is destitute of constituted Government, it is impossible to offend against its principles, or to be with justice accused of wishing to subvert what has no real existence. If a man was accused of setting fire to a house, which house never existed, and from the nature of things could not have existed, it is impossible that a jury in their senses would find him guilty of arson. The English constitution, then, could not be offended by the principles of virtue and freedom. In fact, the manner in which the Government of England has varied since its earliest establishment proves that its present form is the result of a progressive accommodation to existing principles. It has been a continual

struggle for liberty on the part of the people, and an uninterrupted attempt at tightening the reins of oppression and encouraging ignorance and imposture by the oligarchy to whom the first William parcelled out the property of the aborigines at the conquest of England by the Normans. I hear much of its being a tree so long growing which to cut down is as bad as cutting down an oak where there are no more. But the best way, on topics similar to these, is to tell the plain truth, without the confusion and ornament of metaphor. I call expressions similar to these political cant, which, like the songs of *Rule, Britannia* and *God Save the King* are but abstracts of the caterpillar creed of courtiers, cut down to the taste and comprehension of a mob; the one to disguise to an alehouse politician the evils of that devilish practice of war, and the other to inspire among clubs of all descriptions a certain feeling which some call loyalty and others servility. A philanthropic association has nothing to fear from the English constitution, but it may expect danger from its government. So far, however, from thinking this an argument against its institution, establishments, and augmentation, I am inclined to rest much of the weight of the cause which my duties call upon me to support, on the very fact that government forcibly interferes when the opposition that is made to its proceedings is professedly and undeniably nothing but intellectual. A good cause may be shown to be good; violence instantly renders bad what might before have been good. "Weapons that falsehood can use are unfit for the hands of truth." Truth can reason, and falsehood cannot.

A political or religious system may burn and imprison those who investigate its principles; but it is an invariable proof of their falsehood and hollowness. Here then is another reason for the necessity of a Philanthropic Association, and I call upon any fair and rational opponent to controvert the

11. This discussion of governments and constitutions is a recasting of Paine's ideas in *The Rights of Man* (Everyman edition), pp. 48-49.

argument which it contains, for there is no one who even calls himself a philanthropist that thinks personal danger or dishonor terrible in any other light than as it affects his usefulness.

Man has a heart to feel, a brain to think, and a tongue to utter. The laws of his moral as of his physical nature are immutable, as is everything of nature; nor can the ephemeral institutions of human society take away those rights, annihilate or strengthen the duties that have for their basis the imperishable relations of his constitution.

Though the Parliament of England were to pass a thousand bills to inflict upon those who determined to utter their thoughts a thousand penalties, it could not render that criminal which was in its nature innocent before the passing of such bill.

Man has a right to feel, to think, and to speak, nor can any acts of legislature destroy that right. He will feel, he must think, and he *ought* to give utterance to those thoughts and feelings with the readiest sincerity and the strictest candor. A man must have a right to do a thing before he can have a duty; this right must permit before his duty can enjoin him to any act. Any law is bad which attempts to make it criminal to do what the plain dictates within the breast of every man tells him that he ought to do.

The English Government permits a fanatic to assemble any number of persons to teach them the most extravagant and immoral systems of faith; but a few men meeting to consider its own principles are marked with its hatred and pursued by its jealousy.

The religionist who agonizes the deathbed of the cottager, and by picturing the hell which hearts black and narrow as his own alone could have invented and which exists but in their cores, spreads the uncharitable doctrines which devote *heretics* to eternal torments, and represents heaven to be what earth is, a monopoly in the hands of certain favored ones whose merit consists in slavishness, whose success is the reward of syco-phancy. Thus much is permitted, but a public inquiry that involves any doubt of their rectitude into the principles of government is not permitted. When Jupiter and a countryman were one day walking out, conversing familiarly on the affairs of earth, the countryman listened to Jupiter's assertions on the subject for some time in acquiescence; at length happening to hint a doubt, Jupiter threatened him with his thunder; "Ah, ah," says the countryman, "now, Jupiter, I know that you are wrong; you are always wrong when you appeal to your thunder." The essence of virtue is disinterestedness. Disinterestedness is the quality which preserves the character of virtue distinct from that of either innocence or vice. This, it will be said, is mere assertion. It is so, but it is an assertion, whose truth, I believe, the hearts of philanthropists are disinclined to deny. Those who have been convinced by their grandam of the doctrine of an original hereditary sin, or by the apostles of a degrading philosophy of the necessary and universal selfishness of man cannot be philanthropists. Now, as an action, or a motive to action, is only virtuous so far as it is disinterested, or partakes (I adopt this mode of expression to suit the taste of some) of the nature of generalized self-love, then reward or punishment, attached even by omnipotence to any action, can in no wise make it either good or bad.

It is no crime to act in contradiction to an English judge or an English legislator, but it is a crime to transgress the dictates of a monitor which feels the spring of every motive, whose throne is the human sensorium, whose empire the human conduct. Conscience is a Government before which all others sink into nothingness; it surpasses, and, where it can act, supersedes all other, as nature surpasses art, as God surpasses man.

In the preceding pages during the course of an investigation of the possible objections which might be urged by philanthropy to an association such as I recommend, as I have rather sought to bring forward than conceal my principles, it will appear that they have their origin from the discoveries in the sciences of politics and morals which preceded and occasioned the revolutions of America and France. It is with openness that I confess, nay with pride I assert, that they are so. The names of Paine and Lafayette will outlive the poetic aristocracy of an expatriated Jesuit[12] as the executive of a bigoted policy will die before the disgust at the sycophancy of their eulogists can subside.

It will be said, perhaps, that much as principles such as these may appear marked on the outside with peace, liberty, and virtue, that their ultimate tendency is to a revolution, which, like that of France, will end in bloodshed, vice, and slavery. I must offer, therefore, my thoughts on that event, which so suddenly and so lamentably extinguished the overstrained hopes of liberty which it excited. I do not deny that the Revolution of France was occasioned by the literary labors of the Encyclopaedists. When we see two events together, in certain cases, we speak of one as the cause, the other the effect. We have no other idea of cause and effect, but that which arises from necessary connection;[13] it is, therefore, still doubtful whether D'Alembert, Boulanger, Condorcet, and other celebrated characters were the causes of the overthrow of the ancient monarchy of France. Thus much is certain, that they contributed greatly to the extension and diffusion of knowledge, and that knowledge is incompatible with slavery.[14] The French nation was bowed to the dust by ages of uninterrupted despotism. They were plundered and insulted by a succession of oligarchies, each more bloodthirsty and unrelenting than the foregoing. In a state like this, her soldiers learned to fight for freedom on the plains of America, while at this very conjuncture a ray of science burst through the clouds of bigotry that obscured the moral day of Europe. The French were in the lowest state of human degradation, and when the truth, unaccustomed to their ears, that they were men and equals was promulgated, they were the first to vent their indignation on the monopolizers of earth, because they were most glaringly defrauded of the immunities of nature.

Since the French were furthest removed by the sophistications of political institution from the genuine condition of human beings, they must have been most unfit for that happy state of equal law which proceeds from consummated civilization and which demands habits of the strictest virtue before its introduction.

The murders during the period of the French Revolution, and the despotism which has since been established, prove that the doctrines of philanthropy and freedom were but shallowly understood. Nor was it until after that period that their principles became clearly to be explained and unanswerably to be established.

Voltaire was the flatterer of kings, though in his heart he despised them—so far has he been instrumental in the present slavery of his country.[15] Rousseau gave license by his writings to passions that only incapacitate and contract the human heart. So far hath he prepared the necks of his fellow-beings for that yoke of galling and dishonorable servitude which at this moment it bears. Helvetius and Condorcet established principles, but if they drew conclusions, their conclusions were unsystematical and devoid of the luminousness and energy of method; they were little understood in the Revolution. But this age of ours is not stationary. Philosophers have not developed the great principles of the human mind that conclusions from them should be unprofitable and

---

12. See *Mémoires . . . du Jacobinisme*, par l'abbé Barruel. [Shelley's Note.]

13. This idea is probably from Hume's *An Enquiry Concerning Human Understanding*, Secs. V and VI.

14. This paragraph is a recasting of one in Paine's *The Rights of Man* (Everyman edition), pp. 74-75.

15. See Paine's *The Rights of Man* (Everyman edition), p. 75, for a similar idea.

impracticable. We are in a state of continually progressive improvement. One truth that has been discovered can never die, but will prevent the revivification of its apportioned opposite falsehood. By promoting truth and discouraging its opposite, the means of philanthropy are principally to be forwarded. Godwin wrote during the Revolution of France, and certainly his writings were totally devoid of influence, with regard to its purposes. Oh! that they had not! In the Revolution of France were engaged men whose names are inerasible from the records of Liberty. Their genius penetrated with a glance the gloom and glare which Churchcraft and State-craft had spread before the imposture and villainy of their establishments. They saw the world. Were they men? Yes! They felt for it! They risked their lives and happiness for its benefit! Had there been more of those men France would not now be a beacon to warn us of the hazard and horror of Revolutions, but a pattern of society rapidly advancing to a state of perfection and holding out an example for the gradual and peaceful regeneration of the world. I consider it to be one of the effects of a philanthropic association to assist in the production of such men as these, in an extensive development of those germs of excellence, whose favorite soil is the cultured garden of the human mind.

Many well-meaning persons may think that the attainment of the good which I propose as the ultimatum of philanthropic exertion is visionary and inconsistent with human nature; they would tell me not to make people happy, for fear of overstocking the world, and to permit those who found dishes placed before them on the table of partial nature to enjoy their superfluities in quietness, though millions of wretches crowded around but to pick a morsel,[16] which morsel was still refused to the prayers of agonizing famine.

I cannot help thinking this an evil, nor help endeavoring by the safest means that

I can devise to palliate at present and in fine to eradicate this evil; war, vice, and misery are undeniably bad—they embrace all that we can conceive of temporal and eternal evil. Are we to be told that these are remediless, because the earth would, in case of their remedy, be overstocked? That the rich are still to glut, that the ambitious are still to plan, that the fools whom these knaves mould are still to murder their brethren and call it glory, and that the poor are to pay with their blood, their labor, their happiness, and their innocence, for the crimes and mistakes which the hereditary monopolists of earth commit? Rare sophism! How will the heartless rich hug thee to their bosoms and lull their conscience into slumber with the opiate of thy reconciling dogmas! But when the philosopher and philanthropist contemplates the universe, when he perceives existing evils that admit of amendment, and hears tell of other evils, which, in the course of sixty centuries, may again derange the system of happiness which the amendment is calculated to produce, does he submit to prolong a positive evil, because, if that were eradicated, after a millennium of 6000 years (for such space of time would it take to people the earth) another evil would take place.

To how contemptible a degradation of grossest credulity will not prejudice lower the human mind! We see in winter that the foliage of the trees is gone, that they present to the view nothing but leafless branches; we see that the loveliness of the flower decays, though the root continues in the earth. What opinion should we form of that man who, when he walked in the freshness of the spring, beheld the fields enamelled with flowers and the foliage bursting from the buds, should find fault with this beautiful order, and murmur his contemptible discontents because winter must come, and the landscape be robbed of its beauty for a while again? Yet this man is Mr. Malthus. Do we not see that the laws of nature perpetually

16. See Malthus on *Population*. [Shelley's Note.]

act by disorganization and reproduction, each alternately becoming cause and effect. The analysis that we can draw from physical to moral topics are of all others the most striking.

Does any one yet question the possibility of inducing radical reform of moral and political evil? Does he object, from that impossibility, to the association which I propose, which I frankly confess to be one of the means whose instrumentality I would employ to attain this reform? Let them look to the methods which I use. Let me put my object out of their view and propose their own, how would they accomplish it? By diffusing virtue and knowledge, by promoting human happiness. Palsied be the hand, forever dumb be the tongue that would by one expression convey sentiments differing from these; I will use no bad means for any end whatever. Know then, ye philanthropists—to whatever profession of faith, or whatever determination of principles, chance, reason, or education may have conducted you—that the endeavors of the truly virtuous necessarily converge to one point, though it be hidden from them what point that is; they all labor for one end, and that controversies concerning the nature of that end serve only to weaken the strength which for the interest of virtue should be consolidated.

The diffusion of true and virtuous principles (for in the first principles of morality *none* disagree) will produce the best of possible terminations.

I invite to an Association of Philanthropy those of whatever ultimate expectations, who will employ the same means that I employ; let their designs differ as much as they may from mine, I shall rejoice at their co-operation; because if the ultimatum of my hopes be founded on the unity of truth, I shall then have auxiliaries in its cause, and if it be false I shall rejoice that means are not neglected for forwarding that which is true.

The accumulation of evil which Ireland has for the last twenty years sustained, and considering the unremittingness of its pressure I may say patiently sustained; the melancholy prospect which the unforeseen conduct of the Regent of England holds out of its continuance demands of every Irishman whose pulses have not ceased to throb with the life-blood of his heart, that he should individually consult and unitedly determine on some measures for the liberty of his countrymen. That those measures should be pacific though resolute, that their movers should be calmly brave, and temperately unbending, though the whole heart and soul should go with the attempt, is the opinion which my principles command me to give.

And I am induced to call an Association such as this occasion demands an Association of Philanthropy, because good men ought never to circumscribe their usefulness by any name which denotes their exclusive devotion to the accomplishment of its signification.

When I began the preceding remarks I conceived that on the removal of the restrictions from the Regent a ministry less inimical than the present to the interests of liberty would have been appointed. I am deceived and the disappointment of the hopes of freedom on this subject afford an additional argument towards the necessity of an Association.

I conclude these remarks, which I have indited principally with a view of unveiling my principles, with a proposal for an association for the purposes of Catholic Emancipation, a repeal of the Union Act, and grounding upon the attainment of these objects a reform of whatever moral or political evil may be within its compass of human power to remedy.

Such as are favorably inclined towards the institution would highly gratify the proposer, if they would personally communicate with him on this important subject by which means the plan might be matured, errors in the proposer's original system be detected, and a meeting for the purpose convened with that resolute expedition which the nature of the present crisis demands.

A DECLARATION OF RIGHTS

[While in Dublin in the spring of 1812, Shelley composed the *Declaration of Rights* as a broadside to be posted on the walls of public buildings of Dublin to further his campaign for the freedom of Ireland. Did not the French revolutionists do that very thing? Did not Franklin employ similar means to enlighten his fellow Americans? It consists for the most part in succinct statements of the main arguments of *An Address to the Irish People* and the *Proposals for an Association of Philanthropists*. Shelley's plan for distribution of the broadside went awry when he felt it wise to leave Ireland. Nothing daunted by his unhappy experience in Erin, Shelley, on arrival in England, determined to post his broadside on the walls of Barnstaple. His servant Daniel Hill (or Healey) was arrested and fined £200 (or sentenced to two months in prison) for attempting its distribution. These interesting facts were first told by J. R. Chanter in the *Sketches of the Literary History of Barnstaple* (1866). W. M. Rossetti in the *Fortnightly Review* in his article "Shelley in 1812-1813" first printed the broadside. For further details of Shelley's schemes at this period see his letters.]

I. Government has no rights; it is a delegation from several individuals for the purpose of securing their own. It is therefore just only so far as it exists by their consent, useful only so far as it operates to their well-being.

II. If these individuals think that the form of government which they or their forefathers constituted is ill adapted to produce their happiness, they have a right to change it.

III. Government is devised for the security of rights. The rights of man are liberty and an equal participation of the commonage of Nature.

IV. As the benefit of the governed is, or ought to be, the origin of government, no men can have any authority that does not expressly emanate from *their* will.

V. Though all governments are not so bad as that of Turkey, yet none are so good as they might be. The majority of every country have a right to perfect their government. The minority should not disturb them; they ought to secede and form their own system in their own way.

VI. All have a right to an equal share in the benefits and burdens of Government. Any disabilities for opinion imply, by their existence, bare-faced tyranny on the side of Government, ignorant slavishness on the side of the governed.

VII. The rights of man, in the present state of society, are only to be secured by some degree of coercion to be exercised on their violator. The sufferer has a right that the degree of coercion employed be as slight as possible.

VIII. It may be considered as a plain proof of the hollowness of any proposition if power be used to enforce instead of reason to persuade its admission. Government is never supported by fraud until it cannot be supported by reason.

IX. No man has a right to disturb the public peace by personally resisting the execution of a law, however bad. He ought to acquiesce, using at the same time the utmost powers of his reason to promote its repeal.

X. A man must have a right to act in a certain manner, before it can be his duty. He may, before he ought.[1]

XI. A man has a right to think as his reason directs; it is a duty he owes to himself to think with freedom, that he may act from conviction.

XII. A man has a right to unrestricted liberty of discussion. Falsehood is a scorpion that will sting itself to death.

XIII. A man has not only a right to express his thoughts, but it is his duty to do so.

XIV. No law has a right to discourage the practice of truth. A man ought to speak the truth on every occasion. A duty can never be criminal; what is not criminal cannot be injurious.

XV. Law cannot make what is in its nature virtuous or innocent to be criminal, any more than it can make what is criminal to be innocent. Government cannot make a law; it can only pronounce that which was the law before its organization; viz., the moral result of the imperishable relations of things.

XVI. The present generation cannot bind their posterity. The few cannot promise for the many.[2]

XVII. No man has a right to do an evil thing that good may come.

XVIII. Expediency is inadmissible in morals. Politics are only sound when conducted on principles of morality. They are, in fact, the morals of the nations.

XIX. Man has no right to kill his brother. It is no excuse that he does so in uniform; he only adds the infamy of servitude to the crime of murder.

XX. Man, whatever be his country, has the same rights in one place as another—the rights of universal citizenship.

XXI. The government of a country ought to be perfectly indifferent to every opinion. Religious differences, the bloodiest and most rancorous of all, spring from partiality.

XXII. A delegation of individuals, for the purpose of securing their rights, can have no undelegated power of restraining the expression of their opinion.

XXIII. Belief is involuntary; nothing involuntary is meritorious or reprehensible. A man ought not to be considered worse or better for his belief.[3]

XXIV. A Christian, a Deist, a Turk, and a Jew, have equal rights: they are men and brethren.

XXV. If a person's religious ideas correspond not with your own, love him nevertheless. How different would yours have been had the chance of birth placed you in Tartary or India!

XXVI. Those who believe that Heaven is, what earth has been, a monopoly in the hands of a favored few, would do well to reconsider their opinion; if they find that it came from their priest or their grandmother, they could not do better than reject it.

XXVII. No man has a right to be respected for any other possessions but those of virtue and talents. Titles are tinsel, power a corrupter, glory a bubble, and excessive wealth a libel on its possessor.

XXVIII. No man has a right to monopolize more than he can enjoy; what the rich give to the poor, whilst millions are starving, is not a perfect favor, but an imperfect right.

XXIX. Every man has a right to a certain degree of leisure and liberty, because it

---

1. For a probable source of this conception of rights and duties, see Godwin, op. cit., 1.148-157; 158-169; see especially Paine's The Rights of Man (Everyman edition), pp. 94-100.

2. This is one of Paine's major contentions in the The Rights of Man—one which he used with devastating effect against the reactionary philosophy of Burke (Reflections on the Revolution in France).

3. This is a cardinal idea in Shelley's philosophy.

is his duty to attain a certain degree of knowledge. He may, before he ought.[4]

XXX. Sobriety of body and mind is necessary to those who would be free; because, without sobriety, a high sense of philanthropy cannot actuate the heart, nor cool and determined courage execute its dictates.

XXXI. The only use of government is to repress the vices of man. If man were today sinless, tomorrow he would have a right to demand that government and all its evils should cease.[5]

Man! thou whose rights are here declared, be no longer forgetful of loftiness of thy destination. Think of thy rights, of those possessions which will give thee virtue and wisdom, by which thou mayest arrive at happiness and freedom. They are declared to thee by one who knows thy dignity,[6] for every hour does his heart swell with honorable pride in the contemplation of what thou mayest attain—by one who is not forgetful of thy degeneracy, for every moment brings home to him the bitter conviction of what thou art.

Awake!—arise!—or be forever fallen.[7]

4. Compare Godwin's similar idea in *Political Justice* and Paine's, *The Rights of Man.* See Footnote 1.
5. Note how this reflection on the sinfulness of man refutes those who maintain that Shelley un-

realistically trusted in the absolute goodness of men.
6. Shelley firmly believed in the essential dignity of man, and vehemently rejected the doctrine of total depravity.
7. Milton's *Paradise Lost*, 1.330.

A LETTER TO LORD ELLENBOROUGH[1]

[It was on March 6, 1812, that Daniel Isaac Eaton, a liberal London bookseller and publisher, was brought to trial for the publication of Part Three of Paine's *The Age of Reason.* On May 15, Lord Ellenborough sentenced him to the pillory and to one year and six months' imprisonment. On June 11, Shelley wrote to Godwin: "What do you think of Eaton's trial and sentence? I mean not to insinuate that this poor bookseller has any characteristics in common with Socrates or Jesus Christ, still the spirit that pillories and imprisons him is the same that brought them to an untimely end. Still, even in this enlightened age, the moralist and reformer may expect coercion analogous to that used with the humble, zealous imitator of their endeavors. I have thought of addressing the public on the subject and indeed have begun an outline of the address. May I be favored with your remarks on it before I send it to the world?"

1. The remainder of the title page is: Occasioned by the sentence which he passed on Mr. D. I. Eaton, as publisher of the third part of Paine's *Age of Reason.* Deorum offensa, Diis curae. "It is contrary to the mild spirit of the Christian religion, for no sanction can be found under that dispensation which will warrant a government to impose disabilities and penalties upon any man, on account of his religious opinions." [*Hear, Hear.*] Marquis Wellesley's Speech, Globe, July 2.

Advertisement: *I have waited impatiently for these last four months, in the hopes that some pen, fitter for the important task, would have spared me the perilous pleasure of becoming the champion of an innocent man. This may serve as an excuse for the delay, to those who think that I have let pass the aptest opportunity, but it is not to be supposed that in four short months the public indignation, raised by Mr. Eaton's unmerited suffering, can have subsided.*

Shelley must have proceeded at once with the composition, for on July 29 he wrote to Thomas Hookham, a London bookseller, that the printer had finished the *Letter* and that twenty-five copies were being sent to Hookham. Only one copy—that in the Bodleian Library—is known to exist.

For the *Letter* Shelley drew on *The Necessity of Atheism,* on Paine's *The Age of Reason,* and also from Hume's *Essays.* The central theme of the *Letter,* an argument for the freedom of the press and of speech, is the contention that the right to print or to speak should not in any way be denied or abridged, as free press and free speech are absolute essentials to the full development of an individual as of a nation. Coercion is a sign of weakness, not of strength. Shelley maintained that one should not be persecuted on merely ideological grounds, that policy and morality should go hand in hand, that Eaton had violated no moral or legal principle, and that the leaders of Christianity, instead of following the example of its meek founder, adopted a course of coercion, and that Eaton had been sentenced because he was a Deist and the judge a Christian. Like Socrates, Jesus, Galileo, Vanini, and Voltaire, Eaton was persecuted because he opposed the dominant thought of the day. This *Letter* was greatly expanded and used as a note in *Queen Mab* to the line, "I will beget a Son." See Shelley's letter to Hunt, November 3, 1819, for a repetition of this argument occasioned by the trial of Richard Carlile on a similar charge.]

My Lord,

As the station to which you have been called by your country is important, so much the more awful is your responsibility, so much the more does it become you to watch lest you inadvertently punish the virtuous and reward the vicious.

You preside over a court which is instituted for the suppression of crime, and to whose authority the people submit on no other conditions than that its decrees should be conformable to justice.

If it should be demonstrated that a judge had condemned an innocent man, the bare existence of laws in conformity to which the accused is punished would but little extenuate his offense. The inquisitor when he burns an obstinate heretic may set up a similar plea, yet few are sufficiently blinded by intolerance to acknowledge its validity. It will less avail such a judge to assert the policy of punishing one who has committed no crime. Policy and morality ought to be deemed synonymous in a court of justice, and he whose conduct has been regulated by the latter principle is not justly amenable to any penal law for a supposed violation of the former. It is true, my Lord, laws exist which suffice to screen you from the animadversion of any constituted power, in consequence of the unmerited sentence which you have passed upon Mr. Eaton; but there are no laws which screen you from the reproof of a nation's disgust, none which ward off the just judgment of posterity, if that posterity will deign to recollect you.

By what right do you punish Mr. Eaton? What but antiquated precedents, gathered from times of priestly and tyrannical domination, can be adduced in palliation of an outrage so insulting to humanity and justice? Whom has he injured? What crime has he committed? Wherefore may he not walk abroad like other men and follow his accustomed pursuits? What end is proposed in confining this man, charged with the commission of no dishonorable action? Wherefore did his aggressor avail himself of popular prejudice, and return no answer but one of common place contempt to a defence of plain and simple sincerity? Lastly, when the prejudices of the jury, as Christians, were strongly and unfairly inflamed[2] against this injured man as a Deist, wherefore did not you, my Lord, check such unconstitutional pleading, and desire the jury to pronounce the accused innocent or criminal[3] without reference to the particular faith which he professed?

In the name of justice, what answer is there to these questions? The answer which heathen Athens made to Socrates is the same with which Christian England must attempt to silence the advocates of this injured man: "He has questioned established opinions." Alas! the crime of inquiry is one which religion never has forgiven. Implicit faith and fearless inquiry have in all ages been irreconcilable enemies. Unrestrained philosophy has in every age opposed itself to the reveries of credulity and fanaticism. The truths of astronomy demonstrated by Newton have superseded astrology; since the modern discoveries in chemistry the philosopher's stone has no longer been deemed attainable. Miracles of every kind have become rare in proportion to the hidden principles which those who study nature have developed. That which is false will ultimately be controverted by its own falsehood. That which is true needs but publicity to be acknowledged. It is ever a proof that the falsehood of a proposition is felt by those who use power and coercion, not reasoning and persuasion, to procure its admission.[4] Falsehood skulks in holes and corners, "it lets I dare not wait upon I would, Like the poor cat in the adage,"[5] except when it has power, and then, as it was a coward, it is a tyrant; but the eagle-eye of truth darts through the undazzling sunbeam of the immutable and just, gathering thence wherewith to vivify and illuminate a universe!

Wherefore, I repeat, is Mr. Eaton punished? Because he is a Deist? And what are you, my Lord? A Christian. Ha then! the mask is fallen off; you persecute him because his faith differs from yours. You copy the persecutors of Christianity in your actions and are an additional proof that your religion is as bloody, barbarous, and intolerant as theirs.[6] If some deistical bigot in power (supposing such a character for the sake of illustration) should in dark and barbarous ages have enacted a statute making the profession of Christianity criminal, if you, my Lord, were a Christian bookseller and Mr. Eaton a judge, those arguments which you consider adequate to justify yourself for the sentence which you have passed must likewise suffice, in this suppositionary case to justify Mr. Eaton, in sentencing you to Newgate and the pillory for being a Christian. Whence is any right derived but that which power confers for persecution? Do you think to convert Mr. Eaton to your religion by embittering his existence? You might force him by torture to profess your tenets, but he could not believe them, except you should make them credible, which perhaps exceeds your power. Do you think to please the God you worship by this exhibition of your zeal? If so, the demon to whom some nations offer human hecatombs is less barbarous than the deity of civilized society.

You consider man as an accountable being—but he can only be accountable for those actions which are influenced by his will.[7]

Belief and disbelief are utterly distinct from and unconnected with volition. They are the apprehension of the agreement or dis-

2. See the Attorney-General's speech. [Shelley's Note.]
3. By Mr. Fox's bill (1791) juries are in cases of *libel* judges both of the law and the fact. [Shelley's Note.]
4. Much of this paragraph was used in the Note on *Queen Mab* to the line, "I will beget a Son."

5. Shakespeare's *Macbeth*, 1.7.44-45.
6. Shelley many times in his writings condemns the militant spirit of Christianity as inconsonant with the teachings of its meek founder.
7. This is a cardinal point in Shelley's philosophy of morals.

agreement of the ideas which compose any proposition. Belief is an involuntary operation of the mind, and, like other passions, its intensity is purely proportionate to the degrees of excitement. Volition is essential to merit or demerit. How then can merit or demerit be attached to what is distinct from that faculty of the mind whose presence is essential to their being? I am aware that religion is founded on the voluntariness of belief, as it makes it a subject of reward and punishment; but before we extinguish the steady ray of reason and common sense, it is fit that we should discover, which we cannot do without their assistance, whether or no there be any other which may suffice to guide us through the labyrinth of life.[8]

If the law de heretico comburendo[9] has not been formally repealed, I conceive that, from the promise held out by your Lordship's zeal, we need not despair of beholding the flames of persecution rekindled in Smithfield. Even now the lash that drove Descartes[10] and Voltaire[11] from their native country, the chains which bound Galileo,[12] the flames which burned Vanini,[13] again resound. And where? In a nation that presumptuously calls itself the sanctuary of freedom. Under a government which, whilst it infringes the very right of thought and speech, boasts of permitting the liberty of the press; in a civilized and enlightened country, a man is pilloried and imprisoned because he is a Deist, and no one raises his voice in the indignation of outraged humanity.[14] Does the Christian God, whom his followers eulogize as the Deity of humil-

ity and peace; he, the regenerator of the world, the meek reformer, authorize one man to rise against another, and, because lictors are at his beck, to chain and torture him as an Infidel?

When the Apostles went abroad to convert the nations, were they enjoined to stab and poison all who disbelieved the divinity of Christ's mission? Assuredly, they would have been no more justifiable in this case than he is at present who puts into execution the law which inflicts pillory and imprisonment on the Deist.

Has not Mr. Eaton an equal right to call your Lordship an Infidel, as you have to imprison him for promulgating a different doctrine from that which you profess? What do I say! Has he not even a stronger plea? The word Infidel can only mean anything when applied to a person who professes that which he disbelieves. The test of truth is an undivided reliance on its inclusive powers; the test of conscious falsehood is the variety of the forms under which it presents itself, and its tendency towards employing whatever coercive means may be within its command in order to procure the admission of what is unsusceptible of support from reason or persuasion. A dispassionate observer would feel himself more powerfully interested in favor of a man who, depending on the truth of his opinions, simply stated his reasons for entertaining them than in that of his aggressor who, daringly avowing his unwillingness to answer them by argument, proceeded to repress the activity and break the spirit of their promulgator by that

8. The substance of this paragraph is in the Note to Queen Mab for the line, "There is no God" and a Treatise on Morals. Compare also The Necessity of Atheism, and A Refutation of Deism for this important principle in Shelley's philosophy.
9. "On the burning of heretics."
10. Rène Descartes (1596-1650) was a distinguished French philosopher. For an excellent brief account of his ideas, see the article on him in the Encyclopaedia Britannica.
11. Francois Marie Arouet de Voltaire (1694-1778), a distinguished French philosopher and man of letters, who waged constant and fearless war upon all forms of sham and superstition. The

famous saying, "I may not believe a word that you have said, but I will defend to the death your right to say it," though not found verbatim in Voltaire, is a reasonably accurate paraphrase of the theme of his Essay on Tolerance, with which Shelley was probably familiar.
12. Galileo Gallilei (1564-1642) was a noted Italian astronomer whose distinguished work in science won him the condemnation of the church.
13. Lucilio Vanini (1585-1619), an Italian sceptic who was burned at the stake as an atheist.
14. This sentence is in the Note on Queen Mab to the line, "I will beget a Son."

torture and imprisonment whose infliction he could command.[15]

I hesitate not to affirm that the opinions which Mr. Eaton sustained, when undergoing that mockery of a trial at which your Lordship presided, appear to me more true and good than those of his accuser; but were they false as the visions of a Calvinist, it still would be the duty of those who love liberty and virtue to raise their voice indignantly against a reviving system of persecution, against the coercively repressing any opinion, which, if false, needs but the opposition of truth; which, if true, in spite of force, must ultimately prevail.

Mr. Eaton asserted that the scriptures were, from beginning to end, a fable and imposture,[16] that the Apostles were liars and deceivers. He denied the miracles, the resurrection, and ascension of Jesus Christ. He did so, and the Attorney General denied the propositions which he asserted, and asserted those which he denied. What singular conclusion is deducible from this fact? None, but that the Attorney General and Mr. Eaton sustained two opposite opinions. The Attorney General puts some obsolete and tyrannical laws in force against Mr. Eaton, because he publishes a book tending to prove that certain supernatural events, which are supposed to have taken place eighteen centuries ago, in a remote corner of the world, did not actually take place. But how are [is] the truth or falsehood of the facts in dispute relevant to the merit or demerit attachable to the advocates of the two opinions? No man is accountable for his belief, because no man is capable of directing it. Mr. Eaton is therefore totally blameless. What are we to think of the justice of a sentence which punishes an individual against whom it is not even attempted to attach the slightest stain of criminality?[17]

It is asserted that Mr. Eaton's opinions are calculated to subvert morality. How? What moral truth is spoken of with irreverence or ridicule in the book which he published? Morality, or the duty of a man and a citizen, is founded on the relations which arise from the association of human beings, and which vary with the circumstances produced by the different states of this association. This duty in similar situations must be precisely the same in all ages and nations. The opinion contrary to this has arisen from a supposition that the will of God is the source or criterion of morality. It is plain that the utmost exertion of Omnipotence could not cause that to be virtuous which actually is vicious. An all-powerful Demon might, indubitably, annex punishments to virtue and reward to vice, but could not by these means effect the slightest change in their abstract and immutable natures. Omnipotence could vary by a providential interposition the relations of human society; in this latter case, what before was virtuous would become vicious according to the necessary and natural result of the alteration; but the abstract natures of the opposite principles would have sustained not the slightest change; for instance, the punishment with which society restrains the robber, the assassin, and the ravisher is just, laudable, and requisite. We admire and respect the institutions which curb those who would defeat the ends for which society was established; but, should a precisely similar coercion be exercised against one who merely expressed his disbelief of a system admitted by those entrusted with the executive power, using at the same time no methods of promulgation but those afforded by reason, certainly this coercion would be eminently inhuman and immoral; and the supposition that any revelation from an unknown power avails to palliate a persecution so senseless, unprovoked, and indefensible is at once to destroy the barrier which reason places between vice and virtue, and

---

15. This sentence is in the Note in *Queen Mab* to the line, "I will beget a Son."
16. See the Attorney-General's speech. [Shelley's Note.]

17. See paragraph three of the Note to *Queen Mab* to the line, "There is no God," and also *The Necessity of Atheism* for similar ideas.

leave to unprincipled fanaticism a plea whereby it may excuse every act of frenzy which its own wild passions and the inspirations of the Deity have engendered.

Moral qualities are such as only a human being can possess. To attribute them to the Spirit of the Universe, or to suppose that it is capable of altering them, is to degrade God into man and to annex to this incomprehensible being qualities incompatible with any *possible* definition of its nature. It may here be objected—ought not the Creator to possess the perfections of the creature? No. To attribute to God the moral qualities of man is to suppose him susceptible of passions which, arising out of corporeal organization, it is plain that a pure spirit cannot possess. A bear is not perfect except he is rough, a tiger is not perfect if he be not voracious, an elephant is not perfect if otherwise than docile. How *deep* an argument must that not be which proves that the Deity is as rough as a bear, as voracious as a tiger, and as docile as an elephant! But even suppose with the vulgar that God is a venerable old man, seated on a throne of clouds, his breast the theatre of various passions, analogous to those of humanity, his will changeable and uncertain as that of an earthly king; still goodness and justice are qualities seldom nominally denied him, and it will be admitted that he disapproves of any action incompatible with these qualities. Persecution for opinion is unjust. With what consistency, then, can the worshippers of a Deity whose benevolence they boast, embitter the existence of their fellow being, because his ideas of that Deity are different from those which they entertain? Alas! there is no consistency in those persecutors who worship a benevolent Deity; those who worship a Demon would alone act consonantly to these principles, by imprisoning and torturing in his name.

Persecution is the only name applicable to punishment inflicted on an individual in consequence of his opinions. What end is persecution designed to answer? Can it convince him whom it injures? Can it prove to the people the falsehood of his opinions? It may make him a hypocrite, and them cowards, but bad means can promote no good end. The unprejudiced mind looks with suspicion on a doctrine that needs the sustaining hand of power.

Socrates was poisoned because he dared to combat the degrading superstitions in which his countrymen were educated. Not long after his death, Athens recognized the injustice of his sentence; his accuser Melitus was condemned, and Socrates became a demigod.

Jesus Christ was crucified because he attempted to supersede the ritual of Moses with regulations more moral and humane—his very judge made public acknowledgment of his innocence, but a bigoted and ignorant mob demanded the deed of horror. Barabbas, the murderer and traitor, was released. The meek reformer Jesus was immolated to the sanguinary Deity of the Jews. Time rolled on, time changed the situations, and with them, the opinions of men.[18]

The vulgar, ever in extremes, became persuaded that the crucifixion of Jesus was a supernatural event, and testimonies of miracles, so frequent in unenlightened ages, were not wanting to prove that he was something divine. This belief, rolling through the lapse of ages, acquired force and extent, until the divinity of Jesus became a dogma, which to dispute was death, which to doubt was infamy.[19]

Christianity is now the established religion; he who attempts to disprove it must behold murderers and traitors take precedence of him in public opinion, though, if his genius be equal to his courage, and as-

18. This paragraph was greatly expanded in the Note to *Queen Mab* to the line, "I will beget a Son."
19. This paragraph was used in the Note to the line in *Queen Mab*, "I will beget a Son." The Note

adds the phrase, "met with the reveries of Plato and the reasonings of Aristotle," following the word *ages.*

sisted by a peculiar coalition of circumstances, future ages may exalt him to a
divinity, and persecute others in his name,
as he was persecuted in the name of his
predecessor in the homage of the world.[20]

The same means that have supported
every other popular belief have supported
Christianity. War, imprisonment, murder,
and falsehood; deeds of unexampled and
incomparable atrocity have made it what it
is. We derive from our ancestors a belief
thus fostered and supported.[21] We quarrel,
persecute, and hate for its maintenance.
Does not analogy favor the opinion that as
like other systems it has arisen and augmented, so like them it will decay and
perish; that, as violence and falsehood, not
reasoning and persuasion, have procured
its admission among mankind; so, when
enthusiasm has subsided, and time, that
infallible controverter of false opinions, has
involved its pretended evidences in the darkness of antiquity, it will become obsolete,
and that men will then laugh as heartily at
grace, faith, redemption, and original sin,
as they now do at the metamorphoses of
Jupiter, the miracles of Romish saints, the
efficacy of witchcraft, and the appearance of
departed spirits.

Had the Christian religion commenced
and continued by the mere force of reasoning and persuasion, by its self-evident excellence and fitness, the preceding analogy
would be inadmissible. We should never
speculate upon the future obsoleteness of a
system perfectly comformable to nature and
reason. It would endure as long as they endured, it would be a truth as indisputable
as the light of the sun, the criminality of
murder, and other facts, physical and moral,
which, depending on our organization, and
relative situations, must remain acknowledged so long as man is man. It is an incontrovertible fact, the consideration of
which ought to repress the hasty conclusions

of credulity, or moderate its obstinacy in
maintaining them, that, had the Jews not
been a barbarous and fanatical race of men,
had even the resolution of Pontius Pilate
been equal to his candor, the Christian religion never could have prevailed, it could
not even have existed. Man! the very existence of whose most cherished opinions depends from a thread so feeble arises out of
a source so equivocal, learn at least humility;
own at least that it is possible for thyself
also to have been seduced by education and
circumstance into the admission of tenets
destitute of rational proof, and the truth of
which has not yet been satisfactorily demonstrated.[22] Acknowledge at least that the
falsehood of thy brother's opinions is no
sufficient reason for his meriting thy hatred.
What! because a fellow being disputes the
reasonableness of thy faith, wilt thou punish
him with torture and imprisonment? If
persecution for religious opinions were admitted by the moralist, how wide a door
would not be opened by which convulsion-
ists of every kind might make inroads on
the peace of society! How many deeds of
barbarism and blood would not receive a
sanction! But I will demand, if that man is
not rather entitled to the respect than the
discountenance of society, who, by disputing a received doctrine, either proves its
falsehood and inutility, thereby aiming at
the abolition of what is false and useless, or
giving to its adherents an opportunity of
establishing its excellence and truth. Surely
this can be no crime. Surely the individual
who devotes his time to fearless and unrestricted inquiry into the grand questions
arising out of our moral nature ought rather
to receive the patronage than encounter the
vengeance of an enlightened legislature. I
would have you to know, my Lord, that
fetters of iron cannot bind or subdue the
soul of virtue. From the damps and solitude
of its dungeon it ascends free and un-

---

20. Large portions of this and the next paragraph
are common to both the Note to the line "I will
beget a Son" in *Queen Mab* and the *Letter*.

21. These first two sentences are in the Note in
Queen Mab to the line, "I will beget a Son."
22. This paragraph to this point is in the Note
to *Queen Mab* to the line, "I will beget a Son."

daunted, whither thine, from the pompous seat of judgment, dare not soar. I do not warn you to beware lest your profession as a Christian should make you forget that you are a man; but I warn you against festinating that period, which, under the present coercive system, is too rapidly maturing, when the seats of justice shall be the seats of venality and slavishness, and the cells of Newgate become the abode of all that is honorable and true.

I mean not to compare Mr. Eaton with Socrates or Jesus; he is a man of blameless and respectable character; he is a citizen unimpeached with crime; if, therefore, his rights as a citizen and a man have been infringed, they have been infringed by illegal and immoral violence. But I will assert that should a second Jesus arise among men; should such a one as Socrates again enlighten the earth, lengthened imprisonment and infamous punishment (according to the regimen of persecution revived by your Lordship) would effect, what hemlock and the cross have heretofore effected, and the stain on the national character, like that on Athens and Judea, would remain indelible, but by the destruction of the history in which it is recorded. When the Christian religion shall have faded from the earth, when its memory like that of polytheism now shall remain, but remain only as the subject of ridicule and wonder, indignant posterity would attach immortal infamy to such an outrage; like the murder of Socrates, it would secure the execration of every age.

The horrible and wide-wasting enormities which gleam like comets through the darkness of gothic and superstitious ages are regarded by the moralist as no more than the necessary effects of known causes; but, when an enlightened age and nation signalizes itself by a deed becoming none but barbarians and fanatics philosophy itself is even induced to doubt whether human nature will

ever emerge from the pettishness and imbecility of its childhood. The system of persecution at whose new birth, you, my Lord, are one of the presiding midwives, is not more impotent and wicked than inconsistent. The press is loaded with what are called (ironically, I should conceive) *proofs* of the Christian religion; these books are replete with invective and calumny against Infidels; they presuppose that he who rejects Christianity must be utterly divested of reason and feeling. They advance the most unsupported assertions and take as first principles the most revolting dogmas. The inferences drawn from these assumed premises are imposingly logical and correct; but if a foundation is weak, no architect is needed to foretell the instability of the superstructure. If the truth of Christianity is not disputable, for what purpose are these books written? If they are sufficient to prove it, what further need of controversy? *If God has spoken, why is the universe not convinced?*[23] If the Christian religion needs deeper learning, more painful investigation, to establish its genuineness, wherefore attempt to accomplish that by force which the human mind can alone effect with satisfaction to itself? If, lastly, its truth *cannot* be demonstrated, wherefore impotently attempt to snatch from God the government of his creation and impiously assert that the Spirit of Benevolence has left that knowledge most essential to the well being of man, the only one which, since its promulgation, has been the subject of unceasing cavil, the cause of irreconcilable hatred? Either the Christian religion is true, or it is not. If true, it comes from God, and its authenticity can admit of doubt and dispute no further than its Omnipotent Author is willing to allow;[24] if true, it admits of rational proof and is capable of being placed equally beyond controversy, as the principles which have been established concerning

23. From Holbach's *Système de la Nature*, quoted at length in the Note on *Queen Mab* to the line, "There is no God."

24. This sentence to this point is in *Queen Mab* to the line, "I will beget a Son."

matter and mind, by Locke and Newton; and in proportion to the usefulness of the fact in dispute, so must it be supposed that a benevolent being is anxious to procure the diffusion of its knowledge on the earth. If false, surely no enlightened legislature would punish the reasoner who opposes a system so much the more fatal and pernicious as it is extensively admitted; so much the more productive of absurd and ruinous consequences, as it is entwined by education with the prejudices and affections of the human heart in the shape of a popular belief.[25]

Let us suppose that some half-witted philosopher should assert that the earth was the centre of the universe, or that ideas could enter the human mind independently of sensation or reflection. This man would assert what is demonstrably incorrect; he would promulgate a false opinion. Yet, would he therefore deserve pillory and imprisonment? By no means; probably few would discharge more correctly the duties of a citizen and a man. I admit that the case above stated is not precisely in point. The thinking part of the community has not received as indisputable the truth of Christianity as they have that of the Newtonian system. A very large portion of society, and that powerfully and extensively connected, derives its sole emolument from the belief of Christianity as a popular faith.

To torture and imprison the asserter of a dogma, however ridiculous and false, is highly barbarous and impolitic. How, then, does not the cruelty of persecution become aggravated when it is directed against the opposer of an opinion *yet under dispute* and which men of unrivalled acquirements, penetrating genius, and stainless virtue, have spent, and at last sacrificed, their lives in combating.

The time is rapidly approaching, I hope, that you, my Lord, may live to behold its arrival, when the Mahometan, the Jew, the Christian, the Deist, and the Atheist will live together in one community, equally sharing the benefits which arise from its association, and united in the bonds of charity and brotherly love. My Lord, you have condemned an innocent man—no crime was imputed to him—and you sentenced him to torture and imprisonment. I have not addressed this letter to you with the hopes of convincing you that you have acted wrong. The most unprincipled and barbarous of men are not unprepared with sophisms to prove that they would have acted in no other manner, and to show that vice is virtue. But I raise my solitary voice to express my disapprobation, so far as it goes, of the cruel and unjust sentence you passed upon Mr. Eaton; to assert, so far as I am capable of influencing, those rights of humanity which you have wantonly and unlawfully infringed.[26]

My Lord,

Yours, &c

---

25. The Note in *Queen Mab* draws heavily on this paragraph of the *Letter*.

26. Shelley's *Letter*, with its powerful and irrefutable argument for toleration and for freedom of speech and press, was reprinted in New York in 1879, on the occasion of D. M. Bennett's being sentenced to thirteen months' imprisonment, and again in 1883 in London, when George William Foote, editor of *The Freethinker*, was likewise sentenced for his radical opinions. See Cameron, *op. cit.*, p. 186, for further information on this point.

A VINDICATION OF NATURAL DIET

[The Greek quotation on title page and translation are in Appendix D(g). Shelley adopted a vegetarian diet early in March, 1812, and held consistently to it the remainder of his life. That he was convinced of the importance of it may be inferred from the emphasis he gave the matter, making no fewer than four separate attempts to put the case for a vegetable diet. There have been many erroneous statements and no little fun-poking at Shelley's expense about his vegetarianism and the sources of his ideas. It is my belief—the basis of which is fully set forth in my article in *Studies in Philology* for January, 1939—that the Shelleys began a strict vegetarian diet in March, 1812, several months before Shelley had met John Frank Newton—his alleged inspirer— and nearly one year before he wrote the Note in *Queen Mab*. On March 14, 1812, Harriet wrote to Elizabeth Hitchener that "we have forsworn meat, and adopted the Pythagorean system. About a fortnight has elapsed since the change. . . . We are delighted with it." This letter, it seems to me, definitely dates the composition as November, 1812, for the last paragraph of the essay informs us that "the author and his wife have lived on vegetables for eight months"—that is, from March, 1812. This statement in the essay and Harriet's in the letter of March 14 are in agreement. Thus the *Vindication* appears to have been written before the Note in *Queen Mab*. It will be observed that the statement at the end of the essay about the author's having lived eight months on vegetables does not appear in the Note. The principal change introduced by the Note is a paragraph admitting that there are other causes of mental and physical derangements than dietary. Apparently, since writing the *Vindication* Shelley had read other advocates of vegetarianism— among them probably Joseph Ritson, to whose *An Essay on the Abstinence from Animal Food* (London, 1802) I have pointed out in the article referred to above, Shelley probably was considerably indebted.

The interest in the *Vindication* as in Shelley's other attempts to put the case for vegetarianism lies in the typical Shelleyan theme: the nature and cause of evil. To man's unnatural diet must be ascribed *one* cause for the ills of the world. It cannot be maintained that Shelley here says, indeed ever said, that all mental and physical diseases are traceable to flesh-eating. In fact in the Note he specifically disavows any such claim. As fantastic as some of his statements are, his general position is unassailable.]

I hold that the depravity of the physical and moral nature of man originated in his unnatural habits of life. The origin of man, like that of the universe of which he is a part, is enveloped in impenetrable mystery. His generations either had a beginning, or they had not. The weight of evidence in favor of each of these suppositions seems tolerably equal; and it is perfectly unimportant to the present argument which is assumed.[1] The language spoken, however, by the mythology of nearly all religions seems to prove that at some distant period man forsook the path of nature and sacrificed the purity and happiness of his being to unnatural appetites.[2] The date of this event seems to have been that of some great change in the climates of the earth, with which it has an obvious correspondence. The allegory of Adam and Eve eating of the tree of evil, and entailing upon their posterity the wrath of God and the loss of everlasting life, admits of no other explanation than the disease and crime that have flowed from unnatural diet. Milton was so well aware of this that he makes Raphael[3] thus exhibit to Adam the consequence of his disobedience.

> Immediately a place,
> Before his eyes appeared: sad, noisome,
> dark:
> A lazar-house it seem'd; wherein were
> laid
> Numbers of all diseased: all maladies
> Of ghastly spasm, or racking torture,
> qualms
> Of heart-sick agony, all feverous kinds,
> Convulsions, epilepsies, fierce catarrhs,
> Intestine stone and ulcer, cholic pangs,
> Daemoniac frenzy, moping melancholy,
> And moon-struck madness, pining
> atrophy,
> Marasmus, and wide-wasting pestilence,
> Dropsies, and asthmas, and joint-
> racking rheums.

And how many thousands more might not be added to this frightful catalogue![4]

The story of Prometheus is one likewise which, although universally admitted to be allegorical, has never been satisfactorily explained. Prometheus stole fire from heaven and was chained for this crime to mount Caucasus, where a vulture continually devoured his liver, that grew to meet its hunger. Hesiod says that before the time of Prometheus mankind were exempt from suffering; that they enjoyed a vigorous youth, and that death, when at length it came, approached like sleep and gently closed their eyes.[5] Again, so general was this opinion, that Horace, a poet of the Augustan age, writes,

> Audax omnia perpeti,
> Gens humana ruit per vetetum nefas,
> Audax Iapeti genus,
> Ignem fraude mala gentibus intulit,
> Post ignem aetheria domo,
> Subductum, macies et nova febrium,
> Terris incubuit cohors
> Semotique prius tarda necessitas,
> Lethi corripuit gradum.[6]

How plain a language is spoken by all this. Prometheus (who represents the human race) effected some great change in the condition of his nature and applied fire to culinary purposes—thus inventing an expedient for screening from his disgust the horrors of the shambles. From this moment his vitals were devoured by the vulture of disease. It consumed his being in every shape of its loathsome and infinite variety, inducing the soul-quelling sinkings of premature and violent death. All vice arose

1. Shelley's mature belief was that the universe was never created; it always existed. All we see or experience is its modification or change. It can be shown, I believe, that Shelley in this idea is following the persuasive argument of Holbach. See *Système de la Nature*, 1.22-23.
2. This is the idea of the Golden Age in man's past, emphasized in nearly all religions.
3. Shelley should have said Michael.
4. *Paradise Lost*, 11.477-488. The opening paragraph of the essay while compounded of many simples is probably gathered from Joseph Ritson's *An Essay on the Abstinence from Animal Food*, London, 1802, pp. 6, 11, 39, 58, 163-165.

5. This is a paraphrase of the quotation from Hesiod in Newton.
6. From Book I, Ode III.

> Daring all chances to endure,
> The race of man from crime to crime is driven.
> Prometheus thus for men did lure,
> With evil-fated cunning, fire from Heaven.
>
> Once fire from its true home on high
> Was filched, slow Canker and a dismal band
> Of Fevers to the world drew nigh.
> And Death, though sure yet far, came nearer
> hand.

(Translation by John Marshall)

from the ruin of healthful innocence. Tyranny, superstition, commerce, and inequality were then first known when reason vainly attempted to guide the wanderings of exacerbated passion. I conclude this part of the subject with an extract from Mr. Newton's *Defence of Vegetable Regimen,* from which I have borrowed this interpretation of the fable of Prometheus.

"Making allowances for such transposition of the events of the allegory as time might produce after the important truths were forgotten, which this portion of the ancient mythology was intended to transmit, the drift of the fable seems to be this: Man at his creation was endowed with the gift of perpetual youth; that is, he was not formed to be a sickly, suffering creature as we now see him, but to enjoy health and to sink by slow degrees into the bosom of his parent earth without disease or pain. Prometheus first taught the use of animal food (primus boven occidit Prometheus) and of fire with which to render it more digestible and pleasing to the taste. Jupiter and the rest of the gods foreseeing the consequences of these inventions were amused or irritated at the short-sighted devices of the newly-formed creature and left him to experience the sad effects of them. Thirst, the necessary concomitant of a flesh diet," (perhaps of all diet vitiated by culinary preparation) "ensued; water was resorted to and man forfeited the inestimable gift of health which he had received from heaven; he became diseased, the partaker of a precarious existence, and no longer descended slowly to his grave."[7]

But just disease to luxury succeeds,
And every death its own avenger breeds;
The fury passions from that blood began,

And turn'd on man a fiercer savage
—Man.[8]

Man and the animals whom he has infected with his society, or depraved by his dominion, are alone diseased. The wild hog, the mouflon,[9] the bison, and the wolf are perfectly exempt from malady, and invariably die either from external violence, or natural old age. But the domestic hog, the sheep, the cow, and the dog are subject to an incredible variety of distempers; and, like the corrupters of their nature, have physicians who thrive upon their miseries. The supereminence of man is like Satan's a supereminence of pain; and the majority of his species, doomed to penury, disease, and crime, have reason to curse the untoward event that, by enabling him to communicate his sensations, raised him above the level of his fellow animals. But the steps that have been taken are irrevocable. The whole of human science is comprised in one question: How can the advantages of intellect and civilization be reconciled with the liberty and pure pleasures of natural life? How can we take the benefits and reject the evils of the system which is now interwoven with all the fibres of our being? I believe that abstinence from animal food and spirituous liquors would in a great measure capacitate us for the solution of this important question.[10]

Comparative anatomy teaches us that man resembles frugivorous animals in everything, and carnivorous in nothing; he has neither claws wherewith to seize his prey, nor distinct and pointed teeth to tear the living fibre. A Mandarin of the first class, with nails two inches long, would probably find them alone inefficient to hold even a hare. After every subterfuge of gluttony, the bull must be degraded into the ox, and the ram into the wether, by an unnatural and

7. Pliny's *Natural History*, Bk. 7, Sec. 57. Shelley has not quoted Newton accurately, injecting extraneous matter.
8. Newton had quoted 153 lines from Pope's *Es-*

say on Man—the last four of which Shelley uses.
9. Mouflon, a wild sheep.
10. A paragraph in the Note to *Queen Mab* is omitted here.

inhuman operation that the flaccid fibre may offer a fainter resistance to rebellious nature. It is only by softening and disguising dead flesh by culinary preparation that it is rendered susceptible of mastication or digestion, and that the sight of its bloody juices and raw horror does not excite intolerable loathing and disgust. Let the advocate of animal food force himself to a decisive experiment on its fitness, and as Plutarch recommends, tear a living lamb with his teeth and, plunging his head into its vitals, slake his thirst with the steaming blood; when fresh from the deed of horror let him revert to the irresistible instincts of nature that would rise in judgment against it, and say, Nature formed me for such work as this. Then, and then only, would he be consistent.[11]

Man resembles no carnivorous animal. There is no exception, except[12] man be one, to the rule of herbivorous animals having cellulated colons.

The orang-outang perfectly resembles man both in the order and number of his teeth. The orang-outang is the most anthropomorphous of the ape tribe, all of which are strictly frugivorous. There is no other species of animals[13] in which this analogy exists.[14] In many frugivorous animals the canine teeth are more pointed and distinct than those of man. The resemblance also of the human stomach to that of the orang-outang is greater than to that of any other animal.

The intestines are also identical with those of herbivorous animals, which present a larger surface for absorption and have ample and cellulated colons. The caecum also, though short, is larger than that of carnivorous animals; and even here the orang-outang retains its accustomed similarity.[15] The structure of the human frame, then, is that of one fitted to a pure vegetable diet in every essential particular. It is true that the reluctance to abstain from animal food in those who have been long accustomed to its stimulus is so great in some persons of weak minds as to be scarcely overcome; but this is far from bringing any argument in its favor. A lamb which was fed for some time on flesh by a ship's crew refused its natural diet at the end of the voyage. There are numerous instances of horses, sheep, oxen, and even wood-pigeons having been taught to live upon flesh until they have loathed their natural aliment. Young children evidently prefer pastry, oranges, apples, and other fruit to the flesh of animals until, by the gradual depravation of the digestive organs, the free use of vegetables has for a time produced serious inconveniences; *for a time,* I say, since there never was an instance wherein a change from spirituous liquors and animal food to vegetables and pure water has failed ultimately to invigorate the body by rendering its juices bland and consentaneous and to restore to the mind that cheerfulness and elasticity which not one in fifty possess[16] on the present system. A love of strong liquors is also with difficulty taught to infants. Almost every one remembers the wry faces which the first glass of port produced. Unsophisticated instinct is invariably unerring; but to decide on the fitness of animal food from the perverted appetites which its constrained adoption produces is to make the criminal a judge of[17] his own cause; it is even worse, it is appealing to the infatuated drunkard in a question of the salubrity of brandy.[18]

11. This paragraph derives largely from Joseph Ritson's *Essay.*

12. *Unless* in the Note to *Queen Mab.*

13. The Note has "animals, which live on different food."

14. Cuvier, *Leçons d'Anat. Comp.* tom. iii. pp. 169, 373, 448, 465, 480. *Rees's Cyclopaedia,* article "Man." [Shelley's Note.]

15. A new paragraph begins here in the Note.

16. *Possesses* in the Note.

17. The Note has *in.*

18. This long paragraph on the similarity to the frugivorous animals comes in part from Plutarch, but primarily from Ritson, pp. 33-34, 42, 47-48; on p. 48 is Ritson's translation of Plutarch's first essay on flesh-eating, from which Shelley appears to have garnered many phrases.

What is the cause of morbid action in the animal system? Not the air we breathe, for our fellow denizens of nature breathe the same uninjured; not the water we drink, (if remote from the pollutions of man and his inventions[19]) for the animals drink it too; not the earth we tread upon; not the unobscured sight of glorious nature, in the wood, the field, or the expanse of sky and ocean; nothing that we are or do in common with the undiseased inhabitants of the forest. Something then wherein we differ from them: our habit of altering our food by fire so that our appetite is no longer a just criterion for the fitness of its gratification. Except in children there remain no traces of that instinct which determines in all other animals what aliment is natural or otherwise, and so perfectly obliterated are they in the reasoning adults of our species that it has become necessary to urge considerations drawn from comparative anatomy to prove that we are naturally frugivorous.

Crime is madness. Madness is disease.[20] Whenever the cause of disease shall be discovered, the root from which all vice and misery have so long overshadowed the globe will lay[21] bare to the axe. All the exertions of man from that moment may be considered as tending to the clear profit of his species. No sane mind in a sane body resolves upon a real crime.[22] It is a man of violent passions, blood-shot eyes, and swollen veins that alone can grasp the knife of murder. The system of a simple diet promises no Utopian advantages.[23] It is no mere reform of legislation, while the furious passions and evil propensities of the human

heart in which it had its origin are still unassuaged. It strikes at the root of all evil and is an experiment which may be tried with success, not alone by nations, but by small societies, families, and even individuals. In no cases has a return to vegetable diet produced the slightest injury; in most it has been attended with changes undeniably beneficial. Should ever a physician be born with the genius of Locke, I am persuaded that he might trace all bodily and mental derangements to our unnatural habits as clearly as that philosopher has traced all knowledge to sensation. What prolific sources of disease are not those mineral and vegetable poisons that have been introduced for its extirpation! How many thousands have become murderers and robbers, bigots and domestic tyrants, dissolute and abandoned adventurers, from the use of fermented liquors—who, had they slaked their thirst only at the mountain stream,[24] would have lived but to diffuse the happiness of their own unperverted feelings. How many groundless opinions and absurd institutions have not received a general sanction from the sottishness and intemperance of individuals! Who will assert that had the populace of Paris drunk at the pure source of the Seine and[25] satisfied their hunger at the ever-furnished table of vegetable nature that[26] they would have lent their brutal suffrage to the proscription list of Robespierre? Could a set of men whose passions were not perverted by unnatural stimuli look with coolness on an *auto da fé*?[27] Is it to be believed that a being of gentle feelings, rising from his meal of roots, would take delight in sports of blood? Was Nero a man of tem-

19. The necessity of resorting to some means of purifying water, and the disease which arises from its adulteration in civilized countries, is sufficiently apparent. See Dr. Lambe's *Reports on Cancer*. I do not assert that the use of water is in itself unnatural, but that the unperverted palate would swallow no liquid capable of occasioning disease. [Shelley's Note.]
20. This, and the three succeeding paragraphs forming the main *moral* argument, seem to come from Ritson, pp. 83, 86, 88, 146, 159, 206-212. Recall that the subtitle of Ritson's book is *As a Moral Duty.*

21. The Note has "lie."
22. This conception agrees closely with the most informed and humane views of the penologists of the twentieth century.
23. This note of caution and commonsense is often overlooked by Shelley commentators.
24. The Note has "with pure water," for the last four words.
25. The words "drunk . . . Seine and," are not in the Note.
26. "That" is not in the Note.
27. *Auto da fé*, a term used in the Inquisition, meaning the execution or burning of a heretic.

perate life? Could you read calm health in his cheek, flushed with governable[28] propensities of hatred for the human race? Did Muley Ismael's[29] pulse beat evenly, was his skin transparent, did his eyes beam with healthfulness, and its invariable concomitants cheerfulness and benignity? Though history has decided none of these questions, a child could not hesitate to answer in the negative. Surely the bile-suffused cheek of Buonaparte, his wrinkled brow, and yellow eye, the ceaseless inquietude of his nervous system speak no less plainly the character of his unresting ambition than his murders and his victories. It is impossible that had Buonaparte descended from a race of vegetable feeders that he could have had either the inclination or the power to ascend the throne of the Bourbons. The desire of tyranny could scarcely be excited in the individual; the power to tyrannize would certainly not be delegated by a society, neither frenzied by inebriation, nor rendered impotent and irrational by disease. Pregnant indeed with inexhaustible calamity is the renunciation of instinct as it concerns our physical nature; arithmetic cannot enumerate nor reason perhaps suspect the multitudinous sources of disease in civilized life. Even common water, that apparently innoxious pabulum, when corrupted by the filth of populous cities, is a deadly and insidious destroyer.[30] Who can wonder that all the inducements held out by God himself in the Bible to virtue should have been vainer than a nurse's tale; and that those dogmas, apparently favorable to the intolerant and angry passions,[31] should have alone been deemed essential; while Christians are in the daily practice of all those habits which have infected with disease and crime not only the reprobate sons but these favored children of the common Father's love. Omnipotence itself could not save them from the consequences of this original and universal sin.

There is no disease, bodily or mental, which adoption of vegetable diet and pure water has not infallibly mitigated wherever the experiment has been fairly tried. Debility is gradually converted into strength, disease into healthfulness; madness in all its hideous variety, from the ravings of the fettered maniac, to the unaccountable irrationalities of ill temper that make a hell of domestic life into a calm and considerate evenness of temper that alone might offer a certain pledge of the future moral reformation of society. On a natural system of diet old age would be our last and our only malady; the term of our existence would be protracted; we should enjoy life and no longer preclude others from the enjoyment of it. All sensational delights would be infinitely more exquisite and perfect. The very sense of being would then be continued pleasure, such as we now feel it in some few and favored moments of our youth. By all that is sacred in our hopes for the human race, I conjure those who love happiness and truth to give a fair trial to the vegetable system. Reasoning is surely superfluous on a subject whose merits an experience of six months would set forever at rest. But it is only among the enlightened and benevolent that so great a sacrifice of appetite and prejudice can be expected even though its ultimate excellence should not admit of dispute. It is found easier by the short-sighted victims of disease to palliate their torments by medicine than to prevent them by regimen. The vulgar of all ranks are invariably sensual and indocile; yet I cannot but feel myself persuaded that when the benefits of vegetable diet are mathematically proved; when it is as clear that those who live naturally are exempt from premature death as that nine is not one, the most sottish of mankind will feel a preference towards a long

28. "Ungovernable" in the Note.
29. Muley Ismael (1672-1727) was Sultan of Morocco, and because of his cruelty as conqueror was surnamed, the Blood-thirsty.

30. Lambe's *Reports on Cancer*. [Shelley's Note.]
31. The Note has these additional words following *dogmas*, "by which He has there excited and justified the most ferocious propensities."

and tranquil, contrasted with a short and painful life. On the average, out of sixty persons, four die in three years. In April, 1814, a statement will be given that sixty persons, all having lived more than three years on vegetables and pure water, are then in *perfect health*.[32] More than two years have now elapsed;[33] *not one of them has died*; no such example will be found in any sixty persons taken at random. Seventeen persons of all ages (the families of Dr. Lambe and Mr. Newton) have lived for seven years on this diet, without a death and almost without the slightest illness.[34] Surely when we consider that some of these were infants and one a martyr to asthma now nearly subdued, we may challenge any seventeen persons taken at random in this city to exhibit a parallel case. Those who may have been excited to question the rectitude of established habits of diet by these loose remarks should consult Mr. Newton's luminous and eloquent essay.[35] It is from that book and from the conversation of its excellent and enlightened author that I have derived the materials which I here present to the public.[36]

When these proofs come fairly before the world and are clearly seen by all who understand arithmetic, it is scarcely possible that abstinence from aliment demonstrably pernicious should not become universal. In proportion to the number of proselytes, so will be the weight of evidence, and when a thousand persons can be produced living on vegetables and distilled water, who have to dread no disease but old age, the world will be compelled to regard animal flesh and fermented liquors as slow but certain poisons. The change which would be produced by simpler habits on political economy is sufficiently remarkable. The monopolizing eater of animal flesh would no longer destroy his constitution by devouring an acre at a meal, and many loaves of bread would cease to contribute to gout, madness, and apoplexy, in the shape of a pint of porter, or a dram of gin, when appeasing the long-protracted famine of the hard-working peasant's hungry babes. The quantity of nutritious vegetable matter consumed in fattening the carcase of an ox would afford ten times the sustenance, undepraving indeed and incapable of generating disease, if gathered immediately from the bosom of the earth. The most fertile districts of the habitable globe are now actually cultivated by men for animals at a delay and waste of aliment absolutely incapable of calculation. It is only the wealthy that can to any great degree, even now, indulge the unnatural craving for dead flesh and they pay for the greater license of the privilege by subjection to supernumerary diseases. Again, the spirit of the nation that should take lead in this great reform would insensibly become agricultural; commerce, with all its vices,[37] selfishness, and corruption would gradually decline; more natural habits would produce gentler manners, and the excessive complication of political relations would be so far simplified that every individual might feel and understand why he loved his country and took a personal interest in its welfare. How would England, for example, depend on the caprices of foreign rulers, if she contained within herself all the necessaries and despised whatever they possessed of the luxuries of life? How could they starve her into compliance with their views? Of what consequence would it be that they refused to take her woollen manufactures, when large and fertile tracts of the island ceased to be allotted to the waste of pasturage? On a natural system of diet, we should require no spices from India; no wines from Portu-

---

32. The Note has here, "Hopes are entertained that" to introduce the sentence.
33. This statement seems to contradict the argument of the Headnote as to the date of composition.
34. Shelley met Newton early in November, 1812, and the two became at once close friends.

35. *Return to Nature, or Defence of Vegetable Regimen.* (Cadell, 1811.) [Shelley's Note.]
36. No doubt Shelley is here paying an exaggerated compliment to his friend. The last sentence of this paragraph is not in the Note.
37. The Note has "vice."

gal, Spain, France, or Madeira; none of those multitudinous articles of luxury for which every corner of the globe is rifled and which are the causes of so much individual rivalship, such calamitous and sanguinary national disputes. In the history of modern times the avarice of commercial monopoly, no less than the ambition of weak and wicked chiefs, seems to have fomented the universal discord, to have added stubbornness to the mistakes of cabinets, and indocility to the infatuation of the people. Let it ever be remembered that it is the direct influence of commerce to make the interval between the richest and the poorest man wider and more unconquerable. Let it be remembered that it is a foe to everything of real worth and excellence in the human character. The odious and disgusting aristocracy of wealth is built upon the ruins of all that is good in chivalry or republicanism; and luxury is the forerunner of a barbarism scarce capable of cure.[38] Is it impossible to realize a state of society where all the energies of man shall be directed to the production of his solid happiness? Certainly if this advantage (the object of all political speculation) be in any degree attainable, it is attainable only by a community which holds no factitious incentives to the avarice and ambition of the few and which is internally organized for the liberty, security, and comfort of the many. None must be entrusted with power (and money is the completest species of power) who do not stand pledged to use it exclusively for the general benefit.[39] But the use of animal flesh and fermented liquors directly militates with this equality of the rights of man. The peasant cannot gratify these fashionable cravings without leaving his family to starve. Without dis-

ease and war, those sweeping curtailers of population, pasturage would include a waste too great to be afforded. The labor requisite to support a family is far lighter than is usually supposed.[40] The peasantry work not only for themselves but for the aristocracy, the army, and the manufacturers.

The advantage of a reform in diet is obviously greater than that of any other. It strikes at the root of the evil. To remedy the abuses of legislation before we annihilate the propensities by which they are produced is to suppose that by taking away the effect the cause will cease to operate. But the efficacy of this system depends entirely on the proselytism of individuals, and grounds its merits as a benefit to the community upon the total change of the dietetic habits in its members. It proceeds securely from a number of particular cases to one that is universal and has this advantage over the contrary mode that one error does not invalidate all that has gone before.

Let not too much, however, be expected from this system. The healthiest among us is not exempt from hereditary disease.[41] The most symmetrical, athletic, and long-lived is a being inexpressibly inferior to what he would have been had not the unnatural habits of his ancestors accumulated for him a certain portion of malady and deformity. In the most perfect specimen of civilized man something is still found wanting by the physiological critic. Can a return to nature, then, instantaneously eradicate predispositions that have been slowly taking root in the silence of innumerable ages? Indubitably not. All that I contend for is that from the moment of relinquishing all unnatural habits, no new disease is generated; and that the predisposition to hereditary maladies

38. This early view of commerce and wealth is in complete accord with that expressed in the late *A Philosophical View of Reform.*
39. Shelley would, for the most part, be happy with the present British "welfare state."
40. It has come under the author's experience that some of the workmen on an embankment in North Wales, who, in consequence of the inability of the proprietor to pay them, seldom received their

wages, have supported large families by cultivating small spots of sterile ground by moonlight. In the notes to Pratt's Poem, *Bread, or the Poor,* is an account of an industrious laborer who by working in a small garden before and after his day's task attained to an enviable state of independence. [Shelley's Note.]
41. Again Shelley warns his reader not to overemphasize the theme of his essay.

gradually perishes for want of its accustomed supply. In cases of consumption, cancer, gout, asthma, and scrofula, such is the invariable tendency of a diet of vegetables and pure water.

Those who may be induced by these remarks to give the vegetable system a fair trial should, in the first place, date the commencement of their practice from the moment of their conviction. All depends upon breaking through a pernicious habit, resolutely and at once. Dr. Trotter[42] asserts that no drunkard was ever reformed by gradually relinquishing his dram. Animal flesh in its effects on the human stomach is analogous to a dram. It is similar in the kind though differing in the degree of its operation. The proselyte to a pure diet must be warned to expect a temporary diminution of muscular strength. The subtraction of a powerful stimulus will suffice to account for this event. But it is only temporary and is succeeded by an equable capability for exertion far surpassing his former various and fluctuating strength. Above all he will acquire an easiness of breathing, by which the same[43] exertion is performed, with a remarkable exemption from that painful and difficult panting now felt by almost every one after hastily climbing an ordinary mountain. He will be equally capable of bodily exertion, or mental application, after as before his simple meal. He will feel none of the narcotic effects of ordinary diet. Irritability, the direct consequence of exhausting stimuli, would yield to the power of natural and tranquil impulses. He will no longer pine under the lethargy of ennui, that unconquerable weariness of life more dreaded[44] than death itself. He will escape the epidemic madness that broods over its own injurious notions of the Deity, and "realizes the hell that priests and beldams feign." Every man forms as it were his god from his own character; to the divinity of one of simple habits, no offering would be more acceptable than the happiness of his creatures. He would be incapable of hating or persecuting others for the Love of God. He will find, moreover, a system of simple diet to be a system of perfect epicurism. He will no longer be incessantly occupied in blunting and destroying those organs from which he expects his gratification. The pleasures of taste to be derived from a dinner of potatoes, beans, peas, turnips, lettuce,[45] with a dessert of apples, gooseberries, strawberries, currants, raspberries, and in winter, oranges, apples, and pears is far greater than is supposed. Those who wait until they can eat this plain fare, with the sauce of appetite, will scarcely join with the hypocritical sensualist at a lord mayor's feast who declaims against the pleasures of the table. Solomon kept a thousand concubines and owned in despair that all was vanity. The man whose happiness is constituted by the society of one amiable woman would find some difficulty in sympathizing with the disappointment of this venerable debauchee.

I address myself not only to the young enthusiast, the ardent devotee of truth and virtue, the pure and passionate moralist yet unvitiated by the contagion of the world. He will embrace a pure system from its abstract truth, its beauty, its simplicity, and its promise of wide-extended benefit; unless custom has turned poison into food, he will hate the brutal pleasures of the chase by instinct; it will be a contemplation full of horror and disappointment to his mind that beings capable of the gentlest and most admirable sympathies should take delight in the death-pangs and last convulsions of dying animals. The elderly man whose youth has been poisoned by intemperance, or who has lived with apparent moderation, and is afflicted with a variety of painful maladies would find his account in a beneficial change produced without the risk of poisonous medi-

42. See *Trotter on the Nervous Temperament.* [Shelley's Note.]

43. "Such" in the Note.

44. The Note has "more to be dreaded."

45. The Note reads "lettuces."

cines. The mother, to whom the perpetual restlessness of disease and unaccountable deaths incident to her children are the causes of incurable unhappiness, would on this diet experience the satisfaction of beholding their perpetual healths and natural playfulness.[46] The most valuable lives are daily destroyed by diseases that it is dangerous to palliate and impossible to cure by medicine. How much longer will man continue to pimp for the gluttony of death, his most insidious, implacable, and eternal foe?[47]

The proselyte to a simple and natural diet who desires health must from the moment of his conversion attend to these rules:

NEVER TAKE ANY SUBSTANCE INTO THE STOMACH THAT ONCE HAD LIFE.

DRINK NO LIQUID BUT WATER RESTORED TO ITS ORIGINAL PURITY BY DISTILLATION.

APPENDIX[48]

Persons on vegetable diet have been remarkable for longevity. The first Christians practised abstinence from animal flesh, on a principle of self-mortification. Old Parr, 152;

Mary Patten, 136; a shepherd in Hungary, 126; Patrick O'Neale, 113; Joseph Elkins, 103; Elizabeth de Val, 101; Aurungzebe, 100; St. Anthony, 105; James the Hermit, 104; Arsenius, 120; St. Epiphanius, 115; Simeon, 112; Rombald, 120.[49]

Mr. Newton's mode of reasoning on longevity is ingenious and conclusive: "Old Parr, healthy as the wild animals, attained to the age of 152 years. All men might be as healthy as the wild animals. Therefore all men might attain to the age of 152 years."[50] The conclusion is sufficiently modest. Old Parr cannot be supposed to have escaped the inheritance of disease, amassed by the unnatural habits of his ancestors. The term of human life may be expected to be infinitely greater, taking into the consideration all the circumstances that must have contributed to abridge even that of Parr.

It may be here remarked that the author and his wife have lived on vegetables for eight months. The improvements of health and temper here stated is [are] the result of his own experience.

46. See Mr. Newton's book. His children are the most beautiful and healthy creatures it is possible to conceive; the girls are perfect models for a sculptor; their dispositions are also the most gentle and conciliating; the judicious treatment which they experience in other points may be a correlative cause of this. In the first five years of their life of 18,000 children that are born, 7,500 die of various diseases; and how many more of those that survive are not rendered miserable by maladies not immediately mortal? The quality and quantity of a woman's milk are materially injured by the use of dead flesh. In an island near Iceland where no vegetables are to be got, the children invariably die of tetanus, before they are three weeks old, and the population is supplied from the mainland. Sir G. McKenzie's *History of Iceland*. See also *Emile*, Chap. i, pp. 53, 54, 56. [Shelley's Note.]

47. Shelley ends his Note with a passage from Plutarch on flesh-eating. This much garbled quotation he probably took from Ritson—it is not in Newton. It consists of detached and non-consecutive sentences from Plutarch's *two* essays instead of from the first as has been usually thought.

48. This Appendix is not in the Note on *Queen Mab.*

49. For the first seven of these persons Shelley cites, respectively, the following information: Cheyne's *Essay on Health,* p. 62; *Gentleman's Magazine,* VII, 449; *Morning Post,* January 28, 1800; *Emile,* 1.44; he died at Coombe in Northumberland; *Scot's Magazine,* XXXIV, 696; Aurungzebe, from the time of his usurpation adhered strictly to the Vegetable System.

50. From a *Return to Nature.* [Shelley's Note.]

ESSAY ON THE VEGETABLE SYSTEM OF DIET

[The date of this essay is unknown. It has the appearance of being a redaction of the earlier attempts to put the case for a vegetarian system of diet. It was printed for private circulation (1929) by Ingpen, and first published in the Julian Editions (1929). The essay is in a more temperate vein than Shelley's earlier statements on the same subject. He puts more emphasis on the close dependence of mind upon body, of a sound mind in a sound body. Mind and morals to a large degree are conditioned by bodily health or bodily weakness. The central theme of the essay is that unnatural habits cause diseases—that a flesh diet, most unnatural for man, is a prolific cause of diseases.]

The wisest of the moral philosophers have justly remarked that man is the willing victim of innumerable errors, the habitual slave of a thousand perverse propensities. The madness of ambition and the abject idiotism of slavery, the impudence of imposture, and the ignorance of credulity have furnished inexhaustible themes for the indignant reprobation of enlightened virtue. Moralists have contented themselves, however, with tracing these evils to the defective institutions of human society. They have shown that the narrow and malignant passions which have turned man against man as a beast of blood, the unenlightened brutality of the multitude, and the profligate selfishness of courts are *cherished* by errors which have been rendered venerable by antiquity and consecrated by custom. This, however, is a loose and superficial estimate of the case. These pernicious institutions derive their origin from human error. This therefore is the legitimate object of scientific disquisition. This is the cause as well as the consequence of what we seek to remedy. The source of the errors of mankind is to be found not only in the external circumstances of his situation but in these peculiarities of internal organization which modify the operation. It is surprising that philosophers have never been induced to ascribe much of the violent and unreasonable conduct of human beings to diseased organization. They admit the influence of body on mind, they admit that the flames of a fever will calcine the brazen vase of our knowledge, that old age will extinguish the enthusiasm of virtue and of science; and that the faculties of the mind are so connected with the organs of the body that they sympathize minutely in its infancy and perfection, in its decrepitude and decay. Does then a slighter degree of bodily derangement fail to limit in some degree the energies of intellect and to excite some slighter perversities of passion? Is idiotism and frenzy to be traced to one cause, ill temper and stupidity the result of another? A certain degree of violent and injudicious conduct has been invariably ascribed to organic derangement, while the cause of those slighter specimens of folly and malignity which constitute the mass of human misery, have never been the subject to philosophical investigation. Moral inspiration has been thought a sufficient antidote to a malady which is the inevitable result of physical derangement. The speculative truths of moral sciences when perceived never fail perhaps to acquire an empire over the conduct; the difficulty consists in impressing them durably on the conviction of men, and this can only be effected by previously securing an understanding, unvitiated by bodily disease. With arguments shall philosophy assail superstition, so long as terrifying phantoms crowd round the couch of its pale and prostrate victim, refuting with the indisputable evidence of sense the metaphysical scepticism of reason, while politicians' dreams and reveries of indescribable horror testify?

How shall we inspire the miserable man with kindness and humanity whose social feelings are jaundiced by a torture that lurks within his vitals (*esse omnia providentem et cogitantem et animadvertem et omnia ad se pertinere putantem, curiosum et plenum negotii deum*)[1] and forces him to contemplate every cheerful sight and sound as a bitter mockery of his own intolerable anguish? How will you inspire that imbecile being with a persuasion of the importance of active virtue and the faithful discharge of the numerous duties of social life who is constituted by the physical imperfections of his nature into the canting nurse of his own morbid sensibilities? The attempt is more common, but scarcely less absurd than to reason with a lunatic, or to require from a dying man the exertion of that mental power and enlightened subtlety of research, for which when in health he had been conspicuous.

The use of ardent spirits and irritating food deranges in a *greater or less degree the mental faculties* as is evident to daily experience. Not only is inebriety temporarily laborious of the understanding, and gluttony productive of immediate grossness of perception (the benevolent, the selfish, the slave of the passions, the malignant, and the morbid), but habits of indigestion are peculiarly favorable to stupidity, and the consequences of a fit of drunkenness are inimical to intellectual exertion. It is impossible to dispute a fact of which every fire-side circle affords more than one melancholy example, but it belongs to philosophy alone to trace the remote effects of mistakes consecrated by habit, to mark their influence on individual character, to estimate the sum of a thousand unregarded events as affecting the welfare of society, and to trace to the influence of unnatural habits of life hatred, murder and rapine, wars, massacres, and revolutions.

A poet dear to every lover of Nature[2] has illustrated this fact with his exquisite and original pencil:

> . . . Ladurlad hears their distant
> voices
> And with their joy no more his heart
> rejoices:
> And how their old companion now
> may fare
> Little they know, and less they care
> The torment he is doomed to hear
> Was but to them the wonder of a day
> A burthen of sad thoughts soon put
> away.
> They knew not that the wretched man
> was near
> And yet it seemed to his distempered ear
> As if they wronged him with their
> merriment.
> Resentfully he turned away his eyes.
>
> *Curse of Kehama, IX*

A popular objection which never fails to be opposed to every reasoning of this nature is that it is incorrect to ascribe such mighty effect to causes so comparatively trivial. Such nevertheless are the laws of the world which we inhabit. A spark well kindled will consume the most sumptuous palace; some slight derangement in the association of a monarch's ideas may involve his subjects in a long and sanguinary war. The dream of a frantic woman has lighted the piles of persecution in every corner of the civilized globe. Man is a whole the complicated parts of which are so interwoven with each other that the most remote and subtle springs of his machine are connected with those which are more gross and obvious and reciprocally act and react upon each other. The conclusion then to which we have arrived and which is neither contradicted by the experience of daily life, nor the more simple speculations of profane philosophy is that much

---

1. Shelley used this quotation in *A Refutation of Deism;* for a translation see Footnote 39 in that essay.

2. This praise of Southey points to an early date, before Shelley had lost faith in Southey (c. 1815). This praise is indeed strong argument for the early dating of this essay.

of the violent and unreasonable conduct of human beings is to be ascribed to diseased organization.

The vital principle by some inexplicable process influences and is influenced by the nerves and muscles of the body. The flesh is wasted by an excess of grief and passion. Thought is suspended by the langor of a lethargy and deranged by the excitement of a fever.

The establishment of this axiom is of considerable moment to the subject of the present investigation. It attaches a degree of importance to the issue of the enquiry which would scarcely seem to belong to a mere question of dietetics. Much of that spirit in which human beings persecute and destroy each other arises from the morbid disquietude of their physical constitutions. It is not easy to conceive an object more worthy of the philanthropist and the philosopher than to investigate the nature and to oppose the influence of a principle thus eminently hostile to the peace and welfare of mankind.

It will readily be admitted that *disease* is not a natural state of the human frame; that there are certain habits which have a tendency to preserve health, and others on the practice of which organic derangement inevitably ensues. It will not be disputed that there is a peculiar mode of life which would effectually secure the human race from the invasions of malady. The assertion, therefore, that disease is the consequence of unnatural habits of life is liable to no conceivable objection. To every species of animal, excepting man, and those miserable creatures whom he has subjected to his contaminating dominion, there is an average period of existence which few exceed, but which few fail to attain. But no hour of the life of man is exempt from the dreaded invasion of a mortal malady. (One half of every generation perishes.) Some isolated instances of longevity stand upon record as proof of the natural term[3] of human life.

But death ordinarily seizes alike upon old age and childhood, vigor and debility; not innocence of infancy, the strength of manhood, the bloom of dawning youth; nay, not the strictest individual temperance can guard against the secret wiles of this insidious destroyer. Human beings possessed of the most admirable and glorious propensities are suddenly cut off in their full career of usefulness. Beings to whom nations have turned anxiously as to their expected saviors, whom families have regarded as their only comfort and support, who have dispensed concord, happiness, and hope throughout the sphere of their exertions, are abruptly swept away by that mysterious principle which visits the sins of the fathers on the children.

Hospitals are filled with a thousand screaming victims; the palaces of luxury and the hovels of indigence resound alike with the bitter wailings of disease; idiotism and madness grin and rave among us, and all these complicated calamities result from those unnatural habits of life to which the human race has addicted itself during innumerable ages of mistake and misery.

By an unnatural habit is to be understood such a habit as is manifestly inconsistent with the conformation of any animal; and this inconsistency is to be esteemed a sufficient evidence of its pernicious consequences. It is probable that no anatomist will be inclined to deny that if a lion were fed on grass, or a cow on flesh, the health of these animals would be materially injured. In fact the experiment has been tried and has uniformly been attended with the consequences here alleged. The wild bear is healthy and active and one of the most formidable of the beasts of the forests. In his natural state he is frugivorous; domestication has reduced him omnivorous, has rendered him in consequence miserable, languid, and filthy [and] inflicted on him an immense variety of diseases. The argali, or wild sheep, is an animal of remarkable

3. Easton. [Shelley's Note.]

sagacity and strength and attains the age of fourteen years; the domestic sheep is weak, timorous, and would be devoured by innumerable diseases long before the natural term of its existence if the butcher's knife does not anticipate its miserable end. Many similar facts might be adduced if the fact that disease is the result of unnatural habits of life required any additional confirmation.

The object of the present enquiry is to prove that one of these unnatural habits which produce disease is the use of animal food.

The substances which we take into the stomach constitute one of the principal sources of malady. The remotest parts of the body sympathize with the stomach. Groundless terrors, vertigo, and delirium are frequently consequent upon a disease of the digestive organs; tremors and spasmodic affections, remote both in their nature[4] and position from disorders of the stomach, are yet in many cases to be traced to its derangement; and those whose digestive powers are strongly and regularly exerted are particularly exempt from illness. If, therefore, the cause of the disorders of the digestive organs be discovered, disease may be successfully assailed in its source by a system of diet, the reverse of that by which it is produced.[5]

That man is naturally a frugivorous animal numerous considerations conspire to demonstrate. The most obvious of these has not failed to suggest itself to the ancient advocates of simple diet. The manifest natural disqualification of the human frame for rapine and destruction, his want of those instruments of offence with which the carnivorous animals are furnished, sufficiently evinces how ill he is adapted to provide himself with the flesh of animals without the artifices which result from the experience of many centuries. It demanded surely no great profundity of anatomical research to perceive that man has neither the fangs

of a lion nor the claws of a tiger, that his instincts are inimical to bloodshed, and that the food which is not to be eaten without the most intolerable loathing until it is altered by the action of fire and disguised by the addition of condiments, is not that food for which he is adapted by his physical constitutions. The bull must be degraded into the ox, the ram into the wether by an unnatural and inhuman operation that the flaccid fiber may offer less resistance to [a nature]. . . . Sows big with young are indeed no longer stamped upon [to death] and sucking pigs roasted alive; but lobsters are slowly boiled to death and express by their inarticulate cries the dreadful agony they endure; chickens are mutilated and imprisoned until they fatten; calves are bled to death that their flesh may appear white; and a certain horrible process of torture furnishes brawn for the gluttonous repasts with which Christians celebrate the anniversary of their Savior's birth. What beast of prey compels its victim to undergo such protracted, such severe and such degrading torments? The single consideration that man cannot swallow a piece of raw flesh would be sufficient to prove that the natural diet of the human species did not consist in the carcasses of butchered animals.

Custom has been found to reconcile the animal system to habits the most unnatural and pernicious. Narcotic poisons have been gradually swallowed until they have ceased to produce their accustomed effect, although they have never failed eventually to produce disease and death. Every being with which we are acquainted invariably attempts to accommodate itself to the circumstances of its situation; it nevertheless exhausts in the effort much of its vital energy. A willow will attain to its perfection by the bank of a river, because this situation is analogous to its nature; place it [in] that soil which is congenial to the fir tree, and it will live indeed if it survive the shock of

4. See Abernathy. [Shelley's Note.]
5. It is not here asserted that mental and bodily

derangement, etc. See *Queen Mab*, p. 223. [Shelley's Note.]

transplantation and it will become a diseased and stunted shrub. [Lambs have eaten flesh until they have refused their natural diet.] Horses, sheep, oxen, and even wood pigeons have been taught to live upon flesh until they have loathed their natural aliment. No argument therefore can be adduced in favor of any system of diet from the mere fact of its being generally used, so long as disease and meagerness and misery are observed among its unfailing concomitants. . . .[6]

Here then lies exposed one of the most important sources of the wretchedness of man. If then reasoning have any force, mankind is in the daily practice of an unnatural habit, the consequences of which cannot fail to be eminently pernicious. It is a duty which every individual owes to himself, to posterity, to those who are influenced by his example, and to those who depend in any manner on his health and existence for any portion of their happiness, resolutely to break this unnatural practice thus pregnant with inexhaustible calamity. Those who are persuaded of the point which it is the object of this enquiry to establish are bound by the most sacred obligations of morality to adopt in practice what he admits in theory. He is bound to disregard the seductive titillations of a perverted appetite, to despise that false and hollow-hearted conviviality which is founded on intemperance and to control himself with those purer and more consistent elations of nature which invariably accompany a virtuous mind and an unvitiated body. Before the human race shall be capable of any considerable advance towards that happiness which is the ultimate object of all human exertion, habits demonstrably unnatural must be unsparingly discarded. Let not, however, the expectations which may reasonably be indulged from the dereliction of a destructive custom be

exaggerated. Disease is hereditary and the mass which is now existing in the world has been produced by a mistake of unfathomable antiquity. With what rapidity the adoption of vegetable food might diminish this accumulation it is impossible to predict. We are authorized only to assert that it would in some degree be diminished by the use of aliment to which man is adapted by his construction in every essential particular.

Meanwhile facts are not wanting which may serve to show that the vegetable system of diet is innocent and even salutary; and may reconcile it to the selfishness of some by the promise of immediate advantages. Specimens of longevity have been far more common among vegetable eaters in proportion to their numbers than among those who use animal food. The philosophers of ancient Greece[7] and the hermits of primitive Christianity adopted a rigid system of diet from which flesh of animals was almost entirely excluded; they afford numerous examples of longevity. Constitutional diseases which have resisted every other method have yielded to vegetable diet.

Whoever fairly makes the experiment of the change here recommended will speedily perceive the benefit of his abstinence. He will find himself equally capable of bodily or intellectual exertion after, as before his simple meal. His spirits will be more equally constant and less subject to those invincible depressions by which the lightest heart is so frequently invaded. Such are the recommendations of the vegetable system and such are the arguments upon which it is founded. . . . So far as just philosophy and natural sentiments shall prevail among mankind so far I am persuaded the practice of destroying and devouring animals will be contemplated in the light of an unnatural and pernicious outrage.

6. Ritson. [Shelley's Note.] The brackets in the last two paragraphs indicate Shelley's cancellations.
7. See *Return to Nature,* and Dr. Lambe on *Constitutional Diseases.*
Old Parr 152, Mary Patten 136, A shepherd in Hungary 126, Patric O'Neale 113, Joseph Eldems 103, Elizabeth De Val 101, Aurungzebe 100, Rom-

bold 120, Asenius 120, Epiphanius 115, Simeon 112, St. Anthony 105, James the Hermit 104. See Essay. Many other instances (of longevity) are to be found in Easton's catalogue of longevity, in which, however, the habits of life of the individuals are incorrectly omitted. These examples are produced from another source. [Shelley's Notes.]

The mere destruction of any sentiment being abstractedly considered is perhaps an event of exceedingly minute importance. It is of little moment to the welfare of animated beings that a volcano burst out in Kanstashka and destroyed some villages and some heads of cattle. It is because a malevolent and ferocious disposition is generated by the commission of murder that this crime is so tremendous and detestable. Who that is accustomed to the sight of wounds and anguish will scruple to inflict them when he shall deem it expedient? With what measure of evil is anger, vengeance, and malignity contented? How interminable is the series of calamity which that man who first slew his brother unthinkingly produced? It is evident that those who are necessitated by their profession to trifle with the sacredness of life and think lightly of the agonies of living beings are unfit for the benevolence and justice which is required for the performance of the offices of civilized society. They are by necessity brutal, coarse, turbulent, and sanguinary. Their habits form admirable apprenticeship to the more wasting wickedness of war, in which men are hired to mangle and murder their fellow beings, that tyrants and countries may profit by thousands. How can he be expected to preserve a vivid sensibility to the benevolent sympathies of our nature, who is familiar with carnage, agony, and groans? The very sight of animals in the fields who are destined to the axe must encourage obduracy if it fails to awaken compassion. The butchering of harmless animals cannot fail to produce much of that spirit of insane and hideous exultation in which news of a victory is related although purchased by the massacre of a hundred thousand men. If the use of animal food be in consequence subversive to the peace of human society, how unwarrantable is the injustice and barbarity which is exercised toward these miserable victims. They are called into existence by human artifice *that they may drag out a short and miserable existence of slavery and disease, that their bodies may be mutilated, their social feelings outraged.* It were much better that a sentient being should never have existed than that it should have existed only to endure unmitigated misery.[8]

8. The attachment of animals to their young is very strong. The monstrous sophism that beasts are pure unfeeling machines and do not reason scarcely requires a confutation. [Shelley's Note.] This idea of the intellectual powers of animals is fully discussed in Holbach's *Système de la Nature*, 1.81.

"THERE IS NO GOD"

[This essay is a redaction of Shelley's first pamphlet, *The Necessity of Atheism* (1811) to serve as a note to the line in *Queen Mab,* "There is no God" (1813). *The Necessity of Atheism* is greatly expanded and considerably modified in thought and style. A careful study of the two essays will throw some light on Shelley's developing mind during the two crowded years between them. Locke's influence dominates *The Necessity* while Hume and Holbach are the important sources of the Note.]

This negation must be understood solely to affect a *creative* Deity. The hypothesis of a pervading Spirit co-eternal with the universe remains unshaken.

A close examination of the validity of the proofs adduced to support any proposition is the only secure way of attaining truth, on the advantages of which it is unnecessary to descant; our knowledge of the existence of a Deity is a subject of such importance that it cannot be too minutely investigated; in consequence of this conviction we proceed briefly and impartially to examine the proofs which have been adduced. It is necessary first to consider the nature of belief.

When a proposition is offered to the mind, it perceives the agreement or disagreement of the ideas of which it is composed. A perception of their agreement is termed *belief.* Many obstacles frequently prevent this perception from being immediate; these the mind attempts to remove in order that the perception may be distinct. The mind is active in the investigation in order to perfect the state of perception of the relation which the component ideas of the proposition bear to each, which is passive. The investigation being confused with the perception has induced many falsely to imagine that the mind is active in belief—that belief is an act of volition—in consequence of which it may be regulated by the mind. Pursuing, continuing this mistake, they have attached a degree of criminality to disbelief; of which, in its nature, it is incapable; it is equally incapable of merit.

Belief, then, is a passion the strength of which, like every other passion, is in pre-cise proportion to the degrees of excitement.

The degrees of excitement are three:

The senses are the sources of all knowledge to the mind; consequently their evidence claims the strongest assent.

The decision of the mind, founded upon our own experience, derived from these sources, claims the next degree.

The experience of others, which addresses itself to the former one, occupies the lowest degree.

(A graduated scale, on which should be marked the capabilities of propositions to approach to the test of the senses, would be a just barometer of the belief which ought to be attached to them.)

Consequently no testimony can be admitted which is contrary to reason; reason is founded on the evidence of our senses.

Every proof may be referred to one of these three divisions: it is to be considered what arguments we receive from each of them, which should convince us of the existence of a Deity.

1st. The evidence of the senses. If the Deity should appear to us, if He should convince our senses of His existence, this revelation would necessarily command belief. Those to whom the Deity has thus appeared have the strongest possible conviction of His existence. But the God of theologians is incapable of local visibility.

2nd. Reason. It is urged that man knows that whatever is must either have had a beginning, or have existed from all eternity; he also knows that whatever is not eternal must have had a cause. When this reasoning is applied to the universe, it is necessary to prove that it was created—until that is clearly demonstrated we may reasonably suppose that it has endured from all eternity. We must prove design before we can infer a designer. The only idea which we can form of causation is derivable from the constant conjunction of objects, and the consequent inference of one from the other. In a case where two propositions are diametrically opposite, the mind believes that which is least incomprehensible; it is easier to suppose that the universe has existed from all eternity than to conceive a being beyond its limits capable of creating it; if the mind sinks beneath the weight of one, is it an alleviation to increase the intolerability of the burden?[1]

The other argument, which is founded on a man's knowledge of his own existence, stands thus: A man knows not only that he now is, but that once he was not; consequently there must have been a cause. But our idea of causation is alone derivable from the constant conjunction of objects and the consequent inference of one from the other; and, reasoning experimentally, we can only infer from effects causes exactly adequate to those effects. But there certainly is a generative power which is effected by certain instruments; we cannot prove that it is inherent in these instruments; nor is the contrary hypothesis capable of demonstration. We admit that the generative power is incomprehensible; but to suppose that the same effect is produced by an eternal, omniscient, omnipotent being leaves the cause in the same obscurity, but renders it more incomprehensible.

3rd. Testimony. It is required that testimony should not be contrary to reason. The testimony that the Deity convinces the senses of men of His existence can only be admitted by us if our mind considers it less probable that these men should have been deceived than that the Deity should have appeared to them. Our reason can never admit the testimony of men who not only declare that they were eye-witnesses of miracles but that the Deity was irrational; for He commanded that He should be believed; He proposed the highest rewards for faith, eternal punishments for disbelief. We can only command voluntary actions; belief is not an act of volition; the mind is even passive, or involuntarily active; from this it is evident that we have no sufficient testimony, or rather that testimony is insufficient, to prove the being of a God. It has been before shown that it cannot be deduced from reason. They alone, then, who have been convinced by the evidence of the senses can believe it.

Hence it is evident that, having no proofs from either of the three sources of conviction, the mind *cannot* believe the existence of a creative God; it is also evident that, as belief is a passion of the mind, no degree of criminality is attachable to disbelief; and that they only are reprehensible who neglect to remove the false medium through which their mind views any subject of discussion. Every reflecting mind must acknowledge that there is no proof of the existence of a Deity.

God is an hypothesis and, as such, stands in need of proof: the *onus probandi* rests on the theist. Sir Isaac Newton says: *Hypotheses non fingo, quicquid enim ex phaenomenis non deducitur hypothesis vocanda est, et hypothesis vel metaphysicae, vel physicae, vel qualitatum occultarum, seu mechanicae, in philosophia locum non habent.*[2] To all proofs of the existence of a creative God apply this valuable rule. We see a variety of bodies possessing a variety of powers; we merely know their effects; we are in a state of ignorance with respect to their essences and causes. These Newton calls the phenomena of things; but the pride of philosophy is unwilling to admit its ignorance of their causes. From the phenomena, which are the objects of our senses,

1. See Holbach's *Système*, 1.31-39, for a similar argument.
2. "I do not invent hypotheses, for whatever is not deduced from phenomena should be called an hypothesis; and an hypothesis, whether of metaphysics, or physics, or occult qualities, or mechanics, have [*sic*] no place in philosophy."

we attempt to infer a cause, which we call God, and gratuitously endow it with all negative and contradictory qualities. From this hypothesis we invent this general name to conceal our ignorance of causes and essences. The being called God by no means answers with the conditions prescribed by Newton; it bears every mark of a veil woven by philosophical conceit to hide the ignorance of philosophers even from themselves. They borrow the threads of its texture from the anthropomorphism of the vulgar. Words have been used by sophists for the same purposes, from the occult qualities of the peripatetics to the *effluvium* of Boyle and *crinities* or *nebulae* of Herschel. God is represented as infinite, eternal, incomprehensible; He is contained under every *predicate in non* that the logic of ignorance could fabricate. Even His worshippers allow that it is impossible to form any idea of Him; they exclaim with the French poet,

Pour dire ce qu'il est, il faut être lui-même.[3]

Lord Bacon says that atheism leaves to man reason, philosophy, natural piety, laws, reputation, and everything that can serve to conduct him to virtue; but superstition destroys all these, and erects itself into a tyranny over the understandings of men; hence atheism never disturbs the government, but renders man more clear-sighted, since he sees nothing beyond the boundaries of the present life.

Bacon's *Moral Essays*
[A paraphrase from "Of Superstition."]

La première théologie de l'homme lui fit d'abord craindre et adorer les élémens même, des objets matériels et grossiers; il rendit ensuite ses hommages a des agens présidens aux élémens, à des génies inférieurs, à des héros, ou à des hommes doués de grands qualités. A force de réfléchir il crut simplifier les choses en soumettant la nature

entière à un seul agent, a un esprit, à une âme universelle, qui mettoit cette nature et ses parties en mouvement. En remontant des causes en causes, les mortels ont fini par ne rien voir; et c'est dans cette obscurité qu'ils ont place leur Dieu; c'est dans cette obscurité qu'ils ont placé leur Dieu; c'est dans cette abîme ténébreux que leur imagination inquiète travaille toujours à se fabriquer des chimères, qui les affligeront jusqu'à ce que la connoissance de la nature les détrompe des fantômes qu'ils ont toujours si vainement adorés.

Si nous voulons nous rendre compte de nos idées sur la Divinité, nous serons obligés de convenir que, par le mot *Dieu,* les hommes n'ont jamais pu désigner que la cause la plus cachée, la plus éloignée, la plus inconnue des effets qu'ils voyoient: ils ne font usage de ce mot, que lorsque le jeu des causes naturelles et connues cesse d'être visible pour eux; dès qu'ils perdent le fil de ces causes, ou dès que leur esprit ne peut plus en suivre la chaîne, ils tranchent leur difficulté, et terminent leur recherches en appellant Dieu la dernière des causes, c'est-à-dire celle qui est au-delà de toutes les causes qu'ils connoissent; ainsi ils ne font qu'assigner une dénomination vague à une cause ignorée, à laquelle leur paresse ou les bornes de leurs connoissances les forcent de s'arrêter. Toutes les fois qu'on nous dit que Dieu est l'auteur de quelque phénomène, cela signifie qu'on ignore comment un tel phénomène a pu s'opérer par le sécours des forces ou des causes que nous connoissons dans la nature. C'est ainsi que le commun des hommes, dont l'ignorance est le partage, attribue à la Divinité non seulement les effets inusités qui les frappent, mais encore les événemens les plus simples, dont les causes sont les plus faciles à connoître pour quiconque a pu les

---

3. "To say what he is, one would have to be he."

méditer. En un mot, l'homme a toujours respecté les causes inconnues des effets surprenans, que son ignorance l'empêchoit de démêler. Ce fut sur les débris de la nature que les hommes élevèrent le colosse imaginaire de la Divinité.

Si l'ignorance de la nature donna la naissance aux dieux, la connoissance de la nature est faite pour les detruire. A mésure que l'homme s'instruit, ses forces et ses ressources augmentent avec ses lumières; les sciences, les arts conservateurs, l'industrie, lui fournissent des secours; l'expérience le rassûre, ou lui procure des moyens de résister aux efforts de bien des causes qui cessent de l'alarmer dès qu'il les a connues. En un mot, ses terreurs se dissipent dans la même proportion que son esprit s'éclaire. L'homme instruit cesse d'être superstitieux.

Ce n'est jamais que sur parole que des peuples entiers adorent le Dieu de leurs pères et de leurs prêtres: l'autorité, la confiance, la soumission, et l'habitude leur tiennent lieu de conviction et de preuves; ils se prosternent et prient, parce que leurs pères leur ont appris à se prosterner et à prier: mais pourquoi ceux-ci se sont-ils mis à genoux? C'est que dans les temps éloignés leurs legislateurs et leurs guides leur en ont fait un devoir. "Adorez et croyez," ont-ils dit, "des dieux que vous ne pouvez comprendre; rapportez-vous en a notre sagesse profonde; nous en savons plus que vous sur la divinité." "Mais pourquoi m'en rapporterai-je à vous?" "C'est que Dieu le veut ainsi; c'est que Dieu vous punira si vous osez résister:" "Mais ce Dieu n'est-il donc pas la chose en question?" Cependant les hommes se sont toujours payés de ce cercle vicieux; la paresse de leur esprit leur fit trouver plus court de s'en rapporter au jugement des autres. Toutes les notions religieuses sont fondées uniquement sur l'autorité; toutes les religions du monde défendent l'examen et ne veulent pas que l'on raisonne; c'est l'autorité qui veut qu'on croie en Dieu; ce Dieu n'est lui-même fondé que sur l'autorité de quelques hommes qui prétendent le connoître, et venir de sa part pour l'annoncer à la terre. Un Dieu fait par les hommes a sans doute besoin des hommes pour se faire connoître au monde.

Ne seroit-ce donc que pour des prêtres, des inspirés, des métaphysiciens que seroit reservée la conviction de l'existence d'un Dieu, que l'on dit néanmoins si necessaire à toute le genre humain? Mais trouvons-nous de l'harmonie entre les opinions théologiques des différens inspirés, ou des penseurs répandus sur la terre? Ceux même qui font profession d'adorer le même Dieu, sont-ils d'accord sur son compte? sont'ils contents des preuves que leurs collègues apportent de son existence? Souscrivent-ils unanimement aux idées qu'ils présentent sur sa nature, sur sa conduite, sur la façon d'entendre ses prétendus oracles? Est-il une contrée sur la terre où la science de Dieu se soit réellement perfectionnée? A-t-elle pris quelque part la consistance et l'uniformité que nous voyons prendre aux connoissances humaines, aux arts les plus futiles, aux métiers les plus meprisés? les mots d'*esprit*, d'*immatérialité*, de *création*, de *prédestination*, de *grace;* cette foule de distinctions subtiles dont la théologie s'est partout remplie; dans quelques pays, ces inventions si ingénieuses, imaginées par des penseurs qui se sont succédés depuis tant de siècles, n'ont fait, helas! qu'embrouiller les choses, et jamais la science la plus nécessaire aux hommes n'a jusqu' ici pu acquérir la moindre fixité. Depuis des milliers d'années des rêveurs oisifs se sont perpétuellement relayés pour méditer la Divinité, pour deviner ses voies cachées, pour inventer des hypothèses propres à développer cette énigme importante. Leur peu de succès n'a point découragé la vanité théologique; tou-

jours on a parlé de Dieu: on s'est dis-
puté, l'on s'est égorgé pour lui, et cet
être sublime demeure toujours le plus
ignoré et le plus discuté.

Les hommes auroient été trop heu-
reux, si se bornant aux objets visibles
qui les intéressent, ils eussent employé à
perfectionner leurs sciences réelles, leurs
lois, leur morale, leur éducation, la moi-
tié des efforts qu'ils ont mis dans leurs
recherches sur la Divinité. Ils auroient
été bien plus sages encore, et plus for-
tunés, s'ils eussent pu consentir à laisser
leurs guides désoeuvrés se quereller entre eux, et sonder des profondeurs capa-
bles de les étourdir, sans se mêler de
leurs disputes insensées. Mais il est de
l'essence de l'ignorance d'attacher de
l'importance à ce qu'elle ne comprend
pas. La vanité humaine fait que l'esprit
se roidit contre les difficultés. Plus un
objet se dérobe à nos yeux, plus nous
faisons d'efforts pour le saisir, parce que
dès-lors il aiguillone notre orgueil, il
irrite notre curiosité, il nous paroît in-
téressant. En combattant pour son Dieu,
chacun ne combattit en effet que pour
les intérêts de sa propre vanité, qui de
toutes les passions humaines est la plus
prompte à s'alarmer, et la plus propre à
produire de très grandes folies.

Si, écartant pour un moment les idées
fâcheuses que la théologie nous donne
d'un Dieu capricieux, dont les décrets
partiaux et despotiques décident du sort
des humains, nous ne voulons fixer nos
yeux que sur la bonté prétendue, que
tous les hommes, même en tremblant
devant ce Dieu, s'accordent à lui don-
ner; si nous lui supposons le project
qu'on lui prête, de n'avoir travaillé que
pour sa propre gloire, d'exiger les hommages des êtres intelligens; de ne cher-
cher dans ses oeuvres que le bien-être
du genre humain; comment concilier
ces vues et ces dispositions avec l'ignorance vraiment invincible dans laquelle
ce Dieu, si glorieux et si bon, laisse la
plupart des hommes sur son compte? Si
Dieu veut être connu, chéri, remercié,

que ne se montre-t-il sous des traits fa-
vorables à tous ces êtres intelligens dont
il veut être aimé et adoré? Pourquoi ne
point se manifester à toute la terre d'une
façon non équivoque, bien plus capable
de nous convaincre, que ces révélations
particulières qui semblent accuser la
Divinité d'une partialité fâcheuse pour
quelques-unes de ses créatures? Le tout-
puissant n'auroit-il pas donc des moyens
plus convaincans de se montrer aux
hommes, que ces métamorphoses ridicules, ces incarnations prétendues, qui
nous sont attestées par des écrivains si
peu d'accord entre eux dans les récits
qu'ils en font? Au lieu de tant de miracles, inventés pour prouver la mission
divine de tant de législateurs, révé-
rés par les différens peuples du monde,
le souverain des esprits ne pouvoit-il
pas convaincre tout d'un coup l'esprit
humain des choses qu'il vouloit lui faire
connoître? Au lieu de suspendre un so-
leil dans la voûte du firmament; au lieu
de répandre sans ordre les étoiles, et les
constellations qui remplissent l'espace,
n'eut-il pas été plus conforme aux vues
d'un Dieu si jaloux de sa gloire et si
bien intentionné pour l'homme; d'écrire
d'une façon non sujette à dispute, son
nom, ses attributs, ses volontés perma-
nentes, en caractères ineffaçables, et lisi-
bles également pour tous les habitants
de la terre? Personne alors n'auroit pu
douter de l'existence d'un Dieu, de ses
volontés claires, de ses intentions visibles. Sous les yeux de ce Dieu si sensible,
personne n'auroit eu l'audace de violer
ses ordonnances; nul mortel n'eût osé
se mettre dans le cas d'attirer sa colère:
enfin nul homme n'eût eu le front d'en
imposer en son nom, ou d'interpréter ses
volontés suivant ses propres fantaisies.

En effet, quand même on supposeroit
l'existence du Dieu théologique, et la
réalité des attributs si discordans qu'on
lui donne, l'on ne peut en rien conclure,
pour autoriser la conduite ou les cultes
qu'on prescrit de lui rendre. La théologie est vraiment *le tonneau des Danaï-*

des. A force de qualités contradictoires et d'assertions hazardées, elle a, pour ainsi dire, tellement garroté son Dieu qu'elle l'a mis dans l'impossibilité d'agir. S'il est infiniment bon, quelle raison aurions-nous de le craindre? S'il est infiniment sage, de quoi nous inquiéter sur notre sort? S'il sait tout, pourquoi l'avertir de nos besoins, et le fatiguer de nos prières? S'il est partout, pourquoi lui élever des temples? S'il est le maître de tout, pourquoi lui faire des sacrifices et des offrandes? S'il est juste, comment croire qu'il punisse des créatures qu'il a remplies de foiblesses? Si la grace fait tout en elles, quelle raison auroit-il de les récompenser? S'il est tout-puissant, comment l'offenser, comment lui résister? S'il est raisonnable, comment se mettroit-il en colère contre des aveugles, à qui il a laissé la liberté de déraisonner? S'il est immuable, de quel droit prétendrions-nous faire changer ses décrets? S'il est inconcevable, pourquoi nous en occuper? S'IL A PARLÉ, POURQUOI L'UNIVERS N'EST-IL PAS CONVAINCU? Si la connoissance d'un Dieu est la plus nécessaire, pourquoi n'est-elle pas la plus évidente, et la plus claire.—*Système de la Nature, London,* 1781.[4] [Shelley quotes verbatim, errors and all, scattered paragraphs from Volume Two, London edition (1771), principally from pages 16-18, 27, 319-326, as though they were consecutive.]

The enlightened and benevolent Pliny thus publicly professes himself an atheist: Quapropter effigiem Dei formamque quaerere inbecillitatis humanae reor. Quisquis est Deus (si modo est alius) et qua cunque in parte, totus est sensus, totus est visus, totus auditus, totus animae, totus animi, totus sui. . . . Imperfectae vero in homine naturae praecipua solatia ne deum quidem

posse omnia. Namque nec sibi potest mortem consciscere, si velit, quod homini dedit optimum in tantis vitae poenis: nec mortales aeternitate donare, aut revocare defunctos; nec facere ut qui vixit non vixerit, qui honores gessit non gesserit, nullumque habere in praeteritum ius, praeterquam oblivionis, atque (ut facetis quoque argumentis societas haec cum deo copuletur) ut bis dena viginti non sint, et multa similiter efficere non posse. Per quae declaratur haud dubie naturae potentiam id quoque esse quod Deum vocamus.[5]
　　Plin. *Nat. Hist.,* cap. de Deo.

The consistent Newtonian is necessarily an atheist. See Sir W. Drummond's *Academical Questions,* Chapter iii.

Sir W. seems to consider the atheism to which it leads as a sufficient presumption of the falsehood of the system of gravitation; but surely it is more consistent with the good faith of philosophy to admit a deduction from facts than an hypothesis incapable of proof, although it might militate with the obstinate preconceptions of the mob. Had this author, instead of inveighing against the guilt and absurdity of atheism, demonstrated its falsehood, his conduct would have been more suited to the modesty of the sceptic and the toleration of the philosopher.

Omnia enim per Dei potentiam facta sunt: imo quia naturae potentia nulla est nisi ipsa Dei potentia. Certum est nos eatenus Dei potentiam non intelligere, quatenus causas naturales ignoramus; adeoque stulte ad eandem Dei potentiam recurritur, quando rei alicuius causam naturalem, sive est, ipsam Dei potentiam ignoramus.[6]
　　Spinoza, *Tract. Theologico-Pol.* chap. i, p. 14. [Shelley's Note.]

4. For a translation of this quotation see Appendix D(a).
5. For the translation of the quotation see Appendix D(b). Shelley's text differs slightly from

the Loeb. This quotation, lacking the first sentence, is given in *A Refutation of Deism.*
6. For a collation of Shelley's text with that of Spinoza and translation see Appendix D(c).

"I WILL BEGET A SON"

[During 1811-12 Shelley ordered from London booksellers the works of the leading scientists, historians, and philosophers—ancient and modern. These he read assiduously in preparation for his avowed purpose of reforming the world. He put the ideas thus gained to immediate use in the Notes to *Queen Mab,* for the most part written during the first three months of 1813. Among the Notes is one to the line, "I will beget a Son," which statement I shall use as a title for this essay. This Note is essentially a redaction of the *Letter to Lord Ellenborough.*

In the Note Shelley maintained that the leaders of Christianity, throughout its history, had adopted a course of coercion rather than one of persuasion to gain control over the minds of the people as if *belief* were a voluntary act, as unbelief and criminality were synonymous terms. Had Christianity been freely adopted by the people and in harmony with the moral and social teachings of Jesus, its influence would, Shelley urged, have been salutary. But in allying itself with kings and warriors and wealth and greed, it became the champion not of the poor and oppressed—the especial concern of Jesus—but of the oppressor.

Shelley's profound and life-long admiration for the character and teachings of Jesus and his even profounder conviction that organized Christianity has betrayed the moral leadership of its founder is a fact that cannot be overstressed.]

A book is put into our hands when children, called the Bible, the purpose of whose history is briefly this: that God made the earth in six days, and there planted a delightful garden, in which he placed the first pair of human beings; [that] in the midst of the garden he planted a tree whose fruit, although within their reach, they were forbidden to touch; that the Devil in the shape of a snake persuaded them to eat of this fruit; in consequence of which God condemned both them and their posterity yet unborn to satisfy his justice by their eternal misery; that, four thousand years after these events (the human race in the meanwhile having gone unredeemed to perdition), God engendered with the betrothed wife of a carpenter in Judea (whose virginity was nevertheless uninjured), and begat a Son, whose name was Jesus Christ; and who was crucified and died, in order that no more men might be devoted to hell-fire, he bearing the burden of his Father's displeasure by proxy.

The book states, in addition, that the soul of whoever disbelieves this sacrifice will be burned with everlasting fire.[1]

During many ages of misery and darkness this story gained implicit belief; but at length men arose who suspected that it was a fable and imposture, and that Jesus Christ, so far from being a God, was only a man like themselves. But a numerous set of men who derived and still derive emoluments from this opinion in the shape of a popular belief told the vulgar that if they did not believe in the Bible, they would be damned to all eternity—and burned, imprisoned, and poisoned all the unbiassed and unconnected inquirers who occasionally arose. They still oppress them so far as the people—now become more enlightened—will allow.[2]

The belief in all that the Bible contains is called Christianity. A Roman governor of Judea at the instance of a priest-led mob crucified a man called Jesus eighteen centuries ago. He was a man of pure life, who

1. For a similar statement about the Bible, see Paine's *The Age of Reason,* H. H. Clark edition, American Writers Series, 1944, pp. 236-262.

2. Compare this paragraph with paragraph twelve of the *Letter to Lord Ellenborough* for a similar idea.

desired to rescue his countrymen from the tyranny of their barbarous and degrading superstitions. The common fate of all who desire to benefit mankind awaited him. The rabble at the instigation of the priests demanded his death, although his very judge made public acknowledgment of his innocence. Jesus was sacrificed to the honor of that God with whom he was afterwards confounded.[3] It is of importance, therefore, to distinguish between the pretended character of this being as the Son of God and the Saviour of the world and his real character as a man who for a vain attempt to reform the world paid the forfeit of his life to that overbearing tyranny which has since so long desolated the universe in his name. While the one is a hypocritical demon, who announces himself as the God of compassion and peace even while he stretches forth his blood-red hand with the sword of discord to waste the earth, having confessedly devised this scheme of desolation from eternity; the other stands in the foremost list of those true heroes who have died in the glorious martyrdom of liberty and have braved torture, contempt, and poverty in the cause of suffering humanity.[4]

The vulgar, ever in extremes, became persuaded that the crucifixion of Jesus was a supernatural event. Testimonies of miracles, so frequent in unenlightened ages, were not wanting to prove that he was something divine. This belief, rolling through the lapse of ages, met with the reveries of Plato and the reasonings of Aristotle and acquired force and extent until the divinity of Jesus became a dogma which to dispute was death, which to doubt was infamy.[5]

Christianity is now the established religion; he who attempts to impugn it must be contented to behold murderers and traitors take precedence of him in public opinion; though, if his genius be equal to his courage, and assisted by a peculiar coalition of circumstances, future ages may exalt him to a divinity, and persecute others in his name, as he was persecuted in the name of his predecessor in the homage of the world.

The same means that have supported every other popular belief have supported Christianity. War, imprisonment, assassination, and falsehood; deeds of unexampled and incomparable atrocity have made it what it is.[6] The blood shed by the votaries of the God of mercy and peace, since the establishment of his religion, would probably suffice to drown all other sectaries now on the habitable globe. We derive from our ancestors a faith thus fostered and supported; we quarrel, persecute, and hate for its maintenance. Even under a government which, while it infringes the very right of thought and speech, boasts of permitting the liberty of the press, a man is pilloried and imprisoned because he is a deist, and no one raises his voice in the indignation of outraged humanity. But it is ever a proof that the falsehood of a proposition is felt by those who use coercion, not reasoning, to procure its admission; and a dispassionate observer would feel himself more powerfully interested in favor of a man who, depending on the truth of his opinions, simply stated his reasons for entertaining them than in that of his aggressor who, daringly avowing his unwillingness or incapacity to answer them by argument, proceeded to repress the ener-

3. Shelley could have found this account in Part One of Paine's *The Age of Reason*; see Chaps. II and III, especially p. 239.
4. "Since writing this note, I have some reason to suspect that Jesus was an ambitious man who aspired to the throne of Judea." [Shelley's Note.] Shelley probably found this idea in Paine's *The Age of Reason*. At the end of Chapter III, it is said: "Neither is it improbable that Jesus Christ had in

contemplation the delivery of the Jewish Nation from the bondage of the Romans." The idea of this Note has been unduly stressed by Shelley critics.
5. This entire paragraph is in the *Letter to Lord Ellenborough* (1812), as are the next five with slight variations.
6. Shelley could have found this idea in Paine's *The Age of Reason*, and also in Hume's *Dialogues Concerning Natural Religion*.

gies and break the spirit of their promulgator by that torture and imprisonment whose infliction he could command.[7]

Analogy seems to favor the opinion that as, like other systems, Christianity has arisen and augmented, so like them it will decay and perish; that, as violence, darkness, and deceit, not reasoning and persuasion, have procured its admission among mankind so, when enthusiasm has subsided, and time, that infallible controverter of false opinions, has involved its pretended evidences in the darkness of antiquity, it will become obsolete; that Milton's poem alone will give permanency to the remembrance of its absurdities; and that men will laugh as heartily at grace, faith, redemption, and original sin, as they now do at the metamorphoses of Jupiter, the miracles of Romish saints, the efficacy of witchcraft, and the appearance of departed spirits.

Had the Christian religion commenced and continued by the mere force of reasoning and persuasion, the preceding analogy would be inadmissible. We should never speculate on the future obsoleteness of a system perfectly conformable to nature and reason; it would endure so long as they endured; it would be a truth as indisputable as the light of the sun, the criminality of murder, and other facts whose evidence, depending on our organization and relative situations, must remain acknowledged as satisfactory, so long as man is man. It is an incontrovertible fact, the consideration of which ought to repress the hasty conclusions of credulity, or moderate its obstinacy in maintaining them, that had the Jews not been a fanatical race of men, had even the resolution of Pontius Pilate been equal to his candor, the Christian religion never could have prevailed, it could not even have existed; on so feeble a thread hangs the most

cherished opinion of a sixth of the human race! When will the vulgar learn humility? When will the pride of ignorance blush at having believed before it could comprehend?

Either the Christian religion is true, or it is false; if true, it comes from God, and its authenticity can admit of doubt and dispute no further than its omnipotent author is willing to allow. Either the power or the goodness of God is called in question if he leaves those doctrines most essential to the well-being of man in doubt and dispute—the only ones which, since their promulgation, have been the subject of unceasing cavil, the cause of irreconcilable hatred. *If God has spoken, why is the universe not convinced?*[8]

There is this passage in the Christian Scriptures: "Those who obey not God, and believe not the Gospel of his Son, shall be punished with everlasting destruction." This is the pivot upon which all religions turn; they all assume that it is in our power to believe or not to believe; whereas the mind can only believe that which it thinks true. A human being can only be supposed accountable for those actions which are influenced by his will. But belief is utterly distinct from and unconnected with volition: it is the apprehension of the agreement or disagreement of the ideas that compose any proposition. Belief is a passion, or involuntary operation of the mind and, like other passions, its intensity is precisely proportionate to the degrees of excitement. Volition is essential to merit or demerit.[9] But the Christian religion attaches the highest possible degrees of merit and demerit to that which is worthy of neither, and which is totally unconnected with the peculiar faculty of the mind, whose presence is essential to their being.

Christianity was intended to reform the world; had an all-wise Being planned it,

7. This and the next three paragraphs are a recasting of passages in the *Letter to Lord Ellenborough*.

8. This is a sentence from Holbach's *Système de la Nature*.

9. This paragraph in modified form is in *The Necessity of Atheism* and also in the *Letter to Lord Ellenborough*; it is based in part on Locke's *Essay on the Human Understanding*, and on Hume's *Dialogues Concerning Natural Religion*.

nothing is more improbable than that it should have failed; omniscience would infallibly have foreseen the inutility of a scheme which experience demonstrates to this age to have been utterly unsuccessful.

Christianity inculcates the necessity of supplicating the Deity. Prayer may be considered under two points of view: as an endeavor to change the intentions of God, or as a formal testimony of our obedience. But the former case supposes that the caprices of a limited intelligence can occasionally instruct the Creator of the world how to regulate the universe; and the latter, a certain degree of servility analogous to the loyalty demanded by earthly tyrants. Obedience indeed is only the pitiful and cowardly egotism of him who thinks that he can do something better than reason.

Christianity like all other religions rests upon miracles, prophecies, and martyrdoms. No religion ever existed which had not its prophets, its attested miracles, and above all crowds of devotees who would bear patiently the most horrible tortures to prove its authenticity. It should appear that in no case can a discriminating mind subscribe to the genuineness of a miracle. A miracle is an infraction of nature's law by a supernatural cause, by a cause acting beyond that eternal circle within which all things are included. God breaks through the law of nature that he may convince mankind of the truth of that revelation which in spite of his precautions has been since its introduction the subject of unceasing schism and cavil.[10]

Miracles resolve themselves into the following question:[11] Whether it is more probable the laws of nature, hitherto so immutably harmonious, should have undergone violation, or that a man should have told a lie? Whether it is more probable that we are ignorant of the natural cause of an event, or that we know the supernatural one? That, in old times, when the powers of nature were less known than at present, a certain set of men were themselves deceived, or had some hidden motive for deceiving others; or that God begat a son who in his legislation measuring merit by belief, evidenced himself to be totally ignorant of the powers of the human mind—of what is voluntary and what is the contrary?

We have many instances of men telling lies; none of an infraction of nature's laws, those laws of whose government alone we have any knowledge or experience. The records of all nations afford innumerable instances of men deceiving others either from vanity or interest, or themselves being deceived by the limitedness of their views and their ignorance of natural causes; but where is the accredited case of God having come upon earth to give the lie to his own creations? There would be something truly wonderful in the appearance of a ghost. But the assertion of a child that he saw one as he passed through the churchyard is universally admitted to be less miraculous.[12]

But even supposing that a man should raise a dead body to life before our eyes, and on this fact rest his claim to being considered the son of God; the Humane Society restores drowned persons, and because it makes no mystery of the method it employs, its members are not mistaken for the sons of God. All that we have a right to infer from our ignorance of the cause of any event is that we do not know it; had the Mexicans attended to this simple rule when they heard the cannon of the Spaniards, they would not have considered them as gods. The experiments of modern chemistry would have defied the wisest philosophers of ancient Greece and Rome to have accounted for them on natural principles. An author

10. Shelley found this idea in his reading of Paine's *The Age of Reason* and in Hume's *Essays*.

11. See Hume's *Essays*, Vol. II, page 121. [Shelley's Note.]

12. The substance of the last two paragraphs is in Paine's *The Age of Reason*, pp. 283-293, and the paragraph beginning, "We have many instances" and ending, "to be miraculous," is but a paraphrase of one in Paine, p. 289. See also *Letter to Lord Ellenborough* and Hume's *Dialogues Concerning Natural Religion* for similar ideas.

of strong common sense has observed that "a miracle is no miracle at second-hand"; he might have added, that a miracle is no miracle in any case; for until we are acquainted with all natural causes, we have no reason to imagine others.

There remains to be considered another proof of Christianity—prophecy. A book is written before a certain event in which this event is foretold; how could the prophet have foreknown it without inspiration? How could he have been inspired without God? The greatest stress is laid on the prophecies of Moses and Hosea on the dispersion of the Jews, and that of Isaiah concerning the coming of the Messiah. The prophecy of Moses is a collection of every possible cursing and blessing, and it is so far from being marvelous that the one of dispersion should have been fulfilled, that it would have been more surprising if, out of all these, none should have taken effect. In Deuteronomy, chap. xxviii, ver. 64, where Moses explicitly foretells the dispersion, he states that they shall there serve gods of wood and stone: "And the Lord shall scatter thee among all people, from the one end of the earth even to the other, *and there thou shalt serve other gods, which neither thou nor thy fathers have known, even gods of wood and stone.*" The Jews are at this day remarkably tenacious of their religion. Moses also declares that they shall be subjected to these curses for disobedience to his ritual: "And it shall come to pass, if thou wilt not hearken unto the voice of the Lord thy God, to observe to do all the commandments and statutes which I command thee this day, that all these curses shall come upon thee and overtake thee." Is this the real reason? The third, fourth, and fifth chapters of Hosea are a piece of immodest confession. The indelicate type might apply in a hundred senses to a hundred things. The fifty-third chapter of Isaiah is more explicit, yet it does not exceed in clearness the oracles of Del-

phos. The historical proof that Moses, Isaiah, and Hosea did write when they are said to have written is far from being clear and circumstantial.[13]

But prophecy requires proof in its character as a miracle; we have no right to suppose that a man foreknew future events from God until it is demonstrated that he neither could know them by his own exertions, nor that the writings which contain the prediction could possibly have been fabricated after the event pretended to be foretold. It is more probable that writings pretending to divine inspiration should have been fabricated after the fulfillment of their pretended prediction than that they should have really been divinely inspired, when we consider that the latter supposition makes God at once the creator of the human mind and ignorant of its primary powers, particularly as we have numberless instances of false religions and forged prophecies of things long past, and no accredited case of God having conversed with men directly or indirectly. It is also possible that the description of an event might have foregone its occurrence; but this is far from being a legitimate proof of a divine revelation, as many men not pretending to the character of a prophet have nevertheless, in this sense, prophesied.

Lord Chesterfield was never yet taken for a prophet, even by a bishop, yet he uttered this remarkable prediction: "The despotic government of France is screwed up to the highest pitch; a revolution is fast approaching; that revolution, I am convinced, will be radical and sanguinary." This appeared in the letters of the prophet long before the accomplishment of this wonderful prediction. Now, have these particulars come to pass, or have they not? If they have, how could the Earl have foreknown them without inspiration? If we admit the truth of the Christian religion on testimony such as this, we must admit on the same strength of

13. The substance of this paragraph is in Paine's *The Age of Reason.* What Shelley says here about miracles, prophecies, and testimony as proof of the existence of God and the authenticity of the Bible is a recasting of *The Necessity of Atheism* and portions of the *Letter to Lord Ellenborough.*

evidence that God has affixed the highest rewards to belief and the eternal tortures of the never-dying worm to disbelief, both of which have been demonstrated to be involuntary.

The last proof of the Christian religion depends on the influence of the Holy Ghost. Theologians divide the influence of the Holy Ghost into its ordinary and extraordinary modes of operation. The latter is supposed to be that which inspired the Prophets and Apostles; and the former to be the grace of God, which summarily makes known the truth of his revelation to those whose mind is fitted for its reception by a submissive perusal of his word. Persons convinced in this manner can do anything but account for their conviction, describe the time at which it happened, or the manner in which it came upon them. It is supposed to enter the mind by other channels than those of the senses and therefore professes to be superior to reason founded on their experience.

Admitting, however, the usefulness or possibility of a divine revelation, unless we demolish the foundations of all human knowledge, it is requisite that our reason should previously demonstrate its genuineness; for, before we extinguish the steady ray of reason and common sense, it is fit that we should discover whether we cannot do without their assistance, whether or no there be any other which may suffice to guide us through the labyrinth of life:[14] for, if a man is to be inspired upon all occasions, if he is to be sure of a thing because he is sure, if the ordinary operations of the spirit are not to be considered very extraordinary modes of demonstration, if enthusiasm is to usurp the place of proof, and madness that

of sanity, all reasoning is superfluous. The Mahometan dies fighting for his Prophet, the Indian immolates himself at the chariot-wheels of Brahma, the Hottentot worships an insect, the Negro a bunch of feathers, the Mexican sacrifices human victims! Their degree of conviction must certainly be very strong: it cannot arise from reasoning—it must from feelings, the reward of their prayers. If each of these should affirm in opposition to the strongest possible arguments that inspiration carried internal evidence, I fear their inspired brethren, the orthodox missionaries, would be so uncharitable as to pronounce them obstinate.

Miracles cannot be received as testimonies of a disputed fact, because all human testimony has ever been insufficient to establish the possibility of miracles. That which is incapable of proof itself is no proof of anything else. Prophecy has also been rejected by the test of reason. Those, then, who have been actually inspired are the only true believers in the Christian religion.

Mox numine viso
Virginei tumuere sinus, innuptaque
    mater
Arcano stupuit compleri viscera
    partu,
Auctorem paritura suum. Mortalia
    corda
Artificem texere poli, latuitque sub
    uno
Pectore, qui totum late complectitur
    orbem.[15]

CLAUDIAN, *Carmen Paschale.*

Does not so monstrous and disgusting an absurdity carry its own infamy and refutation with itself?

---

14. See Locke's *Essay on the Human Understanding,* book iv, chap. xix, on Enthusiasm. [Shelley's Note.]

15. "Soon after the maiden had seen a god, her breasts became swollen, and the unwed mother, destined to bring forth the author of her own being, was in secret amazed that her womb was filling with child. A mortal covered the maker of the heavens, and beneath one breast he lay concealed who compasses the whole wide universe." This quotation is from Claudian's *De Salvatore,* lines 7-13 with one line omitted, and not from *Carmen Paschale.*

"NECESSITY! THOU MOTHER OF THE WORLD!"

[The following essay, a Note from *Queen Mab,* is important in understanding the development of Shelley's philosophy. It is a blending of the ideas of Spinoza, Hume, and Holbach. Spinoza's vigorous and persuasive exposition of the doctrine of Necessity and its impact on religion and morals powerfully influenced Shelley's youthful mind. It was Spinoza who gave direction to Shelley's thought about Necessity. His reading in Hume on the same subject only confirmed Shelley's growing belief in scientific determinism. But it was perhaps to Holbach's *Système de la Nature* that Shelley owed his greatest and most immediate debt for his ideas of a universe ruled by Necessity. The very phrase, *Thou mother of the world,* comes directly from Holbach, and the idea of a pervading force in nature Holbach discusses at length. The ideas thus early gained underwent but slight change throughout his life, and Necessity under various forms and figures is the key to his fundamental philosophy. Shelley scholars, I am convinced, have overstressed what modification Shelley made in the doctrine of Necessity. The change is more of form than of substance. His study of Plato only accentuated his early leanings toward the doctrine of pantheism, already encountered in Spinoza. It is in the blending of Platonic ideas of Love and Intellectual Beauty and Spinozan pantheism, and their impact upon the cold, impersonal doctrine of Necessity, that we must look for whatever change Shelley's philosophy underwent.

Shelley was never a materialist in the philosophical use of the term, and his conception of Necessity always carried with it a belief in a spiritual or mental element. That is why he defined God as the Soul of the Universe, the animating principle in all forms of matter—both animate and inanimate.]

He who asserts the doctrine of Necessity means that, contemplating the events which compose the moral and material world, he beholds only an immense and uninterrupted chain of causes and effects, no one of which could occupy any other place than it does occupy, or act in any other place than it does act. The idea of Necessity is obtained by our experience of the connection between objects, the uniformity of the operations of nature, the constant conjunction of similar events, and the consequent inference of one from the other. Mankind are therefore agreed in the admission of Necessity, if they admit that these two circumstances take place in voluntary action. Motive is to voluntary action in the human mind what cause is to effect in the material universe. The word *liberty* as applied to mind is analogous to the word *chance* as applied to matter:[1] they spring from the ignorance of the certainty of the conjunction of antecedents and consequents.[2]

Every human being is irresistibly impelled to act precisely as he does act: in the eternity which preceded his birth a chain of causes was generated which, operating under the name of motives, make it impossible that any thought of his mind, or any action of his life, should be otherwise than it is. Were

1. This idea may be found in Hume's *An Enquiry Concerning the Human Understanding. Selections,* Sec. 6, p. 175. All references to Hume unless otherwise indicated are to this edition, edited by Charles W. Hendel, Jr., Scribner's Sons, 1927.

2. Shelley is here drawing heavily on Hume's *An Enquiry Concerning the Human Understanding* and also on Spinoza's *Tractatus Theologico-Politicus,* upon which I am convinced Shelley based his philosophy of Necessity.

SHELLEY'S PROSE   110

the doctrine of Necessity false, the human mind would no longer be a legitimate object of science; from like causes it would be in vain that we should expect like effects; the strongest motive would no longer be paramount over the conduct; all knowledge would be vague and undeterminate; we could not predict with any certainty that we might not meet as an enemy to-morrow him from whom we have parted in friendship to-night; the most probable inducements and the clearest reasonings would lose the invariable influence they possess.[3] The contrary of this is demonstrably the fact. Similar circumstances produce the same unvariable effects. The precise character and motives of any man on any occasion being given, the moral philosopher could predict his actions with as much certainty as the natural philosopher could predict the effects of the mixture of any particular chemical substances.[4] Why is the aged husbandman more experienced than the young beginner? Because there is an uniform, undeniable necessity in the operations of the material universe. Why is the old statesman more skilful than the raw politician? Because, relying on the necessary conjunction of motive and action, he proceeds to produce moral effects by the application of those moral causes which experience has shown to be effectual. Some actions may be found to which we can attach no motives, but these are the effects of causes with which we are unacquainted. Hence the relation which motive bears to voluntary action is that of cause to effect; nor, placed in this point of view, is it, or ever has it been, the subject of popular or philosophical dispute.[5] None but the few fanatics who are engaged in the Herculean task of reconciling

the justice of their God with the misery of man will longer outrage common sense by the supposition of an event without a cause, a voluntary action without a motive. History, politics, morals, criticism, all grounds of reasoning, all principles of science, alike assume the truth of the doctrine of Necessity.[6] No farmer carrying his corn to market doubts the sale of it at the market price. The master of a manufactory no more doubts that he can purchase the human labor necessary for his purposes than that his machines will act as they have been accustomed to act.[7]

But, while none have scrupled to admit Necessity as influencing matter, many have disputed its dominion over mind.[8] Independently of its militating with the received ideas of the justice of God, it is by no means obvious to a superficial inquiry. When the mind observes its own operations, it feels no connection of motive and action; but as we know "nothing more of causation than the constant conjunction of objects and the consequent inference of one from the other, as we find that these two circumstances are universally allowed to have place in voluntary action, we may be easily led to own that they are subjected to the necessity common to all causes."[9] The actions of the will have a regular conjunction with circumstances and characters; motive is to voluntary action what cause is to effect.[10] But the only idea we can form of causation is a constant conjunction of similar objects and the consequent inference of one from the other; wherever this is the case, Necessity is clearly established.[11]

The idea of liberty, applied metaphorically to the will, has sprung from a misconception

3. This idea is the basis of Spinoza's philosophy of scientific determinism. See also Holbach, 1.27-39.
4. Compare this series of statements with similar ones in Hume's *An Enquiry*, Spinoza's *Tractatus*, and Holbach's *Système*.
5. See Hume's *An Enquiry*, Sec. 6.
6. Compare these with like statements in Spinoza's *Tractatus* and the *Ethics*.
7. The last two sentences are a paraphrase of Hume's *An Enquiry*, Part III, Sec. 6, pp. 168-169.

8. Discussed in both Hume and Spinoza, *idem*. See Hume's *An Enquiry*, Part III, Sec. 6.
9. A modified quotation from Hume's *An Enquiry Concerning Human Understanding*, Sec. 6. Similar ideas are found in Holbach's *Système*, Chaps. 1-8, Bk. I.
10. This sentence is a paraphrase of a passage in Hume, *An Enquiry*, Sec. 6, p. 168.
11. This sentence is a recasting of one in Hume, *An Enquiry*, Sec. 6, Part 1, p. 171.

of the meaning of the word *power*. What is power?—*id quod potest,* that which can produce any given effect. To deny power is to say that nothing can or has the power to be or act. In the only true sense of the word *power,* it applies with equal force to the lodestone as to the human will. Do you think these motives which I shall present are powerful enough to rouse him? is a question just as common as, Do you think this lever has the power of raising this weight? The advocates of free-will assert that the will has the power of refusing to be determined by the strongest motive; but the strongest motive is that which, overcoming all others, ultimately prevails; this assertion therefore amounts to a denial of the will being ultimately determined by that motive which does determine it, which is absurd. But it is equally certain that a man cannot resist the strongest motive, as that he cannot overcome a physical impossibility.[12]

The doctrine of Necessity tends to introduce a great change into the established notions of morality and utterly to destroy religion. Reward and punishment must be considered by the Necessarian merely as motives which he would employ in order to procure the adoption or abandonment of any given line of conduct. Desert in the present sense of the word would no longer have any meaning; and he who should inflict pain upon another for no better reason than that he deserved it would only gratify his revenge under pretense of satisfying justice. It is not enough, says the advocate of free-will, that a criminal should be prevented from a repetition of his crime: he should feel pain, and his torments when justly inflicted ought precisely to be proportioned to his fault. But utility is morality; that which is incapable of producing happiness is useless; and though the crime of Damiens must be condemned, yet the frightful torments which revenge, under the name of justice, inflicted

on this unhappy man, cannot be supposed to have augmented, even at the long run, the stock of pleasurable sensation in the world. At the same time the doctrine of Necessity does not in the least diminish our disapprobation of vice.[13] The conviction which all feel that a viper is a poisonous animal and that a tiger is constrained by the inevitable condition of his existence to devour men does not induce us to avoid them less sedulously, or, even more, to hesitate in destroying them; but he would surely be of a hard heart, who, meeting with a serpent on a desert island, or in a situation where it was incapable of injury, should wantonly deprive it of existence. A Necessarian is inconsequent to his own principles, if he indulges in hatred or contempt; the compassion which he feels for the criminal is unmixed with a desire of injuring him; he looks with an elevated and dreadless composure upon the links of the universal chain as they pass before his eyes; while cowardice, curiosity, and inconsistency only assail him in proportion to the feebleness and indistinctness with which he has perceived and rejected the delusions of free-will.

Religion is the perception of the relation in which we stand to the principle of the universe. But if the principle of the universe be not an organic being, the model and prototype of man, the relation between it and human beings is absolutely none. Without some insight into its will respecting our actions, religion is nugatory and vain. But will is only a mode of animal mind; moral qualities also are such as only a human being can possess; to attribute them to the principle of the universe is to annex to it properties incompatible with any possible definition of its nature.[14] It is probable that the word *God* was originally only an expression denoting the unknown cause of the known events which men perceived in the universe. By the vulgar mistake of a metaphor for a real be-

---

12. This idea is common to Hume, Spinoza, and Holbach.

13. Compare these statements with similar ones

in Hume's *Treatise on Human Nature,* Part III, Sec. 1, and the *Enquiry,* p. 171.

14. Shelley is here building on Spinoza's ethics. See also Holbach's *Système,* 1.1-116.

ing, of a word for a thing, it became a man endowed with human qualities and governing the universe as an earthly monarch governs his kingdom. Their addresses to this imaginary being, indeed, are much in the same style as those of subjects to a king. They acknowledge his benevolence, deprecate his anger, and supplicate his favor.[15]

But the doctrine of Necessity teaches us that in no case could any event have happened otherwise than it did happen, and that, if God is the author of good, he is also the author of evil; that, if he is entitled to our gratitude for the one, he is entitled to our hatred for the other; that, admitting the existence of this hypothetic being, he is also subjected to the dominion of an immutable Necessity. It is plain that the same arguments which prove that God is the author of food, light, and life prove him also to be the author of poison, darkness, and death. The wide-wasting earthquake, the storm, the battle, and the tyranny are attributable to this hypothetic being in the same degree as the fairest forms of nature, sunshine, liberty, and peace.[16]

But we are taught by the doctrine of Necessity that there is neither good nor evil in the universe, otherwise than as the events to which we apply these epithets have relation to our own peculiar mode of being.[17] Still less than with the hypothesis of a God will the doctrine of Necessity accord with

the belief of a future state of punishment. God made man such as he is and then damned him for being so; for to say that God was the author of all good, and man the author of all evil is to say that one man made a straight line and a crooked one, and another man made the incongruity.

A Mahometan story, much to the present purpose, is recorded, wherein Adam and Moses are introduced disputing before God in the following manner. Thou, says Moses, art Adam, whom God created, and animated with the breath of life, and caused to be worshipped by the angels, and placed in Paradise, from whence mankind have been expelled for thy fault. Whereto Adam answered, Thou art Moses, whom God chose for his apostle, and entrusted with his word, by giving thee the tables of the law, and whom he vouchsafed to admit to discourse with himself. How many years dost thou find the law was written before I was created? Says Moses, Forty. And dost thou not find, replied Adam, these words therein, And Adam rebelled against his Lord and transgressed? Which Moses confessing, Dost thou therefore blame me, continued he, for doing that which God wrote of me that I should do, forty years before I was created, nay, for what was decreed concerning me fifty thousand years before the creation of heaven and earth?[18]

15. See the letters for 1811-13 for a similar idea of God.

16. The thought in this paragraph is in Hume's *Essays* 2:81-82, and Spinoza's *Tractatus.*

17. This idea is common to both Spinoza and Hume. For a discussion of Shelley's idea of the doctrine of Necessity see article by F. B. Evans,

Shelley, Godwin, Hume, and the Doctrine of Necessity, Studies in Philology (1940), 37:632-640. Holbach's influence is not mentioned, and Spinoza is ignored.

18. Sale's *Prelim. Disc. to the Koran,* p. 164. [Shelley's Note.]

"AND STATESMEN BOAST OF WEALTH"

[This essay is a Note in *Queen Mab* (1813). It stems from *Political Justice* (1793) and *Enquirer* (1797) by William Godwin. But Shelley was familiar with Adam Smith's *The Wealth of Nations* (1776). From it he almost certainly got the idea of the opening paragraph that labor is the sole source of wealth. Smith maintained that the labor of man is the real measure of the commercial value of any commodity. "It is their real price; money is their nominal price only," said Smith. The remainder of the essay holds rather closely to Godwin's ideas.]

There is no real wealth but the labor of man. Were the mountains of gold and the valleys of silver, the world would not be one grain of corn the richer; no one comfort would be added to the human race. In consequence of our consideration for the precious metals, one man is enabled to heap to himself luxuries at the expense of the necessaries of his neighbor—a system admirably fitted to produce all the varieties of disease and crime which never fail to characterize the two extremes of opulence and penury. A speculator takes pride to himself as the promoter of his country's prosperity who employs a number of hands in the manufacture of articles avowedly destitute of use, or subservient only to the unhallowed cravings of luxury and ostentation. The nobleman who employs the peasants of his neighborhood in building his palaces until *"jam pauca aratro jugera regiae moles relinquunt,"*[1] flatters himself that he has gained the title of a patriot by yielding to the impulses of vanity. The show and pomp of courts adduce the same apology for its continuance and many a fête has been given, many a woman has eclipsed her beauty by her dress, to benefit the laboring poor and to encourage trade. Who does not see that this is a remedy which aggravates while it palliates the countless diseases of society? The poor are set to labor—for what? Not the food for which they famish; not the blankets for want of which their babes are frozen by the cold of their miserable hovels; not those comforts of civilization without which civilized man is far more miserable than the meanest savage—oppressed as he is by all its insidious evils within the daily and taunting prospect of its innumerable benefits assiduously exhibited before him—no; for the pride of power, for the miserable isolation of pride, for the false pleasures of the hundredth part of society. No greater evidence is afforded of the wide extended and radical mistakes of civilized man than this fact: those arts which are essential to his very being are held in the greatest contempt; employments are lucrative in an inverse ratio to their usefulness;[2] the jeweler, the toyman, the actor gains fame and wealth by the exercise of his useless and ridiculous art; while the cultivator of the earth, he without whom society must cease to subsist, struggles through contempt and penury and perishes by that famine which but for his unceasing exertions would annihilate the rest of mankind.

I will not insult common sense by insisting on the doctrine of the natural equality of man. The question is not concerning its desirableness, but its practicability; so far as it is practicable, it is desirable. That state of human society which approaches nearer to an equal partition of its benefits and evils should, *caeteris paribus*, be preferred; but so long as we conceive that a wanton expenditure of human labor, not for the necessities, not even for the luxuries of the mass of society, but for the egotism and ostentation of a few of its members, is defensible on the ground of public justice, so long we

---

1. Translation: "Now the royal palaces leave few acres for the plow."

2. See Rousseau, *De l'inégalité parmi les Hommes*, note 7. [Shelley's Note.]

neglect to approximate to the redemption of the human race.

Labor is required for physical, and leisure for moral improvement; from the former of these advantages the rich, and from the latter the poor, by the inevitable conditions of their respective situations, are precluded. A state which should combine the advantages of both would be subjected to the evils of neither. He that is deficient in firm health or vigorous intellect is but half a man; hence it follows that to subject the laboring classes to unnecessary labor is wantonly depriving them of any opportunities of intellectual improvement and that the rich are heaping up for their own mischief the disease, lassitude, and ennui by which their existence is rendered an intolerable burden.

English reformers exclaim against sinecures, but the true pension list is the rent-roll of the landed proprietors; wealth is a power usurped by the few to compel the many to labor for their benefit. The laws which support this system derive their force from the ignorance and credulity of its victims; they are the result of a conspiracy of the few against the many, who are themselves obliged to purchase this pre-eminence by the loss of all real comfort.

"The commodities that substantially contribute to the subsistence of the human species form a very short catalogue; they demand from us but a slender portion of industry. If these only were produced, and sufficiently produced, the species of man would be continued. If the labor necessarily required to produce them were equitably divided among the poor, and still more, if it were equitably divided among all, each man's share of labor would be light, and his portion of leisure would be ample. There was a time when this leisure would have been of small comparative value; it is to be hoped that the time will come when it will be applied to the most important purposes. Those hours which are not required for the production of the necessaries of life may be devoted to the cultivation of the understanding, the enlarging our stock of knowledge, the refining our taste, and thus opening to us new and more exquisite sources of enjoyment. . . .

"It was perhaps necessary that a period of monopoly and oppression should subsist before a period of cultivated equality could subsist. Savages perhaps would never have been excited to the discovery of truth and the invention of art but by the narrow motives which such a period affords. But surely, after the savage state has ceased, and men have set out in the glorious career of discovery and invention, monopoly and oppression cannot be necessary to prevent them from returning to a state of barbarism."[3]

It is a calculation of this admirable author that all the conveniences of civilized life might be produced if society would divide the labor equally among its members, by each individual being employed in labor two[4] hours during the day.

3. Godwin's *Enquirer*, Essay ii. See also *Pol. Jus.*, book VIII, chap. ii. [Shelley's Note.]

4. Godwin changed this to *three* in the second edition of *Political Justice*.

"EVEN LOVE IS SOLD"

[The following essay is a Note from *Queen Mab*. Much of the material may be found in Godwin's chapter on divorce in *Political Justice*. But Shelley's greatest debt is to Sir James Henry Lawrence's *Empire of the Nairs* and Mary Wollstonecraft's *The Rights of Woman*. For confirmation of this statement see Shelley's letter, August 17, 1812, to Lawrence. The views expressed in this Note were pretty generally held by the enlightened thinkers of Shelley's day. It seems to me a distortion of the facts to argue that Shelley is here an advocate for lax divorce laws, much less for free love in its present-day connotation or for promiscuous sexual relations. His letters of this period and his remarks in subsequent prose and verse—despite the well-known passage in *Epipsychidion* to the contrary—prove that Shelley would suffer the social and legal inequities in the existing matrimonial system—bad as they were—until the moral and educational character of mankind were much improved. Shelley's own life would seem to confirm this contention. In this Note the author is pleading for a saner, juster, more realistic system of matrimony. It is a condemnation of the tyranny in the existing marriage tie and its natural offspring—prostitution.

For a different interpretation of this Note, see Cameron's *The Young Shelley*, pp. 264-274.]

Not even the intercourse of the sexes is exempt from the despotism of positive institution. Law pretends even to govern the indisciplinable wanderings of passion, to put fetters on the clearest deductions of reason, and by appeals to the will, to subdue the involuntary affections of our nature. Love is inevitably consequent upon the perception of loveliness. Love withers under constraint; its very essence is liberty; it is compatible neither with obedience, jealousy, nor fear; it is there most pure, perfect, and unlimited, where its votaries live in confidence, equality, and unreserve.

How long then ought the sexual connection to last? What law ought to specify the extent of the grievances which should limit its duration? A husband and wife ought to continue so long united as they love each other; any law which should bind them to cohabitation for one moment after the decay of their affection would be a most intolerable tyranny, and the most unworthy of toleration. How odious an usurpation of the right of private judgment should that law be considered which should make the ties of friendship indissoluble, in spite of the caprices, the inconstancy, the fallibility, and capacity for improvement of the human mind. And by so much would the fetters of love be heavier and more unendurable than those of friendship, as love is more vehement and capricious, more dependent on those delicate peculiarities of imagination, and less capable of reduction to the ostensible merits of the object.[1]

The state of society in which we exist is a mixture of feudal savageness and imperfect civilization. The narrow and unenlightened morality of the Christian religion is an aggravation of these evils. It is not even until lately that mankind have admitted that happiness is the sole end of the science of ethics, as of all other sciences; and that the fanatical idea of mortifying the flesh for the love of God has been discarded.

1. The denunciation of matrimony in the first two paragraphs follows Godwin rather closely.

I have heard, indeed, an ignorant collegian adduce in favor of Christianity its hostility to every worldly feeling![2]

But if happiness be the object of morality, of all human unions and disunions; if the worthiness of every action is to be estimated by the quantity of pleasurable sensation it is calculated to produce, then the connection of the sexes is so long sacred as it contributes to the comfort of the parties, and is naturally dissolved when its evils are greater than its benefits. There is nothing immoral in this separation. Constancy has nothing virtuous in itself, independently of the pleasure it confers, and partakes of the temporizing spirit of vice in proportion as it endures tamely moral defects of magnitude in the object of its indiscreet choice. Love is free; to promise for ever to love the same woman is not less absurd than to promise to believe the same creed; such a vow in both cases excludes us from all inquiry. The language of the votarist is this: the woman I now love may be infinitely inferior to many others; the creed I now profess may be a mass of errors and absurdities; but I exclude myself from all future information as to the amiability of the one and the truth of the other, resolving blindly and in spite of conviction to adhere to them: Is this the language of delicacy and reason? Is love of such a frigid heart of more worth than its belief?[3]

The present system of constraint does no more in the majority of instances than make hypocrites or open enemies. Persons of delicacy and virtue, unhappily united to one whom they find it impossible to love, spend the loveliest season of their life in unproductive efforts to appear otherwise than they are, for the sake of the feelings of their partner or the welfare of their mutual offspring; those of less generosity and refinement openly avow their disappointment, and linger out the remnant of that union, which only death can dissolve, in a state of incurable bickering and hostility. The early education of their children takes its color from the squabbles of the parents; they are nursed in a systematic school of ill-humor, violence, and falsehood. Had they been suffered to part at the moment when indifference rendered their union irksome, they would have been spared many years of misery; they would have connected themselves more suitably, and would have found that happiness in the society of more congenial partners which is for ever denied them by the despotism of marriage. They would have been separately useful and happy members of society, who, while united, were miserable and rendered misanthropical by misery. The conviction that wedlock is indissoluble holds out the strongest of all temptations to the perverse; they indulge without restraint in acrimony and all the little tyrannies of domestic life, when they know that their victim is without appeal. If this connection were put on a rational basis, each would be assured that habitual ill-temper would terminate in separation and would check this vicious and dangerous propensity.[4]

Prostitution is the legitimate offspring of marriage and its accompanying errors. Women, for no other crime than having followed the dictates of a natural appetite, are driven with fury from the comforts and sympathies of society. It is less venial than murder; and the punishment which is inflicted on her who destroys her child to escape reproach is lighter than the life of agony and disease to which the prostitute

---

2. The first Christian emperor made a law by which seduction was punished with death; if the female pleaded her own consent, she also was punished with death; if the parents endeavored to screen the criminals, they were banished and their estates were confiscated; the slaves who might be accessory were burned alive, or forced to swallow melted lead. The very offspring of an illegal love were involved in the consequences of the sentence.

Gibbon's *Decline and Fall*, etc., vol. ii, p. 210. See also, for the hatred of the primitive Christians toward love and even marriage, p. 269. [Shelley's Note.]

3. This paragraph has echoes from Godwin, and especially from Lawrence.

4. This paragraph is based on Mary Wollstonecraft's *Rights of Woman*.

is irrecoverably doomed. Has a woman obeyed the impulse of unerring nature, society declares war against her, pitiless and eternal war; she must be the tame slave; she must make no reprisals; theirs is the right of persecution, hers the duty of endurance. She lives a life of infamy; the loud and bitter laugh of scorn scares her from all return. She dies of long and lingering disease; yet *she* is in fault; *she* is the criminal; *she* is the froward and untamable child; and society, forsooth, the pure and virtuous matron, who casts her as an abortion from her undefiled bosom! Society avenges herself on the criminals of her own creation; she is employed in anathematizing the vice today, which yesterday she was the most zealous to teach. Thus is formed one-tenth of the population of London; meanwhile the evil is twofold. Young men, excluded by the fanatical idea of chastity from the society of modest and accomplished women, associate with these vicious and miserable beings, destroying thereby all those exquisite and delicate sensibilities whose existence cold-hearted worldlings have denied; annihilating all genuine passion, and debasing that to a selfish feeling which is the excess of generosity and devotedness. Their body and mind alike crumble into a hideous wreck of humanity; idiocy and disease become perpetuated in their miserable offspring, and distant generations suffer for the bigoted

morality of their forefathers. Chastity is a monkish and evangelical superstition, a greater foe to natural temperance even than unintellectual sensuality; it strikes at the root of all domestic happiness, and consigns more than half of the human race to misery that some few may monopolize according to law. A system could not well have been devised more studiously hostile to human happiness than marriage.[5]

I.conceive that from the abolition of marriage the fit and natural arrangement of sexual connection would result. I by no means assert that the intercourse would be promiscuous; on the contrary, it appears, from the relation of parent to child that this union is generally of long duration and marked above all others with generosity and self-devotion. But this is a subject which it is perhaps premature to discuss. That which will result from the abolition of marriage will be natural and right, because choice and change will be exempted from restraint.

In fact, religion and morality, as they now stand, compose a practical code of misery and servitude; the genius of human happiness must tear every leaf from the accursed book of God ere man can read the inscription on his heart. How would morality, dressed up in stiff stays and finery, start from her own disgusting image should she look in the mirror of nature!

5. Both Mary Wollstonecraft and Lawrence have contributed to this paragraph.

A REFUTATION OF DEISM

[*A Refutation of Deism* was probably composed in 1812-1813. It was published, privately, in 1814. After Shelley's expulsion from Oxford in March, 1811, his letters for the next two years show him feverishly reading religious, metaphysical, and scientific writers, and formulating his own philosophy of life. He plans ambitious works in prose and in poetry on moral and social problems. One of these is a long philosophical poem *Queen Mab,* in which he endeavors to show the evil effects of church and state in the slow progress of mankind toward civilization. Another work is *A Refutation of Deism,* in which Shelley points out that the prevailing philosophical religion of the day, deism, is untenable. Having struck at the taproot of Christianity in *The Necessity of Atheism* and in the Notes to *Queen Mab,* Shelley now proposes to destroy the foundation of all theism by showing that neither Christianity nor deism is based solidly in fact and reason, and that, on the contrary, atheism is so grounded.

Making extensive use of *The Necessity of Atheism* in *A Refutation of Deism,* Shelley goes far beyond that single pamphlet, however, and assails the fundamental doctrines of deism. Calling to his aid the highest authorities from Locke to Hume, he appeals to common sense and reason. Restating, for most part approvingly, Locke's theory of knowledge; advancing Paine's arguments in *The Age of Reason* against the historicity, the accuracy, and the inspiration of the Bible; following closely Hume's agnostic course of reasoning, and embracing Spinoza's pantheistic position, Shelley questions not only the biblical account of the origin of the universe, and the deist's arguments for the existence of a God from final causes or design in nature, but also the very basis of all knowledge—experience. Sceptical as he assuredly is, Shelley, following Spinoza's philosophy, leaves a place for God as the soul of the universe—the animating principle of all life.

In a letter to Elizabeth Hitchener, June 11, 1811, Shelley states succinctly the main arguments set forth in *A Refutation of Deism.*

Shelley ends his dialogue, as Hume before him had done in *The Dialogues Concerning Natural Religion,* in a note of cautious scepticism. In *A Refutation of Deism* as in *The Necessity of Atheism* Shelley is quite sincere in his endeavor to arrive at the truth.]

PREFACE

The object of the following dialogue is to prove that the system of Deism is untenable. It is attempted to show that there is no alternative between atheism and Christianity; that the evidences of the Being of a God are to be deduced from no other principles than those of divine revelation.

The author endeavors to show how much the cause of natural and revealed religion has suffered from the mode of defense adopted by theosophistical Christians. How far he will accomplish what he proposed to himself in the composition of this dialogue the world will finally determine.

The mode of printing this little work may appear too expensive, either for its merits or its length. However inimical this practice confessedly is to the general diffusion of knowledge, yet it was adopted in this instance with a view of excluding the multitude from the abuse of a mode of reasoning liable to misconstruction on account of its novelty.

EUSEBES AND THEOSOPHUS

Eusebes

O Theosophus, I have long regretted and observed the strange infatuation which has blinded your understanding. It is not without acute uneasiness that I have beheld the progress of your audacious scepticism trample on the most venerable institutions of our forefathers, until it has rejected the salvation which the only begotten Son of God deigned to proffer in person to a guilty and unbelieving world. To his excess, then, has the pride of the human understanding at length arrived? To measure itself with Omniscience! To scan the intentions of Inscrutability!

You can have reflected but superficially on this awful and important subject. The love of paradox, an affectation of singularity, or the pride of reason has seduced you to the barren and gloomy paths of infidelity. Surely you have hardened yourself against the truth with a spirit of coldness and cavil.

Have you been wholly inattentive to the accumulated evidence which the Deity has been pleased to attach to the revelation of his will; the ancient books in which the advent of the Messiah was predicted, the miracles by which its truth has been so conspicuously confirmed, the martyrs who have undergone every variety of torment in attestation of its veracity? You seem to require mathematical demonstration in a case which admits of no more than strong moral probability.[1] Surely the merit of that faith which we are required to repose in our Redeemer would be thus entirely done away. Where is the difficulty of according credit to that which is perfectly plain and

evident? How is he entitled to a recompense who believes what he cannot disbelieve?

When there is satisfactory evidence that the witnesses of the Christian miracles passed their lives in labors, dangers, and sufferings, and consented severally to be racked, burned, and strangled in testimony of the truth of their account, will it be asserted that they were actuated by a disinterested desire of deceiving others? That they were hypocrites for no end but to teach the purest doctrine that ever enlightened the world, and martyrs without any prospect of emolument or fame? The sophist who gravely advances an opinion thus absurd certainly sins with gratuitous and indefensible pertinacity.

The history of Christianity is itself the most indisputable proof of those miracles by which its origin was sanctioned to the world. It is itself one great miracle. A few humble men established it in the face of an opposing universe. In less than fifty years an astonishing multitude was converted, as Suetonius, Pliny, Tacitus, and Lucian attest;[2] and shortly afterwards thousands who had boldly overturned the altars, slain the priests, and burned the temples of paganism, were loud in demanding the recompense of martyrdom from the hands of the infuriated heathens. Not until three centuries after the coming of the Messiah did his holy religion incorporate itself with the institutions of the Roman empire and derive support from the visible arm of fleshly strength. Thus long without any assistance but that of its omnipotent author, Christianity prevailed in defiance of incredible persecutions, and drew fresh vigor from circumstances the most desperate and unpromising. By what process of sophistry can a rational being persuade himself to reject a religion, the original propagation of which is an event wholly unparalleled in the sphere of human experience?

1. This thought, found in Locke's *Essay Concerning the Human Understanding,* 12th edition, London, 1741, Vol. 2, p. 263, appealed to Shelley, for

he used it later in *A Treatise on Morals.*
2. Shelley's quotations from these authors with translations are in Appendix D(d).

The morality of the Christian religion is as original and sublime as its miracles and mysteries are unlike all other portents. A patient acquiescence in injuries and violence; a passive submission to the will of sovereigns; a disregard of those ties by which the feelings of humanity have ever been bound to this unimportant world; humility and faith are doctrines neither similar nor comparable to those of any other system.[3] Friendship, patriotism, and magnanimity; the heart that is quick in sensibility, the hand that is inflexible in execution; genius, learning, and courage are qualities which have engaged the admiration of mankind, but which we are taught by Christianity to consider as splendid and delusive vices.

I know not why a theist should feel himself more inclined to distrust the historians of Jesus Christ than those of Alexander the Great. What do the tidings of redemption contain which render them peculiarly obnoxious to discredit? It will not be disputed that a revelation of the divine will is a benefit to mankind.[4] It will not be asserted that, even under the Christian revelation, we have too clear a solution of the vast enigma of the Universe, too satisfactory a justification of the attributes of God. When we call to mind the profound ignorance in which, with the exception of the Jews, the philosophers of antiquity were plunged; when we recollect that men, eminent for dazzling talents and fallacious virtues, Epicurus, Democritus, Pliny, Lucretius, Euripides,[5] and innumerable others, dared publicly to avow their faith in atheism with impunity, and that the theists Anaxagoras, Pythagoras, and Plato vainly endeavored by that human reason, which is truly incommensurate to so vast a purpose, to establish among philosophers the belief in one Almighty God, the creator and preserver of the world; when we recollect that

the multitude were grossly and ridiculously idolatrous, and that the magistrates, if not atheists, regarded the being of a God in the light of an abstruse and uninteresting speculation;[6] when we add to these considerations a remembrance of the wars and the oppressions which, about the time of the advent of the Messiah, desolated the human race, is it not more credible that the Deity actually interposed to check the rapid progress of human deterioration than that he permitted a specious and pestilent imposture to seduce mankind into the labyrinth of a deadlier superstition? Surely the Deity has not created man immortal and left him forever in ignorance of his glorious destination. If the Christian religion is false, I see not upon what foundation our belief in a moral governor of the Universe, or our hopes of immortality, can rest.

Thus, then, the plain reason of the case and the suffrage of the civilized world conspire with the more indisputable suggestions of faith to render impregnable that system which has been so vainly and so wantonly assailed. Suppose, however, it were admitted that the conclusions of human reason and the lessons of worldly virtue should be found, in the detail, incongruous with divine revelation by the dictates of which would it become us to abide? Not by that which errs whenever it is employed, but by that which is incapable of error; not by the ephemeral systems of vain philosophy, but by the word of God, which shall endure forever.

Reflect, O Theosophus, that if the religion you reject be true, you are justly excluded from the benefits which result from a belief in its efficiency to salvation. Be not regardless, therefore, I entreat you, of the curses so emphatically heaped upon infidels by the inspired organs of the will of God—the fire which is never quenched, the worm

3. See the *Internal Evidence of Christianity*; also Paley's *Evidences*, Vol. II, p. 27 [Shelley's Note.]
4. See Paley's *Evidences*, Vol. I, p. 3 [Shelley's Note.]
5. Shelley's quotations from Pliny's *Natural History*, *Bellerophon*, Frag. xxv, of Euripides, and Lucretius's *De Rerum Natura*, Lib. i, 11.147-151, and the translations are in Appendix D(e).
6. See Cicero's *De Natura Deorum*. [Shelley's Note.]

that never dies. I dare not think that the God in whom I trust for salvation would terrify his creatures with menaces of punishment which he does not intend to inflict. The ingratitude of incredulity is, perhaps, the only sin to which the Almighty cannot extend his mercy without compromising his justice. How can the human heart endure, without despair, the mere conception of so tremendous an alternative? Return, I entreat you, to that tower of strength which securely overlooks the chaos of the conflicting opinions of men. Return to that God who is your creator and preserver, by whom alone you are defended from the ceaseless wiles of your eternal enemy. Are human institutions so faultless that the principle upon which they are founded may strive with the voice of God? Know that faith is superior to reason, in as much as the creature is surpassed by the Creator; and that whensoever they are incompatible, the suggestions of the latter, not those of the former, are to be questioned.

Permit me to exhibit in their genuine deformity the errors which are seducing you to destruction. State to me with candor the train of sophisms by which the evil spirit has deluded your understanding. Confess the secret motives of your disbelief; suffer me to administer a remedy to your intellectual disease. I fear not the contagion of such revolting sentiments; I fear only lest patience should desert me before you have finished the detail of your presumptuous credulity.

Theosophus

I am not only prepared to confess but to vindicate my sentiments. I cannot refrain, however, from premising, that in this controversy I labor under a disadvantage from which you are exempt. You believe that incredulity is immoral, and regard him as an object of suspicion and distrust whose creed is incongruous with your own. But truth is the perception of the agreement or disagreement of ideas. I can no more conceive that a man who perceives the disagreement of any ideas should be persuaded of their agreement than that he should overcome a physical impossibility. The reasonableness or the folly of the articles of our creed is therefore no legitimate object of merit or demerit; our opinions depend not on the will, but on the understanding.

If I am in error (and the wisest of us may not presume to deem himself secure from all illusion) that error is the consequence of the prejudices by which I am prevented, of the ignorance by which I am incapacitated, from forming a correct estimation of the subject. Remove those prejudices, dispel that ignorance, make truth apparent, and fear not the obstacles that remain to be encountered. But do not repeat to me those terrible and frequent curses, by whose intolerance and cruelty I have so often been disgusted in the perusal of your sacred books. Do not tell me that the All-Merciful will punish me for the conclusions of that reason by which he has thought fit to distinguish me from the beasts that perish. Above all, refrain from urging considerations drawn from reason to degrade that which you are thereby compelled to acknowledge as the ultimate arbiter of the dispute. Answer my objections as I engage to answer your assertions, point by point, word by word.

You believe that the only and ever-present God begot a Son whom he sent to reform the world and to propitiate its sins; you believe that a book, called the Bible, contains a true account of this event, together with an infinity of miracles and prophecies which preceded it from the creation of the world. Your opinion that these circumstances really happened appears to me, from some considerations which I will proceed to state, destitute of rational foundation.[7]

7. Shelley could have found this idea in Paine's *The Age of Reason*, with which he was familiar. See also the Note to *Queen Mab* to the line, "I will beget a Son." The substance of the last three paragraphs may be found in Hume's *Essays*, and especially his *Dialogues Concerning Natural Religion*.

To expose all the inconsistency, immorality, and false pretensions which I perceive in the Bible demands a minuteness of criticism at least as voluminous as itself.[8] I shall confine myself, therefore, to the confronting of your tenets with those primitive and general principles which are the basis of all moral reasoning.

In creating the Universe, God certainly proposed to himself the happiness of his creatures. It is just, therefore, to conclude that he left no means unemployed which did not involve an impossibility to accomplish this design.[9] In fixing a residence for this image of his own Majesty, he was doubtless careful that every occasion of detriment, every opportunity of evil, should be removed. He was aware of the extent of his powers, he foresaw the consequences of his conduct, and doubtless modelled his being consentaneously with the world of which he was to be the inhabitant and the circumstances which were destined to surround him.

The account given by the Bible has but a faint concordance with the surmises of reason concerning this event.

According to this book, God created Satan, who, instigated by the impulses of his nature, contended with the Omnipotent for the throne of heaven. After a contest for the empire, in which God was victorious, Satan was thrust into a pit of burning sulphur. On man's creation God placed within his reach a tree whose fruit he forbade him to taste on pain of death, permitting Satan at the same time to employ all his artifice to persuade this innocent and wondering creature to transgress the fatal prohibition.

The first man yielded to this temptation; and to satisfy divine justice the whole of his posterity must have been eternally burned in hell, if God had not sent his only Son on earth to save those few whose salvation has been foreseen and determined before the creation of the world.[10]

God is here represented as creating man with certain passions and powers, surrounding him with certain circumstances, and then condemning him to everlasting torments because he acted as omniscience had foreseen, and was such as omnipotence had made him.[11] For to assert that the Creator is the author of all good, and the creature the author of all evil, is to assert that one man makes a straight line and another a crooked one, and that another makes the incongruity.[12]

Barbarous and uncivilized nations have uniformly adored under various names a god of which themselves were the model: revengeful, blood-thirsty, grovelling, and capricious. The idol of a savage is a demon that delights in carnage. The steam of slaughter, the dissonance of groans, the flames of a desolated land are the offerings which he deems acceptable, and his innumerable votaries throughout the world have made it a point of duty to worship him to his taste.[13] The Phoenicians, the Druids, and the Mexicans have immolated hundreds at the shrines of their divinity, and the high and holy name of God has been in all ages the watchword of the most unsparing massacres, the sanction of the most atrocious perfidies.[14]

But I appeal to your candor, O Eusebes, if there exist a record of such grovelling absurdities and enormities so atrocious, a picture of the Deity so characteristic of a demon as that which the sacred writings of the Jews contain. I demand of you whether as a conscientious theist you can reconcile the conduct which is attributed to the God of the Jews with your conceptions of the purity and benevolence of the divine nature.

8. This idea is in Paine's *The Age of Reason,* though not specifically expressed.

9. A similar idea is expressed in Hume's *The Natural History of Religion. Selections,* p. 280.

10. The thought in the last two paragraphs is in Paine's *The Age of Reason,* Part One.

11. This thought is also used in a Note to *Queen Mab,* and is from Holbach's *Système de la Nature.*

12. Hobbes. [Shelley's Note.]

13. See Preface to *Le Bon Sens.* [Shelley's Note.] This point is made in Hume's *Natural History of Religion. Selections,* pp. 260-261.

14. See Hume's *The History of Natural Religion. Selections,* pp. 254-283.

The loathsome and minute obscenities to which the inspired writers perpetually descend, the filthy observances which God is described as personally instituting,[15] the total disregard of truth and contempt of the first principles of morality, manifested on the most public occasions by the chosen favorites of Heaven, might corrupt, were they not so flagitious as to disgust.[16]

When the chief of this obscure and brutal horde of assassins asserts that the God of the Universe was enclosed in a box of shittim wood, "two feet long and three feet wide,"[17] and brought home in a new cart, I smile at the impertinence of so shallow an imposture. But it is blasphemy of a more hideous and unexampled nature to maintain that the Almighty God expressly commanded Moses to invade an unoffending nation; and on account of the difference of their worship, utterly to destroy every human being it con-

tained, to murder every infant and unarmed man in cold blood, to massacre the captives, to rip up the matrons, and to retain the maidens alone for concubinage and violation.[18] At the very time that philosophers of the most enterprising benevolence were founding in Greece those institutions which have rendered it the wonder and luminary of the world, am I required to believe that the weak and wicked king of an obscure and barbarous nation, a murderer, a traitor, and a tyrant was the man after God's own heart? A wretch, at the thought of whose unparalleled enormities, the sternest soul must sicken in dismay! An unnatural monster, who sawed his fellow beings in sunder, harrowed them to fragments under harrows of iron, chopped them to pieces with axes, and burned them in brick-kilns, because they bowed before a different and less bloody idol than his own. It is surely no perverse con-

15. See Hosea, chap. i, chap. ix. Ezekiel, chap. iv, chap. xvi, chap. xxiii. Heyne, speaking of the opinions entertained of the Jews by ancient poets and philosophers, says:—*Meminit quidem superstitionis Judaicae Horatius, verum ut eam risu exploderet.—Heyn. ad Virg. Poll, in Arg.* [Shelley's Note]. Translation: "Horace, in fact, mentions the Jewish superstition but only to ridicule it." The reference is to Horace's *Satires*, 1.5.100.
16. See Paine's *The Age of Reason*, p. 247, for a similar statement.
17. 1st Samuel, 5.8. Wordsworth's *Lyrical Ballads*. [Shelley's Notes.] Misquoted by Shelley.
18. Then Moses stood in the gate of the camp and said, Who is on the Lord's side? Let him come unto me. And all the sons of Levi gathered themselves together unto him. And he said unto them, *Thus saith the Lord God of Israel,* Put every man his sword by his side, and go in and out from gate to gate throughout the camp, *and slay every man his brother, and every man his companion, and every man his neighbor.* And the children of Levi did according to the word of Moses, and there fell of the people that day about twenty-three thousand men. Exodus, chap. xxxii, 26[-28].
And they warred against the Midianites, as the Lord commanded Moses, and they slew all the males. And the children of Israel took all the women of Midian captives, and their little ones, and took the spoil of all their cattle, and all their flocks, and all their goods. And they burned all their huts wherein they dwelt, and their goodly castles, with fire. And Moses, and Eleazar the priest, and all the princes of the congregation went forth to meet them without the camp. And Moses was wroth with the officers of the host, with captains over hundreds,

and captains over thousands, which came from the battle. And Moses said unto them, *Have ye saved all the women alive?* Behold these caused the children of Israel, through the counsel of Balaam, to commit trespass against the Lord in the matter of Peor, and there was a plague among the congregation of the Lord. *Now therefore kill every male among the little ones, and kill every woman that hath known man by lying with him. And all the women-children, that have not known a man by lying with him,* KEEP ALIVE FOR YOURSELVES. Numbers xxxi.
And we utterly destroyed them, as we did unto Sihon, king of Heshbon, utterly destroying the men, women, and children of every city. Deut. iii, 6.
And they utterly destroyed all that was in the city, both man and woman, young and old, and ox and sheep and ass, with the edge of the sword. Joshua [vi, 21.]
So Joshua fought against Debir, and utterly destroyed all the souls that were therein, he left none remaining, but utterly destroyed all that breathed, as the *Lord God of Israel commanded.* Joshua, chap. x. [38-40.]
And David gathered all the people together, and went to Rabbah, and took it. And he brought forth the people therein, and *put them under saws, and under harrows of iron, and made them pass through the brick kiln. This did he also unto all the children of Ammon.* II Sam. xii., 29 [-31]. [Shelley's Note.]

Shelley condensed and transposed much of the material in these excerpts from the Bible without noting omissions, but by so doing he never changed their meaning. The only error is in the record of the number slain as 23,000: The Bible (King James Version) has 3,000.

clusion of an infatuated understanding that the God of the Jews is not the benevolent author of this beautiful world.[19]

The conduct of the Deity in the promulgation of the Gospel appears not to the eye of reason more compatible with his immutability and omnipotence than the history of his actions under the law accords with his benevolence.

You assert that the human race merited eternal reprobation because their common father had transgressed the divine command, and that the crucifixion of the Son of God was the only sacrifice of sufficient efficacy to satisfy eternal justice. But it is no less inconsistent with justice and subversive of morality that millions should be responsible for a crime which they had no share in committing than that, if they had really committed it, the crucifixion of an innocent being could absolve them from moral turpitude. *Ferretne ulla civitas latorem istiusmode legis, ut condemnaretur filius, aut nepos, si pater aut avus deliquisset?*[20] Certainly this is a mode of legislation peculiar to a state of savageness and anarchy; this is the irrefragable logic of tyranny and imposture.

The supposition that God has ever supernaturally revealed his will to man at any other period than the original creation of the human race necessarily involves a compromise of his benevolence. It assumes that he withheld from mankind a benefit which it was in his power to confer; that he suffered his creatures to remain in ignorance of truths essential to their happiness and salvation; that during the lapse of innumerable ages every individual of the human race had perished without redemption from an universal stain which the Deity at length descended in person to erase; that the good

and wise of all ages, involved in one common fate with the ignorant and wicked, have been tainted by involuntary and inevitable error which torments infinite in duration may not avail to expiate.[21]

In vain will you assure me with amiable inconsistency that the mercy of God will be extended to the virtuous and that the vicious will alone be punished. The foundation of the Christian religion is manifestly compromised by a concession of this nature. A subterfuge thus palpable plainly annihilates the necessity of the incarnation of God for the redemption of the human race, and represents the descent of the Messiah as a gratuitous display of Deity, solely adapted to perplex, to terrify, and to embroil mankind.

It is sufficiently evident that an omniscient being never conceived the design of reforming the world by Christianity. Omniscience would surely have foreseen the inefficacy of that system which experience demonstrates not only to have been utterly impotent in restraining but to have been most active in exhaling the malevolent propensities of men. During the period which elapsed between the removal of the seat of empire to Constantinople in 328, and its capture by the Turks in 1453, what salutary influence did Christianity exercise upon that world which it was intended to enlighten? Never before was Europe the theater of such ceaseless and sanguinary wars; never were the people so brutalized by ignorance and debased by slavery.[22]

I will admit that one prediction of Jesus Christ has been indisputably fulfilled: *I come not to bring peace upon earth, but a sword.* Christianity indeed has equalled Judaism in the atrocities and exceeded it in the extent of its desolation. Eleven millions of men,

---

19. This account of the barbarities of the ancient Jews is similar to that in Paine's *The Age of Reason.* See Hume's *The Natural History of Religion* and also Gibbon's *Decline and Fall of the Roman Empire,* Vol. I, Chapter 15.

20. "Would any state endure (tolerate) the enacter of that kind of law that a son or grandson

would be condemned if his father or grandfather had done wrong?"

21. See Paine, *op. cit.,* for the substance of the last two paragraphs.

22. This paragraph is a recasting of material in the Note in *Queen Mab,* to the line, "I will beget a Son."

women, and children have been killed in battle, butchered in their sleep, burned to death at public festivals of sacrifice, poisoned, tortured, assassinated, and pillaged in the spirit of the religion of Peace, and for the glory of the most merciful God.[23]

In vain will you tell me that these terrible effects flow not from Christianity, but from the abuse of it. No such excuse will avail to palliate the enormities of a religion pretended to be divine. A limited intelligence is only so far responsible for the effects of its agency as it foresaw, or might have foreseen them; but Omniscience is manifestly chargeable with all the consequences of its conduct. Christianity itself declares that the worth of the tree is to be determined by the quality of its fruit. The extermination of infidels; the mutual persecutions of hostile sects; the midnight massacres and slow burning of thousands, because their creed contained either more or less than the orthodox standard of which Christianity has been the immediate occasion; and the invariable opposition which philosophy has ever encountered from the spirit of revealed religion, plainly show that a very slight portion of sagacity was sufficient to have estimated at its true value the advantages of that belief to which some theists are unaccountably attached.[24]

You lay great stress upon the originality of the Christian system of morals. If this claim be just, either your religion must be false, or the Deity has willed that opposite modes of conduct should be pursued by mankind at different times, under the same circumstances—which is absurd.

The doctrine of acquiescing in the most insolent despotism, of praying for and loving

our enemies, of faith and humility appears to fix the perfection of the human character in that abjectness and credulity which priests and tyrants of all ages have found sufficiently convenient for their purposes. It is evident that a whole nation of Christians (could such an anomaly maintain itself a day) would become, like cattle, the property of the first occupier. It is evident that ten highwaymen would suffice to subjugate the world if it were composed of slaves who dared not to resist oppression.

The apathy to love and friendship recommended by your creed, would, if attainable, not be less pernicious. This enthusiasm of anti-social misanthropy, if it were an actual rule of conduct, and not the speculation of a few interested persons, would speedily annihilate the human race. A total abstinence from sexual intercourse is not perhaps enjoined, but is strenuously recommended,[25] and was actually practiced to a frightful extent by the primitive Christians.[26]

The penalties inflicted by that monster Constantine, the first Christian emperor, on the pleasures of unlicensed love, are so iniquitously severe that no modern legislator could have affixed them to the most atrocious crimes.[27] This cold-blooded and hypocritical ruffian cut his son's throat, strangled his wife, murdered his father-in-law and his brother-in-law, and maintained at his court a set of blood-thirsty and bigoted Christian priests, one of whom was sufficient to excite the one half of the world to massacre the other.

I am willing to admit that some few axioms of morality which Christianity has borrowed from the philosophers of Greece and India, dictate, in an unconnected state,

---

23. This point is made in Spinoza's *Tractatus*, Hume's *History of Natural Religion*, and Paine's *The Age of Reason*.
24. For a similar idea see letter to Elizabeth Hitchener, June 11, 1811.
25. "Now concerning the things whereof ye wrote to me. It is good for a man not to touch a woman. I say, therefore, to the unmarried and widows, it is good for them if they abide even as I; but if

they cannot contain, let them marry; it is better to marry than burn."—I Corinthians, chap. vii. 1,8,9. [Shelley's Note.]
26. See Gibbon's *Decline and Fall*, vol. ii., p. 210. See Shelley's letter to Elizabeth Hitchener, June 25, 1811, and the Note in *Queen Mab* to the line, "I will beget a Son," for the same idea. Compare Paine's *The Age of Reason* for this general idea.
27. Gibbon, vol. ii., p. 269. [Shelley's Note.]

rules of conduct worthy of regard; but the purest and most elevated lessons of morality must remain nugatory, the most probable inducements to virtue must fail of their effect, so long as the slightest weight is attached to that dogma which is the vital essence of revealed religion.

Belief is set up as the criterion of merit or demerit; a man is to be judged not by the purity of his intentions but by the orthodoxy of his creed; an assent to certain propositions is to outweigh in the balance of Christianity the most generous and elevated virtue.

But the intensity of belief, like that of every other passion, is precisely proportioned to the degrees of excitement. A graduated scale, on which should be marked the capabilities of propositions to approach to the test of the senses, would be a just measure of the belief which ought to be attached to them; and but for the influence of prejudice or ignorance this invariably *is* the measure of belief. That is believed which is apprehended to be true, nor can the mind by any exertion avoid attaching credit to an opinion attended with overwhelming evidence. Belief is not an act of volition, nor can it be regulated by the mind; it is manifestly incapable therefore of either merit or criminality. The system which assumes a false criterion of moral virtue must be as pernicious as it is absurd. Above all, it cannot be divine, as it is impossible that the Creator of the human mind should be ignorant of its primary powers.[28]

The degree of evidence afforded by miracles and prophesies in favor of the Christian religion is lastly to be considered.

Evidence of a more imposing and irresistible nature is required in proportion to the remoteness of any event from the sphere of our experience. Every case of miracles is a contest of opposite improbabilities, whether it is more contrary to experience that a miracle should be true, or that the story on which it is supported should be false; whether the immutable laws of this harmonious world should have undergone violation, or that some obscure Greeks and Jews should have conspired to fabricate a tale of wonder.

The actual appearance of a departed spirit would be a circumstance truly unusual and portentous; but the accumulated testimony of twelve old women that a spirit had appeared is neither unprecedented nor miraculous.

It seems less credible that the God whose immensity is uncircumscribed by space should have committed adultery with a carpenter's wife than that some bold knaves or insane dupes had deceived the credulous multitude.[29] We have perpetual and mournful experience of the latter; the former is yet under dispute. History affords us innumerable examples of the possibility of the one; philosophy has in all ages protested against the probability of the other.

Every superstition can produce its dupes, its miracles, and its mysteries; each is prepared to justify its peculiar tenets by an equal assemblage of portents, prophecies, and martyrdoms.[30]

Prophecies, however circumstantial, are liable to the same objection as direct miracles; it is more agreeable to experience that the historical evidence of the prediction really having preceded the event pretended to be foretold should be false, or that a lucky conjuncture of events should have justified the conjecture of the prophet, than that God

28. The substance of this paragraph with much of the exact philosophy is found in the Note to "There is no God" in *Queen Mab*, and the point is further enlarged upon in the Note "I will beget a Son." The passage beginning, "A graduated scale," is used many times in Shelley's writings.

29. See Paley's *Evidences*, vol. i., chap. I. [Shelley's Note.]

30. Shelley is here repeating much that he had said in the Note to *Queen Mab*, beginning "I will beget a Son."

should communicate to a man the discernment of future events.[31] I defy you to produce more than one instance of prophecy in the Bible wherein the inspired writer speaks so as to be understood, wherein his prediction has not been so unintelligible and obscure as to have been itself the subject of controversy among Christians.

That one prediction which I except is certainly most explicit and circumstantial. It is the only one of this nature which the Bible contains. Jesus himself here predicts His own arrival in the clouds to consummate a period of supernatural desolation, before the generation which he addressed should pass away.[32] Eighteen hundred years have past, and no such event is pretended to have happened. This single plain prophecy, thus conspicuously false, may serve as a criterion of those which are more vague and indirect and which apply in an hundred senses to an hundred things.

Either the pretended predictions in the Bible were meant to be understood, or they were not. If they were, why is there any dispute concerning them; if they were not, wherefore were they written at all? But the God of Christianity spoke to mankind in parables, that seeing they might not see, and hearing they might not understand.

The Gospels contain internal evidence that they were not written by eye-witnesses of the event[s] which they pretend to record. The Gospel of St. Matthew was plainly not written until some time after the taking of Jerusalem—that is, at least forty years after the execution of Jesus Christ; for he makes Jesus say *that upon you may come all the righteous blood shed upon the earth,*

from the blood of righteous Abel unto the blood of Zacharias, son of Barachias, whom ye slew between the altar and the temple.[33] Now Zacharias, son of Barachias, was assassinated between the altar and the temple by a faction of zealots, during the siege of Jerusalem.[34]

You assert that the design of the instances of supernatural interposition which the Gospel records was to convince mankind that Jesus Christ was truly the expected Redeemer. But it is as impossible that any human sophistry should frustrate the manifestation of Omnipotence as that Omniscience should fail to select the most efficient means of accomplishing its design. Eighteen centuries have passed and the tenth part of the human race have a blind and mechanical belief in that Redeemer, without a complete reliance on the merits of whom, their lot is fixed in everlasting misery; surely if the Christian system be thus dreadfully important its Omnipotent author would have rendered it incapable of those abuses from which it has never been exempt and to which it is subject in common with all human institutions, he would not have left it a matter of ceaseless cavil or complete indifference to the immense majority of mankind. Surely some more conspicuous evidences of its authenticity would have been afforded than driving out devils, drowning pigs, curing blind men, animating a dead body, and turning water into wine. Some theatre worthier of the transcendent event than Judea would have been chosen, some historians more adapted by their accomplishments and their genius to record the incarnation of the immutable God. The humane

31. See the Controversy of Bishop Watson and Thomas Paine. Paine's *Criticism on the xixth Chapter of Isaiah.* [Shelley's Note.]

32. Immediately after the tribulation of these days, shall the sun be darkened, and the moon shall not give her light, and the stars shall fall from Heaven, and the powers of the heavens shall be shaken; and then shall appear the sign of the Son of man in Heaven; and then shall all tribes of the earth mourn, and they shall see the Son of man coming in the clouds of heaven with power and great glory; and he shall send his Angel with a

great sound of a trumpet, and they shall gather together his elect from the four winds, from one end of Heaven to the other. *Verily I say unto you: This generation shall not pass, until all these things be fulfilled.* Matt. Chapter xxiv, 29-31, 34. [Shelley's Note.]

33. See Matthew xxiii, 35. [Shelley's Note.] The Bible reads "between the temple and the altar." See Paine's *The Age of Reason* for the germ of this thought.

34. Josephus. [Shelley's Note.]

society restores drowned persons; every empiric can cure every disease; drowning pigs is no very difficult matter, and driving out devils was far from being an original or an unusual occupation in Judea. Do not recite these stale absurdities as proofs of the Divine origin of Christianity.[35]

If the Almighty has spoken, would not the Universe have been convinced?[36] If he had judged the knowledge of his will to have been more important than any other science to mankind, would he not have rendered it more evident and more clear?

Now, O Eusebes, have I enumerated the general grounds of my disbelief of the Christian religion. I could have collated its Sacred Writings with the Brahminical record of the early ages of the world, and identified its institutions with the ancient worship of the sun. I might have entered into an elaborate comparison of the innumerable discordances which exist between the inspired historians of the same event. Enough, however, has been said to vindicate me from the charge of groundless and infatuated scepticism. I trust, therefore, to your candor for the consideration, and to your logic, for the refutation of my arguments.

Eusebes

I will not dissemble, O Theosophus, the difficulty of solving your general objections to Christianity on the grounds of human reason. I did not assist at the councils of the Almighty when he determined to extend his mercy to mankind, nor can I venture to affirm that it exceeded the limits of his power to have afforded a more conspicuous or universal manifestation of his will.

But this is a difficulty which attends Christianity in common with the belief in the being and attributes of God. This whole scheme of things might have been, according to our partial conceptions, infinitely more admirable and perfect. Poisons, earth-

quakes, disease, war, famine, venomous serpents, slavery, and persecution are the consequences of certain causes, which according to human judgment, might well have been dispensed with in arranging the economy of the globe.

Is this the reasoning which the theist will choose to employ? Will he impose limitations on that Deity whom he professes to regard with so profound a veneration? Will he place his God between the horns of a logical dilemma which shall restrict the fulness either of his power or his bounty?

Certainly he will prefer to resign his objections to Christianity than pursue the reasoning upon which they are found to the dreadful conclusions of cold and dreary atheism.

I confess that Christianity appears not unattended with difficulty to the understanding which approaches it with a determination to judge its mysteries by reason. I will even confess that the discourse which you have just delivered ought to unsettle any candid mind engaged in a similar attempt. The children of this world are wiser in their generation than the children of light.

But if I succeed in convincing you that reason conducts to conclusions destructive of morality, happiness, and the hope of futurity, and inconsistent with the very existence of human society, I trust that you will no longer confide in a director so dangerous and faithless.

I require you to declare, O Theosophus, whether you would embrace Christianity or atheism, if no other systems of belief shall be found to stand the touchstone of enquiry.

Theosophus

I do not hesitate to prefer the Christian system, or indeed any system of religion, however rude and gross, to atheism. Here we truly sympathize; nor do I blame, however I may feel inclined to pity, the man

35. Shelley had more fully developed his idea of prophecy in the Note in *Queen Mab*, to the line "I will beget a Son."

36. This line is from Holbach's *Système de la Nature*, and is also found in French in the Note to *Queen Mab*, to the line, "I will beget a Son."

who in his zeal to escape this gloomy faith should plunge into the most abject superstition.

The atheist is a monster among men.[37] Inducements which are omnipotent over the conduct of others are impotent for him. His private judgment is his criterion of right and wrong. He dreads no judge but his own conscience, he fears no hell but the loss of his self-esteem. He is not to be restrained by punishments, for death is divested of its terror, and whatever enters into his heart to conceive, that will he not scruple to execute.[38] *Iste non timet omnia providentem et cogitantem, et animadvertentem, et omnia ad se pertinere putantem, curiosum et plenum negotii Deum.*[39]

This dark and terrible doctrine was surely the abortion of some blind speculator's brain, some strange and hideous perversion of intellect, some portentous distortion of reason. There can surely be no metaphysician sufficiently bigoted to his own system to look upon this harmonious world and dispute the necessity of intelligence; to contemplate the design and deny the designer; to enjoy the spectacle of this beautiful Universe and not feel himself instinctively persuaded to gratitude and adoration. What arguments of the slightest plausibility can be adduced to support a doctrine rejected alike by the instinct of the savage and the reason of the sage?

I readily engage with you to reject reason as a faithless guide, if you can demonstrate that it conducts to atheism. So little, however, do I mistrust the dictates of reason concerning a supreme Being that I promise, in the event of your success, to subscribe the wildest and most monstrous creed which you

can devise. I will call credulity, faith; reason, impiety; the dictates of the understanding shall be the temptations of the Devil, and the wildest dreams of the imagination, the infallible inspirations of Grace.

Eusebes

Let me request you, then, to state concisely the grounds of your belief in the being of a God. In my reply I shall endeavor to controvert your reasoning and shall hold myself acquitted by my zeal for the Christian religion of the blasphemies which I must utter in the progress of my discourse.

Theosophus

I will readily state the grounds of my belief in the being of a God.[40] You can only have remained ignorant of the obvious proofs of this important truth from a superstitious reliance upon the evidence afforded by a revealed religion. The reasoning lies within an extremely narrow compass: *quicquid enim nos vel meliores vel beatiores facturum est, aut in aperto, aut in proximo posuit natura.*[41]

From every design we justly infer a designer. If we examine the structure of a watch, we shall readily confess the existence of a watch-maker. No work of man could possibly have existed from all eternity. From the contemplation of any product of human art, we conclude that there was an artificer who arranged its several parts. In like manner, from the marks of design and contrivance exhibited in the Universe, we are necessitated to infer a designer, a contriver. If the parts of the Universe have been designed, contrived, and adapted, the existence of a God is manifest.

37. See letter to Elizabeth Hitchener, June 25, 1811, for the same statement.

38. For similar ideas see Hume's *Dialogues Concerning Natural Religion* and also Paine's *The Age of Reason.*

39. "He does not fear a god that foresees and considers everything, and furnishes everything, a god that is filled with care and trouble."

40. In this and in several succeeding paragraphs Shelley states the arguments of the deists, from Locke to Hume, for the existence of God. Shelley

is following rather closely Paley's *Natural Theology,* Chapter I, and Stewart's *Outline of Moral Philosophy,* 1. 155-156.

41. This Latin quotation Shelley found in Dugald Stewart's *Outline of Moral Philosophy,* 1.46 as from Seneca's *De Beneficiis,* L. VII. *A Fragment of "A Refutation of Deism"* appears to be the original draft of this portion of *A Refutation.* Translation: "For nature has placed either openly or near at hand whatever will make us either better or happier."

But design is sufficiently apparent. The wonderful adaptation of substances which act to those which are acted upon; of the eye to light, and of light to the eye; the ear to sound, and of sound to the ear; of every object of sensation to the sense which it impresses prove that neither blind chance nor undistinguishing necessity has brought them into being. The adaptation of certain animals to certain climates, the relation borne to each other by animals and vegetables, and by different tribes of animals; the relation, lastly, between man and the circumstances of his external situation are so many demonstrations of Deity.

All is order, design, and harmony, so far as we can descry the tendency of things, and every new enlargement of our views, every new display of the material world affords a new illustration of the power, the wisdom, and the benevolence of God.

The existence of God has never been the topic of a popular dispute. There is a tendency to devotion, a thirst for reliance on supernatural aid inherent in the human mind. Scarcely any people, however barbarous, have been discovered who do not acknowledge with reverence and awe the supernatural causes of the natural effects which they experience. They worship, it is true, the vilest and most inanimate substances, but they firmly confide in the holiness and power of these symbols, and thus own their connection with what they can neither see nor perceive.

If there is motion in the Universe, there is a God.[42] The power of beginning motion is no less an attribute of mind than sensation or thought. Wherever motion exists it is evident that mind has operated. The phenomena of the Universe indicate the agency of powers which cannot belong to inert matter.

Everything which begins to exist must have a cause; every combination, conspiring to an end, implies intelligence.[43]

Eusebes

Design must be proved before a designer can be inferred. The matter in controversy is the existence of design in the Universe, and it is not permitted to assume the contested premises and thence infer the matter in dispute. Insidiously to employ the words contrivance, design, and adaptation before these circumstances are made apparent in the Universe, thence justly inferring a contriver, is a popular sophism against which it behooves us to be watchful.[44]

To assert that motion is an attribute of mind, that matter is inert, that every combination is the result of intelligence is also an assumption of the matter in dispute.

Why do we admit design in any machine of human contrivance? Simply because innumerable instances of machines having been contrived by human art are present to our mind, because we are acquainted with persons who could construct such machines; but if, having no previous knowledge of any artificial contrivance, we had accidentally found a watch upon the ground, we should have been justified in concluding that it was a thing of Nature, that it was a combination of matter with whose cause we were unacquainted, and that any attempt to account for the origin of its existence would be equally presumptuous and unsatisfactory.

The analogy which you attempt to establish between the contrivances of human art and the various existences of the Universe, is inadmissible. We attribute these effects to human intelligence, because we know beforehand that human intelligence is capable of producing them. Take away this knowledge, and the grounds of our reasoning will

42. See Dugald Stewart's *Outlines of Moral Philosophy* and Paley's *Natural Theology*. [Shelley's Note.] This paragraph with the next two which follow seems to have been taken from Stewart's *Outlines of Moral Philosophy*, 1.150. The same idea is discussed in Hume's *Dialogues Concerning Natural Religion. Selections*, p. 347.

43. See Hume, *Selections*, pp. 259, 353, for a similar idea.

44. Compare Hume, *Selections*, pp. 306-311. See also Shelley's Note on "There is no God," in *Queen Mab*.

be destroyed. Our entire ignorance, therefore, of the Divine Nature leaves this analogy defective in its most essential point of comparison.

What consideration remains to be urged in support of the creation of the Universe by a supreme Being? Its admirable fitness for the production of certain effects, that wonderful consent of all its parts, that universal harmony by whose changeless laws innumerable systems of worlds perform their stated revolutions, and the blood is driven through the veins of the minutest animalcule that sports in the corruption of an insect's lymph; on this account did the Universe require an intelligent Creator, because it exists producing invariable effects, and inasmuch as it is admirably organized for the production of these effects, so the more did it require a creative intelligence.[45]

Thus have we arrived at the substance of your assertion, "That whatever exists, producing certain effects, stands in need of a Creator, and the more conspicuous is its fitness for the production of these effects, the more certain will be our conclusion that it would not have existed from eternity, but must have derived its origin from an intelligent creator."

In what respect, then, do these arguments apply to the Universe and not apply to God? From the fitness of the Universe to its end you infer the necessity of an intelligent Creator. But if the fitness of the Universe to produce certain effects be thus conspicuous and evident, how much more exquisite fitness to his end must exist in the author of this Universe? If we find great difficulty from its admirable arrangement, in conceiving that the Universe has existed from all eternity, and to resolve this difficulty suppose a Creator, how much more clearly must we perceive the necessity of this very Crea-

tor's creation whose perfections comprehend an arrangement far more accurate and just.

The belief of an infinity of creative and created gods, each more eminently requiring an intelligent author of his being than the foregoing, is a direct consequence of the premises which you have stated. The assumption that the Universe is a design leads to a conclusion that there are infinity of creative and created gods, which is absurd. It is impossible indeed to prescribe limits to learned error, when philosophy relinquishes experience and feeling for speculation.[46]

Until it is clearly proved that the Universe was created, we may reasonably suppose that it has endured from all eternity. In a case where two propositions are diametrically opposite, the mind believes that which is less incomprehensible; it is easier to suppose that the Universe has existed from all eternity than to conceive an eternal being capable of creating it. If the mind sinks beneath the weight of one, is it an alleviation to increase the intolerability of the burden?[47]

A man knows not only that he now is but that there was a time when he did not exist; consequently there must have been a cause. But we can only infer from effects causes exactly adequate to those effects. There certainly is a generative power which is effected by particular instruments; we cannot prove that it is inherent in these instruments, nor is the contrary hypothesis capable of demonstration. We admit that the generative power is incomprehensible, but to suppose that the same effects are produced by an eternal omnipotent and omniscient Being leaves the cause in the same obscurity, but renders it more incomprehensible.[48]

We can only infer from effects causes exactly adequate to those effects. An infinite

45. See Hume. *Selections*, pp. 303-313.
46. Compare the thought in the last three paragraphs with Hume's *Essay on Polytheism*. See also Shelley's letter to Hogg, January 6, 1811.
47. This paragraph is a revision of a passage in *The Necessity of Atheism*. It is also verbatim with

a passage in the Note to *Queen Mab*, to the line, "There is no God."
48. This thought and indeed much of the exact phraseology are in the Note in *Queen Mab* to the line, "There is no God." See also Shelley's letter to Elizabeth Hitchener, June 20, 1811.

number of effects demand an infinite number of causes, nor is the philosopher justified in supposing a greater connection or unity in the latter than is perceptible in the former. The same energy cannot be at once the cause of the serpent and the sheep; of the blight by which the harvest is destroyed and the sunshine by which it is matured; of the ferocious propensities by which man becomes a victim to himself and of the accurate judgment by which his institutions are improved. The spirit of our accurate and exact philosophy is outraged by conclusions which contradict each other so glaringly.[49]

The greatest, equally with the smallest, motions of the Universe are subjected to the rigid necessity of inevitable laws. These laws are the unknown causes of the known effects perceivable in the Universe. Their effects are the boundaries of our knowledge; their names, the expressions of our ignorance. To suppose some existence beyond, or above them, is to invent a second and superfluous hypothesis to account for what has already been accounted for by the laws of motion and the properties of matter. I admit that the nature of these laws is incomprehensible, but the hypothesis of a Deity adds a gratuitous difficulty, which so far from alleviating those which it is adduced to explain requires new hypotheses for the elucidation of its own inherent contradictions.[50]

The laws of attraction and repulsion, desire and aversion, suffice to account for every phenomenon of the moral and physical world.[51] A precise knowledge of the properties of any object is alone requisite to determine its manner of action. Let the mathematician be acquainted with the weight and volume of a cannon ball, together with the degree of velocity and inclination with which it is impelled, and he will accurately delineate the course it must describe and determine the force with which it will strike an object at a given distance. Let the influencing motive, present to the mind of any person, be given and the knowledge of his consequent conduct will result. Let the bulk and velocity of a comet be discovered, and the astronomer by the accurate estimation of the equal and contrary actions of the centripetal and centrifugal forces will justly predict the period of its return.[52]

The anomalous motions of the heavenly bodies, their unequal velocities and frequent aberrations, are corrected by that gravitation by which they are caused. The illustrious Laplace has shown that the approach of the moon to the earth and the earth to the sun is only a secular equation of a very long period, which has its maximum and minimum. The system of the Universe, then, is upheld solely by physical powers. The necessity of matter is the ruler of the world. It is vain philosophy which supposes more causes than are exactly adequate to explain the phenomena of things. *Hypotheses non fingo: quicquid enim ex phaenomensis non deducitur, hypothesis vocanda est; et hypotheses vel metaphysicae, vel physicae, vel qualitatum occultarum, seu mechanicae, in philosophia locum non habent.*[53]

You assert that the construction of the animal machine, the fitness of certain animals to certain situations, the connection between the organs of perception and that which is perceived; the relation between everything which exists and that which tends to preserve it in its existence imply design. It is manifest that if the eye could not see, nor the stomach digest, the human frame could not preserve its present mode of existence. It is equally certain, however, that the elements of its composition, if they

---

49. This paragraph is a recasting of a passage in a Note in *Queen Mab* to line "Necessity! Thou Mother of the World." Compare also a similar statement in *A Refutation of the Christian Religion.*

50. This idea appears in several places in the writings of Hume.

51. See Stewart's *Philosophy of the Active and Moral Powers of Man,* 1.354, for this idea. For similar ideas see Newton and Kant and Holbach.

52. The same thought is developed in the Note in *Queen Mab,* on "Necessity." See Hume's *An Enquiry Concerning the Human Understanding. Selections,* pp. 167-175.

53. The Latin quotation is from Sir Isaac Newton, and was first used by Shelley in Note to *Queen Mab* to the line, "There is no God." See footnote 2, p. 98.

did not exist in one form, must exist in another; and that the combinations which they would form must, so long as they endured, derive support for their peculiar mode of being from their fitness to the circumstances of their situation.[54]

It by no means follows that because a being exists, performing certain functions, he was fitted by another being to the performance of these functions. So rash a conclusion would conduct, as I have before shown, to an absurdity; and it becomes infinitely more unwarrantable from the consideration that the known laws of matter and motion, suffice to unravel, even in the present imperfect state of moral and physical science, the majority of those difficulties which the hypothesis of a Deity was invented to explain.

Doubtless no disposition of inert matter, or matter deprived of qualities, could ever have composed an animal, a tree, or even a stone. But matter deprived of qualities is an abstraction, concerning which it is impossible to form an idea. Matter, such as we behold it, is not inert. It is infinitely active and subtile. Light, electricity, and magnetism are fluids not surpassed by thought itself in tenuity and activity; like thought they are sometimes the cause and sometimes the effect of motion; and, distinct as they are from every other class of substances with which we are acquainted, seem to possess equal claims with thought to the unmeaning distinction of immateriality.[55]

The laws of motion and the properties of matter suffice to account for every phenomenon, or combination of phenomena exhibited in the Universe. That certain animals exist in certain climates results from the consentaneity of their frames to the circumstances of their situation; let these circumstances be altered to a sufficient degree, and the ele-

ments of their composition must exist in some new combination no less resulting than the former from those inevitable laws by which the Universe is governed.[56]

It is the necessary consequence of the organization of man that his stomach should digest his food; it inevitably results also from his gluttonous and unnatural appetite for the flesh of animals that his frame be diseased and his vigor impaired; but in neither of these cases is adaptation of means to end to be perceived. Unnatural diet and the habits consequent upon its use are the means and every complication of frightful disease is the end, but to assert that these means were adapted to this end by the Creator of the world, or that human caprice can avail to traverse the precautions of Omnipotence, is absurd. These are the consequences of the properties of organized matter; and it is a strange perversion of the understanding to argue that a certain sheep was created to be butchered and devoured by a certain individual of the human species, when the conformation of the latter, as is manifest to the most superficial student of comparative anatomy, classes him with those animals who feed on fruits and vegetables.[57]

The means by which the existence of an animal is sustained requires a designer in no greater degree than the existence itself of the animal. If it exists, there must be means to support its existence. In a world where *omne mutatur nihil interit*,[58] no organized being can exist without a continual separation of that substance which is incessantly exhausted, nor can this separation take place otherwise than by the invariable laws which result from the relations of matter. We are incapacitated only by our ignorance from referring every phenomenon, however unusual, minute or complex, to

54. Hume develops this thought at length in *Dialogues Concerning Natural Religion. Selections,* pp. 302-303, 350.

55. A portion of this paragraph is in Shelley's *Essay on a Future State.*

56. Compare this paragraph with Hume's *Dialogues Concerning Natural Religion. Selections,* p. 350.

57. See Cuvier, *Leçons d'Anat. Comp.* tom, iii. pp. 169-373, 448, 465, 480. Rees's *Cyclopaedia,* Art. "Man." [Shelley's Note.] Compare Shelley's essays on vegetarianism. Shelley here again quotes from Plutarch on flesh-eating. For details see *A Vindication,* note 47.

58. "Everything changes; nothing perishes."

the laws of motion and the properties of matter; and it is an egregious offense against the first principles of reason to suppose an immaterial creator of the world, *in quo omnia moventur sed sine mutua passione:*[59] which is equally a superfluous hypothesis in the mechanical philosophy of Newton and a useless excrescence on the inductive logic of Bacon.

What, then, is this harmony, this order which you maintain to have required for its establishment, what it needs not for its maintenance, the agency of a supernatural intelligence? Inasmuch as the order visible in the Universe requires one cause, so does the disorder whose operation is not less clearly apparent, demand another. Order and disorder are no more than modifications of our own perceptions of the relations which subsist between ourselves and external objects, and if we are justified in inferring the operation of a benevolent power from the advantages attendant on the former, the evils of the latter bear equal testimony to the activity of a malignant principle, no less pertinacious in inducing evil out of good than the other is unremitting in procuring good from evil.[60]

If we permit our imagination to traverse the obscure regions of possibility, we may doubtless imagine, according to the complexion of our minds, that disorder may have a relative tendency to unmingled good, or order be relatively replete with exquisite and subtle evil. To neither of these conclusions, which are equally presumptuous and unfounded, will it become the philosopher to assent. Order and disorder are expressions denoting our perceptions of what is injurious or beneficial to ourselves, or to the beings in whose welfare we are compelled to sympathize by the similarity of their conformation to our own.[61]

A beautiful antelope panting under the fangs of a tiger, a defenseless ox groaning beneath the butcher's axe, is a spectacle which instantly awakens compassion in a virtuous and unvitiated breast. Many there are, however, sufficiently hardened to the rebukes of justice and the precepts of humanity as to regard the deliberate butchery of thousands of their species as a theme of exultation and a source of honor and to consider any failure in these remorseless enterprises as a defect in the system of things. The criteria of order and disorder are as various as those beings from whose opinions and feelings they result.

Populous cities are destroyed by earthquakes and desolated by pestilence. Ambition is everywhere devoting its millions to incalculable calamity. Superstition, in a thousand shapes, is employed in brutalizing and degrading the human species and fitting it to endure without a murmur the oppression of its innumerable tyrants. All this is abstractedly neither good nor evil, because good and evil are words employed to designate that peculiar state of our own perceptions resulting from the encounter of any object calculated to produce pleasure or pain. Exclude the idea of relation, and words *good* and *evil* are deprived of import.[62]

Earthquakes are injurious to the cities which they destroy, beneficial to those whose commerce was injured by their prosperity, and indifferent to others which are too remote to be affected by their influence. Famine is good to the corn-merchant, evil to the poor, and indifferent to those whose fortunes can at all times command a superfluity. Ambition is evil to the restless bosom it inhabits, to the innumerable victims who are dragged by its ruthless thirst for infamy to expire in every variety of anguish, to the inhabi-

---

59. "In whom all things move, without affecting each other." The substance of this paragraph Shelley could have found in Holbach's *Système de la Nature*, 1.11-39.
60. The idea in the last sentence of this paragraph is also developed in Shelley's *Essay on Christianity*.

61. See Godwin's *Political Justice*, vol. i., p. 449. [Shelley's Note.]
62. Shelley maintains this same opinion of good and evil in *A Treatise on Morals*. Compare this with a slightly different opinion in *Essay on Christianity*.

tants of the country it depopulates, and to the human race whose improvement it retards; it is indifferent with regard to the system of the Universe, and is good only to the vultures and the jackalls that track the conqueror's career, and to the worms who feast in security on the desolation of his progress. It is manifest that we cannot reason with respect to the universal system from that which only exists in relation to our own perceptions.

You allege some considerations in favor of a Deity from the universality of a belief in his existence.

The superstitions of the savage and the religion of civilized Europe appear to you to conspire to prove a first cause. I maintain that it is from the evidence of revelation alone that this belief derives the slightest countenance.[63]

That credulity should be gross in proportion to the ignorance of the mind which it enslaves is in strict consistency with the principles of human nature. The idiot, the child, and the savage agree in attributing their own passions and propensities[64] to the inanimate substances by which they are either benefited or injured. The former become gods and the latter demons; hence prayers and sacrifices, by the means of which the rude theologian imagines that he may confirm the benevolence of the one, or mitigate the malignity of the other. He has averted the wrath of a powerful enemy by supplications and submission; he has secured the assistance of his neighbor by offerings; he has felt his own anger subside before the entreaties of a vanquished foe, and has cherished gratitude for the kindness of another. Therefore, does he believe that the elements will listen to his vows. He is capable of love and hatred towards his fel-

low beings, and is variously impelled by those principles to benefit or injure them. The source of his error is sufficiently obvious. When the winds, the waves, and the atmosphere act in such a manner as to thwart or forward his designs, he attributes to them the same propensities of whose existence within himself he is conscious when he is instigated by benefits to kindness, or by injuries to revenge.[65] The bigot of the woods can form no conception of beings possessed of properties differing from its own; it requires, indeed, a mind considerably tinctured with science and enlarged by cultivation to contemplate itself, not as the center and model of the Universe, but as one of the infinitely various multitude of beings of which it is actually composed.

There is no attribute of God which is not either borrowed from the passions and powers of the human mind, or which is not a negation. Omniscience, omnipotence, omnipresence, infinity, immutability, incomprehensibility, and immateriality are all words which designate properties and powers peculiar to organized beings, with the addition of negations, by which the idea of limitation is excluded.[66]

That the frequency of a belief in God (for it is not universal) should be any argument in its favor, none to whom the innumerable mistakes of men are familiar will assert. It is among men of genius and science that atheism alone is found, but among these alone is cherished an hostility to those errors with which the illiterate and vulgar are infected.

How small is the proportion of those who really believe in God to the thousands who are prevented by their occupations from ever bestowing a serious thought upon the subject, and the millions who worship but-

---

63. See Hume, *Selections*, p. 192, for a similar idea.

64. See Southey's *History of Brazil*, p. 255. [Shelley's Note.] It should be pointed out that Shelley, in the *Fragment of "A Refutation of Deism"* did not cite Southey's *History*, vol. 1, which was published in 1810. This fact would seem to

indicate that Shelley had possibly not at the time of composing the fragment seen the history.

65. This paragraph to this point is in the *Fragment of "A Refutation of Deism."*

66. "See *Le Système de la Nature:* this book is one of the most eloquent vindications of atheism." [Shelley's Note.] Shelley read this book in 1812.

terflies, bones, feathers, monkeys, calabashes, and serpents. The word *God,* like other abstractions, signifies the agreement of certain propositions rather than the presence of any idea. If we found our belief in the existence of God on the universal consent of mankind, we are duped by the most palpable of sophisms. The word *God* cannot mean at the same time an ape, a snake, a bone, a calabash, a trinity, and a unity.[67] Nor can that belief be accounted universal against which men of powerful intellect and spotless virtue have in every age protested. *Non pudet igitur physicum, id est speculatorem venatoremque naturae, ex animis consuetudine imbutis petere testimonium veritatis?*[68]

Hume has shown to the satisfaction of all philosophers that the only idea which we can form of causation is derivable from the constant conjunction of objects and the consequent inference of one from the other. We denominate that phenomenon the cause of another which we observe with the fewest exceptions to precede its occurrence. Hence it would be inadmissible to deduce the being of a God from the existence of the Universe, even if this mode of reasoning did not conduct to the monstrous conclusion of an infinity of creative and created gods, each more eminently requiring a Creator than its predecessor.[69]

If Power[70] be an attribute of existing substance, substance could not have derived its origin from power. One thing cannot be at the same time the cause and the effect of another. The word *power* expresses the capability of anything to be or act. The human mind never hesitates to annex the idea of power to any object of its experience. To deny that *power* is the attribute of being

is to deny that being can be. If power be an attribute of substance, the hypothesis of a God is a superfluous and unwarrantable assumption.

Intelligence is that attribute of the Deity which you hold to be most apparent in the Universe. Intelligence is only known to us as a mode of animal being. We cannot conceive intelligence distinct from sensation and perception, which are attributes to organized bodies. To assert that God is intelligent is to assert that he has ideas; and Locke has proved that ideas result from sensation. Sensation can exist only in an organized body; an organized body is necessarily limited both in extent and operation. The God of the rational theosophist is a vast and wise animal.[71]

You have laid it down as a maxim that the power of beginning motion is an attribute of mind as much as thought and sensation.[72]

Mind cannot create, it can only perceive. Mind is the recipient of impressions made on the organs of sense, and without the action of external objects we should not only be deprived of all knowledge of the existence of mind but totally incapable of the knowledge of anything. It is evident, therefore, that mind deserves to be considered as the effect rather than the cause of motion. The ideas which suggest themselves, too, are prompted by the circumstances of our situation; these are the elements of thought, and from the various combinations of these our feelings, opinions, and volitions inevitably result.[73]

That which is infinite necessarily includes that which is finite. The distinction, therefore, between the Universe and that by

67. This paragraph to this point is in the *Fragment of "A Refutation of Deism."*
68. "Is not the physicist [natural scientist], that is, the investigator and searcher out of nature ashamed to seek the proof [witness] of truth from minds that are imbued with custom [habit]?"
69. The thought of this paragraph can be found in various places in the writings of Hume. Most of the paragraph is in Shelley's *Fragment of "A Refutation of Deism."*

70. For a very profound disquisition on this subject, see Sir William Drummond's *Academical Questions,* chap. i., p. 1. [Shelley's Note.]
71. For a discussion of this idea see Hume's *History of Natural Religion* and *Dialogues Concerning Natural Religion.*
72. This statement is fully analyzed in Hume's *Dialogues Concerning Natural Religion.*
73. The thought of this paragraph is expanded in Hume's *Dialogues,* p. 347, and Shelley uses it in other writings, notably in the *Essay on Life.*

which the Universe is upheld is manifestly erroneous. To devise the word *God* that you may express a certain portion of the universal system can answer no good purpose in philosophy; in the language of reason, the words *God* and *universe* are synonymous. *Omnia enim per Dei potentiam facta sunt; imo quia naturae potentia nulla est nisi ipsa Dei potentia, certem est nos eatenus Dei potentiam non intelligere, quatenus causas naturales ignoramus; adeoque stultè ad eandam Dei potentiam recurritur, quando rei alicujus causam naturalem, hoc est ipsam Dei potentiam ignoramus.*[74]

Thus, from the principles of that reason to which you so rashly appealed as the ultimate arbiter of our dispute, have I shown that the popular arguments in favor of the being of a God are totally destitute of color. I have shown the absurdity of attributing intelligence to the cause of those effects which we perceive in the Universe and the fallacy which lurks in the argument from design. I have shown that order is no more than a peculiar manner of contemplating the operation of necessary agents, that mind is the effect, not the cause of motion, that power is the attribute, not the origin of Being. I have proved that we can have no evidence of the existence of a God from the principles of reason.

You will have observed, from the zeal with which I have urged arguments so revolting to my genuine sentiments, and conducted to a conclusion in direct contradiction to that faith which every good man must eternally preserve, how little I am inclined to sympathize with those of my religion who have pretended to prove the existence of God by the unassisted light of reason. I confess that the necessity of a revelation has been compromised by treacherous friends to Christianity, who have maintained that the sublime mysteries of the being of a God and the immortality of the soul are discoverable from other sources than itself.

I have proved that on the principles of that philosophy to which Epicurus, Lord Bacon, Newton, Locke, and Hume were addicted, the existence of God is a chimera.[75]

The Christian religion, then, alone affords indisputable assurance that the world was created by the power, and is preserved by the Providence of an Almighty God, who, in justice, has appointed a future life for the punishment of the vicious and the remuneration of the virtuous.

Now, O Theosophus, I call upon you to decide between atheism and Christianity; to declare whether you will pursue your principles to the destruction of the bonds of civilized society, or wear the easy yoke of that religion which proclaims "peace upon earth, good-will to all men."

Theosophus

I am not prepared at present, I confess, to reply clearly to your unexpected arguments. I assure you that no considerations, however specious, should seduce me to deny the existence of my Creator.

I am willing to promise that if, after mature deliberation, the arguments which you have advanced in favor of atheism should appear incontrovertible, I will endeavor to adopt so much of the Christian scheme as is consistent with my persuasion of the goodness, unity, and majesty of God.

---

74. Spinoza's *Tractatus Theologico-Politicus*, chap. i., p. 14. [Shelley's Note.] This passage from Spinoza is also quoted in the Note to *Queen Mab*, to the line "There is no God." See Appendix D(c) for the translation and the corrected text.

75. This statement is true in the sense in which Shelley uses the word *God*, as an anthropomorphic, creative deity.

A FRAGMENT OF
A REFUTATION OF DEISM

[This is apparently a fragment of an early draft of a portion of *A Refutation of Deism*. An examination of the speech of Eusebes on Design will establish this fact. It is in the Notebook containing the *Essay on Christianity,* and was first published by A. H. Koszul in *Shelley's Prose in the Bodleian Manuscripts* (1910). The two pages are mutilated exactly as shown in Koszul. For a detailed description of the manuscript see Koszul, pages 126-127. In the present text the broken or incomplete line is indicated by a slant line (/).]

The word *God* signifies an intelligent Creator & / he any force in terms, or discrimination in / of Nature. Nature is the mass of events, / all things which by means of our ser / and which is therefore the only legitim / deductions are founded upon their evidence / some Being above, or beyond Nature, its A / & whose intelligence is the guide of its / -tinged God from Nature, that the mis / have fallen be confounding them, may / The attributes of God are usually supposed / omnipresence, infinite goodness, & immutab / of his existence are supposed to be afforded / displayed in the Universe . . . It is propo / these proofs, & then to discuss the p / universe, & how far the qualities usual / compatible with each other. / [The following portion of the fragment is in pencil.] in favor of the existence of a Deity. / a Deity. / ine the structure of a / aker. No work of Man / the contemplation of / was an artificer / the Universe is / shall be proved / signed, adapted / philosophical / inferred. The / erse; and it / infer a / e, design and / parent in the / a popular / ntrivance? /

Simply because innumerable instances of machines having been contrived by human art are present to our mind, because we are acquainted with persons who could construct such machines; but if, having no previous knowledge of any contrivance of art, we had accidentally found a watch upon the ground, we should have been justified in concluding that it was a thing of Nature, that it was a combination of matter with whose cause we were unacquainted, and that the attempt to account for the origin of its existence would be equally presumptuous and unsatisfactory.

The analogy which some philosophers have attempted to establish between the contrivances of human art and the various existences of the Universe is inadmissible. We attribute these effects to human intelligence, because we know beforehand that human intelligence is capable of producing them. Take away this knowledge and the grounds of our reasoning will be destroyed. But our entire ignorance of the Divine Nature leaves this analogy defective in its most essential point of comparison.

What consideration then remains to be urged by the Deist in support of the creation of the Universe by a supreme Being? Its admirable fitness for the production of certain effects, that wonderful consent of all its parts, that universal harmony by whose invariable laws innumerable systems of worlds perform their stated revolutions, and the blood is driven thro' the veins of the minutest animalcule that sports in the corruption of an insect's lymph; on this account did the Universe require an intelligent Creator, because it exists producing invariable effects, and inasmuch as it is admirably organized for the production of these effects, so the more did it require a creative intelligence.

Thus we have arrived at the Deist's true proposition, "That whatever exists, producing certain effects, stands in need of a Creator, and the more conspicuous is its fitness for the production of these effects, the more certain will be our conclusion that it could not have existed from eternity, but derives its origin from an intelligent creator."

In what respects then does God differ from the Universe? From the admirable fitness of the Universe to its end, the Deist infers that it must have been created. How much more fitness to his end must exist in the author of this Universe? If we find great difficulty from its admirable arrangement in conceiving that the Universe has existed from all eternity, and to resolve this difficulty suppose a Creator, how much more clearly must we perceive the necessity of this very Creator's creation whose perfections comprehend an arrangement far more accurate and just.

The belief of an infinity of creative and created Gods, each more eminently requiring an intelligent author of their being than the foregoing, is a direct consequence of these premises. It is impossible indeed to prescribe limits to learned error when philosophy relinquishes experience for speculation. The assumption that the Universe is a design leads to a conclusion that there are an infinity of creative and created Gods, which is absurd.[1]

Until it is clearly proved that the Universe was created, we may reasonably suppose that it has endured from all eternity. In a case where two propositions are diametrically opposite, the mind believes that which is less incomprehensible; it is easier to suppose that the Universe has existed from all eternity than to conceive an eternal being capable of creating it. If the mind sinks beneath the weight of one, is it an alleviation to increase the intolerability of the burden?

A man knows, not only that he now is, but that there was a time when he did not exist; consequently there must have been a cause. But we can only infer from effects causes exactly adequate to those effects.

There certainly is a generative power which is effected by particular instruments; we cannot prove that it is inherent in these instruments; nor is the contrary hypothesis capable of demonstration. We admit that the generative power is incomprehensible, but to suppose that the same effects are produced by an eternal Omniscient and Omnipotent Being leaves the cause in the same obscurity, but renders it more incomprehensible.

Of the argument in favor of a Deity from the universality of a belief in his existence. God may be defined to be the intelligent Creator and Preserver of the Universe. How small is the proportion of those who believe in this Being to the thousands who are prevented by their occupations from ever bestowing one thought upon the subject, to the millions who worship butterflies, bones, feathers, monkeys, calabashes and serpents. The word *God,* like other abstractions, signifies the agreement of certain propositions rather than the presence of any idea. Certainly not the half of mankind ever heard the reasoning on which philosophers ground the existence of God; nor has an idea of the Cause of all things yet been received into any human mind. If we found our belief in the existence of God on the universal consent of mankind, we are duped by the most palpable of sophisms. The word *God* cannot mean at the same time a snake, an ape, a bone, a calabash, a Trinity and a Unity. The universal belief of mankind in the divinity of a calabash would afford no proof of the Trinity; nor from the simple fact that few nations have neglected to endow real or imaginary beings with human qualities could we justly infer an Intelligent and supreme First Cause.

But there is a tendency to devotion in the human mind. Scarcely any people however barbarous have been discovered, who do not acknowledge with reverence and

1. Compare Hume's *History of Natural Religion* and Holbach's *Système de la Nature,* Chapters 1-8.

awe the supernatural causes of the natural effects which they experience. They worship, it is true, the vilest and more inanimate substance, but they believe firmly in their holiness and power, owning thus their dependence on what they can neither see nor conceive.

That credulity should be gross in proportion to the ignorance of the mind which it enslaves is strictly consistent with the principles of human Nature. The idiot, the child, and the savage agree in attributing their own passions and propensities to those inanimate substances by which they are either benefited or injured. The former become Gods and the latter Demons; hence sacrifices and prayers by the means of which the rude theologian imagines that he may confirm the beneficence of the one or mitigate the malevolence of the other. He has averted the wrath of a powerful enemy by supplications and submission, he has secured the assistance of his neighbor by offerings, he has felt his own fury subside before the entreaties of a vanquished foe, and has cherished gratitude for the kindness of another. Therefore does he believe that the elements will listen to his vows. He is capable of love and hatred towards his fellow beings, and is variously impelled by these principles to benefit or injure them. The source then of his error is sufficiently obvious: when the winds, the waves, and the atmosphere act in such a manner as to thwart or forward his designs, he attributes to them the same propensities of whose existence in his own mind he is conscious, when he is instigated by benefits to kindness, or by injuries to revenge. The only knowledge at which we are capable of arriving of cause and effect is the knowledge of their necessary connection and the subsequent inference of one to the other. We call that event the cause of another which invariably precedes and is connected with it. Much science and experience is required to ascertain the true cause of any event, or that circumstance which is found with the fewest exceptions to precede its occurrence.[2]

2. The thought of this paragraph comes from Hume's *An Enquiry Concerning the Human Understanding. Selections*, pp. 146-175.

[A REFUTATION OF
THE CHRISTIAN RELIGION]

[This fragment on the Christian religion is in Mary Shelley's Notebook of seventy-four pages, now in the Library of Congress; inscribed on the back cover is "Mary Wollstonecraft Godwin, May 16, 1814." The fragment bears no title in the manuscript; the title *A Refutation of the Christian Religion* is my own. In thought it shows some affinity with *A Refutation of Deism,* the *Letter to Lord Ellenborough,* and the Note in *Queen Mab* to the line, "I will beget a Son." The fragment may well be a note to Mary, at her request, for Shelley's opinion of the Christian religion. Indeed, the opening phrase, "At your request I shall endeavor to state . . . ." lends support to this suggestion. On the other hand it has the appearance of being a part of an intended essay on miracles. The piece was first published in *Studies in Philology* (45. No 3. pp. 472-476) for July, 1948, with a brief note by F. L. Jones.]

At your request I shall endeavor to state, in the form of remarks on Leslie's short method[1] with the Deists, a few of the most obvious [arguments][2] reasons for considering that system of opinions most erroneously called the Christian religion as false.

And first, [we ought to reflect] let us observe that this religion, although the established one of the country in which we live, is by no means the only religion in the world which lays claim to a divine origin. There are and have been an incalculable number of others; and at this day, out of the [1 000 000 000] thousand million of [human] persons who form the entire population of the globe, less than a fifth part profess this system of faith, and [that] since its promulgation and diffusion, another religion, that of Mahomet, has been preached and [that] the number of its disciples greatly exceed that of the followers of Christ. If a belief in the Christian religion had been necessary to what is called the eternal welfare of men, it is scarcely to be believed that it would have been communicated to so small a portion of mankind, and after so great a lapse of years, or that, at length, having been communicated, another religion [should] might have arisen near to the birthplace of the former, attended with sufficient evidence [such as it was which] to persuade[d] the [whole] populous nations of Asia to admit its author as divine, and which prevailed in those very countries where the Christian religion had obtained the authority of the state for more than 400 years. [That] According to the theory of every religion, the universe is governed by an intelligent power infinitely benevolent and wise; had [this] a Being of this character interested itself in instructing and benefiting mankind it is probably it would have [accompanied any] devised means [mo] less inadequate to such an end than the system [called the Christian Religion] of doctrines so truly, so inefficacious, and so partial as the Christian religion. [The whole system is founded on a mistake.]

[The fundamental foundation of the whole system is weak.]

The basis of the entire system is founded on [a mistake][3] error. If all the miracles

---

1. Leslie, Charles (1650-1722), a nonjuring English divine, whose chief work was *A Short and Easy Method with the Deists* (1697).

2. Shelley's cancellations in the manuscript are in brackets in this transcription.

3. Shelley made three attempts to achieve a satisfactory wording for beginning his paragraph. He first wrote: "The whole system is founded on a mistake." Next he wrote, "The fundamental foundation of the whole system is weak."

related from the beginning of the Bible to the end had actually taken place, we should still not have approached a jot [towards] nearer the consequences attempted to be established by the advocates of Christianity. [We will] Let us suppose that the Red Sea was [divided and that dried up and] divided; [so that the water] that the Jews found an unusual quantity of quails and manna in the desert; that Joshua caused the sun to [stop] stand still—it would have been a greater miracle to have caused it to move; that the iron head of an axe floated on the Jordan; that a herd of swine were driven into a lake; that water was turned into wine; [and even that a dead man or] that extraordinary cures were performed by contact; and even that in a dead man, or a man apparently dead, the functions of life were restored—I do not see what events of this sort have in common with the prodigious superstructure attempted to be raised upon them. Certainly they exceed and contradict the accustomed lessons of experience and of consequence require more direct and unimpeachable testimony than is [required] demanded for events consistent with the order in which we have been accustomed to observe the phenomena of the universe [appear] succeed each other. But admitting that we are in possession of such evidence; that we see with our own eyes the Thames divided by the stroke of a preacher's wand; [and] that we see a dead man restored to life; water turned to wine, and pigs run violently into the sea; what follows: That the omnipotent author of the universe has entrusted the person who exhibits those singular [powers] with a [divine] special mission to [reform to] declare his will to Mankind? That he is a divine person, and that the doctrines he promulgates are necessarily true and useful? [That] No. These phenomena, like all others, prove no more than [that this person has more than] the existence of causes precisely adequate to their production. They may result from the superior insight of the operator into the laws of nature, from the knowledge of contingencies which he might convert to the profit of his pretensions, or from the creative activity of the imagination of his followers.[4] They may have been produced by a peculiar direction of [natural peculiar] natural yet inexplicable faculties analogous to what we read of animal magnetism and . . . .[5] They might have resulted from the agency of supernatural intelligences, good, bad, or indifferent, who from caprice or motives inconceivable to us, [might] may have chosen to sport with the astonishment of mortals. They *might* have been produced by the Devil—for it seems this personage is not understood to be idle in human affairs—in order to embarrass and annoy his adversary.[6] But it is a strange presumption to attribute them to the [direct, special] agency of the omnipotent God [God Almighty]—unless in as much as every event is. . . .[7]

4. This idea is found in many of Shelley's essays. See especially the Note on *Queen Mab* to the line, "There is no God."

5. Word in manuscript illegible, probably *subdemonism.*
6. See the *Essay on the Devil and Devils.*
7. The fragment ends here.

A FRAGMENT ON MIRACLES

[This fragment is from a manuscript now in the Bodleian Library at Oxford, and was first published in the Julian Editions, 7.147-148, in 1930. The fragment bears a close affinity in thought and style to a portion of *A Refutation of Deism,* the Note in *Queen Mab* to the line "I will beget a Son"—both of 1813—and to the fragment printed in this text under the title of *A Refutation of the Christian Religion.* The work is without title in the manuscript. It was probably composed in 1813-1815—a period in which Shelley was endeavoring to establish his religious ideas on solid ground. For his sources Shelley went to Hume's *Essays* and to Spinoza's *Tractatus,* and especially to Paine's *The Age of Reason.*]

. . . ultimately referable to the First Cause) . . . every event which exceeds one's powers to produce—as if whatever exceeded our own powers was necessarily the effect of Omnipotence. Their argument stands thus: nobody but God can do what I cannot do. But we have no right to suppose a greater cause for an event than one precisely sufficient to produce that event. Supposing also God to be benevolent as well as all powerful, it is not only absurd but impious to impute to his special agency the production of the events called miracles; because if his purpose had been to extirpate error by means of the doctrines recommended by them and contained in the Christian scriptures that purpose has failed and from the nature of things could not but have failed as the Deity must have known beforehand as well as we now learn from history and experience.

I am inclined to think the miracles related in the Bible sprang from the three great sources: of imposture, fabrication, and a heated imagination. But I am open to conviction; and if it can be proved that they were produced by some extraordinary powers inherent in those who exhibited them, I shall [be] willing to admit causes precisely adequate to whatever events can be proved to be historically true. But could it even be proved to me that the Sun actually moved from its place at the command of Joshua, I should no more admit as a consequence that the Author of the Universe had especially enjoined the extirpation of the Canaanites

than if the motion of a drop of dew [or] sunshine from a flower had been alleged us as a guarantee of a similar communication. Still less would it persuade me of the truth of the impudent contradictions and stupendously absurd assertions which the teachers of the Christian religion pretend to deduce from the Old and New Testament.

This objection, which was foreseen by Jesus Christ himself and is felt by the teachers of Christianity, has been met by the assertion that the truth of the doctrines must prove the truth of the miracles. This is both uncandid and absurd. What then do we want with the miracles, for if the miracles require the sanction of the truth of the doctrines—that is, these doctrines are the immediate inspiration of God arising from their conformity to what we reasonably concur. How can they communicate to the doctrines that credibility which the miracles need to receive from these doctrines? How can they confer that [quality] which it is necessary, before their genuineness as miracles can be acknowledged, that they should receive from the doctrine whose sole established claim to be divine rests upon that genuineness which thus they can never acquire? Jesus Christ assures us that Christians will be in the greatest danger of being duped by imposters, and recommends them not to be led astray by miracles, but to try them by the doctrines of the performers. This method would serve very well to determine whether those doctrines agreed with his own or not, but could never conduct to any decision as to whether the doctrines were divine or no, or the miracles the works of God. For if the miracle which accompanies the doctrine be not in itself sufficient to authenticate the doctrine, [how should the] doctrine of which every man must judge according to his own reason possibly suffice to authenticate the miracle. And if even in the opinion of a person who should think the doctrine conformable to reason (and many such are to be found in the New Testament) the miracle should require this authentication, the miracle would have been totally superfluous, without import as without purpose, confirming and testifying in favor of nothing, deducting by the support which it would itself demand from that credence which a doctrine agreeable to reason might have otherwise obtained. Surely this pretense is solemn trifling.

A doctrine pretending to be divine, and therefore true, may assert the most extravagant positions, and as there is no test of it except a miracle, of which as it appears it is itself the test, it follows that there can be no test at all. A doctrine pretending to be true may be brought to the test of logic and dialectics which though not infallible often leaves us in a possession of a probability sufficiently strong to assist us in confirming our actions and sentiments to it. But this sort of doctrine only claims precisely that degree of belief which the proof alleged in its establishment will authorize and may from time to time be suspended.

THE ASSASSINS (1814)

(A Fragment of a Romance)

[*The Assassins* was begun by Shelley, August 25, 1814, during his flight to the Continent with Mary Wollstonecraft Godwin. He worked at it intermittently for a month, leaving it finally in an unfinished state. It is the story of a devout band of Christians—the Assassins—who fled from Jerusalem when the Romans besieged that city, and settled in a peaceful vale in the Lebanon Mountains. They were bent upon establishing their Utopian, communistic society upon the moral principles of Jesus. They lived close to nature, taking reason for their guide. "Attached from principle to peace, despising and hating the pleasures and customs of the degenerate mass of mankind," they hoped to realize an earthly paradise in their new abode.]

CHAPTER I

Jerusalem, goaded on to resistance by the incessant usurpations and insolence of Rome, leagued together its discordant factions to rebel against the common enemy and tyrant. Inferior to their foe in all but the uncon- querable hope of liberty, they surrounded their city with fortifications of uncommon strength, and placed in array before the temple a band rendered desperate by patriotism and religion. Even the women preferred to die rather than survive the ruin of their country. When the Roman army approached the walls of the sacred city, its preparations, its discipline, and its numbers evinced the conviction of its leader, that he had no common barbarians to subdue. At the approach of the Roman army, the strangers withdrew from the city.

Among the multitudes which from every nation of the East had assembled at Jerusalem was a little congregation of Christians. They were remarkable neither for their numbers nor their importance. They contained among them neither philosophers nor poets. Acknowledging no laws but those of God, they modelled their conduct towards their fellow-men by the conclusions of their individual judgment on the practical application of these laws. And it was apparent from the simplicity and severity of their manners that this contempt for human institutions had produced among them a character superior in singleness and sincere self-apprehension to the slavery of pagan customs and the gross delusions of antiquated superstition. Many of their opinions considerably resembled those of the sect afterwards known by the name of Gnostics.[1] They esteemed the human understanding to be the paramount rule of human conduct; they maintained that the obscurest religious truth required for its complete elucidation no more than the strenuous application of the energies of mind. It appeared impossible to them that any doctrine could be subversive of social happiness which is not capable of being confuted by arguments derived from the nature of existing things. With the devoutest submission to the law of Christ, they united an intrepid spirit of inquiry as to the correctest mode of acting in particular instances of conduct that occur among men. Assuming the doctrines of the Messiah concerning benevolence and justice for the regulation of their actions, they could not be persuaded to acknowledge that there was apparent in the divine code any prescribed rule whereby,

for its own sake, one action rather than another, as fulfilling the will of their great Master, should be preferred.

The contempt with which the magistracy and priesthood regarded this obscure community of speculators had hitherto protected them from persecution. But they had arrived at that precise degree of eminence and prosperity which is peculiarly obnoxious to the hostility of the rich and powerful. The moment of their departure from Jerusalem was the crisis of their future destiny. Had they continued to seek a precarious refuge in a city of the Roman empire, this persecution would not have delayed to impress a new character on their opinions and their conduct; narrow views and the illiberality of sectarian patriotism would not have failed speedily to obliterate the magnificence and beauty of their wild and wonderful condition.

Attached from principle to peace, despising and hating the pleasures and the customs of the degenerate mass of mankind, this unostentatious community of good and happy men fled to the solitudes of Lebanon. To Arabians and enthusiasts the solemnity and grandeur of these desolate recesses possessed peculiar attractions. It well accorded with the justice of their conceptions on the relative duties of man towards his fellow in society that they should labor in unconstrained equality to dispossess the wolf and the tiger of their empire and establish on its ruins the dominion of intelligence and virtue. No longer would the worshippers of the God of Nature be indebted to a hundred hands for the accommodation of their simple wants. No longer would the poison of a diseased civilization embrue their very nutriment with pestilence. They would no longer owe their very existence to the vices, the fears, and the follies of mankind. Love, friendship, and philanthropy would now be the characteristic disposers of their indus-

---

1. The Gnostics—a mystic religious sect of the first three centuries of the Christian era—had considerable influence in shaping the thought of early Christendom, particularly in its dualistic or Manichaean aspects.

try. It is for his mistress or his friend that the laborer consecrates his toil; others are mindful, but he is forgetful, of himself. "God feeds the hungry ravens, and clothes the lilies of the fields, and yet Solomon in all his glory is not like to one of these." [Shelley misquotes. See Matt. 6.28-29; Luke 12.27.]

Rome was now the shadow of her former self. The light of her grandeur and loveliness had passed away. The latest and the noblest of her poets and historians had foretold in agony her approaching slavery and degradation. The ruins of the human mind, more awful and portentous than the desolation of the most solemn temples, threw a shade of gloom upon her golden palaces which the brutal vulgar could not see, but which the mighty felt with inward trepidation and despair. The ruins of Jerusalem lay defenceless and uninhabited upon the burning sands; none visited, but in the depth of solemn awe, this accursed and solitary spot. Tradition says that there was seen to linger among the scorched and shattered fragments of the temple, one being, whom he that saw dared not to call man, with clasped hands, immovable eyes, and a visage horribly serene. Not on the will of the capricious multitude, nor the constant fluctuations of the many and the weak, depends the change of empires and religions. These are the mere insensible elements from which a subtler intelligence moulds its enduring statuary. They that direct the changes of this mortal scene breathe the decrees of their dominion from a throne of darkness and of tempest. The power of man is great.

After many days of wandering the Assassins pitched their tents in the valley of Bethzatanai. For ages had this fertile valley lain concealed from the adventurous search of man among mountains of everlasting snow. The men of elder days had inhabited this spot. Piles of monumental marble and fragments of columns that in their integrity almost seemed the work of some intelligence more sportive and fantastic than the gross conceptions of mortality, lay in heaps beside the lake and were visible beneath its transparent waves. The flowering orange-tree, the balsam, and innumerable odoriferous shrubs grew wild in the desolated portals. The fountain tanks had overflowed; and, amid the luxuriant vegetation of their margin, the yellow snake held its unmolested dwelling. Hither came the tiger and the bear to contend for those once domestic animals who had forgotten the secure servitude of their ancestors. No sound, when the famished beast of prey had retreated in despair from the awful desolation of this place, at whose completion he had assisted, but the shrill cry of the stork, and the flapping of his heavy wings from the capital of the solitary column, and the scream of the hungry vulture baffled of its only victim. The lore of ancient wisdom was sculptured in mystic characters on the rocks. The human spirit and the human hand had been busy here to accomplish its profoundest miracles. It was a temple dedicated to the God of knowledge and of truth. The palaces of the Caliphs and the Caesars might easily surpass these ruins in magnitude and sumptuousness; but they were the design of tyrants and the work of slaves. Piercing genius and consummate prudence had planned and executed Bethzatanai. There was deep and important meaning in every lineament of its fantastic sculpture. The unintelligible legend, once so beautiful and perfect, so full of poetry and history, spoke, even in destruction, volumes of mysterious import and obscure significance.

But in the season of its utmost prosperity and magnificence, art might not aspire to vie with nature in the valley of Bethzatanai. All that was wonderful and lovely was collected in this deep seclusion. The fluctuating elements seemed to have been rendered everlastingly permanent in forms of wonder and delight. The mountains of Lebanon had been divided to their base to form this happy valley; on every side their icy summits darted their white pinnacles into the clear blue sky, imaging, in their grotesque outline, minarets, and ruined domes, and columns worn with time. Far below the silver clouds rolled their bright volumes in many beautiful shapes and fed the eternal springs that, spanning the dark chasms like a thousand radiant rainbows, leaped into the quiet vale, then, lingering in many a dark glade among the groves of cypress and of palm, lost themselves in the lake. The immensity of these precipitous mountains, with their starry pyramids of snow, excluded the sun, which overtopped not, even in its meridian, their overhanging rocks. But a more heavenly and serener light was reflected from their icy mirrors, which, piercing through the many-tinted clouds, produced lights and colors of inexhaustible variety. The herbage was perpetually verdant and clothed the darkest recesses of the caverns and the woods.

Nature, undisturbed, had become an enchantress in these solitudes; she had collected here all that was wonderful and divine from the armory of her omnipotence. The very winds breathed health and renovation and the joyousness of youthful courage. Fountains of crystalline water played perpetually among the aromatic flowers and mingled a freshness with their odor. The pine boughs became instruments of exquisite contrivance, among which every varying breeze waked music of new and more delightful melody. Meteoric shapes, more effulgent than the moonlight, hung on the wandering clouds and mixed in discordant dance around the spiral fountains. Blue vapors assumed strange lineaments under the rocks and among the ruins, lingering like ghosts with slow and solemn step. Through a dark chasm to the east, in the long perspective of a portal glittering with the unnumbered riches of the subterranean world, shone the broad moon, pouring in one yellow and unbroken stream her horizontal beams. Nearer the icy region, autumn and spring held an alternate reign. The sere leaves fell and choked the sluggish brooks;

the chilling fogs hung diamonds on every spray; and in the dark cold evening the howling winds made melancholy music in the trees. Far above shone the bright throne of winter, clear, cold, and dazzling. Sometimes there was seen the snow-flakes to fall before the sinking orb of the beamless sun, like a shower of fiery sulphur. The cataracts, arrested in their course, seemed with their transparent columns to support the dark-browed rocks. Sometimes the icy whirlwind scooped the powdery snow aloft to mingle with the hissing meteors, and scatter spangles through the rare and rayless atmosphere.

Such strange scenes of chaotic confusion and harrowing sublimity, surrounding and shutting in the vale, added to the delights of its secure and voluptuous tranquillity. No spectator could have refused to believe that some spirit of great intelligence and power had hallowed these wild and beautiful solitudes to a deep and solemn mystery.

The immediate effect of such a scene, suddenly presented to the contemplation of mortal eyes, is seldom the subject of authentic record. The coldest slave of custom cannot fail to recollect some few moments in which the breath of spring or the crowding clouds of sunset, with the pale moon shining through their fleecy skirts, or the song of some lonely bird perched on the only tree of an unfrequented heath, has awakened the touch of nature. And they were Arabians who entered the valley of Bethzatanai—men who idolized nature and the God of nature, to whom love and lofty thoughts and the apprehensions of an uncorrupted spirit were sustenance and life. Thus securely excluded from an abhorred world, all thought of its judgment was cancelled by the rapidity of their fervid imaginations. They ceased to acknowledge, or deigned not to advert to, the distinctions with which the majority of base and vulgar minds control the longings and struggles of the soul towards its place of rest. A new and sacred fire was kindled in their hearts and sparkled in their eyes. Every gesture, every feature, the minutest action was modelled to beneficence and beauty by the holy inspiration that had descended on their searching spirits. The epidemic transport communicated itself through every heart with the rapidity of a blast from heaven. They were already disembodied spirits; they were already the inhabitants of paradise. To live, to breathe, to move was itself a sensation of immeasurable transport. Every new contemplation of the condition of his nature brought to the happy enthusiast an added measure of delight and impelled to every organ where mind is united with external things a keener and more exquisite perception of all that they contain of lovely and divine. To love, to be loved, suddenly became an insatiable famine of his nature, which the wide circle of the universe, comprehending beings of such inexhaustible variety and stupendous magnitude of excellence, appeared too narrow and confined to satiate.

Alas, that these visitings of the spirit of life should fluctuate and pass away! That the moments when the human mind is commensurate with all that it can conceive of excellent and powerful should not endure with its existence and survive its most momentous change! But the beauty of a vernal sunset, with its overhanging curtains of empurpled cloud, is rapidly dissolved to return at some unexpected period and spread an alleviating melancholy over the dark vigils of despair.

It is true the enthusiasm of overwhelming transport which had inspired every breast among the Assassins is no more. The necessity of daily occupation and the ordinariness of that human life, the burthen of which it is the destiny of every human being to bear had smothered, not extinguished, that divine and eternal fire. Not the less indelible and permanent were the impressions communicated to all; not the more unalterably were the features of their social character modelled and determined by its influence.[2]

CHAPTER II

Rome had fallen. Her senate-house had become a polluted den of thieves and liars; her solemn temples, the arena of theological disputants, who made fire and sword the missionaries of their inconceivable beliefs. The city of the monster Constantine, symbolizing, in the consequences of its foundation, the wickedness and weakness of his successors, feebly imaged with declining power the substantial eminence of the Roman name. Pilgrims of a new and mightier faith crowded to visit the lonely ruins of Jerusalem and weep and pray before the sepulchre of the Eternal God. The earth was filled with discord, tumult, and ruin. The spirit of disinterested virtue had armed one-half of the civilized world against the other. Monstrous and detestable creeds poisoned and blighted the domestic charities. There was no appeal to natural love, or ancient faith, from pride, superstition, and revenge.

Four centuries had passed thus terribly characterized by the most calamitous revolutions. The Assassins, meanwhile, undisturbed by the surrounding tumult, possessed and cultivated their fertile valley. The gradual operation of their peculiar condition had matured and perfected the singularity and excellence of their character. That cause, which had ceased to act as an immediate and overpowering excitement, became the unperceived law of their lives and sustenance of their natures. Their religious tenets had also undergone a change, corresponding with the exalted condition of their moral being. The gratitude which they owed to the benignant Spirit by which their limited intelligences had not only been created but redeemed was less frequently adverted to, became less the topic of comment or contemplation; not, therefore, did it cease to be their presiding guardian, the guide of their inmost thoughts, the tribunal of appeal for the minutest particulars of their conduct.

---

2. Compare this description of the vale with that in Johnson's *Rasselas*, to which Shelley owed no small debt. See Professor White's *Shelley* 1.357; 683, for Shelley's probable debt to Johnson.

They learned to identify this mysterious benefactor with the delight that is bred among the solitary rocks and has its dwelling alike in the changing colors of the clouds and the inmost recesses of the caverns. Their future also no longer existed but in the blissful tranquillity of the present. Time was measured and created by the vices and the miseries of men, between whom and the happy nation of the Assassins, there was no analogy nor comparison. Already had their eternal peace commenced. The darkness had passed away from the open gates of death.

The practical results produced by their faith and condition upon their external conduct were singular and memorable. Excluded from the great and various community of mankind, these solitudes became to them a sacred hermitage in which all formed, as it were, one being, divided against itself by no contending will or factious passions. Every impulse conspired to one end and tended to a single object. Each devoted his powers to the happiness of the other. Their republic was the scene of the perpetual contentions of benevolence; not the heartless and assumed kindness of commercial man, but the genuine virtue that has a legible superscription in every feature of the countenance and every motion of the frame. The perverseness and calamities of those who dwelt beyond the mountains that encircled their undisturbed possessions were unknown and unimagined. Little embarrassed by the complexities of civilized society, they knew not to conceive any happiness that can be satiated without participation, or that thirsts not to reproduce and perpetually generate itself. The path of virtue and felicity was plain and unimpeded. They clearly acknowledged in every case that conduct to be entitled to preference which would obviously produce the greatest pleasure. They could not conceive an instance in which it would be their duty to hesitate in causing, at whatever expense, the greatest and most unmixed delight.

Hence arose a peculiarity which only failed to germinate in uncommon and mo-mentous consequences, because the Assassins had retired from the intercourse of mankind, over whom other motives and principles of conduct than justice and benevolence prevail. It would be a difficult matter for men of such a sincere and simple faith to estimate the final results of their intentions among the corrupt and slavish multitude. They would be perplexed also in their choice of the means whereby their intentions might be fulfilled. To produce immediate pain or disorder for the sake of future benefit is consonant, indeed, with the purest religion and philosophy, but never fails to excite invincible repugnance in the feelings of the many. Against their predilections and distastes an Assassin, accidentally the inhabitant of a civilized community, would wage unremitting hostility from principle. He would find himself compelled to adopt means which they would abhor, for the sake of an object which they could not conceive that he should propose to himself. Secure and self-enshrined in the magnificence and preeminence of his conceptions, spotless as the light of heaven, he would be the victim among men of calumny and persecution. Incapable of distinguishing his motives, they would rank him among the vilest and most atrocious criminals. Great beyond all comparison with them they would despise him in the presumption of their ignorance. Because his spirit burned with an unquenchable passion for their welfare, they would lead him like his illustrious master amidst scoffs, and mockery, and insult to the remuneration of an ignominious death.

Who hesitates to destroy a venomous serpent that has crept near his sleeping friend, except the man who selfishly dreads lest the malignant reptile should turn his fury on himself? And if the poisoner has assumed a human shape, if the bane be distinguished only from the viper's venom by the excess and extent of its devastation will the savior and avenger here retract and pause entrenched behind the superstition of the indefeasible divinity of man? Is the human form, then, the mere badge of a prerogative for unlicensed wickedness and mischief? Can the power derived from the weakness of the oppressed, or the ignorance of the deceived, confer the right in security to tyrannize and defraud?

The subject of regular governments and the disciple of established superstition dares not to ask this question. For the sake of the eventual benefit, he endures what he esteems a transitory evil and the moral degradation of man disquiets not his patience. But the religion of an Assassin imposes other virtues than endurance when his fellow-men groan under tyranny, or have become so bestial and abject that they cannot feel their chains. An Assassin believes that man is eminently man, and only then enjoys the prerogatives of his privileged condition when his affections and his judgment pay tribute to the God of Nature. The perverse, and vile, and vicious—what were they? Shapes of some unholy vision, moulded by the spirit of Evil, which the sword of the merciful destroyer should sweep from this beautiful world. Dreamy nothings; phantasms of misery and mischief, that hold their death-like state on glittering thrones, and in the loathsome dens of poverty. No Assassin would submissively temporize with vice, and in cold charity become a pander to falsehood and desolation. His path through the wilderness of civilized society would be marked with the blood of the oppressor and the ruiner. The wretch whom nations tremblingly adore would expiate in his throttling grasp a thousand licensed and venerable crimes.

How many holy liars and parasites, in solemn guise, would his savior arm drag from their luxurious couches, and plunge in the cold charnel, that the green and many-legged monsters of the slimy grave might eat off at their leisure the lineaments of rooted malignity and detested cunning. The respectable man—the smooth, smiling, polished villain whom all the city honors; whose very trade is lies and murder; who buys his daily bread with the blood and tears of men—would feed the ravens with his limbs. The Assassin would cater nobly for the eyeless worms of earth and the carrion fowls of heaven.

Yet here religion and human love had imbued the manners of those solitary people with inexpressible gentleness and benignity. Courage and active virtue, and the indignation against vice, which becomes a hurrying and irresistible passion, slept like the imprisoned earthquake, or the lightning shafts that hang in the golden clouds of evening. They were innocent, but they were capable of more than innocence; for the great principles of their faith were perpetually acknowledged and adverted to; nor had they forgotten, in this uninterrupted quiet, the author of their felicity.

Four centuries had thus worn away without producing an event. Men had died, and natural tears had been shed upon their graves in sorrow that improves the heart. Those who had been united by love had gone to death together leaving to their friends the bequest of a most sacred grief, and of a sadness that is allied to pleasure. Babes that hung upon their mothers' breasts had become men; men had died; and many a wild luxuriant weed that overtopped the habitations of the vale had twined its roots around their disregarded bones. Their tranquil state was like a summer sea whose gentle undulations disturb not the reflected stars and break not the long still line of the rainbow hues of sunrise.

CHAPTER III

Where all is thus calm, the slightest circumstance is recorded and remembered. Before the sixth century had expired one incident occurred remarkable and strange. A young man named Albedir, wandering in the woods, was startled by the screaming of a bird of prey and, looking up, saw blood fall, drop by drop, from among the intertwined boughs of a cedar. Having climbed the tree, he beheld a terrible and dismaying spectacle. A naked human body was impaled on the broken branch. It was maimed and mangled horribly; every limb bent and bruised into frightful distortion and exhibiting a breathing image of the most sickening mockery of life. A monstrous snake had scented its prey from among the mountains —and above hovered a hungry vulture. From amidst this mass of desolated humanity, two eyes, black and inexpressibly brilliant, shone with an unearthly lustre. Beneath the blood-stained eye-brows their steady rays manifested the serenity of an immortal power, the collected energy of a deathless mind, spell-secured from dissolution. A bitter smile of mingled abhorrence and scorn distorted his wounded lip—he appeared calmly to observe and measure all around—self-possession had not deserted the shattered mass of life.

The youth approached the bough on which the breathing corpse was hung. As he approached, the serpent reluctantly unwreathed his glittering coils and crept towards his dark and loathsome cave. The vulture, impatient of his meal, fled to the mountain, that re-echoed with his hoarse screams. The cedar branches creaked with their agitating weight, faintly, as the dismal wind arose. All else was deadly silent.

At length a voice issued from the mangled man. It rattled in hoarse murmurs from his throat and lungs—his words were the conclusion of some strange mysterious soliloquy. They were broken, and without apparent connection, completing wide intervals of inexpressible conceptions.

"The great tyrant is baffled even in success. Joy! joy! to his tortured foe! Triumph to the worm whom he tramples under his feet! Ha! His suicidal hand might dare as well abolish the mighty frame of things! Delight and exultation sit before the closed gates of death! I fear not to dwell beneath their black and ghastly shadow. Here thy power may not avail! Thou createst—'tis mine to ruin and destroy. I was thy slave— I am thy equal, and thy foe. Thousands tremble before thy throne who, at my voice,

shall dare to pluck the golden crown from thine unholy head!" He ceased. The silence of noon swallowed up his words. Albedir clung tighter to the tree—he dared not for dismay remove his eyes. He remained mute in the perturbation of deep and creeping horror.

"Albedir!" said the same voice, "Albedir! in the name of God, approach. He that suffered me to fall watches thee; the gentle and merciful spirits of sweet human love delight not in agony and horror. For pity's sake approach, in the name of thy good God, approach, Albedir!" The tones were mild and clear as the responses of Aeolian music. They floated to Albedir's ear like the warm breath of June that lingers in the lawny groves, subduing all to softness. Tears of tender affection started into his eyes. It was as the voice of a beloved friend. The partner of his childhood, the brother of his soul, seemed to call for aid and pathetically to remonstrate with delay. He resisted not the magic impulse, but advanced towards the spot and tenderly attempted to remove the wounded man. He cautiously descended the tree with his wretched burthen and deposited it on the ground.

A period of strange silence intervened. Awe and cold horror were slowly succeeding to the softer sensations of tumultuous pity, when again he heard the silver modulations of the same enchanting voice. "Weep not for me, Albedir! What wretch so utterly lost but might inhale peace and renovation from this paradise! I am wounded and in pain; but having found a refuge in this seclusion, and a friend in you, I am worthier of envy than compassion. Bear me to your cottage secretly; I would not disturb your gentle partner by my appearance. She must love me more dearly than a brother. I must be the playmate of your children; already I regard them with a father's love. My arrival must not be regarded as a thing of mystery and wonder. What, indeed, but that men are prone to error and exaggeration is less inexplicable, than that a stranger, wandering on

Lebanon, fell from the rocks into the vale? Albedir," he continued, and his deepening voice assumed awful solemnity, "in return for the affection with which I cherish thee and thine, thou owest this submission."

Albedir implicitly submitted; not even a thought had power to refuse its deference. He reassumed his burthen and proceeded towards the cottage. He watched until Khaled should be absent and conveyed the stranger into an apartment appropriated for the reception of those who occasionally visited their habitation. He desired that the door should be securely fastened and that he might not be visited until the morning of the following day.

Albedir waited with impatience for the return of Khaled. The unaccustomed weight of even so transitory a secret hung on his ingenuous and unpracticed nature like a blighting, clinging curse. The stranger's accents had lulled him to a trance of wild and delightful imagination. Hopes so visionary and aerial that they had assumed no denomination had spread themselves over his intellectual frame, and, phantoms as they were, had modelled his being to their shape. Still his mind was not exempt from the visitings of disquietude and perturbation. It was a troubled stream of thought over whose fluctuating waves unsearchable fate seemed to preside, guiding its unforeseen alternations with an inexorable hand. Albedir paced earnestly the garden of his cottage, revolving every circumstance attendant on the incident of the day. He reimaged with intense thought the minutest recollections of the scene. In vain—he was the slave of suggestions not to be controlled. Astonishment, horror, and awe—tumultuous sympathy and a mysterious elevation of soul hurried away all activity of judgment and overwhelmed with stunning force every attempt at deliberation or inquiry.

His reveries were interrupted at length by the return of Khaled. She entered the cottage, that scene of undisturbed repose, in the confidence that change might as soon overwhelm the eternal world as disturb this inviolable sanctuary. She started to behold Albedir. Without preface or remark, he recounted with eager haste the occurrences of the day. Khaled's tranquil spirit could hardly keep pace with the breathless rapidity of his narration. She was bewildered with staggering wonder even to hear his confused tones and behold his agitated countenance.

CHAPTER IV

On the following morning Albedir arose at sunrise and visited the stranger. He found him already risen and employed in adorning the lattice of his chamber with flowers from the garden. There was something in his attitude and occupation singularly expressive of his entire familiarity with the scene. Albedir's habitation seemed to have been his accustomed home. He addressed his host in a tone of gay and affectionate welcome, such as never fails to communicate by sympathy the feelings from which it flows.

"My friend," said he, "the balm of the dew of our vale is sweet; or is this garden the favored spot where the winds conspire to scatter the best odors they can find? Come, lend me your arm awhile, I feel very weak." He motioned to walk forth, but, as if unable to proceed, rested on the seat beside the door. For a few moments they were silent, if the interchange of cheerful and happy looks is to be called silence. At last he observed a spade that rested against the wall. "You have only one spade, brother," said he; "you have only one, I suppose, of any of the instruments of tillage. Your garden ground, too, occupies a certain space which it will be necessary to enlarge. This must be quickly remedied. I cannot earn my supper of tonight, nor of tomorrow; but thenceforward, I do not mean to eat the bread of idleness. I know that you would willingly perform the additional labor which my nourishment would require; I know, also, that you would feel a degree of pleasure in the fatigue arising from this employment, but I shall contest with you such pleasures as these, and such pleasures as these alone." His eyes were somewhat wan, and the tone of his voice languid as he spoke.

As they were thus engaged Khaled came towards them. The stranger beckoned to her to sit beside him, and taking her hands within his own, looked attentively on her mild countenance. Khaled inquired if he had been refreshed by sleep. He replied by a laugh of careless and inoffensive glee; and placing one of her hands within Albedir's, said, "If this be sleep, here in this odorous vale where these sweet smiles encompass us and the voices of those who love are heard —if these be the visions of sleep, sister, those who lie down in misery shall arise lighter than the butterflies. I came from amid the tumult of a world, how different from this! I am unexpectedly among you, in the midst of a scene such as my imagination never dared to promise. I must remain here—I must not depart." Khaled, recovering from the admiration and astonishment caused by the stranger's words and manner, assured him of the happiness which she should feel in such an addition to her society. Albedir, too, who had been more deeply impressed than Khaled by the event of his arrival earnestly re-assured him of the ardor of the affection with which he had inspired them. The stranger smiled gently to hear the unaccustomed fervor of sincerity which animated their address, and was rising to retire, when Khaled said, "You have not yet seen our children, Maimuna and Abdallah. They are by the water-side, playing with their favorite snake. We have only to cross yonder little wood and wind down a path cut in the rock that overhangs the lake and we shall find them beside a recess which the shore makes there and which a chasm, as it were, among the rocks and woods, encloses. Do you think you could walk there?" "To see your children, Khaled? I think I could with the assistance of Albedir's arm and yours." So they went

through the wood of ancient cypress, intermingled with the brightness of many-tinted blooms, which gleamed like stars through its romantic glens. They crossed the green meadow, and entered among the broken chasms, beautiful as they were in their investiture of odoriferous shrubs. They came at last, after pursuing a path which wound through the intricacies of a little wilderness, to the borders of the lake. They stood on the rock which overhung it, from which there was a prospect of all the miracles of nature and of art which encircled and adorned its shores. The stranger gazed upon it with a countenance unchanged by any emotion, but, as it were, thoughtfully and contemplatingly. As he gazed, Khaled ardently pressed his hand, and said, in a low yet eager voice, "Look, look, lo there!" He turned towards her, but her eyes were not on him. She looked below—her lips were parted by the feelings which possessed her soul—her breath came and went regularly but inaudibly. She leaned over the precipice and her dark hair hanging beside her face gave relief to its fine lineaments, animated by such love as exceeds utterance. The stranger followed her eyes and saw that her children were in the glen below; then raising his eyes exchanged with her affectionate looks of congratulation and delight. The boy was apparently eight years old; the girl about two years younger. The beauty of their form and countenance was something so divine and strange, as overwhelmed the senses of the beholder like a delightful dream, with insupportable ravishment. They were arrayed in a loose robe of linen, through which the exquisite proportions of their form appeared. Unconscious that they were observed, they did not relinquish the occupation in which they were engaged. They had constructed a little boat of the bark of trees and had given it sails of interwoven feathers and launched it on the water. They sat beside a white flat stone, on which a small snake lay coiled and, when their work was finished, they arose and called to the snake in melodious tones, so that it understood their language. For it unwreathed its shining circles and crept to the boat, into which no sooner had it entered, than the girl loosened the band which held it to the shore, and it sailed away. Then they ran round and round the little creek, clapping their hands, and melodiously pouring out wild sounds which the snake seemed to answer by the restless glancing of his neck. At last a breath of wind came from the shore, and the boat changed its course, and was about to leave the creek, which the snake perceived and leaped into the water, and came to the little children's feet. The girl sang to it, and it leaped into her bosom, and she crossed her fair hands over it, as if to cherish it there. Then the boy answered with a song, and it glided from beneath her hands and crept towards him. While they were thus employed, Maimuna looked up and, seeing her parents on the cliff ran to meet them up the steep path that wound around it; and Abdallah, leaving his snake, followed joyfully.[3]

3. The symbolism of the snake in this story throws light on the snake-eagle episode in *Laon and Cythna*.

ESSAY ON THE PUNISHMENT OF DEATH

[The date of this essay is unknown. It is by some authorities dated as 1815 on the assumption that Shelley was inspired to write it by his reading of Beccaria's *Dei delitti e delle pene (On Crimes and Punishments)*[1] on March 16, 1814. An examination of that work, however, will show that Shelley was not influenced by it. In fact in his letters of 1811-1814, and in *An Address to the Irish People, Proposals for an Association of Philanthropists,* and *Letter to Lord Ellenborough*—all composed in 1812—Shelley had expressed substantially the same ideas on crime and punishment as those in the essay. I believe that this essay was probably written in 1813-1814.

·In the essay Shelley called for the abolition of capital punishment because of the evil effect of public executions upon both criminal and spectators. The spectacle brutalizes the spectators and the criminal. The author advocated the prevention rather than the punishment of crime. He condemned torture.

Probably the most significant portion of the essay is the consideration of the moral and metaphysical nature of death. Shelley asks: Is death good or evil, a punishment or a reward? Does the mind, or that within us which thinks, survive death? His answer is, "No man can take upon himself to assert," and in his comments on these issues Shelley adopts the scepticism of Hume.]

1. Beccaria, Cesare Bonesana (1738-1794), was an Italian mathematician, economist, and social philosopher, whose advanced ideas spread rapidly throughout Europe. Shelley said that he forced himself to read his famous book.

The first law which it becomes a reformer to propose and support, at the approach of a period of great political change, is the abolition of the punishment of death.

It is sufficiently clear that revenge, retaliation, atonement, expiation are rules and motives so far from deserving a place in any enlightened system of political life that they are the chief sources of a prodigious class of miseries in the domestic circles of society. It is clear that however the spirit of legislation may appear to frame institutions upon more philosophical maxims, it has hitherto, in those cases which are termed criminal, done little more than palliate the spirit by gratifying a portion of it and afforded a compromise between that which is best—the inflicting of no evil upon a sensitive being without a decisively beneficial result in which he should at least participate and that which is worse that he should be put to torture for the amusement of those whom he may have injured or may seem to have injured.

Omitting these remoter considerations, let us inquire what *death* is. [It is] that punishment which is applied as a measure of transgressions of indefinite shades of distinction, so soon as they shall have passed that degree and color of enormity with which it is supposed no inferior infliction is commensurate.

And first, whether death is good or evil, a punishment or a reward, or whether it be wholly indifferent, no man can take upon himself to assert. That that within us which thinks and feels continues to think and feel after the dissolution of the body has been the almost universal opinion of mankind, and the accurate philosophy of what I may be permitted to term the modern Academy, by showing the prodigious depth and extent of our ignorance respecting the causes and nature of sensation, renders probable the affirmative of a proposition, the negative of which it is so difficult to conceive, and the popular arguments

against which, derived from what is called the atomic system, are proved to be applicable only to the relation which one object bears to another, as apprehended by the mind, and not to existence itself, or the nature of that essence which is the medium and receptacle of objects.[2]

The popular system of religion suggests the idea that the mind, after death, will be painfully or pleasurably affected according to its determinations during life. However ridiculous and pernicious we must admit the vulgar accessories of this creed to be, there is a certain analogy, not wholly absurd, between the consequences resulting to an individual during life from the virtuous or vicious, prudent or imprudent, conduct of his external actions, to those consequences which are conjectured to ensue from the discipline and order of his internal thoughts, as affecting his condition in a future state. They omit, indeed, to calculate upon the accidents of disease, and temperament, and organization, and circumstance, together with the multitude of independent agencies which affect the opinions, the conduct, and the happiness of individuals, and produce determinations of the will, and modify the judgment so as to produce effects the most opposite in natures considerably similar. These are those operations in the order of the whole of nature, tending, we are prone to believe, to some definite mighty end to which the agencies of our peculiar nature are subordinate; nor is there any reason to suppose that in a future state they should become suddenly exempt from that subordination. The philosopher is unable to determine whether our existence in a previous state has affected our present condition and abstains from deciding whether our present condition will affect us in that which may be future. That, if we continue to exist, the manner of our existence will be such as no inferences nor conjectures afforded by a consideration of our earthly experience can elucidate, is suf-

2. The substance of this paragraph is found in Hume's essays on Immortality, Death, etc.

ficiently obvious. The opinion that the vital principle within us, in whatever mode it may continue to exist, must lose that consciousness of definite and individual being which now characterizes it and become a unit in the vast sum of action and of thought which disposes and animates the universe, and is called God, seems to belong to that class of opinion which has been designated as indifferent.

To compel a person to know all that can be known by the dead concerning that which the living fear, hope, or forget; to plunge him into the pleasure or pain which there awaits him; to punish or reward him in a manner and in a degree incalculable and incomprehensible by us; to disrobe him at once from all that intertexture of good and evil[3] with which Nature seems to have clothed every form of individual existence is to inflict on him the doom of death.

A certain degree of pain and terror usually accompany the infliction of death. This degree is infinitely varied by the infinite variety in the temperament and opinions of the sufferers. As a measure of punishment, strictly so considered, and as an exhibition which, by its known effects on the sensibility of the sufferer, is intended to intimidate the spectators from incurring a similar liability, it is singularly inadequate.[4]

Firstly, persons of energetic character, in whom, as in men who suffer for political crimes, there is a large mixture of enterprise, and fortitude, and disinterestedness, and the elements, though misguided and disarranged, by which the strength and happiness of a nation might have been cemented, die in such a manner as to make death appear not evil, but good. The death of what is called a traitor, that is, a person who, from whatever motive, would abolish the government of the day, is as often a triumphant exhibition of suffering virtue as the warning of a culprit. The mutitude,

instead of departing with a panic-stricken approbation of the laws which exhibited such a spectacle, are inspired with pity, admiration, and sympathy, and the most generous among them feel an emulation to be the authors of such flattering emotions as they experience stirring in their bosoms. Impressed by what they see and feel, they make no distinction between the motives which incited the criminals to the actions for which they suffer, or the heroic courage with which they turned into good that which their judges awarded to them as evil, or the purpose itself of those actions, though that purpose may happen to be eminently pernicious. The laws in this case lose that sympathy, which it ought to be their chief object to secure, and in a participation of which consists their chief strength in maintaining those sanctions by which the parts of the social union are bound together so as to produce, as nearly as possible, the ends for which it is instituted.

Secondly, persons of energetic character, in communities not modelled with philosophical skill to turn all the energies which they contain to the purposes of common good, are prone also to fall into the temptation of undertaking, and are peculiarly fitted for despising the perils attendant upon consummating the most enormous crimes. Murder, rapes, extensive schemes of plunder are the actions of persons belonging to this class; and death is the penalty of conviction. But the coarseness of organization peculiar to men capable of committing acts wholly selfish is usually found to be associated with a proportionate insensibility to fear or pain. Their sufferings communicate to those of the spectators who may be liable to the commission of similar crimes, a sense of the lightness of that event when closely examined, which, at a distance, as uneducated persons are accustomed to do, probably they regarded with horror. But a great

3. Shelley believed that there is not anything absolute about good or evil. They are relative terms and are intermixed in all things. Hume had said as much. See *A Treatise on Human Nature*, the third book, dealing with morals.

4. Shelley's thought here is consonant with that of his day. Compare Paine's similar ideas.

majority of the spectators are so bound up in the interests and the habits of social union that no temptation would be sufficiently strong to induce them to a commission of the enormities to which this penalty is assigned. The more powerful, and the richer among them—and a numerous class of little tradesmen are richer and more powerful than those who are employed by them, and the employer, in general, bears this relation to the employed—regard their own wrongs as in some degree avenged and their own rights secured by this punishment, inflicted as the penalty of whatever crime. In cases of murder or mutilation, this feeling is almost universal. In those, therefore, whom this exhibition does not awaken to the sympathy which extenuates crime and discredits the law which restrains it, it produces feelings more directly at war with the genuine purposes of political society. It excites those emotions which it is the chief object of civilization to extinguish forever, and in the extinction of which alone there can be any hope of better institutions than those under which men now misgovern one another. Men feel that their revenge is gratified, and that their security is established by the extinction and the sufferings of beings, in most respects resembling themselves; and their daily occupations constraining them to a precise form in all their thoughts, they come to connect inseparably the idea of their own advantage with that of the death and torture of others. It is manifest that the object of sane polity is directly the reverse; and that laws founded upon reason should accustom the gross vulgar to associate their ideas of security and of interest with the reformation and the strict restraint, for that purpose alone, of those who might invade it.

The passion of revenge is orginally nothing more than an habitual perception of the ideas of the sufferings of the person who inflicts an injury, as connected as they are in a savage state, or in such portions of society as are yet undisciplined to civilization, with security that that injury will not be repeated in future. This feeling, engrafted upon superstition and confirmed by habit, at last loses sight of the only object for which it may be supposed to have been implanted and becomes a passion and a duty to be pursued and fulfilled, even to the destruction of those ends to which it originally tended. The other passions, both good and evil—avarice, remorse, love, patriotism—present a similar appearance; and to this principle of the mind overshooting the mark at which it aims, we owe all that is eminently base or excellent in human nature; in providing for the nutriment or the extinction of which consists the true art of the legislator.[5]

Nothing is more clear than that the infliction of punishment in general, in a degree which the reformation and the restraint of those who transgress the laws does not render indispensable, and none more than death, confirms all the inhuman and unsocial impulses of men. It is almost a proverbial remark that those nations in which the penal code has been particularly mild have been distinguished from all others by the rarity of crime.[6] But the example

---

5. The savage and the illiterate are but faintly aware of the distinction between the future and the past; they make actions belonging to periods so distinct, the subjects of similar feelings; they live only in the present, or in the past, as it is present. It is in this that the philosopher excels one of the many; it is this which distinguishes the doctrine of philosophic necessity from fatalism; and that determination of the will, by which it is the active source of future events, from that liberty or indifference, to which the abstract liability of irremediable actions is attached, according to the notions of the vulgar.

This is the source of the erroneous excesses of remorse and revenge; the one extending itself over the future, and the other over the past; provinces in which their suggestions can only be the sources of evil. The purpose of a resolution to act more wisely and virtuously in future, and the sense of a necessity of caution in repressing an enemy, are the sources from which the enormous superstitions implied in the words cited have arisen. [Shelley's Note.]

6. Paine and others had noted this fact.

is to be admitted to be equivocal. A more decisive argument is afforded by a consideration of the universal connection of ferocity of manners and a contempt of social ties, with the contempt of human life. Governments which derive their institutions from the existence of circumstances of barbarism and violence, with some rare exceptions perhaps, are bloody in proportion as they are despotic, and form the manners of their subjects to a sympathy with their own spirit.

The spectators who feel no abhorrence at a public execution, but rather a self-applauding superiority and a sense of gratified indignation, are surely excited to the most inauspicious emotions. The first reflec-

tion of such a one is the sense of his own internal and actual worth as preferable to that of the victim whom circumstances have led to destruction. The meanest wretch is impressed with a sense of his own comparative merit. He is one of those on whom the tower of Siloam fell not—he is such a one as Jesus Christ found not in all Samaria, who, in his own soul, throws the first stone at the woman taken in adultery. The popular religion of the country takes its designation from that illustrious person whose beautiful sentiment I have quoted. Any one who has stript from the doctrines of this person the veil of familiarity will perceive how adverse their spirit is to feelings of this nature.[7]

7. This idea of Jesus and of Christianity is that which Shelley held throughout his life. In compiling his *Biblical Extracts* in 1812, Shelley, like Thomas Jefferson, in compiling his version of the Bible, stripped from the doctrines of Jesus the mystery and immorality. In his letter to Elizabeth Hitchener,

February 27, 1812, Shelley said, "I have often thought that the moral sayings of Jesus Christ might be very useful if selected from the mystery and immorality which surrounds them. It is a little work I have in contemplation."

A PROPOSAL FOR PUTTING REFORM
TO THE VOTE THROUGHOUT THE KINGDOM

[This pamphlet was composed in February, 1817, and distributed in March to a large number of distinguished public men. But its influence seems to have been inconsiderable. It grew out of and was Shelley's contribution to the widespread agitation for social, economic, and political reforms made necessary by the rapid changes in the social structure of the state incident to the Industrial Revolution and the revolution in France.

Shelley, in the same moderation which characterized his earlier political pamphlet, *An Address to the Irish People,* urged the formation of plans to ascertain the will of the whole nation as to parliamentary reform. He advised open, but cautious action. Shelley would limit the suffrage until the voters were better educated and informed in political procedures. The social and political wisdom shown in this and other political pamphlets refutes the widespread conception of Shelley as an impractical and radical thinker.]

A great question is now agitating in this nation which no man or party of men is competent to decide; indeed there are no materials of evidence which can afford a foresight of the result. Yet on its issue depends whether we are to be slaves or freemen.

It is needless to recapitulate all that has been said about *reform*. Every one is agreed that the House of Commons is not a representation of the people. The only theoretical question that remains is whether the people ought to legislate for themselves, or be governed by laws and impoverished by taxes originating in the edicts of an assembly which represents somewhat less than a thousandth part of the entire community. I think they ought not to be so taxed and governed. An hospital for lunatics is the only theatre where we can conceive so mournful a comedy to be exhibited as this mighty nation now exhibits: a single person bullying and swindling a thousand of his comrades out of all they possessed in the world and then trampling and spitting upon them though he were the most contemptible and degraded of mankind and they had strength in their arms and courage in their hearts. Such a parable realized in political society is a spectacle worthy of the utmost indignation and abhorrence.

The prerogatives of Parliament constitute a sovereignty which is exercised in contempt of the people, and it is in strict consistency with the laws of human nature that it should have been exercised for the people's misery and ruin. Those whom they despise, men instinctively seek to render slavish and wretched that their scorn may be secure. It is the object of the reformers to restore the people to a sovereignty thus held in their contempt. It is my object, or I would be silent now.

Servitude is sometimes voluntary. Perhaps the people choose to be enslaved; perhaps it is their will to be degraded and ignorant and famished; perhaps custom is their only God, and they its fanatic worshippers will shiver in frost and waste in famine rather than deny that idol; perhaps the majority of this nation decree that they will not be represented in Parliament, that they will not deprive of power those who have reduced them to the miserable condition in which they now exist. It is *their* will—it is their own concern. If such be their decision, the champions of the rights and the mourners over the errors and calamities of man must retire to their homes in silence until accumulated sufferings shall have produced the effect of reason.

The question now at issue is whether the majority of the adult individuals of the United Kingdom of Great Britain and Ireland desire or no a complete representation in the legislative assembly.

I have no doubt that such is their will, and I believe this is the opinion of most persons conversant with the state of the public feeling. But the fact ought to be formally ascertained before we proceed. If the majority of the adult population should solemnly state their desire to be that the representatives whom they might appoint should constitute the Commons House of Parliament, there is an end to the dispute. Parliament would then be required, not petitioned, to prepare some effectual plan for carrying the general will into effect; and if Parliament should then refuse, the consequences of the contest that might ensue would rest on its presumption and temerity. Parliament would have rebelled against the people then.

If the majority of the adult population shall, when seriously called upon for their opinion, determine on grounds however erroneous that the experiment of innovation by reform in Parliament is an evil of greater magnitude than the consequences of misgovernment to which Parliament has afforded a constitutional sanction, then it becomes us to be silent; and we should be guilty of the great crime which I have conditionally imputed to the House of Commons if after unequivocal evidence that it was the national will to acquiesce in the existing system we should by partial assemblies of the multitude, or by any party acts, excite the minority to disturb this decision.

The first step towards reform is to ascertain this point. For which purpose I think the following plan would be effectual:

That a meeting should be appointed to be held at the *Crown and Anchor Tavern* on the ———— of ————, to take into consideration the most effectual measures for ascertaining whether or no a reform in Parliament is the will of the majority of the individuals of the British nation.

That the most eloquent, and the most virtuous, and the most venerable among the Friends of Liberty should employ their authority and intellect to persuade men to lay aside all animosity and even discussion respecting the topics on which they are disunited and by the love which they bear to their suffering country conjure them to contribute all their energies to set this great question at rest—whether the nation desires a reform in Parliament or no.

That the friends of reform residing in any part of the country be earnestly entreated to lend perhaps their last and the decisive effort to set their hopes and fears at rest; that those who can should go to London and those who cannot, but who yet feel that the aid of their talents might be beneficial, should address a letter to the Chairman of the meeting, explaining their sentiments; let these letters be read aloud, let all things be transacted in the face of day. Let resolutions of an import similar to those that follow be proposed.

1. That those who think that it is the duty of the people of this nation to exact such a reform in the Commons House of Parliament as should make that House a complete representation of their will and that the people have a right to perform this duty assemble here for the purpose of collecting evidence as to how far it is the will of the majority of the people to acquit themselves of this duty and to exercise this right.

2. That the population of Great Britain and Ireland be divided into three hundred distinct portions, each to contain an equal number of inhabitants, and three hundred persons be commissioned, each personally to visit every individual within the district named in his commission, and to inquire whether or no that individual is willing to sign the declaration contained in the third Resolution, requesting him to annex to his signature any explanation or exposure of his sentiments which he might choose to place on record. That the following Declaration be proposed for signature:

3. That the House of Commons does not represent the will of the People of the British nation; we the undersigned therefore declare, and publish, and our signatures annexed shall be evidence of our firm and solemn conviction that the liberty, the happiness, and the majesty of the great nation to which it is our boast to belong have been brought into danger and suffered to decay through the corrupt and inadequate manner in which members are chosen to sit in the Commons House of Parliament; we hereby express, before God and our country, a deliberate and unbiassed persuasion that it is our duty, if we shall be found in the minority in this great question, incessantly to petition; if among the majority, to require and exact that that House should originate such measure of reform as would render its members the actual representatives of the nation.

4. That this meeting shall be held day after day until it determines on the whole detail of the plan for collecting evidence as to the will of the nation on the subject of a reform in Parliament.

5. That this meeting disclaims any design, however remote, of lending their sanction to the revolutionary and disorganizing schemes which have been most falsely imputed to the Friends of Reform, and declares that its object is purely constitutional.

6. That a subscription be set on foot to defray the expenses of this plan.

In the foregoing proposal of resolutions to be submitted to a National Meeting of the Friends of Reform, I have purposely avoided detail. If it shall prove that I have in any degree afforded a hint to men who have earned and established their popularity by personal sacrifices and intellectual eminence such as I have not the presumption to rival, let it belong to them to pursue and develop all suggestions relating to the great cause of liberty which has been nurtured (I am scarcely conscious of a metaphor) with their very sweat, and blood, and tears; some have tended it in dungeons, others have cherished it in famine, all have been constant to it amidst persecution and calumny and in the face of the sanctions of power; so accomplish what ye have begun.

I shall mention therefore only one point relating to the practical part of my Proposal. Considerable expenses according to my present conception would be necessarily incurred; funds should be created by subscription to meet these demands. I have an income of a thousand a year, on which I support my wife and children in decent comfort, and from which I satisfy certain large claims of general justice. Should any plan resembling that which I have proposed be determined on by you, I will give £100, being a tenth part of one year's income, towards its object; and I will not deem so proudly of myself as to believe that I shall stand alone in this respect when any rational and consistent scheme for the public benefit shall have received the sanction of those great and good men who have devoted themselves for its preservation.

A certain degree of coalition among the sincere Friends of Reform, in whatever shape, is indispensable to the success of this proposal. The friends of universal or of limited suffrage, of annual or triennial Parliaments ought to settle these subjects on which they disagree when it is known whether the nation desires that measure on which they are all agreed. It is trivial to discuss what species of reform shall have place when it yet remains a question whether there will be any reform or no.

Meanwhile, nothing remains for me but to state explicitly my sentiments on this subject of reform. The statement is indeed quite foreign to the merits of the proposal in itself, and I should have suppressed it until called upon to subscribe such a requisition as I have suggested if the question which it is natural to ask as to what are the sentiments of the person who originates the scheme, could have received in any other manner a more simple and direct reply. It appears to me that annual Parliaments ought to be adopted as an immediate measure, as one which strongly tends to preserve the liberty and happiness of the nation; it would enable men to cultivate those energies on which the performance of the political duties belonging to the citizen of a free state as the rightful guardian of its prosperity essentially depends; it would familiarize men with liberty by disciplining them to an habitual acquaintance with its forms. Political institution is undoubtedly susceptible of such improvements as no rational person can consider possible so long as the present degraded condition to which the vital imperfections in the existing system of government has reduced the vast multitude of men shall subsist. The securest method of arriving at such beneficial innovations is to proceed gradually and with caution; or in the place of that order and freedom which the Friends of Reform assert to be violated now anarchy and despotism will follow. Annual Parliaments have my entire assent. I will not state those general reasonings in their favor, which Mr. Cobbett[1] and other writers have already made familiar to the public mind.

With respect to universal suffrage, I confess I consider its adoption in the present unprepared state of public knowledge and feeling a measure fraught with peril. I think that none but those who register their names as paying a certain small sum in *direct taxes* ought, at present, to send members to Parliament. The consequences of the immediate

1. William Cobbett (1763-1835), English author and journalist, alternately conservative and liberal, and finally a radical.

extension of the elective franchise to every male adult would be to place power in the hands of men who have been rendered brutal and torpid and ferocious by ages of slavery.[2] It is to suppose that the qualities belonging to a demagogue are such as are sufficient to endow a legislator. I allow Major Cartwright's[3] arguments to be unanswerable; abstractedly it is the right of every human being to have a share in the government. But Mr. Paine's[4] arguments are also unanswerable[5]; a pure republic may be

shown by inferences the most obvious and irresistible to be that system of social order the fittest to produce the happiness and promote the genuine eminence of man. Yet, nothing can less consist with reason, or afford smaller hopes of any beneficial issue than the plan which should abolish the regal and the aristocratical branches of our constitution before the public mind through many gradations of improvement shall have arrived at the maturity which can disregard these symbols of its childhood.

2. Perhaps Shelley had observed what had happened in France when the franchise was too rapidly liberalized.

3. John Cartwright (1740-1824), elder brother of Edmund, inventor of the power-loom, was an early advocate of parliamentary reform, a staunch friend of American independence.

4. Thomas Paine (1737-1809), British-born world

citizen, and as we have already seen, the most distinguished radical reformer of his day.

5. After "unanswerable" Shelley cancelled the following words: *and who is bold enough to say that he would abolish the Lords and pull down the King, careless of all the ruin and bloodshed that must ensue. I am intimately persuaded that theoretically a pure republic is the.*

AN ADDRESS TO THE PEOPLE ON
THE DEATH OF THE PRINCESS CHARLOTTE[1]

[On Sunday, the 9th of November, 1817, the Shelleys visited the Hunts and other friends in London, among them William Godwin and Charles Ollier; on November 10 and 11 two serious subjects engaged their conversation: the death of the Princess Charlotte on November 6, and the serious unrest among the poor laborers, and especially the recent judicial murder of three of their members. In the insane old King, George III, or in his profligate son, the Prince of Wales, liberals saw no hope for much needed reforms in the government; the young Princess, who might succeed to the throne, was, however, considered to be more sympathetic toward reforms. Thus her death occasioned rather general mourning among the friends of liberty. Shelley began *An Address* on November 11 and finished it on November 12.

But her death was only the occasion for Shelley's *Address:* its real purpose was to arouse the nation to a sympathetic understanding of the intolerable plight of the poor, and to call attention to the fact that Englishmen had lost their

1. " 'We Pity the Plumage, but Forget The Dying Bird'; *An Address to the People on the Death of the Princess Charlotte*, by The Hermit of Marlow,"

is the full title-page. The quotation is adapted from Paine's *The Rights of Man* (Everyman edition), p. 24.

time-honored freedom to write and speak and to petition freely about their grievances.

Shelley then proceeded to draw a deadly parallel between the mourning for a beautiful Princess and what should be the deep grief of a whole nation for the hanging and quartering of three poor laborers on frame-up charges by the government. With a persuasive and eloquent pen Shelley insisted that in their shameful execution Freedom itself was murdered. "Let us follow," he dramatically put it, "the corpse of British Liberty slowly and reverently to the tomb."

The subtitle, which expressed the central theme of the *Address,* carried a stinging application of Paine's famous rebuke to Burke's puerile and sentimental lament over the death of Marie Antoinette: "We pity the plumage, but forget the dying bird."

This *Address* is vigorous in style, forthright in approach, dignified in thought, eloquent, if not poetic in phrasing, and powerful in its simple-hearted pleading for just treatment of the oppressed. Let those critics of Shelley who see him solely as an impractical dreamer contemplate the sage and sound social and political philosophy in this essay—and then reassess their ideas.]

I. The Princess Charlotte is dead. She no longer moves, nor thinks, nor feels. She is as inanimate as the clay with which she is about to mingle. It is a dreadful thing to know that she is a putrid corpse who but a few days since was full of life and hope; a woman young, innocent, and beautiful, snatched from the bosom of domestic peace, and leaving that single vacancy which none can die and leave not.

II. Thus much the death of the Princess Charlotte has in common with the death of thousands. How many women die in childbed and leave their families of motherless children and their husbands to live on blighted by the remembrance of that heavy loss? How many women of active and energetic virtues, mild, affectionate, and wise, whose life is as a chain of happiness and union which, once being broken, leaves those whom it bound to perish, have died and have been deplored with bitterness, which is too deep for words?[2] Some have perished in penury or shame, and their orphan baby has survived, a prey to the scorn and neglect of strangers. Men have

watched by the bedside of their expiring wives and have gone mad when the hideous death-rattle was heard within the throat, regardless of the rosy child sleeping in the lap of the unobservant nurse. The countenance of the physician had been read by the stare of this distracted husband, until the legible despair sunk into his heart. All this has been and is. You walk with a merry heart through the streets of this great city and think not that such are the scenes acting all around you. You do not number in your thought the mothers who die in childbed. It is the most horrible of ruins: in sickness, in old age, in battle, death comes as to his own home; but in the season of joy and hope, when life should succeed to life, and the assembled family expects one more, the youngest and the best beloved—that the wife, the mother—she for whom each member of the family was so dear to one another should die! Yet thousands of the poorest poor whose misery is aggravated by what cannot be spoken now suffer this. And have they no affections? Do not their hearts beat in their bosoms and the tears gush from

2. An echo of the last line of Wordsworth's *Intimations of Immortality:* "thoughts that do often lie too deep for tears."

their eyes? Are they not human flesh and blood? Yet none weep for them—none mourn for them—none when their coffins are carried to the grave (if indeed the parish furnishes a coffin for all) turn aside and moralize upon the sadness they have left behind.

III. The Athenians did well to celebrate with public mourning the death of those who had guided the republic with their valor and their understanding, or illustrated it with their genius. Men do well to mourn for the dead: it proves that we love something besides ourselves; and he must have a hard heart who can see his friend depart to rottenness and dust and speed him without emotion on his voyage to "that bourne whence no traveller returns."[3] To lament for those who have benefited the state is a habit of piety yet more favorable to the cultivation of our best affections. When Milton died it had been well that the universal English nation had been clothed in solemn black and that the muffled bells had tolled from town to town. The French nation should have enjoined a public mourning at the deaths of Rousseau and Voltaire. We cannot truly grieve for every one who dies beyond the circle of those especially dear to us; yet in the extinction of the objects of public love and admiration and gratitude, there is something, if we enjoy a liberal mind, which has departed from within that circle. It were well done also that men should mourn for any public calamity which has befallen their country or the world, though it be not death. This

helps to maintain that connection between one man and another, and all men considered as a whole, which is the bond of social life. There should be public mourning when those events take place which make all good men mourn in their hearts—the rule of foreign or domestic tyrants, the abuse of public faith, the wresting of old and venerable laws to the murder of the innocent, the established insecurity of all those the flower of the nation who cherish an unconquerable enthusiasm for public good. Thus, if Horne Tooke[4] and Hardy[5] had been convicted of high treason, it had been good that there had been not only the sorrow and the indignation which would have filled all hearts but the external symbols of grief. When the French Republic was extinguished, the world ought to have mourned.

IV. But this appeal to the feelings of men should not be made lightly, or in any manner that tends to waste on inadequate objects those fertilizing streams of sympathy which a public mourning should be the occasion of pouring forth. This solemnity should be used only to express a wide and intelligible calamity and one which is felt to be such by those who feel for their country and for mankind; its character ought to be universal, not particular.

V. The news of the death of the Princess Charlotte, and of the execution of [Jeremiah] Brandreth, [Isaac] Ludlam, and [William] Turner,[6] arrived nearly at the same time. If beauty, youth, innocence, amiable manners, and the exercise of the domestic virtues could alone justify public

3. A misquotation from Shakespeare's *Hamlet*, 3.1.79-80: "the undiscovered country, from whose bourn no traveller returns."

4. John Horne Tooke (1736-1812), son of John Horne, was an English philologist and radical reformer, founder of the Constitutional Society to agitate for reform in England. He was imprisoned for collecting funds for the relief for relatives of the Americans "murdered by the King's troops at Lexington and Concord." After a checkered political career, he was indicted for high treason; was acquitted in 1794 and won a seat in Parliament in 1801, but after one session he was ejected.

5. Thomas Hardy (1752-1832), a radical English reformer, founder of the London Correspondence Society to promote political reform. Because of his activity in the Society he was arrested in 1794 and charged with treason. After a short trial he and other distinguished members were cleared of the charges.

6. Three laborers who, it seems, had been framed by the government in its policy of suppression. They were made to appear as dangerous agitators for reform or revolution. They were tried, publicly hanged, and quartered. For details see *The Dictionary of National Biography*.

sorrow when they are extinguished forever, this interesting Lady would well deserve that exhibition. She was the last and the best of her race. But there were thousands of others equally distinguished as she for private excellencies who have been cut off in youth and hope. The accident of her birth neither made her life more virtuous nor her death more worthy of grief. For the public she had done nothing either good or evil; her education had rendered her incapable of either in a large and comprehensive sense. She was born a princess, and those who are destined to rule mankind are dispensed with acquiring that wisdom and that experience which is necessary even to rule themselves. She was not like Lady Jane Grey, or Queen Elizabeth, a woman of profound and various learning. She had accomplished nothing, and aspired to nothing, and could understand nothing respecting those great political questions which involve the happiness of those over whom she was destined to rule. Yet this should not be said in blame, but in compassion; let us speak no evil of the dead. Such is the misery, such the impotence of royalty. Princes are prevented from the cradle from becoming anything which may deserve that greatest of all rewards next to a good conscience, public admiration and regret.

VI. The execution of Brandreth, Ludlam, and Turner is an event of quite a different character from the death of Princess Charlotte. These men were shut up in a horrible dungeon for many months, with the fear of a hideous death and of everlasting hell thrust before their eyes; and at last were brought to the scaffold and hung. They too had domestic affections and were remarkable for the exercise of private virtues. Perhaps their low station permitted the growth of those affections in a degree not consistent with a more exalted rank. They had sons, and brothers, and sisters, and fathers, who loved them, it should seem, more than the Princess Charlotte could be loved by those whom the regulations of her rank had held in perpetual estrangement from her. Her husband was to her as father, mother, and brethren. Ludlam and Turner were men of mature years, and the affections were ripened and strengthened within them. What these sufferers felt shall not be said. But what must have been the long and various agony of their kindred may be inferred from Edward Turner, who, when he saw his brother dragged along upon the hurdle, shrieked horribly and fell in a fit and was carried away like a corpse by two men. How fearful must have been their agony, sitting in solitude on that day when the tempestuous voice of horror from the crowd told them that the head so dear to them was severed from the body! Yes—they listened to the maddening shriek which burst from the multitude; they heard the rush of ten thousand terror-stricken feet, the groans and the hootings which told them that the mangled and distorted head was then lifted into the air. The sufferers were dead. What is death? Who dares to say that which will come after the grave?[7] Brandreth was calm and evidently believed that the consequences of our errors were limited by that tremendous barrier. Ludlam and Turner were full of fears lest God should plunge them in everlasting fire. Mr. Pickering, the clergyman, was evidently anxious that Brandreth should not by a false confidence lose the single opportunity of reconciling himself with the Ruler of the future world. None knew what death was, or could know. Yet these men were presumptuously thrust into that unfathomable gulf by other men who knew as little and who reckoned not the present or the future sufferings of their victims. Nothing is more horrible than that man should for any cause shed the life of man. For all other calamities there is a remedy or a consolation. When that Power through which we live ceases to maintain the

---

7. "Your death has eyes in his head—mine is not painted so." Shakespeare's *Cymbeline*. [Shelley's Note.]

life which it has conferred, then is grief and agony, and the burthen which must be borne; such sorrow improves the heart. But when man sheds the blood of man, revenge, and hatred, and a long train of executions, and assassinations, and proscriptions is perpetuated to remotest time.

VII. Such are the particular and some of the general considerations depending on the death of these men. But however deplorable, if it were a mere private or customary grief, the public, as the public, should not mourn. But it is more than this. The events which led to the death of those unfortunate men are a public calamity. I will not impute blame to the jury who pronounced them guilty of high treason; perhaps the law requires that such should be the denomination of their offence. Some restraint ought indeed to be imposed on those thoughtless men who imagine they can find in violence a remedy for violence, even if their oppressors had tempted them to this occasion of their ruin. They are instruments of evil, not so guilty as the hands that wielded them, but fit to inspire caution. But their death by hanging and beheading, and the circumstances of which it is the characteristic and the consequence constitute a calamity such as the English nation ought to mourn with an unassuageable grief.

VIII. Kings and their ministers have in every age been distinguished from other men by a thirst for expenditure and bloodshed. There existed in this country until the American war a check, sufficiently feeble and pliant indeed, to this desolating propensity. Until America proclaimed itself a republic, England was perhaps the freest and most glorious nation subsisting on the surface of the earth. It was not what is to the full desirable that a nation should be, but all that it can be, when it does not govern itself. The consequences, however, of that fundamental defect soon became evident.

The government which the imperfect constitution of our representative assembly threw into the hands of a few aristocrats improved the method of anticipating the taxes by loans, invented by the ministers of William III, until an enormous debt had been created. In the war against the Republic of France, this policy was followed up, until now, the *mere interest* of the public debt amounts to more than twice as much as the lavish expenditure of the public treasure for maintaining the standing army, and the royal family, and the pensioners, and the placemen. The effect of this debt is to produce such an unequal distribution of the means of living as saps the foundation of social union and civilized life. It creates a double aristocracy, instead of one which was sufficiently burdensome before, and gives twice as many people the liberty of living in luxury and idleness on the produce of the industrious and the poor. And it does not give them this because they are more wise and meritorious than the rest, or because their leisure is spent in schemes of public good, or in those exercises of the intellect and the imagination whose creations ennoble or adorn a country. They are not like the old aristocracy men of pride and honor, *sans peur et sans tache,*[8] but petty piddling slaves who have gained a right to the title of public creditors, either by gambling in the funds,[9] or by subserviency to government, or some other villainous trade. They are not the "Corinthian capital of polished society," but the petty and creeping weeds which deface the rich tracery of its sculpture. The effect of this system is that the day-laborer gains no more now by working sixteen hours a day than he gained before by working eight. I put the thing in its simplest and most intelligible shape. The laborer, he that tills the ground and manufactures cloth, is the man who has to provide out of what he would bring home to his wife and children for the luxuries and comforts of those whose claims are repre-

8. "Without fear and without stain."

9. In English usage the word means public securities or national stock or holdings.

sented by an annuity of forty-four millions a year levied upon the English nation. Before, he supported the army and the pensioners, and the royal family, and the landholders; and this is a hard necessity to which it was well that he should submit. Many and various are the mischiefs flowing from oppression, but this is the representative of them all; namely, that one man is forced to labor for another in a degree not only not necessary to the support of the subsisting distinctions among mankind but so as by the excess of the injustice to endanger the very foundations of all that is valuable in social order and to provoke that anarchy which is at once the enemy of freedom and the child and the chastiser of misrule. The nation tottering on the brink of two chasms began to be weary of a continuance of such dangers and degradations and the miseries which are the consequence of them; the public voice loudly demanded a free representation of the people. It began to be felt that no other constituted body of men could meet the difficulties which impend. Nothing but the nation itself dares to touch the question as to whether there is any remedy or no to the annual payment of forty-four millions a year beyond the necessary expenses of state, forever and forever. A nobler spirit also went abroad, and the love of liberty, and patriotism, and the self-respect attendant on those glorious emotions, revived in the bosoms of men. The government had a desperate game to play.

IX. In the manufacturing districts of England discontent and disaffection had prevailed for many years; this was the consequence of that system of double aristocracy produced by the causes before mentioned. The manufacturers,[10] the helots of luxury, are left by this system famished, without affections, without health, without leisure or opportunity for such instruction as might counteract those habits of turbulence and dissipation produced by the precariousness and insecurity of poverty. Here was a ready

field for any adventurer who should wish for whatever purpose to incite a few ignorant men to acts of illegal outrage. So soon as it was plainly seen that the demands of the people for a free representation must be conceded, if some intimidation and prejudice were not conjured up, a conspiracy of the most horrible atrocity was laid in train. It is impossible to know how far the higher members of the government are involved in the guilt of their infernal agents. It is impossible to know how numerous or how active they have been, or by what false hopes they are yet inflaming the untutored multitude to put their necks under the axe and into the halter. But thus much is known that so soon as the whole nation lifted up its voice for parliamentary reform, spies were sent forth. These were selected from the most worthless and infamous of mankind and dispersed among the multitude of famished and illiterate laborers. It was their business, if they found no discontent, to create it. It was their business to find victims, no matter whether right or wrong. It was their business to produce upon the public an impression that, if any attempt to attain national freedom, or to diminish the burdens of debt and taxation under which we groan, were successful the starving multitude would rush in and confound all orders and distinctions, and institutions and laws in common ruin. The inference with which they were required to arm the ministers was that despotic power ought to be eternal. To produce this salutary impression, they betrayed some innocent and unsuspecting rustics into a crime whose penalty is a hideous death. A few hungry and ignorant manufacturers, seduced by the splendid promises of these remorseless blood-conspirators, collected together in what is called rebellion against the state. All was prepared, and the eighteen dragoons assembled in readiness, no doubt, conducted their astonished victims to that dungeon which they left only to be mangled by the executioner's

10. "Manufacturers"—daily laborers in the mills.

hand. The cruel instigators of their ruin retired to enjoy the great revenues which they had earned by a life of villainy. The public voice was overpowered by the timid and the selfish, who threw the weight of fear into the scale of public opinion, and parliament confided anew to the executive government those extraordinary powers which may never be laid down, or which may be laid down in blood, or which the regularly constituted assembly of the nation must wrest out of their hands. Our alternatives are a despotism, a revolution, or reform.[11]

X. On the 7th of November, Brandreth, Turner, and Ludlam ascended the scaffold. We feel for Brandreth the less, because it seems he killed a man. But recollect who instigated him to the proceedings which led to murder. On the word of a dying man, Brandreth tells us, that "OLIVER *brought him to this*"—that, *"but for* OLIVER, *he would not have been there."* See, too, Ludlam and Turner, with their sons and brothers and sisters, how they kneel together in a dreadful agony of prayer. Hell is before their eyes, and they shudder and feel sick with fear lest some unrepented or some wilful sin should seal their doom in everlasting fire. With that dreadful penalty before their eyes—with that tremendous sanction for the truth of all he spoke, Turner exclaimed loudly and distinctly *while the executioner was putting the rope round his neck,* "THIS IS ALL OLIVER AND THE GOVERNMENT." What more he might have said we know not, because the chaplain prevented any further observations. Troops of horse, with keen and glittering swords, hemmed in the multitudes collected to witness this abominable exhibition. "When the stroke of the axe was heard, there was a burst of horror from the crowd. The instant the head was exhibited, there was a tremendous shriek set up, and the multitude ran violently in all directions, as if under the impulse of sudden frenzy.

Those who resumed their stations, groaned and hooted."[12] It is a national calamity that we endure men to rule over us who sanction for whatever ends a conspiracy which is to arrive at its purpose through such a frightful pouring forth of human blood and agony. But when that purpose is to trample upon our rights and liberties forever, to present to us the alternatives of anarchy and oppression, and triumph when the astonished nation accepts the latter at their hands, to maintain a vast standing army, and add year by year to a public debt, which, already they know, cannot be discharged, and which, when the delusion that supports it fails, will produce as much misery and confusion through all classes of society as it has continued to produce of famine and degradation to the undefended poor; to imprison and calumniate those who may offend them, at will; when this, if not the purpose, is the effect of that conspiracy, how ought we not to mourn?

XI. Mourn then, People of England. Clothe yourselves in solemn black. Let the bells be tolled. Think of mortality and change. Shroud yourselves in solitude and the gloom of sacred sorrow. Spare no symbol of universal grief. Weep—mourn—lament. Fill the great City—fill the boundless fields with lamentation and the echo of groans. A beautiful Princess is dead: she who should have been the Queen of her beloved nation and whose posterity should have ruled it forever. She loved the domestic affections, and cherished arts which adorn, and valor which defends. She was amiable and would have become wise, but she was young, and in the flower of youth the despoiler came. LIBERTY is dead. Slave! I charge thee disturb not the depth and solemnity of our grief by any meaner sorrow. If One has died who was like her that should have ruled over this land, like Liberty, young, innocent, and lovely, know that the power through which that one perished

---

11. Liberals in England, fearing a revolution, pleaded for reform as the only wise alternative.

12. These expressions are taken from *The Examiner,* Sunday, November 9th. [Shelley's Note.]

was God, and that it was a private grief. But *man* has murdered Liberty, and while the life was ebbing from its wound, there descended on the heads and on the hearts of every human thing the sympathy of an universal blast and curse. Fetters heavier than iron weigh upon us, because they bind our souls. We move about in a dungeon more pestilential than damp and narrow walls, because the earth is its floor and the heavens are its roof. Let us follow the corpse of British Liberty slowly and reverentially to its tomb; and if some glorious Phantom should appear and make its throne of broken swords and sceptres and royal crowns trampled in the dust, let us say that the Spirit of Liberty has arisen from its grave and left all that was gross and mortal there, and kneel down and worship it as our Queen.

ESSAY ON LOVE

[The date of this essay is unknown; Shelley scholars date it anywhere from 1815 to 1819. But for the reason given below I believe it was composed in 1814-1815. See especially the article on "The Dating of Shelley's Prose," *PMLA,* 58:488. The essay is perhaps a by-product of his marital troubles of 1814. It appears to be a plea for understanding by Harriet and their friends. The poems to her during the early summer of 1814 lend support to this idea.

Indeed the close affinity between the *Essay on Love* and the Preface to *Alastor* is striking and suggestive. In phrase and in thought they complement and explain each other. The closeness of the theme of each to the treatment of the passion of sympathy by the philosophers of Shelley's day suggests a probable indebtedness not before suspected. Further study might be fruitful.

But whatever its date of composition the essay has as its central theme the conception of love as *sympathy,* a thirsting after its likeness by the soul of man. The theme had undoubtedly as its immediate inspiration the extended treatment of the idea of *sympathy* by the moral philosophers which Shelley had just read—Hume, Dugald Stewart, Reid, and Adam Smith. Shelley's *Alastor* (1815) has the same theme as this essay. For an extended treatment of this theme see Roy R. Male's *Shelley: The Power of Sympathy* (1950), a University of Texas doctoral dissertation.]

What is love? Ask him who lives, what is life? Ask him who adores, what is God?

I know not the internal constitution of other men, nor even yours whom I now address. I see that in some external attributes they resemble me, but when misled by that appearance I have thought to appeal to something in common and unburden my inmost soul to them, I have found my language misunderstood like one in a distant and savage land. The more opportunities they have afforded me for experience, the wider has appeared the interval between us, and to a greater distance have the points of sympathy been withdrawn. With a spirit ill fitted to sustain such proof, trembling and feeble through its tenderness, I have everywhere sought sympathy and found only repulse and disappointment.[1]

Thou demandest, What is Love? It is that powerful attraction towards all that we conceive, or fear, or hope beyond ourselves, when we find within our own thoughts the chasm of an insufficient void and seek to awaken in all things that are a community with what we experience within ourselves.[2] If we reason, we would be understood; if we imagine, we would that the airy children of our brain were born anew within another's; if we feel, we would that another's nerves should vibrate to our own, that the beams of their eyes should kindle at once and mix and melt into our own, that lips of motionless ice should not reply to lips quivering and burning with the heart's best blood. This is Love. This is the bond and the sanction which connects not only man with man but with everything which exists.[3] We are born into the world, and there is something within us which, from the instant that we live, more and more thirsts after its likeness. It is probably in correspondence with this law that the infant drains milk from the bosom of its mother; this propensity develops itself with the development of our nature.[4] We dimly see within our intellectual nature a miniature as it were of our entire self, yet deprived of all that we condemn or despise, the ideal prototype of every thing excellent or lovely that we are capable of conceiving as belonging to the nature of man.[5] Not only the portrait of our external being but an assemblage of the minutest particles of which our nature is composed;[6] a mirror whose surface reflects only the forms of purity and brightness; a soul within our soul that describes a circle around its proper paradise which pain, and sorrow, and evil dare not overleap.[7] To this we eagerly refer all sensations, thirsting that they should resemble or correspond with it. The discovery of its anti-type; the meeting with an understanding capable of clearly estimating our own; an imagination which should enter into and seize upon the subtle and delicate peculiarities which we have delighted to cherish and unfold in secret; with a frame whose nerves, like the chords of two exquisite lyres, strung to the accompaniment of one delightful voice, vibrate with the vibrations of our own; and of a combination of all these in such proportion as the type within demands; this is the invisible and unattainable point to which Love tends; and to attain which, it urges forth the powers of man to arrest the faintest shadow of that without the possession of which there is no rest nor respite to the heart over which it rules.[8] Hence in solitude, or in that deserted state when we are surrounded by human beings, and yet they sympathize not with us, we love the flowers, the grass, and the waters, and the sky. In the motion of the very leaves of spring, in the blue air, there is then found a secret correspondence with our heart. There is eloquence in the tongueless wind, and a melody in the flowing brooks and the rustling of the reeds beside them, which by their inconceivable relation to something within the soul, awaken the spirits to a dance of breathless rapture, and bring tears of mysterious tenderness to the eyes, like the enthusiasm of patriotic success, or the voice of one beloved singing

1. The thought of this paragraph is very similar to that in the Preface to *Alastor, or the Spirit of Solitude* (1815). See Dugald Stewart's *Philosophy of the Active and Moral Powers of Man*. Complete Works, 6.140-142.

2. Stewart, *ibid.*, p. 140: "When in solitude he languishes, and by making comparisons of the lower animals or by attaching himself to inanimate objects, strives to fill up the *void* of which he is conscious."

3. Stewart, *ibid.*, p. 140: "Were I in a desert, I would find out wherewith in it to call forth my affections. If I could do no better, I would fasten them upon some sweet myrtle, or seek some melancholy cypress to connect myself to. . . ."

4. This is an eighteenth century doctrine.

5. See letter to Hogg, January 12, 1811, for a similar idea.

6. "These words are ineffectual and metaphorical. Most words are so—No help!" [Shelley's Note.]

7. Compare *Epipsychidion*, i.e., the meaning of the title word.

8. For a slightly divergent discussion on love, see Shelley's letters to Elizabeth Hitchener, November 12 and 24, 1811.

to you alone.[9] Sterne says that, if he were in a desert, he would love some cypress. So soon as this want or power is dead, man becomes the living sepulchre of himself, and what yet survives is the mere husk of what once he was.[10]

9. The thought and many of the words and phrases are almost identical with lines 475-510 of *Alastor*.

10. See Dugald Stewart's *The Philosophy of the Active and Moral Powers of Man* for the probable source of this idea.

ESSAY ON LIFE

[The exact date of this essay is unknown, but in thought it is consistent with material composed in 1812-1814. The work was first published in the *Athenaeum* for September 29, 1832. The essay, although a complete unit, is so condensed as to appear fragmentary. Speculative and metaphysical, the essay is difficult to interpret. Shelley is apparently trying to reconcile Berkeleian idealism with the scepticism of Hume, but with little success.

Much of the difficulty of interpretation lies in the use, or misuse, of such loaded words as *mind, thought, create,* and *exist.* In the philosophy of Locke and Hume the mind is essentially a passive, a perceiving function of the brain, with imagination as the creative "faculty." Then, there is the Berkeleian identification of thought and the objects of thought, each being *immaterial.* At times Shelley seems to accept Berkeley's position, but Humean scepticism concerning the ability of the mind to understand the sensible world raises doubts about the truth of Berkeley's doctrine of immaterialism. Shelley had at an early period embraced a crude sort of materialism which a reading of Berkeley had made him relinquish for a subtler view. But at the time of this essay Shelley found Berkeley's conception unsatisfactory. In a letter to Godwin, July 29, 1812, he said, "Immaterialism seems to me nothing but a simple denial of the presence of matter, of the presence of all forms of being with which our senses are acquainted, and it surely is somewhat inconsistent to assign real existence to what is a mere negation of all that actual world to which our senses introduce us. I have read Berkeley, and the perusal of his arguments tended more than anything to convince me that immaterialism, and other words of general usage deriving their force from mere *predicates in non,* were invented by the pride of philosophers to conceal their ignorance, even from themselves." Apparently Shelley has misunderstood Berkeley, for that philosopher did not deny the real existence of the external world: he merely asserts that we cannot *know* that objects do exist; all the mind has is an *image* of the various sensible objects. Then, there must be a mind to perceive them, but all that mind can perceive are images or impressions, which may or may not correspond to reality. Thus, Berkeley's main doctrine—that the mind cannot create; it can only perceive—Shelley for a time conditionally accepted.]

Life and the world, or whatever we call that which we are and feel, is an astonishing thing. The mist of familiarity obscures from us the wonder of our being. We are struck with admiration at some of its transient modifications, but it is itself the great miracle. What are changes of empires, the wreck of dynasties, with the opinions which supported them; what is the birth and the extinction of religious and of political systems, to life? What are the revolutions of the globe which we inhabit, and the operations of the elements of which it is composed, compared with life? What is the universe of stars, and suns, of which this inhabited earth is one, and their motions, and their destiny, compared with life? Life, the great miracle, we admire not, because it is so miraculous. It is well that we are thus shielded by the familiarity of what is at once so certain and so unfathomable from an astonishment which would otherwise absorb and overawe the functions of that which is its object.

If any artist, I do not say had executed, but had merely conceived in his mind the system of the sun, and the stars, and planets, they not existing, and had painted to us in words, or upon canvas, the spectacle now afforded by the nightly cope of heaven, and illustrated it by the wisdom of astronomy, great would be our admiration. Or had he imagined the scenery of this earth, the mountains, the seas, and the rivers; the grass, and the flowers, and the variety of the forms and masses of the leaves of the woods, and the colors which attend the setting and the rising sun, and the hues of the atmosphere, turbid or serene, these things not before existing, truly we should have been astonished, and it would not have been a vain boast to have said of such a man, "Non merita nome di creatore, se non Iddio ed il Poeta."[1] But now these things are looked on with little wonder, and to be conscious of them with intense delight is esteemed to be the distinguishing mark of a refined and extraordinary person. The multitude of men care not for them. It is thus with Life—that which includes all.

What is life? Thoughts and feelings arise, with or without our will, and we employ words to express them. We are born, and our birth is unremembered, and our infancy remembered but in fragments; we live on, and in living we lose the apprehension of life. How vain is it to think that words can penetrate the mystery of our being! Rightly used they may make evident our ignorance to ourselves, and this is much.[2] For what are we? Whence do we come? And whither do we go? Is birth the commencement, is death the conclusion of our being? What is birth and death?

1. Translation: "None merits the name of Creator but God and the poet." Shelley had first used this quotation in a letter to Peacock, August 16, 1818, and again with variations, in the *Essay on Life,* in *The Defence of Poetry,* and finally in a letter to Leigh Hunt, November, 1819. This quotation is not in Tasso, verbatim, but in substance it is in *Discorsi del Poema Eroico.* Apparently it was first published in Abate Pierantonio Serassi's *Life of Tasso* (Second edition, 1790), but there is no record that Shelley ever read Serassi. During the spring and summer of 1818 Shelley was reading widely in Tasso, including Manso's life of the poet, preparatory to composing his tragedy on Tasso's madness. Shelley could have seen the quotation in John Black's *Life of Tasso* (1810), which on page 326 contains a literal translation into English. But there can be no reasonable doubt that Shelley first saw the quotation, together with the Italian account of Tasso's reputed utterance of it, in John Cam Hobhouse's *Historical Illustrations of the Fourth Canto of*

Childe Harold (1818), one of the guide books which the Shelleys used in their tours of Italy. There on page 26 of this work Shelley read the Italian quotation, together with the circumstances of its utterance: "Il Tasso si levò in collera, e disse . . . che il poeta era cosa divina, e i Greci il chiamano con un' attributo che si da a Dio, quasi volendo inferire, che nel mondo non ci è chi meriti il nome di creatore, che Dio e il Poeta." See La Vita, &c. lib. iii. p. 262. Monsignor de Nores asked him who he thought deserved the first place, "fra i nostri poeti . . . mi ripose, 'al mio giudizio all' Ariosto si deve il secondo,' e soggiungendogli io subito, 'e il primo?' Sorrise, e mi voltò le spalle, volendo credo io che intendessi, che il primo lo riserbava a sè." See La Vita &c. lib. iii. p. 262. tom. ii.

(For another conclusion see C. B. Beall, "A Tasso Quotation in Shelley," *Modern Language Quarterly,* II, no. 4 (1941), pp. 609-610.)

2. A similar idea is found in Shelley's letter to Godwin, July 29, 1812.

The most refined abstractions of logic conduct to a view of life which, though startling to the apprehension, is in fact that which the habitual sense of its repeated combinations has extinguished in us. It strips, as it were, the painted curtain from this scene of things.[3] I confess that I am one of those who am unable to refuse my assent to the conclusions of those philosophers who assert that nothing exists but as it is perceived.[4]

It is a decision against which all our persuasions struggle, and we must be long convicted before we can be convinced that the solid universe of external things is "such stuff as dreams are made of."[5] The shocking absurdities of the popular philosophy of mind and matter, its fatal consequences in morals, and their violent dogmatism concerning the source of all things, had early conducted me to materialism.[6] This materialism is a seducing system to young and superficial minds. It allows its disciples to talk and dispenses them from thinking. But I was discontented with such a view of things as it afforded; man is a being of high aspirations, "looking both before and after,"[7] whose "thoughts wander through eternity," disclaiming alliance with transience and decay; incapable of imagining to himself annihilation; existing but in the future and the past; being, not what he is, but what he has been and shall be. Whatever may be his true and final destination, there is a spirit within him at enmity with nothingness and dissolution.[8] This is the character of all life and being. Each is at once the centre and the circumference, the point to which all things are referred, and the line in which all things are contained. Such

contemplations as these, materialism and the popular philosophy of mind and matter alike forbid; they are only consistent with the intellectual system.

It is absurd to enter into a long recapitulation of arguments sufficiently familiar to those inquiring minds whom alone a writer on abstruse subjects can be conceived to address. Perhaps the most clear and vigorous statement of the intellectual system is to be found in Sir William Drummond's *Academical Questions*. After such an exposition, it would be idle to translate into other words what could only lose its energy and fitness by the change. Examined point by point, and word by word, the most discriminating intellects have been able to discern no train of thoughts in the process of reasoning which does not conduct inevitably to the conclusion which has been stated.

What follows from the admission? It establishes no new truth, it gives us no additional insight into our hidden nature, neither its action nor itself. Philosophy, impatient as it may be to build, has much work yet remaining as pioneer for the overgrowth of ages. It makes one step towards this object: it destroys error and the roots of error. It leaves, what it is too often the duty of the reformer in political and ethical questions to leave, a vacancy. It reduces the mind to that freedom in which it would have acted but for the misuse of words and signs, the instruments of its own creation. By signs, I would be understood in a wide sense, including what is properly meant by that term, and what I peculiarly mean. In this latter sense, almost all familiar objects are signs, standing not for themselves but for others in their capacity of suggesting one

3. This imagery is common to Shelley's poetry.
4. This is a fundamental concept of Berkeley's philosophy.
5. The quotation is from Shakespeare's *The Tempest*, 4.1.156-158, which reads *on* instead of *of*.
6. This reference is to the so-called intellectual philosophy advocated by Locke, Hume, Hartley, Priestley, and the philosophers of the French Enlightenment, particularly Holbach and Cabanis. Compare this passage with a divergent statement

in the letter to Godwin, July 29, 1812. But perhaps the immediate source of this statement is a passage in Stewart's *Outlines of Moral Philosophy*, 6.70-75. At the end of this paragraph Shelley declares that neither materialism nor immaterialism is satisfactory.
7. The quotation is a paraphrase of Shakespeare's *Hamlet*, 4.4.37. Compare *The Essay on Christianity* and Godwin's *Essay on Sepulchres*.
8. For a probable source of this idea see Stewart's *Outlines of Moral Philosophy*, 6.68-76.

thought which shall lead to a train of thoughts. Our whole life is thus an education of error.

Let us recollect our sensations as children. What a distinct and intense apprehension had we of the world and of ourselves! Many of the circumstances of social life were then important to us which are now no longer so. But that is not the point of comparison on which I mean to insist. We less habitually distinguished all that we saw and felt, from ourselves. They seemed, as it were, to constitute one mass. There are some persons who in this respect are always children. Those who are subject to the state called reverie feel as if their nature were dissolved into the surrounding universe, or as if the surrounding universe were absorbed into their being. They are conscious of no distinction. And these are states which precede, or accompany, or follow an unusually intense and vivid apprehension of life. As men grow up this power commonly decays, and they become mechanical and habitual agents.[9] Thus feelings and then reasonings are the combined result of a multitude of entangled thoughts and of a series of what are called impressions, planted by reiteration.[10]

The view of life presented by the most refined deductions of the intellectual philosophy is that of unity. Nothing exists but as it is perceived. The difference is merely nominal between those two classes of thought which are vulgarly distinguished by the names of ideas and of external objects.[11] Pursuing the same thread of reasoning, the existence of distinct individual minds, similar to that which is employed in now questioning its own nature, is likewise found to be a delusion. The words I, you, they are not signs of any actual difference subsisting between the assemblage of thoughts thus indicated, but are merely marks employed to denote the different modifications of the one mind.

Let it not be supposed that this doctrine conducts to the monstrous presumption that I, the person who now write and think, am that one mind. I am but a portion of it. The words I and you and they are grammatical devices invented simply for arrangement, and totally devoid of the intense and exclusive sense usually attached to them. It is difficult to find terms adequate to express so subtle a conception as that to which the Intellectual Philosophy has conducted us. We are on that verge where words abandon us, and what wonder if we grow dizzy to look down the dark abyss of how little we know.

The relations of things remain unchanged, by whatever system. By the word things is to be understood any object of thought— that is, any thought upon which any other thought is employed with an apprehension of distinction. The relations of these remain unchanged; and such is the material of our knowledge.[12]

What is the cause of life? That is, how was it produced, or what agencies distinct from life have acted or act upon life? All recorded generations of mankind have wearily busied themselves in inventing answers to this question; and the result has been—Religion. Yet, that the basis of all things cannot be, as the popular philosophy alleges, mind, is sufficiently evident.[13] Mind, as far as we have any experience of its properties, and beyond that experience how vain is argument! cannot create, it can only perceive.[14] It is said also to be the cause. But cause is only a word expressing a certain state of the human mind with regard to the manner in which two thoughts are appre-

9. Compare this thought with Wordsworth's *Ode on Intimations of Immortality.*

10. This notion is fully developed in Hume's philosophy. See especially *A Treatise,* 2.13-14 (Everyman edition). See also the letter to Godwin, July 29, 1812.

11. For a probable source for this statement see Berkeley's third dialogue of *Hylas and Philonous* (Everyman edition, p. 289.)

12. Berkeley, *Ibid.,* p. 289. (Everyman edition.)

13. In this statement Shelley is following Hume, *Essays,* 2.50-79.

14. For a discussion of this idea see Hume's *An Enquiry Concerning the Human Understanding* (Everyman edition), 2.14; also pp. 50-79.

hended to be related to each other. If any one desires to know how unsatisfactorily the popular philosophy employs itself upon this great question, they need only impartially reflect upon the manner in which thoughts develop themselves in their minds. It is infinitely improbable that the cause of mind, that is, of existence, is similar to mind.[15]

15. See Hume's *Dialogues Concerning Natural Religion. Selections*, pp. 302-311, for the substance of this paragraph. Shelley uses the same argument in *A Refutation of Deism*, pp. 132-136. Compare his statements on the same subject in letters June 11 and 20, 1811. Holbach develops the same thought in his *Système de la Nature*, Chaps. 1-8.

ESSAY ON A FUTURE STATE

[The date of this essay is unknown, but the fact that almost every idea in it is found in Shelley's letters for 1811-1813, and repeated in his *A Refutation of Deism* (1813) and in the Notes to *Queen Mab* (1813), would seem to indicate that it was among those metaphysical essays Shelley is known to have composed in 1812. The work was first published by Mrs. Shelley in 1840, though a portion of it had appeared in the *Athenaeum*, September 29, 1832.

With Spinoza, Holbach, and Hume, primarily, as his authority Shelley rather objectively states the various arguments for the belief in a future state of existence of the soul or thinking principle (mind). He concludes that there is no evidence for immortality other than the desire to be forever as we are. That is the secret of man's belief in immortality.]

It has been the persuasion of an immense majority of human beings in all ages and nations that we continue to live after death —that apparent termination of all the functions of sensitive and intellectual existence. Nor has mankind been contented with supposing that species of existence which some philosophers have asserted—namely, the resolution of the component parts of the mechanism of a living being into its elements and the impossibility of the minutest particle of these sustaining the smallest diminution. They have clung to the idea that sensibility and thought, which they have distinguished from the objects of it, under the several names of spirit and matter, is, in its own nature, less susceptible of division and decay, and that when the body is resolved into its elements the principle which animated it will remain perpetual and unchanged. Some philosophers, and those to whom we are indebted for the most stupendous discoveries in physical science, suppose on the other hand that intelligence is the mere result of certain combinations among the particles of its objects;[1] and those among them who believe that we live after death recur to the interposition of a supernatural power which shall overcome the tendency inherent in all material combination to dissipate and be absorbed into other forms.

Let us trace the reasonings which in one and the other have conducted to these two opinions, and endeavor to discover what we

1. The reference here is perhaps to Hobbes, Spinoza, Hume, and particularly the natural (physical) scientists—Priestley and Hartley, and French materialists Holbach, Condorcet, Volney, and Cabanis.

ought to think on a question of such momentous interest. Let us analyze the ideas and feelings which constitute the contending beliefs and watchfully establish a discrimination between words and thoughts. Let us bring the question to the test of experience and fact, and ask ourselves, considering our nature in its entire extent, what light we derive from a sustained and comprehensive view of its component parts which may enable us to assert with certainty that we do or do not live after death.

The examination of this subject requires that it should be stript of all those accessory topics which adhere to it in the common opinion of men. The existence of a God and a future state of rewards and punishments are totally foreign to the subject. If it be proved that the world is ruled by a divine power, no inference necessarily can be drawn from that circumstance in favor of a future state.[2] It has been asserted, indeed, that as goodness and justice are to be numbered among the attributes of the Deity, he will undoubtedly compensate the virtuous who suffer during life and that he will make every sensitive being who does not deserve punishment happy forever. But this view of the subject, which it would be tedious as well as superfluous to develop and expose, satisfies no person and cuts the knot which we now seek to untie. Moreover, should it be proved on the other hand that the mysterious principle which regulates the proceedings of the universe is neither intelligent nor sensitive, yet it is not an inconsistency to suppose at the same time that the animating power survives the body which it has animated by laws as independent of any supernatural agent as those through which it first became united with it. Nor, if a future state be clearly proved, does it follow that it will be a state of punishment or reward.

By the word *death* we express that condition in which natures resembling ourselves apparently cease to be that which they were. We no longer hear them speak, nor see them move. If they have sensations and apprehensions, we no longer participate in them. We know no more than that those external organs and all that fine texture of material frame, without which we have no experience that life or thought can subsist, are dissolved and scattered abroad. The body is placed under the earth, and after a certain period there remains no vestige even of its form. This is that contemplation of inexhaustible melancholy whose shadow eclipses the brightness of the world. The common observer is struck with dejection at the spectacle. He contends in vain against the persuasion of the grave that the dead indeed cease to be.[3] The corpse at his feet is prophetic of his own destiny. Those who have preceded him, and whose voice was delightful to his ear; whose touch met his like sweet and subtle fire; whose aspect spread a visionary light upon his path—these he cannot meet again. The organs of sense are destroyed and the intellectual operations dependent on them have perished with their sources. How can a corpse see or feel? Its eyes are eaten out, and its heart is black and without motion. What intercourse can two heaps of putrid clay and crumbling bones hold together? When you can discover where the fresh colors of the faded flower abide, or the music of the broken lyre, seek life among the dead. Such are the anxious and fearful contemplations of the common observer, though the popular religion often prevents him from confessing them even to himself.[4]

The natural philosopher, in addition to the sensations common to all men inspired by the event of death, believes that he sees with more certainty that it is attended with the annihilation of sentiment and thought. He observes the mental powers increase and fade with those of the body and even ac-

2. For a similar position see Hume's *Essay on the Immortality of the Soul.*
3. A similar statement is in Hume's *A Treatise*

on *Human Nature* (Everyman edition), 2.318.
4. For a discussion of the same thought see letters for August 19 and November 24, 1811.

commodate themselves to the most transitory changes of our physical nature. Sleep suspends many of the faculties of the vital and intellectual principles; drunkenness and disease will either temporarily or permanently derange them. Madness or idiocy may utterly extinguish the most excellent and delicate of those powers. In old age the mind gradually withers, and as it grew and was strengthened with the body, so does it together with the body sink into decrepitude. Assuredly these are convincing evidences that so soon as the organs of the body are subjected to the laws of inanimate matter, sensation, and perception, and apprehension are at an end.[5] It is probable that what we call thought is not an actual being, but no more than the relation between certain parts of that infinitely varied mass of which the rest of the universe is composed and which ceases to exist so soon as those parts change their position with regard to each other. Thus color, and sound, and taste, and odor exist only relatively. But let thought be considered as some peculiar substance which permeates and is the cause of the animation of living beings. Why should that substance be assumed to be something essentially distinct from all others and exempt from subjection to those laws from which no other substance is exempt? It differs, indeed, from all other substances, as electricity, and light, and magnetism, and the constituent parts of air and earth severally differ from all others.[6] Each of these is subject to change and to decay and to conversion into other forms. Yet the difference between light and earth is scarcely greater than that which exists between life, or thought, and fire. The difference between the two former was never alleged as an argument for the eternal permanence of either in that form under which they first might offer themselves to our notice. Why should the difference between the two latter substances be an argument for the pro-

longation of the existence of one and not the other when the existence of both has arrived at their apparent termination? To say that fire exists without manifesting any of the properties of fire, such as light, heat, &c., or that the principle of life exists without consciousness, or memory, or desire, or motive is to resign, by an awkward distortion of language, the affirmative of the dispute. To say that the principle of life *may* exist in distribution among various forms is to assert what cannot be proved to be either true or false, but which, were it true, annihilates all hope of existence after death in any sense in which that event can belong to the hopes and fears of men. Suppose, however, that the intellectual and vital principle differs in the most marked and essential manner from all other known substances; that they have all some resemblance between themselves which it in no degree participates. In what manner can this concession be made an argument for its imperishability? All that we see or know perishes and is changed. Life and thought differ indeed from everything else. But that it survives that period beyond which we have no experience of its existence, such distinction and dissimilarity affords no shadow of proof and nothing but our own desires could have led us to conjecture or imagine.

Have we existed before birth? It is difficult to conceive the possibility of this. There is in the generative principle of each animal and plant a power which converts the substances by which it is surrounded into a substance homogeneous with itself. That is, the relation between certain elementary particles of matter undergo a change and submit to new combinations. For when we use the words *principle, power, cause,* &c., we mean to express no real being, but only to class under those terms a certain series of co-existing phenomena; but let it be supposed that this principle is a certain sub-

---

5. This point is made by Hume in his *Essay on Immortality of the Soul*. See also Shelley's letters for June 20, 25, and November 24, 1811, for similar statements. But its primary source is probably

Holbach's *Système de la Nature*, 1.116-129.
6. This point of view is more fully discussed in *A Refutation of Deism* (1814), and in Holbach, 1.116-129.

stance which escapes the observation of the chemist and anatomist. It certainly *may be* though it is sufficiently unphilosophical to allege the possibility of an opinion as a proof of its truth. Does it see, hear, feel, before its combination with those organs on which sensation depends? Does it reason, imagine, apprehend, without those ideas which sensation alone can communicate? If we have not existed before birth; if, at the period when the parts of our nature on which thought and life depend seem to be woven together, they are woven together; if there are no reasons to suppose that we have existed before that period at which our existence apparently commences, then there are no grounds for supposition that we shall continue to exist after our existence has apparently ceased. So far as thought and life is concerned, the same will take place with regard to us, individually considered, after death as had place before our birth.[7]

It is said that it is possible that we should continue to exist in some mode totally inconceivable to us at present. This is a most unreasonable presumption. It casts on the adherents of annihilation the burthen of proving the negative of a question, the affirmative of which is not supported by a single argument, and which, by its very nature, lies beyond the experience of the human understanding. It is sufficiently easy, indeed, to form any proposition concerning which we are ignorant just not so absurd as not to be contradictory in itself, and defy refutation. The possibility of whatever enters into the wildest imagination to conceive is thus triumphantly vindicated. But it is enough that such assertions should be either contradictory to the known laws of nature, or exceed the limits of our experience, that their fallacy or irrelevancy to our consideration should be demonstrated. They persuade, indeed, only those who desire to be persuaded.

This desire to be for ever as we are, the reluctance to a violent and unexperienced change which is common to all the animated and inanimate combinations of the universe is, indeed, the secret persuasion which has given birth to the opinions of a future state.

7. This idea is discussed in letters for June 11, 20, and November 24 and 26, 1811.

ESSAY ON THE REVIVAL OF LITERATURE

[The date of this fragment is not known. It was first published by Thomas Medwin in the *Athenaeum* for November 24, 1832, and reprinted in his *Shelley Papers* the following year. The composition of the essay probably dates from 1815. But the subject-matter has close affinity with portions of the *Discourse on the Manners of the Ancient Greeks*, and of the beginning of *A Philosophical View of Reform*.

The essay is a brief account of the revival of learning, or the Renaissance, of how the spark of Greek thought showed through the Dark Ages, not being completely extinguished by the ravages of war or by the absurd mixture of pagan and Christian philosophy; or how superstition—that enemy of all progress—will gradually be dissipated in minds nurtured on Greek philosophy. When emancipated from superstition and free of all religious and governmental restraints, mind, and mind alone, can achieve virtue and happiness. Shelley is still a vigorous opponent of priests and organized church, and the Bible in his opinion is essentially a record of tribal wars and rank superstitions.]

In the fifteenth century of the Christian era a new and extraordinary event roused Europe from her lethargic state and paved the way to her present greatness. The writings of Dante in the thirteenth and of Petrarch in the fourteenth were the bright luminaries which had afforded glimmerings of literary knowledge to the almost benighted traveller toiling up the hill of fame. But on the taking of Constantinople, a new and sudden light appeared; the dark clouds of ignorance rolled into distance, and Europe was inundated by learned monks, and still more by the quantity of learned manuscripts which they brought with them from the scene of devastation. The Turks settled themselves in Constantinople, where they adopted nothing but the vicious habits of the Greeks; they neglected even the small remains of its ancient learning which, filtered and degenerated as it was by the absurd mixture of Pagan and Christian philosophy, proved on its retirement to Europe the spark which spread gradually and successfully the light of knowledge over the world.

Italy, France, and England—for Germany still remained many centuries less civilized than the surrounding countries—swarmed with monks and cloisters. Superstition of whatever kind, whether earthly or divine, has hitherto been the weight which clogged man to earth and prevented his genius from soaring aloft amid its native skies. The enterprises and the effects of the human mind are something more than stupendous; the works of nature are material and tangible; we have a half insight into their kind and in many instances we predict their effects with certainty. But mind seems to govern the world without visible or substantial means. Its birth is unknown; its action and influence unperceived; and its being seems eternal. To the mind both humane and philosophical there cannot exist a greater subject of grief than the reflection of how much superstition has retarded the progress of intellect and consequently the happiness of man.

The monks in their cloisters were engaged in trifling and ridiculous disputes; they contented themselves with teaching the dogmas of their religion and rushed impatiently forth to the colleges and halls, where they disputed with an acrimony and meanness little befitting the resemblance of their pretended holiness. But the situation of a monk is a situation the most unnatural that bigotry, proud in the invention of cruelty, could conceive; and their vices may be pardoned as resulting from the wills and devices of a few proud and selfish bishops who enslaved the world that they might live at ease.

The disputes of the schools were mostly scholastical; it was the discussion of words and had no relation to morality. Morality—the great means and end of man—was contained, as they affirmed, in the extent of a few hundred pages of a certain book which others have since contended were but scraps of martyrs' last dying words collected together and imposed on the world. In the refinements of the scholastic philosophy the world seemed in danger of losing the little real wisdom that still remained as her portion; and the only valuable part of their disputes was such as tended to develop the system of the Peripatetic philosophers.[1] Plato, the wisest, the profoundest, and Epicurus, the most humane and gentle among the ancients, were entirely neglected by them.[2] Plato interfered with their peculiar mode of thinking concerning heavenly matters, and Epicurus, maintaining the rights of man to pleasure and happiness, would have afforded a seducing contrast to their

dark and miserable code of morals. It has been asserted that these holy men solaced their lighter moments in a contraband worship of Epicurus and profaned the philosophy which maintained the rights of all by a selfish indulgence of the rights of a few. Thus it is: the laws of nature are invariable, and man sets them aside that he may have the pleasure of travelling through a labyrinth in search of them again.[3]

Pleasure, in an open and innocent garb, by some strange process of reasoning is called vice; yet man (so closely is he linked to the chains of necessity—so irresistibly is he impelled to fulfil the end of his being) must seek her at whatever price: he becomes a hypocrite and braves damnation with all its pains.

Grecian literature—the finest the world has ever produced—was at length restored; its form and mode we obtained from the manuscripts which the ravages of time, of the Goths, and of the still more savage Turks, had spared. The burning of the library at Alexandria was an evil of importance.[4] This library is said to have contained volumes of the choicest Greek authors.

1. The followers of Aristotle. Chief among them were Theophrastus, Strabo, and Andronicus, who emphasized naturalism and logic. The overemphasis on the latter led eventually to the hairsplitting of the schoolmen of the Middle Ages.
2. This statement is not strictly correct, for the schoolmen did make use of the more mystical ideas in Plato, which had been made prominent by the Neo-Platonists.

3. A characteristic Shelleyan statement.
4. The library was founded under Ptolemy the First, c. 250 B.C. and developed until it became the greatest library of the ancient world. It contained 700,000 volumes in 47 B.C., at the time of Caesar's visit, when with the burning of the fleet in the Alexandrian harbor, most of the library was accidentally destroyed.

A TREATISE ON MORALS

(A Fragment)

[The date of the composition of the two fragments usually referred to as Speculations on Metaphysics and Morals is unknown. They are found amidst materials written as early as 1815 and as late as 1821. But in thought and style they belong to Shelley's early prose, probably dating from 1812-1815. For a detailed statement of the condition and whereabouts of the various manuscripts in which the fragments occur, see the Julian Editions, 7.341-345, and A. H. Koszul's *Shelley Prose in the Bodleian Manuscripts*. The material of these fragments is scattered, disordered, inconclusive, and without title. Mary Shelley attempted to rearrange it, taking material logically belonging to one section and placing it in another, and then in 1840 she published it under two separate and distinct headings as the *Speculations on Metaphysics* and *Speculations on Morals*. After careful study of the manuscripts, I am convinced that the work was meant to be an extended treatise on morals and that Shelley wrote the sections on metaphysics to give emphasis to his ideas on morals. It was his expressed desire—see the Preface to *Prometheus Unbound*—to write a treatise on morals, "a history of the genuine elements of human society."

I have arranged these fragments into one continuous whole under the title of *A Treatise on Morals* because Shelley himself in the text refers to this work as a "little treatise." The section on "dreams" which Mary Shelley inserted into the *Speculations on Metaphysics* has been put at the end of the essay because it is not in the manuscript with the other sections and because it has slight connection with the body of the treatise.

It is difficult to know from this disordered material what the completed work would have been. As Shelley left the material, the main theme cannot be definitely stated. But fragmentary as it is one can gain from it considerable insight into Shelley's philosophy at this important period of his life.

The source of Shelley's ideas for the portion on metaphysics is definitely Lockean, with enough of Hume's scepticism to give the work soundness; his principles of morals come directly from Hume and Adam Smith. The reader will search in vain for any modifying influence of Platonic or Neo-Platonic ideas. Following his sources Shelley contended that metaphysics has been, unfortunately, lost in a mirage of learned words, and thus it had nothing but negative truth to contribute to the advancement of knowledge. The design of his treatise Shelley said, "is restricted to the development of the elementary principles of morals," and in the achievement of his purpose metaphysics would be considered only as an adjunct.

Moral science, on the other hand, Shelley insisted "is the doctrine of the voluntary actions of man as a sentient and social being." The author aligned himself squarely with the utilitarian school of his day, maintaining that the happiness of the individual is the only conceivable, logical end of organized society, and thus the greatest happiness to the greatest number of individuals should be the end of all moral activity. We must regulate our living, Shelley said, on the principle that that which produces pleasure is good and that which produces pain is bad. We must be guided by the principles of benevolence and justice, and these in turn must be directed by those principles of the human mind, equally great: *sympathy* and *imagination*. Sympathy born of the imagination is the great civilizing force in social life. This idea is the keynote to all that Shelley thought and to all that he wrote; and it is the basic principle of his treatise on morals.]

PLAN OF A TREATISE ON MORALS

That great science which regards the nature and the operations of the human mind is popularly divided into morals and metaphysics. The latter relates to a just classification and the assignment of distinct names to its ideas; the former regards simply the determination of that arrangement of them which produces the greatest and most solid happiness.[1] It is admitted that a virtuous or moral action is that action which, when considered in all its accessories and consequences, is fitted to produce the highest pleasure to the greatest number of sensitive beings.[2] The laws according to which all pleasure, since it cannot be equally felt by all sensitive beings, ought to be distributed by a voluntary agent, [are] reserved for [a separate] chapter.

The design of this little treatise is restricted to the development of the elementary principles of morals. As far as regards that purpose, metaphysical science will be treated merely so far as a source of negative truth; while morality will be considered as a science respecting which we can arrive at positive conclusions.[3]

THE SCIENCE OF METAPHYSICS

The Mind

It is an axiom in mental philosophy that we can think of nothing which we have not perceived. When I say we can think of nothing, I mean, we can imagine nothing, we can reason of nothing, we can remember nothing, we can foresee nothing. The most astonishing combinations of poetry, the subtlest deductions of logic and mathematics are no other than combinations which the intellect makes of sensations according to its own laws.[4] A catalogue of all the thoughts of the mind and of all their possible modifications is a cyclopaedic history of the Universe.[5]

But, it will be objected, the inhabitants of the various planets of this and other solar systems, and the existence of a Power bearing the same relation to all that we perceive and are, as what we call a cause does to what we call effect, were never subjects of sensation, and yet the laws of mind almost universally suggest, according to the various dispositions of each, a conjecture, a persuasion, or a conviction of their existence. The

1. Shelley had already made a similar statement in the Note to *Queen Mab* to the line, "Even love is sold."
2. This concept is associated with the philosophy of Bentham. See also Beccaria's *Dei delitti e delle Pene.* See Shelley's treatment of it in *Letter to Lord Ellenborough.*

3. See Hume's *An Enquiry Concerning the Principles of Morals,* Sec. 1, for a similar statement of the design of his treatise.
4. This echoes Hume's *An Enquiry Concerning the Human Understanding* (Everyman edition), 2.50-84.
5. See Thomas Reid's *Active Powers of Man,* 1.28 and 1.99 for similar ideas.

reply is simple: these thoughts are also to be included in the catalogue of existence; they are modes in which thoughts are combined; the objection only adds power to the conclusion that beyond the limits of perception and thought nothing can exist.[6]

Thoughts, or ideas, or notions, call them what you will, differ from each other, not in kind, but in force. It has commonly been supposed that those distinct thoughts which affect a number of persons at regular intervals during the passage of a multitude of other thoughts, which are called *real, or external objects,* are totally different in kind from those which affect only a few persons and which recur at irregular intervals and are usually more obscure and indistinct, such as hallucinations, dreams, and the ideas of madness. No essential distinction between any one of these ideas, or any class of them, is founded on a correct observation of the nature of things, but merely on a consideration of what thoughts are most invariably subservient to the security and happiness of life; and if nothing more were expressed by the distinction, the philosopher might safely accommodate his language to that of the vulgar. But they pretend to assert an essential difference, which has no foundation in truth and which suggests a narrow and false conception of universal nature, the parent of the most fatal errors in speculation. A specific difference between every thought of the mind is indeed a necessary consequence of that law by which it perceives diversity and number; but a generic or essential difference is wholly arbitrary. The principle of the agreement and similarity of all thoughts is that they are all thoughts; the principle of their disagreement consists in the variety and irregularity of the occasions on which they arise in the mind. That in which they agree to that in which they differ is as everything to nothing. Important distinctions of various degrees of force indeed are to be established between them, if they were as they may be, subjects of ethical and economic discussion. But that is a question altogether distinct.[7]

By considering all knowledge as bounded by perception, whose operations may be indefinitely combined, we arrive at a conception of Nature inexpressibly more magnificent, simple and true, than accord[s with] the ordinary systems of complicated and partial consideration. Nor does a contemplation of the Universe in this comprehensive and synthetical view exclude the subtlest analysis of its modifications and parts.[8]

A scale might be formed, graduated according to the degrees of a combined ratio of intensity, duration, connection, periods of recurrence, and utility which would be the standard according to which all ideas might be measured and an uninterrupted chain of nicely shadowed distinctions would be observed, from the faintest impression on the senses to the most distinct combination of those impressions; from the simplest of those combinations to that mass of knowledge which, including our own nature, constitutes what we call the universe.[9]

We are intuitively conscious of our own existence and of that connection in the train of our successive ideas which we term our identity. We are conscious also of the existence of other minds; but not intuitively. Our evidence with respect to the existence

6. Shelley seems to owe much to Hume in this paragraph. See *A Treatise of Human Nature. Selections,* pp. 1-21.

7. The theme of this paragraph is discussed at length in Locke's *Essay on the Human Understanding,* Bk. IV, and repeated with variations in Hume's *Enquiry Concerning the Human Understanding,*

with both of which Shelley was familiar.

8. This paragraph seems to derive from Hume's *A Treatise on Human Nature,* Bk. I, Secs. 1-3.

9. This idea in slightly different words first appeared in Shelley's Note to *Queen Mab* to line, "There is no God." It is repeated in *A Refutation,* p. 126. See Reid, 1.488.

of other minds is founded upon a very complicated relation of ideas, which it is foreign to [the] purpose of this treatise to anatomize.[10] The basis of this relation is undoubtedly a periodical recurrence of masses of ideas which our own voluntary determinations have in one peculiar direction no power to circumscribe or to arrest, and against the recurrence of which they can only imperfectly provide. The irres[is]tible laws of thought constrain us to believe that the precise limits of our actual ideas are not the actual limits of possible ideas; the law, according to which these deductions are drawn, is called analogy; and this is the foundation of all our inferences from one idea to another inasmuch as they resemble each other.

We see trees, houses, fields, living beings in our own shape, and in shapes more or less analogous to our own. These are perpetually changing the mode of their existence relatively to us. To express the varieties of these modes, we say, *we move, they move*; and as this motion is continual, though not uniform, we express our conception of the diversities of its course by, *it has been, it is, it shall be*. These diversities are events or objects and are essential, considered relatively to human identity, for the existence of the human mind. For if the inequalities produced by what has been termed the operations of the external universe were levelled by the perception of our being uniting and filling up their interstices, motion, and mensuration, and time, and space; the elements of the human mind being thus abstracted, sensation and imagination cease. Mind cannot be considered pure.[11]

WHAT METAPHYSICS ARE. ERRORS IN THE USUAL METHODS OF CONSIDERING THEM

We do not attend sufficiently to what passes within ourselves. We combine words, combined a thousand times before. In our minds we assume entire opinions; and in the expression of those opinions, entire phrases, when we would philosophize. Our whole style of expression and sentiment is infected with the tritest plagiarisms. Our words are dead, our thoughts are cold and borrowed. . . .

Let us contemplate facts; let us in the great study of ourselves resolutely compel the mind to a rigid consideration of itself. We are not content with conjecture, and inductions, and syllogisms in sciences regarding external objects. As in these, let us also, in considering the phenomena of mind, severely collect those facts which cannot be disputed. Metaphysics will thus possess this conspicuous advantage over every other science that each student by attentively referring to his own mind may ascertain the authorities upon which any assertions regarding it are supported. There can thus be no deception, we ourselves being the depositaries of the evidence of the subject we consider.

Metaphysics may be defined as an inquiry concerning those things belonging to, or connected with, the internal nature of man.

It is said that mind produces motion; and it might as well have been said that motion produces mind.[12]

. . . more than suggest an association of words, or the remembrance of external ob-

10. Locke's *Essay*, 2.177, says "We have an intuitive knowledge of our own existence." See Berkeley's third dialogue (Everyman edition, p. 267). Hume also discusses this point, and Reid analyzes it at length, 1.126-130.

11. For a similar statement see Hume's *An Enquiry Concerning the Human Understanding. Selections*, pp. 175-182.

12. This is Spinoza's position. See *The Philosophy of Spinoza*, Modern Library, p. 200. Hume agrees by implication with this concept (*Selections*), pp. 59-61, and Locke fully discusses this point in the *Essay on the Human Understanding*, 2.247-249. It is also stated in *A Refutation of Deism*. The remainder of the material in this section was first published by H. Buxton Forman in his Library edition of *Shelley's Works*, VI, 287-290.

jects distinct from the conceptions which the mind exerts relatively to them. They are about these conceptions. They perpetually awaken the attention of their reader to the consideration of their intellectual nature. They make him feel that his mind is not merely impelled or organized by the adhibition of events proceeding from what has been termed the mechanism of the material universe.

That which the most consummate intelligences that have adorned this mortal scene inherit as their birthright, let us acquire (for it is within our grasp) by caution, by strict scepticism concerning all assertions, all expressions, by scrupulous and strong attention to the mysteries of our own nature.

Let us contemplate facts. Let me repeat that in the great study of ourselves we ought resolutely to compel the mind to a rigid examination of itself. Let us in the science which regards those laws by which the mind acts, as well as in those which regard the laws by which it is acted upon, severely collect those facts.

Metaphysics is a word which has been so long applied to denote an inquiry into the phenomena of mind that it would justly be considered presumptuous to employ another. But etymologically considered it is very ill adapted to express the science of mind. It asserts a distinction between the moral and the material universe which it is presumptuous to assume. Metaphysics may be defined as the science of all that we know, feel, remember, and believe inasmuch as our knowledge, sensations, memory, and faith constitute the universe considered relatively to human identity. Logic, or the science of words, must no longer be confounded with metaphysics or the science of facts. Words are the instruments of mind whose capacities it becomes the metaphysician accurately to know, but they are not mind, nor are they portions of mind. The discoveries of Horne Tooke in philology do not, as he has asserted, throw light upon metaphysics: they only render the instruments requisite to its

perception more exact and accurate. Aristotle and his followers, Locke and most of the modern philosophers gave logic the name of metaphysics. Nor have those who are accustomed to profess the greatest veneration for the inductive system of Lord Bacon adhered with sufficient scrupulousness to its regulations. They have professed indeed (and who have not professed?) to deduce their conclusions from indisputable facts. How came many of those facts to be called indisputable? What sanctioning correspondence unites a concatenation of syllogisms? Their promises of deducing all systems from facts has [have] too often been performed by appealing in favor of these pretended realities to the obstinate preconceptions of the multitude; or by the most preposterous mistake of a name for a thing they . . . .

The science of mind possesses eminent advantages over every other with regard to the certainty of the conclusions which it affords. It requires indeed for its entire development no more than a minute and accurate attention to facts. Every student may refer to the testimonials which he bears within himself to ascertain the authorities upon which any assertion rests. It requires no more than attention to perceive perfect sincerity in the relation of what is perceived, and care to distinguish the arbitrary marks by which [blank] are designated from the [blank] themselves. . . .

We are ourselves then depositories of the evidence of the subject which we consider.

DIFFICULTY OF ANALYZING THE HUMAN MIND

If it were possible that a person should give a faithful history of his being from the earliest epochs of his recollection, a picture would be presented such as the world has never contemplated before. A mirror would be held up to all men in which they might behold their own recollections and, in dim perspective, their shadowy hopes and fears—all that they dare not, or that daring and desiring, they could not expose to the open eyes of day. But thought can with difficulty visit the intricate and winding chambers which it inhabits. It is like a river whose rapid and perpetual stream flows outwards—like one in dread who speeds through the recesses of some haunted pile and dares not look behind. The caverns of the mind are obscure and shadowy; or pervaded with a lustre, beautifully bright indeed, but shining not beyond their portals. If it were possible to be where we have been, vitally and indeed—if, at the moment of our presence there, we could define the results of our experience—if the passage from sensation to reflection—from a state of passive perception to voluntary contemplation were not so dizzying and so tumultuous, this attempt would be less difficult.

HOW THE ANALYSIS SHOULD BE CARRIED ON

Most of the errors of philosophers have arisen from considering the human being in a point of view too detailed and circumscribed. He is not a moral and an intellectual—but also and pre-eminently an imaginative being.[13] His own mind is his law; his own mind is all things to him. If we would arrive at any knowledge which should be serviceable from the practical conclusions to which it leads, we ought to consider the mind of man and the universe as the great whole on which to exercise our speculations. Here, above all, verbal disputes ought to be laid aside, though this has long been their chosen field of battle. It imports little to inquire whether thought be distinct from the objects of thought.[14] The use of the words *external* and *internal,* as applied to the establishment of this distinction, has been the symbol and the source of much dispute. This is merely an affair of words and

as the dispute deserves, to say, that when speaking of the objects of thought, we indeed only describe one of the forms of thought— or that, speaking of thought, we only apprehend one of the operations of the universal system of beings. Among the great philosophers who . . . .

THE SCIENCE OF MORALS

The misguided imaginations of men have rendered the ascertaining of what *is not true* the principal direct service which metaphysical enquiry can bestow upon moral science. Moral science itself is the doctrine of the voluntary actions of man as a sentient and social being. These actions depend on the thoughts in his mind. But there is a mass of popular opinion from which the most enlightened persons are seldom wholly free, into the truth or falsehood of which, it is incumbent on us to inquire before we can arrive at any firm conclusions as to the conduct which we ought to pursue in the regulation of our own minds, or toward our fellow-beings or before we can ascertain the elementary laws according to which these thoughts from which these actions flow are originally combined.

The object of the forms according to which human society is administered is the happiness of the individuals composing the communities which they regard, and these forms are perfect or imperfect in proportion to the degree in which they promote this end.[15]

This object is not merely the quantity of happiness enjoyed by individuals as sensitive beings but the mode in which it should be distributed among them as social beings. It is not enough, if such a coincidence can be conceived of as possible, that one person or class of persons should enjoy the highest happiness, while another is suffering a dis-

---

13. Hume exalts the imagination over the understanding. See *An Enquiry Concerning the Human Understanding. Selections,* pp. 107-115. Also pp. 137-143. See also the same author *A Treatise* (Everyman edition), 2.135-142.

14. See Hume, *Selections,* pp. 175-182.
15. For a similar idea see Hume's *An Enquiry Concerning the Principles of Morals,* Sec. III. The same thought is expressed by Paine in *The Rights of Man.* See also Godwin's *Political Justice,* 1.1-119.

proportionate degree of misery. It is necessary that material happiness produced by the common efforts and preserved by the common care should be distributed according to the just claims of each individual; if not, although the quantity produced should be the same, the end of society would remain unfulfilled. The object is in a compound proportion to the quantity of happiness produced, and the correspondence of the mode in which it is distributed to the elementary feelings of man as a social being.[16]

The disposition in an individual to promote this object is called virtue; and the two constituent parts of virtue, benevolence and justice, are correlative with these two portions of the only true object of all the voluntary actions of a human being. Benevolence is the desire to be the author of good, and justice the apprehension of the manner in which good ought to be done.[17]

Justice and benevolence result from the elementary laws of the human mind.[18]

ON THE NATURE OF VIRTUE

Sect. 1. General View of the Nature and Objects of Virtue. (2) The Origin and Basis of Virtue as founded on the elementary Principles of Mind. (3) The Laws which flow from the nature of Mind regulating the application of those principles to human actions. (4) Virtue, a possible attribute of man.

We exist in the midst of a multitude of beings like ourselves, upon whose happiness most of our actions exert some obvious and decisive influence.

The regulation of this influence is the object of moral science.

We know that we are susceptible of receiving painful or pleasurable impressions of greater or less intensity and duration. That is called good which produces pleasure; that is called evil which produce pain.[19] These are general names, applicable to every class of causes, from which an overbalance of pain or pleasure may result. But when a human being is the active instrument of generating or diffusing happiness, the principle through which it is most effectually instrumental to that purpose is called virtue. And benevolence, or the desire to be the author of good, united with justice, or an apprehension of the manner in which that good is to be done, constitutes virtue.

But, wherefore should a man be benevolent and just? The immediate emotions of his nature, especially in its most inartificial state, prompt him to inflict pain and to arrogate dominion. He desires to heap superfluities to his own store, although others perish with famine. He is propelled to guard against the smallest invasion of his own liberty, though he reduces others to a condition of the most pitiless servitude. He is revengeful, proud, and selfish. Wherefore should he curb these propensities?

It is inquired for what reason a human being should engage in procuring the happiness, or refrain from producing the pain, of another? When a reason is required to prove

16. This paragraph appears to be a recasting of a portion of the Note on "Even love is sold," in *Queen Mab*. Compare this with the Marxist philosophy.

17. This idea of benevolence and justice follows Hume very closely. See *An Enquiry Concerning the Principles of Morals*, Secs. II and III. Note that Shelley was also acquainted with similar treatments by Reid and Stewart. Cf. Shelley's discussion of the same subject in *Proposals for An Association* and *Letter to Lord Ellenborough*.

18. At this point in the manuscript Shelley jotted down the following note: "An essay on the progressive excellence perceptible in the expressions— of Solomon, Homer, Bion and the Seven Sages, Socrates, Plato, Theodorus, Zeno, Carneades, Aris-

totle, Epicurus, Pythagoras, Cicero, Tacitus, Jesus Christ, Virgil, Lucan, Seneca, Epictetus, Antoninus . . . Sulpicius, Severus, Mahomet, Manes, The Fathers—Ari[o]sto, Tasso, Petrarch, Dante, Abeillard, Thomas Aquinas—The Schoolmen. The reformers. Spinoza, Bayle, Paschal, Locke, Berkeley, Leibnitz, Malebranche. The French Philosophers, Voltaire, Rousseau, the Germans—the Illuminati —Hume. Godwin—State of General Society. Perfectibility."

19. Shelley perhaps found this simple definition in Locke's *Essay*, 1.185; 210; 325. Of course, many of the later philosophers held the same idea. See Hume's *Treatise* (Everyman edition), 2.178-190. Shelley makes use of the same concept in *A Refutation of Deism*.

the necessity of adopting any system of conduct, what is it that the objector demands?
He requires proof of that system of conduct
being such as will most effectually promote
the happiness of mankind. To demonstrate
this is to render a moral reason. Such is the
object of virtue.

A common sophism which, like many
others, depends on the abuse of a metaphorical expression to a literal purpose, has produced much of the confusion which has
involved the theory of morals. It is said that
no person is bound to be just or kind, if, on
his neglect, he should fail to incur some
penalty. Duty is obligation. There can be
no obligation without an obliger. Virtue is
a law to which it is the will of the lawgiver
that we should conform, which will we
should in no manner be bound to obey,
unless some dreadful punishment were attached to disobedience. This is the philosophy of slavery and superstition.[20]

In fact no person can be *bound* or *obliged*
without some power preceding to bind and
oblige.[21] If I observe a man bound hand
and foot, I know that some one bound him.
But if I observe him returning self-satisfied
from the performance of some action by
which he has been the willing author of
extensive benefit, I do not infer that the
anticipation of hellish agonies, or the hope
of heavenly reward, has constrained him to
sacrifice. . . . [A leaf of the manuscript is
missing here.]

. . . question itself proceeds upon a mistake of the terms of the proposition which it
contains. It remains to be stated in what
manner the sensations which constitute the
basis of virtue originate in the human mind;
what are the laws which it receives there;
how far the principles of mind allow it to
be an attribute of a human being; and, lastly,
what is the probability of persuading mankind to adopt it as a universal and systematic
motive of conduct.

20. See Reid, *Philosophy of the Active Powers*,
2.643, for a similar discussion.

BENEVOLENCE

There is a class of emotions which we instinctively avoid. A human being, such as is
man considered in his origin, a child a
month old, has a very imperfect consciousness of the existence of other natures resembling itself. All the energies of its being are
directed to the extinction of the pains with
which it is perpetually assailed. At length
it [attains to a knowledge] that it is surrounded by natures susceptible of sensations
similar to its own. It is very late before children attain to this knowledge. If a child
observes, without emotion, its nurse or its
mother suffering acute pain, it is attributable
rather to ignorance than insensibility. So
soon as the accents and gestures, significant
of pain, are referred to the feelings which
they express, they awaken in the mind of
the beholder a desire that they should cease.
Pain is thus apprehended to be evil for its
own sake, without any other necessary reference to the mind by which [its existence is
perceived than] such as is indispensable to its
perception. The tendencies of our original
sensations, indeed, all have for their object
the preservation of our individual being. But
these are passive and unconscious. In proportion as the mind acquires an active
power, the empire of these tendencies becomes limited. (Everyone has experience of
the fact that to sympathize with the sufferings of another is to enjoy a transitory oblivion of his own.) Thus an infant, a savage,
and a solitary beast is selfish, because its
mind is incapable [of] receiving an accurate
intimation of the nature of pain as existing
in beings resembling itself. The inhabitant
of a highly civilized community will more
acutely sympathize with the sufferings and
enjoyments of others than the inhabitant of
a society of a less degree of civilization. He
who shall have cultivated his intellectual
powers by familiarity with the finest speci-

21. See Hume's *A Treatise on Human Nature*
(Everyman edition), 2.221.

mens of poetry and philosophy will usually [sympathize more] than one engaged in the less refined functions of manual labor.

The imagination thus acquires by exercise a habit as it were of perceiving and abhorring evil, however remote from the immediate sphere of sensations with which that individual mind is conversant. Imagination or mind employed in prophetically [imaging forth] its objects is that faculty of human nature on which every gradation of its progress, nay, every, the minutest, change depends. Pain or pleasure, if subtly analyzed, will be found to consist entirely in prospect. The only distinction between the selfish man and the virtuous man is that the imagination of the former is confined within a narrow limit, while that of the latter embraces a comprehensive circumference. In this sense wisdom and virtue may be said to be inseparable and criteria of each other. Selfishness is thus the offspring of ignorance and mistake; it is the portion of unreflecting infancy and savage solitude, or of those whom toil or evil occupations have [blunted and rendered torpid]; disinterested benevolence is the product of a cultivated imagination and has an intimate connection with all the arts which add ornament, or dignity, or power, or stability to the social state of man. Virtue is thus entirely a refinement of civilized life, a creation of the human mind, or, rather a combination which it has made according to elementary rules contained within itself of the feelings suggested by the relations established between man and man.

All the theories which have refined and exalted humanity, or those which have been devised as alleviations of its mistakes and evils, have been based upon [the elementary emotions of] disinterestedness which we feel to constitute the majesty of our nature. Patriotism, as it existed in the ancient republics, was never as has been supposed a calculation of personal advantages. When Mutius Scaevola thrust his hand into the burning coals, and Regulus returned to Carthage, and Epicharis sustained the rack silently, in the torments of which she knew that she would speedily perish rather than betray the conspirators to the tyrant; these illustrious persons certainly made [a] small estimate of their private interest. If it be said that they sought posthumous fame, instances are not wanting in history which prove that men have even defied infamy for the sake of good. But there is a great error in the world with respect to the selfishness of fame. It is certainly possible that a person should seek distinction as a medium of personal gratification. But the love of fame is frequently no more than a desire that the feelings of others should confirm, illustrate, and sympathize with our own.[22] In this respect it is allied with all that draws us out of ourselves. It is the "last infirmity of noble minds."[23] Chivalry was likewise founded on the theory of self-sacrifice. Love possesses so extraordinary a power over the human heart, only because disinterestedness is united with the natural propensities. These propensities themselves are comparatively impotent in cases where the imagination of pleasure to be given, as well as to be received, does not enter into the account. Let it not be objected that patriotism, and chivalry, and sentimental love, have been the fountains of enormous mischief. They are cited only to establish the proposition that according to the elementary principles of mind man is capable of desiring and pursuing good for its own sake.

JUSTICE

The benevolent propensities are thus inherent in the human mind. We are impelled to seek the happiness of others.[24] We experience a satisfaction in being the authors of

22. Compare this sentence with the *Essay on Love*, paragraph 2.
23. Misquoted from Milton's *Lycidas*. Correct:
"That last infirmity of noble mind."
24. See Stewart's *Outlines of Moral Philosophy*, 1.79.

that happiness. Everything that lives is open to impressions of pleasure and pain. We are led by our benevolent propensities to regard every human being indifferently with whom we come in contact. They have preference only with respect to those who offer themselves most obviously to our notice. Human beings are indiscriminating and blind; they will avoid inflicting pain, though that pain should be attended with eventual benefit; they will seek to confer pleasure without calculating the mischief that may result. They benefit one at the expense of many.

There is a sentiment in the human mind that regulates benevolence in its application as a principle of action. This is the sense of justice. Justice, as well as benevolence, is an elementary law of human nature. It is through this principle that men are impelled to distribute any means of pleasure which benevolence may suggest the communication of to others, in equal portions among an equal number of applicants. If ten men are shipwrecked on a desert island, they distribute whatever subsistence may remain to them into equal portions among themselves. If six of them conspire to deprive the remaining four of their share, their conduct is termed unjust.

The existence of pain has been shown to be a circumstance which the human mind regards with dissatisfaction, and of which it desires the cessation. It is equally according to its nature to desire that the advantages to be enjoyed by a limited number of persons should be enjoyed equally by all. This proposition is supported by the evidence of indisputable facts. Tell some ungarbled tale of a number of persons being made the victims of the enjoyments of one, and he who would appeal in favor of any system which might produce such an evil to the primary emotions of our nature would have nothing to reply. Let two persons, equally strangers, make application for some benefit in the possession of the other to bestow, and

he feels that they have equal claim. They are both sensitive beings; pleasure and pain affect them alike.

[THE GENERAL SCOPE OF THIS TREATISE]

It is foreign to the general scope of this little Treatise to encumber a simple argument by controverting any of the trite objections of habit or fanaticism. But there are two: the first, the basis of all political mistake, and the second, the prolific cause and effect of religious error, which it seems useful to refute.

First, it is enquired, ["Wherefore should a man be benevolent and just?" The answer has been given in the preceding chapter]. If a man persists to inquire why he ought to promote the happiness of mankind, he demands a mathematical or metaphysical reason for a moral action.[25] The absurdity of this scepticism is more apparent, but not less real than the exacting a moral reason for a mathematical or metaphysical fact. If any person should refuse to admit that all the radii of a circle are of equal length, or that human actions are necessarily determined by motives, until it could be proved that these radii and these actions uniformly tended to the production of the greatest general good, who would not wonder at the unreasonable and capricious association of his ideas?

The writer of a philosophical treatise may, I imagine, at this advanced era of human intellect be held excused from entering into a controversy with those reasoners, if such there are, who would claim an exemption from its decrees in favor of any one among those diversified systems of obscure opinion respecting morals which, under the name of religions, have in various ages and countries obtained among mankind. Besides that if, as these reasoners have pretended, eternal torture or happiness will ensue as the conse-

---

25. This sentence with slight changes is in

A Refutation of Deism. See Locke's *Essay,* 2.263, for a similar idea.

quence of certain actions, we should be no nearer the possession of a standard to determine what actions were right and wrong, even if this pretended revelation, which is by no means the case, had furnished us with a complete catalogue of them. The character of actions, as virtuous or vicious, would by no means be determined alone by the personal advantage or disadvantage of each moral agent individually considered. Indeed, an action is often virtuous in proportion to the greatness of the personal calamity which the author willingly draws upon himself by daring to perform it. It is because an action produces an overbalance of pleasure or pain to sentient beings, and not merely because its consequences are beneficent or injurious to the author of that action that it is good or evil.[26] Nay, this latter consideration has a tendency to pollute the purity of virtue, inasmuch as it consists in the motive rather than in the consequences of an action. A person who should labor for the happiness of mankind lest he should be tormented eternally in Hell would with reference to that motive possess as little claim to the epithet of virtuous as he who should torture, imprison, and burn them alive, a more usual and natural consequence of such principles, for the sake of the enjoyments of Heaven.[27]

My neighbor presuming on his strength may direct me to perform or to refrain from a particular action indicating a certain arbitrary penalty in the event of disobedience within his power to inflict. My action if modified by his menaces can in no degree participate in virtue. He has afforded me no criterion as to what is right or wrong. A king, or an assembly of men, may publish a proclamation affixing any penalty to any particular action, [but that is not immoral because such penalty is affixed]. Nothing is more evident than that the epithet of virtue is inapplicable to the refraining from

that action on account of the evil arbitrarily attached to it. If the action is in itself beneficial, virtue would rather consist in not refraining from it, but in firmly defying the personal consequences attached to its performance.

Some usurper of supernatural energy might subdue the whole globe to his power; he might possess new and unheard-of resources for induing his punishments with the most terrible attributes of pain. The torments of his victims might be intense in their degree and protracted to an infinite duration. Still the "will of the lawgiver" would afford no surer criterion as to what actions were right or wrong. It would only increase the possible virtue of those who refuse to become the instruments of his [tyranny].[28]

MORAL SCIENCE CONSISTS IN CONSIDERING THE DIFFERENCE, NOT THE RESEMBLANCE, OF PERSONS

The internal influence derived from the constitution of the mind from which they flow produces that peculiar modification of actions which makes them intrinsically good or evil. [The manuscript at this point is fragmentary and shows considerable revision.]

To attain an apprehension of the importance of this distinction, let us visit in imagination the proceedings of some metropolis. Consider the multitude of human beings who inhabit it and survey in thought the actions of the several classes into which they are divided. Their obvious actions are apparently uniform; the stability of human society seems to be maintained sufficiently by the uniformity of the conduct of its members, both with regard to themselves, and with regard to others. The laborer arises at

26. Compare Spinoza's *Ethics* (Everyman edition), p. 149.
27. This idea is in the letter to Hogg, April 24, 1811, and those to Elizabeth Hitchener, November 12 and December 11, 1811.

28. The substance of the last two paragraphs may be found in *A Refutation of Deism* and the *Letter to Lord Ellenborough*. The letters for the last six months of 1811 contain the same ideas as those in this treatise on morals.

a certain hour and applies himself to the task enjoined him. The functionaries of government and law are regularly employed in their offices and courts. The trader holds a train of conduct from which he never deviates. The ministers of religion employ an accustomed language and maintain a decent and equable regard. The army is drawn forth; the motions of every soldier are such as they were expected to be; the general commands, and his words are echoed from troop to troop. The domestic actions of men are, for the most part, undistinguishable one from the other, at a superficial glance. The actions which are classed under the general appellation of marriage, education, friendship, &c., are perpetually going on and, [on] a superficial glance, are similar one to the other.

But, if we would see the truth of things, they must be stripped of this fallacious appearance of uniformity. In truth no one action has, when considered in its whole extent, an essential resemblance with any other. Each individual who composes the vast multitude which we have been contemplating has a peculiar frame of mind, which, while the features of the great mass of his actions remain uniform, impresses the minuter lineaments with its peculiar hues. Thus, while his life, as a whole, is like the lives of other men, in detail it is most unlike; and the more sub-divided the actions become, that is, the more they enter into that class which have a vital influence on the happiness of others and his own, so much the more are they distinct from those of other men.

"Those little, nameless, unremembered acts Of kindness and of love,"[29] as well as those deadly outrages which are inflicted by a look, a word—or less—the very refraining from some faint and most evanescent expression of countenance; these flow from a profounder source than the series of our habitual conduct, which, it has been already said, derives its origin from without. These are the actions and such as these which make human life what it is and are the fountains of all the good and evil with which its entire surface is so widely and impartially overspread, and though they are called minute, they are called so in compliance with the blindness of those who cannot estimate their importance. It is in the due appreciating the general effects of their peculiarities and in cultivating the habit of acquiring decisive knowledge respecting the tendencies arising out of [them] in particular cases that the most important part of moral science consists. [The] deepest abyss of this vast and multitudinous cavern, it is necessary that we should visit.

This is the difference between social and individual man. Not that this distinction is to be considered definite, or characteristic of one human being as compared with another. It denotes rather two classes of agency common in a degree to every human being. None is exempt indeed from that species of influence which affects, as it were the surface of his being and gives the specific outline to his conduct. Almost all that which is ostensible submits to that legislature created by the general representation of the past feelings of mankind—imperfect as it is from a variety of causes, as it exists in the government, the religion, and domestic habits—those who do not nominally, yet actually, submit to the same power. The external features of their conduct, indeed, can no more escape it than the clouds can escape from the stream of the wind; and his opinion which he often hopes he has dispassionately secured from all contagion of prejudice and vulgarity would be found on examination to be the inevitable excrescence of the very usages from which he vehemently dissents. Internally all is conducted otherwise; the efficiency, the essence, the vitality [of actions,] derives its color from what is no wise contributed to from any external source. Like the plant which, while it derives the accident of its size and shape from the soil

29. From Wordsworth's *Tintern Abbey*, lines 34-35.

in which it springs and is cankered, or distorted, or inflated, [yet] retains those qualities which essentially divide it from all others; so that hemlock continues to be poison, and the violet does not cease to emit its odor in whatever soil it may grow.

We consider our own nature too superficially. We look on all that in ourselves with which we can discover a resemblance in others and consider those resemblances as the materials of moral knowledge. It is in the differences that it actually consists.

CATALOGUE OF THE PHENOMENA OF DREAMS, AS CONNECTING SLEEPING AND WAKING

[The fragment on Dreams is not in the Bodleian manuscript containing the fragments on morals and metaphysics, but Mary Shelley in her 1840 edition inserted the piece as an integral part of the essay. It is here placed at the end of the *Treatise* as having some possible connection with that work. Mrs. Shelley's note at the end—following Shelley's own note that, "Here I was obliged to leave off, overcome by thrilling horrors,"—records: "This remark closes this fragment, which was written in 1815."]

I. Let us reflect on our infancy, and give as faithfully as possible a relation of the events of sleep.

And first I am bound to present a faithful picture of my own peculiar nature relative to sleep. I do not doubt that were every individual to imitate me, it would be found that among many circumstances peculiar to their individual nature, a sufficiently general resemblance would be found to prove the connection existing between those peculiarities and the most universal phenomena. I shall employ caution, indeed, as to the facts which I state, that they contain nothing false or exaggerated. But they contain no more than certain elucidations of my own nature; concerning the degree in which it resembles, or differs from, that of others, I am by no means accurately aware. It is sufficient, however, to caution the reader against drawing general inferences from particular instances.

I omit the general instances of delusion in fever or delirium, as well as mere dreams considered in themselves. A delineation of this subject, however inexhaustible and interesting, is to be passed over.

What is the connection of sleeping and of waking?

II. I distinctly remember dreaming three several times, between intervals of two or more years, the same precise dream. It was not so much what is ordinarily called a dream; the single image, unconnected with all other images, of a youth who was educated at the same school with myself, presented itself in sleep. Even now, after the lapse of many years, I can never hear the name of this youth, without the three places where I dreamed of him presenting themselves distinctly to my mind.

III. In dreams, images acquire association peculiar to dreaming; so that the idea of a particular house, when it recurs a second time in dreams, will have relation with the idea of the same house, in the first time, of a nature entirely different from that which the house excites, when seen or thought of in relation to waking ideas.

IV. I have beheld scenes, with the intimate and unaccountable connection of which with the obscure parts of my own nature, I have been irresistibly impressed. I have beheld a scene which has produced no unusual effect on my thoughts. After the lapse of many years I have dreamed of this scene. It has hung on my memory; it has haunted my thoughts at intervals with the pertinacity of an object connected with human affections. I have visited this scene again. Neither the dream could be dissociated from the landscape, not the landscape from the dream, nor feelings, such as neither singly could have awakened, from both. But the most remarkable event of this nature which ever occurred to me happened five years ago at Oxford. I was walking with a friend in the neighborhood of that city engaged in earnest and interesting conversation. We suddenly turned the corner of a lane, and the view which its high banks and hedges had concealed presented itself. The view consisted of a windmill, standing in one among many plashy meadows, inclosed with stone walls; the irregular and broken ground between the wall and the road on which we stood; a long low hill behind the windmill, and a grey covering of uniform cloud spread over the evening sky. It was that season when the last leaf had just fallen from the scant and stunted ash. The scene surely was a common scene; the season and the hour little calculated to kindle lawless thought; it was a tame uninteresting assemblage of objects, such as would drive the imagination for refuge in serious and sober talk, to the evening fireside and the dessert of winter fruits and wine. The effect which it produced on me was not such as could have been expected. I suddenly remembered to have seen that exact scene in some dream of long[1]—.

1. *Here I was obliged to leave off, overcome by thrilling horror.* This remark closes this fragment, which was written in 1815. I remember well his coming to me from writing it, pale and agitated, to seek refuge in conversation from the fearful emotions it excited. No man, as these fragments prove, had such keen sensations as Shelley. His nervous temperament was wound up by the delicacy of his health to an intense degree of sensibility, and while his active mind pondered for ever upon, and drew conclusions from his sensations, his reveries increased their vivacity, till they mingled with, and made one with thought, and both became absorbing and tumultous, even to physical pain. [Mary Shelley's Note.]

THE ELYSIAN FIELDS: A LUCIANIC FRAGMENT

[The date of *The Elysian Fields: A Lucianic Fragment* is unknown, but it was probably 1818-1820. It gives an account of what the departed dead in their Elysian abode are contemplating. They are concerned there as they were here with the same problems and ideas which disturbed them on earth—death, immortality, religion, and politics. There can be little doubt that Shelley intended the essay to be a warning to the Prince of Wales, soon to be King of England, to do something about the deplored social and political conditions of his country.]

I am not forgetful in this dreary scene of the country which whilst I lived in the upper air, it was my whole aim to illustrate and render happy. Indeed, although immortal, we are not exempted from the enjoyments and the sufferings of mortality. We sympathize in all the proceedings of mankind and we experience joy or grief in all intelligence from them according to our various opinions and views. Nor do we resign those opinions, even those which the grave has utterly refuted. Frederick of Prussia has lately arrived among us and persists in maintaining that "death is an eternal sleep," to the great discomfiture of Philip the Second of Spain who on the furies refusing to apply the torture, expects the roof of Tartarus to fall upon his head, and laments that at least in his particular instances the doctrine shall be false. Religion is more frequently the subject of discussion among the departed dead than any other topic, for we know as little which mode of faith is true as you do. Every one maintains the doctrine he maintained on Earth and accommodates the appearances which surround us to his peculiar tenets.

I am one of those who esteeming political science capable of certain conclusions have ever preferred it to these airy speculations which, when they assume an empire over the passions of mankind, render them so mischievous and unextinguishable that they subsist even among the dead. The art of employing the power entrusted to you for the benefit of those who entrust it is something more definite and subject as all its details must ever be to innumerable limitations and exceptions arising out of the change in the habits, opinions of mankind, is the noblest, and the greatest, and the most universal of all. It is not as a queen, but as a human being that this science must be learned; the same discipline which contributes to domestic happiness and individual distinction secures true welfare and genuine glory to a nation.

You will start, I do not doubt, to hear the language of philosophy.[1] You will have been informed that those who approach sovereigns with warnings that they have duties to perform, that they are elevated above the rest of mankind simply to prevent their tearing one another to pieces, and for the purpose of putting into effect all practical equality and justice, are insidious traitors who devise their ruin. But if the character which I bore on earth should not reassure you, it would be well to recollect the circumstances under which you will ascend the throne of England, and what is the spirit of the times. These are better examples to emulate than those who have only refrained from depraving or tyrannizing over their subjects, because they remembered the fates of Pisistratus and Tarquin. If generosity and virtue should have dominion over your actions, my lessons can hardly be needed; but if the discipline of a narrow education may have extinguished all thirst of genuine excellence, all desire of becoming illustrious for the sake of the illustriousness of the actions which I would incite you to perform—should you be thus—and no pains have been spared to make you so—make your account with holding your crown on this condition: of deserving it alone. And that this may be evident I will expose to you the state in which the nation will be found at your accession, for the very dead know more than the counsellors by whom you will be surrounded.

The English nation does not, as has been imagined, inherit freedom from its ancestors. Public opinion rather than positive institution maintains it in whatever portion it may now possess, which is in truth the acquirement of their own incessant struggles. And yet the gradations by which this freedom has advanced have been contested step by step.

---

1. If this is addressed to the Prince of Wales on the occasion of his approaching the accession to the throne, then our date above seems correct. The Prince succeeded to the throne on January 29, 1820, as George IV.

ESSAY ON CHRISTIANITY

[The date of composition of this essay is unknown. The fragment—the work was never completed—is in a notebook, now in the Bodleian Library, amidst materials known to have been written between 1813 *(A Refutation of Deism)* and 1819 *(A Passage of the Apennines).* Both internal and external evidence points to an early date, probably 1812-1815. The subject-matter and the peculiarities of style very closely parallel the letters and other productions known to have been written in that period. Most Shelley scholars, however, give dates ranging from 1815-1819.

Since the material in the manuscript notebook and in the published version is not in orderly sequence, I have endeavored to give the whole as logical order as the fragmentary nature of the work would permit. For a detailed statement of the condition of the manuscript, see A. H. Koszul's *Shelley's Prose in the Bodleian Manuscripts* (Oxford Press, 1910). Two fragments closely related to the Essay are here placed at the end of the main essay.

It was first published by Lady Shelley in *Shelley Memorials* in 1859 as *Essay on Christianity.* It is my opinion that the essay is an early draft of the *Biblical Extracts,* which Shelley is known to have composed and sent to Hookham in 1812. We learn of *Biblical Extracts* first in a letter to Miss Hitchener, February 27, 1812, just after his first arrival in Ireland. He writes: "I have met with some waverers between Christianity and Deism. I shall attempt to make them reject all the bad, and take all the good, of the Jewish books. I have often thought that the moral sayings of Jesus Christ might be very useful, if selected from the mystery and immorality which surround them; it is a little work I have in contemplation." The "little work" was done by December 17, when he wrote to Hookham: "You will receive the 'Biblical Extracts' in a day or two." And on January 2, 1813, he was urging his publisher to hasten with the work, for "small Christmas or *Easter offering* of a neat little book have frequently a surprising effect."

We hear no more of the *Biblical Extracts.* Hookham would hardly have dared to publish it as Christmas or Easter offerings, for there was too much dynamite in it. The essay is mainly a compilation of eleven extracts from the moral teachings of Jesus. Each extract is followed by a commentary in which Shelley strips away "the mystery and immorality," and frequently bolsters up a statement by Jesus with substantiating evidence from some great philosopher. Clearly the essay answers to a compilation of the sayings of Jesus, and not to an essay on Christianity. It is a curious fact that no one has apparently ever suspected that the so-called essay and the *Biblical Extracts* might be identical. In an article of mine in *Modern Language Notes* LXVI, (Nov. 1951, 435-441), I give support to this theory by pointing out that the thought and phraseology of the letters and pamphlets of 1810-1813 closely parallel those of the essay. Furthermore, in that article I endeavor to show that the ideas of the essay come more or less directly from the authors which Shelley was known to be reading during 1810-1813.

Shelley's early letters and essays are replete with statements that the only true religion is that of philanthropy and benevolence. "Anything short of complete charity with all men," wrote Shelley in *An Address* (1812), "on which . . . Jesus Christ principally insisted, is wrong." The early Christians practiced this creed, but after the first glow of enthusiasm faded, people again became envious and avaricious. It failed because moral improvement did not precede the system. Shelley in his letters and pamphlets of 1811-1813 insisted that a *moral* revolution must precede political improvement.

"Such," then, says Shelley, "appear to have been the fundamental doctrines of Jesus Christ. It is not too much to assert that they have been the doctrines of every just and compassionate mind that ever speculated on the social nature of man."

We see in this essay that Shelley was concerned, as he knew Jesus had been primarily concerned, with the social and moral welfare of the people. He everywhere insisted that love and sympathy are the basis of all right living. This, Shelley maintained, is the central ethical doctrine of Jesus.]

The Being who has influenced in the most memorable manner the opinions and the fortunes of the human species is Jesus Christ. At this day his name is connected with the devotional feelings of two hundred millions of the race of man. The institutions of the most civilized portion of the globe derive their authority from the sanction of his doctrines. He is the God of our popular religion. His extraordinary genius, the wide and rapid effect of his unexampled doctrines, his invincible gentleness and benignity, the devoted love borne to him by his adherents suggested a persuasion to them that he was something divine. The supernatural events which the historians of this wonderful man subsequently asserted to have been connected with every gradation of his career established the opinion. His death is said to have been accompanied by an accumulation of tremendous prodigies. Utter darkness fell upon the earth, blotting the noonday sun, dead bodies arising from their graves walked through the public streets, and an earthquake shook the astonished city, rending the rocks of the surrounding mountains. The philosophers may attribute the application of these events *to*

the death of a reformer or the events themselves to a visitation of that Universal Pan who [At this point are two blank pages in the manuscript. What follows here through the paragraph beginning "The national religion" is in Julian, 6.227-228.] may be a God or man. It is the profound wisdom and the comprehensive morality of his doctrines which essentially distinguished him from the crowd of martyrs and of patriots who have exulted to devote themselves for what they conceived would contribute to the benefit of their fellowmen.

The birth of Christ occurred at a period which may be considered as a crisis the most stupendous and memorable in the progress of the human race. The splendor of the Roman name, the vital spirit of the Roman power had vanished. A race of despicable usurpers had assumed the dominion of the world power and was no longer distributed but as the price of the basest artifices of slavery. Sentiments of liberty and heroism no longer lived but in the lamentations of those who had felt, but had survived their influence. Even from these they were speedily effaced. Accumulations of wealth and power were inordinately great. The most abject of mankind, freedmen, eunuchs, and every species of satellite attendant on a court became invested with inexhaustible resources. The consequences of this system speedily became manifest, and they accurately corresponded to the pernicious character of their cause. Refinement in arts and letters, distorted from its national tendency to promote benevolence and truth, became subservient to lust and luxury. All communication among human beings was vitiated and polluted in its sources. The prosperity of the republic no longer excited disinterested care. The intercourse of man with man was that of tyrant with slave, the one stipulating as the price of his submission, the other as the prerogation of his superiority, some personal advantage. Selfishness became a system whose gradations were so nicely ascertained that the balance never unturned to the smallest disadvantage of the estimator. And as intellectual objects betray their presence more readily in situations of self-sacrifice, sensual pleasures occupied the interest of mankind. Hence those persons who occupied the most eminent stations in society, public opinions having lost its value, became habituated to the most monstrous and complicated perversities of appetite and sentiment. The national affections were first destroyed, the domestic affections now vanished away; man lived like a beast of prey among his fellowmen, uniting more than a serpent's cunning to its deadliest malignity and venom.

The meanwhile other effects indirectly favorable to the progress of mankind sprung from the same causes.[1] Good and evil subsist in so intimate an union that few situations of human affairs can be affirmed to contain either of the principles in an unconnected state.

The national religion of the Roman republic perished when Rome lost the character and privileges of a nation. It was incorporated with the ceremonies and institutions of a free people, and disjoined from these lost the. . . .

It cannot be precisely ascertained [in] what degree Jesus Christ accommodated his doctrines to the opinions of his auditors, or in what degree he really said all that he is related to have said. He has left no written record of himself and we are compelled to judge from the imperfect and obscure information which his biographers, persons certainly of very undisciplined and undiscriminating minds, have transmitted to posterity. These writers, our only guides, impute sentiments to Jesus Christ which flatly contradict each other. They represent him as narrow, superstitious, or exquisitely vindictive and malicious. They insert in the midst of a strain of impassioned eloquence, or sagest exhortation, a sentiment only remarkable for its naked and drivelling folly. But it is not difficult to distinguish the inventions by which these historians have filled up the interstices of tradition, or corrupted the simplicity of truth, from the real character of the object of their rude amazement. They have left sufficiently clear indications of the genuine character of Jesus Christ to rescue it forever from the imputations cast upon it by their ignorance and fanaticism. We discover that he is the enemy of oppression and of falsehood, that he is the advocate of equal justice, that he is neither disposed to sanction bloodshed or deceit under whatsoever pretences their practice may be vindicated. We discover that he was a man of meek and majestic demeanor, calm in danger, of natural and simple thought and habits, beloved to adoration by his adherents, unmoved and solemn and serene. It is utterly incredible that this man said that if you hated your enemy you would find it to your account to return him good for evil, since by such temporary oblivion of vengeance you would heap coals of fire upon his head. Where such contradictions occur, a favorable construction is

1. The dominion which Rome had usurped over the civilized world was essentially iniquitious. It was procured by a series of aggressions, and preserved by sanguinary despotism. [Shelley's Note.]

warranted by the general innocence of manners and comprehensiveness of views which he is represented to possess.[2]

The rule of criticism to be adopted in judging of the life, actions, and words of a man who has acted any conspicuous part in the revolutions of the world should not be narrow. We ought to form a general image of his character and of his doctrines, and refer to this whole the distinct portions of actions and of speech by which they are diversified. It is not here asserted that no contradictions are to be admitted to have place in the system of Jesus Christ, between doctrines promulgated in different states of feeling or information, or even such as are implied in the enunciation of a scheme of thought various and obscure through its immensity and depth. It is not asserted that no degree of human indignation ever hurried him beyond the limits which his calmer mood had placed to disapprobation against vice and folly. Those deviations from the history of his life are alone to be vindicated which represent his own essential character in contradiction with itself. Every human mind has what Lord Bacon calls its *idola specus*,[3] peculiar images which reside in the inner cave of thought. These constitute the essential and distinctive character of every human being, to which every action and every word bears intimate relation, and by which in depicturing a character the genuineness and meaning of those words and actions are to be determined. Every fanatic or enemy of virtue is not at liberty to misrepresent the greatest geniuses and the most heroic defenders of all that is valuable in this mortal world. His story to gain any credit must contain some truth, and that truth shall thus be made a sufficient indication of his prejudice and his deceit.

With respect to the miracles which these biographers have related, I have already declined to enter into any discussion on their

nature or their existence. The supposition of their falsehood or their truth would modify in no degree the hues of the picture which is attempted to be delineated. To judge truly of the moral and philosophical character of Socrates it is not necessary to determine the question of the familiar Spirit which it is supposed that he believed to attend him. The power of the human mind relatively to intercourse with or dominion over the invisible world is doubtless an interesting theme of discussion, but the connection of the instance of Jesus Christ with the established religion of the country in which I write renders it dangerous to subject oneself to the imputation of introducing new gods or abolishing old ones, nor is the duty of mutual forbearance sufficiently understood to render it certain that the metaphysician and the moralist, even though he carefully sacrifice a cock to Esculapius, may not receive something analogous to the bowl of hemlock for the reward of his labors.

Much, however, of what his biographers have asserted is not to be rejected merely because inferences inconsistent with the general spirit of his system are to be deduced from its admission. Jesus Christ did what every other reformer who has produced any considerable effect upon the world has done. He accommodated his doctrines to the prepossessions of those whom he addressed.[4] He used a language for this view sufficiently familiar to our comprehensions. He said, however new or strange my doctrines may appear to you, they are, in fact only the restoration and re-establishment of those original institutions and ancient customs of your own law and religion. The constitution of your faith and policy, although perfect in their origin, have become corrupt and altered, and have fallen into decay. I profess to restore them to their pristine authority and splendor. "Think not that I am come to destroy the law and the prophets. I am not

---

2. See Paine's *The Age of Reason* for a similar discussion. This is precisely what Shelley proposed to do in *Biblical Extracts*.

3. From Bacon *Novum Organum*, App. 53—*De Aug. Scien.*, lib. V c. 4. [Shelley's Note.]
4. Spinoza in *The Tractatus* makes a similar remark about Jesus.

come to destroy but to fulfill. Till Heaven and Earth pass away, one jot or one title shall in no wise pass from the Law till all be fulfilled." [Misquotes Matt. 5.17-18]. Thus like a skilful orator (see Cicero's *De Oratore*), he secures the prejudices of his auditors and induces them by his professions of sympathy with their feelings to enter with a willing mind into the exposition of his own. The art of persuasion differs from that of reasoning, and it is of no small moment to the success even of a true cause that the judges who are to determine on its merits should be free from those national and religious predilections which render the multitude both deaf and blind. Let not this practice be considered as an unworthy artifice. It were best for the cause of reason that mankind should acknowledge no authority but its own, but it is useful to a certain extent that they should not consider those institutions which they have been habituated to reverence as opposing an obstacle to its admission. All reformers have been compelled to practice this misrepresentation of their own true feelings and opinions. It is deeply to be lamented that a word should ever issue from human lips which contains the minutest alloy of dissimulation, or simulation, or hypocrisy, or exaggeration, or anything but the precise and rigid image which is present to the mind and which ought to dictate the expression. But this practice of entire sincerity towards other men would avail to no good end, if they were incapable of practicing it towards their own minds. In fact, truth cannot be communicated until it is perceived. The interests, therefore, of truth required that an orator should so far as possible produce in his hearers that state of mind in which alone his exhortations could fairly be contemplated and examined.

Having produced this favorable disposition of mind Jesus Christ proceeds to qualify and finally to abrogate the system of the Jewish law. He descants upon its insuffi-

ciency as a code of moral conduct, which it professed to be, and absolutely selects the law of retaliation as an instance of the absurdity and immorality of its institutions.[5] The conclusion of the speech is in a strain of most daring and most impassioned speculation. He seems emboldened by the success of his exculpation to the multitude to declare in public the utmost singularity of his faith. He tramples upon all received opinions, on all the cherished luxuries and superstitions of mankind. He bids them cast aside the chains of custom and blind faith by which they have been encompassed from the very cradle of their being, and become the imitators and ministers of the Universal God. [Here follows a blank page in the manuscript.]

GOD

The thoughts which the word *God* suggests to the human mind are susceptible of as many variations as human minds themselves. The Stoic, the Platonist, and the Epicurean, the polytheist, the dualist, and the trinitarian differ infinitely in their conceptions of its meaning. They agree only in considering it the most awful and most venerable of names, as a common term devised to express all of mystery or majesty or power which the invisible world contains.[6] And not only has every sect distinct conceptions of the application of this name but scarcely two individuals of the same sect who exercise in any degree the freedom of their judgment, or yield themselves with any candor of feeling to the influencings of the visible world find perfect coincidence of opinion to exist between them. It is interes [-ting] to inquire in what acceptation Jesus Christ employed this term.

We may conceive his mind to have been predisposed on this subject to adopt the opinions of his countrymen. Every human being is indebted for a multitude of his sentiments to the religion of his early years.

5. See Matt. V. verse 21, 27, 31, 33, 38. [Shelley's Note.]

6. Compare these ideas with similar statements in *A Refutation of Deism* and *Letter to Lord Ellenborough*.

Jesus Christ probably studied the historians of his country with the ardor of a spirit seeking after truth. They were undoubtedly the companions of his childish years, the food and nutriment and materials of his youthful meditations. The sublime dramatic poem entitled Job had familiarized his imagination with the boldest imagery afforded by the human mind and the material world. Ecclesiastes had diffused a seriousness and solemnity over the frame of his spirit glowing with youthful hope and made audible to his listening heart:

> The still, sad music of humanity,
> Not harsh or grating, but of ample
> power
> To chasten and subdue.[7]

He had contemplated this name as having been profanely perverted to the sanctioning of the most enormous and abominable crimes.[8] We can distinctly trace in the tissue of his doctrines the persuasion that God is some universal being, differing both from man and from the mind of man. According to Jesus Christ, God is neither the Jupiter who sends rain upon the earth, nor the Venus through whom all living things are produced, nor the Vulcan who presides over the terrestrial element of fire, nor the Vesta that preserves the light which is enshrined in the sun and moon and stars. He is neither the Proteus [n]or the Pan of the material world. But the word God according to the acceptation of Jesus Christ unites all the attributes which these denominations contain and is the interfused and overruling Spirit of all the energy and wisdom included within the circle of existing things.[9] It is important to observe that the author of the Christian system had a conception widely differing from the gross imaginations of the vulgar relatively to the ruling Power of the universe. He everywhere represents this power as something mysteriously and illimitably pervading the frame of things.[10] Nor do his doctrines practically assume any proposition which they theoretically deny. They do not represent God as a limitless and inconceivable mystery, affirming at the same time his existence as a being subject to passion and capable. . . . [There is here a gap in the manuscript.]

[THE DOCTRINES OF JESUS]

"Blessed are the pure in heart, for they shall see God"—blessed are those who have preserved internal sanctity of soul, who are conscious of no secret deceit, who are the same in act as they are in desire, who conceal no thought, no tendencies of thought from their own conscience, who are faithful and sincere witnesses before the tribunal of their own judgment of all that passes within their mind. Such as these shall see God. What! after death, shall their awakened eyes behold the King of Heaven? Shall they stand in awe before the golden throne on which he sits, and gaze upon the venerable countenance of the paternal Monarch? Is this the reward of the virtuous and the pure? These are the idle dreams of the visionary or the pernicious representations of impostors, who have fabricated from the very materials of wisdom a cloak for their own dwarfish or imbecile conceptions. Jesus Christ has said no more than the most excellent philosophers have felt and expressed —that virtue is its own reward. It is true that such an expression as he has used was prompted by the energy of genius, it was the overflowing enthusiasm of a poet, but it is the less literally true, clearly repugnant to the mistaken conceptions of the multitude. God, it has been asserted, was contemplated by Jesus Christ as every poet and every

7. Shelley inaccurately quotes—the second line should be "Nor harsh, nor grating though." Wordsworth's *Lines Composed a Few Miles above Tintern Abbey*, lines 91-93.
8. Compare this with a similar thought in *A Refutation of Deism*, pp. 122-124.
9. See *A Refutation of Deism*, p. 131, for a similar idea. Compare also the letter to Elizabeth Hitchener, June 11, 1811; see Spinoza's *Tractatus*, Chap. vi on Miracles. See also the *Ethics* (Everyman edition), pp. 1-81.
10. Compare this statement with Spinoza's conception in the *Tractatus*. See also the *Essay on the Punishment of Death*, p. 156.

philosopher must have contemplated that mysterious principle. He considered that venerable word to express the overruling Spirit of the collective energy of the moral and material world.[11] He affirms therefore no more than that a simple and sincere mind is an indispensable requisite of true science and true happiness. He affirms that a being of pure and gentle habits will not fail in every thought, in every object of every thought, to be aware of benignant visitings from the invisible energies by which he is surrounded. Whosoever is free from the contamination of luxury and license may go forth to the fields and to the woods, inhaling joyous renovation from the breath of spring, or catching from the odors and the sounds of autumn some diviner mood of sweetest sadness, which improves the [solitary] heart. Whosoever is no deceiver or destroyer of his fellowmen—no liar, no flatterer, no murderer—may walk among his species, deriving from the communion with all which they contain of beautiful or of majestic, some intercourse with the Universal God. Whoever has maintained with his own heart the strictest correspondence of confidence, who dares to examine and to estimate every imagination which suggests itself to his mind, who is that which he designs to become, and only aspires to that which the divinity of his own nature shall consider and approve—he has already seen God. We live and move and think, but we are not the creators of our own origin and existence; we are not the arbiters of every motion of our own complicated nature; we are not the masters of our own imaginations and moods of mental being.[12] There is a Power by which we are surrounded, like the atmosphere in which some motionless lyre is suspended, which visits with its breath our silent chords at will. Our most imperial and stupendous qualities—those on which the majesty and the power of humanity is erected—are, relatively to the inferior portion of its mechanism, indeed active and imperial; but they are the passive slaves of some higher and more omnipresent Power. This Power is God. And those who have seen God, have, in the period of their purer and more perfect nature, been harmonized by their own will to so exquisite [a] consentaneity of powers as to give forth divinest melody when the breath of universal being sweeps over their frame.[13]

That those who are pure in heart shall see God, and that virtue is its own reward, may be considered as equivalent assertions. The former of these propositions is a metaphorical repetition of the latter. The advocates of literal interpretation have been the most efficacious enemies of those doctrines whose institutor they profess to venerate.[14] Thucydides, in particular, affords a number of instances calculated to establish this opinion. . . .

Tacitus says, that "the Jews hold God to be something eternal and supreme, neither subject to change nor to decay. Therefore, they permit no statues in their cities or their temples." The Universal Being can only be described or defined by negatives which deny his subjection to the laws of all inferior existences. Where indefiniteness ends idolatry and anthropomorphism begin. God is, as Lucan has expressed,

Quodcunque vides quodcunque moveris,
Et coelum et virtus.[15]

The doctrine of what some fanatics have termed a peculiar Providence, that is of

---

11. See letter to Elizabeth Hitchener, January 2, 1812, for the same idea.

12. Apparently Shelley is here influenced by Hume.

13. The thought of this sentence suggests that of a passage in *Hymn to Intellectual Beauty* (1816).

14. Both Spinoza and Paine make this point. See also *A Refutation of Deism*.

15. Lucan's *Pharsalia*, 9.578-580. Shelley has misquoted. The two lines should read "Et Caelum et Virtus? Superos quid quaerimus ultra? Jupiter est quodcunque vides, quocunque moveris." Shelley, perhaps, found this in Stewart's *The Philosophy of the Active and Moral Powers of Man*, 7.83. Translation of the quotation: "Does heaven exist, does Virtue? Why ask further of the gods above? Jupiter is whatever you see, whatever (impulse) by which you are moved."

some power beyond and superior to that which ordinarily guides the operations of the Universe, interfering to punish the vicious and reward the virtuous, is explicitly denied by Jesus Christ. The absurd and execrable doctrine of vengeance seems to have been contemplated in all its shapes by this great moralist with the profoundest disapprobation.[16] Nor would he permit the most venerable of names to be perverted into a sanction for the meanest and most contemptible propensities incident to the nature of man. "Love your enemies, bless those who curse you that ye may be the sons of your Heavenly Father who makes the sun to shine on the good and on the evil, and the rain to fall on the just and the unjust." [Misquotes Matt. 5.44-45.] How monstrous a calumny have not impostors dared to advance against the mild and gentle author of this just sentiment, and against the whole tenor of his doctrines and his life overflowing with benevolence and forbearance and compassion! They have represented him asserting that the Omnipotent God, that merciful and benignant power who scatters equally upon the beautiful earth all the elements of security and happiness, whose influencings are distributed to all whose natures admit of a participation in them, who sends to the weak and vicious creatures of his will all the benefits which they are capable of sharing, that this God has devised a scheme whereby the body shall live after its apparent dissolution and be rendered capable of indefinite torture. He is said to have compared the agonies which the vicious shall then endure to the excruciations of a living body bound among the flames and being consumed sinew by sinew and bone by bone. And this is to be done, not because it is supposed (and the supposition would be sufficiently detestable) that the moral nature of the sufferer would be improved by his tortures. It is done because it *is just* to be done. My neighbor or my servant or my

child has done me an injury, and it is just that he should suffer an injury in return. Such is the doctrine which Jesus Christ summoned his whole resources of persuasion to oppose. "Love your enemy, bless those who curse you. . . ." [There is a blank here in the manuscript] such he says is the practice of God, and such must you imitate if you would be the children of God. Jesus Christ would hardly have cited as an example of all that is gentle and beneficent and compassionate a being who shall deliberately scheme to inflict on a large portion of the human race tortures indescribably intense and indefinitely protracted; who shall inflict them too without any mistake as to the true nature of pain, without any view to future good, merely because it *is just.* This, and no other is justice. To consider under all the circumstances and consequences of a particular case, how the greatest quantity and purest quality of happiness will ensue from any action is to be just, and there is no other justice. The distinction between justice and mercy was first imagined in the courts of tyrants. Enslaved by the usurpation of these rulers mankind receives every relaxation of their tyranny as a circumstance of grace or favor. Such was the clemency of Julius Caesar who, having achieved by a series of treachery and bloodshed the ruin of the liberties of his country, receives the fame of mercy because, possessing the power to slay and torture the noblest men of Rome, he restrained his sanguinary soul arrogating to himself as a merit an abstinence from actions which if he had committed, he would only have added one other atrocity to his [enormous] deeds. His assassins understood justice better. They saw the most virtuous and civilized community of mankind under the insolent dominion of one wicked man, and they murdered him. They destroyed the usurper of the liberties of their countrymen, not because they hated him, not because they would revenge the wrongs which they had

16. Very similar ideas are expressed in *A Refu-*

tation of Deism. Compare Holbach's *Système de la Nature.* Chaps. 1-8.

sustained. Brutus, it is said, was his most familiar friend; most of the conspirators were habituated to domestic intercourse with the man whom they destroyed. It was in affection, in inextinguishable love for all that is venerable and dear to the human heart, in the names of country, liberty, and virtue; it was in serious and solemn and reluctant mood that these holy patriots murdered their father and their friend. They would have spared his violent death if he could have deposited the rights which he had assumed. His own selfish and narrow nature necessitated the sacrifice they made. They required that he should change all those habits which debauchery and bloodshed had twined around the fibres of his inmost frame of thought, that he should participate with them and with his country those privileges which, having corrupted by assuming to himself, he would no longer value. They would have sacrificed their lives if they could have made him worthy of the sacrifice. Such are the feelings which Jesus Christ asserts to belong to the ruling Power of the world. He desires not the death of a sinner; he makes the sun to shine upon the just and upon the unjust.

The nature of a narrow and malevolent spirit is so essentially incompatible with happiness as to render it inaccessible even to the influencings of the benignant God. All that his own perverse propensities will permit him to receive, that God abundantly pours forth upon him. If there is the slightest overbalance of happiness which can be allotted to the most atrocious offender consistently with the nature of things, that is rigidly made his portion by the ever watchful power of good. In every case the human mind enjoys the utmost pleasure which it is capable of enjoying. God is represented by Jesus Christ as the Power from which or

through which the streams of all that is excellent and delightful flow; the Power which models, as they pass, all the elements of this mixed universe to the purest and most perfect shape which it belongs to their nature to assume; Jesus Christ attributes to this power the faculty of will.[17] How far such a doctrine in its ordinary sense may be philosophically true, or how far Jesus Christ intentionally availed himself of a metaphor easily understood, is foreign to the subject to consider. Thus much is certain that Jesus Christ represents God as the fountain of all goodness, the eternal enemy of pain and evil, the uniform and unchanging motive of the salutary operations of the material world. The supposition that this cause is excited to action by some principle analogous to the human will adds weight to the persuasion that it is foreign to its benevolent nature to inflict the slightest pain. According to Jesus Christ, and according to the indisputable facts of the case, some evil Spirit has dominion in this imperfect world.[18] But there will come a time when the human mind shall be visited exclusively by the influences of the benignant power.[19] Men shall die and their bodies shall rot under the ground; all the organs through which their knowledge and their feelings have flowed, or in which they have originated, shall assume other forms and become ministrant to purposes the most foreign from their former tendencies. There is a time when we shall neither hear nor see, neither be heard [n]or be seen by the multitude of beings like ourselves by whom we have been so long surrounded. They shall go [to] the grave where "there is. . . ." It appears that we moulder to a heap of senseless dust, a few worms that arise and perish like ourselves.[20] Jesus Christ asserts that these appearances are fallacious, and that a gloomy and cold imagination

17. For the same idea see the letter to Elizabeth Hitchener, November 24, 1811.

18. This thought is developed at length in *A Refutation of Deism*. See the letter for May 8, 1811. See also *Essay on the Devil and Devils*.

19. Is this power intellectual beauty of the poems? See *Adonais*, stanza 42.

20. The passage is more fully discussed in the letter for June 20 and 25, 1811. See also the *Essay on a Future State* and the *Essay on Life* for further development. Compare Plutarch's *Moralia*, 5.111-115. Shelley no doubt meant to quote *Ecclesiastes* 9.10.

alone suggests the conception that thought can cease to be.[21]

Another and a more extensive state of being, rather than the complete extinction of being, will follow from that mysterious change which we call death. There shall be no misery, no pain, no fear. The empire of the evil spirit extends not beyond the boundaries of the grave. The unobscured irradiations from the fountain-fire of all goodness shall reveal all that is mysterious and unintelligible until the mutual communications of knowledge and of happiness throughout all thinking natures constitute a harmony of good that ever varies and never ends. This is Heaven when pain and evil cease, and when the benignant principle untrammelled and uncontrolled visits in the fulness of its power the universal frame of things.[22] Human life with all its unreal ills and transitory hopes is as a dream which departs before the dawn leaving no trace of its evanescent hues. All that it contains of pure or of divine visits the passive mind in some serenest mood.[23] Most holy are the affections through which our fellow-beings are rendered dear and venerable to the heart; the remembrance of their sweetness and the completion of the hopes which they did excite constitute, when we awaken from the sleep of life,[24] the fulfilment of the prophecies of its most majestic and beautiful visions. We die, says Jesus Christ, and when we awaken from the langor of disease the glories and the happiness of Paradise are around us.[25] All evil and pain have ceased forever. Our happiness also corresponds [with] and is adapted to, the nature of what is most excellent in our being. We see God, and we see that he is good. How delightful a picture even if it be not true! How magnificent and illustrious is the conception which this bold theory suggests to the contemplation, even if it be

no more than the imagination of some sublimest and most holy poet who, impressed with the loveliness and majesty of his own nature, is impatient and discontented with the narrow limits which this imperfect life and the dark grave have assigned forever as his melancholy portion.[26]

It is not to be believed that hell or punishment was the conception of this daring mind. It is not to be believed that the most prominent group of this picture which it framed so heart-moving and lovely, the accomplishment of all human hope, the extinction of all mortal fear and anguish would consist of millions of sensitive beings enduring in every variety of torture which omniscient vengeance could invent, immortal agony.

Jesus Christ opposed with earnest eloquence the panic fears and hateful superstitions which have enslaved mankind for ages. Nations had risen against nations employing the subtlest devices of mechanism and mind to waste and excruciate and overthrow. The great community of mankind had been subdivided into ten thousand communities each organized for the ruin of the other. Wheel within wheel the vast machine was instinct with the restless spirit of desolation. Pain has been inflicted; therefore pain should be inflicted in return. Retaliation is the only remedy which can be applied to violence, because it teaches the injurer the true nature of his own conduct, and operates as a warning against its repetition. Nor must the same measure of calamity be returned as was received. If a man borrows a certain sum from me, he is bound to repay that sum. Shall no more be required from the enemy who destroys my reputation or ravages my fields? It is just that he should suffer ten times the loss which he has inflicted that the legitimate consequences of

---

21. For a similar idea see the *Essay on a Future State*, pp. 175-178.
22. This is probably the Platonic spirit of beauty as seen in the *Hymn to Intellectual Beauty*. See *Adonais*, stanza 54, for a similar idea.
23. See *The Hymn* for this thought.

24. Compare this to line 344 in *Adonais*, "He hath awakened from the dream of life."
25. For a similar idea compare stanza 42 of *Adonais*.
26. The identical thought is in the *Essay on Life*.

his deed may never be obliterated from his remembrance, and that others may clearly discern and feel the danger of invading the peace of human society. Such reasonings and the impetuous feelings arising from them have armed nation against nation, family against family, man against man. An Athenian soldier in the Ionian army which had assembled for the purpose of vindicating the liberty of the Asiatic Greeks, accidentally set fire to Sardis. The city being composed of combustible materials was burned to the ground. The Persians believed that this circumstance of aggression made it their duty to retaliate on Athens. They assembled successive expeditions on the most extensive scale. Every nation of the East was united to ruin the Grecian States. Athens was burned to the ground, the whole territory laid waste, and every living thing which it contained [destroyed]. After suffering and inflicting incalculable mischiefs they desisted from their purpose only when they became impotent to effect it. The desire of revenge for the aggression of Persia outlived among the Greeks that love of liberty which had been their most glorious distinction among the nations of mankind, and Alexander became the instrument of its completion. The mischiefs attendant on this consummation of fruitless ruin are too manifold and too tremendous to be related. If all the thought which had been expended on the construction of engines of agony and death, the modes of aggression and defense, the raising of armies, and the acquirement of those arts of tyranny and falsehood without which mixed multitudes deluded and goaded to mutual ruin could neither be led nor governed, had been employed to promote the true welfare and extend the real empire of man how different would have been the present situation of human society! How different the state of knowledge on physical and moral science, on which the power and happiness of mankind essentially depend! What nation has the example of the desolation of Attica by Mardonius and Xerxes, or the extinction of the Persian empire by Alexander of Macedon, restrained from outrage? Was not the pretext of this latter system of spoliation derived immediately from the former? Had revenge in this instance any other effect than to increase, instead of diminishing, the mass of malice and evil already existing in the world?

The emptiness and folly of retaliation is apparent from every example which can be brought forward. Not only Jesus Christ but the most eminent professors of every sect of philosophy have reasoned against this futile superstition. Legislation is, in one point of view, to be considered as an attempt to provide against the excesses of this deplorable mistake. It professes to assign the penalty of all private injuries and denies to individuals the right of vindicating their proper cause. This end is certainly not attained without some accommodation to the propensities which it desires to destroy. Still, it professes to recognize no principle but the production of the greatest eventual good with the least immediate injury, and to regard the torture or the death of any human being as unjust, of whatever mischief he may have been the author, so long as the result shall not more than compensate for the immediate pain. Such are the only justifiable principles and such is the [true] reason of law.[27] [There is a blank here in the manuscript.]

Mankind, transmitting from generation to generation the horrible legacy of accumulated vengeances and pursuing with the feelings of duty the misery of their fellow-beings, have not failed to attribute to the universal cause a character analogous with their own. The image of this invisible, mysterious being is more or less excellent and perfect, resembles more or less its original in proportion to the perfectness of the mind on which it is impressed. Thus, the nation which has arrived at the highest step in the scale of moral progression will believe most

---

27. There is a similar discussion of retaliation in the *Essay on the Punishment of Death*, pp. 155, 157-158.

purely in that God the knowledge of whose real attributes [has] been considered as the firmest basis of the true religion. The reason of the belief of each individual also will be so far regulated by his conceptions of what is good. Thus, the conceptions which any nation or individual entertains of the God of its popular worship may be inferred from their own actions and opinions which are the subjects of their approbation among their fellow-men. Jesus Christ instructed his disciples to be perfect as their father in Heaven is perfect, declaring at the same time his belief that human perfection required the refraining from revenge or retribution in any of its various shapes. The perfection of the human and the divine character is thus asserted to be the same: man by resembling God fulfils most accurately the tendencies of his nature, and God comprehends within itself all that constitutes human perfection. Thus God is a model through which the excellence of man is to be estimated, while the *abstract* perfection of the human character is the type of the *actual* perfection of the divine.[28] It is not to [be] believed that a person of such comprehensive views as Jesus Christ could have fallen into so manifest a contradiction as to assert that men would be tortured after death by that being whose character is held up as a model to human kind, because he is incapable of malevolence or revenge. All the arguments which have been brought forward to justify retribution fail when retribution is destined neither to operate as an example to other agents, nor to the offender himself. How feeble such reasoning is to be considered has been already shown; but it is the character of an evil daemon to consign the beings whom he has endowed with sensation to improfitable anguish. The peculiar circumstances attendant on the conception of God casting sinners to burn in hell forever combine to render that conception the most perfect specimen of the greatest imaginable crime. Jesus Christ

represented God as the principle of all good, the source of all happiness, the wise and benevolent creator and preserver of all living things. But the interpreters of his doctrine have confounded the good and the evil principle. They observed the emanations of their universal natures to be inextricably intangled in the world, and trembling before the power of the cause of all things addressed to it such flattery as is acceptable to the ministers of human tyranny, attributing love and wisdom to those energies which they felt to be exerted indifferently for the purposes of benefit and calamity. Jesus Christ expressly asserts that distinction between the good and evil principle which it has been the practice of all theologians to confound. How far his doctrines, or their interpretation, may be true, it would scarcely have been worth while to inquire, if the one did not afford an example and an incentive to the attainment of true virtue, while the other holds out a sanction and apology for every species of mean and cruel vice.

EQUALITY OF MANKIND

"The spirit of the Lord is upon me because he hath chosen me to preach the gospel to the poor, he hath sent me to heal the broken-hearted, to preach deliverance to the captives, and recovery of sight to the blind, and to set at liberty them that are bruised."[29]

This is an enunciation of all that Plato and Diogenes have speculated upon of the equality of mankind. They saw that the great majority of the human species were reduced to the situation of squalid ignorance and moral imbecility, for the purpose of purveying for the luxury of a few and contributing to the satisfaction of their thirst for power. Too mean-spirited and too feeble in resolve to attempt the conquest of their own evil passions and of the difficulties of the material world men sought dominion over their fellow-men as an easy method to gain that apparent majesty and power which

28. See the discussion in *Letter to Lord Ellenborough* for a slightly divergent point of view.

29. Luke 4.18. [Shelley's Note.]

the instinct of their nature requires. Plato wrote the scheme of a republic in which law should watch over the equal distribution of the external instruments of unequal power: honors, property and [a blank here in the manuscript]. Diogenes devised a nobler and more worthy system of opposition to the system of slave and tyrant. He said,[30] "It is in the power of each individual to level the inequality which is the topic of the complaint of mankind. Let him be aware of his own worth and the station which he really occupies in the scale of moral beings. Diamonds and gold, palaces and sceptres, derive their value from the opinion of mankind. The only sumptuary law which can be imposed on the use and fabrication of these instruments of mischief and deceit, these symbols of successful injustice, is the law of opinion. Every man possesses .the power in this respect to legislate for himself. Let him be well aware of his own worth and moral dignity. Let him yield in [Blank here in manuscript] to any wiser or worthier than he so long as he accords no veneration to the splendor of his apparel, the luxury of his food, the multitude of his flatterers and slaves. It is because, O mankind, ye value and seek the empty pageantry of wealth and social power that ye are enslaved to its possessions. Decrease your physical wants, learn to live, so far as nourishment and shelter are concerned like the beasts of the forest and the birds of the air;[31] you will need not to complain that other individuals of your species are surrounded by the diseases of luxury and the vices of subserviency. With all those who are truly wise, there will be an entire community, not only of thoughts and feelings but also of external possessions." Insomuch, therefore, as you love one another, you may enjoy the community of whatsoever benefits arise from the inventions of civilized life. They are of value only for purposes of mental power; they are of value only as they are capable of being shared and applied to the common advantage of philosophy, and if there be no love among men, whatever institutions they may frame must be subservient to the same purpose: to the continuance of inequality. If there be no love among men, it is best that he who sees through the hollowness of their professions should fly from their society and suffice to his own soul. In wisdom he will thus lose nothing; in peace, he will gain everything. In proportion to the love existing among men, so will be the community of property and power. Among true and real friends all is common, and were ignorance and envy and superstition banished from the world, all mankind would be as friends. The only perfect and genuine republic is that which comprehends every living being. Those distinctions which have been artificially set up of nations and cities and families and religions are only general names expressing the abhorrence and contempt with which men blindly consider their fellowmen. I love my country; I love the city in which I was born, my parents and my wife and the children of my care, and to this city, this woman, and this nation, it is incumbent on me to do all the benefit in my power. To what do these distinctions point, but to an indirect denial of the duty which humanity imposes on you of doing every possible good to every individual under whatever denomination he may be comprehended, to whom you have the power of doing it. You ought to love all mankind, nay, every individual of mankind; you ought not to love the individuals of your domestic circle less, but to love those who exist beyond it, more. Once make the feelings of confidence and affection universal and the distinctions of property and power will vanish; nor are they to be abolished without substituting something equivalent in mischief to them, until all mankind shall acknowledge an entire

30. There are no quotation marks to indicate what Shelley has Diogenes say.

31. Compare this with letter to Elizabeth Hitchener, July 25, 1811, and also a passage in *An Address to the Irish People* for a similar idea.

community of rights.[32] But, as the shades of night are dispelled by the faintest glimmerings of dawn, so shall the minutest progress of the benevolent feelings disperse in some degree the gloom of tyranny and slavery—ministers of mutual suspicion and abhorrence.

Your physical wants are few, while those of your mind and heart cannot be numbered or described from their multitude and complication. To secure the gratification of the former, men have made themselves the bond-slaves of each other. They have cultivated these meaner wants to so great an excess as to judge nothing valuable or desirable but what relates to their gratification. Hence has arisen a system of passions which loses sight of the end which they were originally awakened to attain. Fame, power, and gold are loved for their own sakes, are worshipped with a blind and habitual idolatry. The pageantry of empire and the fame of irresistible might is contemplated by its possessor with unmeaning complacency, without a retrospect to the properties which first made him consider them of value. It is from the cultivation of the most contemptible properties of human nature that the discord and torpor and [blank] by which the moral universe is disordered essentially depend. So long as these are the ties by which human society is connected, let it not be admired that they are fragile.

Before man can be free and equal and truly wise he must cast aside the chains of habit and superstition; he must strip sensuality of its pomp and selfishness of its excuses, and contemplate actions and objects as they really are. He will discover the wisdom of universal love. He will feel the meanness and the injustice of sacrificing the leisure and the liberty of his fellowmen to the indulgence of his physical appetites and becoming a party to their degradation by the consummation of his own. He will consider

Ευγενειας δε και δοξας προσκοσμηματα κακιας ειναι, μονην τε ορθην πολιτειαν ειναι την εν κοσμω.[33]

Such, with those differences only incidental to the age and the state of society in which they were promulgated, appear to have been the doctrines of Jesus Christ. It is not too much to assert that they have been the doctrines of every just and compassionate mind that ever speculated on the social nature of man. The dogma of the equality of mankind has been advocated with various success in different ages of the world. It was imperfectly understood, but a kind of instinct in its favor influenced considerably on the practice of ancient Greece and Rome. Attempts to establish usages founded on this dogma have been made in modern Europe, in several instances since the revival of literature and the arts. Rousseau has vindicated this opinion with all the eloquence of sincere and earnest faith and is perhaps the philosopher among the moderns who in the structure of his feelings and understanding resembles most nearly the mysterious sage of Judaea. It is impossible to read those passionate words in which Jesus Christ upbraids the pusillanimity and sensuality of mankind, without being strongly reminded of the more connected and systematic enthusiasm of Rousseau. "No man," says Jesus Christ, "can serve two masters. . . . [A blank of half a page here.] Take, therefore, no thought for the morrow; for the morrow shall take thought for the things of itself. Sufficient unto the day is the evil thereof." If we would profit by the wisdom of a sublime and poetical mind, we must beware of the vulgar error of interpreting literally every expression which it employs. Nothing can well be more remote from truth than the literal and strict construction of such expressions as Jesus Christ delivers, or than it were best for man that he should abandon

32. This is a fundamental idea in Shelley. Compare *An Address to the Irish People* and see letters in 1811-12 to Hogg and Elizabeth Hitchener.

33. "He will consider the additional ornaments are evils, and that the only true republic is the one that has ideal beauty."

all his acquirements in physical and intellectual science and depend on the spontaneous productions of Nature for his subsistence.[34] Nothing is more obviously false than that the remedy for the inequality among men consists in their return to the condition of savages and beasts. Philosophy will never be understood if we approach the study of its mysteries with so narrow and illiberal conceptions of its universality. Rousseau certainly did not mean to persuade the immense population of his country to abandon all the arts of life, destroy their habitations and their temples and become the inhabitants of the woods. He addressed the most enlightened of his compatriots, and endeavored to persuade them to set the example of a pure and simple life, by placing in the strongest point of view his conceptions of the calamitous and diseased aspect which, overgrown as it is with the vices of sensuality and selfishness, is exhibited by civilized society. Nor can it be believed that Jesus Christ endeavored to prevail on the inhabitants of Jerusalem neither to till their fields nor to frame a shelter against the sky, nor to provide food for the morrow. He simply exposes with the passionate rhetoric of enthusiastic love towards all human beings the miseries and mischiefs of that system which makes all things subservient to the subsistence of the material frame of man. He warns them that no man can serve two masters, God and Mammon; that it is impossible at once to be high-minded and just and wise, and comply with the accustomed forms of human society, seek honor, wealth, or empire either from the idolatry of habit or as the direct instruments of sensual gratification. He instructs them that clothing and food and shelter are not, as they suppose, the true end of human life, but only certain means to be valued in proportion to their subserviency to that end. These means it is the right of every human being to possess, and that in the same degree. In this respect

the fowls of the air and the lilies of the field are examples for the imitation of mankind. They are clothed and fed by the Universal God. Permit, therefore, the spirit of this benignant principle to visit your intellectual frame, or, in other words, become just and pure. When you understand the degree of attention which the requisitions of your physical nature demand, you will perceive how little labor suffices for their satisfaction. Your heavenly father knows that you have need of these things. The universal Harmony or Reason which makes your passive frame of thought its dwelling in proportion to the purity and majesty of its nature, will instruct you, if you are willing to attain that exalted condition, in what manner to possess all the objects necessary for your material subsistence. All men are invocated to become thus pure and happy. All men are called to participation in the community of nature's gifts. The man who has fewest bodily wants approaches nearest to the divine nature.[35] Satisfy these wants, at the cheapest rate, and expend the remaining energies of your nature in the attainment of virtue and knowledge. The mighty frame of the wonderful and lovely world is the food of your contemplation, and living beings who resemble your own nature and are bound to you by similarity of sensations are destined to be the nutriment of your affections; united they are the consummation of the widest hopes that your mind can contain. You can expend thus no labor on mechanism consecrated to luxury and pride. How abundant will not be your progress in all that truly ennobles and extends human nature! By rendering yourselves thus worthy, you will be as free in your imaginations as the swift and many-colored fowls of the air, and as beautiful in your simplicity as the lilies of the field.

In proportion as mankind becomes wise, yes, in exact proportion to that wisdom should be the extinction of the unequal

34. The same idea is in *An Address to the Irish People*, p. 52.

35. This idea appears in many of Shelley's writings.

system under which they now subsist. Government is in fact the mere badge of their depravity.[36] They are so little aware of the inestimable benefits of mutual love as to indulge without thought and almost without motive in the worst excesses of selfishness and malice. Hence without graduating human society into a scale of empire and subjection, its very existence has become impossible. It is necessary that universal benevolence should supersede the regulations of precedent and prescription before these regulations can safely be abolished. Meanwhile their very subsistence depends on the system of injustice and violence which they have been devised to palliate. They suppose men endowed with the power of deliberating and determining for their equals; while these men, as frail and as ignorant as the multitude whom they rule, possess, as a practical consequence of this power, the right which they of necessity exercise to pervert, together with their own the physical and moral and intellectual nature of all mankind. It is the object of wisdom to equalize the distinctions on which this power depends, by exhibiting in their proper worthlessness the objects, a contention concerning which renders its existence a necessary evil. The evil in fact is virtually abolished wherever *justice* is practised, and it is abolished in precise proportion to the prevalence of true virtue. The whole frame of human things is infected by the insidious poison. Hence it is that man is blind in his understanding, corrupt in his moral sense, and diseased in his physical functions. The wisest and most sublime of the ancient poets saw this truth and embodied their conception of its value in retrospect to the earliest ages of mankind. They represented equality as the reign of Saturn and taught that mankind had gradually degenerated from the virtue which enabled them to enjoy or maintain this happy state. Their doctrine was philosophically false. Later and

more correct observations have instructed us that uncivilized man is the most pernicious and miserable of beings and that the violence and injustice which are the genuine indications of real inequality obtain in the society of these beings without mixture and without palliation. Their imaginations of a happier state of human society were referred indeed to the [Saturnian was inserted here by Lady Shelley in *Shelley Memorials,* (1859).] period; they ministered indeed to thoughts of despondency and sorrow. But they were the children of airy hope, the prophets and parents of mysterious futurity. Man was once as a wild beast; he has become a moralist, a metaphysician, a poet, and an astronomer. Lucretius or Virgil might have referred the comparison to themselves, and, as a proof of this progress of the nature of man, challenged a comparison with the cannibals of Scythia.[37] The experience of the ages which have intervened between the present period and that in which Jesus Christ taught tends to prove his doctrine and to illustrate theirs. There is more equality, because there is more justice among mankind and there is more justice because there is more universal knowledge.[38]

To the accomplishment of such mighty hopes were the views of Jesus Christ extended; such did he believe to be the tendency of his doctrines: the abolition of artificial distinctions among mankind so far as the love which it becomes all human beings to bear towards each other, and the knowledge of truth from which that love will never fail to be produced avail to their destruction.

A young man came to Jesus Christ struck by the miraculous dignity and simplicity of his character and attracted by the words of power which he uttered. He demanded to be considered as one of the followers of his creed. "Sell all that thou hast," replied the philosopher, "give it to the poor, and

36. This statement is a paraphrase of a sentence from Paine's *Common Sense* (American Writers Series, edited by H. H. Clark), p. 4.

37. Jesus Christ foresaw what these poets retrospectively imagined. [Shelley's Note.]
38. A similar idea is in *An Address to the Irish People,* pp. 45-49.

follow me." But the young man had large possessions, and he [went away sorrowing.] [A blank of one-half page here.]

The system of equality was attempted, after Jesus Christ's death, to be carried into effect by his followers. "They that believed had all things common: they sold their possessions and goods and parted them to all men as every man had need, and they continued daily with one accord in the temple and breaking bread from house to house did eat their meat with gladness and singleness of heart."[39] The practical application of the doctrines of strict justice to a state of society established in its contempt was such as might have been expected. After the transitory glow of enthusiasm had faded from the minds of men, precedent and habit resumed their empire, broke like a universal deluge on one shrinking and solitary island. Men to whom birth had allotted these possessions looked with complacency on sumptuous apartments and luxurious food, and those ceremonials of delusive majesty which surround the throne of power and the court of wealth. Men from whom these things were withheld by their condition began again to gaze with stupid envy on their pernicious splendor and, by desiring the false greatness of another's state, to sacrifice the intrinsic majesty of their own. The demagogues of the infant republic of the Christian sect attaining through eloquence or artifice to influence among its members, first violated, under the pretence of watching over their integrity, the institutions established for the common and equal benefit of all. These demagogues artfully silenced the voice of the moral sense among them by engaging them to attend not so much to the cultivation of a virtuous and happy life in this mortal scene as to the attainment of a fortunate condition after death; not so much to the consideration of those means by which the state of man is adorned and improved

as an enquiry into the secrets of the connection between God and the world, things which they well knew were not to be explained or even to be conceived. The system of equality which they established necessarily fell to the ground, because it is a system that must result from rather than precede the moral improvement of human kind. It was a circumstance of no moment that the first adherents of the system of Jesus Christ cast their property into a common stock. The same degree of real community of property could have subsisted without this formality, which served only to extend a temptation of dishonesty to the treasures of so considerable a patrimony. Every man in proportion to his virtue considers himself with respect to the great community of mankind as the steward and guardian of their interests in the property which he chances to possess. Every man in proportion to his wisdom sees the manner in which it is his duty to employ the resources which the consent of mankind has entrusted to his discretion. Such is the annihilation of the unjust inequality of powers and conditions existing in the world, so gradually and inevitably is the progress of equality accommodated to the progress of wisdom and of virtue among mankind. Meanwhile some benefit has not failed to flow from the imperfect attempts which have been made to erect a system of equal rights to property and power upon the basis of arbitrary institutions. They have undoubtedly in every case, from the very instability of their foundation, failed. Still they constitute a record of those epochs at which a true sense of justice suggested itself to the understandings of men so that they consented to forego all the cherished delights of luxury, all the habitual gratifications arising out of the possession or the expectations of power, all the superstitions which the accumulated authority of ages had made dear and venerable to them. They are so

---

39. Acts, chap. 2, v. 44. [Shelley's Note.] Shelley here misquotes Acts 2.44-46.

many trophies erected in the enemy's land to mark the limits of the victorious progress of truth and justice.

Jesus Christ did not fail to advert to the—[Left blank].

THE DOCTRINES OF CHRIST[40]

No mistake is more to be deplored than the conception that a system of morals and religion should derive any portion of its authority either from the circumstance of its novelty or its antiquity, that it should be judged excellent, not because it is reasonable or true, but because no person has ever thought of it before, or because it has been thought of from the beginning of time. The vulgar mind delights to [abstract?] from the most useful maxims or institutions the true reasons for their preferableness and to accommodate to the loose inductions of their own indisciplinable minds. . . . Thus mankind is governed by precedents for actions which were never, or are no longer, useful . . . . Such has been, most unfortunately, the process of the human mind relative to the doctrines of Jesus Christ. Their original promulgation was authorized by an appeal to the antiquity of the institutions of Judea; and in vindication of superstitions professing to be founded on them, it is asserted that nothing analogous to their tenor was ever before produced. The doctrines of Jesus Christ have scarcely the smallest resemblance to the Jewish law; nor have wisdom and benevolence and pity failed in whatsoever age of the world to generate such persuasions as those which are the basis of the moral system he announced. The most eminent philosophers of Greece had long been familiarized to the boldest and most sublime speculations on God, on the visible world, and on the moral and intellectual nature of man. The universality and

unity of God, the omnipotence of the mind of man, the equality of human beings, and the duty of internal purity, is [are] either asserted by Pythagoras, Plato, Diogenes, Zeno, and their followers, or may be directly inferred from their assertions. Nothing would be gained by the establishment of the originality of Jesus Christ's doctrines but the casting a suspicion upon its practicability. Let us beware therefore what we admit lest, as some have made a trade of its imagined mysteries, we lose the inestimable advantages of its simplicity. Let us beware, if we love liberty and truth, if we loathe tyranny and imposture, if, imperfect ourselves, we still aspire to the freedom of internal purity and cherish the elevated hope that mankind may not be everlastingly condemned to the bondage of their own passions and the passions of their fellow beings, let us beware. An established religion returns to deathlike apathy the sublimest ebullitions of most exalted genius and the spirit-stirring truths of a mind inflamed with the desire to benefiting mankind. It is the characteristic of a cold and tame spirit to imagine that such doctrines as Jesus Christ promulgated are destined to follow the fortunes and share the extinction of a popular religion.

THE MORAL TEACHING
OF JESUS CHRIST[41]

The preachers of the Christian religion urge the morality of Jesus Christ as being itself miraculous and stamped with the impression of divinity. Mahomet advanced the same pretensions respecting the composition of the Koran and, if we consider the number of his followers, with greater success. But these gentlemen condemn themselves, for in their admiration they prefer

---

40. The following fragment was first published in St. James's Magazine, March 1876, by Townsend Meyer. It was reprinted by Forman as part of Essay on Christianity.

41. This fragment is closely related in thought

to the Essay on Christianity though it is not found in the same note-book containing the Essay. The fragment was first published in the Julian Editions (6.255-256). The manuscript is in the Bodleian Library at Oxford.

the comment to the text. Read the words themselves of this extraordinary person, and weigh their import well. The doctrines indeed, in my judgment, are excellent and strike at the root of moral evil. If acted upon, no political or religious institution could subsist a moment. Every man would be his own magistrate and priest; the change so long desired would have attained its consummation, and man exempt from the external evils of his own choice would be left free to struggle with the physical evils which exist in spite of him. But these are the very doctrines which, in another shape, the most violent asserters of Christianity denounce as impious and seditious; who are such earnest champions for social and political disqualification as they? This alone would be a demonstration of the falsehood of Christianity, that the religion so called is the strongest ally and bulwark of that system of successful force and fraud and of the selfish passions from which it has derived its origin and permanence, against which Jesus Christ declared the most uncompromising war, and the extinction of which appears to have been the great motive of his life. We are called upon to believe in the divinity of a doctrine the effect of which

has been to establish more firmly than [that] which it was promulgated to destroy, and that they who invite us to . . . our reason with envious priests and tyrannical princes, whose [existence] is an everlasting answer to the pretensions of Christianity. Doctrines of reform were never carried to so great a length as by Jesus Christ. The *Republic* of Plato and the *Political Justice* of Godwin are probable and practical systems in the comparison.

The doctrines of Jesus Christ though excellent are not new. The immortality of the soul was already a dogma, familiar from all antiquity to every nation of the earth except the Jews. Plato said all that could be said on this subject, and whoever had aspired to excel this mighty mind ought to have sought their information from undoubted sources. Jesus claimed no pretension of the kind, and the Christian knows as little, as did the Pagan, of the foundation of this notion. The idea of forgiveness of injuries, the error of revenge, and the immorality and inutility of punishment considered as punishment, (for these correlative doctrines) are stated by Plato in the first book of the *Republic*; and . . . .

ESSAY ON MARRIAGE

(A Fragment)

[This fragment was first published by Koszul in *Shelley's Prose in the Bodleian Manuscripts* (1910). It is contained in the same notebook as the *Essay on Christianity,* and seems to be related directly to that essay. The author is indebted to Hume's *Essay on Polygamy and Divorce* and to Godwin's *Political Justice* for the thought content of the essay.]

Before the commencement of human society, if such a state can be conceived to have existed, it is probable that men like other animals used promiscuous concubinage. Force or persuasion regulated the particular instances of this general practice. No moral affections arose from the indulgence of a physical impulse; nor did the relations of parent and child endure longer than is essential for the preservation of the latter. The circumstance of the pleasure being attached to the fulfilment of the sexual functions rendered that which was the object of their exercise a possession analogous in value to those articles of luxury or necessity which maintain or delight the existence of a savage. The superiority of strength inherent in the male rendered him the possessor and the female the possession in the same manner as beasts are the property of men through their pre-eminence of reason and never are the property of each other through the inequality of opportunity and the success of fraud. Women, therefore, in rude ages and in rude countries have been considered as the property of men, because they are the materials of usefulness or pleasure. They were valuable to them in the same manner as their flocks and herds were valuable, and its was as important to their interests that they should retain undisturbed possession. The same dread of insecurity which gave birth to those laws or opinions which defend the security of property suggested also the institution of marriage: that is, a contrivance to prevent others from deriving advantage from that which any individual has succeeded in pre-occupying. I am aware that this institution has undergone essential modifications from an infinite multitude of circumstances which it is unnecessary to enumerate: such [undubitably] was however the original spirit of marriage.

If any assemblage of men agree to command or prohibit any action with reference to their society the omission of the commission of this action is to be called criminal. If it be an action manifestly and most extensively beneficial such is nevertheless the denomination under which, by the universal function of language, it is to be ranged. To consider whether any particular action of any human being is really right or wrong we must estimate that action by a standard strictly universal. We must consider the degree of substantial advantage which the greatest number of the worthiest beings are intended to derive from that action. I say thus much to distinguish what is really right and wrong from that which from the equivocal application of the idea of criminality has been falsely called right and wrong. The ideas are sufficiently distinguishable from the circumstance of one being measured by a standard common to all human beings; the other by a standard peculiar only to a portion of mankind. A superficial observer considers the laws of his own society universal in the same manner and with the same justice as all that to which no limits have been discovered is called infinite. The origin of law therefore was the origin of crime, although the ideas of right and wrong must have subsisted from the moment that one human being could sympathize in the pains and pleasure of another. Every law supposes the criminality of its own infraction. If it be a law which has a tendency to produce in every case the greatest good, this supposition and even the consideration of what is lawful as what is right is salutary and may be innocent. If it is partial and unjust the greatest evils would flow from the abolition of this distinction. Such in fact is the unhappy cause whence all the doctrinal perversions of ethical science have arisen.

A DISCOURSE ON THE MANNERS
OF THE ANCIENT GREEKS
RELATIVE TO THE SUBJECT OF LOVE

[Two excerpts from this essay were published by Thomas Medwin in the *Athenaeum* for September, 1832, the first consisting of the first two paragraphs of the essay, and the second, from "the mind," in the last paragraph but one, to "social beings." These were republished in *Shelley Papers* (1833) as *The Age of Pericles* and *Reflections on Love,* respectively. The essay was published in a fragmentary form by Mary Shelley in 1840. That portion of the essay beginning with the paragraph, "From this distinction" to the end Mary had been forced by Shelley's father and her publisher, Moxon, to suppress because of its bearing on homosexual love. The complete essay was first published in *Plato's Banquet, translated from the Greek, A Discourse on the Manners of Antient Greeks Relative to the subject of Love,* etc. *Revised and Enlarged, by Roger Ingpen, from the MSS. in the Possession of Sir John C. E. Shelley-Rolls.* Privately printed, London, 1931. For details and complete text see *The Platonism of Shelley* (pp. 375-413) by James A. Notopoulos.

The date of composition is 1818. The first reference to the work, probably, was in a letter to Peacock, August 16, 1818, in which Shelley said, "I am proceeding to employ myself on a discourse upon the subject of which the *Symposium* treats, considering the subject with reference to the difference of sentiment respecting it existing between the Greeks and Modern Nations; a subject to be handled with that delicate caution which either I cannot or will not practice in other matters, but which I here acknowledge to be necessary."

As the essay stood in Mary Shelley's 1840 edition it was merely the introduction to the subject, which was to be Love. As it now stands the essay is complete and intelligible. The last part—that suppressed in 1840—is little more than Plato's own discussion in the *Symposium* and in the *Phaedrus.* Shelley had translated the *Symposium* of Plato during the week of July 9, 1818, completing it on July 17, "only as an exercise or perhaps to give Mary some idea of the manners and feelings of the Athenians," as he put it in a letter to the Gisbornes on July 16.

It was no doubt this work on the *Symposium* that led Shelley to begin this essay on Love. The introduction is an appraisal of the literature, the arts, and the manners of the Athenians, but the body of the essay has for its theme the different ideas of love among the ancients and the moderns. Shelley pointed out the great progress made by modern nations in respect to women and love as compared with those ideas held by the Greeks. The essay shows how conversant Shelley was with Greek literature and life and thought, how discriminating his judgment in evaluating the ideals of the Greeks and the moderns, and how penetrating his insight into the essentials of great art and the social conditions necessary for the good life. There is, of course, no attempt on Shelley's part to advocate or condone homosexuality. He is merely explaining the well-known Greek practice.]

The period which intervened between the birth of Pericles and the death of Aristotle[1] is undoubtedly, whether considered in itself or with reference to the effects which it had produced upon the subsequent destinies of civilized man, the most memorable in the history of the world. What was the combination of moral and political circumstances which produced so unparalleled a progress during that period in literature and the arts—why that progress, so rapid and so sustained, so soon received a check, and became retrograde—are problems left with the wonder and conjecture of posterity. The wrecks and fragments of those subtle and profound minds, like the ruins of a fine statue, obscurely suggest to us the grandeur and perfection of the whole. Their very language—a type of the understandings of which it was the creation and the image—in variety, in simplicity, in flexibility, and in copiousness, excels every other language of the western world.[2] Their sculptures are such as we in our presumption assume to be the models of ideal truth and beauty, and to which no artist of modern times can produce forms in any degree comparable. Their paintings, according to Pliny and Pausanias, were full of delicacy and harmony; and some even were powerfully pathetic, so as to awaken like tender music or tragic poetry the most overwhelming emotions. We are accustomed to conceive the painters of the sixteenth century as those who have brought their art to the highest perfection, probably because none of the ancient paintings have been preserved. For all the inventive arts maintain, as it were, a sympathetic connection between each other, being no more than various expressions of one internal power, modified by different circumstances, either of an individual, or of society. The paintings of that period would probably bear the same relation as is confessedly borne by the sculptures to all succeeding ones. Of their music we know little; but the effects which it is said to have produced, whether they be attributed to the skill of the composer, or the sensibility of his audience, are far more powerful than any which we experience from the music of our own times; and if, indeed, the melody of their compositions were more tender and delicate and inspiring than the melodies of some modern European nations, their superiority in this art must have been something wonderful and wholly beyond conception.

Their poetry seems to maintain a very high, though not so disproportionate a rank, in the comparison. Perhaps Shakespeare, from the variety and comprehension of his genius, is to be considered on the whole as the greatest individual mind of which

1. That is, between c. 490 and 322 B.C.
2. Compare this statement with that in a letter to Godwin, July 29, 1812, as contradictory to the general tone of this essay. On this subject Shelley's mind underwent considerable change.

we have specimens remaining. Perhaps Dante created imaginations of greater loveliness and energy than any that are to be found in the ancient literature of Greece. Perhaps nothing has been discovered in the fragments of the Greek lyric poets equivalent to the sublime and chivalric sensibility of Petrarch. But, as a poet, Homer must be acknowledged to excel Shakespeare in the truth, the harmony, the sustained grandeur, the satisfying completeness of his images, their exact fitness to the illustration, and to that to which they belong. Nor could Dante, deficient in conduct, plan, nature, variety, and temperance, have been brought into comparison with these men but for those fortunate isles laden with golden fruit which alone could tempt any one to embark in the misty ocean of his dark and extravagant fiction.

But, omitting the comparison of individual minds, which can afford no general inference, how superior was the spirit and system of their poetry to that of any other period! So that had any genius equal in other respects to the greatest that ever enlightened the world arisen in that age, he would have been superior to all from this circumstance alone—that his conceptions would have assumed a more harmonious and perfect form. For it is worthy of observation that whatever the poets of that age produced is as harmonious and perfect as possible. If a drama, for instance, were the composition of a person of inferior talent, it was still homogeneous and free from inequalities; it was a whole, consistent with itself. The compositions of great minds bore throughout the sustained stamp of their greatness. In the poetry of succeeding ages the expectations are often exalted on Icarian wings, and fall too much disappointed to give a memory and a name to the oblivious pool in which they fell.

In physical knowledge Aristotle and Theophrastus had already—no doubt assisted by the labors of those of their predecessors whom they criticize—made [advances] worthy of the maturity of science. The astonishing invention of geometry, that series of discoveries which have enabled man to command the elements and foresee future events before the subjects of his ignorant wonder and has opened as it were the doors of the mysteries of nature, had already been brought to great perfection. Metaphysics, the science of man's intimate nature, and logic, or the grammar and elementary principles of that science,[3] received from the latter philosophers of the Periclean age a firm basis. All our more exact philosophy is built upon the labors of these great men, and many of the words which we employ in metaphysical distinctions were invented by them to give accuracy and system to their reasonings. The science of morals, or the voluntary conduct of men in relation to themselves or others, dates from this epoch. How inexpressibly bolder and more pure were the doctrines of those great men in comparison with the timid maxims which prevail in the writings of the most esteemed modern moralists. They were such as Phocion, and Epaminondas, and Timoleon, who formed themselves on their influence, were to the wretched heroes of our own age.

Their political and religious institutions were more difficult to bring into comparison with those of other times. A summary idea may be formed of the worth of any political and religious system by observing the comparative degree of happiness and of intellect produced under its influence. And while many institutions and opinions which, in ancient Greece were obstacles to the improvement of the human race, have been abolished among modern nations, how many pernicious superstitions and new contrivances of misrule and unheard-of complications of public mischief have not been invented among them by the ever-watchful spirit of avarice and tyranny!

The modern nations of the civilized world owe the progress which they have made—

3. Compare *A Treatise on Morals.*

as well in those physical sciences in which they have already excelled their masters as in the moral and intellectual inquiries in which, with all the advantage of their experience of the latter, it can scarcely be said that they have yet equalled them—to what is called the revival of learning; that is, the study of the writers of the age which preceded and immediately followed the government of Pericles, or of subsequent writers, who were, so to speak, the rivers flowing from those immortal fountains. And though there seems to be a principle in the modern world which, should circumstances analogous to those which modelled the intellectual resources of the age to which we refer into so harmonious a proportion again arise, would arrest and perpetuate them and consign their results to a more equal, extensive, and lasting improvement of the condition of man—though justice and the true meaning of human society is, if not more accurately, more generally understood; though perhaps men know more, and therefore are more as a mass, yet this principle has never been called into action and requires indeed a universal and an almost appalling change in the system of existing things. The study of modern history is the study of kings, financiers, statesmen, and priests. The history of ancient Greece is the study of legislators, philosophers, and poets; it is the history of men, compared with the history of titles. What the Greeks were was a reality, not a promise. And what we are and hope to be is derived, as it were, from the influence and inspiration of these glorious generations.

Whatever tends to afford a further illustration of the manners and opinions of those to whom we owe so much and who were perhaps on the whole the most perfect specimens of humanity of whom we have authentic record were infinitely valuable.

Let us see their errors, their weaknesses, their daily actions, their familiar conversation and catch the tone of their society. When we discover how far the most admirable community ever formed was removed from that perfection to which human society is impelled by some active power within each bosom to aspire, how great ought to be our hopes, how resolute our struggles! For the Greeks of the Periclean age were widely different from us. It is to be lamented that no modern writer has hitherto dared to show them precisely as they were. Barthélemy cannot be denied the praise of industry and system; but he never forgets that he is a Christian and a Frenchman.[4] Wieland,[5] in his delightful novels, makes indeed a very tolerable Pagan, but cherishes too many political prejudices and refrains from diminishing the interest of his romances by painting sentiments in which no European of modern times can possibly sympathize. There is no book which shows the Greeks precisely as they were; they seem all written for children, with the caution that no practice or sentiment highly inconsistent with our present manners should be mentioned, lest those manners should receive outrage and violation. But there are many to whom the Greek language is inaccessible who ought not to be excluded by this prudery to possess an exact and comprehensive conception of the history of man; for there is no knowledge concerning what man has been and may be from partaking of which a person can depart without becoming in some degree more philosophical, tolerant, and just.

One of the chief distinctions between the manners of ancient Greece and modern Europe consisted in the regulations and the sentiments respecting sexual intercourse. Whether this difference arises from some imperfect influence of the doctrines of Jesus

4. Jean Jacques Barthélemy (1716-1795), French author whose *Voyage du jeune Anacharsis en Grece vers le milieu du quatrieme siecle avant l'ere chietienne* appeared in 1787. This work Shelley read at Bracknell in 1813.

5. Christoph Martin Wieland (1733-1813), distinguished German man of letters, whom Shelley read in 1813-1814.

Christ, who alleges the absolute and unconditional equality of all human beings, or from the institutions of chivalry, or from a certain fundamental difference of physical nature existing in the Celts, or from a combination of all or any of these causes acting on each other is a question worthy of voluminous investigation. The fact is that the modern Europeans have in this circumstance and in the abolition of slavery made an improvement the most decisive in the regulation of human society; and all the virtue and the wisdom of the Periclean age arose under other institutions in spite of the diminution which personal slavery and the inferiority of women, recognized by law and by opinion, must have produced in the delicacy, the strength, the comprehensiveness, and the accuracy of their conceptions in moral, political, and metaphysical science and perhaps in every other art and science.

The women, thus degraded, became such as it was expected they would become. They possessed, except with extraordinary exceptions, the habits and the qualities of slaves. They were probably not extremely beautiful; at least there was no such disproportion in the attractions of the external form between the female and male sex among the Greeks as exists among the modern Europeans. They were certainly devoid of that moral and intellectual loveliness with which the acquisition of knowledge and the cultivation of sentiment animates as with another life of overpowering grace the lineaments and the gestures of every form which it inhabits. Their eyes could not have been deep and intricate from the workings of the mind and could have entangled no heart in soul-enwoven labyrinths.

Let it not be imagined that because the Greeks were deprived of its legitimate object, [they] were incapable of sentimental love; and that this passion is the mere child of chivalry and the literature of modern times. This object or its archetype forever exists in the mind which selects among those who resemble it that which most resembles it[6] and instinctively fills up the interstices of the imperfect image in the same manner as the imagination moulds and completes the shapes in clouds, or in the fire, into the resemblances of whatever form, animal, building, &c., happens to be present to it. Man is in his wildest state a social being;[7] a certain degree of civilization and refinement ever produces the want of sympathies still more intimate and complete; and the gratification of the senses is no longer all that is sought in sexual connection.[8] It soon becomes a very small part of that profound and complicated sentiment which we call love, which is rather the universal thirst for a communion not merely of the senses but of our whole nature, intellectual, imaginative, and sensitive, and which, when individualized, becomes an imperious necessity, only to be satisfied by the complete or partial, actual or supposed fulfilment of its claims. This want grows more powerful in proportion to the development which our nature receives from civilization, for man never ceases to be a social being. The sexual impulse, which is only one and often a small part of these claims, serves from its obvious and external nature as a kind of type or expression of the rest, as common basis, an acknowledged and visible link. Still it is a claim which even derives a strength not its own from the accessory circumstances which surround it and one which our nature thirsts to satisfy. To estimate this, observe the degree of intensity and durability of the love of the male towards the female in animals and savages; and acknowledge all the duration and intensity observable in the love of civi-

6. Compare this statement with a similar one in the *Essay on Love*.
7. This idea is emphasized by Hume, as by Shelley in many places.
8. This conception is fundamental in Shelley's philosophy. See his note to *Queen Mab* to the line,

"Even love is sold." Shelley probably borrowed much from Gibbon's *Decline and Fall of the Roman Empire* for his notion of the attitude of Christianity to the problems of sex. See also Hume's *Essays*, 1.237.

lized beings beyond that of savages to be produced from other causes. In the susceptibility of the external senses there is probably no important difference.

Among the ancient Greeks the male sex, one half of the human race, received the highest cultivation and refinement; while the other, so far as intellect is concerned, were educated as slaves and were raised but few degrees in all that related to moral or intellectual excellence above the condition of savages. The gradations in the history of man present us with a slow improvement in this respect. The Roman women held a higher consideration in society and were esteemed almost as the equal partners with their husbands in the regulation of domestic economy and the education of their children. The practices and customs of modern Europe are essentially different from and incomparably less pernicious than either, however remote from what an enlightened mind cannot fail to desire as the future destiny of human beings.

From this distinction arose that difference of manners which subsists between the ancient Greeks and the modern Europeans. They both had arrived at that epoch of refinement, when sentimental love becomes an imperious want of the heart and of the mind. The senses of both sought with the same impatient eagerness that gratification upon which the perpetuity of our species depends. In modern Europe the sexual and intellectual claims of love, by the more equal cultivation of the two sexes, so far converge towards one point as to produce, in the attempt to unite them, no gross violation in the established nature of man.

Among the Greeks these feelings, being thus deprived of their natural object, sought a compensation and a substitute. The men of Greece corresponded in external form to the models which they have left as specimens of what they were. The firm yet flowing proportion of their forms; the winning unreserve and facility of their manners; the eloquence of their speech, in a language which is itself music and persuasion; their gestures animated at once with the delicacy

and the boldness which the perpetual habit of persuading and governing themselves and others; and the poetry of their religious rites, inspired into their whole being—rendered the youth of Greece a race of beings something widely different from that of modern Europe. If my observation be correct, the word καλος (beautiful) is more frequently applied to the male sex, while ευειδης (handsome) denoted the attractiveness of a female. Whether the cause is to be sought in the climate, in the original constitution of the peculiar race of the Greeks, or in the institutions and system of society, or in the mutual action of these several circumstances, such is the effect. And as a consequence of those causes, beautiful persons of the male sex became the object of that sort of feelings, which are only cultivated at present as towards females.

An enlightened philosophy, although it must condemn the laws by which an indulgence in the sexual instinct is usually regulated, suggests, however, the propriety of habits of chastity in like manner with those of temperance. It regards the senses as but a minute and subordinate portion of our complicated nature, and it deems the pleasures to be derived from their exercise such as are rather weakened, not enhanced by repetition, especially if unassociated with some principle from which they may participate in permanency and excellence. Few characters are more degraded than that of an habitual libertine; that is, a person who is in the custom of seeking a relief from the impulse of the sexual instinct, divested of those associated sentiments which in a civilized state precede, accompany, or follow such an act.

The act itself is nothing. The sources of condemnation to be pronounced against the indulgence in this gratification are twofold: first, as it regards the complicated and arbitrary distinctions of society; and the other as it regards the indestructible laws of human nature.

With respect to the first, the one general law applicable to all other actions is applicable also to this: that nothing is to be done which, including your own being in the estimate, will produce, on the whole, greater pain than pleasure—in this sense adultery, seductions, etc., until mankind shall have enough. With respect to the second, the following propositions may be established as applications of this general law.

First, that the person selected as the subject of this gratification should be as perfect and beautiful as possible, both in body and in mind, so that all sympathies may be harmoniously blended, and the moments of abandonment be prepared by the entire consent of all the conscious portions of our being; the perfection of intercourse consisting, not perhaps in a total annihilation of the instinctive sense, but in the reducing it to as minute a proportion as possible, compared with those higher faculties of our nature, from which it derives a value.

Secondly, temperance in pleasure. This prevents the act which ought always to be the link and type of the highest emotions of our nature from degenerating into a diseased habit, equally pernicious to body and mind. Everyone will recollect Mrs. Shandy's clock; and after the customary smile has passed, cannot but be shocked at the picture it affords of the brutal prostitution of the most sacred impulses of our being.

Thirdly, this act ought to be indulged *according to nature*. A volume of definitions and limitations belong to this maxim, which here may be passed over.

To apply these propositions to the Greeks. The passion which their poets and philosophers described and felt seems inconsistent with this latter maxim, in a degree inconceivable to the imagination of a modern European. But let us not exaggerate the matter. We are not exactly aware—and the laws of modern composition scarcely permit a modest writer to investigate the subject with philosophical accuracy—what that action was by which the Greeks expressed this passion. I am persuaded that it was totally

different from the ridiculous and disgusting conceptions which the vulgar have formed on the subject, at least except among the more debased and abandoned of mankind. It is impossible that a lover could usually have subjected the object of his attachment to so detestable a violation or have consented to associate his own remembrance in the beloved mind with images of pain and horror. If we consider the facility with which certain phenomena connected with sleep, at the age of puberty, associate themselves with those images which are the objects of our waking desires; and even that in some persons of an exalted state of sensibility that a similar process may take place in reverie, it will not be difficult to conceive the almost involuntary consequences of a state of abandonment in the society of a person of surpassing attractions, when the sexual connection cannot exist, to be such as to preclude the necessity of so operose and diabolical a machination as that usually described. This is the result apparently alluded to by Plato.[9] That it could seldom have approached to a resemblance the vulgar imputation, with even among the more gross and unrefined Romans, I appeal to a passage of Petronius, well known to every scholar, in which Giton, the pathic, is represented to talk the language of a woman receiving pleasure from the embraces of Encolpius. This, even as a piece of meretricious flattery, is wholly inconsistent with the vulgar notion.

But let us not measure the Greeks of the age to which I refer with our own feeble conceptions of the intensity of distinterested love; or according to the horrible commentary which the imitation of their manners by the licentious Romans, who had contributed to the overthrow of the Republic, produced upon the text. Probably there were innumerable instances among that exalted and refined people, in which never any circumstance happens [to] the lover and his beloved by which natural modesty was

9. In *Phaedrus*.

wronged. The lover appeased his physical instinct with his wife or his slave; or was engrossed in such lofty thoughts and feelings as admitted of no compromise between them and less intense emotions. Thus much is to be admitted that, represent this passion as you will, there is something totally irreconcilable in its cultivation to the beautiful order of social life, to an equal participation in which all human beings have an indefeasible claim and from which half of the human race by the Greek arrangement were excluded. This invidious distinction of humankind as a class of beings [of] intellectual nature into two sexes is a remnant of savage barbarism which we have less excuse than they for not having totally abolished.

The action by which this passion was expressed, taken in its grossest sense, is indeed sufficiently detestable. But a person must be blinded by superstition to conceive of it as more horrible than the usual intercourse endured by almost every youth of England with a diseased and insensible prostitute. It cannot be more unnatural, for nothing defeats and violates nature, or the purposes for which the sexual instincts are supposed to have existed, than prostitution.[10] Nor is it possible that the society into which the one plunges its victim should be more pernicious than the other. Nothing is at the same time more melancholy and ludicrous than to observe that the inhabitants of one epoch or of one nation harden themselves to all amelioration of their own practices and institutions and soothe their consciences by heaping violent invectives upon those of others while in the eye of sane philosophy their own are no less deserving of censure. If it be inquired how an individual ought to act in the—the reply is—make the best of a bad matter.

The ideas suggested by Catullus, Martial, Juvenal, and Suetonius never occur among the Greeks; or even among those Romans who, like Lucretius, Virgil, Horace, imitated them. The Romans were brutally obscene; the Greeks seemed hardly capable of obscenity in a strict sense. How innocent is even the Lysistrata of Aristophanes compared with the infamous perversions of Catullus! The earlier dramatic English writers are often frightfully obscene, exceeding even the Romans. I should consider obscenity to consist in a capability of associating disgusting images with the act of the sexual instinct. Luxury produced for the Romans what the venereal disease did for the writers of James, and after the redeeming interval over which Milton presided the effects of both were united under Charles II to infect literature.

It may blunt the harshness of censure also to reflect that in the golden age of our own literature a certain sentimental attachment towards persons of the same sex was not uncommon. Shakespeare has devoted the impassioned and profound poetry of his sonnets to commemorate an attachment of this kind, which we cannot question was wholly divested of any unworthy alloy. Towards the age of Charles II it is said that this romantic friendship degenerated into licentiousness, and this latter age bears the same relation to the former as the first of the Roman Empire to . . . .

Thus far the translator has thought it his duty to overstep the jealous limits between what the learned and the unlearned know of the Greeks, and to indicate a system of reasoning which may enable the reader to form a liberal, consistent, and just judgment of the peculiarities of their domestic manners. This slight sketch was undertaken to induce the reader to cast off the cloak of his self-flattering prejudices and forbid the distinction of manners, which he has endeavored to preserve in the translation of the ensuing piece, interfere with his delights or his instruction.

10. Compare this statement with a similar one in Shelley's review of *Alexy Haimatoff*.

THE COLOSSEUM

[This fragmentary sketch was begun on November 25, 1818, on the Shelleys' first visit to Rome. They returned to Rome on February 28, and for the next month made almost daily visits to the Colosseum. See Shelley's letter of December 22, 1818, to Peacock for a vivid description of the Colosseum. To Shelley that ruin was a symbol of the power as of the weakness of man. But in its unfinished state the work has no well-defined theme. As it now stands the fragment is little more than a story of great human interest. Although Shelley's early editors, and apparently Shelley himself, used the Italianate spelling of the word for the Flavian amphitheatre, Coliseum, I have deliberately adopted the more accurate Latin form, *Colosseum*.]

At the hour of noon, on the feast of the Passover, an old man, accompanied by a girl, apparently his daughter, entered the Colosseum at Rome. They immediately passed through the Arena, and seeking a solitary chasm among the arches of the southern part of the ruin, selected a fallen column for their seat, and clasping each other's hands, sat as in silent contemplation of the scene. But the eyes of the girl were fixed upon her father's lips, and his countenance, sublime and sweet, but motionless as some Praxitelean image of the greatest of poets, filled the silent air with smiles, not reflected from external forms.

It was the great feast of the Resurrection, and the whole native population of Rome, together with all the foreigners who flock from all parts of the earth to contemplate its celebration, were assembled around the Vatican. The most awful religion of the world went forth surrounded by emblazonry of mortal greatness, and mankind had assembled to wonder at and worship the creations of their own power. No straggler was to be met with in the streets and grassy lanes which led to the Colosseum. The father and daughter had sought this spot immediately on their arrival.

A figure only visible at Rome in night or solitude, and then only to be seen amid the desolated temples of the Forum, or gliding among the weed-grown galleries of the Colosseum crossed their path. His form, which, though emaciated, displayed the elementary outlines of exquisite grace, was enveloped in an ancient chlamys,[1] which half concealed his face; his snow-white feet were fitted with ivory sandals, delicately sculptured in the likeness of two female figures, whose wings met upon the heel, and whose eager and half-divided lips seemed quivering to meet: It was a face once seen, never to be forgotten. The mouth and the moulding of the chin resembled the eager and impassioned tenderness of the statues of Antinous; but instead of the effeminate sullenness of the eye, and the narrow smoothness of the forehead, shone an expression of profound and piercing thought; the brow was clear and open, and his eyes deep, like two wells of crystalline water which reflect the all-beholding heavens. Over all was spread a timid expression of womanish tenderness and hesitation, which contrasted, yet intermingled strangely, with the abstracted and fearless character that predominated in his form and gestures.

He avoided, in an extraordinary degree, all communication with the Italians, whose language he seemed scarcely to understand, but was occasionally seen to converse with some accomplished foreigner, whose gestures and appearance might attract him amid his solemn haunts. He spoke Latin, and especially Greek, with fluency and with a peculiar but sweet accent; he had apparently

---

1. A short mantle fastened at the front or at the shoulder.

acquired a knowledge of the northern languages of Europe. There was no circumstance connected with him that gave the least intimation of his country, his origin, or his occupation. His dress was strange, but splendid and solemn. He was forever alone. The literati of Rome thought him a curiosity, but there was something in his manner unintelligible but impressive which awed their obtrusions into distance and silence. The countrymen, whose path he rarely crossed, returning by starlight from their market at Campo Vaccino, called him, with that strange mixture of religious and historical ideas so common in Italy, *Il Diavolo di Bruto*.[2]

Such was the figure which interrupted the contemplations, if they were so engaged, of the strangers, by addressing them in the clear, and exact, but unidiomatic phrases of their native language: "Strangers, you are two; behold the third in this great city, to whom alone the spectacle of these mighty ruins is more delightful than the mockeries of a superstition which destroyed them."[3]

"I see nothing," said the old man.

"What do you here, then?"

"I listen to the sweet singing of the birds, and the sound of my daughter's breathing composes me like the soft murmur of water —and I feel the sunwarm wind—and this is pleasant to me."

"Wretched old man, know you not that these are the ruins of the Colosseum?"

"Alas! stranger," said the girl, in a voice like mournful music, "speak not so—he is blind."

The stranger's eyes were suddenly filled with tears, and the lines of his countenance became relaxed. "Blind!" he exclaimed, in a tone of suffering which was more than an apology, and seated himself apart on a flight of shattered and mossy stairs which wound up among the labyrinths of the ruin.

"My sweet Helen," said the old man, "you did not tell me that this was the Colosseum?"

"How should I tell you, dearest father, what I knew not? I was on the point of inquiring the way to that building when we entered this circle of ruins and, until the stranger accosted us I remained silent, subdued by the greatness of what I see."

"It is your custom, sweetest child, to describe to me the objects that give you delight. You array them in the soft radiance of your words, and while you speak I only feel the infirmity which holds me in such dear dependence as a blessing. Why have you been silent now?"

"I know not, first the wonder and pleasure of the sight, then the words of the stranger, and then thinking on what he had said, and how he had looked—and now, beloved father, your own words."

"Well, tell me now, what do you see?"

"I see a great circle of arches built upon arches, and shattered stones lie around, that once made a part of the solid wall. In the crevices and on the vaulted roofs grow a multitude of shrubs, the wild olive and the myrtle—and intricate brambles and entangled weeds and plants I never saw before. The stones are immensely massive, and they jut out one from the other. There are terrible rifts in the wall, and broad windows through which you see the blue heaven. There seems to be more than a thousand arches, some ruined, some entire, and they are all immensely high and wide. Some are shattered, and stand forth in great heaps, and the underwood is tufted on their crumbling summits. Around us lie enormous columns, shattered and shapeless—and fragments of capitals and cornice, fretted with delicate sculptures."

"It is open to the blue sky?" said the old man.

"Yes. We see the liquid depth of heaven above through the rifts and the windows; and the flowers, and the weeds, and the grass and creeping moss are nourished by its unforbidden rain. The blue sky is above—

2. "The Devil of a brute."

3. Shelley always condemned Christianity for destroying the beautiful Greek myths.

the wide, bright, blue sky—it flows through the great rents on high, and through the bare boughs of the marble rooted fig-tree, and through the leaves and flowers of the weeds, even to the dark arcades beneath. I see—I feel its clear and piercing beams fill the universe and impregnate the joy-inspiring wind with life and light, and casting the veil of its splendor over all things —even me. Yes, and through the highest rift the noonday waning moon is hanging, as it were, out of the solid sky, and this shows that the atmosphere has all the clearness which it rejoices me that you feel."

"What else see you?"

"Nothing."

"Nothing?"

"Only the bright-green mossy ground, speckled by tufts of dewy clovergrass that run into the interstices of the shattered arches, and round the isolated pinnacles of the ruin."

"Like the lawny dells of soft short grass which wind among the pine forests and precipices in the Alps of Savoy?"

"Indeed, father, your eye has a vision more serene than mine."

"And the great wrecked arches, the shattered masses of precipitous ruin, overgrown with the younglings of the forest, and more like chasms rent by an earthquake among the mountains than like the vestige of what was human workmanship—what are they?"

"Things awe-inspiring and wonderful."

"Are they not caverns such as the untamed elephant might choose, amid the Indian wilderness, wherein to hide her cubs;

such as, were the sea to overflow the earth, the mightiest monsters of the deep would change into their spacious chambers?"

"Father, your words image forth what I would have expressed, but alas! could not."

"I hear the rustling of leaves, and the sound of waters, but it does not rain—like the faint drops of fountain among woods."

"It falls from among the heaps of ruin over our heads—it is, I suppose, the water collected in the rifts by the showers."

"A nursling of man's art, abandoned by his care, and transformed by the enchantment of Nature into a likeness of her own creations, and destined to partake their immortality! Changed into a mountain cloven with woody dells which overhang its labyrinthine glade, and shattered into toppling precipices. Even the clouds, intercepted by its craggy summit, feed its eternal fountains with their rain. By the column on which I sit, I should judge that it had once been crowned by a temple or a theater, and that on sacred days the multitude wound up its craggy path to the spectacle or the sacrifice. It was such itself!4 Helen, what sound of wings is that?"

"It is the wild pigeons returning to their young. Do you not hear the murmur of those that are brooding in their nests?"

"Ay, it is the language of their happiness. They are as happy as we are, child, but in a different manner. They know not the sensations which this ruin excites within us. Yet it is pleasure to them to inhabit it; and the succession of its forms as they pass is connected with associations in their minds,

4. Nor does a recollection of the use to which it may have been destined interfere with these emotions. Time has thrown its purple shadow athwart this scene, and no more is visible than the broad and everlasting character of human strength and genius, that pledge of all that is to be admirable and lovely in ages yet to come. Solemn temples, where the senate of the world assembled, palaces, triumphal arches, and cloud-surrounded columns, loaded with the sculptured annals of conquest and domination—what actions and deliberations have they been destined to enclose and commemorate? Superstitious rites, which in their mildest form, outrage reason, and obscure the moral sense of mankind; schemes for wide-extended murder, and devas-

tation, and misrule, and servitude; and, lastly, these schemes brought to their tremendous consummations, and a human being returning in the midst of festival and solemn joy, with thousands and thousands of his enslaved and desolated species chained behind his chariot, exhibiting, as titles to renown, the labor of ages, and the admired creations of genius, overthrown by the brutal force which was placed as a sword within his hand and, contemplation fearful and abhorred!—he himself a being capable of the gentlest and best emotions, inspired with the persuasion that he has done a virtuous deed! We do not forget these things. . . . [Shelley's Note.]

sacred to them, as these to us. The internal nature of each being is surrounded by a circle, not to be surmounted by his fellows; and it is this repulsion which constitutes the misfortune of the condition of life. But there is a circle which comprehends, as well as one which mutually excludes, all things which feel. And, with respect to man, his public and his private happiness consists in diminishing the circumference which includes those resembling himself, until they become one with him and he with them. It is because we enter into the meditations, designs, and destinies of something beyond ourselves that the contemplation of the ruins of human power excites an elevating sense of awfulness and beauty. It is therefore that the ocean, the glacier, the cataract, the tempest, the volcano have each a spirit which animates the extremities of our frame with tingling joy. It is therefore that the singing of birds, and the motion of leaves, the sensation of the odorous earth beneath, and the freshness of the living wind around is sweet. And this is Love.[5] This is the religion of eternity, whose votaries have been exiled from among the multitude of mankind. O Power!" cried the old man, lifting his sightless eyes towards the undazzling sun, "thou which interpenetratest all things, and without which this glorious world were a blind and formless chaos, Love, Author of Good, God, King, Father! Friend of these thy worshippers! Two solitary hearts invoke thee, may they be divided never! If the contentions of mankind have been their misery; if to give and seek that happiness which thou art has been their choice and destiny; if, in the contemplation of these majestic records of the power of their kind, they see the shadow and the prophecy of that which thou mayst have decreed that he should become; if the justice, the liberty, the loveliness, the truth, which are thy footsteps have been sought by them, divide them not! It is thine to unite, to eternize; to make outlive the limits of the grave those who have left

among the living memorials of thee. When this frame shall be senseless dust, may the hopes, and the desires, and the delights which animate it now, never be extinguished in my child; even as, if she were borne into the tomb, my memory would be the written monument of all her nameless excellencies!"

The old man's countenance and gestures, radiant with the inspiration of his words, sunk, as he ceased, into more than its accustomed calmness, for he heard his daughter's sobs, and remembered that he had spoken of death. "My father, how can I outlive you?" said Helen.

"Do not let us talk of death," said the old man, suddenly changing his tone. "Heraclitus, indeed, died at my age, and if I had so sour a disposition, there might be some danger. But Democritus reached a hundred and twenty by the mere dint of a joyous and unconquerable mind. He only died at last, because he had no gentle and beloved ministering spirit like my Helen for whom it would have been his delight to live. You remember his gay old sister requested him to put off starving himself to death until she had returned from the festival of Ceres alleging that it would spoil her holiday if he refused to comply, as it was not permitted to appear in the procession immediately after the death of a relation; and how good-temperedly the sage acceded to her request."

The old man could not see his daughter's grateful smile, but he felt the pressure of her hand by which it was expressed. "In truth," he continued, "that mystery, death, is a change which neither for ourselves nor for others is the just object of hope or fear. We know not if it be good or evil; we only know it is. The old, the young may alike die; no time, no place, no age, no foresight exempts us from death and the chance of death. We have no knowledge if death be a state of sensation, or any precaution that can make those sensations fortunate, if the existing series of events shall not produce that effect. Think not of death, or think of it as some-

5. Compare this idea with that on the same subject in his *Essay on Love.*

thing common to us all. It has happened," said he, with a deep and suffering voice, "that men have buried their children."

"Alas! then, dearest father, how I pity you. Let us speak no more."

They arose to depart from the Colosseum, but the figure which had first accosted them interposed itself: "Lady," he said, "if grief be an expiation of error, I have grieved deeply for the words which I spoke to your companion. The men who anciently inhabited this spot and those from whom they learned their wisdom respected infirmity and age. If I have rashly violated that venerable form, at once majestic and defenceless, may I be forgiven?"

"It gives me pain to see how much your mistake afflicts you," she said; "if you can forget, doubt not that we forgive."

"You thought me one of those who are blind in spirit," said the old man, "and who deserve, if any human being can deserve, contempt and blame. Assuredly, contemplating this monument as I do, though in the mirror of my daughter's mind, I am filled with astonishment and delight; the spirit of departed generations seems to animate my limbs and circulate through all the fibres of my frame. Stranger, if I have expressed what you have ever felt, let us know each other more."

"The sound of your voice and the harmony of your thoughts are delightful to me," said the youth, "and it is a pleasure to see any form which expresses so much beauty and goodness as your daughter's; if you reward me for my rudeness, by allowing me to know you, my error is already expiated, and you remember my ill words no more. I live a solitary life, and it is rare that I encounter any stranger with whom it is pleasant to talk; besides, their meditations, even though they be learned, do not always agree with mine; and, though I can pardon this difference, they cannot. Nor have I ever explained the cause of the dress I wear, and the difference which I perceive between my language and manners, and those with whom I have intercourse—not but that it is painful to me to live without communion with intelligent and affectionate beings. You are such, I feel."

A PHILOSOPHICAL VIEW OF REFORM

[*A Philosophical View of Reform* had its inception in the political unrest and the imminence of revolution in the closing days of 1819. The first reference to the essay is in a letter to the Gisbornes on November 6. Shelley remarks that he "has deserted the odorous gardens of literature to journey across the great sandy desert of politics." Earlier in the letter is a rough outline of the contents of the essay. On December 15 in a letter to Charles Ollier, Shelley writes, "I am preparing an octavo on reform. . . . I intend it to be an instructive and readable book, appealing from the passions to the reason of men." And on May 26, 1820, to Hunt: "Do you know any bookseller who would publish for me an octavo volume entitled *A Philosophical View of Reform?* It is boldly but temperately written, and I think readable. It is intended for a kind of standard book for the philosophical reformers, politically considered." It is not known why Ollier did not offer to publish it.

In preparing the prose for publication in her 1839-40 edition, Mary Shelley copied it with the apparent intention of publishing it, but she did not include it, perhaps fearing complications with Sir Timothy Shelley, whose heavy hand was laid on her every effort to do justice to the memory of her husband.

The original manuscript, in a two-hundred page Italian notebook, was presented by Lady Shelley to the Reverend Stopford A. Brooke. On his death in 1916, it passed to his daughter. Her husband, T. W. Rolleston, edited the work and published it in 1920, just one hundred years after its composition. The manuscript is now in possession of Mr. Carl Pforzheimer of New York, and Mary's transcript is in the Bodleian Library at Oxford. The work was left unfinished, with many gaps in the text, yet it is remarkably well unified, and readable. See Julian Editions 7.333 for further details.

As the essay now stands it is divided into three chapters: the first hastily outlines the rise of despotic states in link with the Catholic Church to the fall of the Roman Empire. The wise social teachings of Jesus, Shelley says, were distorted by the Church for the sole purpose of gaining temporal power and enslaving the people. The Reformation renewed something of the spirit of Jesus in that the poor and the oppressed gained a modicum of relief from their natural enemies, the rich. With the Reformation the freedom and dignity of man were strongly asserted, and the history of man for the next two hundred years was a record of the struggle of the spirit of freedom against entrenched authority in church and state. The final triumph of liberty found complete expression in the revolutions in America and France. In all this struggle it was the spirit of the great philosophers, Berkeley, Hume, Hartley, Spinoza, and Lord Bacon that led the advance, thus giving to practical reform a philosophical base and ethical foundation.

Chapter two traces rapidly the history of England from Charles First to Shelley's own day with the rise of political parties and the enslavement of the masses to the God of Greed. In this chapter Shelley insists on the necessity of change. The third and last chapter outlines the means by which necessary reforms might be achieved. Shelley here maintains that a gradual and peaceable change is desirable. He decries revolution or the use of force except as a final and only means of bringing about salutary and necessary reforms. "The first principle of political reform is the natural equality of men, not with relation to their property but to their rights. That equality in property which Jesus Christ so passionately taught is a moral rather than a political truth and is such as social institutions cannot without mischief inflexibly secure. Morals and politics can only be considered as portions of the same science . . . equality in possessions must be the last result of the utmost refinements of civilization." This is the ultimate, but remote, goal of all reform; the immediate goal is for gradual reforms in the tax and franchise systems. At the bottom of all wholesome change is freedom of speech and press and assembly. While Shelley recommends passive resistance to constituted authority, that alone will not suffice, for the good life can be achieved only by active and courageous minds. In the van of this onward march of civilization are the poet, the prophet, the philosopher, for it is they who are the free men—they who must teach enslaved minds *how* to be free.

There is nothing mystical or impractical or starry-eyed in this essay. It is everywhere informed with common sense and clear-eyed wisdom.]

[FOREWORD]

Those who imagine that their personal interest is directly or indirectly concerned in maintaining the power in which they are clothed by the existing institutions of English Government do not acknowledge the necessity of a material change in those institutions . . . . With this exception, there is no inhabitant of the British Empire of mature age and perfect understanding not fully persuaded of the necessity of Reform. Let us believe not only that [it] is necessary because it is just and ought to be, but necessary because it is inevitable and must be.

[OUTLINE]

1st. Sentiment of the necessity of change.

2nd. Practicability and utility of such a change.

3rd. State of parties as regards it.

4th. Probable mode—desirable mode.

CHAPTER I

Introduction

From the dissolution of the Roman Empire, that vast and successful scheme for the enslaving [of] the most civilized portion of mankind, to the epoch of the present year have succeeded a series of schemes on a smaller scale, operating to the same effect.[1] Names borrowed from the life and opinions of Jesus Christ were employed as symbols of domination and imposture, and a system of liberty and equality (for such was the system preached by that great Reformer) was perverted to support oppression—not his doctrines, for they are too simple and direct to be susceptible of such perversion, but the mere names.[2] Such was the origin of the Catholic Church, which, together with the several dynasties then beginning to consolidate themselves in Europe, means, being interpreted, a plan according to which the

1. Compare this statement with one at the beginning of the *Essay on Revival of Literature*, which indeed may be a fragment of the unfinished *Philo-sophical View of Reform*.

2. This view of Jesus is one which Shelley held consistently throughout his life.

cunning and selfish few have employed the fears and hopes of the ignorant many to the establishment of their own power and the destruction of the real interest of all.

The republics and municipal governments of Italy opposed for some time a systematic and effectual resistance to the all-surrounding tyranny. The Lombard League defeated the armies of the despot in open field, and until Florence was betrayed to those flattered traitors [and] polished tyrants, the Medici, Freedom had one citadel wherein it could find refuge from a world which was its enemy. Florence long balanced, divided, and weakened the strength of the Empire and the Popedom. To this cause, if to anything, was due the undisputed superiority of Italy in literature and the arts over all its contemporary nations, that union of energy and of beauty which distinguish[es] from all other poets the writings of Dante, that restlessness of fervid power which expressed itself in painting and sculpture and in daring architectural forms, and from which, and conjointly from the creations of Athens, its predecessor and its image, Raphael and Michel Angelo drew the inspiration which created those forms and colors now the astonishment of the world.[3] The father of our own literature, Chaucer, wrought from the simple and powerful language of a nursling of this republic the basis of our own literature. And thus we owe among other causes the exact condition belonging to [our own] intellectual existence to the generous disdain of submission which burned in the bosoms of men who filled a distant generation and inhabited another land.[4]

When this resistance was overpowered (as what resistance to fraud and [tyranny] has not been overpowered?) another was even then maturing. The progress of philosophy and civilization which ended in that imperfect emancipation of mankind from the yoke of priests and kings called the Reformation had already commenced. Exasperated by

their long sufferings, inflamed by the spark of that superstition from the flames of which they were emerging, the poor rose against their natural enemies, the rich, and repaid with bloody interest the tyranny of ages. One of the signs of the times was that the oppressed peasantry rose like the negro slaves of West Indian plantations and murdered their tyrants when they were unaware. For so dear is power that the tyrants themselves neither then, nor now, nor ever, left or leave a path to freedom but through their own blood. The contest then waged under the names of religion—which have seldom been any more [than] the popular and visible symbols which express the degree of power in some shape or other asserted by one party and disclaimed by the other—ended; and the result, though partial and imperfect, is perhaps the most animating that the philanthropist can contemplate in the history of man. The Republic of Holland, which has been so long an armory of the arrows of learning by which superstition has been wounded even to death, was established by this contest. What though the name of Republic—and by whom but by conscience-stricken tyrants could it be extinguished—is no more? The Republics of Switzerland derived from this event their consolidation and their union. From England then first began to pass away the strain of conquest. The exposition of a certain portion of religious imposture drew with it an inquiry into political imposture and was attended with an extraordinary exertion of the energies of intellectual power. Shakespeare and Lord Bacon and the great writers of the age of Elizabeth and James the 1st were at once the effects of the new spirit in men's minds and the causes of its more complete development. By rapid gradation the nation was conducted to the temporary abolition of aristocracy and episcopacy, and [to] the mighty example which, "in teaching nations how to live," England afforded to the world—of bringing

3. Similar ideas are stated in *A Defence of Poetry* and *A Discourse on the Manners of the Ancient Greeks.*

4. See *A Defence of Poetry* for a similar discussion.

to public justice one of those chiefs of a conspiracy of privileged murderers and robbers whose impunity has been the consecration of crime.[5]

After the selfish passions and compromising interests of men had enlisted themselves to produce and establish the restoration of Charles the 2nd the unequal combat was renewed under the reign of his successor,[6] and that compromise between the unextinguishable spirit of Liberty and the ever-watchful spirit of fraud and tyranny, called the Revolution, had place. On this occasion monarchy and aristocracy and episcopacy were at once established and limited by law. Unfortunately they lost no more in extent of power than they gained in security of possession. Meanwhile those by whom they were established acknowledged and declared that the will of the people was the source from which these powers, in this instance, derived the right to subsist.[7] A man has no right to be a king or lord or a bishop but so long as it is for the benefit of the people and so long as the people judge that it is for their benefit that he should impersonate that character. The solemn establishment of this maxim as the basis of our constitutional law more than any beneficial and energetic application of it to the circumstances of this era of its promulgation was the fruit of that vaunted event. Correlative with this series of events in England was the commencement of a new epoch in the history of the progress of civilization and society.

That superstition which has disguised itself under the name of the religion of Jesus subsisted under all its forms, even where it had been separated from those things especially considered as abuses by the multitude, in the shape of intolerant and oppressive hierarchies. Catholics massacred Protestants and Protestants proscribed Catholics,

and extermination was the sanction of each faith within the limits of the power of its professors.[8] The New Testament is in everyone's hand, and the few who ever read it with the simple sincerity of an unbiased judgment may perceive how distinct from the opinions of any of those professing themselves establishers[9] were the doctrines and the actions of Jesus Christ. At the period of the Reformation this test was applied, and this judgment formed of the then existing hierarchy, and the same compromise was then made between the spirit of truth and the spirit of imposture after [the] struggle which ploughed up the area of the human mind as was made in the particular instance of England between the spirit of freedom and the spirit of tyranny at that event called the Revolution.[10] In both instances the maxims so solemnly recorded remain as trophies of our difficult and incomplete victory, planted in the enemies' land. *The will of the people to change their government is an acknowledged right in the Constitution of England.* The protesting against religious dogmas which present themselves to his mind as false is the inalienable prerogative of every human being.

The new epoch was marked by the commencement of deeper inquiries into the forms of human nature than are compatible with an unreserved belief in any of those popular mistakes upon which popular systems of faith with respect to the cause and agencies of the universe, with all their superstructure of political and religious tyranny, are built.[11] Lord Bacon, Spinoza, Hobbes, Bayle, Montaigne regulated the reasoning powers, criticized the past history, exposed the errors by illustrating their causes and their connection, and anatomized the inmost nature of social man. Then, with a less interval of time than of genius followed

---

5. The execution of Charles I.
6. James II (1685-1688).
7. John Locke in his tracts on civil government became the spokesman of this philosophy.
8. Compare similar statements in *An Address to the Irish People* (1812).

9. The Pope, Luther, Calvin, and others.
10. The Revolution of 1688.
11. As knowledge increases, organized religion (superstition) decreases—this was a firm belief held by Shelley.

[Locke] and the philosophers of his exact and intelligible but superficial school. Their illustrations of some of the minor consequences of the doctrines established by the sublime genius of their predecessors were correct, popular, simple, and energetic. Above all, they indicated inferences the most incompatible with the popular religions and the established governments of Europe. [Philosophy went forth into the enchanted forest of the demons of worldly power as the pioneer of the over-growth of ages.] Berkeley, and Hume, [and] Hartley [at a] later age, following the traces of these inductions, have clearly established the certainity of our ignorance with respect to those obscure questions which under the name of religious truths have been the watch-words of contention and the symbols of unjust power ever since they were distorted by the narrow passions of the immediate followers of Jesus from that meaning to which philosophers are even now restoring them. A crowd of writers in France seized upon the most popular portions of the new philosophy which conducted to inferences at war with the dreadful oppressions under which the country groaned made familiar to mankind the falsehood of their religious mediators and political oppressors. Considered as philosophers their error seems to have consisted chiefly of a limitedness of view; they told the truth, but not the whole truth. This might have arisen from the terrible sufferings of their countrymen inviting them rather to apply a portion of what had already been discovered to their immediate relief than to pursue one interest, the abstractions of thought, as the great philosophers who preceded them had done, for the sake of a future and more universal advantage. While that philosophy which, burying itself in the obscure part of our nature, regards the truth and falsehood of dogmas relating to the cause of the universe and the nature and manner of man's relation with it, was thus stripping power of its darkest mask, political philosophy, or that which considers the relations of man as a social

being, was assuming a precise form. This philosophy indeed sprang from and maintained a connection with that other as its parent. What would Swift and Bolingbroke and Sidney [Algernon] and Locke and Montesquieu, or even Rousseau, not to speak of political philosophers of our own age, Godwin and Bentham, have been but for Lord Bacon, Montaigne, and Spinoza, and the other great luminaries of the preceding epoch? Something excellent and eminent, no doubt, the least of these would have been, but something different from and inferior to what they are. A series of these writers illustrated with more or less success the principles of human nature as applied to man in political society. A thirst for accommodating the existing forms according to which mankind are found divided to those rules of freedom and equality which are thus discovered as being the elementary principles according to which the happiness resulting from the social union ought to be produced and distributed was kindled by these inquiries. Contemporary with this condition of the intellect all the powers of man seemed, though in most cases under forms highly inauspicious, to develop themselves with uncommon energy. The mechanical sciences attained to a degree of perfection which, though obscurely foreseen by Lord Bacon, it had been accounted madness to have prophesied in a preceding age. Commerce was pursued with a perpetually increasing vigor, and the same area of the earth was perpetually compelled to furnish more and more subsistence. The means and sources of knowledge were thus increased together with knowledge itself and the instruments of knowledge. The benefit of this increase of the powers of man became, in consequence of the inartificial forms into which society came to be distributed, an instrument of his additional evil. The capabilities of happiness were increased and applied to the augmentation of misery. Modern society is thus an engine assumed to be for useful purposes, whose force is by a system of subtle mechanism augmented to the highest pitch, but which, instead of grinding corn or raising water, acts against itself and is perpetually wearing away or breaking to pieces the wheels of which it is composed. The result of the labors of the political philosophers has been the establishment of the principle of utility as the substance and liberty and equality as the forms, according to which the concerns of human life ought to be administered. By this test the various institutions regulating political society have been tried and, as the undigested growth of the private passions, errors, and interests of barbarians and oppressors have been condemned. And many new theories, more or less perfect, but all superior to the mass of evil which they would supplant, have been given to the world.

The system of government in the United States of America was the first practical illustration of the new philosophy. Sufficiently remote, it will be confessed, from the accuracy of ideal excellence is that representative system which will soon cover the extent of that vast Continent. But it is scarcely less remote from the insolent and contaminating tyrannies under which, with some limitation of these terms as regards England, Europe groaned at the period of the successful rebellion of America. America holds forth the victorious example of an immensely populous[12] and, as far as the external arts of life are concerned, a highly civilized community administered according to republican forms. It has no king; that is, it has no officer to whom wealth and from whom corruption flows. It has no hereditary oligarchy; that is, it acknowledges no order of men privileged to cheat and insult the rest of the members of the state and who inherit a right of legislating and judging which the principles of human nature compel them to exercise to their own profit and to the detriment of those not included within their peculiar class. It has no established church; that is, it has no system of opinions respecting the abstrusest questions which can be topics of human thought founded in an age of error and fanaticism and opposed by law to all other opinions, defended by prosecutions and sanctioned by enormous bounties given to idle priests and forced through the unwilling hands of those who have an interest in the cultivation and improvement of the soil. It has no false representation, whose consequences are captivity, confiscation, infamy, and ruin, but a true representation. The will of the many is represented by the few in the assemblies of legislation and by the officers of the executive entrusted with the administration of the executive power almost as directly as the will of one person can be represented by the will of another. [This is not the place for dilating upon the inexpressible advantages (if such advantages require any manifestation) of a self-governing society, or one which approaches it in the degree of the Republic of the United States.] Lastly, it has an institution by which it is honorably distinguished from all other governments which ever existed. It constitutionally acknowledges the progress of human improvement and is framed under the limitation of the probability of more simple views of political science being rendered applicable to human life. There is a law by which the constitution is reserved for revision every ten years.[13] Every other set of men who have assumed the office of legislation and framing institutions for future ages, with far less right to such an assumption than the founders of the American Republic, assumed that their work was the wisest and the best that could possibly have been produced; these illustrious men[14] looked upon the past history of their species and saw that

12. At the time Shelley wrote this sentence the population of the United States of America was approximately nine million.
13. Shelley is in error here. It is true, however, that while such a clause was proposed, it was never adopted. Jefferson did argue that there should be a revolution every twenty years. Compare Jefferson's liberal views with that of the witchhunters today.
14. The framers of the Constitution.

it was the history of his mistakes and his sufferings arising from his mistakes; they observed the superiority of their own work to all the works which had preceded it, and they judged it probable that other political institutions would be discovered bearing the same relation to those which they had established which they bear to those which have preceded them. They provided therefore for the application of these contingent discoveries to the social state without the violence and misery attendant upon such change in less modest and more imperfect governments. The United States, as we would have expected from theoretical deduction, affords an example, compared with the old governments of Europe and Asia, of a free, happy, and strong people. Nor let it be said that they owe their superiority rather to the situation than to their government. Give them a king, and let that king waste in luxury, riot, and bribery the same sum which now serves for the entire expenses of their government. Give them an aristocracy, and let that aristocracy legislate for the people. Give them a priesthood, and let them bribe with a tenth of the produce of the soil a certain set of men to say a certain set of words.[15] Pledge the larger part of them by financial subterfuges to pay the half of their property or earnings to another portion, and let the proportion of those who enjoy the fruits of the toil of others without toiling themselves be three instead of one. Give them a Court of Chancery, and let the property, the liberty, and the interest in the dearest concerns of life, the exercise of the most sacred rights of a social being, depend upon the will of one of the most servile creature[s] of that kingly and oligarchical and priestly power to which every man in proportion as he is of an inquiring and philosophical mind and of a sincere and honorable disposition is a natural, a necessary enemy. Give them, as you must if you give them these things, a great standing army to cut down the people if they murmur. If any American should see these words, his blood would run cold at the imagination of such a change. He well knows that the prosperity and happiness of the United States if subjected to such institutions [would] be no more.[16]

The just and successful revolt[17] of America corresponded with a state of public opinion in Europe of which it was the first result. The French Revolution was the second. The oppressors of mankind had enjoyed (O that we could say suffered) a long and undisturbed reign in France, and to the pining famine, the shelterless destitution of the inhabitants of that country had been added and heaped-up insult harder to endure than misery. For the feudal system (the immediate causes and conditions of its institution having become obliterated) had degenerated into an instrument not only of oppression but of contumely, and both were unsparingly inflicted. Blind in the possession of strength, drunken as with the intoxication of ancestral greatness, the rulers perceived not that increase of knowledge in their subjects which made its exercise insecure. They called soldiers to hew down the people when their power was already past. The tyrants were, as usual, the aggressors. Then the oppressed, having been rendered brutal, ignorant, servile, and bloody by long slavery, having had the intellectual thirst excited in them by the progress of civilization, satiated from fountains of literature poisoned by the spirit and the form of monarchy, arose and took a dreadful revenge on their oppressors. Their desire to wreak revenge to this extent, in itself a mistake, a crime, a calamity, arose from the same source as their other miseries and errors and affords an additional proof of the necessity of that long-delayed change which it accompanied and disgraced. If a just and necessary revolution could have

15. Shelley's war on priests and on legislators as the source of most of the world's troubles was both persistent and consistent throughout his life.
16. But we have fallen victims to many of the

evils Shelley lamented in his own country.
17. Shelley is using his words very exactly when he speaks of *revolt* in America, and *revolution* in France.

been accomplished with as little expense of happiness and order in a country governed by despotic as [in] one governed by free laws, equal liberty and justice would lose their chief recommendations and tyranny be divested of its most revolting attributes. Tyranny entrenches itself within the existing interests of the most refined citizens of a nation and says, "If you dare trample upon these, be free." Though this terrible condition shall not be evaded, the world is no longer in a temper to decline the challenge.

The French were what their literature is (excluding Montaigne and Rousseau, and some few leaders of the . . .) weak, superficial, vain, with little imagination, and with passions as well as judgments cleaving to the external form of things. Not that [they] are organically different from the inhabitants of the nations who have become . . . or rather not that their organical differences, whatever they may amount to, incapacitate them from arriving at the exercise of the highest powers to be attained by man. Their institutions made them what they were. Slavery and superstition, contumely and the tame endurance of contumely, and the habits engendered from generation to generation out of this transmitted inheritance of wrong, created this thing which has extinguished what has been called the likeness of God in man. The Revolution in France overthrew the hierarchy, the aristocracy, and the monarchy, and the whole of that peculiarly insolent and oppressive system on which they were based. But as it only partially extinguished those passions which are the spirit of these forms a reaction took place which has restored in a certain limited degree the old system—in a degree, indeed, exceedingly limited, and stript of all its ancient terrors. The hope of the monarchy of France, with his teeth drawn and his claws pared, was its maintaining the formal likeness of most imperfect and insecure dominion. The usurpation of Bonaparte, and

then the Restoration of the Bourbons were the shapes in which this reaction clothed itself, and the heart of every lover of liberty was struck as with palsy by the succession of these events. But reversing the proverbial expression of Shakespeare, it may be the good which the Revolutionists did lives after them, their ills are interred with their bones.[18] But the military project of government of the great tyrant having failed, and there being even no attempt—and, if there were any attempt, there being not the remotest possibility of re-establishing the enormous system of tyranny ·abolished by the Revolution—France is, as it were, regenerated. Its legislative assemblies are in a certain limited degree representations of the popular will, and the executive power is hemmed in by jealous laws. France occupies in this respect the same situation as was occupied by England at the restoration of Charles the 2nd. It has undergone a revolution (unlike in the violence and calamities which attended it, because unlike in the abuses which it was excited to put down) which may be paralleled with that in our own country which ended in the death of Charles the 1st. The authors of both revolutions proposed a greater and more glorious object than the degraded passions of their countrymen permitted them to attain. But in both cases abuses were abolished which never since have dared to show their face.[19] There remains in the natural order of human things that the tyranny and perfidy of the reigns of Charles the 2nd and James the 2nd (for these were less the result of the disposition of particular men than the vices which would have been engendered in any but an extraordinary man by the natural necessities of their situation) perhaps under a milder form and within a shorter period should produce the institution of a government in France which may bear the same relation to the state of political knowledge existing at the present day, as the Revolution

18. *Julius Caesar,* 3.2.81-82.
19. See the Preface to *Laon and Cythna* for an earlier, though similar statement concerning the

cause, the course, and the apparent failure of the Revolution.

under William the 3rd bore to the state of political knowledge existing at that period.

Germany, which is among the great nations of Europe one of the latest civilized with the exception of Russia, is rising with the fervor of a vigorous youth to the assertion of those rights for which it has that desire arising from knowledge, the surest pledge of victory. The deep passion and the bold and Aeschylean vigor of the imagery of their poetry; the enthusiasm, however distorted, of their religious sentiments; the flexibility and comprehensiveness of their language, which is a many-sided mirror of every changing thought; their severe, bold, and liberal spirit of criticism; their subtle and deep philosophy, however erroneous and illogical [in] mingling fervid intuitions into truth with obscure error (for the period of just distinction is yet to come), and their taste and power in the plastic arts, prove that they are a great people. And every great people either has been, or is, or will be free. The panic-stricken tyrants of that country promised to their subjects that their governments should be administered according to republican forms, they retaining merely the right of hereditary chief magistracy in their families. This promise, made in danger, the oppressors dream that they can break in security. And everything in consequence wears in Germany the aspect of rapidly maturing revolution.[20]

In Spain and in the dependencies of Spain good and evil in the forms of despair and tyranny are struggling foot to foot. That great people have been delivered bound hand and foot to be trampled upon and insulted by a traitorous and sanguinary tyrant, a wretch who makes credible all that might have been doubted in the history of Nero, Christiern,[21] Muley Ismael,[22] or Ezzelin[23]—the persons who have thus delivered them were that hypocritical knot of conspiring tyrants who proceeded upon the credit they gained by putting down the only tyrant among them who was not a hypocrite to undertake the administration of those *arrondissements* of consecrated injustice and violence which they deliver to those who the nearest resemble them under the name of the "kingdoms of the earth." This action signed a sentence of death, confiscation, exile, or captivity against every philosopher and patriot in Spain. The tyrant Ferdinand, he whose name is changed into a proverb of execration, found natural allies in all the priests and a few of the most dishonorable military chiefs of that devoted country. And the consequences of military despotism and the black, stagnant, venomous hatred which priests in common with eunuchs seek every opportunity to wreak upon the portion of mankind exempt from their own unmanly disqualifications is slavery. And what is slavery—in its mildest form hideous and, so long as one amiable or great attribute survives in its victims, rankling and intolerable, but in its darkest shape [as] it now exhibits itself in Spain it is the presence of all and more than all the evils for the sake of an exemption from which mankind submit to the mighty calamity of government. It is a system of insecurity of property, and of person, of prostration of conscience and understanding, of famine heaped upon the greater number, and contumely heaped upon all, defended by unspeakable tortures employed not merely as punishments but as precautions, by want, death, and captivity, and the application to political purposes of the execrated and enormous instruments of religious cruelty. Those men of understanding, integrity, and courage who rescued their country from one tyrant are exiled from it by his successor and his enemy and their

<hr/>

20. The revolution—a minor one—did come twenty-eight years later. This evaluation of the government and people of Germany is penetrating.

21. Christiern was Christian II of Sweden, who ordered in 1520 the Massacre of Stockholm.

22. Ismael, Emperor of Morocco (1673-1727), put his son to a slow death.

23. Ezzelin, Lord of Padua, in the thirteenth century was the greatest tyrant of his age.

legitimate king.[24] Tyrants, however they may squabble among themselves, have common friends and foes. The taxes are levied at the point of the sword. Armed insurgents occupy all the defensible mountains of the country. The dungeons are peopled thickly, and persons of every sex and age have the fibres of their frame torn by subtle torments. Boiling water (such is an article in the last news from Spain) is poured upon the legs of a noble Spanish Lady newly delivered, slowly and cautiously, that she may confess what she knows of a conspiracy against the tyrant, and she dies, as constant as the slave Epicharis, imprecating curses upon her torturers and passionately calling upon her children. These events, in the present condition of the understanding and sentiment of mankind, are the rapidly passing shadows which forerun successful insurrection, the ominous comets of our republican poet[25] perplexing great monarchs with fear of change.[26] Spain, having passed through an ordeal severe in proportion to the wrongs and errors which it is kindled to erase, must of necessity be renovated. [The country which] produced Calderon and Cervantes, what else did it but breathe through the tumult of the despotism and superstition which invested them, the prophecy of a glorious consummation?[27]

The independents of South America are as it were already free. Great republics are about to consolidate themselves in a portion of the globe sufficiently vast and fertile to nourish more human beings than at present occupy, with the exception perhaps of China, the remainder of the inhabited earth. Some indefinite arrears of misery and blood remain to be paid to the Moloch of oppression. These, to the last drop and groan, it will implacably exact. But not the less are [they] inevitably enfranchised. The great monarchies of Asia cannot, let us confidently hope, remain unshaken by the earthquake which shatters to dust the "mountainous strongholds" of the tyrants of the western world.

Revolutions in the political and religious state of the Indian peninsula seem to be accomplishing, and it cannot be doubted but the zeal of the missionaries of what is called the Christian faith will produce beneficial innovation there, even by the application of dogmas and forms of what is here an outworn incumbrance.[28] The Indians have been enslaved and cramped in the most severe and paralyzing forms which were ever devised by man; some of this new enthusiasm ought to be kindled among them to consume it and leave them free, and even if the doctrines of Jesus do not penetrate through the darkness of that which those who profess to be his followers call Christianity,[29] there will yet be a number of social forms modelled upon those European feelings from which it has taken its color substituted to those according to which they are at present cramped, and from which, when the time for complete emancipation shall arrive, their disengagement may be less difficult, and under which their progress to it may be the less imperceptibly slow. Many native Indians have acquired, it is said, a competent knowledge in the arts and philosophy of Europe, and Locke and Hume and Rousseau are familiarly talked of in Brahminical society. But the thing to be sought is that they should as they would if they were free attain to a system of arts and literature of their own. Of Persia we know little but that it has been the theater of sanguinary contests for power, and that it is now at peace. The Persians appear to be from organization a beautiful, refined, and impassioned people and would probably soon be infected by the contagion

24. Spain still lies prostrate and ignorant under the twin tyrannies of Church and State.

25. Milton.

26. Compare *Paradise Lost*, 1.597-598 "With fear of change Perplexing Monarchs."

27. For a poetic expression of these ideas see Shelley's *Ode to Liberty* (1820).

28. This is a nice distinction which Shelley here makes.

29. It is a fundamental Shelleyan philosophy to distinguish between the teachings of Jesus and the distortions of those teachings in institutionalized Christianity.

of good. The Jews, that wonderful people which has preserved so long the symbols of their union, may reassume their ancestral seats,[30] and—the Turkish Empire is in its last stage of ruin, and it cannot be doubted but that the time is approaching when the deserts of Asia Minor and of Greece will be colonized by the overflowing population of countries less enslaved and debased, and that the climate and the scenery which was the birthplace of all that is wise and beautiful will not remain forever the spoil of wild beasts and unlettered Tartars. In Syria and Arabia the spirit of human intellect has roused a sect of people called Wahabees,[31] who maintain the Unity of God, and the equality of man, and their enthusiasm must go on "conquering and to conquer" even if it must be repressed in its present shape. Egypt having but a nominal dependence upon Constantinople is under the government of Ottoman Bey,[32] a person of enlightened views who is introducing European literature and arts, and is thus beginning that change which Time, the great innovator, will accomplish in that degraded country; [and] by the same means its sublime enduring monuments may excite lofty emotions in the hearts of the posterity of those who now contemplate them without admiration.

Lastly, in the West Indian islands, first from the disinterested yet necessarily cautious measures of the English nation, and then from the infection of the spirit of Liberty in France, the deepest stain upon civilized man is fading away. Two nations of free negroes are already established; one, in pernicious mockery of the usurpation over

France, an empire, the other a republic—both animating yet terrific spectacles to those who inherit around them the degradation of slavery and the peril of dominion.[33]

Such is a slight sketch of the general condition of the human race to which they have been conducted after the obliteration of the Greek republics by the successful external tyranny of Rome—its internal liberty having been first abolished—and by those miseries and superstitions consequent upon this event which compelled the human race to begin anew its difficult and obscure career of producing, according to the forms of society, the great portion of good.[34]

Meanwhile England, the particular object for the sake of which these general considerations have been stated on the present occasion, has arrived like the nations which surround it at a crisis in its destiny. The literature of England, an energetic development of which has ever followed or preceded a great and free development of the national will, has arisen, as it were, from a new birth. In spite of that low-thoughted envy which would undervalue, through a fear of comparison with its own insignificance, the eminence of contemporary merit, it is *felt by the British* [that] ours is in intellectual achievements a memorable age, and we live among such philosophers and poets as surpass beyond comparison any who have appeared in our nation since its last struggle for liberty.[35] For the most unfailing herald, or companion, or follower, of an universal employment of the sentiments of a nation to the production of beneficial change is poetry, meaning by poetry an intense and impassioned power of communicating in-

30. But they had to wait another hundred and thirty years.
31. A liberal reforming sect in Arabia, named after Abd Wahhab (1691-1787), their founder and leader. They overran all of Arabia, but were finally put down by the Turks by 1818 after years of bloody war.
32. This person sent his nephew to Lucca to study European learnings, and when his nephew asked with reference to some branch of study at enmity with Mahometanism whether he was permitted to engage in it, he replied, "You are at liberty to do anything which will not injure another." [Shelley's Note.]
33. Shelley here refers in part to the astonishing fight put up by the Negroes under the leadership of Toussaint L'Ouverture (1743-1803). See Wordsworth's sonnet to him.
34. See *A Discourse on the Manners of the Ancient Greeks* and *A Defence of Poetry* for similar statements.
35. That is, since the Renaissance and the religious struggles which followed.

tense and impassioned impressions respecting man and nature. The persons in whom this power takes its abode may often, as far as regards many portions of their nature, have little tendency [to] the spirit of good of which it is the minister. But although they may deny and abjure, they are yet compelled to serve that which is seated on the throne of their own soul.[36] And whatever systems they may [have] professed by support, they actually advance the interests of liberty. It is impossible to read the productions of our most celebrated writers, whatever may be their system relating to thought or expression, without being startled by the electric life which there is in their words. They measure the circumference or sound the depths of human nature with a comprehensive and all-penetrating spirit at which they are themselves perhaps most sincerely astonished, for it [is] less their own spirit than the spirit of their age. They are the priests of an unapprehended inspiration, the mirrors of gigantic shadows which futurity casts upon the present; the words which express what they conceive not; the trumpet which sings to battle and feels not what it inspires; the influence which is moved not, but moves. Poets and philosophers are the unacknowledged legislators of the world.[37]

But, omitting these more abstracted considerations, has there not been and is there not in England a desire of change arising from the profound sentiment of the exceeding inefficiency of the existing institutions to provide for the physical and intellectual happiness of the people? It is proposed in this work (1) to state and examine the present condition of this desire, (2) to elucidate its causes and its object, (3) to then show the practicability and utility, nay the necessity of change, (4) to examine the state of parties as regards it, and (5) to state the

probable, the possible, and the desirable mode in which it should be accomplished.

CHAPTER II

On the Sentiment of the Necessity of Change

Two circumstances arrest the attention of those who turn their regard to the present political condition of the English nation—first, that there is an almost universal sentiment of the approach of some change to be wrought in the institutions of the government, and secondly, the necessity and desirableness of such a change.[38] From the first of these propositions, it being matter of fact, no person addressing the public can dissent. The latter, from a general belief in which the former flows and on which it depends, is matter of opinion, but [one] which to the mind of all, excepting those interested in maintaining the contrary is a doctrine so clearly established that even they, admitting that great abuses exist, are compelled to impugn it by insisting upon the specious topic, that popular violence, by which they alone could be remedied, would be more injurious than the continuance of these abuses. But as those who argue thus derive for the most part great advantage and convenience from the continuance of these abuses, their estimation of the mischiefs of uprising [and] popular violence as compared with the mischiefs of tyrannical and fraudulent forms of government are likely, from the known principles of human nature [*The following passage is omitted in Mary Shelley's transcription:* According to the principles of human nature as modified by the existing opinions and institutions of society a man loves himself with an overweaning love. The generous emotions of disinterested affection which the records of human

36. Compare this idea with parallel statements in *A Defence of Poetry.*
37. That portion of the essay beginning with "the literature of England" and ending "legislators of the world," was later used almost verbatim as the closing paragraph of *A Defence of Poetry.* For the

idea of poets as prophets and as the first legislators, see Puttenham's *Arte of English Poesie* (c. 1585), Chap. III.
38. Compare this with the *Two Fragments on Reform,* at the end of this essay.

nature and our experience teach us that the human heart is highly susceptible of are confined within the narrow circle of our kindred and friends. And therefore there is a class of men considerable from talents, influence, and station who of necessity are enemies to Reform.

For Reform would benefit the nation at their expense instead of suffering them to benefit themselves at the expense of the nation. If a reform however mild were to take place, they must submit to a diminution of those luxuries and vanities in the idolatry of which they have been trained. Not only they, but what in most cases would be esteemed a harder necessity their wives and children and dependents must be comprehended in the same restrictions. That degree of pain which however it is to be regretted is necessarily attached to the relinquishment of the habits of particular persons at war with the general permanent advantage, must be inflicted by the mildest reform. It is not alleged that every person whose interest is directly or indirectly concerned in the maintaining things as they are, is therefore necessarily interested. There are individuals who can be just judges even against themselves, and by study and self-examination have established a severe tribunal within themselves to which these principles which demand the advantages of the greater number are admitted to appeal. With some it assumes the mark of fear, with others that of hope — with all it is expectation.] to be exaggerated. Such an estimate comes too with a worse grace from them who, if they would in opposition to their own unjust advantage take the lead in reform, might spare the nation from the inconveniences of the temporary dominion of the poor who by means of that degraded condition which their insurrection would be designed to ameliorate are sufficiently incapable of discerning their own genuine and permanent advantage, though surely less incapable than those whose interests consist in proposing to themselves an object perfectly

opposite [to] and wholly incompatible with that advantage: all public functionaries who are overpaid either in money or in power for their public services, beginning with the person invested with the royal authority and ending with the turnkey who extorts his last shilling from his starving prisoner; all members of the House of Lords who tremble lest the annihilation of their borough interest might not involve the risk of their hereditary legislative power and of those distinctions which considered in a pecuniary point of view are injurious to those beyond the pale of their caste in proportion as they are beneficial to those within; an immense majority of the assembly called the House of Commons, who would be reduced, if they desired to administer public business, to consult the interest of their electors and conform themselves. The functionaries who know that their claims to several millions yearly of the produce of the soil for the services of certain dogmas, which if necessary other men would enforce as effectually for as many thousands, would undergo a very severe examination [in the event of a general Reform]. These persons propose to us the dilemma of submitting to a despotism which is notoriously gathering like an avalanche year by year, or taking the risk of something which it must be confessed bears the aspect of revolution. To this alternative we are reduced by the selfishness [*The following passage is omitted in Mary Shelley's transcription*: It is of no avail that they call this selfishness principle or that they are self-deluded by the same sophism with which they would deceive others. To attach another name to the same idea to which those principles which demand the advantage of the greater number are admitted to appeal may puzzle the hearer but can in no manner change the import of it. But these, even should they be few would yet be few among the many.] of those who taunt us with it. And the history of the world teaches us not to hesitate an instant in the decision, if indeed the power of decision be not already past.

The establishment of King William III on the throne of England has already been referred to as a compromise between liberty and despotism. The Parliament of which that event was the act had ceased to be in an emphatic sense a representation of the people. The Long Parliament, questionless, was the organ of the will of all classes of people in England since it effected the complete revolution in a tyranny consecrated by time. But since its meeting and since its dissolution a great change had taken place in England. Feudal manners and institutions having become obliterated, monopolies and patents having been abolished, property and personal liberty having been rendered secure, the nation advanced rapidly towards the acquirement of the elements of national prosperity. Population increased, a greater number of hands were employed in the labors of agriculture and commerce, towns arose where villages had been, and the proportion borne by those whose labor produces the materials of subsistence and enjoyment to those who claim for themselves a superfluity of these materials began to increase indefinitely. A fourth class therefore appeared in the nation, the unrepresented multitude. Nor was it so much that villages which sent no members to Parliament became great cities, and that towns which had been considerable enough to send members dwindled from local circumstances into villages. This cause no doubt contributed to the general effect of rendering the Commons House a less complete representation of the people. Yet had this been all, though it had ceased to be a legal and actual, it might still have been a virtual representation of the people. But the nation universally became multiplied into a denomination which had no constitutional presence in the state. This denomination had not existed before, or had existed only to a degree in which its interests were sensibly interwoven with that of those who enjoyed a constitutional presence. Thus, the proportion borne by the Englishmen who possessed [the] faculty of suffrage

to those who were excluded from that faculty at the several periods of 1641 and 1688 had changed by the operation of these causes from 1 to 8 to 1 to 20. The rapid and effectual progress by which it changed from 1 to 20 to one to many hundreds in the interval between 1688 and 1819 is a process, to those familiar with the history of the political economy of that period, which is rendered by these principles sufficiently intelligible. The number therefore of those who have influence on the government, even if numerically the same as at the former period, was relatively different. And a sufficiently just measure is afforded of the degree in which a country is enslaved or free by the consideration of the relative number of individuals who are admitted to the exercise of political rights. Meanwhile another cause was operating of a deeper and more extensive nature. The *class* who compose the Lords must, by the advantage of their situation as the great landed proprietors, possess a considerable influence over nomination to the Commons. This influence from an original imperfection in the equal distribution of suffrage was always enormous, but it is only since it has been combined with the cause before stated that it has appeared to be fraught with consequences incompatible with public liberty. In 1641 this influence was almost wholly [inoperative to] pervert the counsels of the nation from its own advantage. But at that epoch the enormous tyranny of the agents of the royal power weighed equally upon all denominations of men and united all counsels to extinguish it; add to which, the nation was as stated before in a very considerable degree fairly represented in Parliament. [The] common danger which was the bond of union between the aristocracy and the people having been destroyed, the former systematized their influence through the permanence of hereditary right, while the latter were losing power by the inflexibility of the institutions which forbade a just accommodation to their numerical increase. After the operations of these causes had commenced, the accession of William the III placed a seal upon forty years of Revolution.

The government of this country at the period of 1688 was regal, tempered by aristocracy, for what conditions of democracy attach to an assembly one portion of which [was] imperfectly nominated by less than a twentieth part of the people, and another perfectly nominated by the nobles? For the nobility, having by the assistance of the people imposed close limitations upon the royal power, finding that power to be its natural ally and the people (for the people from the increase of their numbers acquired greater and more important rights while the organ through which those rights might be asserted grew feebler in proportion to the increase of the cause of those rights and of their importance) its natural enemy, made the Crown the mask and pretence of their own authority. At this period began that despotism of the oligarchy of party, and under color of administering the executive power lodged in the king, represented in truth the interests of the rich. When it is said by political reasoners, speaking of the interval between 1688 and the present time, that the royal power progressively increased, they use an expression which suggests a very imperfect and partial idea. The power which has increased is that entrusted with the administration of affairs, composed of men responsible to the aristocratic assemblies, or to the reigning party in those assemblies which represents those orders of the nation which are privileged, and will retain power as long as it pleases them and must be divested of power as soon as it ceases to please them. The power which has increased therefore is the [pow]er of the rich. The name and office of king is merely the mask of this power and is a kind of stalking-horse used to conceal these "catchers of men," while they lay their nets. Monarchy is only the string which ties the robber's bundle. Though less contumelious and ab-

horrent from the dignity of human nature than an absolute monarchy, an oligarchy of this nature exacts more of suffering from the people because it reigns both by the opinion generated by imposture and the force which that opinion places within its grasp.

At the epoch adverted to, the device of public credit was first systematically applied as an instrument of government. It was employed at the accession of William III less as a resource for meeting the financial exigencies of the state than as a bond to connect those in the possession of property with those who had, by taking advantage of an accident of party, acceded to power. In the interval elapsed since that period it has accurately fulfilled the intention of its establishment and has continued to add strength to the government even until the present crisis. Now this device is one of those execrable contrivances of misrule which overbalance the materials of common advantage produced by the progress of civilization and increase the number of those who are idle in proportion to those who work, while it increases, through the factitious wants of those indolent, privileged persons, the quantity of work to be done. The rich, no longer being able to rule by force, have invented this scheme that they may rule by fraud.

The most despotic governments of antiquity were strangers to this invention, which is a compendious method of extorting from the people far more than praetorian guards and arbitrary tribunals and excise officers, created judges in the last resort, could ever wring. Neither the Persian monarchy nor the Roman empire, where the will of one person was acknowledged as unappealable law, ever extorted a twentieth part the proportion now extorted from the property and labor of the inhabitants of Great Britain. The precious metals have been from the earliest records of civilization employed as the signs of labor and the titles to an unequal distribution of its produce. The [government of] a country is necessarily entrusted with the affixing to certain portions of these metals a stamp by which to mark their genuineness; no other is considered as current coin, nor can be a legal tender. The reason for this is that no alloyed coin should pass current and thereby depreciate the genuine and by augmenting the price of the articles which are the produce of labor, defraud the holders of that which is genuine of the advantages legally belonging to them. If the government itself abuses the trust reposed in it to debase the coin in order that it may derive advantage from the unlimited multiplication of the mark entitling the holder to command the labor and property of others, the gradations by which it sinks, as labor rises, to the level of their comparative values, produces public confusion and misery. The foreign exchange meanwhile instructs the government how temporary was its resource. This mode of making the distribution of the sign of labor a source of private aggrandisement at the expense of public confusion and loss was not wholly unknown to the nations of antiquity.

But the modern scheme of public credit is a far subtler and more complicated contrivance of misrule. All great transactions of personal property in England are managed by signs and that is by the authority of the possessor expressed upon paper, thus representing in a compendious form his right to so much gold, which represents his right to so much labor. A man may write on a piece of paper what he pleases; he may say he is worth a thousand when he is not worth a hundred pounds. If he can make others believe this, he has credit for the sum to which his name is attached. And so long as this credit lasts, he can enjoy all the advantages which would arise out of the actual possession of the sum he is believed to possess. He can lend two hundred to this man and three to that other, and his bills, among those who believe that he possesses this sum, pass like money. Of course in the same proportion as bills of this sort, beyond the actual goods or gold and silver possessed by the drawer, pass current, they defraud those who have gold and silver and goods of the advantages legally attached to the possession of them, and they defraud the laborer and artizan of the advantage attached to increasing the nominal price of labor, and such a participation in them as their industry *might* command, while they render wages fluctuating and add to the toil of the cultivator and manufacturer.

The existing government of England in substituting a currency of paper [for] one of gold has had no need to depreciate the currency by alloying the coin of the country; they have merely fabricated pieces of paper on which they promise to pay a certain sum. The holders of these papers came for payment in some representation of property universally exchangeable. They then declared that the persons who held the office for that payment could not be forced by law to pay. They declared subsequently that these pieces of paper were the legal coin of the country. Of this nature are all such transactions of companies and banks as consist in the circulation of promissory notes to a greater amount than the actual property possessed by those whose names they bear. They have the effect of augmenting the prices of provision and of benefiting at the expense of the community the speculators in this traffic. One of the vaunted effects of this system is to increase the national industry: that is, to increase the labors of the poor and those luxuries of the rich which they supply; to make a manufacturer work 16 hours where he only worked 8; to turn children into lifeless and bloodless machines at an age when otherwise they would be at play before the cottage doors of their parents; to augment indefinitely the proportion of those who enjoy the profit of the labor of others as compared with those who exercise this labor. . . .

The consequences of this transaction have been the establishment of a new aristocracy, which has its basis in fraud as the old one has its basis in force. The hereditary landowners in England derived their title from royal grants—they are fiefs bestowed by conquerors, or church-lands, or they have been bought by bankers and merchants from those persons. Now bankers and merchants are persons whose. . . . Since usage has consecrated the distinction of the word aristocracy from its primitive meaning. . . . Let me be assumed to employ the word *aristocracy* in that ordinary sense which signifies that class of persons who possess a right to the produce of the labor of others, without dedicating to the common service any labor in return. This class of persons, whose existence is a prodigious anomaly in the social system, has ever constituted an inseparable portion of it, and there has never been an approach in practice towards any plan of political society modelled on equal justice, at least in the complicated mechanism of modern life. Mankind seem to acquiesce, as in a necessary condition of the imbecility of their own will and reason, in the existence of an aristocracy. With reference to this imbecility, it has doubtless been the instrument of great social advantage, although that advantage would have been greater which might have been produced according to the forms of a just distribution of the goods and evils of life. The object therefore of all enlightened legislation and administration is to enclose within the narrowest practicable limits this order of drones. The effect of the financial impostures of the modern rulers of England has been to increase the numbers of the drones. Instead of one aristocracy the condition [to] which, in the present state of human affairs, the friends of justice and liberty are willing to subscribe as to an inevitable evil, they have supplied us with two aristocracies: the one, consisting [of] great land proprietors and merchants who receive and interchange the produce of this country with the produce of other countries; in this, because all other great communities have as yet acquiesced in it, we acquiesce. Connected with the members of [it] is a certain generosity and refinement of manners and opinion which, although neither philosophy nor virtue has been that acknowledged substitute for them, which at least is a religion which makes respected those venerable names. The other is an aristocracy of attorneys and excisemen and directors and government pensioners, usurers, stock jobbers, country bankers, with their dependents and descendants. These are a set of pelting wretches in whose employment there is nothing to exercise, even to their distortion, the more majestic faculties of the soul. Though at the bottom it is all trick, there is something frank and magnificent in the chivalrous disdain of infamy connected with a gentleman. There is something to which —until you see through the base falsehood upon which all inequality is founded—it is difficult for the imagination to refuse its respect in the faithful and direct dealings of the substantial merchant. But in the habits and lives of this new aristocracy created out of an increase [in] the public calamities, and whose existence must be determined by their termination, there is nothing to qualify our disapprobation. They eat and drink and sleep and, in the intervals of those things performed with most ridiculous ceremony and accompaniments, they cringe and lie. They poison the literature of the age in which they live by requiring either the antitype of their own mediocrity in books, or such stupid and distorted and inharmonious idealisms as alone have the power to stir their torpid imaginations. Their hopes and fears are of the narrowest description. Their domestic affections are feeble, and they have no others. They think of any commerce with their species but as a means, never as an end, and as a means to the basest forms of personal advantage.[39]

If this aristocracy had arisen from a false and depreciated currency to the exclusion of the other, its existence would have been a

---

39. The substance of the last few paragraphs is found in Shelley's *An Address to the People on the Death of the Princess Charlotte.*

moral calamity and disgrace, but it would not have constituted an oppression. But the hereditary aristocracy who held the political administration of affairs took the measures which created this other for purposes peculiarly its own. Those measures were so contrived as in no manner to diminish the wealth and power of the contrivers. The lord does not spare himself one luxury, but the peasant and artizan are assured of many needful things. To support the system of social order according to its supposed unavoidable constitution, those from whose labor all those external accommodations which distinguish a civilized being from a savage arise, worked, before the institution of this double aristocracy, eight hours. And of these only the healthy were compelled to labor, the efforts of the old, the sick, and the immature being dispensed with, and they maintained by the labor of the sane, for such is the plain English of the poor-rates. That labor procured a competent share of the decencies of life, and society seemed to extend the benefits of its institution even to its most unvalued instruments. Although deprived of those resources of sentiment and knowledge which might have been their lot could the wisdom of the institutions of social forms have established a system of strict justice, yet they earned by their labor a competency in those external materials of life which, and not the loss of moral and intellectual excellence, is supposed to be the legitimate object of the desires and murmurs of the poor. Since the institution of this double aristocracy, however, they have often worked not ten but twenty hours a day. Not that all the poor have rigidly worked twenty hours, but that the worth of the labor of twenty hours now, in food and clothing, is equivalent to the worth of ten hours then. And because twenty hours' labor cannot, from the nature of the human frame, be exacted from those who before performed ten, the aged and the sickly are compelled

either to work or starve. Children who were exempted from labor are put in requisition, and the vigorous promise of the coming generation blighted by premature exertion. For fourteen hours' labor which they do perform, they receive—no matter in what nominal amount—the price of seven. They eat less bread, wear worse clothes, are more ignorant, immoral, miserable, and desperate. This, then, is the condition of the lowest and the largest class from whose labor the whole materials of life are wrought, of which the others are only the receivers or the consumers.[40] They are more superstitious, for misery on earth begets a diseased expectation and panic-stricken faith in miseries beyond the grave. "God," they argue, "rules this world as well as that; and assuredly since his nature is immutable, and his powerful will unchangeable, he rules them by the same laws." The gleams of hope which speak of Paradise seem like the flames in Milton's hell only to make darkness visible, and all things take [their] color from what surrounds them. They become revengeful . . . .

But the condition of all classes of society, excepting those within the privileged pale, is singularly unprosperous, and even they experience the reaction of their own short-sighted tyranny in all those sufferings and deprivations which are not of a distinctly physical nature, in the loss of dignity, simplicity, and energy, and in the possession of all those qualities which distinguish a slave-driver from a proprietor. Right government being an institution for the purpose of securing such a moderate degree of happiness to men as has been experimentally practicable, the sure character of misgovernment is misery, and first discontent and, if that be despised, then insurrection, as the legitimate expression of that misery. The public ought to demand happiness; the laboring classes, when they cannot get food for their labor, are impelled to take it by force. Laws and

40. Shelley here is in general agreement with Adam Smith's view that labor is the sole source of wealth. See the Note on labor in *Queen Mab*.

assemblies and courts of justice and delegated powers placed in balance or in opposition are the means and the form, but public happiness is the substance and the end of political institution. Whenever this is attained in a nation, not from external force but from the internal arrangement and divisions of the common burthens of defence and maintenance, then there is oppression. And then arises an alternative between reform and the institution of a military despotism, or a revolution in which these two parties, one striving after ill-digested systems of democracy, and the other clinging to the outworn abuses of power, leave the few who aspire to more than the former and who would overthrow the latter at whatever expense to wait until that modified advantage which results from this conflict produces a small portion of that social improvement which, with the temperance and the toleration which both regard as a crime, might have resulted from the occasion which they let pass in a far more signal manner.

The propositions which are the consequences or the corollaries to which the preceding reasoning seems to have conducted us are:

That the majority [of] the people of England are destitute and miserable, ill-clothed, ill-fed, ill-educated.

That they know this, and that they are impatient to procure a reform of the cause of their abject and wretched state.

That the cause of this peculiar misery is the unequal distribution which, under the form of the national debt, has been surreptitiously made of the products of their labor and the products of the labor of their ancestors; for all property is the produce of labor.

That the cause of that cause is a defect in the government.

That if they knew nothing of their condition, but believed that all they en-

dured and all [they] were deprived of arose from the unavoidable condition of human life, this belief being an error, and [one] the endurance of [which] enforces an injustice, every enlightened and honorable person, whatever may be the imagined interest of his peculiar class, ought to excite them to the discovery of the true state of the case and to the temperate but irresistible vindication of their rights.

It is better that they should be instructed in the whole truth, that they should see the clear grounds of their rights, the objects to which they ought to tend; and be impressed with the first persuasion that patience and reason and endurance, and a calm yet invisible progress. . . .

A reform in England is most just and necessary. What ought to be that reform?

A writer of the present day (a priest of course, for his doctrines are those of a eunuch and of a tyrant) has stated that the evils of the poor arise from an excess of population,[41] and that after they have been stript naked by the tax-gatherer and reduced to bread and tea and fourteen hours of hard labor by their masters, and after the frost has bitten their defenceless limbs, and the cramp has wrung like a disease within their bones, and hunger—and the suppressed revenge of hunger—has stamped the ferocity of want like the mark of Cain upon their countenance, that the last tie by which Nature holds them to benignant earth whose plenty is garnered up in the strongholds of their tyrants, is to be divided; that the single alleviation of their sufferings and their scorns, the one thing which made it impossible to degrade them below the beasts, which amid all their crimes and miseries yet separated a cynical and unmanly contamination, an anti-social cruelty, from all the soothing, elevating, and harmonious gentleness of the sexual intercourse and the hu-

41. Thomas Robert Malthus (1766-1834), a British economist, whose *Essay on the Principles of Population* (1798), called forth by Godwin's *Politi-* *cal Justice* (1793), aroused the ire of Shelley, Godwin, and other liberals.

manizing charities of domestic life which are its appendages—that this is to be obliterated. They are required to abstain from marrying under penalty of starvation.[42] And it is threatened to deprive them of that property which is as strictly their birthright as a gentleman's land is his birthright, without giving them any compensation but the insulting advice to conquer, with minds undisciplined in the habits of higher gratification, a propensity which persons of the most consummate wisdom have been unable to resist, and which it is difficult to admire a person for having resisted. The doctrine of this writer is that the principle of population when under no dominion of moral restraint [is] outstripping the sustenance produced by the labor of man, and that not in proportion to the number of inhabitants, but operating equally in a thinly peopled community as in one where the population is enormous, being not a prevention but a check. So far a man might have been conducted by a train of reasoning which, though it may be shown to be defective, would argue in the reasoner no selfish and slavish feelings. But he has the hardened insolence to propose as a remedy that the poor should be compelled (for what except compulsion is a threat of the confiscation of those funds which by the institutions of their country had been set apart for their sustenance in sickness or destitution?) to abstain from sexual intercourse, while the rich are to be permitted to add as many mouths to consume the products of the labor of the poor as they please. The rights of all men are intrinsically and originally equal and they forgo the assertion of all of them only that they may the more securely enjoy a portion. If any new disadvantages are found to attach to the condition of social existence, those disadvantages ought not to be borne exclusively by one class of men, nor especially by that class whose ignorance leads them to exaggerate the advantages of

sensual enjoyment, whose callous habits render domestic endearments more important to dispose them to resist the suggestions to violence and cruelty by which their situation ever exposes them to be tempted, and all whose other enjoyments are limited and few, while their sufferings are various and many. In this sense I cannot imagine how the advocates of equality would so readily have conceded that the unlimited operation of the principle of population affects the truth of these theories. On the contrary, the more heavy and certain are the evils of life, the more injustice is there in casting the burden of them exclusively on one order in the community. They seem to have conceded it merely because their opponents have insolently assumed it. Surely it is enough that the rich should possess to the exclusion of the poor all other luxuries and comforts, and wisdom, and refinement, the least envied but the most deserving of envy among all their privileges.

What is the reform that we desire? Before we aspire after theoretical perfection in the amelioration of our political state, it is necessary that we possess those advantages which we have been cheated of and to which the experience of modern times has proved that nations even under the present [conditions] are susceptible: first, we would regain these; second, we would establish some form of government which might secure us against such a series of events as have conducted us to a persuasion that the forms according to which it is now administered are inadequate to that purpose.

We would abolish the national debt.

We would disband the standing army.

We would, with every possible regard to the existing interests of the holders, abolish sinecures.

We would, with every possible regard to the existing interests of the holders, abolish tithes, and make all religions, all forms of

---

42. Malthus maintained that the means of subsistence increases in arithmetical, and population in geometrical progression—thus there could not be any permanent amelioration of the lot of the poor; thus the necessity of war and poverty and disease to keep population in check.

opinion respecting the origin and government of the universe, equal in the eye of the law.

We would make justice cheap, certain, and speedy, and extend the institution of juries to every possible occasion of jurisprudence.[43]

The national debt was chiefly contracted in two liberticide wars, undertaken by the privileged classes of the country[44]—the first, for the ineffectual purpose of tyrannizing over one portion of their subjects; the second, in order to extinguish the resolute spirit of obtaining their rights, in another. The labor which this money represents, and that which is represented by the money wrung for purposes of the same detestable character, out of the people since the commencement of the American war would, if properly employed, have covered our land with monuments of architecture exceeding the sumptuousness and the beauty of Egypt and Athens; it might have made every peasant's cottage, surrounded with its garden, a little paradise of comfort, with every convenience desirable in civilized life; neat tables and chairs, and good beds, and a nice collection of useful books; and our ships manned by sailors well-paid and well-clothed might have kept watch round this glorious island against the less enlightened nations which assuredly would have envied, until they could have imitated, its prosperity. But the labor which is expressed by these sums has been diverted from these purposes of human happiness to the promotion of slavery, or the attempt at dominion, and a great portion of the sum in question is debt and must be paid. Is it to remain unpaid forever, an eternal rent-charge upon the sacred soil from which the inhabitants of these islands draw their subsistence? This were to pronounce the perpetual institution of two orders of aristocracy, and men are in a temper to endure one with some reluctance. Is it to be paid now? If so what are the funds, or when

and how is it to be paid? The fact is that the national debt is a debt not contracted by the whole nation towards a portion of it, but a debt contracted by the whole mass of the privileged classes towards one particular portion of those classes. If the principal were paid, the whole property of those who possess property must be valued and the public creditor, whose property would have been included in this estimate, satisfied out of the proceeds. It has been said that all the land in the nation is mortgaged for the amount of the national debt. This is a partial statement; not only all the land in the nation but all the property of whatever denomination, all the houses and the furniture and the goods and every article of merchandise, and the property which is represented by the very money lent by the fund-holder, who is bound to pay a certain portion as debtor while he is to receive another certain portion as creditor. The property of the rich is mortgaged: to use the language of the law, let the mortgagee foreclose.

If the principal of this debt were paid, after such reductions had been made so as to make an equal value, taking corn for the standard, be given as was received, it would be the rich who alone could, as justly they ought to pay it. It would be a mere transfer among persons of property. Such a gentleman must lose a third of his estate, such a citizen a fourth of his money in the funds; the persons who borrowed would have paid, and the juggling and complicated system of paper finance be suddenly at an end. As it is, the interest is chiefly paid by those who had no hand in the borrowing and who are sufferers in other respects from the consequences of those transactions in which the money was spent.[45]

The payment of the principal of what is called the national debt, which it is pretended is so difficult a problem, is only difficult to those who do not see who is the

---

43. It is interesting to note how many of these reforms here suggested have been achieved, particularly in England.

44. For a similar idea see Godwin's *Political Justice,* Book V, Chap. XVI.

45. This is tantamount to saying that if *profit* is taken out of war there will be no war.

creditor and who the debtor, and who the wretched sufferers from whom they both wring the taxes which under the form of interest is given by the former [latter] and accepted by the latter [former]. It is from the labor of those who have no property that all the persons who possess property think to extort the perpetual interest of a debt, the whole of them to the part, which the latter [former] know they could not persuade the former [latter] to pay, but by conspiring with them in an imposture which makes the third class pay what the first [second] neither received by their sanction nor spent for their benefit, and what the second [first] never lent to them. They would both shift to the labor of the present and of all succeeding generations the payment of the interest of their own debt, from themselves and their posterity, because the payment of the principal would be no more than a compromise and transfer of property between each other by which the nation would be spared forty-four millions a year, which now is paid to maintain in luxury and indolence the public debtors and to protect them from the demand of their creditors upon them, who, being part of the same body and owing as debtors while they possess a claim as creditors, agree to abstain from demanding the principal which they must all unite to pay, for the sake of receiving an enormous interest which is principally wrung out of those who had no concern whatever in the transaction. One of the first acts of a reformed government would undoubtedly be an effectual scheme for compelling these to compromise their debt between themselves.

When I speak of persons of property I mean not every man who possesses any right of property; I mean the rich. Every man whose scope in society has a plebeian and intelligible utility, whose personal exertions are more valuable to him than his capital; every tradesman who is not a monopolist, all surgeons and physicians and those mechanics and editors and literary men and artists, and farmers, all those persons whose profits spring from honorably and honestly exerting their own skill and wisdom or strength in greater abundance than from the employment of money to take advantage of the necessity of the starvation of their fellow citizens for their profit, or those who pay, as well as those more obviously understood by the laboring classes, the interest of the national debt. It is the interest of all these persons as well as that of the poor to insist upon the payment of the principal.

For this purpose the form ought to be as simple and succinct as possible. The operations deciding who was to pay, at what time, and how much, and to whom are divested of financial chicanery, problems readily to be determined. The common tribunals may possess a legal jurisdiction to award the proportion due upon the several claim of each.[46]

There are two descriptions of property which, without entering into the subtleties of a more refined moral theory as applicable to the existing forms of society, are entitled to two very different measures of forbearance and regard. And this forbearance and regard have by political institutions usually been accorded in an inverse reason from what is just and natural. Labor, industry, economy, skill, genius, or any similar powers honorably and innocently exerted are the foundations of one description of property, and all true political institutions ought to defend every man in the exercise of his discretion with respect to property so acquired. Of this kind is the principal part of the property enjoyed by those who are but one degree removed from the class which subsists by daily labor. Yet there are instances of persons in this class who have procured their property by fraudulent and violent means, as there are instances in the other of persons who have acquired their property

46. Is this proposal a forerunner of the graduated income tax? Compare Paine on this subject.

by innocent or honorable exertion. All political science abounds with limitations and exceptions. Property thus acquired men leave to their children. Absolute right becomes weakened by descent, first because it is only to avoid the greater evil of arbitrarily interfering with the discretion of any man in matters of property that the great evil of acknowledging any person to have an exclusive right to property who has not created it by his skill or labor is admitted, and secondly because the mode of its having been originally acquired is forgotten, and it is confounded with the property acquired in a very different manner; and the principle upon which all property justly rests, after the great principle of the general advantage, becomes thus disregarded and misunderstood. Yet the privilege of disposing of property by will is one necessarily connected with the existing forms of domestic life, and exerted merely by those who have acquired property by industry or who have preserved it by economy, would never produce any great and invidious inequality of fortune. A thousand accidents would perpetually tend to level the accidental elevation, and the signs of property would perpetually recur to those whose deserving skill might attract or whose labor might create it.

But there is another species of property which has its foundation in usurpation, or imposture, or violence, without which, by the nature of things, immense possessions of gold or land could never have been accumulated. Of this nature is the principal part of the property enjoyed by the aristocracy and by the great fund-holders, the great majority of whose ancestors never either deserved it by their skill and talents or acquired and created it by their personal labor. It could not be that they deserved it, for if the honorable exertion of the most glorious imperial faculties of our nature had been the criterion of the possession of property, the posterity of Shakespeare, of Milton, of Hampden, of Lor[d Bacon] would be the wealthiest proprietors in England. It could

not be that they acquired it by legitimate industry, for, besides that the real mode of acquisition is matter of history, no honorable profession or honest trade, nor the hereditary exercise of it, ever in such numerous instances accumulated masses of property so vast as those enjoyed by the ruling orders in England. They were either grants from the feudal sovereigns whose right to what they granted was founded upon conquest or oppression, both a denial of all right; or they were the lands of the ancient Catholic clergy which, according to the most acknowledged principles of public justice, reverted to the nation at their suppression, or they were the products of patents and monopolies, an exercise of sovereignty most pernicious that direct violence to the interests of a commercial nation; or in later times such property has been accumulated by dishonorable cunning and the taking advantage of a fictitious paper currency to obtain an unfair power over labor and the fruits of labor.

Property thus accumulated being transmitted from father to son acquires, as property of the more legitimate kind loses, force and sanction, but in a more limited manner. For not only on an examination and recurrence to first principles is it seen to have been founded on a violation of all that to which the latter owes its sacredness, but it is felt in its existence and perpetuation as a public burthen, and known as a rallying point to the ministers of tyranny, having the property of a snowball, gathering as it rolls, and rolling until it bursts. [It] is astonishing that political theorists have not branded [it] as the most pernicious and odious. [Yet] there are three sets of people, one who can place a thing to another in an intelligible light, another who can understand it when so communicated, and a third who can neither discover [n]or understand it.

Labor and skill and the immediate wages of labor and skill is a property of the most sacred and indisputable right and the foundation of all other property. And the right of a man [to] property in the exertion of his own bodily and mental faculties, or to the produce and free reward from and for that exertion is the most [inalienable of rights]. If, however, he takes by violence or appropriates to himself through fraudulent cunning, or receives from another property so acquired, his claim to that property is of a far inferior force. We may acquiesce, if we evidently perceive an overbalance of public advantage in submission under this claim; but if any public emergency should arise, at which it might be necessary as at present by a tax on capital to satisfy the claims of a part of the nation by a contribution from such national resources as may with the least injustice be appropriated to that purpose, assuredly it would not be on labor and skill, the foundation of all property, nor on the profits and savings of labor and skill, which are property itself, but on such possession which can only be called property in a modified sense, as have from their magnitude and their nature an evident origin in violence or imposture.[47]

The national debt, as has been stated, is a debt contracted by the whole of a particular class in the nation towards a portion of that class. It is sufficiently clear that this debt was not contracted for the purpose of the public advantage. Besides there was no authority in the nation competent to a measure of this nature. The usual vindication of national debts is that, [since] they are contracted in an overwhelming measure for the purpose of defence against a common danger, for the vindication of the rights and liberties of posterity, it is just that posterity should bear the burthen of payment. This reasoning is most fallacious. The history of nations presents us with a succession of extraordinary emergencies, and through their present imperfect organization their existence is perpetually threatened by new and unexpected combinations and developments of foreign or internal force. Imagine a situation of equal emergency to occur to

England as that which the ruling party assume to have occurred as their excuse for burthening the nation with the perpetual payment of £45,000,000 annually. Suppose France, Russia, and America were to enter into a league against England, the first to revenge [avenge] its injuries, the second to satisfy its ambition, the third to soothe its jealousy. Could the nation bear £90,000,000 of yearly interest? Must there be twice as many luxurious and idle persons? Must the laborer receive for twenty-eight hours' work what he now receives for fourteen, as he now receives for fourteen what he once received for seven? But this argument . . . .

What is meant by a reform of Parliament? If England were a republic governed by one assembly; if there were no chamber of hereditary aristocracy which is at once an actual and a virtual representation of all who claim through rank or wealth superiority over their countrymen; if there were no king who is as the rallying point of those whose tendency is at once to [gather] and to confer that power which is consolidated at the expense of the nation, then . . . .

The advocates of universal suffrage have reasoned correctly that no individual who is governed can be denied a direct share in the government of his country without supreme justice. If we pursue the train of reasonings which have conducted to this conclusion, we discover that systems of social order still more incompatible than universal suffrage with any reasonable hope of instant accomplishment appear to be that which should result from a just combination of the elements of social life. I do not understand why those reasoners who propose at any price an immediate appeal to universal suffrage, because it is that which it is injustice to withhold, do not insist on the same ground on the immediate abolition, for instance, of monarchy and aristocracy, and the levelling of inordinate wealth, and an agrarian distribution, including the parks and chases of the rich, of

47. Shelley was far out in front of leading tax economists in his day, or even in our day, in his philosophy of taxation.

the uncultivated districts of the country. No doubt the institution of universal suffrage would by necessary consequence *immediately* tend to the *temporary* abolition of these forms; because it is impossible that the people, having attained power, should fail to see what the demagogues now conceal from them the legitimate consequence of the doctrines through which they had attained it. A republic, however just in its principle and glorious in its object, would through violence and sudden change which must attend it incur a great risk of being as rapid in its decline as in its growth. It is better that they should be instructed in the whole truth; that they should see the clear grounds of their rights, the objects to which they ought to tend; and be impressed with the just persuasion that patience and reason and endurance [are the means of] a calm yet irresistible progress. A civil war, which might be engendered by the passions attending on this mode of reform, would confirm in the mass of the nation those military habits which have been already introduced by our tyrants and with which liberty is incompatible. From the moment that a man is a soldier, he becomes a slave. He is taught obedience; his will is no longer, which is the most sacred prerogative of man, guided by his own judgment. He is taught to despise human life and human suffering; this is the universal distinction of slaves. He is more degraded than a murderer; he is like the bloody knife which has stabbed and feels not; a murderer we may abhor and despise, a soldier is by profession beyond abhorrence and below contempt.

CHAPTER III

Probable Means

That Commons should reform itself, uninfluenced by any fear that the people would, on their refusal, assume to itself that office, seems a contradiction. What need of reform if it expresses the will and watches over the interests of the public? And if, as is sufficiently evident, it despises that will and neglects that interest, what motives would incite it to institute a reform which the aspect of the times renders indeed sufficiently perilous, but without which there will speedily be no longer anything in England to distinguish it from the basest and most abject community of slaves that ever existed.

The great principle of reform consists in every individual of mature age and perfect understanding giving his consent to the institution and the continued existence of the social system which is instituted for his advantage and for the advantage of others in his situation. As in a great nation this is practically impossible, masses of individuals consent to qualify other individuals, whom they delegate to superintend their concerns. These delegates have constitutional authority to exercise the functions of sovereignty; they unite in the highest degree the legislative and executive functions. A government that is founded on any other basis is a government of fraud or force and ought on the first convenient occasion to be overthrown. The broad principle of political reform is the natural equality of men, not with relation to their property but to their rights. That equality in possessions which Jesus Christ so passionately taught[48] is a moral rather than political truth and is such as social institutions cannot without mischief inflexibly secure. Morals and politics can only be considered as portions of the same science, with relation to a system of such absolute perfection as Christ and Plato and Rousseau and other reasoners have asserted, and as Godwin has, with irresistible eloquence, systematized and developed. Equality in possessions must be the last result of the utmost refinements of civilization; it is one of the conditions of that system of society towards which with whatever hope of ultimate success, it is our

---

48. Shelley was fond of reminding his readers of the communistic or socialistic philosophy of Jesus. But he considered this condition as the ultimate refinement of any nation, the goal toward which we should exert every effort.

duty to tend. We may and ought to advert to it as to the elementary principle, as to the goal, unattainable perhaps by us, but which, as it were, we revive in our posterity to pursue. We derive tranquillity and courage and grandeur of soul from contemplating an object which is, because we will it, and may be because we hope and desire it, and must be if succeeding generations of the enlightened sincerely and earnestly seek it. We should with sincere and patient as . . . .

But our present business is with the difficult and unbending realities of actual life, and when we have drawn inspiration from the great object of our hopes it becomes us with patience and resolution to apply ourselves to accommodating our theories to immediate practice.[49]

That representative assembly called the House of Commons ought questionless to be *immediately* nominated by the great mass of the people. The aristocracy and those who unite in their own persons the vast privileges conferred by the possession of inordinate wealth are sufficiently represented by the House of Peers and by the King. Those theorists who admire and would put into action the mechanism of what is called the British Constitution would acquiesce in this view of the question. For if the House of Peers be a permanent representative of the privileged classes, if the regal power be no more than another form and a form still more jealously to be regarded, of the same representation, while the House of Commons be not chosen by the mass of the population, what becomes of that democratic element, upon the presence of which it has been supposed that the waning superiority of England over the surrounding nations has depended?

Any sudden attempt at universal suffrage would produce an immature attempt at a republic. It [is better] that [an] object so

inexpressibly great and sacred should never have been attempted than that it should be attempted and fail. It is no prejudice to the ultimate establishment of the boldest political innovations that we temporize so as, when they shall be accomplished, they may be rendered permanent.

Considering the population of Great Britain and Ireland as twenty millions and the representative assembly as five hundred, each member ought to be the expression of the will of 40,000 persons; of these two-thirds would [consist of] women and children and persons under age; the actual number of voters therefore for each member would be 13,333. The whole extent of the empire might be divided into five hundred electoral departments or parishes, and the inhabitants assemble on a certain day to exercise their rights of suffrage.

Mr. Bentham and other writers have urged the admission of females to the right of suffrage; this attempt seems somewhat immature. Should my opinion be the result of despondency, the writer of these pages would be the last to withhold his vote from any system which might tend to an equal and full development of the capacities of all living beings.

The system of voting by ballot which some reasoners have recommended is attended with obvious inconveniences. [It withdraws the elector from the regard of his country, and] his neighbors, and permits him to conceal the motives of his vote, which, if concealed, cannot but be dishonorable; when, if he had known that he had to render a public account of his conduct, he would have never permitted them to guide him.[50] There is in this system of voting by ballot and of electing a member of the *Representative Assembly* as a churchwarden is elected something too mechanical. The elector and the elected ought to meet one another face to face and interchange the

---

49. Those interpreters of Shelley who see him as a starry-eyed impractical, radical reformer should ponder such statements as these—the whole essay in fact.

50. This argument appears logically valid, but a secret ballot is the only means of protecting the voter from intimidation.

meanings of actual presence and share some common impulses and, in a degree, understand each other.[51] There ought to be the common sympathy of the excitements of a popular assembly among the electors themselves. The imagination would thus be strongly excited, and a mass of generous and enlarged and popular sentiments be awakened, which would give the vitality of . . . .

That republican boldness of censuring and judging one another, which has indeed [been] exerted in England under the title of 'public opinion,' though perverted from its true uses into an instrument of prejudice and calumny, would then be applied to its genuine purposes. Year by year the people would become more susceptible of assuming forms of government more simple and beneficial.

It is in this publicity of the exercise of sovereignty that the difference between the republics of Greece and the monarchies of Asia consisted. The actions of the times . . . .

If the existing government shall compel the nation to take the task of reform into its own hands, one of the most obvious consequences of such a circumstance would be the abolition of monarchy and aristocracy. Why, it will then be argued, if the subsisting condition of social forms is to be thrown into confusion, should these things be endured? Then why do we now endure them? Is it because we think that an hereditary King is cheaper and wiser than an elected President, or a House of Lords and a Bench of Bishops are institutions modelled by the wisdom of the most refined and civilized periods, beyond which the wit of mortal man can furnish nothing more perfect? In case the subsisting government should compel the people to revolt to establish a representative assembly in defiance of them and to assume in that assembly an attitude of resistance and defence, this question would probably be answered in a very summary manner. No

friend of mankind and of his country can desire that such a crisis should suddenly arrive; but still less, once having arrived, can he hesitate under what banner to array his person and his power. At the peace, the people would have been contented with strict economy and severe retrenchment, and some direct and intelligible plan for producing that equilibrium between the capitalists and the landholders which is delusively styled the payment of the national debt; had this system been adopted, they probably would have refrained from exacting Parliamentary reform, the only secure guarantee that it would have been pursued. Two years ago it might still have been possible to have commenced a system of gradual reform. The people were then insulted, tempted, and betrayed, and *the petitions of a million* of men rejected with disdain. Now they are more miserable, more hopeless, more impatient of their misery. Above all, they have become more universally aware of the true sources of their misery. It is possible that the period of conciliation is past, and that after having played with the confidence and cheated the expectations of the people, their passions will be too little under discipline to allow them to wait the slow, gradual, and certain operation of such a reform as we can imagine the constituted authorities to concede.

Upon the issue of this question depends the species of reform which a philosophical mind should regard with approbation. If reform shall be begun by the existing government, let us be contented with a limited *beginning,* with any whatsoever opening; let the rotten boroughs be disfranchised and their rights transferred to the unrepresented cities and districts of the nation; it is no matter how slow, gradual, and cautious be the change; we shall demand more and more with firmness and moderation, never anticipating, but never deferring the moment of successful opposition, so that the people may become habituated [to] exer-

51. Ideally this is true, but with large populations it is impractical. See Godwin's *Political Justice.*

cising the functions of sovereignty, in proportion as they acquire the possession of it. If reform could begin from within the Houses of Parliament, as constituted at present, it appears to me that what is called moderate reform, that is a suffrage whose qualification should be the possession of a certain small property, and triennial parliaments, would be principles—a system in which, for the sake of obtaining without bloodshed or confusion ulterior improvements of a more important character, all reformers ought to acquiesce. Not that such are first principles, or that they would produce a system of perfect social institutions or one approaching to [such]. But nothing is more idle than to reject a limited benefit because we cannot without great sacrifices obtain an unlimited one. We might thus reject a representative republic, if it were obtainable, on the plea that the imagination of man can conceive of something more absolutely perfect. Towards whatsoever we regard as perfect, undoubtedly it is no less our duty than it is our nature to press forward; this is the generous enthusiasm which accomplishes not indeed the consummation after which it aspires, but one which approaches it in a degree far nearer than if the whole powers had not been developed by a delusion. It is in politics rather than in religion that faith is meritorious.

If the Houses of Parliament obstinately and perpetually refuse to concede any reform to the people, my vote is for universal suffrage and equal representation. My vote is—but, it is asked, how shall this be accomplished, in defiance of and in opposition to the constituted authorities of the nation, they who possess whether with or without its consent the command of a standing army and of a legion of spies and police officers and hold all the strings of that complicated mechanism with which the hopes and fears of men are moved like puppets? They would disperse any assembly really chosen by the people; they would shoot and hew down any multitude without regard to sex or age as the Jews did the Canaanites, which might be collected in its defence; they would calumniate, imprison, starve, ruin, and expatriate every person who wrote or acted, or thought, or might be suspected to think against them; misery and extermination would fill the country from one end to another . . . .

This question I would answer by another.

Will you endure to pay the half of your earnings to maintain in luxury and idleness the confederation of your tyrants as the reward of a successful conspiracy to defraud and oppress you? Will you make your tame cowardice and the branding record of it the everlasting inheritance of your posterity? Not only this: will you render by your torpid endurance this condition of things as permanent as the system of castes in India by which the same horrible injustice is perpetrated under another form?

Assuredly no Englishmen by whom these propositions are understood will answer in the affirmative; and the opposite side of the alternative remains.

When the majority in any nation arrive at a conviction that it is their duty and their interest to divest the minority of a power employed to their disadvantage, and the minority are sufficiently mistaken as to believe that their superiority is tenable, a struggle must ensue.

If the majority are enlightened, united, impelled by a uniform enthusiasm and animated by a distinct and powerful apprehension of their object—and full confidence in their undoubted power—the struggle is merely nominal. The minority perceive the approaches of the development of an irresistible force. By the influence of the public opinion of their weakness on those political forms of which no government but an absolute despotism is devoid. They divest themselves of their usurped distinctions; the public tranquillity is not disturbed by the revolution.

But these conditions may only be imperfectly fulfilled by the state of a people grossly oppressed and impotent to cast off the load. Their enthusiasm may have been subdued by the killing weight of toil and suffering; they may be panic-stricken and disunited by their oppressors and the demagogues, the influence of fraud may have been sufficient to weaken the union of classes which compose them by suggesting jealousies, and the position of the conspirators, although it is to be forced by repeated assaults, may be tenable until the siege can be vigorously urged. The true patriot will endeavor to enlighten and to unite the nation and animate it with enthusiasm and confidence. For this purpose he will be indefatigable in promulgating political truth. He will endeavor to rally round one standard the divided friends of liberty and make them forget the subordinate objects with regard to which they differ by appealing to that respecting which they are all agreed. He will promote such open confederations among men of principle and spirit as may tend to make their intentions and their efforts converge to a common center. He will discourage all secret associations which have a tendency, by making national will develop itself in a partial and premature manner, to cause tumult and confusion. He will urge the necessity of exciting the people frequently to exercise their right of assembling in such limited numbers as that all present may be actual parties to the proceedings of the day. Lastly, if circumstances had collected a more considerable number as at Manchester on the memorable 16th of August, if the tyrants command their troops to fire upon them or cut them down unless they disperse, he will exhort them peaceably to risk the danger, and to expect without resistance the onset of the cavalry, and wait with folded arms the event of the fire of the artillery and receive with unshrinking bosoms the bayonets of the charging battalions. Men are every day persuaded to incur greater perils for a less

manifest advantage. And this, not because active resistance is not justifiable when all other means shall have failed, but because in this instance temperance and courage would produce greater advantages than the most decisive victory. In the first place the soldiers are men and Englishmen, and it is not to be believed that they would massacre an unresisting multitude of their countrymen drawn up in unarmed array before them and bearing in their looks the calm, deliberate resolution to perish rather than abandon the assertion of their rights. In the confusion of flight the ideas of the soldier become confused and he massacres those who fly from him by the instinct of his trade. In the struggle of conflict and resistance he is irritated by a sense of his own danger; he is flattered by an apprehension of his magnanimity in incurring it; he considers the blood of his countrymen at once the price of his valor, the pledge of his security. He applauds himself by reflecting that these base and dishonorable motives will gain him credit among his comrades and his officers, who are animated by the same as if they were something the same. But if he should observe neither resistance nor flight he would be reduced to impotence and indecision. Thus far, his ideas were governed by the same law as those of a dog who chases a flock of sheep to the corner of a field and keeps aloof when they make the firm parade of resistance. But the soldier is a man and an Englishman. This unexpected reception would probably throw him back upon a recollection of the true nature of the measures of which he was made the instrument, and the enemy might be converted into the ally.

The patriot will be foremost to publish the boldest truths in the most fearless manner, yet without the slightest tincture of personal malignity. He would encourage all others to the same efforts and assist them to the utmost of his power with the resources both of his intellect and fortune. He would call upon them to despise imprisonment and persecution and lose no opportunity of bringing public opinion and the power of the tyrants into circumstances of perpetual contest and opposition.

All might, however, be ineffectual to produce so uniform an impulse of the national will as to preclude a further struggle. The strongest argument, perhaps, for the necessity of reform is the inoperative and unconscious abjectness to which the purposes of a considerable mass of the people are reduced. They neither know nor care. They are sinking into a resemblance with the Hindoos and the Chinese, who were once men as they are. Unless the cause which renders them passive subjects instead of active citizens be removed, they will sink with accelerated gradations into that barbaric and unnatural civilization which destroys all the differences among men. It is in vain to exhort us to wait until all men shall desire freedom whose real interest will consist in its establishment. It is in vain to hope to enlighten them while their tyrants employ the utmost artifices of all their complicated engine to perpetuate the infection of every species of fanaticism and error from generation to generation. The advocates of reform ought indeed to leave no effort unexerted, and they ought to be indefatigable in exciting all men to examine.

But if they wait until those neutral politicians, a class whose opinions represent the actions of this class, are persuaded that so soon [as] effectual reform is necessary, the occasion will have passed or will never arrive, and the people will have exhausted their strength in ineffectual expectation and will have sunk into incurable supineness. It was principally the [effect of] a similar quietism that the populous and extensive nations of Asia have fallen into their existing decrepitude; and that anarchy, insecurity, ignorance, and barbarism, the symptoms of the confirmed disease of monarchy, have reduced nations of the most delicate physical and intellectual organization and under the most fortunate climates of the globe to a blank in the history of man. The manufacturers to a man are persuaded of the necessity of reform; an immense majority of the inhabitants of London. . . .

The reasoners who incline to the opinion that it is not sufficient that the innovators should produce a majority in the nation, but that we ought to expect such an unanimity as would preclude anything amounting to a serious dispute, are prompted to this view of the question by the dread of anarchy and massacre. Infinite and inestimable calamities belong to oppression, but the most fatal of them all is that mine of unexploded mischief which it has practiced beneath the foundations of society, and with which, "pernicious to one touch" it threatens to involve the ruin of the entire building together with its own. But delay merely renders these mischiefs more tremendous, not the less inevitable. For the utmost may now be the crisis of the social disease [which] is rendered thus periodical, chronic, and incurable.

The savage brutality of the populace is proportioned to the arbitrary character of their government, and tumults and insurrections soon, as in Constantinople, become consistent with the permanence of the causing evil, of which they might have been the critical determination.

The public opinion in England ought first to [be] excited to action, and the durability of those forms within which the oppressors intrench themselves brought perpetually to the test of its operation. No law or institution can last if this opinion be distinctly pronounced against it. For this purpose government ought to be defied, in cases of questionable result, to prosecute for political libel. All questions relating to the jurisdiction of magistrates and courts of law respecting which any doubt could be raised ought to be agitated with indefatigable pertinacity. Some two or three of the popular leaders have shown the best spirit in this respect; they only want system and co-operation. The tax-gatherer ought to be compelled in every practicable instance to distrain while the right to impose taxes, as was the case in the beginning of the resistance to the tyranny of Charles the 1st, is formally contested by an overwhelming multitude of defendants before the courts of common law. Confound the subtlety of lawyers with the subtlety of the law. All of the nation would thus be excited to develop itself and to declare whether it acquiesced in the existing forms of government. The manner in which all questions of this nature might be decided would develop the occasions and afford a prognostic as to the success of more decisive measures. Simultaneously with this active and vigilant system of opposition means ought to be taken of solemnly conveying the sense of large bodies and various denominations of the people in a manner the most explicit to the existing depositaries of power. Petitions, couched in the actual language of the petitioners, and emanating from distinct assemblies ought to load the tables of the House of Commons. The poets, philosophers, and artists ought to remonstrate, and the memorials entitled their petitions might show the diversity [of] convictions they entertain of the inevitable connection between national prosperity and freedom, and the cultivation of the imagination and the cultivation of scientific truth, and the profound development of moral and metaphysical enquiry. Suppose these memorials to be severally written by Godwin, Hazlitt, Bentham, and Hunt, they would be worthy of the age and of the cause; these, radiant and irresistible like the meridian sun, would strike all but the eagles who dared to gaze upon its beams, with blindness and confusion. These appeals of solemn and emphatic argument from those who have already a predestined existence among posterity would appal the enemies of mankind by their echoes from every corner of the world in which the majestic literature of England is cultivated; it would be like

a voice from beyond the dead of those who will live in the memories of men, when they must be forgotten; it would be Eternity warning Time.

Let us hope that at this stage of the progress of reform, the oppressors would feel their impotence and reluctantly and imperfectly concede some limited portion of the rights of the people and disgorge some morsels of their undigested prey. In this case the people ought to be exhorted by everything ultimately dear to them to pause until by the exercise of those rights which they have regained they become fitted to demand more. It is better that we gain what we demand by a process of negotiation which would occupy twenty years than that by communicating a sudden shock to the interests of those who are the depositaries and dependents of power we should incur the calamity which their revenge might inflict upon us by giving the signal of civil war. If, after all, they consider the chance of personal ruin and the infamy of figuring on the page of history as the promoters of civil war preferable to resigning any portion how small soever of their usurped authority, we are to recollect that we possess a right beyond remonstrance. It has been acknowledged by the most approved writers on the English constitution, which is in this instance merely [a] declaration of the superior decisions of eternal justice, that we possess a right of resistance. The claim of the [reigning] family is founded upon a memorable exertion of this solemnly recorded right.

The last resort of resistance is undoubtedly insurrection. The right of insurrection is derived from the employment of armed force to counteract the will of the nation. Let the government disband the standing army, and the purpose of resistance would be sufficiently fulfilled by the incessant agitation of the points of dispute before the courts of common law and by an unwarlike display of the irresistible number and union of the people.

Before we enter into a consideration of the measures which might terminate in civil war, let us for a moment consider the nature and the consequences of war. This is the alternative which the unprincipled cunning of the tyrants has presented to us, from which we must not sh[rink]. There is secret sympathy between destruction and power, between monarchy and war; and the long experience of the history of all recorded time teaches us with what success they have played into each other's hands. War is a kind of superstition; the pageantry of arms and badges corrupts the imagination of men. How far more appropriate would be the symbols of an inconsolable grief—muffled drums, and melancholy music, and arms reversed, and the livery of sorrow rather than of blood. When men mourn at funerals, for what do they mourn in comparison with the calamities which they hasten with all circumstance of festivity to suffer and to inflict! Visit in imagination the scene of a field of battle or a city taken by assault, collect into one group the groans and the distortions of the innumerable dying, the inconsolable grief and horror of their surviving friends, the hellish exultation, and unnatural drunkenness of destruction of the conquerors, the burning of the harvests and the obliteration of the traces of cultivation. To this, in civil war is to be added the sudden disruption of the bonds of social life, and "father against son."

If there had never been war, there could never have been tyranny in the world; tyrants take advantage of the mechanical organization of armies to establish and defend their encroachments. It is thus that the mighty advantages of the French Revolution have been almost compensated by a succession of tyrants (for demagogues, oligarchies, usurpers, and legitimate kings are merely varieties of the same class) from Robespierre to Louis 18. War, waged from whatever motive, extinguishes the sentiment of reason and justice in the mind. The motive is forgotten, or only adverted to in a mechanical and habitual manner.

A sentiment of confidence in brute force and in a contempt of death and danger is considered as the highest virtue, when in truth and however indispensable they are merely the means and the instruments, highly capable of being perverted to destroy the cause they were assumed to promote. It is a foppery the most intolerable to an amiable and philosophical mind. It is like what some reasoners have observed of religious faith; no false and indirect motive to action can subsist in the mind without weakening the effect of those which are genuine and true. The person who thinks it virtuous to believe will think a less degree of virtue attaches to good actions than if he had considered it as indifferent. The person who has been accustomed to subdue men by force will be less inclined to the trouble of convincing or persuading them.

These brief considerations suffice to show that the true friend of mankind and of his country would hesitate before he recommended measures which tend to bring down so heavy a calamity as war.

I imagine, however, that before the English nation shall arrive at that point of moral and political degradation now occupied by the Chinese, it will be necessary to appeal to an exertion of physical strength. If the madness of parties admits no other mode of determining the question at issue. . . .

When the people shall have obtained, by whatever means, the victory over their oppressors and when persons appointed by them shall have taken their seats in the Representative Assembly of the nation and assumed the control of public affairs according to constitutional rules, there will remain the great task of accommodating all that can be preserved of ancient forms with the improvements of the knowledge of a more enlightened age in legislation, jurisprudence, government, and religious and academical institutions. The settlement of the national debt is on the principles before elucidated merely circumstance of form, and however necessary and important is an affair of mere arithmetical proportions readily determined;

nor can I see how those, who being deprived of their unjust advantages will probably inwardly murmur, can oppose one word of open expostulation to a measure of such inescapable justice.

There is one thing which certain vulgar agitators endeavor to flatter the most uneducated part of the people by assiduously proposing, which they ought not to do nor to require: and that is, Retribution. Men having been injured desire to injure in return. This is falsely called an universal law of human nature; it is a law from which many are exempt, and all in proportion to their virtue and cultivation. The savage is more revengeful than the civilized man, the ignorant and uneducated than the person of a refined and cultivated intellect; the generous and . . . .

[The work was left incomplete].

TWO FRAGMENTS ON REFORM

[These fragments seem to be related to *A Philosophical View of Reform*.]

A. That our country is on the point of submitting to some momentous change in its internal government is a fact which few who observe and compare the [blank] of human society will dispute.[52] The distribution of wealth no less than the spirit by which it is upheld and that by which it is assailed render the event inevitable. Call it reform or revolution, as you will, a change must take place; one of the consequences of which will be the wresting of political power from those who are at present the depositories of it. A strong sentiment [prevails] in the nation at large that they have been guilty of enormous malversations of their trust. It is a commonplace of political reformers to say that it is the measures, not the men, they abhor; and it is a general practice, so soon as the party shall have gained the victory, to inflict the severest punishments upon their predecessors and to pursue measures not less selfish and pernicious than those a protest against which was the ladder that conducted them to power. The people sympathize with the passions of their liberators without reflecting that these in turn may become their tyrants, and without perceiving that the same motives and excitements to act or to feel can never, except by a perverse imitation, belong to both.[53]

B. The hopes of the world were bound up in the claims which the people of England made, to be delivered from the oppression under which they groaned and to abolish the symbols of those impostures which surrounded their tyrants with sanctity. The claim on the part of the people was that the institutions of government should be provided for at certain limited periods by the people themselves; those for whose benefit alone it was declared or declaimed that any of the regulations of social life ought to be permitted to subsist. The voice of public opinion had by no means decided as to the precise form of the political institutions which should supersede that already existing; but a general persuasion prevailed that the multitude was deluded and oppressed by its rulers; thousands of miserable men and women and children wandered through the streets famished, naked, and homeless, [and] the cottages and farm houses became tenanted whilst . . . .[54]

52. Compare this idea with one in the Preface to *Laon and Cythna*: "I am aware, methinks, of a slow, gradual, silent change."

53. This fragment was first published by Garnett in *Relics of Shelley* (1862).

54. This fragment was first published in the Julian Editions, 6.295-296.

A SYSTEM OF GOVERNMENT BY JURIES

[A fragment, whose date is probably 1819-20. It seems to bear some relation to *A Philosophical View of Reform.* The fragment was first published by Medwin in the *Athenaeum,* April 20, 1833.]

Government, as it now subsists, is perhaps an engine at once the most expensive and inartificial that could have been devised as a remedy for the imperfections of society. Immense masses of the product of labor are committed to the discretion of certain individuals for the purpose of executing its intentions, or interpreting its meaning. These have not been consumed, but wasted, in the principal part of the past history of political society.

Government may be distributed into two parts: first, the fundamental—that is, the permanent forms which regulate the deliberation or the action of the whole, from which it results that a state is democratical, or aristocratical, or despotic, or a combination of all these principles.

And secondly—the necessary or accidental —that is, those that determine *not* the forms according to which the deliberation or the action of the mass of the community is to be regulated, but the opinions or moral principles which are to govern the particular instances of such action or deliberation. These may be called, with little violence to the popular acceptation of those terms, Constitution and Law: understanding by the former, the collection of those written institutions or traditions which determine the individuals who are to exercise, in a nation, the discretionary right of peace and war, of death or imprisonment, fines and penalties, and the imposition and collection of taxes, and their application, thus vested in a king, or an hereditary senate, or in a representative assembly, or in a combination of all; and by the latter, the mode of determining those opinions, according to which the constituted authorities are to decide on any action; for law is either a collection of opinions expressed by individuals without constitutional authority, or the decision of a constitutional body of men, the opinion of some of all of whom it expresses—and no more.

To the former, or constitutional topics, this treatise has no direct reference. Law may be considered, simply—an opinion regulating political power. It may be divided into two parts—General Law, or that which relates to the external and integral concerns of a nation, and decides on the competency of a particular person or collection of persons to discretion in matters of war and peace—the assembling of the representative body—the time, place, manner, form, of holding judicial courts, and other concerns enumerated before, and in reference to which this community is considered as a whole; and Particular Law, or that which decides upon contested claims of property, which punishes or restrains violence and fraud, which enforces compacts and preserves to every man that degree of liberty and security, the enjoyment of which is judged not to be inconsistent with the liberty and security of another.

To the former, or what is here called general law, this treatise has no direct reference. How far law, in its general form or constitution, as it at present exists in the greater part of the nations of Europe, may be affected by inferences from the ensuing reasonings, it is foreign to the present purpose to inquire—let us confine our attention to particular law, or law strictly so termed.

The only defensible intention of law, like that of every other human institution, is very simple and clear—the good of the whole. If law is found to accomplish this object very imperfectly, that imperfection makes no part of the design with which men submit to its institution. Any reasonings which tend to throw light on a subject hitherto so dark and intricate cannot fail, if distinctly stated, to impress mankind very deeply, because it is a question in which the life and property and liberty and reputation of every man are vitally involved.

For the sake of intelligible method, let us assume the ordinary distinctions of law, those of civil and criminal law, and of the objects of it, private and public wrongs. The author of these pages ought not to suppress his conviction that the principles on which punishment is usually inflicted are essentially erroneous; and that, in general, ten times more is apportioned to the victims of law than is demanded by the welfare of society under the shape of reformation or example. He believes that, although universally disowned, the execrable passion of vengeance, exasperated by fear, exists as a chief source among the secret causes of this exercise of criminal justice. He believes also that in questions of property there is a vague but most effective favoritism in courts of law and among lawyers against the poor to the advantage of the rich—against the tenant in favor of the landlord—against the creditor in favor of the debtor; thus enforcing and illustrating that celebrated maxim against which -moral science is a perpetual effort: *To whom much is given, of him shall much be required; and to whom men have committed much, of him they will ask the more.* But the present purpose is, not the exposure of such mistakes as actually exist in public opinion, but an attempt to give to public opinion its legitimate dominion and an uniform and unimpeded influence to each particular case which is its object.

When law is once understood to be no more than the recorded opinion of men, no more than the apprehensions of individuals on the reasoning of a particular case, we may expect that the sanguinary or stupid mistakes which disgrace the civil and criminal jurisprudence of civilized nations will speedily disappear. How long under its present sanctions do not the most exploded violations of humanity maintain their ground in courts of law after public opinion has branded them with reprobation; sometimes even until by constantly maintaining their post under the shelter of venerable names, they out-weary the very scorn and abhorrence of mankind, or subsist unrepealed and silent, until some check in the progress of human improvement awakens them, and that public opinion from which they should have received their reversal is infected by their influence. Public opinion would never long stagnate in error were it not fenced about and frozen over by forms and superstitions. If men were accustomed to reason and to hear the arguments of others upon each particular case that concerned the life, or liberty, or property, or reputation of their peers, those mistakes which at present render these possessions so insecure to all but those who enjoy enormous wealth never could subsist. If the administration of law ceased to appeal from the common sense, or the enlightened minds of twelve contemporary *good and true men,* who should be the peers of the accused, or, in cases of property, of the claimant, to the obscure records of dark and barbarous epochs, or the precedents of what venal and enslaved judges might have decreed to please their tyrants, or the opinion of any man or set of men who lived when bigotry was virtue, and passive obedience that discretion which is the better part of valor—all those mistakes now fastened in the public opinion, would be brought at each new case to the . . . .

ESSAY ON THE DEVIL AND DEVILS

[*The Essay on the Devil and Devils* because of its charming wit and good-natured sarcasm is one of Shelley's most delightful essays. In spirit, though not in style, it is of an early vintage, and was composed probably in 1819; in any case not later than 1820.

Because of its satiric approach, the reader may mistake its purpose, which is to attack the superstitions and mythologies in the Christian religion. In *The Necessity of Atheism* (1811) and the Notes to *Queen Mab* (1813) Shelley is direct and forthright, but in the present essay, though characteristically Shelleyan in theme, the author's method of approach is subtler. He will disarm the reader by appealing to his sense of the ridiculous. But in the end he will have driven home his point. He makes it clear that a belief in the devil and other Christian myths cannot keep company with science and reason.

Half playfully and charmingly ironic Shelley gives the reader what appears to be a serious account of the life of Mr. Badman, and when one has finished reading the essay, he cannot help chuckling over the stupidity and gullibility of *homo sapiens*.

In this essay Shelley is a consummate realist bent upon exposing man's apparent desire to be fooled. He makes it clear, however, that as knowledge increases superstitions will recede, and the myths by which men live will be eradicated. When science has fully and finally explained the world around us—as it certainly will—man's mind will no longer be enchained by those dark, mysterious forces in nature which give birth to religions and creeds. It is an article of Shelley's faith that knowledge—religious, moral, scientific—is the sole basis of virtuous living. A man can be virtuous and wise and good only through knowledge of himself and the world in which he lives.

Closely linked with his war on superstition is Shelley's serious concern in the essay with the origin and the nature of good and evil. His conception is found in several of his essays and letters. *A Treatise on Morals* is brief but representative. Following Spinoza and Hume, Shelley says, "That is called good which produces pleasure; that is called evil which produces pain." Evil, while real and inextricably intermixed with good, is relative and thus may be eradicated by knowledge. If God is the author of evil, so he is of good. See the *Essay on Christianity* for a divergent view.

When Shelley turned from didactic prose to the idealisms of poetry as the best means of reforming the world, he did not change this conception of evil; he merely resorted to symbolism and myth, the thought remaining the same. This fact has often misled the general reader as well as the mature Shelley scholar into misinterpretations of the poet.]

To determine the nature and functions of the Devil is no contemptible province of the European mythology. Who, or what he is, his origin, his habitation, his destiny, and his power are subjects which puzzle the most acute theologians, and on which no orthodox person can be induced to give a decisive opinion. He is the weak place of the popular religion, the vulnerable belly of the crocodile.

The Manichaean philosophy respecting the origin and government of the world, if not true, is at least an hypothesis conformable to the experience of actual facts. To suppose that the world was created and is superintended by two spirits of a balanced power and opposite dispositions is simply a personification of the struggle which we experience within ourselves, and which we perceive in the operations of external things as they affect us, between good and evil.[1] The supposition that the good spirit is, or hereafter will be, superior, is a personification of the principle of hope and that thirst for improvement without which present evil would be intolerable. The vulgar are all Manichaeans—all that remains of the popular superstition is mere machinery and accompaniment. Nothing is [simpler than to take] from our sensations of pleasure and pain all circumstance and limit—to add those active powers, of whose existence we are conscious within ourselves—to give to that which [is] most pleasing to us a perpetual or an ultimate superiority, with all epithets of honorable addition, and to brand that which is displeasing with epithets ludicrous or horrible, predicting its ultimate defeat, is to pursue the process by which the vulgar arrive at the familiar notions of God and the Devil.

The wisest of the ancient philosophers accounted for the existence without introducing the Devil. The Devil was clearly a Chaldaean invention, for we first hear of him after the return of the Jews from their second Assyrian captivity.[2] He is indeed mentioned in the Book of Job; but, so far from that circumstance affording any denial of that Book having been written at a very early period, it tends rather to show that it was the production of a later age. The

magnificence and purity, indeed, of the poetry and the irresistible grandeur of the poem strongly suggest the idea that it was a birth of the vigorous infancy of some community of men. Assuredly it was not written by a Jew before the period of the second Captivity, because it speaks of the Devil, and there is no other mention of this personage in the voluminous literature of that epoch. [That] it was not written by a Jew at all may be presumed from a perpetual employment and that with the most consummate beauty of imagery belonging to a severer climate than Palestine.

But to return to the Devil. Those among the Greek Philosophers whose poetical imagination suggested a personification of the cause of the Universe seem nevertheless to have dispensed with the agency of the Devil. Democritus, Epicurus, Theodorus, and perhaps even Aristotle, indeed abstained from introducing a living and thinking Agent, analogous to the human mind, as the author or superintendent of the world. Plato, following his master Socrates, who had been struck with the beauty and novelty of the theistical hypothesis as first delivered by the tutor of Pericles, supposed the existence of a God, and accommodated a moral system of the most universal character, including the past, the present, and the future condition of man, to the popular supposition of the moral superintendence of this one intellectual cause. Of the Stoics —it is needless to pursue the modification of this doctrine as it extended among the succeeding sects. These hypotheses, though rude enough, are in no respect very absurd and contradictory. The refined speculations respecting the existence of external objects by which the idea of matter is suggested to which Plato has the merit of first having directed the attention of the thinking part of mankind. . . . A partial interpretation of it has gradually afforded the basis of the

1. Compare this with a similar statement in the *Essay on Christianity*.
2. For an account of the origin of evil (the devil) see Dugald Stewart's *The Philosophy of the Active*

and Moral Powers of Man. Collected Works, Hamilton Edition, 7.129 ff. See Hume's *Dialogues Concerning Natural Religion*, Holbach's *Système*, and Paine's *The Age of Reason* for similar ideas.

least inspired portion of our popular religion.

But the Greek philosophers abstained from introducing the Devil. They accounted for evil by supposing that what is called matter is eternal and that God in making the world made not the best that he, or even inferior intelligence, could conceive; but that he moulded the reluctant and stubborn materials ready to his hand into the nearest arrangement possible to the perfect archetype existing in his contemplation. In the same manner as a skilful watchmaker who, if he had diamonds, and steel, and brass, and gold, can construct a timepiece of the most accurate workmanship, [but] could produce nothing beyond a coarse and imperfect clock if he were restricted to wood as his material. The Christian theologians, however, have invariably rejected this hypothesis on the ground that the eternity of matter is incompatible with the omnipotence of God.

Like panic-stricken slaves in the presence of a jealous and suspicious despot, they have tortured themselves ever to devise any flattering sophism by which they might appease him by the most contradictory praises, endeavoring to reconcile omnipotence, and benevolence, and equity in the Author of an Universe, where evil and good are inextricably entangled, and where the most admirable tendencies to happiness and preservation are forever baffled by misery and decay. The Christians, therefore, invented or adopted the Devil to extricate them from this difficulty.[3]

The account they give us of the origin of the Devil is curious: Heaven, according to the popular creed, is a certain airy region inhabited by the Supreme Being and a multitude of inferior spirits. With respect to the situation of it, theologians are not agreed, but it is generally supposed to be placed beyond that remotest constellation of the visible stars. These spirits are supposed, like those which reside in the bodies of animals and men, to have been created by God with foresight of the consequences which would result from the mechanism of their nature. He made them as good as possible, but the nature of the substance out of which they were formed, or the unconquerable laws according to which that substance when created was necessarily modified, prevented them from being so perfect as he could wish. Some say that he gave them free-will; that is, that he made them without any very distinct apprehension of the results of his workmanship, leaving them an active power which might determine them to this or that action, independently of the motives afforded by the regular operation of those impressions which were produced by the general agencies of the rest of his creation.[4] This he is supposed to have done that he might excuse himself to his own conscience for tormenting and annoying these unfortunate spirits when they provoked him by turning out worse than he expected. This account of the origin of evil, to make the best of it, does not seem more complimentary to the Supreme Being, or less derogatory to his omnipotence and goodness than the Platonic scheme.[5]

They then proceed to relate, gravely, that one fine Morning a chief of these spirits took it into his head to rebel against God, having gained over to his cause a third part of the eternal angels who attended upon

3. This idea of the origin of evil is not really in conflict with the author's moral principles in earlier statements in A Refutation of Deism, Note on Queen Mab, and A Treatise on Morals. See footnote 5 to this essay.

4. This view is in perfect agreement with a statement in the Note on Queen Mab on the line beginning with "Necessity, thou Mother." Most of the ideas in this essay are discussed in Holbach's Système de la Nature, 1.27-187—especially the last fifty pages.

5. This idea is fully discussed in Stewart, op. cit., Book Three, p. 357. See also Reid's Philosophy of the Active and Moral Powers of Man, 2.632-636, and Hume's An Enquiry (Everyman edition), 2.61-84. Plato thought that evil is not a positive something, but merely a negative good, a lesser good, tending to perfection. Indeed, Plato seems uncertain as to the origin and the nature of evil.

the Creator and Preserver of Heaven and Earth. After a series of desperate conflicts between those who remained faithful to the ancient dynasty and the insurgents, the latter were beaten and driven into a place called Hell, which was rather their empire than their prison, and where God reserved them, first to be the tempters and then the jailors and tormentors of a new race of beings whom he created under the same conditions of imperfection and with the same foresight of an unfortunate result. The motive of this insurrection is not assigned by any of the early mythological writers. Milton supposes that, on a particular day, God chose to adopt as his son and *heir,* (the reversion of an estate with an immortal incumbent would be worth little) a being unlike the other spirits, who seems to have been and approved to be a detached portion of himself, and afterwards figured upon the earth in the well-known character of Jesus Christ. The Devil is represented as conceiving high indignation at this preference and as disputing the affair with arms. I cannot discover Milton's authority for this circumstance, but all agree in the fact of the insurrection, and the defeat, and the casting out into Hell. Nothing can exceed the grandeur and the energy of the character of the Devil as expressed in *Paradise Lost.* Here is a Devil very different from the popular personification of evil, malignity, and it is a mistake to suppose that he was intended for an idealism of implacable hate, cunning, and refinement of device to inflict the utmost anguish on an enemy; these, which are venial in a slave, are not to be forgiven in a tyrant; these, which are redeemed by much that ennobles in one subdued, are marked by all that dishonors his conquest in the victor.

Milton's Devil as a moral being is as far superior to his God as one who perseveres in some purpose which he has conceived to be excellent, in spite of adversity and torture, is to one who in the cold security of undoubted triumph inflicts the most horrible revenge upon his enemy—not from any mistaken notion of bringing him to repent of a perseverance in enmity but with the open and alleged design of exasperating him to deserve new torments.

Milton so far violated all that part of the popular creed which is susceptible of being preached and defended in argument as to allege no superiority in moral virtue to his God over his Devil. He mingled as it were the elements of human nature, as colors upon a single palette, and arranged them into the composition of his great picture, according to the laws of epic truth; that is, according to the laws of that principle by which a series of actions of intelligent and ethical beings developed in rhythmical language are calculated to excite the sympathy and [or] antipathy of succeeding generations of mankind. The writer who would have attributed majesty and beauty to the character of victorious and vindictive omnipotence must have been contented with the character of a good Christian; he never could have been a great epic poet. It is difficult to determine, in a country where the most enormous sanctions of opinion and law are attached to a direct avowal of certain speculative notions, whether Milton was a Christian or not at the period of the composition of *Paradise Lost.* Is it possible that Socrates seriously believed that Aesculapius would be propitiated by the offering of a cock? Thus much is certain, that Milton gives the Devil all imaginable advantage; and the arguments with which he exposes the injustice and impotent weakness of his adversary are such as, had they been printed distinct from the shelter of any dramatic order, would have been answered by the most conclusive of syllogisms—persecution.

As it is, *Paradise Lost* has conferred on the modern mythology a systematic form; when the immeasurable and unceasing mutability of time shall have added one more superstition to those which have already arisen and decayed upon the earth, commentators and critics will be learnedly employed in elucidating the religion of ancestral Europe, only not utterly forgotten because it will have participated in the eternity of genius.[6] As to the Devil he owes everything to Milton. Dante and Tasso present us with a very gross idea of him. Milton divested him of a sting, hoofs, and horns, clothed him with the sublime grandeur of a graceful but tremendous spirit—and restored him to the society.

I am afraid there is much laxity among the orthodox of the present day respecting a belief in the Devil. I recommend the Bishops to make a serious charge to their diocesans on this dangerous latitude. The Devil is the outwork of the Christian faith; he is the weakest point—you may observe that infidels in their novitiate always begin by humorously doubting the existence of the Devil.

Depend upon it, that when a person once begins to think that perhaps there is no Devil, he is in a dangerous way. There may be observed in polite society a great deal of coquetting about the Devil, especially among divines, which is singularly ominous. They qualify him as the Evil Spirit; they consider him as synonymous with the flesh. They seem to wish to divest him of all personality; to reduce him from his abstract to his concrete; to reverse the process by which he was created in the mind, which they will by no means bear with respect to God. It is popular and well looked upon, if you deny the Devil "a local habitation and a name." Even the vulgar begin to scout him. Hell is popularly considered as metaphorical of the torments of an evil conscience and by no means capable of being topographically ascertained. No one likes to mention the torments of everlasting fire and the poisonous gnawing of the worm that liveth forever and ever. It is all explained away into the regrets and the reproaches of an evil conscience, and in this respect I think that the most presumptuous among us may safely say:

"One touch of nature makes the whole world kin."[7]

On the other hand, Heaven is supposed to have some settled locality, and the joys of the elect are to be something very positive. This way of talking about a personage whose office in the mythological scheme is so important must lead to disbelief. It is in fact a proof of approaching extinction in any religion when its teachers and its adherents, instead of proudly and dogmatically insisting upon the most invidious or unintelligible articles of their creed, begin to palliate and explain away the doctrines in which their more believing ancestors had shown a reverential acquiescence and an audacious exultation of confidence. It is less the opinion of the person himself than that of those by whom he is surrounded which gives that air of confidence by which the most absurd tenets have been transmitted from generation to generation. A man may in truth never have considered whether there is or is not a Devil; he may be totally indifferent. Yet it may occur to him to state his positive opinion on one side or the other; the air of confidence with which he does this is manifestly determined by the disposition with which he expects his opinion to be received. An illustration of this view of the subject is afforded by a circumstance in the life of Dr. Johnson, the last man of considerable talents who showed any serious attachments to the ancient faith, and whose life and death as compared with that of his contemporary Hume affords a just standard of the consolations of Christianity or the infidel systems. A gentleman inquired of Johnson what he meant by *being damned*. "Sent to Hell and punished everlastingly," he replied. The kingdom of the faithful.

The Devil is Διάβολος, an Accuser. In this character he presented himself among the other sons of God before his Father's throne to request to be allowed to tempt Job by tormenting him so that God might

6. The whole mechanism of the affair—the tempting of Eve—the damnation of the innocent posterity of our first parents. [Shelley's Note.]

7. Shakespeare's *Troilus and Cressida*, 3.3.175.

damn him. God, it seems, had some special reason for patronizing Job; and one does not well see why he spared him at last. The expostulations of Job with God are of the most daring character; it is certain he would not bear them from a Christian. If God were a refined critic, which from his inspiration of Ezechiel would never have been suspected, one might imagine that the profuse and sublime strain of poetry, not to be surpassed by ancient literature, much less modern, had found favor with him. In this view he [the Devil] is at once the informer, the attorney general, and the jailor of the celestial tribunal. It is not good policy, or at least cannot be considered as constitutional practice, to unite these characters. The Devil must have a great interest to exert himself to procure a sentence of guilty from the judge; for I suppose there will be no jury at the resurrection—at least if there is it will be so overawed by the bench and the counsel for the Crown as to ensure whatever verdict the court shall please to recommend. No doubt as an incentive to his exertions, half goes to the informer. What an army of spies and informers all Hell must afford, under the direction of that active magistrate, the Devil! How many plots and conspiracies and . . . .

If the Devil takes but half the pleasure in tormenting a sinner which God does, who took the trouble to create him, and then to invent a system of casuistry by which he might excuse himself for devoting him to external torment, this reward must be considerable. Conceive how the enjoyment of one half of the advantages to be derived from their ruin, whether in person or property, must irritate the activity of a delator. Tiberius, or Bonaparte, or Lord Castlereagh, never affixed any reward to the disclosure or the creation of conspiracies equal to that which God's government has attached to the exertions of the Devil, to tempt, betray, and accuse unfortunate man. These two considerable personages are supposed to have entered into a sort of partnership in which the weaker has consented to bear all the odium of their common actions and to allow the stronger to talk of himself as a very honorable person, on condition of having a participation in what is the especial delight of both of them, burning men to all eternity. The dirty work is done by the Devil in the same manner as some starving wretch will hire himself out to a King or Minister to work with a stipulation that he shall have some portion of the public spoil as an instrument to betray a certain number of other starving wretches into circumstances of capital punishment, when they may think it convenient to edify the rest by hanging up a few of those whose murmurs are too loud.

It is far from inexplicable that earthly tyrants should employ this kind of agents, or that God should have done so with regard to the Devil and his angels; or that any depository of power should take these measures with respect to those by whom he fears lest that power should be wrested from him. But to tempt mankind to incur everlasting damnation must, on the part of God and even on the part of the Devil, arise from that very disinterested love of tormenting and annoying which is seldom observed on earth except from the very old. . . . The thing that comes nearest to it is a troop of idle dirty boys baiting a cat; cooking, skinning eels, and boiling lobsters alive, and bleeding calves, and whipping pigs to death; naturalists anatomizing dogs alive (a dog has as good a right and a better excuse for anatomizing a naturalist) are nothing compared to God and the Devil judging, damning, and then tormenting the soul of a miserable sinner. It is pretended that God dislikes it, but this is mere shamefacedness and coquetting, for he has everything his own way and he need not damn unless he likes. The Devil has a better excuse, for, as he was entirely made by God, he can have no tendency or disposition the seeds of which were not originally planted by his creator; and as everything else was made by God, those seeds can have only developed themselves in the precise degree and manner determined by the impulses arising from the agency of the rest of his creation. It would be as unfair to complain of the Devil for acting ill, as of a watch for going badly; the defects are to be imputed as much to God in the former case, as to the watch-maker in the latter. There is also another view of the subject, suggested by mythologi-cal writers, which strongly recommends the Devil to our sympathy and compassion, though [it] is less consistent with the theory of God's omnipotence than that already stated. The Devil it is said, before his fall, as an angel of the highest rank and the most splendid accomplishments, placed his peculiar delight in doing good. But the in-flexible grandeur of his spirit, mailed and nourished by the consciousness of the purest and loftiest designs, was so secure from the assault of any gross or common torments that God was considerably puzzled to invent what he considered an adequate punishment for his rebellion; he exhausted all the varie-ties of smothering and burning and freezing and cruelly lacerating his external frame, and the Devil laughed at the impotent revenge of his conqueror. At last the benevo-lent and amiable disposition which dis-tinguished his adversary furnished God with the true method of executing an enduring and a terrible vengeance. He turned his good into evil, and, by virtue of his omnipotence, inspired him with such impulses as, in spite of his better nature, irresistibly deter-mined him to act what he most abhorred and to be a minister of those designs and schemes of which he was the chief and the original victim. He is forever tortured with compassion and affection for those whom he betrays and ruins; he is racked by a vain abhorrence for the desolation of which he is the instrument; he is like a man compelled by a tyrant to set fire to his own possession, and to appear as the witness against and the accuser of his dearest friends and most intimate connections, and then to be their executioner and to inflict the most subtle protracted torments upon them. As a man, were he deprived of all other refuge, he might hold his breath and die—but God is represented as omnipotent and the Devil as eternal. Milton has expressed this view of the subject with the sublimest pathos.[8]

It is commonly said that the Devil has only precisely so much power as is allowed him by God's providence. Christians exhort each other to despise his attacks and to trust in God. If this trust has ever been deceived, they seem in a poor way, especially when it is considered that God has arranged it so that the Devil should have no inconsiderable portion of the souls of men. My pious friend Miss ———— tells me that she thinks that about nineteen in twenty will be damned. Formerly it was supposed that all those who were not Christians and even all those who were not of a particular sect of Christians would be damned. At present this doctrine seems abandoned or confined to a few. One does not well see who are to be damned and who not according to the fashionable creed.

The sphere of the operations of the Devil is difficult to determine. The late invention and improvement in telescopes has consider-ably enlarged the notions of men respecting the bounds of the Universe. It is discovered that the earth is a comparatively small globe in a system consisting of a multitude of others which roll round the Sun; and there is no reason to suppose but that all these are inhabited by organized and intelligent be-ings. The fixed stars are supposed to be suns, each of them the center of a system like ours. Those little whitish specks of light that are seen in a clear night are discovered to consist of a prodigious multitude of suns, each probably the center of a system of planets. The system of which our earth is a planet has been discovered to belong to one of those larger systems of suns, which when seen at a distance look like a whitish speck of light; and that lustrous streak called the Milky Way is found to be one of the

8. In *Paradise Lost.*

extremities of the immense group of suns in which our system is placed. The heaven is covered with an incalculable number of these white specks, and the better the telescopes the more are discovered and the more distinctly the confusion of white light is resolved into stars. All this was not known during the gradual invention of the Christian mythology and was never suspected by those barbarians on the obscure extremities of the Roman Empire by whom it was first adopted. If these incalculable millions of suns, planets, satellites, and comets are inhabited, is it to be supposed that God formed their inhabitants better, or less liable to offend him, than those primordial Spirits, those Angels near his throne, those first and most admirable of his creatures who rebelled and were damned? Or has he improved like a proficient in statuary or painting, with rude outlines and imperfect forms, to a more perfect idealism or imitation, so that his latter works are better than his first? Or has some fortunate chance like that which, when the painter despaired of being able to paint the foam of a horse directed the spunge so as to represent it accurately, interfered to confer stability and exactness upon one, or how many, among the numerous systems of animated nature? There is little reason to suppose that any considerable multitude of the planets were tenanted by beings better capable of resisting the temptations of the Devil than ours. But is the Devil, like God, omnipresent? If so, he interpenetrates God, and they both exist together, as metaphysicians have compared the omnipresence of God pervading the infinity of space and being, to salt mixed with water. If not, he must send some inferior angels either to this or some other planet first to tempt the inhabitants to disobey God and secondly to induce them to reject all terms of salvation; for which latter purpose, it seems equally requisite that he should take up his residence on the spot; nor do I see, how he or God, by whose Providence he is permitted—that is to say—compelled to act,

could commit a business of such high moment to an inferior angel. It seems very questionable whether the Devil himself, or only some inferior Devil, tempted and betrayed the people of the earth; or whether Jupiter, a planet capable of containing a hundred times more inhabitants than the earth, to mention only the planets of our own system, or the sun, which would contain a million times more, were not entitled to the preference.

Any objection arising from the multitude of Devils, that I think futile. You may suppose a million times as many devils as there are stars. In fact you may suppose anything you like on such a subject. That there are a great number of Devils, and that they go about in legions of six or seven, or more, at a time, all mythologists are agreed. Christians, indeed, will not admit the substansive presence of Devils upon earth in modern times, or they suppose their agency to be obscure and surreptitious, in proportion as any histories of them approach to the present epoch, or indeed any epoch in which there has been a considerable progress in historical criticism or natural science. There were a number of Devils in Judea in the time of Jesus Christ, and a great reputation was gained both by him and others, by what was called casting them out. A droll story is told us, among others, of Jesus Christ having driven a legion of Devils into a herd of pigs, who were so discomfited with these new enemies that they all threw themselves over a precipice into the lake and were drowned. These were a set of hypochondriacal and high-minded swine, very unlike any others of which we have authentic record; they disdained to live, if they must live in so intimate a society with devils as that which was imposed on them, and the pig-drivers were no doubt confounded at so unusual a resolution. What became of the Devils after the death of the pigs, whether they passed into the fish, and then by digestion, through the stomach, into the brain of the Gadarene Icthyophagists; whether they returned to Hell, or remained in the water, the historian has left as subject for everlasting conjecture. I should be anxious to know whether any half-starved Jew picked up these pigs and sold them at the market of Gadara, and what effect the bacon of a demoniac pig who had killed himself produced upon the consumers. The Devils requested Jesus Christ to send them into the pigs, and the Son of God showed himself more inclined to do what was agreeable to these Devils than what was profitable to the owners of the pigs. No doubt saying: "Poor fellows," the Christians had good reasons [and] were probably ruined by this operation. The Gadarenes evidently disapproved of this method of ejecting Devils—they thought probably that Jesus showed an inequitable preference to the disagreeable beings—and they sent a deputation to him to request that he would depart out of their country. I doubt whether the yeomen of the present day would have treated him with so much lenity but . . . neither, Jesus Christ did not foresee this circumstance. I wonder what Ulysses would have said to Eumanus, if that driven pig herd had informed him on his return that all pigs had drowned themselves in despair because a wandering prophet had driven a legion of Devils into them. If I were a pig herd, I would make any excuse rather than that to a master renowned for subtilty of penetration and extent and variety of experience.

Among the erroneous theories concerning the condition of Devils, some have applied [resorted] to the Pythagorean hypothesis, but in such a manner as to pervert that hypothesis from motives of humanity into an excuse for cruel tyranny. They suppose that the bodies of animals and especially domestic animals are animated by Devils and that the tyranny exercised over these unfortunate beings by man is an unconscious piece of retaliation over the beings who betrayed them into a state of reprobation. On this theory Lord Erskine's Act[9] might have been entitled "An Act for the better protection of Devils." How Devils inhabit the bodies of men is not explained. It cannot be that they animate them like what is called the soul or vital principle, because that is supposed to be already preoccupied. Some have supposed that they exist in the human body in the shape of teniae and hydadits and animalcula; but I know not whether those persons subject to vermicular disease are the most likely to be subject to the incursions of Devils from any reason *a priori*, although they may safely be said to be tormented of the Devils. The pedicular diseases, on this view of the subject, may be the result of a diabolical influence, the sensorium of every separate louse being the habitation of a distinct imp. Some have supposed that the Devils live in the sun, and that glorious luminary is the actual Hell; perhaps that every fixed star is a distinct Hell appropriated for the use of its several systems of planets, so great a proportion of the inhabitants of which are probably devoted to everlasting damnation, if the belief of one particular creed is essential to their escape, and the testimony of its truth so very remote and obscure as in the planet which we inhabit. I do not envy the theologians who first invented this theory. The Magian worship of the sun as the creator and preserver of the world is considerably more to the credit of the inventors. It is in fact a poetical exposition of the matter of fact, before modern science had so greatly enlarged the boundaries of the sensible world, and was, next to pure Deism or a personification of all the powers whose agency we know or can conjecture, the religion of the fewest evil consequences.

If the sun is Hell, the Devil has a magnificent abode, being elevated as it were on the imperial throne of the visible world. If we assign to the Devil the greatest and most glorious habitation within the scope of our

9. Lord Erskine's bill "For the Prevention of Cruelty to Animals," although proposed in 1809, was not finally passed until 1824.

senses, where shall we conceive his mightier adversary to reside? Shall we suppose that the Devil occupies the center and God the circumference of existence, and that one urges inwards with the centripetal, while the other is perpetually struggling outwards from the narrow focus with the centrifugal force, and that from their perpetual conflict results that mixture of good and evil, harmony and discord, beauty and deformity, production and decay, which are the general laws of the moral and material world? Alas, the poor theologian never troubled his fancy with nonsense of so philosophical a form and contented himself with supposing that God was somewhere or other; that the Devil and all his angels, together with the perpetually increasing multitude of the damned, were burning alive to all eternity in that prodigious orb of elemental light which sustains and animates that multitude of inhabited globes, in whose company this earth revolves. Others have supposed Hell to be distributed among the comets, which constitute according to this scheme a number of floating prisons of intense and inextinguishable fire; a great modern poet adopts this idea when he calls a comet

"A wandering Hell in the eternal space."[10]

Misery and injustice contrive to produce very poetical effect, because the excellence of poetry consists in its awakening the sympathy of men which among persons influenced by an abject and gloomy superstition is much more easily done by images of horror than of beauty. It requires a higher degree of skill in a poet to make beauty, virtue, and harmony poetical, that is, to give them an idealized and rhythmical analogy with the predominating emotions of his readers than to make injustice, deformity, and discord and horror poetical. There are fewer Raphaels than Michael Angelos. Bet-

ter verses have been written on Hell than Paradise. How few read the *Purgatorio* or the *Paradiso* of Dante, in the comparison of those who know the *Inferno* well. But yet the *Purgatorio,* with the exception of two famous passages, is a finer poem than the *Inferno.* No poet develops the same power in the heat of his composition when he feels himself insecure of the emotions of his readers, as in those where he knows that he can command their sympathy.

As to the Devil, and the imps, and the damned living in the sun—why there is no great probability of it. The comets are better fitted for this purpose; except that some astronomers have suggested the possibility of their orbits gradually becoming ecliptical, until at last they might arrange themselves in orbits concentric with the planets, lose their heat and their substance, become subject to the same laws of animal and vegetable life as those according to which the substance of the surface of the others is arranged. The Devils and the damned, without some miraculous interposition, would then be the inhabitants of a very agreeable world; and as they probably would have become very good friends from a community of misfortune and the experience which time gives those who live long enough of the folly of quarrelling, would probably administer the affairs of their colony with great harmony and success. But there is an objection to this whole theory of solar and planetary hells— which is, that there is no proof that the sun or that comets are themselves burning. It is the same with fire as with wit: a man may not be witty himself as Falstaff was, although like him he may be the cause of wit in others. So the sun, though the cause of fire, may only develop a limited proportion of that principle on its own surface. Herschel's discoveries[11] incline to a presumption that this is actually the case. He has perceived that the universal cause of light and

10. Byron's *Manfred,* 1.1.46.
11. Sir Frederick Herschel (1738-1822), a distinguished German-born, English astronomer, whose

sublime conceptions of the universe greatly influenced Shelley's thinking. See especially his *Motion of the Solar System in Space* (1783).

heat is not the burning body of the sun itself, but a shell as it were of phosphoric vapors, suspended many thousand miles in the atmosphere of that body. These vapors surround the sphere of the sun at a distance which has not been accurately computed, but which is assuredly very great, encircling and canopying it as with a vault of ethereal splendor whose internal surface may perform the same office to the processes of vital and material action on the body of the sun as its external one does on those of the planets. A certain degree of plausibility is inferred in this notion by the observation that the interior surface, as far as can be attested from a view of the sides of the chasm, is of an obscurer color than the external one: what are called spots in the sun being no more than immense rents produced probably by streams of wind in this incumbent mass of vapors which disclose the opaque body of the sun itself. All this diminishes the probability of the sun being a hell, by showing that there is no reason for supposing it considerably hotter than the planets—not to mention that the Devils may be like the animalculae in mutton broth, whom you may boil as much as you please, but they will always continue alive and vigorous.

The idea of the sun being Hell is an attempt at an improvement on the old-established idea of its occupying the center of the earth. The Devils and the damned would be exceedingly crowded in process of ages, if they were confined within so inconsiderable sphere.

The Devil and his angels are called the Powers of the Air, and the Devil himself Lucifer.[12] I cannot discover why he is called Lucifer, except from a misinterpreted passage in Isaiah, where that poet exults over the fall of an Assyrian king, the oppressor of his country: "How art thou fallen, Lucifer, king of Morning!" The Devil after

having gradually assumed the horns, hoofs, tail, and ears of the ancient Gods of the woods, gradually lost them again, although wings had been added. It is inexplicable why men assigned him these additions as circumstances of terror and deformity. The sylvans and fauns with their leader, the great Pan, were most poetical personages and were connected in the imagination of the Pagans with all that could enliven and delight. They were supposed to be innocent beings not greatly different in habits from the shepherds and herdsmen of which they were the patron saints. But the Christians contrived to turn the wrecks of the Greek mythology, as well as the little they understood of their philosophy, to purposes of deformity and falsehood.[13] I suppose the sting with which he was armed gave him a dragon-like and viperous appearance, very formidable.

I can sufficiently understand why the author of evil should have been typified under the image of a serpent—that animal producing merely by its sight so strong an associated recollection of the malignity of many of its species. But this was eminently a practice confined to the Jews, whose earliest mythology suggested this animal as the cause of all evil. Among the Greeks the Serpent was considered as an auspicious and favorable being.[14] He attended on Aesculapius and Apollo. In Egypt the Serpent was an hieroglyphic of eternity. The Jewish account is that the Serpent, that is the animal, persuaded the original pair of human beings to eat of a fruit from which God had commanded them to abstain, and that in consequence God expelled them from the pleasant garden where he had before permitted them to reside. God on this occasion, it is said, assigned a punishment to the Serpent that its motion should be as it now is along the ground upon its belly. We are given to suppose that, before this misconduct, it hopped

12. From the Latin, meaning the bearer of light; the dawn or morning light—thus the dispenser of knowledge.

13. It is a characteristic Shelleyan idea that Christian mythology destroyed the lovely Greek myths.

14. This accords with Shelley's treatment of the serpent myth in *Laon and Cythna,* thus making the symbolism in that poem intelligible. See also *The Assassins.*

along upon its tail, a mode of progression which, if I was a serpent, I should think the severer punishment of the two. The Christians have turned this Serpent into their Devil and accommodated the whole story to their new scheme of sin and propitiation.

A DEFENCE OF POETRY

[Shelley's London publishers, C. and J. Ollier, in 1820 issued the first and only number of Ollier's *Literary Miscellany,* the last article in which was *The Four Ages of Poetry* by Shelley's friend Thomas Love Peacock. After reading the copy which the Olliers had sent to him, Shelley wrote to them on January 20, 1821: "I am enchanted with your *Literary Miscellany,* although the last article it contains has excited my polemical faculties so violently that the moment I get rid of my opthalmia, I mean to set about an answer to it. . . . It is very clever, but I think, very false." To Peacock himself Shelley wrote on February 15: "Your anathemas against poetry itself excited me to a sacred rage. . . . I had the greatest possible desire to break a lance with you . . . in honor of my mistress Urania."

During the closing days of February Shelley began the composition of his *Defence,* but on March 4 he informed the Olliers that the subject "requires more words than I had expected." By March 20, Part One of *A Defence of Poetry* being completed, copied, and dispatched to the Olliers, Shelley informed them that he proposed "to add two other parts." On March 21, he wrote to Peacock: "You will see that I have taken a more general view of what is poetry than you have. . . . But read and judge and do not let us imitate the great founders of the picturesque, Price and Payne Knight, who like two ill-trained beagles began snarling at each other when they could not catch the hare."

The Olliers never published it; but Peacock secured the manuscript from them and consigned it to John Hunt for publication in *The Liberal.* Hunt edited it, omitting the specific allusions (or answers) to the *Four Ages of Poetry,* thus making it not an *answer* to Peacock, but a general defence of poetry. In the meantime *The Liberal* having died a natural death, *A Defence* remained unpublished until Mary Shelley's edition of the prose in 1840.

The Four Ages of Poetry, half-serious, half-playful, maintains that poetry is the natural expression of primitive and untutored peoples, and as man becomes civilized, it should be abandoned for the more worthy and practical pursuits.

Shelley's essay is divided into three sections: the first defines the nature of poetry and the function of the poet; the second insists strongly on the moral

influence of poetry; and the third endeavors to point out the value and significance of poetry in more advanced states of civilization. These divisions are not by
any means airtight, for the material is overlapping and repetitious. But the
work as a whole is unified and orderly.

Shelley mainly insists on the moral value of poetry. Since poetry is fundamentally the product of the *creative imagination* and since a high state of
civilization can be achieved only through insight into the moral problems facing
men, and since sympathy and love are the very basis of moral life, and finally
since love and sympathy can be awakened only by the active imagination, it
follows that poetry, in the broad sense in which Shelley uses the word, is the
sine qua non of the *Good Life*. Thus Shelley, in the main current of thought
in his day, and particularly as seen in the philosophy of Adam Smith and David
Hume, exalts imagination to the level of reason.

There is little or nothing of the mystic, the Platonist, or neo-Platonist in this
essay. Shelley's position is a demonstrable fact, and the present chaotic condition of the world is ample proof of that. Our moral and social sciences have
lagged behind the practical or natural sciences until we have more knowledge
than we know how to use for achieving happiness! The creative imagination
has been lulled to sleep to the persuasive hymns in praise of the active, the practical life. In a most eloquent portion of the essay, the author states his main
theme: "We have more moral, political, and historical wisdom than we know
how to reduce into practice; we have more scientific and economic knowledge
than can be accommodated to the just distribution of the produce which it
multiplies. . . . We want the creative faculty to imagine that which we know;
we want the generous impulse to act that which we imagine; we want the
poetry of life; our calculations have outrun our conception; we have eaten more
than we can digest. . . . Man having enslaved the elements remains himself
a slave." Or in other words in ferreting out the secret of the atom, man has
made the achievement of the Good Life possible, but men lack the imaginative
insight and moral courage to put the atom to work for the happiness of mankind. With "mere reasoners"—as Shelley would say—as our leaders, we have
only the insight of cavemen, preparing for another Dark Ages.

Shelley's sources are general: Plato, Aristotle, Horace, Sidney, but he owed
very little to any of these. *A Defence of Poetry* is fundamentally a product of
Shelley's own thinking. We have seen that he has drawn heavily on his own
writings, taking over ideas, sentences, and whole paragraphs almost verbatim,
making *A Defence* appear like a patchwork. Because of variations in the extant
MSS. of this work a "correct" text is difficult to establish. For details see Julian,
7.350-358.]

According to one mode of regarding those two classes of mental action which are called reason and imagination, the former may be considered as mind contemplating the relations borne by one thought to another, how-ever produced, and the latter, as mind acting upon those thoughts so as to color them with its own light and composing from them, as from elements, other thoughts, each containing within itself the principle of its own integrity. The one is the τὸ ποιεῖν,[1] or the principle of synthesis, and has for its objects those forms which are common to universal nature and existence itself; the other is the τὸ λογίζειν, or principle of analysis, and its action regards the relations of things simply as relations considering thoughts, not in their integral unity but as the algebraical representations which conduct to certain general results. Reason is the enumeration of quantities already known; imagination is the perception of the value of those quantities, both separately and as a whole.[2] Reason respects the differences, and imagination the similitudes of things.[3] Reason is to imagination as the instrument to the agent; as the body to the spirit; as the shadow to the substance.[4]

Poetry, in a general sense, may be defined to be "the expression of the imagination," and poetry is connate with the origin of man. Man is an instrument over which a series of external and internal impressions are driven like the alternations of an ever-changing wind over an Aeolian lyre which move it by their motion to ever-changing melody. But there is a principle within the human being, and perhaps within all sentient beings, which acts otherwise than in a lyre and produces not melody alone but harmony, by an internal adjustment of the sounds and motions thus excited to the impressions which excite them. It is as if the lyre could accommodate its chords to the motions of that which strikes them in a determined proportion of sound, even as the musician can accommodate his voice to the sound of the lyre.[5] A child at play by itself will express its delight by its voice and motions; and every inflection of tone and every gesture will bear exact relation to a corresponding antitype in the pleasurable impressions which awakened it; it will be the reflected image of that impression; and as the lyre trembles and sounds after the wind has died away, so the child seeks, by prolonging in its voice and motions the duration of the effect, to prolong also a consciousness of the cause. In relation to the objects which delight a child, these expressions are what poetry is to higher objects. The savage (for the savage is to ages what

1. Shelley could have found this Greek word describing the poet as a *Maker* in Sidney's *Defence of Poesy*, but he probably already knew this term from his wide reading in classical literature; see especially Aristotle. See also Tasso's *Discorsi del Poema Eroico*, and Chap. I of Puttenham's *Arte of English Poesie* (c. 1585).
2. This is a statement of the new philosophy of the imagination as seen in Adam Smith, David Hume, and Dugald Stewart. See Coleridge and Wordsworth on this subject.
3. This idea appears in various places in Shelley.
4. The three fragments below no doubt belong to an early draft of the essay. It should be noted that Shelley is here giving to the *imagination* an equal place with *reason* in his analysis of the functions of the mind. Some critics have asserted that in his earlier writings, Shelley has exalted reason above imagination. The facts do not sustain this point of view:

In one mode of considering these two classes of action of the human mind which are called reason and imagination, the former may be considered as mind employed upon the relations borne by one thought to another, however produced; and imagination as mind combining the elements of thought itself. It has been termed the power of association; and on an accurate anatomy of the functions of the mind, it would be difficult to assign any other origin to the mass of what we perceive and know than this power. Association is, however, rather a law according to which this power is exerted than the power itself; in the same manner as gravitation is a passive expression of the reciprocal tendency of heavy bodies towards their respective centers. Were these bodies conscious of such a tendency, the name which they would assign to that consciousness would express the cause of gravitation; and it were a vain inquiry as to what might be the cause of that cause. Association bears the same relation to imagination as a mode to a source of action; when we look upon shapes in the fire or the clouds and imagine to ourselves the resemblance of familiar objects, we do no more than seize the relation of certain points of visible objects, and fill up, blend together. . . .

The imagination is a faculty not less imperial and essential to the happiness and dignity of the human being than the reason.

It is by no means indisputable that what is true, or rather that which the disciples of a certain mechanical and superficial philosophy call true, is more excellent than the beautiful.

5. Compare this idea with the following statement in the *Essay on Christianity:* "There is a Power by which we are surrounded, like the atmosphere in which some motionless lyre is suspended, which visits with its breath our silent chords at will."

the child is to years) expresses the emotions produced in him by surrounding objects in a similar manner; and language and gesture, together with plastic or pictorial imitation, become the image of the combined effect of those objects and of his apprehension of them.[6] Man in society, with all his passions and his pleasures, next becomes the object of the passions and pleasures of man; an additional class of emotions produces an augmented treasure of expressions; and language, gesture, and the imitative arts become at once the representation and the medium, the pencil and the picture, the chisel and the statue, the chord and the harmony. The social sympathies, or those laws from which as from its elements society results, begin to develop themselves from the moment that two human beings coexist; the future is contained within the present as the plant within the seed; and equality, diversity, unity, contrast, mutual dependence become the principles alone capable of affording the motives according to which the will of a social being is determined to action inasmuch as he is social, and constitute pleasure in sensation, virtue in sentiment, beauty in art, truth in reasoning, and love in the intercourse of kind. Hence men, even in the infancy of society, observe a certain order in their words and actions, distinct from that of the objects and the impressions represented by them, all expression being subject to the laws of that from which it proceeds. But let us dismiss those more general considerations which might involve an inquiry into the principles of society itself and restrict our view to the manner in which the imagination is expressed upon its forms.[7]

In the youth of the world men dance and sing and imitate natural objects, observing in these actions as in all others a certain rhythm or order. And, although all men observe a similar, they observe not the same order in the motions of the dance, in the melody of the song, in the combinations of language, in the series of their imitations of natural objects. For there is a certain order or rhythm belonging to each of these classes of mimetic representation, from which the hearer and the spectator receive an intenser and purer pleasure than from any other. The sense of an approximation to this order has been called taste by modern writers. Every man in the infancy of art observes an order which approximates more or less closely to that from which this highest delight results; but the diversity is not sufficiently marked, as that its gradations should be sensible except in those instances where the predominance of this faculty of approximation to the beautiful (for so we may be permitted to name the relation between this highest pleasure and its cause) is very great. Those in whom it exists in excess are poets, in the most universal sense of the word; and the pleasure resulting from the manner in which they express the influence of society or nature upon their own minds communicates itself to others and gathers a sort of reduplication from that community. Their language is vitally metaphorical; that is, it marks the before unapprehended relations of things and perpetuates their apprehension until the words which represent them become, through time, signs for portions or classes of thoughts instead of pictures of integral thoughts; and then, if no new poets should arise to create afresh the associations which have been thus disorganized, language will be dead to all the nobler purposes of human intercourse. These similitudes or relations are finely said by Lord Bacon to be "the same footsteps of nature impressed upon the various subjects of the world,"[8] and he considers the faculty which perceives them as the storehouse of axioms common

6. See Wordsworth's conception in *Ode on Intimations of Immortality*.
7. The thought of this paragraph was probably inspired by Hume's *A Treatise on Human Nature*, Book III (*On Morals*).

8. *De Augment. Scient.*, cap. I., lib. iii. [Shelley's Note.] The substance of this long paragraph may have been suggested by Sidney's *Defence of Poesy*, pp. 31-32, A. S. Cook edition.

to all knowledge. In the infancy of society every author is necessarily a poet, because language itself is poetry; and to be a poet is to apprehend the true and the beautiful—in a word, the good which exists in the relation subsisting, first between existence and perception and secondly between perception and expression. Every original language near to its source is in itself the chaos of a cyclic poem; the copiousness of lexicography and the distinctions of grammar are the works of a later age and are merely the catalogue and the form of the creations of poetry.[9]

But poets, or those who imagine and express this indestructible order, are not only the authors of language and of music, of the dance, and architecture, and statuary and painting: they are the institutors of laws and the founders of civil society and the inventors of the arts of life and the teachers, who draw into a certain propinquity with the beautiful and the true that partial apprehension of the agencies of the invisible world which is called religion. Hence all original religions are allegorical, or susceptible of allegory, and like Janus have a double face of false and true.[10] Poets, according to the circumstances of the age and nation in which they appeared, were called in the earlier epochs of the world legislators or prophets; a poet essentially comprises and unites both these characters.[11] For he not only beholds intensely the present as it is and discovers those laws according to which present things ought to be ordered but he beholds the future in the present, and his thoughts are the germs of the flower and the fruit of latest time.[12] Not that I assert poets to be prophets in the gross sense of the word, or that they can foretell the form as surely as they fore-

know the spirit of events: such is the pretence of superstition which would make poetry an attribute of prophecy rather than prophecy an attribute of poetry.[13] A poet participates in the eternal, the infinite, and the one; as far as relates to his conceptions, time and place and number are not.[14] The grammatical forms which express the moods of time, and the difference of persons, and the distinction of place are convertible with respect to the highest poetry without injuring it as poetry; and the choruses of Aeschylus, and the book of Job, and Dante's *Paradiso* would afford more than any other writings examples of this fact, if the limits of this essay did not forbid citation. The creations of sculpture, painting, and music are illustrations still more decisive.

Language, color, form, and religious and civil habits of action are all the instruments and materials of poetry; they may be called poetry by that figure of speech which considers the effect as a synonym of the cause. But poetry in a more restricted sense expresses those arrangements of language and especially metrical language which are created by that imperial faculty whose throne is curtained within the invisible nature of man. And this springs from the nature itself of language, which is a more direct representation of the actions and passions of our internal being and is susceptible of more various and delicate combinations than color, form, or motion, and is more plastic and obedient to the control of that faculty of which it is the creation. For language is arbitrarily produced by the imagination and has relation to thoughts alone; but all other materials, instruments, and conditions of art have relations among each other which

9. This long analysis of taste and the nature of art is in conformity with the new concepts of judgment awakened by the Romantic writers. Its ancestry is long and honorable, beginning with Hume's *Essay on the Standard of Taste* (1757); William Duff's *Essay on Original* [Creative] *Genius* (1767); Sir Joshua Reynold's *Discourses*, No. 15 especially, (1769); Archibald Alison's *Essay on Taste* (1790), on through all the works of Wordsworth and Coleridge. See Sidney, pp. 2-3 for the idea that in the infancy of society every author is necessarily a poet.

10. For a similar notion compare Hume on natural religion. See also Sidney, pp. 2-3.

11. This is essentially Paine's idea as expressed in *The Age of Reason*, Chapter 7.

12. Compare with Wordsworth's Preface to *Lyrical Ballads* (1800).

13. See Paine, *The Age of Reason*, Chapter 7, for a similar statement.

14. Sidney expresses a similar idea in his *Defence of Poesy*.

limit and interpose between conception and expression. The former is as a mirror which reflects, the latter as a cloud which enfeebles the light of which both are mediums of communication. Hence the fame of sculptors, painters, and musicians, although the intrinsic powers of the great masters of these arts may yield in no degree to that of those who have employed language as the hieroglyphic of their thoughts, has never equalled that of poets in the restricted sense of the term, as two performers of equal skill will produce unequal effects from a guitar and a harp. The fame of legislators and founders of religion, so long as their institutions last, alone seems to exceed that of poets in the restricted sense; but it can scarcely be a question whether, if we deduct the celebrity which their flattery of the gross opinions of the vulgar usually conciliates, together with that which belonged to them in their higher character of poets, any excess will remain.

We have thus circumscribed the meaning of the word *poetry* within the limits of that art which is the most familiar and the most perfect expression of the faculty itself. It is necessary, however, to make the circle still narrower and to determine the distinction between measured and unmeasured language, for the popular division into prose and verse is inadmissible in accurate philosophy.[15]

Sounds as well as thought have relation both between each other and towards that which they represent, and a perception of the order of those relations has always been found connected with a perception of the order of those relations of thoughts. Hence the language of poets has ever affected a certain uniform and harmonious recurrence of sound, without which it were not poetry, and which is scarcely less indispensable to the communication of its influence than the

words themselves, without reference to that peculiar order. Hence the vanity of translation; it were as wise to cast a violet into a crucible that you might discover the formal principle of its color and odor, as seek to transfuse from one language into another the creations of a poet. The plant must spring again from its seed, or it will bear no flower—and this is the burthen of the curse of Babel.

An observation of the regular mode of the recurrence of this harmony in the language of poetical minds, together with its relation to music, produced metre; or a certain system of traditional forms of harmony of language. Yet it is by no means essential that a poet should accommodate his language to this traditional form so that the harmony, which is its spirit, be observed. The practice is indeed convenient and popular and to be preferred, especially in such composition as includes much form and action; but every great poet must inevitably innovate upon the example of his predecessors in the exact structure of his peculiar versification.[16] The distinction between poets and prose writers is a vulgar error. The distinction between philosophers and poets has been anticipated. Plato was essentially a poet —the truth and splendor of his imagery and the melody of his language is [are] the most intense that it is possible to conceive.[17] He rejected the harmony of the epic, dramatic, and lyrical forms, because he sought to kindle a harmony in thoughts divested of shape and action, and he forebore to invent any regular plan of rhythm which would include under determinate forms the varied pauses of his style. Cicero sought to imitate the cadence of his periods, but with little success. Lord Bacon was a poet.[18] His language has a sweet and majestic rhythm which satisfies the sense, no less than the

---

15. This idea is in perfect accord with the philosophy of Wordsworth and Coleridge which identifies poetry with order and harmony.

16. Both Coleridge and Wordsworth maintained this idea.

17. Fully discussed in Wordsworth's *Preface* (1800). For a similar idea, see Sidney, p. 3. For a

parallel statement see Shelley's *On the Symposium* or *Preface to the Banquet*.

18. See the *Filum Labyrinthi* and the *Essay on Death* particularly. [Shelley's Note.] Bacon's almost superhuman knowledge and his sympathy with the idea of progress are quite compatible with Shelley's philosophy.

almost superhuman wisdom of his philosophy satisfies the intellect; it is a strain which distends and then bursts the circumference of the hearer's mind and pours itself forth together with it into the universal element with which it has perpetual sympathy. All the authors of revolutions in opinion are not only necessarily poets as they are inventors, nor even as their words unveil the permanent analogy of things by images which participate in the life of truth but as their periods are harmonious and rhythmical and contain in themselves the elements of verse being the echo of the eternal music. Nor are those supreme poets who have employed traditional forms of rhythm on account of the form and action of their subjects less capable of perceiving and teaching the truth of things than those who have omitted that form. Shakespeare, Dante, and Milton (to confine ourselves to modern writers) are philosophers of the very loftiest power.

A poem is the very image of life expressed in its eternal truth.[19] There is this difference between a story and a poem, that a story is a catalogue of detached facts which have no other bond of connection than time, place, circumstance, cause, and effect; the other is the creation of actions according to the unchangeable forms of human nature as existing in the mind of the creator, which is itself the image of all other minds. The one is partial and applies only to a definite period of time and a certain combination of events which can never again recur; the other is universal and contains within itself the germ of a relation to whatever motives or actions have place in the possible varieties of human nature.[20] Time, which destroys the beauty and the use of the story of particular facts stripped of the poetry which should invest them, augments that of poetry

and forever develops new and wonderful applications of the eternal truth which it contains. Hence epitomes have been called the moths of just history; they eat out the poetry of it.[21] A story of particular facts is a mirror which obscures and distorts that which should be beautiful; poetry is a mirror which makes beautiful that which is distorted.[22]

The parts of a composition may be poetical without the composition as a whole being a poem[23] A single sentence may be considered as a whole, though it may be found in the midst of a series of unassimilated portions; a single word even may be a spark of inextinguishable thought. And thus all the great historians, Herodotus, Plutarch, Livy were poets; and although the plan of these writers, especially that of Livy, restrained them from developing this faculty in its highest degree, they make copious and ample amends for their subjection by filling all the interstices of their subjects with living images.[24]

Having determined what is poetry and who are poets, let us proceed to estimate its effects upon society.

Poetry is ever accompanied with pleasure: all spirits upon which it falls open themselves to receive the wisdom which is mingled with its delight. In the infancy of the world neither poets themselves nor their auditors are fully aware of the excellence of poetry, for it acts in a divine and unapprehended manner, beyond and above consciousness; and it is reserved for future generations to contemplate and measure the mighty cause and effect in all the strength and splendor of their union. Even in modern times no living poet ever arrived at the fulness of his fame; the jury which sits in judgment upon a poet, belonging as he does

19. Compare this with various similar statements in Wordsworth and Coleridge.
20. Hume touches briefly on this point in his *An Enquiry Concerning the Human Understanding,* Sections 3 and 4.
21. This is from Bacon's *Advancement of Learning,* II. ii., 4: "As for the corruption and moths of history, which are epitomes, the use of them deserv-

eth to be banished."
22. Shelley may have had this idea from Aristotle, or from Sidney, who borrowed from Aristotle.
23. Compare this statement with Poe's idea of a long poem; see his *The Philosophy of Composition.* Of course the indebtedness, if any, would be Poe's.
24. Aristotle in his *De Poetica* exalts poetry above history, as more philosophical and serious.

to all time, must be composed of his peers;[25] it must be empanelled by time from the selectest of the wise of many generations. A poet is a nightingale, who sits in darkness and sings to cheer its own solitude with sweet sounds; his auditors are as men entranced by the melody of an unseen musician, who feel that they are moved and softened, yet know not whence or why. The poems of Homer and his contemporaries were the delight of infant Greece; they were the elements of that social system which is the column upon which all succeeding civilization has reposed. Homer embodied the ideal perfection of his age in human character; nor can we doubt that those who read his verses were awakened to an ambition of becoming like to Achilles, Hector, and Ulysses; the truth and beauty of friendship, patriotism, and persevering devotion to an object were unveiled to their depths in these immortal creations; the sentiments of the auditors must have been refined and enlarged by a sympathy with such great and lovely impersonations until from admiring they imitated and from imitation they identified themselves with the objects of their admiration. Nor let it be objected that these characters are remote from moral perfection and that they can by no means be considered as edifying patterns for general imitation. Every epoch, under names more or less specious, has deified its peculiar errors; revenge is the naked idol of the worship of a semi-barbarous age; and self-deceit is the veiled image of unknown evil, before which luxury and satiety lie prostrate. But a poet considers the vices of his contemporaries as the temporary dress in which his creations must be arrayed and which cover without concealing the eternal proportions of their beauty. An epic or dramatic personage is understood to wear them around his soul,

as he may the ancient armor or modern uniform around his body while it is easy to conceive a dress more graceful than either. The beauty of the internal nature cannot be so far concealed by its accidental vesture, but that the spirit of its form shall communicate itself to the very disguise and indicate the shape it hides from the manner in which it is worn. A majestic form and graceful motions will express themselves through the most barbarous and tasteless costume. Few poets of the highest class have chosen to exhibit the beauty of their conceptions in its naked truth and splendor; and it is doubtful whether the alloy of costume, habit, &c., be not necessary to temper this planetary music for mortal ears.[26]

The whole objection, however, of the immortality of poetry rests upon a misconception of the manner in which poetry acts to produce the moral improvement of man.[27] Ethical science arranges the elements which poetry has created and propounds schemes and proposes examples of civil and domestic life; nor is it for want of admirable doctrines that men hate, and despise, and censure, and deceive, and subjugate one another. But poetry acts in another and diviner manner. It awakens and enlarges the mind itself by rendering it the receptacle of a thousand unapprehended combinations of thought. Poetry lifts the veil from the hidden beauty of the world and makes familiar objects be as if they were not familiar; it reproduces all that it represents, and the impersonations clothed in its Elysian light stand thenceforward in the minds of those who have once contemplated them as memorials of that gentle and exalted content which extends itself over all thoughts and actions with which it coexists. The great secret of morals is love, or a going out of our own nature and an identification of ourselves

25. Sidney in the *Defence of Poesy* suggests this idea. See Cook's edition, pp. 13-24.

26. Because of its highly wrought imagery, beauty of phrase, and penetrating thought this passage is the essence of poetry. Compare portions of it with *Prometheus Unbound*, Act I.

27. This is Shelley's answer to Plato's criticism of the poet, and more specifically to Peacock's half humorous, half-serious attack on poetry. Here Shelley repeats what he has frequently said, that the function of poetry is to elevate by awakening the sympathy and arousing the mind to great moral courage.

with the beautiful which exists in thought, action, or person, not our own. A man, to be greatly good, must imagine intensely and comprehensively; he must put himself in the place of another and of many others; the pains and pleasures of his species must become his own.[28] The great instrument of moral good is the imagination;[29] and poetry administers to the effect by acting upon the cause. Poetry enlarges the circumference of the imagination by replenishing it with thoughts of ever new delight, which have the power of attracting and assimilating to their own nature all other thoughts and which form new intervals and interstices whose void forever craves fresh food. Poetry strengthens that faculty which is the organ of the moral nature of man in the same manner as exercise strengthens a limb. A poet therefore would do ill to embody his own conceptions of right and wrong, which are usually those of his place and time, in his poetical creations which participate in neither.[30] By this assumption of the inferior office of interpreting the effect in which perhaps after all he might acquit himself but imperfectly, he would resign the glory in a participation in the cause. There was little danger that Homer, or any of the eternal poets, should have so far misunderstood themselves as to have abdicated this throne of their widest dominion. Those in whom the poetical faculty, though great, is less intense, as Euripides, Lucan, Tasso, Spenser, have frequently affected a moral aim, and the effect of their poetry is diminished in exact proportion to the degree in which they compel us to advert to this purpose.[31]

Homer and the cyclic poets were followed at a certain interval by the dramatic and lyrical poets of Athens, who flourished con-temporaneously with all that is most perfect in the kindred expressions of the poetical faculty: architecture, painting, music, the dance, sculpture, philosophy—and we may add—the forms of civil life. For although the scheme of Athenian society was deformed by many imperfections which the poetry existing in chivalry and Christianity has erased from the habits and institutions of modern Europe, yet never at any other period has so much energy, beauty, and virtue been developed; never was blind strength and stubborn form so disciplined and rendered subject to the will of man, or that will less repugnant to the dictates of the beautiful and the true, as during the century which preceded the death of Socrates. Of no other epoch in the history of our species have we records and fragments stamped so visibly with the image of the divinity in man. But it is poetry alone, in form, in action, or in language, which has rendered this epoch memorable above all others and the storehouse of examples to everlasting time. For written poetry existed at that epoch simultaneously with the other arts, and it is an idle inquiry to demand which gave and which received the light which all, as from a common focus, have scattered over the darkest periods of succeeding time. We know no more of cause and effect than a constant conjunction of events; poetry is ever found to co-exist with whatever other arts contribute to the happiness and perfection of man. I appeal to what has already been established to distinguish between the cause and the effect.[32]

It was at the period here adverted to that the drama had its birth; and however a succeeding writer may have equalled or surpassed those few great specimens of the

28. This is Shelley's most persistent and most fundamental philosophy. It is the guiding principle of his entire life and informs all that he wrote.

29. In considering the imagination the civilizing force in society and the great *creative* faculty, Shelley is in the main current of thought of his day; indeed, he goes beyond Adam Smith, Hume, and Alison in assigning to the imagination such an

exalted station. See the Prefaces to *Prometheus Unbound* and *The Cenci*.

30. For similar ideas compare the Prefaces to *Laon and Cythna,* and *Prometheus Unbound.*

31. See Prefaces to *Prometheus Unbound*, and *The Cenci* for an apparent divergent view.

32. The theme of this paragraph is more fully developed in his *Discourse on the Manners of the Ancient Greeks.*

Athenian drama which have been preserved to us, it is indisputable that the art itself never was understood or practiced according to the true philosophy of it, as at Athens. For the Athenians employed language, action, music, painting, the dance, and religious institutions to produce a common effect in the representation of the loftiest idealisms of passion and of power; each division in the art was made perfect in its kind by artists of the most consummate skill and was disciplined into a beautiful proportion and unity one towards another. On the modern stage a few only of the elements capable of expressing the image of the poet's conception are employed at once. We have tragedy without music and dancing; and music and dancing without the highest impersonations of which they are the fit accompaniment, and both without religion and solemnity.[33] Religious institution has indeed been usually banished from the stage. Our system of divesting the actor's face of a mask, on which the many expressions appropriated to his dramatic character might be moulded into one permanent and unchanging expression, is favorable only to a partial and inharmonious effect; it is fit for nothing but a monologue, where all the attention may be directed to some great master of ideal mimicry. The modern practice of blending comedy with tragedy, though liable to great abuse in point of practice, is undoubtedly an extension of the dramatic circle; but the comedy should be as in *King Lear* universal, ideal, and sublime. It is perhaps the intervention of this principle which determines the balance in favor of *King Lear* against the *Oedipus Tyrannus,* or the *Agamemnon,* or, if you will, the trilogies with which they are connected, unless the intense power of the choral poetry, especially that of the latter, should be considered as restoring the equilibrium. *King Lear,* if it can sustain this comparison, may be judged to be the most perfect specimen of the dramatic

art existing in the world, in spite of the narrow conditions to which the poet was subjected by the ignorance of the philosophy of the drama which has prevailed in modern Europe. Calderon in his religious *Autos* has attempted to fulfil some of the high conditions of dramatic representation neglected by Shakespeare, such as the establishing a relation between the drama and religion and the accommodating them to music and dancing; but he omits the observation of conditions still more important, and more is lost than gained by a substitution of the rigidly-defined and ever-repeated idealisms of a distorted superstition for the living impersonations of the truth of human passions.

But we digress. The author of the *Four Ages of Poetry* has prudently omitted to dispute on the effect of the drama upon life and manners. For, if I know the knight by the device of his shield, I have only to inscribe Philoctetes or Agamemnon or Othello upon mine to put to flight the giant sophisms which have enchanted him, as the mirror of intolerable light though on the arm of one of the weakest of the Paladines could blind and scatter whole armies of necromancers and pagans. The connection of scenic exhibitions with the improvement or corruption of the manners of men has been universally recognized; in other words, the presence or absence of poetry, in its most perfect and universal form, has been found to be connected with good and evil in conduct and habit. The corruption which has been imputed to the drama as an effect begins when the poetry employed in its constitution ends; I appeal to the history of manners whether the gradations of the growth of the one and the decline of the other have not corresponded with an exactness equal to any other example of moral cause and effect.

The drama at Athens, or wheresoever else it may have approached to its perfec-

---

33. There is no inconsistency here in Shelley's attitude toward religion, for he always sympathized with genuine religion, but never with institutionalized worship.

tion, ever co-existed with the moral and intellectual greatness of the age. The tragedies of the Athenian poets are as mirrors in which the spectator beholds himself, under a thin disguise of circumstance, stript of all but that ideal perfection and energy which every one feels to be the internal type of all that he loves, admires, and would become. The imagination is enlarged by a sympathy with pains and passions so mighty that they distend in their conception the capacity of that by which they are conceived; the good affections are strengthened by pity, indignation, terror, and sorrow; and an exalted calm is prolonged from the satiety of this high exercise of them into the tumult of familiar life; even crime is disarmed of half its horror and all its contagion by being represented as the fatal consequence of the unfathomable agencies of nature; error is thus divested of its wilfulness; men can no longer cherish it as the creation of their choice. In a drama of the highest order there is little food for censure or hatred; it teaches rather self-knowledge and self-respect. Neither the eye nor the mind can see itself unless reflected upon that which it resembles. The drama, so long as it continues to express poetry, is as a prismatic and many-sided mirror which collects the brightest rays of human nature and divides and reproduces them from the simplicity of these elementary forms and touches them with majesty and beauty, and multiplies all that it reflects and endows it with the power of propagating its like wherever it may fall.

But in periods of the decay of social life, the drama sympathizes with that decay. Tragedy becomes a cold imitation of the form of the great masterpieces of antiquity, divested of all harmonious accompaniment of the kindred arts and often the very form misunderstood, or a weak attempt to teach certain doctrines which the writer considers as moral truths and which are usually no more than specious flatteries of some gross vice or weakness with which the author, in

common with his auditors, are infected. Hence what has been called the classical and domestic drama. Addison's *Cato* is a specimen of the one; and would it were not superfluous to cite examples of the other! To such purposes poetry cannot be made subservient. Poetry is a sword of lightning, ever unsheathed, which consumes the scabbard that would contain it. And thus we observe that all dramatic writings of this nature are unimaginative in a singular degree; they affect sentiment and passion which, divested of imagination, are other names for caprice and appetite. The period in our own history of the grossest degradation of the drama is the reign of Charles II, when all forms in which poetry had been accustomed to be expressed became hymns to the triumph of kingly power over liberty and virtue. Milton stood alone illuminating an age unworthy of him.[34] At such periods the calculating principle pervades all the forms of dramatic exhibition, and poetry ceases to be expressed upon them. Comedy loses its ideal universality; wit succeeds to humor; we laugh from self-complacency and triumph, instead of pleasure; malignity, sarcasm, and contempt succeed to sympathetic merriment; we hardly laugh, but we smile. Obscenity, which is ever blasphemy against the divine beauty in life, becomes from the very veil which it assumes, more active if less disgusting; it is a monster for which the corruption of society forever brings forth new food, which it devours in secret.

The drama being that form under which a greater number of modes of expression of poetry are susceptible of being combined than any other, the connection of poetry and social good is more observable in the drama than in whatever other form. And it is indisputable that the highest perfection of human society has ever corresponded with the highest dramatic excellence; and that the corruption or the extinction of the drama in a nation where it has once flourished is a mark of a corruption of manners and an

34. For a similar idea see *Adonais*, lines 28-35.

extinction of the energies which sustain the soul of social life.[35] But, as Macchiavelli says of political institutions, that life may be preserved and renewed if men should arise capable of bringing back the drama to its principles. And this is true with respect to poetry in its most extended sense; all language, institution, and form require not only to be produced but to be sustained; the office and character of a poet participates in the divine nature as regards providence, no less than as regards creation.

Civil war, the spoils of Asia, and the fatal predominance first of the Macedonian and then of the Roman arms, were so many symbols of the extinction or suspension of the creative faculty in Greece. The bucolic writers,[36] who found patronage under the lettered tyrants of Sicily and Egypt, were the latest representatives of its most glorious reign. Their poetry is intensely melodious; like the odor of the tuberose, it overcomes and sickens the spirit with excess of sweetness,[37] while the poetry of the preceding age was as a meadow-gale of June which mingles the fragrance of all the flowers of the field and adds a quickening and harmonizing spirit of its own which endows the sense with a power of sustaining its extreme delight. The bucolic and erotic delicacy in written poetry is correlative with that softness in statuary, music, and the kindred arts and even in manners and institutions which distinguished the epoch to which we now refer. Nor is it the poetical faculty itself, or any misapplication of it, to which this want of harmony is to be imputed. An equal sensibility to the influence of the senses and the affections is to be found in the writings of Homer and Sophocles; the former, especially, has clothed sensual and pathetic images with irresistible attractions. Their superiority over these succeeding writers consists in the presence of those thoughts which belong to the inner faculties of our nature, not in the absence of those which are connected with the external; their incomparable perfection consists in a harmony of the union of all.[38] It is not what the erotic writers have, but what they have not, in which their imperfection consists. It is not inasmuch as they were poets, but inasmuch as they were not poets, that they can be considered with any plausibility as connected with the corruption of their age. Had that corruption availed so as to extinguish in them the sensibility to pleasure, passion, and natural scenery which is imputed to them as an imperfection, the last triumph of evil would have been achieved. For the end of social corruption is to destroy all sensibility to pleasure; and, therefore, it is corruption. It begins at the imagination and the intellect as at the core and distributes itself thence as a paralyzing venom through the affections into the very appetites, till all become a torpid mass in which sense hardly survives. At the approach of such a period poetry ever addresses itself to those faculties which are the last to be destroyed, and its voice is heard, like the footsteps of Astraea,[39] departing from the world. Poetry ever communicates all the pleasure which men are capable of receiving; it is ever still the light of life—the source of whatever of beautiful or generous or true can have place in an evil time. It will readily be confessed that those among the luxurious citizens of Syracuse and Alexandria who were delighted with the poems of Theocritus were less cold, cruel, and sensual than the remnant of their tribe. But corruption must utterly have destroyed the fabric of human society before poetry can ever cease. The sacred links of that chain have never been entirely disjoined, which descending through the minds of many men is attached to those great minds, whence as from a magnet the invisible effluence is sent forth, which at once connects, animates,

35. A statement that needs substantiation.
36. Theocritus, Bion, and Moschus were the Greek elegiac, or pastoral poets.
37. Compare *The Sensitive Plant*, lines 37-38.

38. For a contrary opinion see Shelley's letter to Godwin, July 29, 1812.
39. Goddess of Justice.

and sustains the life of all. It is the faculty which contains within itself the seeds at once of it own and of social renovation.[40] And let us not circumscribe the effects of the bucolic and erotic poetry within the limits of the sensibility of those to whom it was addressed. They may have perceived the beauty of those immortal compositions simply as fragments and isolated portions; those who are more finely organized, or born in a happier age, may recognize them as episodes to that great poem which all poets, like the co-operating thoughts of one great mind, have built up since the beginning of the world.

The same revolutions within a narrower sphere had place in ancient Rome; but the actions and forms of its social life never seem to have been perfectly saturated with the poetical element. The Romans appear to have considered the Greeks as the selectest treasuries of the selectest forms of manners and of nature and to have abstained from creating in measured language, sculpture, music, or architecture, anything which might bear a particular relation to their own condition, while it might bear a general one to the universal constitution of the world. But we judge from partial evidence, and we judge perhaps partially. Ennius, Varro, Pacuvius, and Accius, all great poets, have been lost. Lucretius is in the highest, and Virgil in a very high sense, a creator. The chosen delicacy of the expressions of the latter are [is] as a mist of light which conceal[s] from us the intense and exceeding truth of his conceptions of nature. Livy is instinct with poetry. Yet Horace, Catullus, Ovid, and generally the other great writers of the Virgilian age, saw man and nature in the mirror of Greece. The institutions also, and the religion of Rome were less poetical than those of Greece, as the shadow is less vivid than the substance. Hence poetry in Rome seemed to follow rather than accom-

pany the perfection of political and domestic society. The true poetry of Rome lived in its institutions; for whatsoever of beautiful, true, and majestic they contained could have sprung only from the faculty which creates the order in which they consist. The life of Camillus, the death of Regulus; the expectation of the senators, in their godlike state, of the victorious Gauls; the refusal of the Republic to make peace with Hannibal after the battle of Cannae were not the consequences of a refined calculation of the probable personal advantage to result from such a rhythm and order in the shows of life to those who were at once the poets and the actors of these immortal dramas. The imagination beholding the beauty of this order created it out of itself according to its own idea; the consequence was empire, and the reward everliving fame. These things are not the less poetry, *quia carent vate sacro*.[41] They are the episodes of that cyclic poem written by Time upon the memories of men. The Past like an inspired rhapsodist fills the theatre of everlasting generations with their harmony.[42]

At length the ancient system of religion and manners had fulfilled the circle of its revolutions. And the world would have fallen into utter anarchy and darkness but that there were found poets among the authors of the Christian and chivalric systems of manners and religion who created forms of opinion and action never before conceived, which copied into the imaginations of men became as generals to the bewildered armies of their thoughts.[43] It is foreign to the present purpose to touch upon the evil produced by these systems, except that we protest on the ground of the principles already established that no portion of it can be imputed to the poetry they contain.

It is probable that the astonishing poetry of Moses, Job, David, Solomon, and Isaiah had produced a great effect upon the mind

40. For this imagery see Plato's *Ion*, which in part Shelley translated. Julian, 7.238-240.

41. From *Ode IV* of Horace: "They lack a sacred poet."

42. See Shelley's translation of *Ion* for this figure.

43. See opening paragraph of the *Essay on the Revival of Literature* for a like idea.

of Jesus and his disciples. The scattered fragments preserved to us by the biographers of this extraordinary person are all instinct with the most vivid poetry.[44] But his doctrines seem to have been quickly distorted.[45] At a certain period after the prevalence of doctrines founded upon those promulgated by him, the three forms into which Plato had distributed the faculties of mind underwent a sort of apotheosis and became the object of the worship of the civilized world.[46] Here it is to be confessed that "Light seems to thicken," and

The crow makes wing to the rooky wood,
Good things of day begin to droop and
      drowse,
And night's black agents to their preys do
      rouse.[47]

But mark how beautiful an order has sprung from the dust and blood of this fierce chaos! How the world as from a resurrection, balancing itself on the golden wings of knowledge and of hope, has reassumed its yet unwearied flight into the heaven of time. Listen to the music, unheard by outward ears, which is as a ceaseless and invisible wind nourishing its everlasting course with strength and swiftness.

The poetry in the doctrines of Jesus Christ and the mythology and institutions of the Celtic conquerors of the Roman empire outlived the darkness and the convulsions connected with their growth and victory and blended themselves into a new fabric of manners and opinion. It is an error to impute the ignorance of the Dark Ages to the Christian doctrines or the predominance of the Celtic nations.[48] Whatever of evil their agencies may have contained sprang from the extinction of the poetical principle connected with the progress of despotism and superstition. Men, from causes too intricate to be here discussed, had become insensible and selfish; their own will had become feeble, and yet they were its slaves, and thence the slaves of the will of others; lust, fear, avarice, cruelty, and fraud characterized a race among whom no one was to be found capable of *creating* in form, language, or institution. The moral anomalies of such a state of society are not justly to be charged upon any class of events immediately connected with them, and those events are most entitled to our approbation which could dissolve it most expeditiously. It is unfortunate for those who cannot distinguish words from thoughts that many of these anomalies have been incorporated into our popular religion.[49]

It was not until the eleventh century that the effects of the poetry of the Christian and chivalric systems began to manifest themselves. The principle of equality had been discovered and applied by Plato in his *Republic* as the theoretical rule of the mode in which the materials of pleasure and of power produced by the common skill and labor of human beings ought to be distributed among them. The limitations of this rule were asserted by him to be determined only by the sensibility of each, or the utility to result to all. Plato, following the doctrines of Timaeus and Pythagoras, taught also a moral and intellectual system of doctrine, comprehending at once the past, the present, and the future condition of man. Jesus Christ divulged the sacred and eternal truths contained in these views to mankind, and Christianity in its abstract purity became the exoteric expression of the esoteric doctrines of the poetry and wisdom of antiquity. The incorporation of the Celtic nations with the exhausted population of the

---

44. Compare *Essay on Christianity*.
45. This is a fundamental belief with Shelley.
46. See the *Timaeus* for the meaning here.
47. *Macbeth*, 3.2.50-53. Shelley does not quote this passage accurately.

48. See the fifteenth chapter of Gibbon's *Decline and Fall of the Roman Empire* for the assertion which Shelley here combats. But this attitude is in no wise a reversal of Shelley's life-long antagonism to institutionalized Christianity.
49. This idea is a commonplace in Shelley.

south impressed upon it the figure of the poetry existing in their mythology and institutions. The result was a sum of the action and reaction of all the causes included in it; for it may be assumed as a maxim that no nation or religion can supersede any other without incorporating into itself a portion of that which it supersedes.[50] The abolition of personal and domestic slavery and the emancipation of women from a great part of the degrading restraints of antiquity were among the consequences of these events.

The abolition of personal slavery is the basis of the highest political hope that it can enter into the mind of man to conceive. The freedom of women produced the poetry of sexual love. Love became a religion the idols of whose worship were ever present. It was as if the statues of Apollo and the Muses had been endowed with life and motion and had walked forth among their worshippers; so that earth became peopled by the inhabitants of a diviner world. The familiar appearance and proceedings of life became wonderful and heavenly, and a paradise was created out of the wrecks of Eden. And as this creation itself is poetry, so its creators were poets; and language was the instrument of their art: "Galeotto fù il libro, e chi lo scrisse."[51] The Provençal Trouveurs, or inventors, preceded Petrarch, whose verses are as spells which unseal the inmost enchanted fountains of the delight which is in the grief of love. It is impossible to feel them without becoming a portion of that beauty which we contemplate;[52] it were superfluous to explain how the gentleness and the elevation of mind connected with these sacred emotions can render men more amiable, and generous, and wise, and lift them out of the dull vapors of the little world of self. Dante understood the secret things

of love even more than Petrarch. His *Vita Nuova* is an inexhaustible fountain of purity of sentiment and language; it is the idealized history of that period and those intervals of his life which were dedicated to love. His apotheosis of Beatrice in Paradise, and the gradations of his own love and her loveliness, by which as by steps he feigns himself to have ascended to the throne of the Supreme Cause, is the most glorious imagination of modern poetry. The acutest critics have justly reversed the judgment of the vulgar and the order of the great acts of the *Divina Commedia* in the measure of the admiration which they accord to the Hell, Purgatory, and Paradise. The latter [last] is a perpetual hymn of everlasting love. Love, which found a worthy poet in Plato alone of all the ancients, has been celebrated by a chorus of the greatest writers of the renovated world; and the music has penetrated the caverns of society and its echoes still drown the dissonance of arms and superstition. At successive intervals Ariosto, Tasso, Shakespeare, Spenser, Calderon, Rousseau, and the great writers of our own age have celebrated the dominion of love, planting as it were trophies in the human mind of that sublimest victory over sensuality and force. The true relation borne to each other by the sexes into which human kind is distributed has become less misunderstood; and if the error which confounded diversity with inequality of the powers of the two sexes has been partially recognized in the opinions and institutions of modern Europe, we owe this great benefit to the worship of which chivalry was the law, and poets the prophets.

The poetry of Dante may be considered as the bridge thrown over the stream of time, which unites the modern and ancient world. The distorted notions of invisible things

---

50. Shelley here shows a deep understanding of the compromise and adjustment in the conflicting social forces which make up any society. For further discussion of this idea see *A Discourse on the Manners of the Ancient Greeks.*

51. This quotation is from Dante's *Divina Commedia* (the *Inferno*, v. 137 ff): "Galeotto was the book, and he who wrote it."
52. A fundamental idea in Shelley. See *Adonais*, XLII-XLIII. See further *A Discourse on the Manners of the Ancient Greeks.*

which Dante and his rival Milton have idealized are merely the mask and the mantle in which these great poets walk through eternity enveloped and disguised. It is a difficult question to determine how far they were conscious of the distinction which must have subsisted in their minds between their own creeds and that of the people. Dante at least appears to wish to mark the full extent of it by placing Riphaeus, whom Virgil calls *justissimus unus,* in Paradise, and observing a most heretical caprice in his distribution of rewards and punishments. And Milton's poem contains within itself a philosophical refutation of that system of which, by a strange and natural antithesis, it has been a chief popular support.[53] Nothing can exceed the energy and magnificence of the character of Satan as expressed in *Paradise Lost.* It is a mistake to suppose that he could ever have been intended for the popular personification of evil. Implacable hate, patient cunning, and a sleepless refinement of device to inflict the extremest anguish on an enemy—these things are evil; and, although venial in a slave are not to be forgiven in a tyrant; although redeemed by much that ennobles his defeat in one subdued are marked by all that dishonors his conquest in the victor. Milton's Devil as a moral being is as far superior to his God as one who perseveres in some purpose which he has conceived to be excellent in spite of adversity and torture is to one who in the cold security of undoubted triumph inflicts the most horrible revenge upon his enemy, not from any mistaken notion of inducing him to repent of a perseverance in enmity but with the alleged design of exasperating him to deserve new torments. Milton has so far violated the popular creed (if this shall be judged to be a violation) as to have alleged no superiority of moral

virtue to his God over his Devil. And this bold neglect of a direct moral purpose is the most decisive proof of the supremacy of Milton's genius. He mingled as it were the elements of human nature as colors upon a single palette and arranged them in the composition of his great picture according to the laws of epic truth; that is, according to the laws of that principle by which series of actions of the external universe and of intelligent and ethical beings is calculated to excite the sympathy of succeeding generations of mankind. The *Divina Commedia* and *Paradise Lost* have conferred upon modern mythology a systematic form; and when change and time shall have added one more superstition to the mass of those which have arisen and decayed upon the earth, commentators will be learnedly employed in elucidating the religion of ancestral Europe, only not utterly forgotten because it will have been stamped with the eternity of genius.[54]

Homer was the first and Dante the second epic poet: that is, the second poet, the series of whose creations bore a defined and intelligible relation to the knowledge and sentiment and religion and political conditions of the age in which he lived and of the ages which followed it, developing itself in correspondence with their development. For Lucretius[55] had limed the wings of his swift spirit in the dregs of the sensible world; and Virgil, with a modesty which ill became his genius, had affected the fame of an imitator, even while he created anew all that he copied; and none among the flock of mockbirds, though their notes were sweet, Apollonius Rhodius, Quintus Calaber Smyrnaeus, Nonnus, Lucan, Statius, or Claudian have sought even to fulfil a single condition of epic truth. Milton was the third epic poet. For if the title of epic in its highest sense

53. That is, a refutation of Christianity. Milton was perhaps at one time a Unitarian.
54. The portion of this paragraph beginning with "Nothing can exceed" and ending with "genius,"

is almost verbatim from the *Essay on the Devil and Devils.*
55. This is a statement of matter of fact, and not an outright condemnation, for Shelley always ranked Lucretius among the very great.

be refused to the *Aeneid*, still less can it be conceded to the *Orlando Furioso*, the *Gerusalemme Liberata*, the *Lusiad*, or the *Fairy Queen*.[56]

Dante and Milton were both deeply penetrated with the ancient religion of the civilized world, and its spirit exists in their poetry probably in the same proportion as its forms survived in the unreformed worship of modern Europe. The one preceded and the other followed the Reformation at almost equal intervals. Dante was the first religious reformer, and Luther surpassed him rather in the rudeness and acrimony than in the boldness of his censures of papal usurpation. Dante was the first awakener of entranced Europe; he created a language, in itself music and persuasion, out of a chaos of inharmonious barbarisms. He was the congregator of those great spirits who presided over the resurrection of learning, the Lucifer of that starry flock which in the thirteenth century shone forth from republican Italy, as from a heaven, into the darkness of the benighted world. His very words are instinct with spirit; each is as a spark, a burning atom of inextinguishable thought; and many yet lie covered in the ashes of their birth and pregnant with a lightning which has yet found no conductor. All high poetry is infinite; it is as the first acorn, which contained all oaks potentially. Veil after veil may be undrawn and the inmost naked beauty of the meaning never exposed. A great poem is a fountain forever overflowing with the waters of wisdom and delight; and after one person and one age has exhausted all of its divine effluence which their peculiar relations enable them to share, another and yet another succeeds, and new relations are ever developed, the source of an unforeseen and an unconceived delight.[57]

The age immediately succeeding to that of Dante, Petrarch, and Boccaccio was characterized by a revival of painting, sculpture,

music, and architecture. Chaucer caught the sacred inspiration, and the superstructure of English literature is based upon the materials of Italian invention.

But let us not be betrayed from a defence into a critical history of poetry and its influence on society. Be it enough to have pointed out the effects of poets, in the large and true sense of the word, upon their own and all succeeding times, and to revert to the partial instances cited as illustrations of an opinion the reverse of that attempted to be established by the author of *The Four Ages of Poetry*.

But poets have been challenged to resign the civic crown to reasoners and mechanists, on another plea. It is admitted that the exercise of the imagination is most delightful, but it is alleged that that of reason is more useful. Let us examine as the grounds of this distinction what is here meant by utility. Pleasure or good, in a general sense, is that which the consciousness of a sensitive and intelligent being seeks and in which, when found, it acquiesces. There are two kinds of pleasure, one durable, universal, and permanent; the other transitory and particular. Utility may either express the means of producing the former or the latter. In the former sense whatever strengthens and purifies the affections, enlarges the imagination, and adds spirit to sense is useful. But the meaning in which the author of *The Four Ages of Poetry* seems to have employed the word *utility* is the narrower one of banishing the importunity of the wants of our animal nature, the surrounding men with security of life, the dispersing the grosser delusions of superstition, and the conciliating such a degree of mutual forbearance among men as may consist with the motives of personal advantage.

Undoubtedly the promoters of utility in this limited sense have their appointed office in society. They follow the footsteps of poets

---

56. Of the last four poems, the first is by Ariosto, the second by Tasso, the third by Camoëns, and the fourth by Spenser.

57. Shelley's evaluation of the work of Dante has never been surpassed for penetration and poetic insight.

and copy the sketches of their creations into the book of common life. They make space and give time. Their exertions are of the highest value so long as they confine their administration of the concerns of the inferior powers of our nature within the limits due to the superior ones. But while the sceptic destroys gross superstitions, let him spare to deface as some of the French writers have defaced, the eternal truths charactered upon the imaginations of men. While the mechanist abridges and the political economist combines labor, let them beware that their speculations, for want of correspondence with those first principles which belong to the imagination, do not tend as they have in modern England to exasperate at once the extremes of luxury and want. They have exemplified the saying, "To him that hath, more shall be given; and from him that hath not, the little that he hath shall be taken away."[58] The rich have become richer and the poor have become poorer, and the vessel of the state is driven between the Scylla and Charybdis of anarchy and despotism. Such are the effects which must ever flow from an unmitigated exercise of the calculating faculty.

It is difficult to define pleasure in its highest sense—the definition involving a number of apparent paradoxes. For, from an inexplicable defect of harmony in the constitution of human nature, the pain of the inferior is frequently connected with the pleasures of the superior portions of our being. Sorrow, terror, anguish, despair itself are often the chosen expressions of an approximation to the highest good. Our sympathy in tragic fiction depends on this principle: tragedy delights by affording a shadow of the pleasure which exists in pain. This is the source also of the melancholy which is inseparable from the sweetest melody.[59] The pleasure that is in sorrow is sweeter than the pleasure of pleasure itself. And hence the saying, "It is better to go to the house of mourning than to the house of mirth"[60]—not that this highest species of pleasure is necessarily linked with pain. The delight of love and friendship, the ecstasy of the admiration of nature, the joy of the perception and still more of the creation of poetry is often wholly unalloyed.[61]

The production and assurance of pleasure in this highest sense is true utility. Those who produce and preserve this pleasure are poets or poetical philosophers.

The exertions of Locke, Hume, Gibbon, Voltaire, Rousseau,[62] and their disciples in favor of oppressed and deluded humanity are entitled to the gratitude of mankind. Yet it is easy to calculate the degree of moral and intellectual improvement which the world would have exhibited had they never lived. A little more nonsense would have been talked for a century or two; and perhaps a few more men, women, and children burnt as heretics. We might not at this moment have been congratulating each other on the abolition of the Inquisition in Spain.[63] But it exceeds all imagination to conceive what would have been the moral condition of the world if neither Dante, Petrarch, Boccaccio, Chaucer, Shakespeare, Calderon, Lord Bacon, nor Milton had ever existed; if Raphael and Michael Angelo had never been born; if the Hebrew poetry had never been translated; if a revival of the study of Greek literature had never taken place; if no monuments of ancient sculpture had been handed down to us; and if the poetry of the religion of the ancient world had been extinguished together

58. Adapted from Matthew, 25.29.

59. Compare *To A Skylark:* "Our sweetest songs are those that tell of saddest thought."

60. Ecclesiastes, 7.2, inaccurately quoted. It should read, "*It is* better to go to the house of mourning than go to the house of feasting; . . . ."

61. Forman in his edition of Shelley's *Prose Works,* 7.130 (1880), gives a slightly different reading for the last three paragraphs, but not enough to call for a reprinting here.

62. I follow the classification adopted by the author of *The Four Ages of Poetry.* Although Rousseau has been thus classed, he was essentially a poet. The others, even Voltaire, were mere reasoners. [Shelley's Note.]

63. The Spanish Inquisition was finally abolished in 1820.

with its belief. The human mind could never, except by the intervention of these excitements, have been awakened to the invention of the grosser sciences and that application of analytical reasoning to the aberrations of society which it is now attempted to exalt over the direct expression of the inventive and creative faculty itself.[64]

We have more moral, political, and historical wisdom than we know how to reduce into practice; we have more scientific and economic knowledge than can be accommodated to the just distribution of the produce which it multiplies.[65] The poetry in these systems of thought is concealed by the accumulation of facts and calculating processes. There is no want of knowledge respecting what is wisest and best in morals, government, and political economy, or at least, what is wiser and better than what men now practice and endure. But we let "*I dare not* wait upon *I would,* like the poor cat i' the adage." We want the creative faculty to imagine that which we know; we want the generous impulse to act that which we imagine; we want the poetry of life; our calculations have outrun our conception; we have eaten more than we can digest. The cultivation of those sciences which have enlarged the limits of the empire of man over the external world has for want of the poetical faculty proportionally circumscribed those of the internal world; and man, having enslaved the elements, remains himself a slave.[66] To what but a cultivation of the mechanical arts in a degree disproportioned to the presence of the creative faculty, which is the basis of all knowledge, is to be attributed the abuse of all invention for abridging and combining labor to the exasperation of the inequality of mankind? From what

other cause has it arisen that the discoveries which should have lightened have added a weight to the curse imposed on Adam? Thus poetry and the principle of self, of which money is the visible incarnation, are the God and Mammon of the world.

The functions of the poetical faculty are twofold: by one it creates new materials of knowledge, and power, and pleasure; by the other it engenders in the mind a desire to reproduce and arrange them according to a certain rhythm and order, which may be called the beautiful and the good. The cultivation of poetry is never more to be desired than at periods when, from an excess of the selfish and calculating principle, the accumulation of the materials of external life exceed the quantity of the power of assimilating them to the internal laws of human nature. The body has then become too unwieldy for that which animates it.[67]

Poetry is indeed something divine. It is at once the center and circumference of knowledge; it is that which comprehends all science and that to which all science must be referred.[68] It is at the same time the root and blossom of all other systems of thought; it is that from which all spring and that which adorns all; and that which, if blighted, denies the fruit and the seed, and withholds from the barren world the nourishment and the succession of the scions of the tree of life. It is the perfect and consummate surface and bloom of all things; it is as the odor and the color of the rose to the texture of the elements which compose it, as the form and the splendor of unfaded beauty to the secrets of anatomy and corruption. What were virtue, love, patriotism, friendship; what were the scenery of this beautiful universe which we inhabit; what were our consolations on this

64. This is not a renunciation of Shelley's youthful ideas as seen in *Queen Mab, Laon and Cythna,* and the early essays, but it is merely an extension of the meaning latent in those works.

65. How profound is this statement. Here is in a nutshell the fundamental trouble with the world today.

66. Again Shelley penetrates to the heart of the world's unrest.

67. The reader should know by now that Shelley's conception of poetry is that it is the harmony, order, beauty, and rhythm in life.

68. Compare these statements with similar remarks by Wordsworth in the Preface to *Lyrical Ballads:* "Poetry is the breath and finer spirit of all knowledge; it is the impassioned expression which is the countenance of all science. . . . Poetry is the first and last of all knowledge." And with Coleridge in the *Biographia Literaria,* Chap. 14.

side of the grave and what were our aspirations beyond it, if poetry did not ascend to bring light and fire from those eternal regions where the owl-winged faculty of calculation dare not ever soar? Poetry is not like reasoning, a power to be exerted according to the determination of the will. A man cannot say, "I will compose poetry." The greatest poet even cannot say it; for the mind in creation is as a fading coal which some invisible influence, like an inconstant wind, awakens to transitory brightness; this power arises from within like the color of a flower which fades and changes as it is developed, and the conscious portions of our natures are unprophetic either of its approach or its departure. Could this influence be durable in its original purity and force, it is impossible to predict the greatness of the results; but when composition begins, inspiration is already on the decline, and the most glorious poetry that has ever been communicated to the world is probably a feeble shadow of the original conceptions of the poet. I appeal to the great poets of the present day, whether it be not an error to assert that the finest passages of poetry are produced by labor and study. The toil and the delay recommended by critics can be justly interpreted to mean no more than a careful observation of the inspired moments and an artificial connection of the spaces between their suggestions by the intertexture of conventional expressions—a necessity only imposed by the limitedness of the poetical faculty itself; for Milton conceived the *Paradise Lost* as a whole before he executed it in portions. We have his own authority also for the muse having "dictated" to him the "unpremeditated song." And let this be an answer to those who would allege the fifty-six various readings of the first line of the *Orlando Furioso*. Compositions so produced are to poetry what mosaic is to painting. This instinct and intuition of the poetical faculty is still more observable in the plastic and pictorial arts: a great statue or picture grows under the power of the artist as a child in the mother's womb; and the very mind which directs the hands in formation is incapable of accounting to itself for the origin, the gradations, or the media of the process.

Poetry is the record of the best and happiest moments of the happiest and best minds. We are aware of evanescent visitations of thought and feeling, sometimes associated with place or person, sometimes regarding our own mind alone, and always arising unforeseen and departing unbidden, but elevating and delightful beyond all expression;[69] so that even in the desire and the regret they leave, there cannot but be pleasure, participating as it does in the nature of its object. It is as it were the interpenetration of a diviner nature through our own; but its footsteps are like those of a wind over the sea, which the coming calm erases, and whose traces remain only as on the wrinkled sand which paves it. These and corresponding conditions of being are experienced principally by those of the most delicate sensibility and the most enlarged imagination; and the state of mind produced by them is at war with every base desire. The enthusiasm of virtue, love, patriotism, and friendship is essentially linked with such emotions; and while they last, self appears as what it is, an atom to a universe. Poets are not only subject to these experiences as spirits of the most refined organization but they can color all that they combine with the evanescent hues of this ethereal world; a word, or a trait in the representation of a scene or a passion, will touch the enchanted chord and reanimate in those who have ever experienced these emotions the sleeping, the cold, the buried image of the past. Poetry thus makes immortal all that is best and most beautiful in the world; it arrests the vanishing apparitions which haunt the interlunations of life and, veiling them, or in language or in form, sends them forth

69. Compare with the *Hymn to Intellectual Beauty,* and the *Essay on Christianity.*

among mankind, bearing sweet news of kindred joy to those with whom their sisters abide—abide, because there is no portal of expression from the caverns of the spirit which they inhabit into the universe of things. Poetry redeems from decay the visitations of the divinity in man.

Poetry turns all things to loveliness; it exalts the beauty of that which is most beautiful and it adds beauty to that which is most deformed; it marries exultation and horror, grief and pleasure, eternity and change; it subdues to union, under its light yoke, all irreconcilable things. It transmutes all that it touches, and every form moving within the radiance of its presence is changed by wondrous sympathy to an incarnation of the spirit which it breathes; its secret alchemy turns to potable gold the poisonous waters which flow from death through life; it strips the veil of familiarity from the world and lays bare the naked and sleeping beauty, which is the spirit of its forms.

All things exist as they are perceived—at least in relation to the percipient. "The mind is its own place, and in itself Can make a Heaven of Hell, a Hell of Heaven."[70] But poetry defeats the curse which binds us to be subjected to the accident of surrounding impressions. And whether it spreads its own figured curtain, or withdraws life's dark veil from before the scene of things, it equally creates for us a being within our being. It makes us the inhabitants of a world to which the familiar world is a chaos. It reproduces the common Universe of which we are portions and percipients, and it purges from our inward sight the film of familiarity which obscures from us the wonder of our being.[71] It compels us to feel that which we perceive, and to imagine that which we know. It creates anew the universe, after it has been annihilated in our minds by the recurrence of impressions blunted by reiteration. It

justifies the bold and true word of Tasso: *Non merita nome di creatore, se non Iddio ed il Poeta.*[72]

A poet, as he is the author to others of the highest wisdom, pleasure, virtue, and glory, so he ought personally to be the happiest, the best, the wisest, and the most illustrious of men. As to his glory, let time be challenged to declare whether the fame of any other institutor of human life be comparable to that of a poet. That he is the wisest, the happiest, and the best, inasmuch as he is a poet, is equally incontrovertible; the greatest poets have been men of the most spotless virtue, of the most consummate prudence, and, if we could look into the interior of their lives, the most fortunate of men; and the exceptions, as they regard those who possessed the imaginative faculty in a high yet inferior degree, will be found on consideration to confirm rather than destroy the rule. Let us for a moment stoop to the arbitration of popular breath, and usurping and uniting in our own persons the incompatible characters of accuser, witness, judge, and executioner, let us without trial, testimony, or form, determine that certain motives of those who are "there sitting where we dare not soar,"[73] are reprehensible. Let us assume that Homer was a drunkard, that Virgil was a flatterer, that Horace was a coward, that Tasso was a madman, that Lord Bacon was a peculator, that Raphael was a libertine, that Spenser was a poet laureate. It is inconsistent with this division of our subject to cite living poets, but posterity has done ample justice to the great names now referred to. Their errors have been weighed and found to have been dust in the balance; if their sins were as scarlet, they are now white as snow: they have been washed in the blood of the mediator and the redeemer, Time. Observe in what a ludicrous chaos the imputations of real or fic-

70. *Paradise Lost*, 1.254-255.
71. Compare Coleridge's *Biographia Literaria*, Chap. 14, for a similar thought.

72. "No one merits the name of Creator but God and the poet." See Footnote 1 in the *Essay on Life*.
73. Compare Milton's *Paradise Lost*, 4.828-829, and *Adonais*, line 337.

titious crime have been confused in the contemporary calumnies against poetry and poets; consider how little is, as it appears— or appears, as it is; look to your own motives, and judge not, lest ye be judged.[74]

Poetry, as has been said, in this respect differs from logic, that it is not subject to the control of the active powers of the mind, and that its birth and recurrence have no necessary connection with consciousness or will. It is presumptuous to determine that these are the necessary conditions of all mental causation, when mental effects are experienced insusceptible of being referred to them. The frequent recurrence of the poetical power, it is obvious to suppose, may produce in the mind a habit of order and harmony correlative with its own nature and with its effects upon other minds. But in the intervals of inspiration, and they may be frequent without being durable, a poet becomes a man and is abandoned to the sudden reflux of the influences under which others habitually live. But as he is more delicately organized than other men and sensible to pain and pleasure both his own and that of others, in a degree unknown to them, he will avoid the one and pursue the other with an ardor proportioned to this difference. And he renders himself obnoxious to calumny when he neglects to observe the circumstances under which these objects of universal pursuit and flight have disguised themselves in one another's garments.

But there is nothing necessarily evil in this error, and thus cruelty, envy, revenge, avarice, and the passions purely evil have never formed any portion of the popular imputations on the lives of poets.

I have thought it most favorable to the cause of truth to set down these remarks according to the order in which they were suggested to my mind, by a consideration of the subject itself, instead of following

that of the treatise that excited me to make them public. Thus although devoid of the formality of a polemical reply, if the view which they contain be just, they will be found to involve a refutation of the doctrines of *The Four Ages of Poetry,* so far at least as regards the first division of the subject. I can readily conjecture what should have moved the gall of the learned and intelligent author of that paper; I confess myself like him unwilling to be stunned by the Theseids of the hoarse Codri [75] of the day. Bavius and Maevius [76] undoubtedly are, as they ever were, insufferable persons. But it belongs to a philosophical critic to distinguish rather than confound.

The first part of these remarks has related to poetry in its elements and principles; and it has been shown, as well as the narrow limits assigned them would permit, that what is called poetry in a restricted sense has a common source with all other forms of order and of beauty, according to which the materials of human life are susceptible of being arranged, and which is poetry in an universal sense.

The second part [77] will have for its object an application of these principles to the present state of the cultivation of poetry and a defence of the attempt to idealize the modern forms of manners and opinions and compel them into a subordination to the imaginative and creative faculty. For the literature of England, an energetic development of which has ever preceded or accompanied a great and free development of the national will, has arisen as it were from a new birth. In spite of the low-thoughted envy which would undervalue contemporary merit, our own will be a memorable age in intellectual achievements, and we live among such philosophers and poets as surpass beyond comparison any who have appeared since the last national struggle for civil and

74. This is perhaps a defense of himself and his contemporaries against the hostile attacks of the reviewers.
75. A dull writer satirized by Juvenal (*First Satire*).

76. Bavius and Maevius were poetasters lampooned by Virgil in his *Third Eclogue.*
77. Shelley never wrote the second part of *A Defence of Poetry.*

religious liberty.[78] The most unfailing herald, companion, and follower of the awakening of a great people to work a beneficial change in opinion or institution is poetry. At such periods there is an accumulation of the power of communicating and receiving intense and impassioned conceptions respecting man and nature. The persons in whom this power resides may often, as far as regards many portions of their nature, have little apparent correspondence with that spirit of good of which they are the ministers. But even while they deny and abjure, they are yet compelled to serve the power which is seated upon the throne of their own soul. It is impossible to read the compositions of the most celebrated writers of the present day without being startled with the electric life which burns within their words. They measure the circumference and sound the depths of human nature with a comprehensive and all-penetrating spirit, and they are themselves perhaps the most sincerely astonished at its manifestations; for it is less their spirit than the spirit of the age.[79] Poets are the hierophants of an unapprehended inspiration; the mirrors of the gigantic shadows which futurity casts upon the present; the words which express what they understand not; the trumpets which sing to battle and feel not what they inspire; the influence which is moved not, but moves. Poets are the unacknowledged legislators of the world.[80]

78. Shelley's judgment has stood the test of time.
79. These remarks do not always agree with the various statements in Shelley's letters, essays, prefaces, and poems on the same subjects.

80. Just as the plowman prepares the soil for the seed, so does the poet prepare mind and heart for the reception of new ideas, and thus for change.

UNA FAVOLA[1]

[This Italian piece was composed in 1820, at the time Shelley's interest in Petrarch was deepest. The fable is closely related in thought to Petrarch's *Trionfi* or Triumphs. In the fable the author represents one in love with two mistresses—Life and Death—and the greater of these is Death, which is the door to the Eternal Verities.]

C'era un giovane il quale viaggiava per paesi lontani, cercando per il mondo una donna, della quale esso fu innamorato. E chi fu quella donna, e come questo giovane s'innamorò di lei, e come e perchè gli cessò l'amore tanto forte che aveva, sono cose degne d'essere conosciute da ogni gentil cuore.

Al spuntare della decima quinta primavera della sua vita, uno chiamandosi Amore gli destava, dicendo che una chi egli aveva molte volte veduto nei sogni gli stava aspettando. Quello fu accompagnato d'una schiera immensa di persone, tutte velate in bianchi veli, e coronate di lauro, ellera e mirto inghirlandite ed intrecciate di viole, rose, a fiordilisi. Cantavano si dolcemente che forse l'armonia delle sfere alla quale le stelle ballano, e meno soave. E le maniere e le parole loro erano cosi lusinghevoli, che il giovane fu allettato, e levandosi del letto, si fece pronto di fare tutto il volere di quello che si chiamava Amore, al di cui cenno lo seguitava per solinghe vie ed eremi e caverne, fino chè tutta la schiera arrivò ad un bosco solitario in una cupa valle per due altissime montagne, il quale fu piantato a guisa di laberinto di pini, cipressi, cedari e tassi, le ombre dei quali destavano un misto di diletto e malinconia. Ed in questo bosco il giovane seguitava per un anno intero i passi incerti di questo compagno e duce suo, come la luna segue la terra; non però tramutandosi come essa. E fu egli nutrito delle fruttà d'un certo albero che crebbe nel mezzo del laberinto, un cibo insieme dolce ed amaro, il quale essendo freddo come ghiaccio sulle labbre, pareva fuoco nelle vene. Le forme velate sempre gli furono intorno, erano servi e ministri ubbidienti al menomo cenno, e

corrieri per lui ed Amore quando per affari suoi l'Amore un poco lo lascierebbe. Ma queste forme, eseguendo ogni altra ordine sua prestamente, mai non vollero svelarsi a lui quantunque le pregasse sollecitamente; eccettuato una, che aveva nome la Vita, ed aveva riputazione di incantatrice gagliarda. Era essa grande di persona e bella, allegra e sciolta, ed ornata riccamente, e, siccome pareva dal suo pronto svelarsi, voleva bene a questo giovane. Ma ben presto la riconobbe d'essere piu finta che alcuna Sirena, poichè per consiglio suo, Amore gli lasciò in questo selvaggio luogo, colla sola compagnia de queste forme velate, le quali per il loro ostinato celarsi sempre gli avevano fatte qualche paura. E, sé quelle forme erano i spettri dei suoi proprii morti pensieri, ovvero le ombre dei vivi pensieri dell' Amore, nessuno può schiarire. La Vita, vergognandosi forse della sua fraude, si celò allora dentro alla spelonca d'una sua sorella abitando colá; ed Amore se ne tornò, sospirando, alla sua terza sfera.

Appena fu partito Amore, quando le mascherate forme, solute della sua legge, si svelarone davanti all' attonito giovane. E per molti giorni le sopradette figure ballavano intorno di lui dovunque andasse—ora motteggiando ed ora minacciandolo, e la notte quando riposava sfilavano in lunga e lenta processione davanti al suo letto, ognuna più schifosa e terribile che l'altra. Il loro orribile aspetto e ria figura gli ingombrava tanto il cuore di tristezza, che il bel cielo, coperto di quella ombra, si vestì di nuvoloso tutto agli occhi suoi; e tanto pianse, che le erbe del suo cammino pasciate di lagrime in vece di rugiada, diventarono come lui, pallide e chinate. Stanco alfine di questo soffrire, veniva alla grotta della Sorella della Vita, in-

[1] For a translation see Appendix D(f).

cantatrice anch'ella e, la trovò seduta davanti un pallido fuoco di odorose legna, cantando lai soavemente dolorosi, e tessendo una bianca mortaia, sopra la quale suo nome era a mezzo intessato, con qualche altro nome oscuro ed imperfetto; ed egli la pregò di dirlo suo nome, ed ella disse con voce fiocca ma dolce—"La Morte;" ed il giovane disse—"O bella Morte, ti prego di aiutarmi contre di queste noiose immagini, compagni della tua sorella, le quali mi tormentano tutta-via." E la Morte lo rassicurò, gli prese la mano, ridendo, e gli baciò la fronte e le guancie, sicchè tremava ogni vena di gioia e di paura; e gli fece stare presso di se, in una camera della sua grotta, dove, disse, fu contro al destino che le rie forme, compagne della Vita, venissero. Il giovane continuamente praticandosi colla Morte, ed ella, coll'animo di sorella, carezzandolo e facendo ogni cortesia di atto e di parola, ben presto s'innamorò di lei; e la Vita stessa, non che alcuna della sua schiera, non gli pareva bella. E tanto lo vinse la passione, che sul ginocchio pregò la Morte di amarlo come egli amava lei, e di voler fare il suo piacere. Ma la Morte disse, "Ardito che tu siei, al desir del quale mai ha la Morte corrisposta? Si tu non mi amasti, io forse ti amerei, amandomi io ti odio, e fuggo." Cosi dicendo, uscì della spelcona, e la sua oscura ed eterea figura fu presto persa fra gli intrecciati rami della selva.

Da quel punto il giovane seguiva le orme della Morte, e si forte fu l'amore chi lo menava, che aveva circuito l'orbe, ed indagato ogni regione; e molti anni erano già spenti, ma le soffranze più che gli anni avevano imbiancita la chioma ed appassito il fiore della forma, quando si trovò sui confini della stessa selva della quale aveva cominciato il suo misero errare. E si gittò sull'erba, e per molte ore pianse; e le lagrime l'accecavano tanto, che per molto tempo non se n'avvidde, che tutte quelle che bagnavano il viso e il petto, non furono sue proprie; ma che una donna chinata dietro di lui pianse per pietà del suo pianto. E levando gli occhi la vidde; e mai gli pareva d'aver veduto

una visione si gloriosa: e dubitava forte si fosse cosa umana. Suo amore per la Morte fu improvvisamente cangiato in odio e sospetto, perche questo nuovo amore fu si forte che vinse ogni altro pensiero. E quella pietosa donna primo gli amava per pietà sola, ma tosto colla compassione crebbe l'amore; e gl'amava schiettamente, non avendo più uopo d'essere compatito alcuno amato da quella. Fu questa la donna, in traccia della quale Amore aveva menato il giovane per quel oscuro laberinto, e fatto tanto errare e soffrire; forse che lo giudicava indegno ancora di tanta gloria, e che lo vedeva debole per toleare si immensa gioia. Dopo avere un poco asciugato il pianto, quei due passeggiavano insieme in questa stessa selva, fin chè la Morte si mise avanti e disse, "Mentre che, o giovane, mi amasti, io ti odiava, ed ora che tu mi odiasti, ti amo, e voglio tanto bene a te ed alla tua sposa che nel mio regno, che tu puoi chiamare Paradiso, ho serbato un eletto luogo, dove voi potete securamente compire i vostri felici amori." E la donna sdegnata, o forse un poco ingelosita per cagione dell'amore passato dello suo sposo, tornò il dosso la Morte, dicendo fra se stesso, "Che vuol questa amante del mio sposo che viene qui turbarci?" e chiamò "Vita, Vita!" e la Vita venne col viso allegro, coronata d'una iride, e vestita in versicolore manto di pelle di cameleone, e la Morte se ni andò piangendo, e partendo disse dolcemente, "Voi mi sospettate, ma io vi lo perdono, e vi aspetto dove bisogna che passiate, perchè io abito coll'Amore e coll'Eternità, con quelle e forza che praticassero quelle anime che eternamente amano. Voi vedrete allora se io ho meritata i vostri dubbj. Intanto vi raccomando alla Vita, e, sorella mia, ti prego per amore di quella Morte della quella tu sei la gemella, di non adoperare contra di questi amanti le tue solite arti, che ti basti il tribute già pagato di sospiri e di lagrime, che sono le ricchezze tue." Il giovane, rammentandosi di quanti mali gli aveva recati in quel bosco, se disfidava della Vita; ma la donna, quantunque in sospetto, essendo pure gelosa della Morte, . . .

APPENDIXES

APPENDIX A: *LITERARY CRITICISM*

[The reviews are Shelley's only direct literary criticisms, and for that fact as for their intrinsic worth and for what they reveal of the author's character and opinions they rightfully deserve a place in this volume.]

REVIEW OF
THOMAS JEFFERSON HOGG'S
MEMOIRS OF
PRINCE ALEXY HAIMATOFF

[This review was composed in November, 1814, and published in *The Critical Review,* December, 1814. The reader should note in particular Shelley's condemnation of sexual immorality.]

Is the suffrage of mankind the legitimate criterion of intellectual energy? Are complaints of the aspirants to literary fame to be considered as the honorable disappointment of neglected genius, or the sickly impatience of a dreamer miserably self-deceived? The most illustrious ornaments of the annals of the human race have been stigmatized by the contempt and abhorrence of entire communities of man; but this injustice arose out of some temporary superstition, some partial interest, some national doctrine. A glorious redemption awaited their remembrance. There is, indeed, nothing so remarkable in the contempt of the ignorant for the enlightened; the vulgar pride of folly delights to triumph upon mind. This is an intelligible process; the infamy or ingloriousness that can be thus explained detracts nothing from the beauty of virtue or the sublimity of genius. But what does utter obscurity express? If the public do not advert even in censure to a performance, has that performance already received its condemnation?

The result of this controversy is important to the ingenuous critic. His labors are indeed miserably worthless if their objects may invariably be attained before their application. He should know the limits of his prerogative. He should not be ignorant, whether it is his duty to promulgate the decisions of others or to cultivate his taste and judgment that he may be enabled to render a reason for his own.

Circumstances the least connected with intellectual nature have contributed for a certain period to retain in obscurity the most memorable specimens of human genius. The author refrains perhaps from introducing his production to the world with all the pomp of empirical bibliopolism. A sudden tide in the affairs of men make the neglect of contradiction of some insignificant doctrine a badge of obscurity and discredit; those even who are exempt from the action of these absurd predilections are necessarily in an indirect manner affected by their influence. It is perhaps the product of an imagination daring and undisciplined; the majority of readers ignorant and disdaining toleration refuse to pardon a neglect of common rules; their canons of criticism are carelessly infringed; it is less religious than a charity sermon, less methodical and cold than a French tragedy where all the unities are preserved; no excellencies where prudish cant and dull regularity are absent can preserve it from the contempt and abhorrence of the multitude. It is evidently not difficult to imagine an instance in which the most elevated genius shall be recompensed with neglect. Mediocrity alone seems unvaryingly to escape rebuke and obloquy; it accommodates its attempts to the spirit of the age which has produced it and adopts with mimic effrontery the cant of the day and hour for which alone it lives.

We think that *The Memoirs of Prince Alexy Haimatoff* deserves to be regarded as an example of the fact, by the frequency of which, criticism is vindicated from the imputation of futility and impertinence. We do not hesitate to consider this fiction as the product of a bold and original mind. We hardly remember ever to have seen surpassed the subtle delicacy of imagination by which the manifest distinctions of character and form are seized and pictured in colors that almost make nature more beautiful than herself. The vulgar observe no resemblance or discrepancies but such as are gross and glaring. The science of mind to which history, poetry, biography serve as the materials consists in the discernment of shades and distinctions where the unenlightened discover nothing but a shapeless and unmeaning mass. The faculty for this discernment distinguishes genius from dulness. There are passages in the production before us which afford instances of just and rapid intuition belonging only to intelligences that possess this faculty in no ordinary degree. As a composition the book is far from faultless. Its abruptness and angularities do not appear to have received the slightest polish or correction. The author has written with fervor, but has disdained to revise at leisure. These errors are the errors of youth and genius and the fervid impatience of sensibilities impetuously disburdening their fulness. The author is proudly negligent of connecting the incidents of his tale. It appears more like the recorded day-dream of a poet, not unvisited by the sublimest and most lovely visions, than the tissue of a romance skilfully interwoven for the purpose of maintaining the interest of the reader and conducting his sympathies by dramatic gradations to the denouement. It is what it professes to be a memoir, not a novel. Yet its claims to the former appellation are established only by the impatience and inexperience of the author, who, possessing in an eminent degree the higher qualifications of a novelist—we had almost said a poet—has neglected the number by which that success would probably have been secured, which,

in this instance, merits of a far nobler stamp have unfortunately failed to acquire. Prince Alexy is by no means an unnatural, although no common character. We think we can discern his counterpart in Alfieri's delineation of himself. The same propensities, the same ardent devotion to his purposes, the same chivalric and unproductive attachment to unbounded liberty characterize both. We are inclined to doubt whether the author has not attributed to his hero the doctrines of universal philanthropy in a spirit of profound and almost unsearchable irony; at least he appears biassed by no peculiar principles, and it were perhaps an insoluble inquiry whether any, and if any, what moral truth he designed to illustrate by his tale. Bruhle, the tutor of Alexy, is a character delineated with consummate skill; the power of intelligence and virtue over external deficiencies is forcibly exemplified. The calmness, patience, and magnanimity of this singular man are truly rare and admirable; his disinterestedness, his equanimity, his irresistible gentleness form a finished and delightful portrait. But we cannot regard his commendation to his pupil to indulge in promiscuous concubinage without horror and detestation. The author appears to deem the loveless intercourse of brutal appetite a venial offense against delicacy and virtue! he asserts that a transient connection with a cultivated female may contribute to form the heart without essentially vitiating the sensibilities. It is our duty to protest against so pernicious and disgusting an opinion. No man can rise pure from the poisonous embraces of a prostitute, or sinless from the desolated hopes of a confiding heart. Whatever may be the claims of chastity, whatever the advantages of simple and pure affection, these ties, these benefits are of equal obligation to either sex. Domestic relations depend for their integrity upon a complete reciprocity of duties. But the author himself has in the adventure of the sultana, Debesh-Sheptuti, afforded a most impressive and tremendous allegory of the cold-blooded and malignant selfishness of sensuality.[1]

We are incapacitated by the unconnected and vague narrative from forming an analysis of the incidents; they would consist indeed simply of a catalogue of events which, divested of the aerial tinge of genius, might appear trivial and common. We shall content ourselves, therefore, with selecting some passages calculated to exemplify the peculiar powers of the author. The following description of the simple and interesting Rosalie is in the highest style of delineation. . . .

[A long description of the heroine follows, which we omit here, as we do all other quotations from the novel as indicated by . . . .].

Alexy's union with Aür-Ahebeh, the Circassian slave, is marked by circumstances of deep pathos, and the sweetest tenderness of sentiment. The description of his misery and madness at her death deserves to be remarked as affording evidence of an imagination vast, profound, and full of energy. . . .

The episode of Viola is affecting, natural, and beautiful. We do not ever remember to have seen the unforgiving fastidiousness of family honor more awfully illustrated. After the death of her lover, Viola still expects that he will esteem, still cherishes the delusion that he is not lost to her for ever. . . .

The character of Mary deserves, we think, to be considered as the only complete failure in the book. Every other female whom the author has attempted to describe is designated by an individuality peculiarly marked and true. They constitute finished portraits of whatever is eminently simple, graceful, gentle, or disgustingly atrocious and vile. Mary alone is the miserable parasite of fashion, the tame slave of drivelling and drunken folly, the cold-hearted coquette, the

lying and meretricious prude. The means employed to gain this worthless prize corresponds exactly with its worthlessness. Sir Fulke Hildebrand is a strenuous Tory; Alexy, on his arrival in England, professes himself inclined to the principles of the Whig party; finding that the Baronet had sworn that his daughter should never marry a Whig, he sacrifices his principles and with inconceivable effrontery thus palliates his apostacy and falsehood. . . .

An instance of more deplorable perversity of the human understanding we do not recollect ever to have witnessed. It almost persuades us to believe that scepticism or indifference concerning certain sacred truths may occasionally produce a subtlety of sophism by which the conscience of the criminal may be bribed to overlook his crime.

Towards the conclusion of this strange and powerful performance it must be confessed that *aliquando bonus dormitat Homerus*.[2] The adventure of the Eleutheri, although the sketch of a profounder project, is introduced and concluded with unintelligible abruptness. Bruhle dies purposely as it should seem that his pupil may renounce the romantic sublimity of his nature, and that his inauspicious union and prostituted character might be exempt from the censure of violated friendship. Numerous indications of profound and vigorous thought are scattered over even the most negligently compacted portions of the narrative. It is an unweeded garden where nightshade is interwoven with sweet jessamine, and the most delicate spices of the East peep over struggling stalks of rank and poisonous hemlock.

In the delineation of the more evanescent feelings and uncommon instances of strong and delicate passion we conceive the author to have exhibited new and unparalleled powers. He has noticed some peculiarities of

---

1. The sentiments expressed in this paragraph seem ample refutation of the charge that Shelley, at the very time that he was composing this condemnation of the lax morality in the novel, was

conniving to share his own wife with Hogg, who was then a frequenter of the Shelley household.

2. "Good Homer sometimes sleeps."

female character, with a delicacy and truth singularly exquisite. We think that the interesting subject of sexual relations requires for its successful development the application of a mind thus organized and endowed. Yet even here how great the deficiencies; this mind must be pure from the fashionable superstitions of gallantry, must be exempt from the sordid feelings which with blind idolatry worship the image and blaspheme the deity, reverence the type, and degrade the reality of which it is an emblem.

We do not hesitate to assert that the author of this volume is a man of ability. His great though indisciplinable energies and fervid rapidity of conception embody scenes and situations and passions affording inexhaustible food for wonder and delight. The interest is deep and irresistible. A moral enchanter seems to have conjured up the shapes of all that is beautiful and strange to suspend the faculties in fascination and astonishment.

PREFACE TO
FRANKENSTEIN; OR, THE
MODERN PROMETHEUS, (1818)

[The Preface was written by Shelley as if he were Mary.]

The event on which this fiction is founded has been supposed, by Dr. Darwin and some of the physiological writers of Germany, as not of impossible occurrence. I shall not be supposed as according the remotest degree of serious faith to such an imagination; yet, as in assuming it as a basis of a work of fancy, I have not considered myself as merely weaving a series of supernatural terrors. The event on which the interest of the story depends is exempt from the disadvantages of a mere tale of spectres or enchantment. It was recommended by the novelty of the situations which it developes; and however impossible as a physical fact, affords a point of view to the imagination for the delineating of human passions more comprehensive and commanding than any which the ordinary relations of interesting events can yield.

I have thus endeavored to preserve the truth of the elementary principles of human nature, while I have not scrupled to innovate upon their combinations. The *Iliad,* the tragic poetry of Greece, Shakespeare in the *Tempest* and *Midsummer Night's Dream,* and most especially Milton in *Paradise Lost* conform to this rule; and the most humble novelist who seeks to confer or receive amusement from his labors may, without presumption, apply to prose fiction a licence, or rather a rule, from the adoption of which so many exquisite combinations of human feeling have resulted in the highest specimens of poetry.

The circumstance on which my story rests was suggested in casual conversation. It was commenced partly as a source of amusement and partly as an expedient for exercising any untried resources of mind. Other motives were mingled with these as the work proceeded. I am by no means indifferent to the manner in which whatever moral tendencies exist in the sentiments or characters it contains shall affect the reader; yet my chief concern in this respect has been limited to the avoiding the enervating effects of the novels of the present day, and to the exhibition of the amiableness of domestic affection, and the excellence of universal virtue. The opinions which naturally spring from the character and situation of the hero are by no means to be conceived as existing always in my own conviction; nor is any inference justly to be drawn from the following pages as prejudicing any philosophical doctrine of whatever kind.

It is a subject also of additional interest to the author that this story was begun in the majestic region where the scene is principally laid and in society which cannot cease to be regretted. I passed the summer of 1816 in the environs of Geneva. The season was cold and rainy, and in the evenings we crowded around a blazing wood fire and occasionally amused ourselves with some German stories of ghosts which happened to fall into our hands. These tales excited in us a playful desire of imitation. Two other friends (a tale from the pen of one of whom would be far more acceptable to the public than anything I can ever hope to produce) and myself agreed to write each a story founded on some supernatural occurrence.

The weather, however, suddenly became serene; and my two friends left me on a journey among the Alps and lost in the magnificent scenes which they present all memory of their ghostly visions. The following tale is the only one which has been completed.

REVIEW OF
MARY SHELLEY'S
FRANKENSTEIN (1817)

[*Frankenstein* is a novel by Mary Shelley. Shelley's review of his wife's novel is done with skill and candor.]

The novel of *Frankenstein, or the Modern Prometheus* is undoubtedly, as a mere story, one of the most original and complete productions of the day. We debate with ourselves in wonder as we read it what could have been the series of thoughts—what could have been the peculiar experiences that awakened them—which conduced in the author's mind to the astonishing combinations of motives and incidents and the startling catastrophe which compose this tale. There are perhaps some points of subordinate importance which prove that it is the author's first attempt. But in this judgment, which requires a very nice discrimination, we may be mistaken; for it is conducted throughout with a firm and steady hand. The interest gradually accumulates and advances towards the conclusion with the ac-

celerated rapidity of a rock rolled down a mountain. We are led breathless with suspense and sympathy and the heaping up of incident on incident and the working of passion out of passion. We cry "hold, hold! enough!" but there is yet something to come; and like the victim whose history it relates we think we can bear no more, and yet more is to be borne. Pelion is heaped on Ossa, and Ossa on Olympus. We climb Alp after Alp until the horizon is seen blank, vacant, and limitless; and the head turns giddy, and the ground seems to fail under our feet.

This novel rests its claim on being a source of powerful and profound emotion. The elementary feelings of the human mind are exposed to view; and those who are accustomed to reason deeply on their origin and tendency will perhaps be the only persons who can sympathize to the full extent in the interest of the actions which are their result. But, founded on nature as they are, there is perhaps no reader who can endure anything beside[s] a new love-story who will not feel a responsive string touched in his inmost soul. The sentiments are so affectionate and so innocent—the characters of the subordinate agents in this strange drama are clothed in the light of such a mild and gentle mind—the pictures of domestic manners are of the most simple and attaching character; the pathos is irresistible and deep. Nor are the crimes and malevolence of the single Being, though indeed withering and tremendous, the offspring of any unaccountable propensity to evil, but flow irresistibly from certain causes fully adequate to their production. They are the children, as it were, of Necessity and Human Nature.[1] In this the direct moral of the book consists, and it is perhaps the most important and of the most universal application of any moral that can be enforced by example—Treat a person ill and he will become wicked. Requite affection with scorn; let one being be selected for whatever cause as the refuse of his kind—

1. Let those who think that Shelley relaxed his belief in Necessity ponder this statement.

divide him, a social being, from society, and you impose upon him the irresistible obligations—malevolence and selfishness. It is thus that too often in society those who are best qualified to be its benefactors and its ornaments are branded by some accident with scorn, and changed by neglect and solitude of heart into a scourge and a curse.

The Being in *Frankenstein* is, no doubt, a tremendous creature. It was impossible that he should not have received among men that treatment which led to the consequences of his being a social nature. He was an abortion and an anomaly; and though his mind was such as its first impressions framed it, affectionate and full of moral sensibility, yet the circumstances of his existence are so monstrous and uncommon that when the consequences of them became developed in action his original goodness was gradually turned into inextinguishable misanthropy and revenge. The scene between the Being and the blind De Lacey in the cottage is one of the most profound and extraordinary instances of pathos that we ever recollect. It is impossible to read this dialogue—and indeed many others of a somewhat similar character—without feeling the heart suspend its pulsations with wonder, and the "tears stream down the cheeks." The encounter and argument between Frankenstein and the Being on the sea of ice almost approaches in effect to the expostulation of Caleb Williams with Falkland. It reminds us indeed somewhat of the style and character of that admirable writer to whom the author has dedicated his work, and whose productions he seems to have studied.

There is only one instance, however, in which we detect the least approach to imitation, and that is the conduct of the incident of Frankenstein's landing in Ireland. The general character of the tale, indeed, resembles nothing that ever preceded it. After the death of Elizabeth, the story, like a stream which grows at once more rapid and profound as it proceeds, assumes an irresistible solemnity and the magnificent energy and swiftness of a tempest.

The churchyard scene, in which Frankenstein visits the tombs of his family, his quitting Geneva, and his journey through Tartary to the shores of the Frozen Ocean resemble at once the terrible reanimation of a corpse and the supernatural career of a spirit. The scene in the cabin of Walton's ship, the more than mortal enthusiasm and grandeur of the Being's speech over the dead body of his victim, is an exhibition of intellectual and imaginative power which, we think, the reader will acknowledge has seldom been surpassed.

REVIEW OF
WILLIAM GODWIN'S
MANDEVILLE

[The text follows Shelley's copy in Hunt's *Examiner,* December 28, 1817, rather than the garbled version of Medwin in the *Athaneaum,* October 27, 1832.]

(To the Editor of *The Examiner*)

Sir, the author of *Mandeville* is one of the most illustrious examples of intellectual power of the present age. He has exhibited that variety and universality of talent which distinguishes him who is destined to inherit lasting renown from the possessors of temporary celebrity. If his claims were to be measured solely by the comprehension and accuracy of his researches into ethical and political science, still it would be difficult to name a contemporary competitor. Let us make a deduction of all those parts of his moral system which are liable to any possible controversy and consider simply those which only to allege is to establish, and which belong to that most important class of truths which he that announces to mankind seems less to teach than to recall.

Political Justice[1] is the first moral system explicitly founded upon the doctrine of the negativeness of rights and the positiveness of duties, an obscure feeling of which has been the basis of all the political liberty and private virtue in the world. But he is also the author of *Caleb Williams;* and if we had no other record of a mind but simply some fragment containing the conception of the character of Falkland, doubtless we should say, "This is an extraordinary mind, and undoubtedly was capable of the very sublimest enterprises of thought."

St. Leon and *Fleetwood*[2] are molded, with somewhat inferior distinctness, in the same character of a union of delicacy and power. The *Essay on Sepulchres* has all the solemnity and depth of passion which belong to a mind that sympathizes, as one man with his friend, in the interests of future ages, and in the concerns of the vanished generations of mankind.

It may be said with truth that Godwin has been treated unjustly by those of his countrymen upon whose favor temporary distinction depends. If he had devoted his high accomplishments to flatter the selfishness of the rich or enforced those doctrines on which the powerful depend for power, they would no doubt have rewarded him with their countenance, and he might have been more fortunate in that sunshine than Mr. Malthus or Dr. Paley. But the difference would still have been as wide as that which must forever divide notoriety from fame. Godwin has been to the present age in moral philosophy what Wordsworth is in poetry. The personal interest of the latter would probably have suffered from his pursuit of the true principles of taste in poetry, as much as all that is temporary in the fame of Godwin has suffered from his daring to announce the true foundation of morals, if servility, and dependence, and superstition

had not been too easily reconcilable with Wordsworth's species of dissent from the opinions of the great and the prevailing. It is singular that the other nations of Europe should have anticipated in this respect the judgment of posterity and that the name of Godwin, and that of his late illustrious and admirable wife, should be pronounced even by those who know but little of English literature with reverence; and that the writings of Mary Wollstonecraft should have been translated and universally read in France and Germany long after the bigotry of faction has stifled them in our own country.

Mandeville is Godwin's last production. The interest of this novel is undoubtedly equal, in some respects superior, to that of *Caleb Williams.* Yet there is no character like Falkland, whom the author, with that sublime casuitry which is the parent of toleration and forbearance, persuades us personally to love, while his actions must forever remain the theme of our astonishment and abhorrence. Mandeville challenges our compassion, and no more. His errors arise from an immutable necessity of internal nature, and from much of a constitutional antipathy and suspicion, which soon sprang up into a hatred and contempt and barren misanthrophy, which, as it had no roots in genius or virtue, produces no fruit uncongenial with the soil wherein it grew. Those of Falkland arose from a high, though perverted conception of the majesty of human nature, from a powerful sympathy with his species, and from a temper which led him to believe that the very reputation of excellence should walk among mankind, unquestioned and undefiled. So far as it was a defect to link the interest of the tale with anything inferior to Falkland, so is *Mandeville* defective. But if the varieties of human character, the depth and complexity of human motive,

---

1. *The Enquiry Concerning Political Justice, and Its Influence on General Virtue and Happiness* (1793), by William Godwin.

2. *Caleb Williams* (1774), *St. Leon* (1799), and *Fleetwood* (1805) are novels by Godwin.

those sources of the union of strength and weakness, those useful occasions for pleading in favor of universal kindness and toleration are just subjects for illustration and development in a work of fiction. *Mandeville* yields in interest and importance to none of the productions of the author.

The language is more rich and various, and the expressions more eloquently sweet, without losing that energy and distinctness which characterizes *Political Justice* and *Caleb Williams*. The moral speculations have a strength and consistency and boldness which have been less clearly aimed at in his other works of fiction. The pleadings of Henrietta to Mandeville, after his recovery from madness, in favor of virtue and benevolent energy, compose in every respect the most perfect and beautiful piece of writing of modern times. It is the genuine doctrine of *Political Justice* presented in one perspicuous and impressive view, and clothed in such enchanting melody of language as seems scarcely less than the writings of Plato to realize those lines of Milton:

How charming is divine Philosophy!
Not harsh and crabbed, as dull fools
    suppose,
But musical as is Apollo's lute.[3]

Clifford's talk, too, about wealth has a beautiful and readily to be disentangled intermixture of truth and error. Clifford is a person who, without those characteristics which usually constitute the sublime, is sublime from the mere excess of loveliness and innocence. Henrietta's first appearance to Mandeville at Mandeville House is an occurrence resplendent with the sunrise of life; it recalls to the memory many a vision, or perhaps but one, which the delusive exhalations of unbaffled hope has invested with a rose-like luster as of morning, yet unlike morning a light which, once extinguished, never can return. Henrietta seems at first to be all that a susceptible heart imagines in the object of its earliest passion. We scarcely can see her, she is so beautiful. There is a mist of dazzling loveliness which encircles her and shuts out from the sight all that is mortal in her transcendent charms. But the veil is gradually withdrawn, and she "fades into the light of common day."[4] Her actions and even her sentiments do not correspond with the elevation of her speculative opinions and the fearless purity which should be and is the accompaniment of truth and virtue. But she has a divided affection, and she is faithful there only where infidelity would have been self-sacrifice. Could the spotless Henrietta have subjected her love for Clifford to the vain and insulting accidents of wealth and reputation and the babbling of a miserable old woman and have proceeded unshrinkingly to her nuptial feast from the expostulations of Mandeville's impassioned and pathetic madness? It might be well in the author to show the foundations of human hope thus overturned, for his picture would otherwise have been illumined with one gleam of light; it was his skill to enforce the moral "that all things are vanity" and that "the house of mourning is better than the house of feasting";[5] and we are indebted to those who make us feel the instability of our nature that we may lay the knowledge which is its foundation deep and make the affections which are its cement strong. But one regrets that Henrietta, who soared far beyond her contemporaries in her opinions, who was so beautiful that she seemed a spirit among mankind should act and feel no otherwise than the least exalted of her sex; and still more that the author capable of conceiving something so admirable and lovely should have been withheld by the tenor of the fiction which he chose from executing it to its full extent. It almost seems in the original conception of the character of Henrietta that something was imagined

3. Milton's *Comus,* lines 476-478.
4. Line 76 of Wordsworth's *Intimations of Immortality* (1803-1806).

5. See Ecclesiastes 7.2. Not accurately quoted: "It is better to go to the house of mourning than to go to the house of feasting."

too vast and too uncommon to be realized; and the feeling weighs like disappointment on the mind.

But these considered with reference to the core of the story are extrinsical. The events of the tale flow on like the stream of fate, regular and irresistible, and growing at once darker and swifter in their progress; there is no surprise; there is no shock; we are prepared for the worst from the very opening scene, though we wonder whence the author drew the shadows which render the moral darkness every instant more profound and at last so appalling and complete. The interest is awfully deep and rapid. To struggle with it would be gossamer attempting to bear up against the tempest. In this respect it is more powerful than *Caleb Williams*—the interest of *Caleb Williams* being as rapid but not so profound as that of *Mandeville*. It is a wind which tears up the deepest waters of the ocean of mind. The reader's mind is hurried on, as he approaches the end, with breathless and accelerated impulse. The noun *Smorfia*[6] comes at last and touches some nerve which jars the inmost soul and grates as it were along the blood; and we can scarcely believe that the grin which must accompany Mandeville to his grave is not stamped upon our own visage.

E. K.[7]

REVIEW OF
THOMAS LOVE PEACOCK'S
RHODODAPHNE, OR THE
THESSALIAN SPELL (1818)

[Shelley's review of this poem by Thomas Love Peacock, though written in 1818, was not published until 1879—by H. Buxton Forman.]

Rhododaphne is a poem of the most remarkable character, and the nature of the

subject no less than the spirit in which it is written forbid us to range it under any of the classes of modern literature. It is a Greek and Pagan poem. In sentiment and scenery it is essentially antique. There is a strong *religio loci* throughout, which almost compels us to believe that the author wrote from the dictation of a voice heard from some Pythian cavern in the solitudes where Delphi stood. We are transported to the banks of the Peneus and linger under the crags of Tempe, and see the water lilies floating on the stream. We sit with Plato by Old Ilissus under the sacred Plane tree among the sweet scent of flowering sallows;[1] and above there is the nightingale of Sophocles in the ivy of the pine, who is watching the sunset so that it may dare to sing; it is the radiant evening of a burning day, and the smooth hollow whirlpools of the river are overflowing with the aerial gold of the level sunlight. We stand in the marble temples of the Gods, and see their sculptured forms gazing and almost breathing around. We are led forth from the frequent pomp of sacrifice into the solitudes of mountains and forests where Pan, "the life, the intellectual soul of grove and stream," yet lives and yet is worshipped. We visit the solitudes of Thessalian magic and tremble with new wonder to hear statues speak and move and to see the shaggy changelings minister to their witch queen with the shape of beasts and the reason of men and move among the animated statues who people her enchanted palaces and gardens. That wonderful overflowing of fancy, the *Syria Dea* of Lucian, and the impassioned and elegant pantomime of Apuleius, have contributed to this portion of the poem. There is here, as in the songs of ancient times, music and dancing and the luxury of voluptuous delight. The Bacchanalians toss on high their leaf-interwoven hair, and the tumult and fervor of the chase is depicted; we hear its clamor gathering among the woods, and she who impels it is so graceful

6. A grimace, or an expression of disgust.
7. E. K. stands for Elfin Knight, one of Mary's pet names for Shelley.

1. The European broad-leaved willow.

and so fearless that we are charmed—and it needs no feeble spell to see nothing of the agony and blood of that royal sport. This it is to be a scholar; this it is to have read Homer and Sophocles and Plato.

Such is the scenery and the spirit of the tale. The story itself presents a more modern aspect, being made up of combinations of human passion which seem to have been developed since the Pagan system has been outworn. The poem opens in a strain of elegant but less powerful versification than that which follows. It is descriptive of the annual festival of Love at his temple in Thespia. Anthemion is among the crowd of votaries, a youth from the banks of Arcadian Ladon:

> The flower of all Arcadia's youth
> Was he: such form and face, in
>   truth,
> As thoughts of gentlest maidens
>   seek
> In their day-dreams: soft glossy hair
> Shadowed his forehead, snowy-fair,
> With many a hyacinthine cluster:
> Lips, that in silence seemed to
>   speak,
> Were his, and eyes of mild blue
>   lustre:
> And even the paleness of his cheek,
> The passing trace of tender care,
> Still shewed how beautiful it were
> If its own natural bloom were there.
>> Canto I, p. 11.

He comes to offer his vows at the shrine for the recovery of his mistress Calliroë, who is suffering under some strange, and as we are led to infer, magical disease. As he presents his wreath of flowers at the altar they are suddenly withered up. He looks and there is standing near him a woman of exquisite beauty, who gives him another wreath, which he places on the altar and it does not wither. She turns to him and bids him wear a flower which she presents, saying, with other sweet words—

> Some meet for once and part for
>   aye,
> Like thee and me, and scarce a day
> Shall each by each remembered be:
> But take the flower I give to thee,
> And till it fades remember me.
>> Canto I, p. 22.

As Anthemion passes from the temple among the sports and dances of the festival "with vacant eye"

> the trains
> Of youthful dancers round him
>   float,
> As the musing bard from his sylvan
>   seat
> Looks on the dance of the noontide
>   heat,
> Or the play of the watery flowers,
>   that quiver
> In the eddies of a lowland river.
>> Canto II, p. 29.

He there meets an old man who tells him that the flower he wears is the profane laurel-rose, which grows in Larissa's unholy gardens; that it is impious to wear it in the temple of Love, and that he who has suffered evils which he dares not tell from Thessalian enchantments knows that the gift of this flower is a spell only to be dissolved by invoking his natal genius and casting the flower into some stream with the caution of not looking upon it after he has thrown it away. Anthemion obeys his direction, but as soon as he has . . . [Part of the manuscript is missing.]

> round his neck
> Are closely twined the silken rings
> Of Rhododaphne's glittering hair,
> And round him her bright arms she
>   flings,
> And cintured thus in loveliest
>   bands
> The charmed waves in safety bear

The youth and the enchantress fair
And leave them on the golden
  sands.

Canto V, pp. 110-11.

They now find themselves on a lonely moor on which stands a solitary cottage—ruined and waste; this scene is transformed by Thessalian magic to a palace surrounded by magnificent gardens. Anthemion enters the hall of the palace where, surrounded by sculptures of divine workmanship, he sees the earthly image of Uranian Love.

Plato says with profound allegory, that Love is not itself beautiful, but seeks the possession of beauty; this idea seems embodied in the deformed dwarf who bids, with a voice as from a trumpet, Anthemion enter. After feast and music the natural result of the situation of the lovers is related by the poet to have place.

The last Canto relates the enjoyments and occupations of the lovers; and we are astonished to discover that anything can be added to the gardens of Armida and Alcina, and the Bower of Bliss; the following description among many of a Bacchanalian dance is a remarkable instance of a fertile and elegant imagination.

Oft 'mid those palace-gardens fair,
The beauteous nymph (her radiant
  hair
With mingled oak and vine-leaves
  crowned)
Would grasp the thyrsus ivy-bound,
And fold, her festal vest around,
The Bacchic nebris, leading thus
The swift and dizzy thiasis:
And as she moves, in all her
  charms,
With springing feet and flowing
  arms,
'Tis strange in one fair shape to see
How many forms of grace can be.
The youths and maids, her beau-
  teous train,
Follow fast in sportive ring,
Some the torch and mystic cane,
Some the vine-bough, brandishing;
Some, in giddy circlets fleeting,
The Corybantic timbrel beating:
Maids, with silver flasks advancing,
Pour the wine's red-sparkling tide,
Which youths, with heads recum-
  bent dancing,
Catch in goblets as they glide:
All upon the odorous air
Lightly toss their leafy hair,
Ever singing, as they move,
  "Io Bacchus! son of Jove!"

Canto VII, pp. 148-50.

APPENDIX B: *PREFACES TO POEMS*

[The Prefaces to poems are included in this edition not because they are inaccessible, but because they are essential to the understanding of the development of Shelley's mind in general, and in its relation to the art of poetry in particular. Then, the inclusion of the Prefaces makes it possible to carry out the avowed purpose of this work—that is, the study of Shelley's ideas in the prose as the best approach to the understanding of his poetry. The Preface to the *Banquet of Plato* is also included here.]

ALASTOR,

OR

THE SPIRIT OF SOLITUDE

(1815)

Preface

The poem entitled *Alastor* may be considered as allegorical of one of the most interesting situations of the human mind. It represents a youth of uncorrupted feelings and adventurous genius led forth by an imagination inflamed and purified through familiarity with all that is excellent and majestic, to the contemplation of the universe. He drinks deep of the fountains of knowledge and is still insatiate. The magnificence and beauty of the external world sinks profoundly into the frame of his conceptions and affords to their modifications a variety not to be exhausted. So long as it is possible for his desires to point towards objects thus infinite and unmeasured, he is joyous, and tranquil, and self-possessed. But the period arrives when these objects cease to suffice. His mind is at length suddenly awakened and thirsts for intercourse with an intelligence similar to itself. He images to himself the Being whom he loves. Conversant with speculations of the sublimest and most perfect natures, the vision in which he embodies his own imaginations unites all of wonderful, or wise, or beautiful, which the poet, the philosopher, or the lover could depicture. The intellectual faculties, the imagination, the functions of sense have their respective requisitions on the sympathy of corresponding powers in other human beings. The Poet is represented as uniting these requisitions and attaching them to a single image. He seeks in vain for a prototype of his conception. Blasted by his disappointment, he descends to an untimely grave.

The picture is not barren of instruction to actual men. The Poet's self-centered seclusion was avenged by the furies of an irresistible passion pursuing him to speedy ruin. But that Power which strikes the luminaries of the world with sudden darkness and extinction by awakening them to too exquisite a perception of its influences dooms to a slow and poisonous decay those meaner spirits that dare to abjure its dominion. Their destiny is more abject and inglorious as their delinquency is more contemptible and pernicious. They who, deluded by no generous error, instigated by no sacred thirst of doubtful knowledge, duped by no illustrious superstition, loving nothing on this earth, and cherishing no hopes beyond, yet keep aloof from sympathies with their kind, rejoicing neither in human joy nor mourning with human grief; these, and such as they, have their apportioned curse. They languish, because none feel with them their common nature. They are morally dead. They are neither friends, nor lovers, nor fathers, nor citizens of the world, nor benefactors of their country. Among those who attempt to exist without human sympathy, the pure and tender-hearted perish through the intensity and passion of their search after its communities, when the vacancy of their spirit suddenly makes itself felt. All else, selfish, blind, and torpid, are those unforeseeing multitudes who constitute, together with their own, the lasting misery and loneliness of the world. Those who love not their fellow-beings live unfruitful lives, and prepare for their old age a miserable grave.

The good die first,
And those whose hearts are dry as summer dust,
Burn to the socket!

LAON AND CYTHNA; OR, THE REVOLUTION OF THE GOLDEN CITY A VISION OF THE NINETEENTH CENTURY[1]

Preface

The poem which I now present to the world is an attempt from which I scarcely dare to expect success, and in which a writer of established fame might fail without disgrace. It is an experiment on the temper of the public mind as how far a thirst for a happier condition of moral and political society survives among the enlightened and refined the tempests which have shaken the age in which we live. I have sought to enlist the harmony of metrical language, the ethereal combinations of the fancy, the rapid and subtle transitions of human passion— all those elements which essentially compose a poem—in the cause of a liberal and comprehensive morality; and in the view of kindling within the bosoms of my readers a virtuous enthusiasm for those doctrines of liberty and justice, that faith and hope in something good, which neither violence nor misrepresentation nor prejudice can ever totally extinguish among mankind.

For this purpose I have chosen a story of human passion in its most universal character, diversified with moving and romantic adventures, and appealing, in contempt of all artificial opinions or institutions, to the common sympathies of every human breast. I have made no attempt to recommend the motives which I would substitute for those at present governing mankind, by methodical and systematic argument. I would only awaken the feelings so that the reader should see the beauty of true virtue and be incited to those inquiries which have led to my moral and political creed, and that of some of the sublimest intellects in the world. The poem therefore (with the exception of the first canto, which is purely introductory) is narrative, not didactic. It is a succession of pictures illustrating the growth and progress of individual mind aspiring after excellence and devoted to the love of mankind; its influence in refining and making pure the most daring and uncommon impulses of the imagination, the understanding, and the senses; its impatience at "all the oppressions which are done under the sun"; its tendency to awaken public hope and to enlighten and improve mankind; the rapid effects of the application of that tendency; the awakening of an immense nation from their slavery and degradation to a true sense of moral dignity and freedom; the bloodless dethronement of their oppressors and the unveiling of the religious frauds by which they had been deluded into submission; the tranquillity of successful patriotism, and the universal toleration and benevolence of true philanthropy; the treachery and barbarity of hired soldiers; vice not the object of punishment and hatred, but kindness and pity; the faithlessness of tyrants; the confederacy of the Rulers of the World[2] and the restoration of the expelled Dynasty by foreign arms; the massacre and extermination of the Patriots and the victory

1. After slight revision, the poem was reissued as *The Revolt of Islam*.
2. The Holy Alliance was a league entered into by Russia, Austria, and Prussia, after Napoleon's de-

feat, to rule the world on the principles of Christian charity, but it resulted in a reign of despotism, and was finally abandoned.

of established power; the consequences of legitimate despotism—civil war, famine, plague, superstition, and an utter extinction of the domestic affections; the judicial murder of the advocates of Liberty; the temporary triumph of oppression that secure earnest of its final and inevitable fall; the transient nature of ignorance and error and the eternity of genius and virtue. Such is the series of delineations of which the poem consists. And, if the lofty passions with which it has been my scope to distinguish this story shall not excite in the reader a generous impulse, an ardent thirst for excellence, and interest profound and strong such as belongs to no meaner desires, let not the failure be imputed to a natural unfitness for human sympathy in these sublime and animating themes. It is the business of the Poet to communicate to others the pleasure and the enthusiasm arising out of those images and feelings in the vivid presence of which within his own mind consists at once his inspiration and his reward.

The panic which, like an epidemic transport, seized upon all classes of men during the excesses consequent upon the French Revolution, is gradually giving place to sanity. It has ceased to be believed that whole generations of mankind ought to consign themselves to a hopeless inheritance of ignorance and misery, because a nation of men who had been dupes and slaves for centuries were incapable of conducting themselves with the wisdom and tranquillity of freemen so soon as some of their fetters were partially loosened. That their conduct could not have been marked by any other characters than ferocity and thoughtlessness is the historical fact from which liberty derives all its recommendations, and falsehood the worst features of its deformity. There is a reflux in the tide of human things which bears the shipwrecked hopes of men into a secure haven after the storms are past. Methinks, those who now live have survived an age of despair.

The French Revolution may be considered as one of those manifestations of a general state of feeling among civilized mankind produced by a defect of correspondence between the knowledge existing in society and the improvement or gradual abolition of political institutions. The year 1788 may be assumed as the epoch of one of the most important crises produced by this feeling. The sympathies connected with that event extended to every bosom. The most generous and amiable natures were those which participated the most extensively in these sympathies. But such a degree of unmingled good was expected as it was impossible to realize. If the Revolution had been in every respect prosperous, then misrule and superstition would lose half their claims to our abhorrence as fetters which the captive can unlock with the slightest motion of his fingers and which do not eat with poisonous rust into the soul. The revulsion occasioned by the atrocities of the demagogues and the re-establishment of successive tyrannies in France was terrible and felt in the remotest corner of the civilized world. Could they listen to the plea of reason who had groaned under the calamities of a social state according to the provisions of which one man riots in luxury while another famishes for want of bread? Can he who the day before was a trampled slave suddenly become liberal-minded, forbearing, and independent? This is the consequence of the habits of a state of society to be produced by resolute perseverance and indefatigable hope, and long-suffering and long-believing courage, and the systematic efforts of generations of men of intellect and virtue. Such is the lesson which experience teaches now. But, on the first reverses of hope in the progress of French liberty, the sanguine eagerness for good overleaped the solution of these questions, and for a time extinguished itself in the unexpectedness of their result. Thus, many of the most ardent and tender-hearted of the worshippers of public good have been morally ruined by what a partial glimpse of the events they deplored appeared to show as the melancholy desolation of all their cherished hopes. Hence gloom and misanthropy have become the characteristics of the age in which we live, the solace of a disappointment that unconsciously finds relief only in the wilful exaggeration of its own despair. This influence has tainted the literature of the age with the hopelessness of the minds from which it flows. Metaphysics,[3] and inquiries into moral and political science, have become little else than vain attempts to revive exploded superstitions, or sophisms like those of Mr. Malthus, calculated to lull the oppressors of mankind into a security of everlasting triumph.[4] Our works of fiction and poetry have been overshadowed by the same infectious gloom. But mankind appear to me to be emerging from their trance. I am aware, methinks, of a slow, gradual, silent change. In that belief I have composed the following Poem.

I do not presume to enter into competition with our greatest contemporary poets. Yet I am unwilling to tread in the footsteps of any who have preceded me. I have sought to avoid the imitation of any style of language or versification peculiar to the original minds of which it is the character—designing that, even if what I have produced be worthless, it should still be properly my own. Nor have I permitted any system relating to mere words to divert the attention of the reader from whatever interest I may have succeeded in creating to my own ingenuity in contriving to disgust them according to the rules of criticism. I have simply clothed my thoughts in what appeared to me the most obvious and appropriate language. A person familiar with nature and with the most celebrated productions of the human mind can scarcely err in following the instinct,

with respect to selection of language, produced by that familiarity.

There is an education peculiarly fitted for a poet, without which genius and sensibility can hardly fill the circle of their capacities. No education, indeed, can entitle to this appellation a dull and unobservant mind, or one, though neither dull nor unobservant, in which the channels of communication between thought and expression have been obstructed or closed. How far it is my fortune to belong to either of the latter classes I cannot know. I aspire to be something better. The circumstances of my accidental education have been favorable to this ambition. I have been familiar from boyhood with mountains and lakes and the sea and the solitude of forests; danger, which sports upon the brink of precipices, has been my playmate. I have trodden the glaciers of the Alps and lived under the eye of Mont Blanc. I have been a wanderer among distant fields. I have sailed down mighty rivers and seen the sun rise and set and the stars come forth while I have sailed night and day down a rapid stream among mountains. I have seen populous cities, and have watched the passions which rise and spread, and sink and change among assembled multitudes of men. I have seen the theater of the more visible ravages of tyranny and war; cities and villages reduced to scattered groups of black and roofless houses, and the naked inhabitants sitting famished upon their desolated thresholds. I have conversed with living men of genius. The poetry of ancient Greece and Rome, and modern Italy, and our own country has been to me, like external nature, a passion and an enjoyment. Such are the sources from which the materials for the imagery of my poem have been drawn. I have considered poetry in its most comprehensive

---

3. I ought to except Sir W. Drummond's *Academical Questions;* a volume of very acute and powerful metaphysical criticism. [Shelley's Note.]

4. It is remarkable, as a symptom of the revival of public hope, that Mr. Malthus has assigned, in the later editions of his work, an indefinite dominion

to moral restraint over the principle of population. This concession answers all the inferences from his doctrine unfavorable to human improvement, and reduces the *Essay on Population* to a commentary illustrative of the unanswerableness of *Political Justice*. [Shelley's Note.]

sense; and have read the poets and the historians and the metaphysicians[5] whose writings have been accessible to me, and have looked upon the beautiful and majestic scenery of the earth as common sources of those elements which it is the province of the Poet to embody and combine. Yet the experience and the feelings to which I refer do not in themselves constitute men poets, but only prepare them to be the auditors of those who are. How far I shall be found to possess that more essential attribute of poetry, the power of awakening in others sensations like those which animate my own bosom, is that which, to speak sincerely, I know not; and which, with an acquiescent and contented spirit, I expect to be taught by the effect which I shall produce upon those whom I now address.

I have avoided, as I have said before, the imitation of any contemporary style. But there must be a resemblance, which does not depend upon their own will, between all the writers of any particular age. They cannot escape from subjection to a common influence which arises out of an infinite combination of circumstances belonging to the times in which they live though each is in a degree the author of the very influence by which his being is thus pervaded. Thus, the tragic poets of the age of Pericles; the Italian revivers of ancient learning; those mighty intellects of our own country that succeeded the Reformation, the translators of the Bible, Shakespeare, Spenser, the dramatists of the reign of Elizabeth and Lord Bacon;[6] the colder spirits of the interval that succeeded—all resemble each other and differ from every other in their several classes. In this view of things, Ford can no more be called the imitator of Shakespeare than Shakespeare the imitator of Ford. There were perhaps few other points of resemblance between these two men than that which the universal and inevitable in-

fluence of their age produced. And this is an influence which neither the meanest scribbler nor the sublimest genius of any era can escape and which I have not attempted to escape.

I have adopted the stanza of Spenser (a measure inexpressibly beautiful), not because I consider it a finer model of poetical harmony than the blank verse of Shakespeare and Milton, but because in the latter there is no shelter for mediocrity; you must either succeed or fail. This perhaps an aspiring spirit should desire. But I was enticed also by the brilliancy and magnificence of sound which a mind that has been nourished upon musical thoughts can produce by a just and harmonious arrangement of the pauses of this measure. Yet there will be found some instances where I have completely failed in this attempt; and one, which I here request the reader to consider as an erratum, where there is left, most inadvertently, an alexandrine in the middle of a stanza.

But in this as in every other respect I have written fearlessly. It is the misfortune of this age that its writers, too thoughtless of immortality, are exquisitely sensible to the temporary praise or blame. They write with the fear of reviews before their eyes. This system of criticism sprang up in that torpid interval when poetry was not. Poetry and the art which professes to regulate and limit its powers cannot subsist together. Longinus could not have been the contemporary of Homer, nor Boileau of Horace. Yet this species of criticism never presumed to assert an understanding of its own; it has always, unlike true science, followed, not preceded, the opinion of mankind, and would even now bribe with worthless adulation some of our greatest poets to impose gratuitous fetters on their own imaginations and become unconscious accomplices in the daily murder of all genius either not so aspiring or not so fortunate as their own. I have sought

5. In this sense there may be such a thing as perfectibility in works of fiction, notwithstanding the concession often made by the advocates of

human improvement, that perfectibility is a term applicable only to science. [Shelley's Note.]

6. Milton stands alone in the age which he illumined. [Shelley's Note.]

therefore to write, as I believe that Homer, Shakespeare, and Milton wrote, with an utter disregard of anonymous censure. I am certain that calumny and misrepresentation, though it may move me to compassion, cannot disturb my peace. I shall understand the expressive silence of those sagacious enemies who dare not trust themselves to speak. I shall endeavor to extract, from the midst of insult and contempt and maledictions, those admonitions which may tend to correct whatever imperfections such censurers may discover in this my first serious appeal to the public. If certain critics were as clear-sighted as they are malignant, how great would be the benefit to be derived from their virulent writings! As it is, I fear I shall be malicious enough to be amused with their paltry tricks and lame invectives. Should the public judge that my composition is worthless, I shall indeed bow before the tribunal from which Milton received his crown of immortality and shall seek to gather, if I live, strength from that defeat, which may nerve me to some new enterprise of thought which may *not* be worthless. I cannot conceive that Lucretius, when he meditated that poem whose doctrines are yet the basis of our metaphysical knowledge and whose eloquence has been the wonder of mankind, wrote in awe of such censure as the hired sophists of the impure and superstitious noblemen of Rome might affix to what he should produce. It was at the period when Greece was led captive, and Asia made tributary to the Republic, fast verging itself to slavery and ruin, that a multitude of Syrian captives, bigoted to the worship of their obscene Ashtaroth and the unworthy successors of Socrates and Zeno, found there a precarious subsistence by administering under the name of freed men to the vices and vanities of the great. These wretched men were skilled to plead with a superficial but plausible set of sophisms in favor of that contempt for virtue which is the portion of slaves and that faith in portents the most

fatal substitute for benevolence in the imaginations of men, which, arising from the enslaved communities of the East, then first began to overwhelm the western nations in its stream. Were these the kind of men whose disapprobation the wise and lofty-minded Lucretius should have regarded with a salutary awe? The latest and perhaps the meanest of those who follow in his footsteps would disdain to hold life on such conditions.

The poem now presented to the public occupied little more than six months in the composition. That period has been devoted to the task with unremitting ardor and enthusiasm. I have exercised a watchful and earnest criticism on my work as it grew under my hands. I would willingly have sent it forth to the world with that perfection which long labor and revision is said to bestow. But I found that if I should gain something in exactness by this method I might lose much of the newness and energy of imagery and language as it flowed fresh from my mind. And, although the mere composition occupied no more than six months, the thoughts thus arranged were slowly gathered in as many years.

I trust that the reader will carefully distinguish between those opinions which have a dramatic propriety in reference to the characters which they are designed to elucidate and such as are properly my own. The erroneous and degrading idea which men have conceived of a Supreme Being, for instance, is spoken against, but not the Supreme Being itself. The belief which some superstitious persons whom I have brought upon the stage entertain of the Deity, as injurious to the character of his benevolence, is widely different from my own. In recommending also a great and important change in the spirit which animates the social institutions of mankind, I have avoided all flattery to those violent and malignant passions of our nature which are ever on the watch to mingle with and to alloy the most beneficial innovations. There is no quarter given to Revenge, or Envy, or Prejudice. Love is celebrated everywhere as the sole law which should govern the moral world.

In the personal conduct of my hero and heroine, there is one circumstance which was intended to startle the reader from the trance of ordinary life. It was my object to break through the crust of those outworn opinions on which established institutions depend. I have appealed therefore to the most universal of all feelings and have endeavored to strengthen the moral sense by forbidding it to waste its energies in seeking to avoid actions which are only crimes of convention. It is because there is so great a multitude of artificial vices that there are so few real virtues. Those feelings alone which are benevolent or malevolent are essentially good or bad. The circumstance of which I speak was introduced, however, merely to accustom men to that charity and toleration which the exhibition of a practice widely differing from their own has a tendency to promote.[7] Nothing indeed can be more mischievous than many actions innocent in themselves, which might bring down upon individuals the bigoted contempt and rage of the multitude.[8]

ROSALIND AND HELEN
(1817-1818)
A MODERN ECLOGUE

Advertisement

The story of *Rosalind and Helen* is, undoubtedly, not an attempt in the highest style of poetry. It is in no degree calculated to excite profound meditation; and if, by interesting the affections and amusing the imagination, it awakens a certain ideal melancholy favorable to the reception of more important impressions, it will produce in the reader all that the writer experienced in the composition. I resigned myself, as I wrote, to the impulse of the feelings which

moulded the conception of the story; and this impulse determined the pauses of a measure, which only pretends to be regular inasmuch as it corresponds with, and expresses, the irregularity of the imaginations which inspired it.

I do not know which of the few scattered poems I left in England will be selected by my bookseller to add to this collection. One, which I sent from Italy, was written after a day's excursion among those lovely mountains which surround what was once the retreat, and where is now the sepulcher, of Petrarch. If any one is inclined to condemn the insertion of the introductory lines, which image forth the sudden relief of a state of deep despondency by the radiant visions disclosed by the sudden burst of an Italian sunrise in autumn on the highest peak of those delightful mountains, I can only offer as my excuse that they were not erased at the request of a dear friend, with whom added years of intercourse only add to my apprehension of its value, and who would have had more right than anyone to complain, that she has not been able to extinguish in me the very power of delineating sadness.

PETER BELL THE THIRD
(1819)
BY MICHING MALLECHO, ESQ.

Dedication

To Thomas Brown, Esq.,
The Younger, H. F.

Dear Tom——Allow me to request you to introduce Mr. Peter Bell to the respectable family of the Fudges. Although he may fall short of those very considerable personages in the more active properties which characterize the Rat and the Apostate, I suspect that even you, their historian, will confess that he surpasses them in the more peculiarly legitimate qualification of intolerable dulness.

7. The sentiments connected with and characteristic of this circumstance have no personal reference to the writer. [Shelley's Note.]

8. This paragraph was omitted in *The Revolt of Islam.*

You know Mr. Examiner Hunt; well—it was he who presented me to two of the Mr. Bells. My intimacy with the younger Mr. Bell naturally sprung from this introduction to his brothers. And in presenting him to you, I have the satisfaction of being able to assure you that he is considerably the dullest of the three.

There is this particular advantage in an acquaintance with any one of the Peter Bells, that if you know one Peter Bell, you know three Peter Bells; they are not one, but three; not three, but one. An awful mystery, which, after having caused torrents of blood, and having been hymned by groans enough to deafen the music of the spheres, is at length illustrated to the satisfaction of all parties in the theological world, by the nature of Mr. Peter Bell.

Peter is a polyhedric Peter, or a Peter with many sides. He changes colors like a chameleon, and his coat like a snake. He is a Proteus of a Peter. He was at first sublime, pathetic, impressive, profound; then dull; then prosy and dull; and now dull—oh so very dull! it is an ultra-legitimate dulness.

You will perceive that it is not necessary to consider Hell and the Devil as supernatural machinery. The whole scene of my epic is in "this world which is"—so Peter informed us before his conversion to *White Obi*—

> The world of all of us, *and where*
> *We find our happiness, or not at all.*

Let me observe that I have spent six or seven days in composing this sublime piece; the orb of my moonlike genius has made the fourth part of its revolution round the dull earth which you inhabit, driving you mad, while it has retained its calmness and its splendor, and I have been fitting this its last phase "to occupy a permanent station in the literature of my country."

Your works, indeed, dear Tom, sell better; but mine are far superior. The public is no judge; posterity sets all to rights.

Allow me to observe that so much has been written of Peter Bell that the present history can be considered only, like the *Iliad*, as a continuation of that series of cyclic poems, which have already been candidates for bestowing immortality upon, at the same time that they receive it from, his character and adventures. In this point of view I have violated no rule of syntax in beginning my composition with a conjunction; the full stop which closes the poem continued by me being, like the full stops at the end of the *Iliad* and *Odyssey,* a full stop of a very qualified import.

Hoping that the immortality which you have given to the Fudges, you will receive from them; and in the firm expectation, that when London shall be an habitation of bitterns; when St. Paul's and Westminster Abbey shall stand, shapeless and nameless ruins, in the midst of an unpeopled marsh; when the piers of Waterloo Bridge shall become the nuclei of islets of reeds and osiers, and cast the jagged shadows of their broken arches on the solitary stream, some transatlantic commentator will be weighing in the scales of some new and now unimagined system of criticism, the respective merits of the Bells and the Fudges, and their historians. I remain, dear Tom, yours sincerely, Miching Mallecho.

December 1, 1819.

P. S. Pray excuse the date of place; so soon as the profits of the publication come in, I mean to hire lodgings in a more respectable street.

THE CENCI (1819)

A Tragedy in Five Acts

Dedication
To Leigh Hunt, Esq.

My Dear Friend——I inscribe with your name, from a distant country and after an absence whose months have seemed years, this latest of my literary efforts.

Those writings which I have hitherto published have been little else than visions which impersonate my own apprehensions of the beautiful and the just. I can also perceive in them the literary defects incidental to youth and impatience; they are dreams of what ought to be, or may be. The drama which I now present to you is a sad reality. I lay aside the presumptuous attitude of an instructor and am content to paint with such colors as my own heart furnishes that which has been.

Had I known a person more highly endowed than yourself with all that it becomes a man to possess, I had solicited for this work the ornament of his name. One more gentle, honorable, innocent, and brave; one of more exalted toleration for all who do and think evil, and yet himself more free from evil; one who knows better how to receive and how to confer a benefit, though he must ever confer far more than he can receive; one of simpler, and, in the highest sense of the word, of purer life and manners I never knew; and I had already been fortunate in friendships when your name was added to the list.

In that patient and irreconcilable enmity with domestic and political tyranny and imposture which the tenor of your life has illustrated, and which, had I health and talents, should illustrate mine, let us, conforting each other in our task, live and die.

All happiness attend you! Your affectionate friend,

Percy B. Shelley.

Rome, May 29, 1819.

Preface

A manuscript was communicated to me during my travels in Italy, which was copied from the archives of the Cenci Palace at Rome and contains a detailed account of the horrors which ended in the extinction of one of the noblest and richest families of that city during the Pontificate of Clement VIII in the year 1599. The story is that an old man having spent his life in debauchery and wickedness, conceived at length an implacable hatred towards his children, which showed itself towards one daughter under the form of an incestuous passion, aggravated by every circumstance of cruelty and violence. This daughter, after long and vain attempts to escape from what she considered a perpetual contamination both of body and mind, at length plotted with her mother-in-law and brother to murder their common tyrant. The young maiden, who was urged to this tremendous deed by an impulse which overpowered its horror, was evidently a most gentle and amiable being, a creature formed to adorn and be admired, and thus violently thwarted from her nature by the necessity of circumstance and opinion. The deed was quickly discovered, and, in spite of the most earnest prayers made to the Pope by the highest persons in Rome, the criminals were put to death. The old man had during his life repeatedly bought his pardon from the Pope for capital crimes of the most enormous and unspeakable kind, at the price of a hundred thousand crowns; the death therefore of his victims can scarcely be accounted for by the love of justice. The Pope, among other motives for severity, probably felt that whoever killed the Count Cenci deprived his treasury of a certain and copious source of revenue.[1] Such a story, if told so as to present to the reader all the feelings of those who once acted it, their hopes and fears, their confidences and misgivings, their various interests, passions, and opinions, acting upon and with each other, yet all conspiring to one tremendous end, would be as a light to make apparent some of the most dark and secret caverns of the human heart.

On my arrival at Rome I found that the story of the Cenci was a subject not to be mentioned in Italian society without awakening a deep and breathless interest; and that the feelings of the company never failed to incline to a romantic pity for the wrongs, and a passionate exculpation of the horrible deed to which they urged her, who has been mingled two centuries with the common

1. The Papal Government formerly took the most extraordinary precautions against the publicity of facts which offer so tragical a demonstration of its own wickedness and weakness; so that the communication of the MS. had become, until very lately, a matter of some difficulty. [Shelley's Note].

dust. All ranks of people knew the outlines of this history and participated in the overwhelming interest which it seems to have the magic of exciting in the human heart. I had a copy of Guido's picture of Beatrice which is preserved in the Colonna Palace, and my servant instantly recognized it as the portrait of *La Cenci*.

This national and universal interest which the story produces and has produced for two centuries and among all ranks of people in a great city, where the imagination is kept forever active and awake, first suggested to me the conception of its fitness for a dramatic purpose. In fact it is a tragedy which has already received, from its capacity of awakening and sustaining the sympathy of men, approbation and success. Nothing remained as I imagined, but to clothe it to the apprehensions of my countrymen in such language and action as would bring it home to their hearts. The deepest and the sublimest tragic compositions, *King Lear* and the two plays in which the tale of Oedipus is told, were stories which already existed in tradition, as matters of popular belief and interest, before Shakespeare and Sophocles made them familiar to the sympathy of all succeeding generations of mankind.

This story of the Cenci is indeed eminently fearful and monstrous; anything like a dry exhibition of it on the stage would be insupportable. The person who would treat such a subject must increase the ideal and diminish the actual horror of the events, so that the pleasure which arises from the poetry which exists in these tempestuous sufferings and crimes may mitigate the pain of the contemplation of the moral deformity from which they spring. There must also be nothing attempted to make the exhibition subservient to what is vulgarly termed a moral purpose. The highest moral purpose aimed at in the highest species of the drama is the teaching the human heart, through its sympathies and antipathies the knowledge of itself; in proportion to the possession of which knowledge, every human being is wise, just, sincere, tolerant, and kind. If

dogmas can do more, it is well; but a drama is no fit place for the enforcement of them. Undoubtedly, no person can be truly dishonored by the act of another; and the fit return to make to the most enormous injuries is kindness and forbearance, and a resolution to convert the injurer from his dark passions by peace and love. Revenge, retaliation, atonement are pernicious mistakes. If Beatrice had thought in this manner she would have been wiser and better; but she would never have been a tragic character; the few whom such an exhibition would have interested could never have been sufficiently interested for a dramatic purpose, from the want of finding sympathy in their interest among the mass who surround them. It is in the restless and anatomizing casuitry with which men seek the justification of Beatrice, yet feel that she has done what needs justification; it is in the superstitious horror with which they contemplate alike her wrongs and their revenge, that the dramatic character of what she did and suffered consists.

I have endeavored as nearly as possible to represent the characters as they probably were, and have sought to avoid the error of making them actuated by my own conceptions of right or wrong, false or true; thus under a thin veil converting names and actions of the sixteenth century into cold impersonations of my own mind. They are represented as Catholics, and as Catholics deeply tinged with religion. To a Protestant apprehension there will appear something unnatural in the earnest and perpetual sentiment of the relations between God and men which pervade the tragedy of the Cenci. It will especially be startled at the combination of an undoubting persuasion of the truth of the popular religion with a cool and determined perseverance in enormous guilt. But religion in Italy is not, as in Protestant countries, a cloak to be worn on particular days; or a passport which those who do not wish to be railed at carry with them to exhibit; or a gloomy passion for penetrating the impenetrable mysteries of our being, which terrifies its possessor at the darkness of the abyss to the brink of which it has conducted him. Religion coexists, as it were, in the mind of an Italian Catholic, with a faith in that of which all men have the most certain knowledge. It is interwoven with the whole fabric of life. It is adoration, faith, submission, penitence, blind admiration—not a rule for moral conduct. It has no necessary connection with any one virtue. The most atrocious villain may be rigidly devout, and without any shock to established faith, confess himself to be so. Religion pervades intensely the whole frame of society, and is according to the temper of the mind which it inhabits, a passion, a persuasion, an excuse, a refuge; never a check. Cenci himself built a chapel in the court of his Palace and dedicated it to St. Thomas the Apostle, and established masses for the peace of his soul. Thus in the first scene of the fourth act Lucretia's design in exposing herself to the consequences of an expostulation with Cenci after having administered the opiate, was to induce him by a feigned tale to confess himself before death—this being esteemed by Catholics as essential to salvation; and she only relinquishes her purpose when she perceives that her perseverance would expose Beatrice to new outrages.

I have avoided with great care in writing this play the introduction of what is commonly called mere poetry, and I imagine there will scarcely be found a detached simile or a single isolated description, unless Beatrice's description of the chasm appointed for her father's murder should be judged to be of that nature.[2]

In a dramatic composition the imagery and the passion should interpenetrate one another, the former being reserved simply for the full development and illustration of the latter. Imagination is as the immortal God which should assume flesh for the redemption of mortal passion. It is thus that the most remote and the most familiar imagery may alike be fit for dramatic purposes when employed in the illustration of strong feeling, which raises what is low, and levels to the apprehension that which is lofty, casting over all the shadow of its own greatness. In other respects, I have written more carelessly, that is, without an over-fastidious and learned choice of words. In this respect I entirely agree with those modern critics who assert that in order to move men to true sympathy we must use the familiar language of men, and that our great ancestors the ancient English poets are the writers, a study of whom might incite us to do that for our own age which they have done for theirs. But it must be the real language of men in general and not that of any particular class to whose society the writer happens to belong. So much for what I have attempted; I need not be assured that success is a very different matter, particularly for one whose attention has but newly awakened to the study of dramatic literature.

I endeavored while at Rome to observe such monuments of this story as might be accessible to a stranger. The portrait of Beatrice at the Colonna Palace is admirable as a work of art; it was taken by Guido during her confinement in prison. But it is most interesting as a just representation of one of the loveliest specimens of the workmanship of Nature. There is a fixed and pale composure upon the features; she seems sad and stricken down in spirit, yet the despair thus expressed is lightened by the patience of gentleness. Her head is bound with folds of white drapery from which the yellow strings of her golden hair escape and fall about her neck. The moulding of her face is exquisitely delicate; the eyebrows are distinct and arched; the lips have that permanent meaning of imagination and sensibility which suffering has not repressed and which it seems as if death scarcely could extinguish. Her forehead is large and clear; her eyes which we are told were remarkable for their

2. An idea in this speech was suggested by a most sublime passage in *El Purgatorio de San Patricio* of Calderon, the only plagiarism which I have intentionally committed in the whole piece. [Shelley's Note].

vivacity, are swollen with weeping and lusterless, but beautifully tender and serene. In the whole mien there is a simplicity and dignity which, united with her exquisite loveliness and deep sorrow, are inexpressibly pathetic. Beatrice Cenci appears to have been one of those rare persons in whom energy and gentleness dwell together without destroying one another; her nature was simple and profound. The crimes and miseries in which she was an actor and a sufferer are as the mask and the mantle in which circumstances clothed her for her impersonation on the scene of the world.

The Cenci Palace is of great extent; and though in part modernized, there yet remains a vast and gloomy pile of feudal architecture in the same state as during the dreadful scenes which are the subject of this tragedy. The Palace is situated in an obscure corner of Rome, near the quarter of the Jews, and from the upper windows you see the immense ruins of Mount Palatine half hidden under their profuse overgrowth of trees. There is a court in one part of the Palace (perhaps that in which Cenci built the Chapel to St. Thomas), supported by granite columns and adorned with antique friezes of fine workmanship, and built up, according to the ancient Italian fashion, with balcony over balcony of open-work. One of the gates of the Palace formed of immense stones and leading through a passage, dark and lofty and opening into gloomy subterranean chambers, struck me particularly.

Of the Castle of Petrella, I could obtain no further information than that which is to be found in the manuscript.

JULIAN AND MADDALO
(1818)
A CONVERSATION

Preface

The meadows with fresh streams,
 the bees with thyme,
The goats with the green leaves of
 budding Spring,

Are saturated not—nor Love with
 tears.

Virgil's *Gallus*.

Count Maddalo is a Venetian nobleman of ancient family and of great fortune, who, without mixing much in the society of his countrymen, resides chiefly at his magnificent palace in that city. He is a person of the most consummate genius, and capable, if he would direct his energies to such an end, of becoming the redeemer of his degraded country. But it is his weakness to be proud: he derives, from a comparison of his own extraordinary mind with the dwarfish intellects that surround him, an intense apprehension of the nothingness of human life. His passions and his powers are incomparably greater than those of other men; and, instead of the latter having been employed in curbing the former, they have mutually lent each other strength. His ambition preys upon itself for want of objects which it can consider worthy of exertion. I say that Maddalo is proud, because I can find no other word to express the concentered and impatient feelings which consume him; but it is on his own hopes and affections only that he seems to trample, for in social life no human being can be more gentle, patient, and unassuming than Maddalo. He is cheerful, frank, and witty. His more serious conversation is a sort of intoxication; men are held by it as by a spell. He has travelled much; and there is an inexpressible charm in his relation of his adventures in different countries.

Julian is an Englishman of good family, passionately attached to those philosophical notions which assert the power of man over his own mind, and the immense improvements of which, by the extinction of certain moral superstitions, human society may be yet susceptible. Without concealing the evil in the world, he is forever speculating how good may be made superior. He is a complete infidel and a scoffer at all things reputed holy; and Maddalo takes a wicked pleasure in drawing out his taunts against religion. What Maddalo thinks on these matters is not exactly known. Julian, in spite of his heterodox opinions, is conjectured by his friends to possess some good qualities. How far this is possible the pious reader will determine. Julian is rather serious.

Of the Maniac I can give no information. He seems, by his own account, to have been disappointed in love. He was evidently a very cultivated and amiable person when in his right senses. His story, told at length, might be like many other stories of the same kind; the unconnected exclamations of his agony will perhaps be found a sufficient comment for the text of every heart.

OEDIPUS TYRANNUS, OR SWELLFOOT THE TYRANT
(1819)

A TRAGEDY IN TWO ACTS
TRANSLATED FROM THE ORIGINAL DORIC

Advertisement

This tragedy is one of a triad, or system of three plays (an arrangement according to which the Greeks were accustomed to connect their dramatic representations), elucidating the wonderful and appalling fortunes of the SWELLFOOT dynasty. It was evidently written by some *learned Theban*, and, from its characteristic dulness, apparently before the duties on the importation of *Attic salt* had been repealed by the Boeotarchs. The tenderness with which he treats the PIGS proves him to have been a *sus Boeotiae*, possibly *Epicuri de grege porcus,* for, as the poet observes,

A fellow feeling makes us wondrous kind.

No liberty has been taken with the translation of this remarkable piece of antiquity except the suppressing a seditious and blasphemous Chorus of the Pigs and Bulls at the last act. The word Hoydipouse (or more

properly Oedipus) has been rendered literally SWELLFOOT, without its having been conceived necessary to determine whether a swelling of the hind or the fore feet of the Swinish Monarch is particularly indicated.

Should the remaining portions of this tragedy be found, entitled *Swellfoot in Angaria* and *Charité,* the translator might be tempted to give them to the reading public.

PROMETHEUS UNBOUND
(1818-1819)
A LYRICAL DRAMA
IN FOUR ACTS

Preface

The Greek tragic writers, in selecting as their subject any portion of their national history or mythology, employed in their treatment of it a certain arbitrary descretion. They by no means conceived themselves bound to adhere to the common interpretation or to imitate in story as in title their rivals and predecessors. Such a system would have amounted to a resignation of those claims to preference over their competitors which incited the composition. The Agamemnonian story was exhibited on the Athenian theatre with as many variations as dramas.

I have presumed to employ a similar licence. The *Prometheus Unbound* of Aeschylus supposed the reconciliation of Jupiter with his victim as the price of the disclosure of the danger threatened to his empire by the consummation of his marriage with Thetis. Thetis, according to this view of the subject, was given in marriage to Peleus, and Prometheus, by the permission of Jupiter, delivered from his captivity by Hercules. Had I framed my story on this model, I should have done no more than have attempted to restore the lost drama of Aeschylus—an ambition which, if my preference to this mode of treating the subject had incited me to cherish, the recollection of the high comparison such an attempt would challenge might well abate. But, in truth, I was averse from a catastrophe so feeble as that of reconciling the Champion with the Oppressor of mankind. The moral interest of the fable, which is so powerfully sustained by the sufferings and endurance of Prometheus, would be annihilated if we could conceive of him as unsaying his high language and quailing before his successful and perfidious adversary. The only imaginary being resembling in any degree Prometheus is Satan; and Prometheus is, in my judgment, a more poetical character than Satan, because in addition to courage and majesty and firm and patient opposition to omnipotent force, he is susceptible of being described as exempt from the taints of ambition, envy, revenge, and a desire for personal aggrandisement, which, in the hero of *Paradise Lost,* interfere with the interest. The character of Satan engenders in the mind a pernicious casuitry which leads us to weigh his faults with his wrongs, and to excuse the former because the latter exceed all measure. In the minds of those who consider that magnificent fiction with a religious feeling it engenders something worse. But Prometheus is, as it were, the type of the highest perfection of moral and intellectual nature, impelled by the purest and the truest motives to the best and noblest ends.

This poem was chiefly written upon the mountainous ruins of the Baths of Caracalla, among the flowery glades, and thickets of odoriferous blossoming trees, which are extended in ever winding labyrinths upon its immense platforms and dizzy arches suspended in the air. The bright blue sky of Rome, and the effect of the vigorous awakening of spring in that divinest climate, and the new life with which it drenches the spirits even to intoxication, were the inspiration of this drama.

The imagery which I have employed will be found, in many instances, to have been drawn from the operations of the human mind, or from those external actions by which they are expressed. This is unusual in modern poetry, although Dante and Shakespeare are full of instances of the same kind; Dante indeed more than any other poet, and with greater success. But the Greek poets, as writers to whom no resource of awakening the sympathy of their contemporaries was unknown, were in the habitual use of this power; and it is the study of their works (since a higher merit would probably be denied me) to which I am willing that my readers should impute this singularity.

One word more is due in candor to the degree in which the study of contemporary writings may have tinged my composition, for such has been a topic of censure with regard to poems far more popular, and indeed more deservedly popular, than mine. It is impossible that any one who inhabits the same age with such writers as those who stand in the foremost ranks of our own, can conscientiously assure himself that his language and tone of thought may not have been modified by the study of the productions of those extraordinary intellects. It is true, that, not the spirit of their genius, but the forms in which it has manifested itself, are due less to the peculiarities of their own minds than to the peculiarity of the moral and intellectual condition of the minds among which they have been produced. Thus a number of writers possess the form, while they want the spirit of those whom, it is alleged, they imitate; because the former is the endowment of the age in which they live, and the latter must be the uncommunicated lightning of their own mind.

The peculiar style of intense and comprehensive imagery which distinguishes the modern literature of England, has not been, as a general power, the product of the imitation of any particular writer. The mass of capabilities remains at every period materially the same; the circumstances which awaken it to action perpetually change. If England were divided into forty republics, each equal in population and extent to Athens, there is no reason to suppose but that, under institutions not more perfect than those of Athens, each would produce philosophers and poets equal to those who (if we except Shakespeare) have never been surpassed. We owe the great writers of the golden age of our literature to that fervid awakening of the public mind which shook to dust the oldest and most oppressive form of the Christian religion. We owe Milton to the progress and development of the same spirit; the sacred Milton was, let it ever be remembered, a republican and a bold inquirer into morals and religion. The great writers of our own age are, we have reason to suppose, the companions and forerunners of some unimagined change in our social condition or the opinions which cement it. The cloud of mind is discharging its collected lightning, and the equilibrium between institutions and opinions is now restoring, or is about to be restored.

As to imitation, poetry is a mimetic art. It creates, but it creates by combination and representation. Poetical abstractions are beautiful and new, not because the portions of which they are composed had no previous existence in the mind of man or in nature, but because the whole produced by their combination has some intelligible and beautiful analogy with those sources of emotion and thought, and with the contemporary condition of them; one great poet is a masterpiece of nature which another not only ought to study but must study. He might as wisely and as easily determine that his mind should no longer be the mirror of all that is lovely in the visible universe, as exclude from his contemplation the beautiful which exists in the writings of a great contemporary. The pretence of doing it would be a presumption in any but the greatest; the effect, even in him, would be strained, unnatural, and ineffectual. A poet is the combined product of such internal powers as modify the nature of others; and of such external influences as excite and sustain these

powers; he is not one, but both. Every man's mind is, in this respect, modified by all the objects of nature and art; by every word and every suggestion which he ever admitted to act upon his consciousness; it is the mirror upon which all forms are reflected, and in which they compose one form. Poets, not otherwise than philosophers, painters, sculptors, and musicians, are, in one sense, the creators, and in another, the creations, of their age. From this subjection the loftiest do not escape. There is a similarity between Homer and Hesiod, between Aeschylus and Euripides, between Virgil and Horace, between Dante and Petrarch, between Shakespeare and Fletcher, between Dryden and Pope; each has a generic resemblance under which their specific distinctions are arranged. If this similarity be the result of imitation, I am willing to confess that I have imitated.

Let this opportunity be conceded to me of acknowledging that I have, what a Scotch philosopher characteristically terms, "a passion for reforming the world"; what passion incited him to write and publish his book, he omits to explain. For my part I had rather be damned with Plato and Lord Bacon than go to Heaven with Paley and Malthus. But it is a mistake to suppose that I dedicate my poetical compositions solely to the direct enforcement of reform or that I consider them in any degree as containing a reasoned system on the theory of human life. Didactic poetry is my abhorrence; nothing can be equally well expressed in prose that is not tedious and supererogatory in verse. My purpose has hitherto been simply to familiarize the highly refined imagination of the more select classes of poetical readers with beautiful idealisms of moral excellence; aware that until the mind can love, and admire, and trust, and hope, and endure, reasoned principles of moral conduct are seeds cast upon the highway of life which the unconscious passenger tramples into dust, although they would bear the harvest of his happiness. Should I live to accomplish what I purpose, that is, produce a systematical history of what appear to me to be the genuine elements of human society, let not the advocates of injustice and superstition flatter themselves that I should take Aeschylus rather than Plato as my model.

The having spoken of myself with unaffected freedom will need little apology with the candid; and let the uncandid consider that they injure me less than their own hearts and minds by misrepresentation. Whatever talents a person may possess to amuse and instruct others, be they ever so inconsiderable, he is yet bound to exert them; if his attempt be ineffectual, let the punishment of an unaccomplished purpose have been sufficient; let none trouble themselves to heap the dust of oblivion upon his efforts; the pile they raise will betray his grave which might otherwise have been unknown.

ADONAIS (1821)

AN ELEGY ON THE DEATH OF
JOHN KEATS, AUTHOR OF
Endymion, Hyperion, ETC.

'Αστὴρ πρὶν μὲν ἔλαμπες ἐνὶ ζωοῖσιν 'Εῷος·
νῦν δὲ θανὼν λάμπεις 'Έσπερος ἐν φθιμένοις.
—Plato.[1]

Preface

Φάρμακον ἦλθε, Βίων, ποτὶ σὸν στόμα,
    φάρμακον εἶδες.
πῶς τευ τοῖς χείλεσσι ποτέδραμε, κοὐκ
    ἐγλυκάνθη;
τίς δὲ βροτὸς τοσσοῦτον ἀνάμερος, ἢ
    κεράσαι τοι,
ἢ δοῦναι λαλέοντι τὸ φάρμακον; ἔκφυγεν
    ᾠδάν.

    —Moschus, Epitaph, Bion.[2]

It is my intention to subjoin to the London edition of this poem a criticism upon the claims of its lamented object to be classed among the writers of the highest genius who have adorned our age. My known repugnance to the narrow principles of taste on which several of his earlier compositions were modelled proves[s] at least that I am an impartial judge. I consider the fragment of Hyperion as second to nothing that was ever produced by a writer of the same years.

John Keats died at Rome of a consumption, in his twenty-fourth year,[3] on the —— of ——— 1821; and was buried in the romantic and lonely cemetery of the Protestants in that city under the pyramid, which is the tomb of Cestius, and the massy walls and towers, now mouldering and desolate, which formed the circuit of ancient Rome. The cemetery is an open space among the ruins, covered in winter with violets and daisies. It might make one in love with death to think that one should be buried in so sweet a place.

The genius of the lamented person to whose memory I have dedicated these unworthy verses was not less delicate and fragile than it was beautiful; and where cankerworms abound, what wonder if its young flower was blighted in the bud? The savage criticism on his Endymion, which appeared in the Quarterly Review, produced the most violent effect on his susceptible mind; the agitation thus originated ended in the rupture of a bloodvessel in the lungs; a rapid consumption ensued, and the succeeding acknowledgements from more candid critics of the true greatness of his powers were ineffectual to heal the wound thus wantonly inflicted.

It may be well said that these wretched men know not what they do. They scatter their insults and their slanders without heed

---

1. Shelley's own translation:
    "Thou wert the morning star among the
      living,
    Ere thy fair light had fled;—
    Now, having died, thou art as Hesperus,
      giving
    New splendor to the dead."
2. "Poison came, Bion, to thy mouth—thou
    didst know poison.

To such life as thine did come and was
    not sweetened.
What mortal was so cruel that could mix
    poison for thee,
Or could give thee the venom that heard
    thy voice?
Surely he had no music in his soul."
             Translation by Andrew Lang
3. Keats died in his twenty-sixth year.

as to whether the poisoned shaft lights on a heart made callous by many blows or one like Keats's composed of more penetrable stuff. One of their associates is, to my knowledge, a most base and unprincipled calumniator. As to *Endymion*, was it a poem, whatever might be its defects, to be treated contemptuously by those who had celebrated, with various degrees of complacency and panegyric, *Paris*, and *Woman*, and a *Syrian Tale*, and Mrs. Lefanu, and Mr. Barrett, and Mr. Howard Payne, and a long list of the illustrious obscure? Are these the men who in their venal good nature presumed to draw a parallel between the Rev. Mr. Milman and Lord Byron? What gnat did they strain at here, after having swallowed all those camels? Against what woman taken in adultery dares the foremost of these literary prostitutes to cast his opprobrious stone? Miserable man! you, one of the meanest, have wantonly defaced one of the noblest specimens of the workmanship of God. Nor shall it be your excuse, that, murderer as you are, you have spoken daggers, but used none.

The circumstances of the closing scene of poor Keats's life were not made known to me until the *Elegy* was ready for the press. I am given to understand that the wound which his sensitive spirit had received from the criticism of *Endymion* was exasperated by the bitter sense of unrequited benefits; the poor fellow seems to have been hooted from the stage of life, no less by those on whom he had wasted the promise of his genius, than those on whom he had lavished his fortune and his care. He was accompanied to Rome and attended in his last illness by Mr. Severn, a young artist of the highest promise, who, I have been informed, "almost risked his own life and sacrificed every prospect to unwearied attendance upon his dying friend." Had I known these circumstances before the completion of my poem, I should have been tempted to add my feeble tribute of applause to the more solid recompense which the virtuous man finds in the recollection of his own motives.

Mr. Severn can dispense with a reward from "such stuff as dreams are made of [on]." His conduct is a golden augury of the success of his future career—may the unextinguished Spirit of his illustrious friend animate the creations of his pencil, and plead against Oblivion for his name!

Cancelled Passages of the Preface

... the expression of my indignation and sympathy. I will allow myself a first and last word on the subject of calumny as it relates to me. As an author I have dared and invited censure. If I understand myself, I have written neither for profit nor for fame. I have employed my poetical compositions and publications simply as the instruments of that sympathy between myself and others which the ardent and unbounded love I cherished for my kind incited me to acquire. I expected all sorts of stupidity and insolent contempt from those ....

... These compositions (excepting the tragedy of *The Cenci*, which was written rather to try my powers than to unburden my full heart) are insufficiently ... commendation than perhaps they deserve, even from their bitterest enemies; but they have not attained any corresponding popularity. As a man, I shrink from notice and regard; the ebb and flow of the world vexes me; I desire to be left in peace. Persecution, contumely, and calumny have been heaped upon me in profuse measure; and domestic conspiracy and legal oppression have violated in my person the most sacred rights of nature and humanity. The bigot will say it was the recompense of my errors; the man of the world will call it the result of my imprudence; but never upon one head ....

... Reviewers, with some rare exception, are a most stupid and malignant race. As a bankrupt thief turns thieftaker in despair, so an unsuccessful author turns critic. But a young spirit panting for fame, doubtful of its powers, and certain only of its aspirations, is ill qualified to assign its true value to the sneer of this world. He knows not that such stuff as this is of the abortive and monstrous births which time consumes as fast as it produces. He sees the truth and falsehood, the merits and demerits, of his case inextricably entangled .... No personal offence should have drawn from me this public comment upon such stuff....

... The offence of this poor victim seems to have consisted solely in his intimacy with Leigh Hunt, Mr. Hazlitt, and some other enemies of despotism and superstition. My friend Hunt has a very hard skull to crack and will take a deal of killing. I do not know much of Mr. Hazlitt, but ....

... I knew personally but little of Keats; but on the news of his situation I wrote to him, suggesting the propriety of trying the Italian climate and inviting him to join me. Unfortunately he did not allow me ....

HELLAS (1821)
A LYRICAL DRAMA
ΜΑΝΤΙΣ 'ΕΙΜ' 'ΕΣΘΛΩΝ 'ΑΓΩΝΩΝ.
—*Oedip. Colon.*

[Translation: "I am a prophet of
a victorious contest."]

To His Excellency
Prince Alexander Mavrocordato
Late Secretary for Foreign Affairs
to the Hospodar of Wallachia
The Drama of Hellas is Inscribed as an
Imperfect Token of the Admiration,
Sympathy, and Friendship of
The Author

Pisa, November 1, 1821.

Preface

The poem of *Hellas,* written at the suggestion of the events of the moment, is a mere improvise, and derives its interest (should it be found to possess any) solely from the intense sympathy which the author feels with the cause he would celebrate.

The subject in its present state is insusceptible of being treated otherwise than lyrically, and if I have called this poem a drama from the circumstance of its being composed in dialogue, the licence is not greater than that which has been assumed by other poets who have called their productions epics, only because they have been divided into twelve or twenty-four books.

The *Persae* of Aeschylus afforded me the first model of my conception, although the decision of the glorious contest now waging in Greece being yet suspended forbids a catastrophe parallel to the return of Xerxes and the desolation of the Persians. I have, therefore, contented myself with exhibiting a series of lyric pictures, and with having wrought upon the curtain of futurity, which falls upon the unfinished scene, such figures of indistinct and visionary delineation as suggest the final triumph of the Greek cause as a portion of the cause of civilization and social improvement.

The drama (if drama it must be called) is, however, so inartificial that I doubt whether, if recited on the Thespian wagon to an Athenian village at the Dionysiaca, it would have obtained the prize of the goat. I shall bear with equanimity any punishment, greater than the loss of such a reward, which the Aristarchi of the hour may think fit to inflict.

The only *goat-song* which I have yet attempted has, I confess, in spite of the unfavorable nature of the subject, received a greater and a more valuable portion of applause than I expected or than it deserved.

Common fame is the only authority which I can allege for the details which form the basis of the poem, and I must trespass upon the forgiveness of my readers for the display of newspaper erudition to which I have been reduced. Undoubtedly, until the conclusion of the war, it will be impossible to obtain an account of it sufficiently authentic for historical materials; but poets have their privilege, and it is unquestionable that actions of the most exalted courage have been performed by the Greeks—that they have gained more than one naval victory, and that their defeat in Wallachia was signalized by circumstances of heroism more glorious even than victory.

The apathy of the rulers of the civilized world to the astonishing circumstance of the descendants of that nation to which they owe their civilization, rising as it were from the ashes of their ruin, is something perfectly inexplicable to a mere spectator of the shows of this mortal scene. We are all Greeks. Our laws, our literature, our religion, our arts have their root in Greece. But for Greece—Rome, the instructor, the conqueror, or the metropolis of our ancestors, would have spread no illumination with her arms, and we might still have been savages and idolators; or what is worse, might have arrived at such a stagnant and miserable state of social institution as China and Japan possess.

The human form and the human mind attained to a perfection in Greece which has impressed its image on those faultless productions, whose very fragments are the despair of modern art, and has propagated impulses which cannot cease, through a thousand channels of manifest or imperceptible operation, to ennoble and delight mankind until the extinction of the race.

The modern Greek is the descendant of those glorious beings whom the imagination almost refuses to figure to itself as belonging to our kind, and he inherits much of their sensibility, their rapidity of conception, their enthusiasm, and their courage. If in many instances he is degraded by moral and political slavery to the practice of the basest vices it engenders—and that below the level of ordinary degradation—let us reflect that the corruption of the best produces the worst, and that habits which subsist only in relation to a peculiar state of social institution may be expected to cease as soon as that relation is dissolved. In fact, the Greeks, since the admirable novel of *Anastasius* could have been a faithful picture of their manners, have undergone most important changes; the flower of their youth, returning to their

country from the universities of Italy, Germany, and France, have communicated to their fellow-citizens the latest results of that social perfection of which their ancestors were the original source. The University of Chios contained before the breaking out of the revolution eight hundred students, and among them several Germans and Americans. The munificence and energy of many of the Greek princes and merchants, directed to the renovation of their country with a spirit and a wisdom which has few examples, is above all praise.

The English permit their own oppressors to act according to their natural sympathy with the Turkish tyrant, and to brand upon their name the indelible blot of an alliance with the enemies of domestic happiness, of Christianity and civilization.

Russia desires to possess, not to liberate Greece, and is contented to see the Turks, its natural enemies, and the Greeks, its intended slaves, enfeeble each other until one or both fall into its net. The wise and generous policy of England would have consisted in establishing the independence of Greece, and in maintaining it both against Russia and the Turk; but when was the oppressor generous or just?

Should the English people ever become free, they will reflect upon the part which those who presume to represent their will have played in the great drama of the revival of liberty, with feelings which it would become them to anticipate. This is the age of the war of the oppressed against the oppressors, and every one of those ringleaders of the privileged gangs of murderers and swindlers, called Sovereigns, look to each other for aid against the common enemy and suspend their mutual jealousies in the presence of a mightier fear. Of this holy alliance all the despots of the earth are virtual members. But a new race has arisen throughout Europe, nursed in the abhorrence of the opinions which are its chains, and she will continue to produce fresh generations to accomplish that destiny which tyrants foresee and dread.[1]

The Spanish Peninsula is already free; France is tranquil in the enjoyment of a partial exemption from the abuses which its unnatural and feeble government are vainly attempting to revive. The seed of blood and misery has been sown in Italy, and a more vigorous race is arising to go forth to the harvest. The world waits only the news of a revolution of Germany to see the tyrants who have pinnacled themselves on its supineness precipitated into the ruin from which they shall never arise. Well do these destroyers of mankind know their enemy, when they impute the insurrection in Greece to the same spirit before which they tremble throughout the rest of Europe, and that enemy well knows the power and the cunning of its opponents, and watches the moment of their approaching weakness and inevitable division to wrest the bloody scepters from their grasp.

NOTES TO HELLAS

(1) *The quenchless ashes of Milan* [1.60].

Milan was the center of the resistance of the Lombard league against the Austrian tyrant. Frederic Barbarossa burnt the city to the ground, but liberty lived in its ashes, and it rose like an exhalation from its ruin. See Sismondi's *Histoire des Républiques Italiennes,* a book which has done much towards awakening the Italians to an imitation of their great ancestors.

(2) *The Chorus.*

The popular notions of Christianity are represented in this chorus as true in their relation to the worship they superseded, and that which in all probability they will supersede, without considering their merits in a relation more universal. The first stanza contrasts the immortality of the living and thinking beings which inhabit the planets, and to use a common and inadequate phrase,

clothe themselves in matter, with the transcience of the noblest manifestations of the external world.

The concluding verses indicate a progressive state of more or less exalted existence, according to the degree of perfection which every distinct intelligence may have attained. Let it not be supposed that I mean to dogmatize upon a subject, concerning which all men are equally ignorant, or that I think the Gordian knot of the origin of evil can be disentangled by that or any similar assertions. The received hypothesis of a Being resembling men in the moral attributes of His nature, having called us out of nonexistence, and after inflicting on us the misery of the commission of error, should superadd that of the punishment and the privations consequent upon it, still would remain inexplicable and incredible. That there is a true solution of the riddle, and that in our present state that solution is unattainable by us, are propositions which may be regarded as equally certain; meanwhile, as it is the province of the poet to attach himself to those ideas which exalt and ennoble humanity, let him be permitted to have conjectured the condition of that futurity towards which we are all impelled by an inextinguishable thirst for immortality. Until better arguments can be produced than sophisms which disgrace the cause, this desire itself must remain the strongest and the only presumption that eternity is the inheritance of every thinking being.

(3) *No hoary priests after that Patriarch* [1.245].

The Greek Patriarch, after having been compelled to fulminate an anathema against the insurgents, was put to death by the Turks.

Fortunately the Greeks have been taught that they cannot buy security by degradation, and the Turks, though equally cruel, are less cunning than the smooth-faced tyrants of Europe. As to the anathema, his Holiness

---

1. This paragraph, suppressed in 1822 by Charles Ollier, was restored in 1892 by Mr. Buxton Forman.

might as well have thrown his mitre at Mount Athos for any effect that it produced. The chiefs of the Greeks are almost all men of comprehension and enlightened views on religion and politics.

(4) *The freedom of a western poet-chief.* [l.563].

A Greek who had been Lord Byron's servant commands the insurgents in Attica. This Greek, Lord Byron informs me, though a poet and an enthusiastic patriot, gave him rather the idea of a timid and unenterprising person. It appears that circumstances make men what they are, and that we all contain the germ of a degree of degradation or of greatness whose connection with our character is determined by events.

(5) *The Greeks expect a Saviour from the West.* [l.598].

It is reported that this Messiah had arrived at a seaport near Lacedaemon in an American brig. The association of names and ideas is irresistibly ludicrous, but the prevalence of such a rumor strongly marks the state of popular enthusiasm in Greece.

(6) *The sound as of the assault of an imperial city* [ll.814-815].

For the vision of Mahmud of the taking of Constantinople in 1453, see Gibbon's *Decline and Fall of the Roman Empire,* vol. xii, p. 223.

The manner of the invocation of the spirit of Mahomet the Second will be censured as over subtle. I could easily have made the Jew a regular conjuror, and the Phantom an ordinary ghost. I have preferred to represent the Jew as disclaiming all pretension, or even belief, in supernatural agency, and as tempting Mahmud to that state of mind in which ideas may be supposed to assume the force of sensations through the confusion of thought with the objects of thought, and the excess of passion animating the creations of imagination.

It is a sort of natural magic, susceptible of being exercised in a degree by any one who should have made himself master of the secret associations of another's thoughts.

(7) *The Chorus.*

The final chorus is indistinct and obscure, as the event of the living drama whose arrival it foretells. Prophecies of wars, and rumors of wars, etc., may safely be made by poet or prophet in any age, but to anticipate however darkly a period of regeneration and happiness is a more hazardous exercise of the faculty which bards possess or feign. It will remind the reader "magno *nec* proximus intervallo"[2] of Isaiah and Virgil, whose ardent spirits overleaping the actual reign of evil which we endure and bewail, already saw the possible and perhaps approaching state of society in which the *"lion shall lie down with the lamb,"* and "omnis feret omnia tellus."[3] Let these great names be my authority and my excuse.

(8) *Saturn and Love their long repose shall burst* [ll.1090-1091].

Saturn and Love were among the deities of a real or imaginary state of innocence and happiness. *All* those *who fell,* or the Gods of Greece, Asia, and Egypt; the *One who rose,* or Jesus Christ, at whose appearance the idols of the Pagan World were amerced of their worship; and *the many unsubdued,* or the monstrous objects of the idolatry of China, India, the Antarctic islands, and the native tribes of America, certainly have reigned over the understandings of men in conjunction or in succession, during periods in which all we know of evil has been in a state of portentous, and, until the revival of learning and the arts, perpetually increasing, activity. The Grecian gods seem indeed to have been personally more innocent, although it cannot be said, that as far as temperance and chastity are concerned, they gave so edifying an example as their successor. The sublime human character of Jesus

2. "Not next, but at a great distance."

3. "Every land shall produce all things."

Christ was deformed by an imputed identification with a Power, who tempted, betrayed, and punished the innocent beings who were called into existence by His sole will; and for the period of a thousand years, the spirit of this most just, wise, and benevolent of men has been propitiated with myriads of hecatombs of those who approached the nearest to His innocence and wisdom, sacrificed under every aggravation of atrocity and variety of torture. The horrors of the Mexican, the Peruvian, and the Indian superstitions are well known.

EPIPSYCHIDION (1821)

Verses Addressed to the Noble and Unfortunate Lady, Emilia V——— Now Imprisoned in the Convent of ———

L'anima amante si slancia fuori del creato, e si crea nell' infinito un Mondo tutto per essa, diverso assai da questo oscuro e paurose baratro.[1]

Her Own Words.

Advertisement

The writer of the following lines died at Florence, as he was preparing for a voyage to one of the wildest of the Sporades, which he had bought, and where he had fitted up the ruins of an old building, and where it was his hope to have realized a scheme of life, suited perhaps to that happier and better world of which he is now an inhabitant, but hardly practicable in this. His life was singular, less on account of the romantic vicissitudes which diversified it, than the ideal tinge which it received from his own character and feelings. The present poem, like the *Vita Nuova* of Dante, is sufficiently intelligible to a certain class of readers without a matter-of-fact history of the circumstances to which it relates; and to a certain other class it must ever remain incomprehensible, from a defect of a common organ of perception for the ideas of which it treats. Not but that *gran vergogna sarebbe a colui, che rimasse cosa sotto veste di figura, o di colore rettorico: e domandato non sapesse denudare le sue parole da cotal veste, in guisa che avessero verace intendimento.*[2]

The present poem appears to have been intended by the Writer as the dedication to some longer one. The stanza on the opposite page is almost a literal translation from Dante's famous Canzonne

> Voi, ch' intendendo, il terzo ciel
>   movete, etc.[3]

The presumptuous application of the concluding lines to his own composition will raise a smile at the expense of my unfortunate friend: be it a smile not of contempt, but pity.   S.

PREFACE TO THE BANQUET OF PLATO (1818)

[This fragment, composed in 1818, was first published by Mary Shelley in *Essays, Letters from Abroad, etc.*]

The dialogue entitled "The Banquet" was selected by the translator as the most beautiful and perfect among all the works of

1. "The loving soul launches itself out from the world and makes itself a world in the infinite, all for itself very different from this dim and fearful abysm."
    From Emilia Viviani's *Il Vero Amore*.
2. Shelley misquotes from Dante's *Vita Nuova* (XXV): *Pero che grande vergogna sarebbe a colui che rimasse cose sotto vesta di figura o di colore rettorico, e poscia, domandato, non sapesse denudare le sue parole da cotale vesta, in guisa che avessero verace intendimento.*
    Translation: "Great were his shame who should rhyme anything under a garb of metaphor or rhetorical color, and then, being asked, should be incapable of stripping his words of this garb so that they might have a veritable meaning." W. M. Rossetti's translation.
3. "Ye who intelligent the Third Heaven move." From Shelley's translation of *The First Canzone of the Convito of Dante.*

Plato.[1] He despairs of having communicated to the English language any portion of the surpassing graces of the composition, or having done more than present an imperfect shadow of the language and the sentiment of this astonishing production.

Plato is eminently the greatest among the Greek philosophers, and from, or, rather perhaps through him, his master Socrates, have proceeded those emanations of moral and metaphysical knowledge, on which a long series and an incalculable variety of popular superstitions have sheltered their absurdities from the slow contempt of mankind. Plato exhibits the rare union of close and subtle logic, with the Pythian enthusiasm of poetry, melted by the splendor and harmony of his periods into one irresistible stream of musical impressions, which hurry the persuasions onward, as in a breathless career. His language is that of an immortal spirit rather than a man. Lord Bacon is, perhaps, the only writer who, in these particulars, can be compared with him; his imitator, Cicero, sinks in the comparison into an ape mocking the gestures of a man. His views into the nature of mind and existence are often obscure, only because they are profound; and though his theories respecting the government of the world, and the elementary laws of moral action are not always correct, yet there is scarcely any of his treatises which do not, however stained by puerile sophisms, contain the most remarkable intuitions into all that can be the subject of the human mind. His excellence consists especially in intuition, and it is this faculty which raises him far above Aristotle, whose genius, though vivid and various, is obscure in comparison with that of Plato.

The dialogue entitled the "Banquet" is called Ερωτικος, or a Discussion upon Love, and is supposed to have taken place at the house of Agathon at one of a series of festivals given by that poet on the occasion of his gaining the prize of tragedy at the Dionysiaca. The account of the debate on this occasion is supposed to have been given by Apollodorus, a pupil of Socrates, many years after it had taken place, to a companion who was curious to hear it. This Apollodorus appears, both from the style in which he is represented in this piece, as well as from a passage in the *Phaedon,* to have been a person of an impassioned and enthusiastic disposition; to borrow an image from the Italian painters, he seems to have been the St. John of the Socratic group. The drama (for so the lively distinction of character and the various and well-wrought circumstances of the story almost entitle it to be called) begins by Socrates persuading Aristodemus to sup at Agathon's, uninvited. The whole of this introduction affords the most lively conception of refined Athenian manners.

[Unfinished]

---

1. *The Republic,* though replete with considerable errors of speculation, is, indeed, the greatest repository of important truths of all the works of Plato. This, perhaps, is because it is the longest. He first, and perhaps last, maintained that a state ought to be governed, not by the wealthiest, or the most ambitious, or the most cunning, but by the wisest; the method of selecting such rulers, and the laws by which such a selection is made, must correspond with and arise out of the moral freedom and refinement of the people. [Shelley's Note.]

APPENDIX C: *FRAGMENTS AND MINOR PIECES*

[In Appendix C will be found a number of minor though significant pieces. They round out and complete the body of Shelley's prose.]

ON POLYTHEISM (1819?)

[In the notebook, in the Bodleian Library, containing the *Essay on Christianity* is a note which reads, "Essay in Favor of Polytheism." The fragment here is in the notebook containing the *Essay on the Devil and Devils* and is also in the Bodleian Library at Oxford. The piece was first published in the Julian Editions, where it is pointed out that it bears some relation to the fragment on Marriage. The fragment is a reflection of the influence of Hume.]

There is a disposition in the human mind to seek the cause of whatever it contemplates. What cause is, no philosopher has succeeded in explaining, and the triumph of the acutest metaphysician has been confined to demonstrating it to be inexplicable. All we know of cause is that one event, or to speak more correctly, one sensation follows another attended with a conviction derived from experience that these sensations will hereafter be similarly connected. This habitual conviction is that to which we appeal when we say that one thing is the cause of another, or has the power of producing certain effects.

The surrounding agencies of the vital and mechanical world which first presented themselves to the notice of men excited their curiosity—that is, impelled them to assign a cause of their original existence and action.

THREE FRAGMENTS ON BEAUTY (1821?)

[These fragments were first published by Richard Garnett in *Relics of Shelley* (1862), and are dated 1821.]

I

Why is the reflection in that canal more beautiful than the objects it reflects? The colors are more vivid and yet blended with more harmony; the openings from within into the soft and tender colors of the distant wood and the intersection of the mountain lines surpass and misrepresent truth.

II

The mountains sweep to the plain like waves that meet in a chasm—the olive woods are as green as a sea and are waving in the wind—the shadows of the clouds are spotting the bosoms of the hills—a heron comes sailing over me—a butterfly flits near—at intervals the pines give forth their sweet and prolonged response to the wind—the myrtle bushes are in bud and the soil beneath me is carpeted with odoriferous flowers.

III

It is sweet to feel the beauties of nature in every pulsation, in every nerve—but it is far sweeter to be able to express this feeling to one who loves you. To feel all that is divine in the green-robed earth and the starry sky is a penetrating yet vivid pleasure which, when it is over, presses like the memory of misfortune; but if you can express those feelings—if, secure of sympathy (for without sympathy it is worse than the taste of those apples whose core is as bitter ashes), if thus secure you can pour forth into another's most attentive ear the feelings by which you are entranced, there is an exultation of spirit in the utterance—a glory of happiness which far transcends all human transports, and seems to invest the soul as the saints are with light, with a halo untainted, holy, and undying.

AN ESSAY
ON FRIENDSHIP (1822?)
(A Fragment)

[The fragment on Friendship was first published by Thomas Jefferson Hogg in his *Life of Shelley* (1858), 1.22-24, where he remarked that it was composed "not long before Shelley's death." The manuscript is in the Bodleian Library.]

The nature of Love and Friendship is very little understood, and the distinctions between them ill established. This latter feeling—at least, a profound and sentimental attachment to one of the same sex, wholly divested of the smallest alloy of sensual intermixture—often precedes the former. It is not right to say, merely, that it is exempt from the smallest alloy of sensuality. It rejects with disdain all thoughts but those of an elevated and imaginative character and the process by which the attachment between two persons of different sexes terminates in a sensual union has not yet begun. I remember forming an attachment of this kind at school. I cannot recall to my memory the precise epoch at which this took place; but I imagine it must have been at the age of eleven or twelve.

The object of these sentiments was a boy about my own age, of a character eminently generous, brave, and gentle; and the elements of human feeling seemed to have been from his birth genially compounded within him. There was a delicacy and a simplicity in his manner, inexpressibly attractive. It has never been my fortune to meet with him since my school-days; but either I confound my present recollections with the delusions of past feelings, or he is now a source of honor and utility to every one around him. The tones of his voice were so soft and winning that every word pierced into my heart, and their pathos was so deep that in listening to him the tears often have involuntarily gushed from my eyes. Such

was the being for whom I first experienced the sacred sentiments of friendship. I remember in my simplicity writing to my mother a long account of his admirable qualities and my own devoted attachment. I suppose she thought me out of my wits, for she returned no answer to my letter. I remember we used to walk the whole play-hours up and down by some moss-covered palings, pouring out our hearts in youthful talk. We used to speak of the ladies with whom we were in love, and I remember that our usual practice was to confirm each other in the everlasting fidelity, in which we had bound ourselves towards them and towards each other. I recollect thinking my friendship exquisitely beautiful. Every night, when we parted to go to bed, I remember we kissed each other.

ADDITIONAL NOTES ON
QUEEN MAB

[The pieces below are short, but suggestive Notes to lines in *Queen Mab*. Though not significant enough to deserve a place in the body of the text, they shed some light on the development of Shelley's mind.]

(a)

"The sun's unclouded orb
Rolled through the black concave."

Beyond our atmosphere the sun would appear a rayless orb of fire in the midst of a black concave. The equal diffusion of its light on earth is owing to the refraction of the rays by the atmosphere and their reflection from other bodies. Light consists either of vibrations propagated through a subtle medium, or of numerous minute particles repelled in all directions from the luminous body. Its velocity greatly exceeds that of any substance with which we are acquainted; observations on the eclipses of Jupiter's satellites have demonstrated that light takes up no more than 8' 7" in passing from the sun to the earth, a distance of 95,000,000 miles. Some idea may be gained of the immense distance of the fixed stars when it is computed that many years would elapse before light could reach this earth from the nearest of them; yet in one year light travels 5,422,-400,000,000 miles, which is a distance of 5,707,600 times greater than that of the sun from the earth.

(b)

> "Whilst round the chariot's way
> Innumerable systems rolled."

The plurality of worlds—the indefinite immensity of the universe—is a most awful subject of contemplation. He who rightly feels its mystery and grandeur is in no danger of seduction from the falsehoods of religious systems, or of deifying the principle of the universe. It is impossible to believe that the Spirit that pervades this infinite machine begat a son upon the body of a Jewish woman, or is angered at the consequences of that necessity which is a synonym of itself. All that miserable tale of the Devil and Eve and an Intercessor with the childish mummeries of the God of the Jews is irreconcilable with the knowledge of the stars. The works of His fingers have borne witness against Him.

The nearest of the fixed stars is inconceivably distant from the earth, and they are probably proportionately distant from each other. By a calculation of the velocity of light, Sirius is supposed to be at least 54,224,-000,000,000 miles from the earth.[1] That which appears only like a thin and silvery cloud streaking the heaven is in effect composed of innumerable clusters of suns, each shining with its own light, and illuminating numbers of planets that revolve around them. Millions and millions of suns are ranged around us, all attended by innumerable worlds, yet calm, regular, and harmonious, all keeping the paths of immutable necessity.

(c)

> "These are the hired bravos who
> defend
> The tyrant's throne."

To employ murder as a means of justice is an idea which a man of an enlightened mind will not dwell upon with pleasure. To march forth in rank and file and all the pomp of streamers and trumpets for the purpose of shooting at our fellowmen as a mark; to inflict upon them all the variety of wound and anguish; to leave them weltering in their blood; to wander over the field of desolation, and count the number of the dying and the dead—are employments which in thesis we may maintain to be necessary, but which no good man will contemplate with gratulation and delight. A battle we suppose is won—thus truth is established; thus the cause of justice is confirmed! It surely requires no common sagacity to discern the connection between this immense heap of calamities and the assertion of truth or the maintenance of justice. [Two paragraphs quoted from Godwin's *Enquirer,* Essay v, are here omitted.]

I will here subjoin a little poem, so strongly expressive of my abhorrence of despotism and falsehood, that I fear lest it never again may be depictured so vividly. This opportunity is perhaps the only one that ever will occur of rescuing it from oblivion. [The poem on *Falsehood and Vice* is here omitted.]

(d)

> "To the red and baleful sun
> That faintly twinkles there."

The north polar star, to which the axis of the earth in its present state of obliquity, points. It is exceedingly probable from many considerations that this obliquity will gradually diminish until the equator coincides with the ecliptic; the nights and days will then become equal on the earth throughout the year, and probably the seasons also.

---

1. See Nicholson's *Encyclopedia,* art. Light. [Shelley's Note.]

There is no great extravagance in presuming that the progress of the perpendicularity of the poles may be as rapid as the progress of intellect; or that there should be a perfect identity between the moral and physical improvement of the human species. It is certain that wisdom is not compatible with disease, and that in the present state of the climates of the earth, health, in the true and comprehensive sense of the word, is out of the reach of civilized man. Astronomy teaches us that the earth is now in its progress and that the poles are every year becoming more and more perpendicular to the ecliptic. The strong evidence afforded by the history of mythology and geological researches that some event of this nature has taken place already affords a strong presumption that this progress is not merely an oscillation as has been surmised by some late astronomers.[1] Bones of animals peculiar to the torrid zone have been found in the north of Siberia and on the banks of the river Ohio. Plants have been found in the fossil state in the interior of Germany which demand the present climate of Hindostan for their production.[2] The researches of M. Bailly[3] establish the existence of a people who inhabited a tract in Tartary 49° north latitude, of greater antiquity than either the Indians, the Chinese, or the Chaldeans, from whom these nations derived their sciences and theology. We find from the testimony of ancient writers that Britain, Germany, and France were much colder than at present and that their great rivers were annually frozen over. Astronomy teaches us also that since this period the obliquity of the earth's position has been considerably diminished.

(e)

"In time-destroying infiniteness."

Time is our consciousness of the succession of ideas in our mind. Vivid sensation of either pain or pleasure makes the time seem long, as the common phrase is, because it renders us more acutely conscious of our ideas. If a mind be conscious of an hundred ideas during one minute by the clock and of two hundred during another, the latter of these spaces would actually occupy so much greater extent in the mind as two exceed one in quantity. If, therefore, the human mind by any future improvement of its sensibility should become conscious of an infinite number of ideas in a minute, that minute would be eternity. I do not hence infer that the actual space between the birth and death of a man will ever be prolonged, but that his sensibility is perfectible and that the number of ideas which his mind is capable of receiving is indefinite. One man is stretched on the rack during twelve hours; another sleeps soundly in his bed; the difference of time perceived by these two persons is immense; one hardly will believe that half an hour has elapsed; the other could credit that centuries had flown during his agony. Thus, the life of a man of virtue and talent who should die in his thirtieth year is with regard to his own feelings longer than that of a miserable priest-ridden slave who dreams out a century of dullness. The one has perpetually cultivated his mental faculties, has rendered himself master of his thoughts, can abstract and generalize amid the lethargy of every-day business; the other can slumber over the brightest moments of his being and is unable to remember the happiest hour of his life. Perhaps the perishing ephemeron enjoys a longer life than the tortoise.

> Dark flood of time!
> Roll as it listeth thee—I measure
>   not
> By months or moments thy ambig-
>   uous course.
> Another may stand by me on the
>   brink

---

1. Laplace, *Système du Monde*. [Shelley's Note.]
2. Cabanis, *Rapports du Physique et du Moral de l'Homme*. [Shelley's Note.]

3. Bailly, *Lettres sur les Sciences, a Voltaire*. [Shelley's Note.]

And watch the bubbles whirled beyond his ken
That pauses at my feet. The sense
of love,
The thirst for action, and the impassioned thought
Prolong my being: if I wake no
more,
My life more actual living will
contain
Than some gray veteran's of the
world's cold school,
Whose listless hours unprofitably
roll,
By one enthusiast feeling unredeemed.[1]

(f)

". . . or religion
Drives his wife raving mad."

I am acquainted with a lady of considerable accomplishments and the mother of a
numerous family whom the Christian religion has goaded to incurable insanity. A
parallel case is, I believe, within the experience of every physician.

Nam iam saepe homines patriam, caros-
que parentes
Prodiderunt, vitare Acherusia templa
petentes.[1]

Lucretius.

"TRUE KNOWLEDGE LEADS
TO LOVE"

[First published by H. Buxton Forman in *Shelley's Prose*, VII.79 (1880).]

True knowledge leads to love. The meanest of our fellow beings contains qualities
which, if developed, we must admire and
adore. The selfish, the hollow, and the base
alone despise and hate. To them I have
erred much.

1. See Godwin's *Pol. Jus.* vol. i, p. 411; And
Condorcet, *Esquisse d'un Tableau Historique des
Progrès de l'Esprit Humain*, époque ix. [Shelley's

NOTE ON THE HUNDRED
AND ELEVENTH SONNET
OF SHAKESPEARE

[This note is on the manuscript of
the Preface to *The Cenci,* which is in
the Bodleian Library at Oxford. It was
first published by Richard Garnett in
Relics of Shelley (1862).]

That famous passage in that pathetic sonnet in which, addressing a dear friend, he
complains of his own situation as an actor,
and says that his nature is (I quote from
memory)

Subdued
To what it works in, like the dyer's
hand.

Observe these images, how simple they are,
and yet animated with what intense poetry
and passion.

ON THE GAME LAWS

[This fragment is in the Mary
Shelley Notebook with the fragment I
have entitled *A Refutation of the
Christian Religion.* It was first published by Professor F. L. Jones in
Studies in Philology for July, 1948.
The main theme is a condemnation of
the House of Commons for its enact-
ment of game laws prejudicial to the
poor and under-privileged people.
Since the opening sentence of this
piece is similar in thought and phrasing to two sentences in paragraph two
of Chapter II of *A Philosophical View
of Reform,* the fragment probably is a
first draft of an intended portion of
that work. The present transcription is
made from the original Notebook
Note.]
1. "For often, in seeking to escape death, men
have betrayed country and loving parents."

now in the Library of Congress. Shelley's cancellations are enclosed in brackets.]

It is said that the House of Commons, though not an actual, is a virtual representation of the people. [It is said that tho' not clearest at what a deception and a shadow If ever] Undoubtedly such cannot be the case. They actually and virtually at present represent none but the powerful and the rich.

If a doubt is ever excited in our minds as to whether that Assembly does or does not provide for the welfare of the community as well as any Assembly more legally constituted, we need only consider the legislative provisions in force in this country for the preservation of game [to contemplate which will expose] to [contemplate] set in [the] its clearest point of view, [a] the despotism which is exercised by an oligarchical minority amongst us. [Which fully to win it was to overthrow.—] We may doubt whether the Parliament repealed the Income Tax because it demanded a tenth of the incomes of its own members; we may doubt whether [the necess] it [taxed] taxed the necessaries [of the] which the laboring poor consume with imposts whilst the most productive as well as the most legitimate object of all taxation is spared [namely its vast accum] namely, vast accumulations of wealth —because it is the species of possession which its own members enjoy, from ignorance or ill-faith; though their conduct would scarcely justify such a question—but the laws which are in force for the preservation of game will admit of no excuse, and bring home to this assembly [which assumes to speak the will of this nation country] a charge of corrupting the tastes and morals sacrificing the lives, [outraging the] imprisoning the persons, and trampling upon the property of the inhabitants of the same country; and that [without] with the barefaced insolence of power, without deigning to allege the remotest pretext of general good, [for] in order that they may indulge themselves in a barbarous and bloody sport, from which

every enlightened and amiable mind [contemplates with] shrinks in abhorrence and disgust.

[First to consider it as a violation of property the]. There is a distinction of ranks; [There are degrees] the inequality of property is established amongst us; [so that] so that one man enjoys all the productions of human art and industry without any exertion of his own, whilst another earns the right of seeing his wife and children famish before his eyes, by providing for the superfluous luxuries of the former. Society submits to this enormous injustice for the sake of an overbalance of what it considers an eventual benefit. It supposes that refinement of sentiment, that literature, that philosophy and the imitative arts are kept alive by the enforcement of this condition of things. To a certain degree this opinion is correct. Gentlemen, or persons of wealth and leisure, are usually found to possess more courage, generosity, and gentleness than men chained to the soil, and occupied in providing for their physical necessities. But the system of the game laws so far as it proceeds is a direct contravention of this compact. It leaves to the poor the same grinding misery as was [been] their lot before, and deprives the community of the contemplation of so much of that moral grace which it has a right to demand in return for a sacrifice so prodigious, and alas, [how] so feebly compensated, as that misery.

Persons of great property nurture animals on their estates for the sake of destroying them. For this they banish, for this they imprison, for this [tort] they persecute and overbear their feebler neighbors, for this they lay in train the whole horrors of that devilish enginery which the law places within the grasp of the wealthy to grind the weak to the dust of the earth. For what?—that they may kill and torture living beings for their sport. When an ox or a sheep is put to death that their flesh may serve for human food the pang to the beast is sudden and unforeseen. The necessity [for] of the action to the very existence of man is supposed to be indispensable. [I am of the most inspired thinkers have ever disputed this necessity. But in theory no one has ever said that to destroy and mangle.] But [But to the destruction of game no]. The [innocence] justifiableness of such action flows directly from the right of self-preservation. Yet the [framers] authors of our common law forbid butchers to decide as jurymen on the life of a [criminal] man because he is familiar, however innocently, with the death of beasts. But how shall those men be considered who go forth not from necessity, not [to] for the preservation, but [to] for the insult and outrage of the rights of their fellowmen to the mangling of living beings. And the case is as widely different between the mode of death of an ox and a sheep, and [that] a pheasant, or a hare, or a deer as [the former] is the [mostly for] are the[1]

NOTES ON SCULPTURES IN ROME AND FLORENCE (1819)

[These notes were composed in 1819, apparently for his own use, and not for publication. They are vigorous, clear-cut observations on the esthetic effects produced on Shelley by these sculptures, thus giving the reader a valuable insight into the author's mental and emotional life. Thomas Medwin published eight of these sketches in the *Athenaeum* (1832). He reprinted them in his *Shelley Papers* (1833), and these with three others in his *Life of Shelley* (1847). The full sixty notes were published by H. B. Forman in *Shelley's Prose* in 1880. Forman's text was from the originals in a Shelley MS. Notebook. Medwin's and Forman's texts differ in numerous details. Our text for the most part follows

1. Here the fragment ends.

Forman's. Breaks in the manuscript are represented by three dots.]

ROME

1. *The Arch of Titus*

On the inner compartment of the Arch of Titus is sculptured in deep relief the desolation of a city. On one side the walls of the Temple, split by the fury of conflagrations, hang tottering in the act of ruin. The accompaniments of a town taken by assault, matrons and virgins and children and old men gathered into groups, and the rapine and licence of a barbarous and enraged soldiery, are imaged in the distance. The foreground is occupied by a procession of the victors, bearing in their profane hands the holy candlesticks and the tables of shewbread and the sacred instruments of the eternal worship of the Jews. On the opposite side the reverse of this sad picture, Titus is represented standing in a chariot drawn by four horses, crowned with laurel, and surrounded by the tumultuous numbers of his triumphant army, and the magistrates, and priests, and generals, and philosophers, dragged in chains beside his wheels. Behind him stands a Victory eagle-winged.

The arch is now mouldering into ruins, and the imagery almost erased by the lapse of fifty generations. Beyond this obscure monument of Hebrew desolation is seen the tomb of the Destroyer's family, now a mountain of ruins.

The Flavian amphitheater has become a habitation for owls and dragons. The power, of whose possession it was once the type, and of whose departure it is now the emblem, is become a dream and a memory. Rome is no more than Jerusalem.

2. *The Laocoön*

The subject of the Laocoön is a disagreeable one, but whether we consider the grouping, or the execution, nothing that remains to us of antiquity can surpass it. It consists of a father and his two sons. Byron thinks that Laocoön's anguish is absorbed in that of his children, that a mortal's agony is blending with an immortal's patience. Not so. Intense physical suffering, against which he pleads with an upraised countenance of despair, and appeals with a sense of its injustice, seems the predominant and overwhelming emotion, and yet there is a nobleness in the expression and a majesty that dignifies torture.

We now come to his children. Their features and attitudes indicate the excess of the filial love and devotion that animates them and swallows up all other feelings. In the elder of the two, this is particularly observable. His eyes are fixedly bent on Laocoön—his whole soul is with—is a part of that of his father. His arm is extended towards him, not for protection, but from a wish as if instinctively to afford it, absolutely speaks. Nothing can be more exquisite than the contour of his form and face and the moulding of his lips that are half open, as if in the act of—not uttering any unbecoming complaint, or prayer or lamentation, which he is conscious are alike useless—but addressing words of consolatory tenderness to his unfortunate parent. The intensity of his bodily torments is only expressed by the uplifting of his right foot, which he is vainly and impotently attempting to extricate from the grasp of the mighty folds in which it is entangled.

In the younger child, surprise, pain, and grief seem to contend for mastery. He is not yet arrived at an age when his mind has sufficient self-possession, or fixedness of reason, to analyze the calamity that is overwhelming himself and all that is dear to him. He is sick with pain and horror. We almost seem to hear his shrieks. His left hand is on the head of the snake that is burying its fangs in his side, and the vain and fruitless attempt he is making to disengage it increases the effect. Every limb, every muscle, every vein of Laocoön expresses with the fidelity of life the working

of the poison and the strained girding round of the inextricable folds, whose tangling sinuosities are too numerous and complicated to be followed. No chisel has ever displayed with such anatomical fidelity and force the projecting muscles of the arm, whose hand clenches the neck of the reptile, almost to strangulation, and the mouth of the enormous asp, and his terrible fangs widely displayed, in a moment to penetrate and meet within its victim's heart, make the spectator of this miracle of sculpture turn away with shuddering and awe, and doubt the reality of what he sees.

3. *Vasa Borghese a Parigi*

A Bronze cast of the Bas relief—a bacchanalian subject—a beautiful reference to Unity. Bacchus with a countenance of calm and majestic beauty surrounded by the tumultuous figures whom the whirlwinds of his Deity are tossing into all attitudes like the sun in the midst of his planets; power calm amid confusion. He leans on a woman with a lyre within her arms, on whom he looks with grand yet gentle love. On one side is a Silenus, who has let fall the cup and hangs heavily his vine-crowned head, supported by another Bacchanal. The contrast between the flowing robe which wraps the lower part of his form and the soft but more defined outline of the leg of the Bacchanal who supports him is in the true harmony of Art.

4. *A Bronze*

A child riding on a swan with a dart in his hand.

5. *A Bacchanal*

.... holding a lion's skin in one hand and a flaming torch in the other, with his muscles starting through his skin, and his hair dishevelled.

6. *An Accouchement: A Bas Relief*

The lady is lying on a couch, supported by a young woman, and looking extremely exhausted and thin; her hair is flowing about her shoulders and she is half-covered with drapery which falls over the couch.

Her tunic is exactly like a shift, only the sleeves are longer, coming halfway down the upper part of the arm. An old wrinkled woman with a cloak over her head and an enormously sagacious look has a most professional appearance and is taking hold of her arm gently with one hand and with the other is supporting it. I think she is feeling her pulse. At the side of the couch sits a woman as in grief, holding her head in her hands. At the bottom of the bed is another old woman tearing her hair and in the act of screaming out most violently, which she seems, however, by the rest of her gestures to do with the utmost deliberation as having come to the conclusion that it was a correct thing to do. Behind is another old woman of the most ludicrous ugliness, crying, I suppose, with her hands crossed upon her neck. There is a young woman also lamenting. To the left of the couch a woman is sitting on the ground, nursing the child, which is swaddled. Behind her is a woman who appears to be in the act of rushing in, with dishevelled hair and violent gestures, and in one hand either a whip or a thunderbolt. She is probably some emblematic person whose personification would be a key to the whole. What they are all wailing at, I don't know; whether the lady is dying, or the father has ordered the child to be exposed: but if the mother be not dead, such a tumult would kill a woman in the straw in these days.

The other compartment or second scene of the drama tells the story of the presentation of the child to its father. An old nurse has it in her arms and with professional and mysterious officiousness is holding it out to the father. The father, a middle-aged and very respectable-looking man, perhaps not married above nine months, is looking with the wonder of a bachelor upon the strange little being which once was himself; his hands are clasped, and his brow wrinkled up with a kind of inexperienced wonder,

and he has gathered up between his arms the folds of his cloak, an emblem of the gathering up of all his faculties to understand so unusual a circumstance.

An old man is standing behind him, probably his own father, with some curiosity and much tenderness in his looks, and around are collected a host of his relations, of whom the youngest seem the most unconcerned. It is altogether an admirable piece quite in the spirit of the comedies of Terence, though I confess I am totally at a loss to comprehend the cause of all that tumult visible in the first scene.

7. A Mercury

A bronze Mercury standing on the wind.

8. An Ox

A most admirable ox in bronze.

9. An Urn

An urn whose ansae are formed of the horned faces of Ammonian Jove and over-sculptured with labyrinth work of leaves and flowers and buds and strange looking insects, and a tablet with this inscription

ΤΩΝ ΑΓΑΘΩΝ Η ΜΝΗΜΗ ΑΕΙ ΘΑΛΗΣ

"The memory of the good is ever green."
And art thou then forgotten?

10. View from the Pitti Gardens

You see below, Florence a smokeless city, its domes and spires occupying the vale; and beyond to the right the Apennines, whose base extends even to the walls, and whose summits were intersected with ashen-colored clouds. The green valleys of these mountains which gently unfold themselves upon the plain, and the intervening hills covered with vineyards and olive plantations are occupied by the villas which are as it were another city—a Babylon of palaces and gardens. In the midst of the picture rolls the Arno, now full with the winter rains through woods and bounded by the aerial snow and summits of the Lucchese Apennines. On the left a magnificent buttress of lofty craggy hills, overgrown with wilderness, juts out in many shapes over a lovely vale, and approaches the walls of the city. Cascini and Ville occupy the pinnacles and the abutments of those hills, over which is seen at intervals the ethereal mountain line hoary with snow and intersected by clouds. The vale below is covered with cypress groves whose obeliskine forms of intense green pierce the grey shadow of the wintry hill that overhangs them. The cypresses too of the garden form a magnificent foreground of accumulated verdure; pyramids of dark leaves and shining cones rising out of a mass, beneath which were cut, like caverns, recesses which conducted into walks. The Cathedral with its gray marble Campanile and the other domes and spires of Florence were at our feet.

11. Victory

Lips of wisdom and arch yet sublime tenderness, a simple yet profound expression of . . . .

12. A Boy

A graceful boy with the skin of a wild beast hanging on his shoulders and a bunch of grapes in his hand. He is crowned with a vine wreath and buds and grapes; the legs are modern, and the face has not an antique . . . but it expresses cheerful and earnest . . . .

13. A Priestess

The drapery beautifully expressed, the face bad.

14. An Athlete

(Curse these fig leaves; why is a round tin thing more decent than a cylindrical marble one?) An exceedingly fine statue—full of graceful strength; the countenance full of sweetness and strength. Its attitude with a staff lifted in one hand and some . . . in the other, expresses serene dignity and power; a personification in the firmness and lightness of its form of that perfection of manhood when the will can be freely com-

municated to every fiber of the body. The muscles are represented how differently from a statue since anatomy has corrupted it.

15. A Pomona

A woman in the act of lightly advancing —much care has been taken to render the effect of the drapery as thrown back by the wind of her motion.

16. An Athlete

In every respect different from and inferior to the first.

17. An Urania

Holding a globe in one hand and compasses in the other; her countenance though not of the highest beauty is beautiful; her drapery drawn closely round shows the conformation of her left side and falls in graceful folds over the right arm.

18. A Vestal

Probably a portrait. This face, which represented a real person, denotes an admirable disposition and mind, and is not beautiful but wise and gentle although with some mixture of severity. Her office might have contributed to this expression.

19. A Venus Genitrix

Remarkable for the voluptuous effect of her finely proportioned form being seen through the folds of a drapery, the original of which must have been the "woven wind" of Chios. There is a softness in the attitude and upper part of the statue—the restoration of the arms and hand truly hideous.

20. A Calliope

Half modern—the drapery rather coarse.

21. A Hercules on an Emblematic Base

The arms probably restored, for the right hand especially is in villainous proportion.

22. A Muse

A statue they call the Muse Polyhymnia— poor Muse—the head which may be a misapplication is of the family likeness of those shrewish and evil-minded Roman women of rank with the busts of whom the Capitol overflows. The form otherwise is too thin and spare for the ideal beauty in which the Muses were clothed. The drapery is very remarkable and very admirable; it is arranged in such large and unrestrained folds as the motions and the shape of a living form naturally forces a form into.

23. Mercury

Another glorious creature of the Greeks. His countenance expresses an imperturbable and god-like self-possession; he seems in the enjoyment of delight which nothing can destroy. His figure, nervous yet light, expresses the animation of swiftness emblemed by the plumes of his sandalled feet. Every muscle and nerve of his frame has tranquil and energetic life.

24. A Venus

with villainous modern arms—this figure is rather too slight and weak—the body is correctly but feebly expressed.

25. Another Venus

A very insipid person in the usual insipid attitude of this lady. The body and hips and where the lines of the . . .   fade into the thighs is exquisitely imagined and executed.

26. An Apollo

with his serpent crawling round a trunk of laurel on which his quiver is suspended. It probably was, when complete, magnificently beautiful. The restorer of the head and arms following the indications of the muscles of the right side has lifted the right arm, as if in triumph, at the success of an arrow— imagining to imitate the Lycian Apollo, or that so finely described by Apollonius Rhodius when the dazzling radiance of his beautiful limbs suddenly shone over the dark Euxine.

27. Another Apollo

In every respect a coarse statue, with a goose or swan who has got the end of his pallium in his bill. Seen on one side the intense energy and god-like animation of those limbs, the spirit which seems as if it would not be contained.

28. A Cupid

Apparently part of a group—as in laughing defiance of those which are lost. It seeks to express what cannot be expressed in sculpture—the coarser and more violent effects of comic feeling cannot be seized by this art. Tenderness, sensibility, enthusiasm, terror, poetic inspiration, the profound, the beautiful, Yes.

29. Bacchus and Ampelus

Less beautiful than that in the royal collection of Naples and yet infinitely lovely. The figures are walking as it were with a sauntering and idle pace and talking to each other as they walk, and this is expressed in the motions of their delicate and flowing forms. One arm of Bacchus rests on the shoulder of Ampelus and the other, the fingers being gently curved as with the burning spirit which animates their flexible joints, is gracefully thrown forward corresponding with the advance of the opposite leg. He has sandals and buskins clasped with two serpent heads, and his leg is cinctured with their skins. He is crowned with vine leaves laden with their crude fruit, and the crisp leaves fall as with the inertness of a lithe and faded leaf over his rich and overhanging hair, which gracefully divided on his forehead falls in delicate wreaths upon his neck and breast. Ampelus with a beast skin over his shoulder holds a cup in his right hand, and with his left half embraces the waist of Bacchus. Just as you may have seen (yet how seldom from their dissevering and tyrannical institutions do you see) a younger and an elder boy at school walking in some remote grassy spot of their playground with that tender friendship towards each other which has so much of love. The countenance of Bacchus is sublimely sweet and lovely, taking a shade of gentle and playful tenderness from the arch looks of Ampelus, whóse cheerful face turned towards him, expresses the suggestions of some droll and merry device. It has a divine and supernatural beauty as one who walks through the world untouched by its corruptions, its corrupting cares; it looks like one who unconsciously yet with delight confers pleasure and peace. The flowing fulness and roundness of the breast and belly, whose lines fading into each other, are continued with a gentle motion as it were to the utmost extremity of his limbs. Like some fine strain of harmony which flows round the soul and enfolds it and leaves it in the soft astonishment of a satisfaction, like the pleasure of love with one whom we most love, which having taken away desire, leaves pleasure, sweet pleasure. The countenance of the Ampelus is in every respect inferior; it has a rugged and unreproved appearance; but the Bacchus is immortal beauty.

30. A Bacchante with a Lynx

The effect of the wind partially developing her young and delicate form upon the light and floating drapery and the aerial motion of the lower part of her limbs are finely imagined. But the inanimate expression of her countenance and the position of her arms are at enmity with these indications.

31. Apollo with a Swan

The arms restored. The same expression of passionate and enthusiastic tenderness seems to have created the intense and sickening beauty by which it is expressed, the same radiance of beauty, arising from lines only less soft and . . . more sublimely flowing than those of Bacchus. This has some resemblance with the Apollo of the Capitol.

32. Leda

A dull thing.

33. Venus Anadyomene

She seems to have just issued from the bath, and yet to be animated with the enjoyment of it. She seems all soft and mild enjoyment, and the curved lines of her fine limbs flow into each other with never-ending continuity of sweetness. Her face expresses a breathless yet passive and innocent voluptuousness without affectation, without doubt; it is at once desire and enjoyment and the pleasure arising from both. Her lips which are without the sublimity of lofty and impetuous passion like . . . or the grandeur of enthusiastic imagination like the Apollo of the Capitol, or an union of both like the Apollo Belvedere, have the tenderness of arch yet pure and affectionate desire, and the mode in which the ends are drawn in yet opened by the smile which forever circles round them, and the tremulous curve into which they are wrought by inextinguishable desire, and the tongue lying against the lower lip as in the listlessness of passive joy, express love, still love.

Her eyes seem heavy and swimming with pleasure, and her small forehead fades on both sides into that sweet swelling and then declension of the bone over the eye and prolongs itself to the cheek in that mode which expresses simple and tender feelings.

The neck is full and swollen as with the respiration of delight and flows with gentle curves into her perfect form.

Her form is indeed perfect. She is half sitting on and half rising from a shell, and the fulness of her limbs, and their complete roundness and perfection, do not diminish the vital energy with which they seem to be embued. The mode in which the lines of the curved back flow into and around the thighs, and the wrinkled muscles of the belly, wrinkled by the attitude, is truly astonishing. The attitude of her arms which are lovely beyond imagination is natural, unaffected, and unforced. This perhaps is the finest personification of Venus, the Deity of superficial desire, in all antique statuary. Her pointed and pear-like bosom ever virgin —the virgin Mary might have this beauty, but alas! . . .

34. A Statue of Minerva

The arm restored. The head is of the very highest beauty. It has a close helmet from which the hair delicately parted on the forehead half escapes. The face uplifted gives entire effect to the perfect form of the neck, and to that full and beautiful moulding of the lower part of the face and the jaw, which is in living beings the seat of the expression of a simplicity and integrity of nature. Her face uplifted to Heaven is animated with a profound, sweet, and impassioned melancholy, with an earnest, fervid, and disinterested pleading against some vast and inevitable wrong; it is the joy and the poetry of sorrow, making grief beautiful, and giving to that nameless feeling which from the imperfection of language we call pain, but which is not all pain, those feelings which make not only the possessor but the spectator of it prefer it to what is called pleasure, in which all is not pleasure. It is difficult to think that the head, though of the highest ideal beauty, is the head of Minerva, although the attributes and attitude of the lower part of the statue certainly suggest that idea. The Greeks rarely in their representations of the Divinities (unless we call the poetic enthusiasm of Apollo, a mortal passion) expressed the disturbance of human feeling; and here is deep and impassioned grief, animating a divine countenance. It is indeed divine, as Wisdom which as Minerva it may be supposed to emblem, pleading earnestly with Power, and invested with the expression of that grief because it must ever plead so vainly. An owl is sitting at her feet. The drapery of the statue, the gentle beauty of the feet, and the grace of the attitude are what may be seen in many other statues belonging to that astonishing era which produced it—such a countenance is seen in few.

This statue happens to be placed on an altar, the subject of the reliefs of which are in a spirit wholly the reverse. It was probably an altar to Bacchus, possibly a funerary urn. It has this inscription: D. M. M. ULPIUS. TERPNUS. FECIT. SIBI ET ULPIAE SE-CUNDILLAE LIBERTAE. B. M. Under the festoons of fruits and flowers . . .   at the corners of the altar with the skulls of goats and in the middle with an inverted flower suspended from a twisted stem are sculptured in moderate relief four figures of Maenads under the inspiration of the God. Nothing can be imagined more wild and terrible than their gestures, touching as they do upon the verge of distortion, in which their fine limbs and lovely forms are thrown. There is nothing however that exceeds the possibility of Nature, although it borders on its utmost line.

The tremendous spirit of superstition aided by drunkenness and producing something beyond insanity seems to have caught them in its whirlwinds and to bear them over the earth as the rapid volutions of a tempest bear the ever-changing trunk of a waterspout, as the torrent of a mountain river whirls the leaves in its full eddies. Their hair loose and floating seems caught in the tempest of their own tumultuous motion, their heads are thrown back leaning with a strange inanity upon their necks, and looking up to Heaven, while they totter and stumble even in the energy of their tempestuous dance. One—perhaps Agave with the head of Pentheus—has a human head in one hand and in the other a great knife; another has a spear with its pine cone, which was their thyrsus; another dances with mad voluptuousness; the fourth is dancing to a kind of tambourine.

This was indeed a monstrous superstition only capable of existing in Greece because there alone capable of combining ideal beauty and poetical and abstract enthusiasm with the wild errors from which it sprung. In Rome it had a more familiar, wicked, and dry appearance—it was not suited to the severe and exact apprehensions of the Romans, and their strict morals once violated by it sustained a deep injury little analogous to its effects upon the Greeks, who turned all things—superstition, prejudice, murder, madness—to Beauty.

35. A Tripod

Said to be dedicated to Mars—three winged figures with emblematic instruments.

36. A Faun

A pretty thing but little remarkable. A lynx is slily peeping round the stem covered with vines on which he leans and gnawing the grapes.

37. A Ganymede

A statue of surpassing beauty. One of the Eagle's wings is half-enfolded round him and one of his arms is placed round the Eagle and his delicate hand lightly touches the wing; the other holds what I imagine to be a representation of the thunder. These hands and fingers are so delicate and light that it seems as if the spirit of pleasure, of light, life, and beauty that lives in them half lifted them, and deprived them of the natural weight of mortal flesh. The roundness and fulness of the flowing perfection of his form is strange and rare. The attitude and form of the legs and the relation borne to each other by his light and delicate feet is peculiarly beautiful. The calves of the legs almost touching each other, one foot is placed on the ground, a little advanced before the other which is raised, the knee being a little bent as those who are slightly, but slightly, fatigued with standing. The face though innocent and pretty has no ideal beauty. It expresses inexperience and gentleness and innocent wonder, such as might be imagined in a rude and lovely shepherd-boy and no more.

38. A Venus

A beautiful Venus, sculptured with great accuracy but without the feeling and the soft and flowing proportions of the Anadyomene. It has great perfection and beauty of form; it is a most admirable piece of sculpture, but hard, angular, and with little of the lithe suppleness or light of life.

39. A Torso of Faunus

(Why I don't know.) The sculpture remarkably good.

40. Two Statues of Marsyas

Two of those hideous St. Sebastians of Antiquity opposite each other—Marsyas: one looks as if he had been flayed, and the other as if he was going to be flayed. This is one of the few abominations of the Greek religion. This is as bad as the everlasting damnation and hacking and hewing between them of Joshua and Jehovah. And is it possible that there existed in the same imagination the idea of that tender and sublime and poetic and life-giving Apollo and of the author of this deed as the same person? It would be worse than confounding Jehovah and Jesus in the same Trinity, which to those who believe in the divinity of the latter, is a pretty piece of blasphemy in any intelligible sense of the word. As to the sculpture of these pieces, it is energetic, especially that of the one already flayed, and moderate. If he knew as much as the moderns about anatomy, which I hope to God he did not, he at least abstained from taking advantage of his subject for making the same absurd display of it. These great artists abstained from overstepping in this particular, except in some cases, as perhaps in the Laocoön, what Shakespeare calls the modesty of nature.

41. Thetis

Thetis on a sea-horse—the face far from idealism seems to be a real face of much energy and goodness. She sits on the curved back of the monster and holds in one hand something like a sponge; in the other, the ears of the head of the sharp beast.

42. Hygieia

An Hygieia with a serpent. A resemblance of the famous Dis— a copy. The forms are soft and flowing but not the most perfect proportion. The head and countenance is of great beauty. There is the serene sweetness of expectation, the gathered firm and yet the calm and gentle lip.

43. Jupiter

A Jupiter in every respect of a very ordinary character.

44. A Minerva

Evidently a production of very great antiquity.

45. A Juno

A statue of great merit. The countenance expresses a stern and unquestioned severity of dominion, with a certain sadness. The lips are beautiful—susceptible of expressing scorn —but not without sweetness in their beauty. Fine lips are never wholly bad and never belong to the expression of emotions completely selfish—lips being the seat of imagination. The drapery is finely conceived, and the manner in which the act of throwing back one leg is expressed in the diverging folds of the drapery of the left breast, fading in bold yet graduated lines into a skirt of it which descends from the right shoulder is admirably imagined.

46. A Wounded Soldier

An unknown figure. His arms are folded within his mantle. His countenance, which may be a portrait, is sad but gentle.

47. A Youth

A youth playing on a lyre—one arm and leg is a restoration and there is no appearance of the head or arm belonging to it. The body and the right leg are of the most consummate beauty. It may or may not be an Apollo.

48. The Figure of a Youth Said To Be Apollo

It was difficult to conceive anything more delicately beautiful than the Ganymede; but the spirit-like lightness, the softness, the flowing perfection of these forms surpass it. The countenance though exquisite, lovely, and gentle is not divine. There is a womanish vivacity of winning yet passive happiness and yet a boyish inexperience exceedingly delightful. Through the limbs there seems to flow a spirit of life which gives them lightness. Nothing can be more perfectly lovely than the legs and the union of the feet with the ankles and the fading away of the lines of the feet to the delicate extremities. It is like a spirit even in dreams. The neck is long yet full and sustains the head with its profuse and knotted hair as if it needed no sustaining.

49. An Aesculapius

A Statue of Aesculapius—the same as in the Borghese Gardens in the temple there.

50. An Aesculapius

A Statue of Aesculapius far superior. It is leaning forward upon a knotty staff imbarked and circled by a viper, with a bundle of plants in one hand and the other with the forefinger in an attitude of instruction. The majestic head, its thick beard, and profuse hair bound by a fillet, leans forward, and the gentle smile of its benevolent lips seems a commentary on his instructions. The upper part of the figure with the exception of the right shoulder is naked, but the rest to the feet is involved in drapery, whose folds flow from the point where the staff confines them sustaining the left arm.

51. Olinthus

(as they call a youth seated). Another of those sweet and gentle figures of adolescent youth in which the Greeks delighted.

52. Marcus Aurelius

A Statue of Marcus Aurelius which is rather without faults than with beauties.

53. Bacchus and Ampelus

A lovely group.

54. Leda

Leda with a very ugly face. I should be a long time before I should make love with her.

55. A Muse

A most hideous thing they call a Muse— evidently the production of some barbarian and of a barbarous age.

56. An Old Cuirass

with all the frogs and fringe complete—a fine piece of antique dandyism.

57. *A Bacchus by Michael Angelo*

The countenance of this figure is the most revolting mistake of the spirit and meaning of Bacchus. It looks drunken, brutal, and narrow-minded and has an expression of dissoluteness the most revolting. The lower part of the figure is stiff, and the manner in which the shoulders are united to the breast, and the neck to the head, abundantly inharmonious. It is altogether without unity, as was the idea of the Deity of Bacchus in the conception of a Catholic. On the other hand, considered merely as a piece of workmanship, it has great merits. The arms are executed in the most perfect and manly beauty; the body is conceived with great energy, and the lines which describe the sides and thighs, and the manner in which they mingle into one another are of the highest order of boldness and beauty. It wants as a work of art unity and simplicity; as a representation of the Greek Deity of Bacchus it wants everything.

58. *Sleep*

A remarkable figure of Sleep as a winged child supine on a lion's skin, sleeping on its great half unfolded wing of black *obsidian* stone. One hand is lightly placed on a horn, with which it might be supposed to call together its wandering dreams, the horn of dreams, and in the other a seedy poppy. The hardness of the stone does not permit the arriving at any great expression.

59. *Copy of the Laocoön*

An admirable copy of the Laocoön in which is expressed with fidelity the agony of the poison and the straining round of the angry serpents. The left hand child seems sick with agony and horror, and the vain and feeble attempt he makes to disentangle himself from its grasp increases the effect. (See Rome.)

60. *The Niobe*

This figure is probably the most consummate personification of loveliness with regard to its countenance as that of the Apollo of the Vatican is with regard to its entire form that remains to us of Greek Antiquity. It is a colossal figure—the size of a work of art rather adds to its beauty, because it allows the spectator the choice of a greater number of points of view in which to catch a greater number of the infinite modes of expression of which any form approaching ideal beauty is necessarily composed—of a mother in the act of sheltering from some divine and inevitable peril, the last, we will imagine, of her surviving children.

The child terrified we may conceive at the strange destruction of all its kindred has fled to its mother and hiding its head in the folds of her robe and casting up one arm as in a passionate appeal for defence from her, where it never before could have been sought in vain, seems in the marble to have scarcely suspended the motion of her terror as though conceived to be yet in the act of arrival. The child is clothed in a thin tunic of delicatest woof, and her hair is gathered on her head into a knot, probably by that mother whose care will never gather it again. Niobe is enveloped in profuse drapery, a portion of which the left hand has gathered up and is in the act of extending it over the child in the instinct of defending her from what reason knows to be inevitable. The right—as the restorer of it has rightly comprehended—is gathering up her child to her and with a like instinctive gesture is encouraging by its gentle pressure the child to believe that it can give security. The countenance which is the consummation of feminine majesty and loveliness, beyond which the imagination scarcely doubts that it can conceive anything, that master-piece of the poetic harmony of marble, expresses other feelings. There is embodied a sense of the inevitable and rapid destiny which is consummating around her as if it were already over. It seems as if despair and beauty had combined and produced nothing but the sublime loveliness of grief. As the motions of the form expressed the instinctive sense of the possibility of protecting the child and the accustomed and affectionate assurance that she would find protection within her arms, so reason and imagination speak in the countenance the certainty that no mortal defence is of avail.

There is no terror in the countenance— only grief—deep grief. There is no anger— of what avail is indignation against what is known to be omnipotent? There is no selfish shrinking from personal pain; there is no panic at supernatural agency—there is no adverting to herself as herself—the calamity is mightier than to leave scope for such emotion.

Every thing is swallowed up in sorrow. Her countenance in assured expectation of the arrow piercing its victim in her embrace is fixed on her omnipotent enemy. The pathetic beauty of the mere expression of her tender and serene despair, which is yet so profound and so incapable of being ever worn away, is beyond any effect of sculpture. As soon as the arrow shall have pierced her last child, the fable that she was dissolved into a fountain of tears will be but a feeble emblem of the sadness of despair, in which the years of her remaining life, we feel, must flow away.

It is difficult to speak of the beauty of her countenance, or to make intelligible in words the forms from which such astonishing loveliness results. The head, resting somewhat backward, upon the full and flowing contour of the neck, is in the act of watching an event momently to arrive. The hair is delicately divided on the forehead, and a gentle beauty gleams from the broad and clear forehead, over which its strings are drawn. The face is altogether broad and the features conceived with the daring harmony of a sense of power. In this respect it resembles the careless majesty which Nature stamps upon those rare masterpieces of her creation, harmonizing them as it were from the harmony of the spirit within. Yet all this not only consists with but is the cause of the subtlest delicacy of that clear and tender beauty which is the expression at once of innocence and sublimity of soul, of purity, and strength, of all that which touches the most removed and divine of the strings of that which makes music within my thoughts, and which shakes with astonishment my most superficial faculties. Compare for this effect the countenance as seen in front and as seen from under the left arm, moving to the right and towards the statue, until the line of the forehead shall coincide with that of the wrist.

APPENDIX D: *TRANSLATIONS OF LONGER FOREIGN LANGUAGE PASSAGES*

[In this Appendix are the longer foreign language passages with their translations, the translations of quotations in Shelley's text, and the translation of his own original story in Italian, *Una Favola*.]

(a) From disconnected passages of Holbach's *Système de la Nature,* 1.1-53.

Man's earliest theology made him at first fear and adore the very elements and material and gross objects; later he rendered homage to the presiding genii of the elements, to the lesser spirits, to heroes, or to men endowed with great qualities. By dint of reflection, he thought he could simplify things by putting all nature under the control of a single force, of a spirit, of a universal soul which was supposed to set this nature and its parts in motion. In ascending from cause to cause, mortals have finished by seeing nothing; and it is in this darkness that they have set up their God; it is in this shadowy abyss that their anxious imagination labors continuously to create for itself chimeras which plague them until their knowledge of nature disabuses them of the fantoms which they have always so vainly adored.

If we are willing to take stock of our ideas upon the Divinity, we will be obliged to admit that, by the word *God*, men have never been able to designate anything but the most hidden, the most distant, the most unknown cause of the effects which they see; they never make use of this word until the play of natural and known causes ceases to be visible to them, until they lose the thread of these causes, or until their minds can no longer follow the chain of them; they hide their confusion and terminate their researches by calling God the last of the causes [First Cause]; that is, that which is beyond all the causes which they know; thus they do nothing but assign a vague name to an unknown cause, at which their laziness or the limits of their understanding force them to stop. Each time someone tells us that God is the author of some phenomenon, that means that he does not know how such a phenomenon could have occurred with only the aid of the forces or the causes which we know in nature. It is thus that the generality of men, whose lot is ignorance, attribute to the Divinity not only unusual effects which strike them but also the most simple events of which the causes are very easily understood by anyone capable of meditating upon them. In a word, man has always reverenced the unknown causes of extraordinary effects, which his ignorance has prevented him from discerning. It was upon the remains of nature that men raised the imaginary colossus of the Divinity.

If ignorance of nature gave birth to the gods, knowledge of nature is made for destroying them. The more man instructs himself, the more his forces and his resources increase with his enlightenment; science, the cumulative arts, industry furnish him aid; experience reassures him or provides him the means of resisting the effects of many of the causes, which cease to alarm him as soon as he has come to know them. In a word, his terrors are dissipated in the same proportion as his mind is enlightened. The educated man ceases to be superstitious.

It is never upon anything but hearsay that entire peoples adore the god of their fathers and their priests; authority, trust, submission, and habit take the place with them of conviction and of proofs; they prostrate themselves and pray because their fathers have taught them to prostrate themselves and to pray; but why did the fathers throw themselves on their knees? It is because in distant times their law-givers and their preceptors charged them with a duty. "Adore and believe in," they said, "Gods whom you cannot understand; rely upon our profound wisdom; we know more than you about divinity." "But why should I rely upon you?" "It is because God wills it thus; it is because God will punish you if you dare refuse." "But this God, is he not then the thing in question?" Nevertheless men have always been satisfied with this vicious circle; the laziness of their minds has made them find it easier to rely upon the judgment of others. All religious notions are founded entirely upon authority; all the religions of the world forbid investigations and are not willing that we reason; it is authority that requires that we believe in God; this God is himself founded solely upon the authority of certain men who claim to know him and to come from him to announce him to the earth. A God made by men undoubtedly needs men to make him known to the world.

Does it not seem to be, then, only for the priests, the zealots, the metaphysicians that the conviction of the existence of a God is reserved, which is said nevertheless to be so necessary to the whole human race? But do we find harmony among the theological opinions of the different zealots or of the thinkers scattered throughout the world? Even those who profess to worship the same God, are they in agreement concerning him? Are they content with the proofs which their colleagues produce of his existence? Do they subscribe unanimously to the ideas which they present upon his nature, upon his conduct, upon the way to understand his alleged oracles? Is there a country on the earth where the science of God is really perfected? Has it taken anywhere the consistency and the uniformity which we see taken by human knowledge, by the most useless arts, by the most despised crafts? The words *spirit, immortality, creation, predestination, grace*— that throng of subtle distinctions of which theology anywhere is full; in every country,

those devices which are so ingenious, conceived by thinkers who have succeeded each other for so many centuries—have only succeeded, alas, in confusing things; and that science which is most necessary to man has been unable so far to achieve the slightest stability. For thousands of years lazy dreamers have perpetually succeeded each other in meditating upon the Divinity, in searching out his hidden ways, in inventing hypotheses suitable for explaining this important enigma. Their small success has not in the least discouraged the theological vanity; we have always talked about God; we have argued, we have slit each other's throats for him, and this sublime being still remains the most unknown and the most debated.

Men would have been too happy, if contenting themselves with the visible objects which interest them, had they used in perfecting their physical science, their laws, their morals, their education, half the efforts they have put into their researches upon the Divinity. They would have been wiser still, and better off, if they had been willing to allow their idle preceptors to quarrel among themselves, and to sound depths fit to make them dizzy, without joining in their senseless disputes. But it is the nature of ignorance to attach importance to that which it does not understand. Human vanity works in such a way that the mind hardens itself against difficulties. The more an object hides itself from our eyes, because from the moment that it pricks our pride it arouses our curiosity, it appears interesting. In contending for his God, one really contends only for the interests of his own vanity, which of all the human passions is the quickest to take alarm and the most likely to produce the greatest follies.

If, putting aside for a moment the troublesome ideas that theology gives us of a capricious God whose partial and despotic decrees decide the fate of human beings, we will fix our eyes only upon the alleged goodness, which all men, even while trembling before this God, agree in attributing to him; if we grant him the purpose that is lent him, of having labored only for his own glory in exacting the homage of intelligent beings, of striving in his works for nothing but the well being of the human race; how reconcile these views and these intentions with the truly invincible ignorance in which this God, so glorious and good, leaves the greater part of men concerning himself? If God wishes to be known, to be loved, to be thanked, why does he not show himself under a favorable guise to all those beings by whom he wants to be loved and adored? Why not manifest himself to the whole earth in an unequivocal manner, which would be much more suitable for convincing us than those private revelations which seem to accuse the Divinity of a vexatious partiality for certain ones of his creatures? Should not the almighty have a more convincing means of revealing himself to men than those ridiculous metamorphoses, those alleged incarnations, which are attested to us by writers so little in accord among themselves in the stories they tell of them? In place of so many miracles invented for proving the divine mission of so many lawgivers, revered by the different peoples of the world, could not the lord of the spirits convince the human mind in an instant of the thing he wants known to it? Instead of suspending a sun in the vault of the firmament, instead of orderlessly scattering the stars and the constellations which fill space, would it not have been more consistent with the picture of a God so jealous of his glory and so well disposed toward men to write in a manner not subject to dispute, his name, his attributes, his immutable will in ineffaceable characters, readable equally by all the inhabitants of the world? No one then would have been able to doubt the existence of God, his clear will, or his visible intentions. Under the eyes of such a sensible God, no one would have had the audacity to violate his commandments; no mortal would have dared put himself in the position of drawing his wrath; finally, no man would

have had the effrontery to impose on anyone in his name, or to interpret his will according to his own fancies. In effect, even if we admit the existence of the God of theology and the reality of the conflicting attributes which we give him, we could not conclude anything therefrom to authorize the conduct or the worship with which we are enjoined to requite him. Theology is truly the *vessel of the Danaides*. By means of contradictory qualities and supposititious assertions, she has, so to speak so trussed up her God that she has made him incapable of acting. If he is infinitely good, what reason would we have to fear him? If he is infinitely wise, why should we be anxious about our fate? If he knows everything, why inform him of our needs and weary him with our prayers? If he is everywhere, why build temples to him? If he is the master of everything, why make him sacrifices and offerings? If he is just, why fear that he will punish creatures he has filled with weakness? If grace does everything in men, what reason would he have for rewarding them? If he is all powerful, how offend him, how resist him? If he is reasonable, why does he become angered against blind people to whom he has given the liberty of being unreasonable? If he is immutable, by what right do we presume to say that his decrees have changed? If he is inconceivable, why concern ourselves about him? IF HE HAS SPOKEN, WHY IS NOT THE UNIVERSE CONVINCED? If the knowledge of God is the most necessary thing, why is it not the most obvious and the most clear?

Translation by E. F. Bennett.

(b) From Pliny's
Natural History, Chapter on God.

"For this reason I deem it a mark of human weakness to seek to discover the shape and form of God. Whoever God is—provided there is a God—and in whatever region he is, he consists wholly of sense, sight, and hearing, wholly of soul, wholly of mind,

357

wholly of himself. . . . But the chief consolations for nature's imperfection in the case of man are that not even for God are all things possible—for he cannot, even if he wishes, commit suicide, the supreme boon that he has bestowed on man among all the penalties of life, nor bestow eternity on mortals or recall the deceased, nor cause a man that has lived not to have lived or one that has held high office not to have held it —and that he has no power over what is past save to forget it, and (to link our fellowship with God by means of frivolous arguments as well) that he cannot cause twice ten not to be twenty or do many things on similar lines: which facts unquestionably demonstrate the power of nature, and prove that it is this that we mean by the word *God*."

Translation from the Loeb edition.

(c) From Spinoza's *Tractatus Theologico-Politicus.*

The Latin passage from Spinoza was first used by Shelley, in a garbled state, in a Note in *Queen Mab* (1813) and repeated, with some variations, the following year in *A Refutation of Deism* (1814). Shelley's text as found in the first edition of *Queen Mab* is here reproduced with the corrections from Spinoza's text in brackets.

"Omnia enim per Dei potentiam facta sunt: imo, quia natura [sunt. Imo naturae] potentia nulla est nisi ipsa Dei potentia, artem [certum] est nos eatenus Dei potentiam non intelligere, quatenus causas naturales ignoramus; adeoque stulte ad eandem Dei potentiam, recurritur, quando rei alicujus, causam naturalem, sive est [hoc est] ipsam Dei potentiam, ignoramus."

Mrs. Shelley in her 1839-1840 edition repeats the errors of the earlier editions. The present edition is the first edition, I believe, which gives Spinoza's original text. The textual notes in the Julian Editions on this passage are inaccurate in some details.

Translation of passage from Spinoza's *Tractatus Theologico-Politicus,* Chapter 1.

"Everything takes place by the power of God: indeed Nature herself is nothing but the power of God. It is certain that our ignorance of the power of God is coextensive with our ignorance of Nature. It is the utmost folly, therefore, to ascribe an event to the power of God when we are ignorant of its natural cause—in other words, the power of God itself."

Translation by Mrs. Minnie Lee Shepard.

(d) From Suetonius, Pliny, and Tacitus.

1. "Judaei, impulsore Chrestus [Christus], turbantes, facile comprimuntur."

Suet. in Tib. [Shelley's Note.]

Translation: The Jews, who rioted at the instigation of Chrestus, were easily suppressed." This quotation is not in Suetonius's *Tiberius,* but from his *Life of Claudius,* chap. 25. Shelley also misquotes. It should be: Suetonius says, "He [Claudius] banished from Rome the Jews, who rioted persistently at the instigation of Chrestus."

2. "Affecti suppliciis Christiani, genus hominum superstitionis novae et maleficae."

Id. in Nerone. [Shelley's Note.]

Translation: "Punishment was inflicted on the Christians, a race of men belonging to a new and mischievous superstition." From Suetonius's *Nerone,* Chap. 16.

3. "Multi omnis aetatis utriusque sexus etiam; neque enim civitates tantum, sed vicos etiam et agros superstitionis istius contagio pervagata est."

Pliny, *Epis.* [Shelley's Note.]

Translation: "Many of every age of both sexes [Here Shelley omits several words— 'are brought into danger,' etc.] for not alone the cities, but even the villages and farms have been overspread by the contagion of this superstition." From Pliny's *Correspondence with Trajan*, 96.9.

Passages 1, 2, 3 translated by H. J. Leon.

4. "Ergo abolendo rumori Nero subdidit reos et quaesitissimis poenis adfecit, quos per flagitia invisos vulgus Christianos appellabat. Auctor nominis eius Christus Tiberio imperitante per procuratorem Pontium Pilatum supplicio adfectus erat; repressaque in praesens exitiabilis superstitio rursum erumpebat, non modo per Iudaeam, originem eius mali, sed per urbem etiam, quo cuncta undique atrocia aut pudenda confluunt celebranturque. Igitur primum correpti qui fatebantur, deinde indicio eorum multitudo ingens haud perinde in crimine incendii quam odio humani generis convicti sunt. Et pereuntibus addita ludibria, ut ferarum tergis contecti laniatu canum interirent, aut crucibus adfixi aut flammandi, atque ubi defecisset dies, in usum nocturni luminis urrentur. Hortos suos ei spectaculo Nero obtulerat et circense ludicrum edebat, habitu aurigae permixtus plebi vel curriculo insistens. Unde quamquam adversus sontis et novissima exempla meritos miseratio oriebatur, tamquam non utilitate publica, sed in saevitiam unius absumerentur." [Shelley's Note.]

From Tacitus, *The Annals*, Bk. XV, Sec. 44.

Translation: "Therefore, to scotch the rumour, Nero substituted as culprits, and punished with the utmost refinements of cruelty, a class of men, loathed for their vices, whom the crowd styled Christians. Christus, the founder of the name, had undergone the death penalty in the reign of Tiberius, by sentence of the procurator Pontius Pilatus, and the pernicious superstition was checked for a moment, only to break out once more, not merely in Judaea, the home of the disease, but in the capital itself, where all things horrible or shameful in the world collect and find a vogue. First, then, the confessed members of the sect were arrested; next, on their disclosures, vast numbers were convicted, not so much on the count of arson as for hatred of the human race. And derision accompanied their end: they were covered with wild beasts' skins and torn to death by dogs; or they were fastened on crosses, and, when daylight failed were burned to serve as lamps by night. Nero had offered his Gardens for the spectacle, and gave an exhibition in his Circus, mixing with the crowd in the habit of a charioteer, or mounted on his car. Hence, in spite of a guilt which had earned the most exemplary punishment, there arose a sentiment of pity, due to the impression that they were being sacrificed not for the welfare of the state but to the ferocity of a single man."

Translation from the Loeb edition.

(e) From Pliny, Euripides, and Lucretius.

1. Shelley again quotes from Pliny's *Natural History*, Chapter on God, beginning with, "imperfectae vero in homine." See the Note on *Queen Mab* to the line, "There is no God," p. 102, for the Latin quotation and Appendix D(b) for the translation.
2. For the source of Shelley's quotation from the Greek see Euripides, *Tragaediae*, Ed. Mauck (Second edition), Vol. iii, Fragment No. 288, quoted in Justin Martyr, *On the Monarchy of God*, as coming from Euripides' *Bellerophon*.

Translation: "Does anybody say that there are gods in heaven? There are not, there are not—if a man will not in folly accept the old tales. Do your own thinking, do not form your opinions on my words. I tell you that absolute power slays many and deprives them of their wealth, that men by breaking their oaths sack cities, and that men who do these things are more prosperous than men who honor the gods and live in peace day by day. And I know of small god-fearing cities that obey larger cities more unrighteous than they, compelled by the numbers of a more powerful army. And I think that if you pray—the gods but live an idle life—

and do not make a living by your toil, you will pile up trouble and ill fortune."

Translation by W. J. Battle.

3. Hunc igitur terrorem animi, tenebrasque
   necesse est
   Non radii solis, neque lucida tela diei
   Discutiant, sed naturae species ratioque:
   Principium hinc cujus nobis exordia
   sumet,
   NULLAM REM NIHILO [E NILO] GIGNI DI-
   VINITUS UNQUAM [UMQUAM].

Luc. de Rer. Nat. Lib. I.
[Shelley's Note.]

Translation:

This terror, then, this darkness of the
   mind,
Not sunrise with its flaring spokes of light,
Nor glittering arrows of morning can
   disperse,
But only Nature's aspect and her law,
Which, teaching us, hath this exordium:
Nothing from nothing ever yet was born.

*Translation by
William Ellery Leonard.*

(f) *A Fable*

There was a youth who travelled through distant lands, seeking throughout the world a lady of whom he was enamored. And who this lady was, and how this youth became enamored of her, and how and why the great love he bore her forsook him are things worthy to be known by every gentle heart.

At the dawn of the fifteenth spring of his life, a certain one calling himself Love awoke him, saying that one whom he had ofttimes beheld in his dreams abode awaiting him. This Love was accompanied by a great troop of female forms, all veiled in white, and crowned with laurel, ivy, and myrtle, garlanded and interwreathed with violets, roses, and lilies. They sang with such sweetness that perhaps the harmony of the spheres, to which the stars dance is not so sweet. And their manners and words were so alluring that the youth was enticed and, arising from his couch, made himself ready to do

all the pleasure of him who called himself Love; at whose behest he followed him by lonely ways and deserts and caverns until the whole troop arrived at a solitary wood in a gloomy valley between two most lofty mountains, which valley was planted in the manner of a labyrinth, with pines, cypresses, cedars, and yews, whose shadows begot a mixture of delight and sadness. And in this wood the youth for a whole year followed the uncertain footsteps of this his companion and guide, as the moons follows the earth, save that there was not change in him, and nourished by the fruit of a certain tree which grew in the midst of the labyrinth—a food sweet and bitter at once, which being cold as ice to the lips, appeared fire in the veins. The veiled figures were continually around him, ministers and attendants obedient to his least gesture, and messengers between him and Love, when Love might leave him for a little on his other errands. But these figures, albeit executing his every other command with swiftness, never would unveil themselves to him, although he anxiously besought them; one only excepted, whose name was Life and who had the fame of a potent enchantress. She was tall of person and beautiful, cheerful and easy in her manners, and richly adorned, and, as it seemed from her ready unveiling of herself, she wished well to this youth. But he soon perceived that she was more false than any Siren, for by her counsel Love abandoned him in this savage place, with only the company of these shrouded figures, who, by their obstinately remaining veiled, had always wrought him dread. And none can expound whether these figures were the spectres of his own dead thoughts, or the shadows of the living thoughts of Love. Then Life, haply ashamed of her deceit, concealed herself within the cavern of a certain sister of hers dwelling there; and Love, sighing, returned to his third heaven.

Scarcely had Love departed, when the masked forms, released from his government, unveiled themselves before the astonished youth. And for many days these figures danced around him whithersoever he went, alternately mocking and threatening him; and in the night while he reposed they defiled in long and slow procession before his couch, each more hideous and terrible than the other. Their horrible aspect and loathsome figure so overcame his heart with sadness that the fair heaven, covered with that shadow, clothed itself in clouds before his eyes; and he wept so much that the herbs upon his path, fed with tears instead of dew, became pale and bowed like himself. Weary at length of this suffering, he came to the grot of the Sister of Life, herself also an enchantress, and found her sitting before a pale fire of perfumed wood, singing laments sweet in their melancholy, and weaving a white shroud, upon which his name was half wrought, with the obscure and imperfect beginning of a certain other name; and he besought her to tell him her own, and she said, with a faint but sweet voice, "Death." And the youth said, "O lovely Death, I pray thee to aid me against these hateful phantoms, companions of thy sister, which cease not to torment me." And Death comforted him and took his hand with a smile and kissed his brow and cheek, so that every vein thrilled with joy and fear, and made him abide with her in a chamber of her cavern, whither, she said, it was against Destiny that the wicked companions of Life should ever come. The youth continually conversing with Death, and she, like-minded to a sister, caressing him and showing him every courtesy both in deed and word, he quickly became enamored of her, and Life herself, far less any of her troop, seemed fair to him no longer; and his passion so overcame him that upon his knees he prayed Death to love him as he loved her and consent to do his pleasure. But Death said, "Audacious that thou art, with whose desire has Death ever complied? If thou lovedst me not, perchance I might love thee—beloved

by thee, I hate thee and I fly thee." Thus saying, she went forth from the cavern, and her dusky and ethereal form was soon lost amid the interwoven boughs of the forest.

From that moment the youth pursued the track of Death; and so mighty was the love that led him that he had encircled the world and searched through all its regions, and many years were already spent, but sorrows rather than years had blanched his locks and withered the flower of his beauty, when he found himself upon the confines of the very forest from which his wretched wanderings had begun. He cast himself upon the grass and wept for many hours, so blinded by his tears that for much time he did not perceive that not all that bathed his face and his bosom were his own, but that a lady bowed behind him wept for pity of his weeping. And lifting up his eyes he saw her, and it seemed to him never to have beheld so glorious a vision, and he doubted much whether she were a human creature. And his love of Death was suddenly changed into hate and suspicion, for this new love was so potent that it overcame every other thought. This compassionate lady at first loved him for mere pity; but love grew up swiftly with compassion, and she loved for Love's own sake, no one beloved by her having need of pity any more. This was the lady in whose quest Love had led the youth through that gloomy labyrinth of error and suffering, haply for that he esteemed him unworthy of so much glory, and perceived him too weak to support such exceeding joy. After having somewhat dried their tears, the twain walked together in that same forest, until Death stood before them, and said, "Whilst, O youth, thou didst love me, I hated thee, and now that thou hatest me, I love thee, and wish so well to thee and thy bride that in my kingdom, which thou mayest call Paradise, I have set apart a chosen spot, where ye may securely fulfill your happy loves." And the lady, offended, and perchance somewhat jealous by reason of the past love of her spouse, turned her back upon Death, saying within herself, "What would this lover of my husband who comes here to trouble us?" and cried, "Life! Life!" and Life came, with a gay visage, crowned with a rainbow, and clad in a various mantle of chameleon skin; and Death went away weeping and, departing, said with a sweet voice, "Ye mistrust me, but I forgive ye, and await ye where ye needs must come, for I dwell with Love and Eternity, with whom the souls whose love is everlasting must hold communion; then will ye perceive whether I have deserved your distrust. Meanwhile I commend ye to Life; and, sister mine, I beseech thee by the love of that Death with whom thou wert twin born not to employ thy customary arts against these lovers, but content thee with the tribute thou hast already received of sighs and tears, which are thy wealth." The youth, mindful of how great evil she had wrought him in that wood, mistrusted Life; but the lady, although she doubted, yet being jealous of Death. . . .

Translation by Richard Garnett.

(g) From Hesiod's *Works and Days:*

Ἰαπετιονίδη, πάντων πέρι μήδεα
   εἰδώς,
χαίρεις πῦρ κλέψας καὶ ἐμὰς φρένας
   ἠπεροπεύσας,
σοί τ' αὐτῷ μέγα πῆμα καὶ ἀνδράσιν
   ἐσσομένοισιν.
τοῖς δ' ἐγὼ ἀντὶ πυρὸς δώσω κακόν, ᾧ
   κεν ἅπαντες
τέρπωνται κατὰ θυμὸν ἑὸν κακὸν ἀμφα-
   γαπῶντες.
Ὣς ἔφατ'· ἐκ δ' ἐγέλασσε πατὴρ ἀν-
   δρῶν τε θεῶν τε.
Ἥφαιστον δ' ἐκέλευσε περικλυτὸν ὅττι
   τάχιστα
γαῖαν ὕδει φύρειν, ἐν δ' ἀνθρώπου
   θέμεν αὐδὴν.

Translation: "You rejoice, O crafty son of Iapetus, that you have stolen fire and deceived Jupiter; but great will thence be the evil both to yourself and to your posterity. To them this gift of fire shall be the gift of woe; in which, while they delight and pride themselves, they shall cherish their own wickedness."

Translated by John Newton and quoted in "The Return to Nature."

BIBLIOGRAPHY

SELECTED BIBLIOGRAPHY

(This bibliography deals primarily with Shelley's Prose.)

EDITIONS

Essays, Letters from Abroad, Translations, and Fragments, edited with invaluable introduction and notes by MARY SHELLEY. London: Edward Moxon, 1840. Several of Shelley's essays were published here for the first time.

Prose Works of Percy Bysshe Shelley, edited by H. BUXTON FORMAN. London: Reeves, 1880. The prose works were re-issued in 1892 in five volumes, with added memoir.

The Prose of Percy Bysshe Shelley, edited by RICHARD HERNE SHEPHERD. 2 vols. London: Chatto and Windus, 1888. These volumes contain the romances, several letters, and several of the essays.

A Defence of Poetry, edited by ALBERT S. COOK. New York: Ginn, 1890. Contains valuable introduction and notes.

Shelley's Literary and Philosophical Criticism, edited by JOHN SHAWCROSS. London: Oxford University Press, 1909. Contains several of the important essays and a valuable introduction on Shelley's ideas of art; on Shelley's philosophy it is in the Victorian tradition.

Shelley's Prose in the Bodleian Manuscripts, edited by ANDRE H. KOSZUL. London: Oxford University Press, 1910. Valuable to the research student for textual criticism.

The Letters of Percy Bysshe Shelley, edited by ROGER INGPEN. 2 vols. New York: Macmillan, 1915. Incomplete, but best readily available edition of the letters.

A Philosophical View of Reform, edited by T. W. ROLLESTON. London: Oxford University Press, 1920. The first edition, and not readily available.

The Complete Works of Percy Bysshe Shelley, edited by ROGER INGPEN and WALTER E. PECK. Julian Editions. 10 vols. New York: Charles Scribner's Sons, 1926-30. The prose is in volumes 5, 6, 7. This is the standard edition, but it is incomplete.

Peacock's Four Ages of Poetry, SHELLEY's *Defence of Poetry,* BROWNING's *Essay on Shelley,* edited by H. F. B. BRET-SMITH. London: Blackwell, 1929. Valuable for the student of Shelley.

Plato's Banquet, Translated from the Greek, A Discourse on the Manners of the Antient Greeks Relative to the Subject of Love, Also a Preface to the Banquet, Revised and Enlarged by Roger Ingpen from MSS in the possession of Sir John C. E. Shelley-Rolls, Bart. Printed for private circulation, 1931. Contains the complete text of Shelley's introductory essay.

Verse and Prose from the Manuscripts of Percy Bysshe Shelley, edited by SIR JOHN C. E. SHELLEY-ROLLS and ROGER INGPEN. Privately printed, 1934. Contains new material.

New Shelley Letters, edited by W. S. SCOTT. London: The Bodley Head, 1948. Corrects from the original manuscripts many errors in the letters as published by Hogg in his *Life of Shelley.*

BIOGRAPHICAL AND CRITICAL

ANGELI, HELEN ROSSETTI. *Shelley and His Friends in Italy.* London: Brentano's, 1911. Contains new material and a sympathetic introduction.

ARNOLD, MATTHEW. "Shelley," *Essays in Criticism.* Second Series. London: Macmillan, 1888. The source of the myth of Shelley as "a beautiful and ineffectual angel."

BAKER, CARLOS. *Shelley's Major Poetry.* Princeton: Princeton University Press, 1948. An excellent survey of Shelley's developing thought.

BALD, MARJORIE A. "The Psychology of Shelley," *Contemporary Review,* CXXXI (March, 1926), 359-366. Brief, but suggestive.

———. "Shelley's Mental Progress," *Essays and Studies by Members of the English Association,* XIII (1928), 112-137. The above expanded.

BARNARD, ELLSWORTH. *Shelley's Religion.* Minneapolis: University of Minnesota Press, 1936. A book with a thesis.

BARRELL, JOSEPH. *Shelley and the Thought of His Time, a Study in the History of Ideas.* New Haven: Yale University Press, 1947. Important in the study of Shelley's relation to Greek philosophy and to the ideas of his age.

BEACH, JOSEPH WARREN. *The Concept of Nature in Nineteenth-Century English Poetry.* New York: Macmillan, 1936. Contains chapters on Shelley's naturalism and Platonism.

BLUNDEN, EDMUND. *Leigh Hunt and His Circle.* New York: Harper, 1930. Sympathetic interpretation of Shelley.
———. *Shelley: A Life Story.* London: Collins, 1946. Well written.

BOWER, GEORGE SPENCER. "The Philosophical Element in Shelley," *Journal of Speculative Philosophy,* XIV (1880), 421-454.

BRADLEY, ANDREW C. "Shelley's View of Poetry," *Oxford Lectures on Poetry.* 2nd edition. London: Macmillan, 1909.

BRAILSFORD, HENRY N. *Shelley, Godwin, and Their Circle.* New York: Holt, 1913. Excellent background study.

BRETT, GEORGE SIDNEY. "Shelley's Relation to Berkeley and Drummond," *Studies in English by Members of the University College.* Toronto: University of Toronto Press, 1931. A valuable study.

BRINTON, CLARENCE CRANE. *The Political Ideas of English Romanticism.* London: Oxford University Press, 1926. Suggestive, but incomplete.

BROWNING, ROBERT. "An Essay on Shelley," *Complete Poetical and Dramatic Works.* Cambridge Edition. Boston and New York: Houghton Mifflin, 1895. Excellent for the beginner.

BUSH, DOUGLAS. *Mythology and the Romantic Tradition in English Poetry.* Cambridge: Harvard University Press, 1937. The chapter on Shelley treats the poet as an impractical dreamer.

CAMERON, KENNETH NEILL. *The Young Shelley.* New York: Macmillan, 1950. A valuable study of Shelley's early life and thought.
———. "The Social Philosophy of Shelley," *Sewanee Review,* L, No. 4 (1942), 457-466.

CAMPBELL, OLWEN WARD. *Shelley and the Unromantics.* New York: Scribner, 1924. A sound, sympathetic study.

CLARK, DAVID LEE. "The Dates and Sources of Shelley's Metaphysical, Moral, and Religious Essays," *Studies in English,* University of Texas, XXVIII (1949), 160-194. No claim to finality.
———. "The Date and Source of Shelley's *A Vindication of Natural Diet,*" *Studies in Philology,* XXXVI (Jan., 1939), 70-76.
———. "Shelley and Bacon," *Publications of the Modern Language Association,* XLVIII, No. 2 (June, 1933), 559-576. Throws light on Shelley's reading and study.
———. "Shelley and *Biblical Extracts,*" *Modern Language Notes,* LXVI (Nov., 1951), 435-441. The author suggests that the so-called *Essay on Christianity* may have been part of the *Biblical Extracts.*
———. "Shelley and Pieces of Irish History," *Modern Language Notes,* LIII (Nov., 1938), 522-525. Sheds light on Shelley's activities in Ireland in 1812.

CLUTTON-BROCK, ARTHUR. *Shelley: The Man and the Poet.* 4th edition. New York: Dutton, 1929.

DOWDEN, EDWARD. *The Life of P. B. Shelley.* 2 vols. London: Kegan Paul, 1886. Until recently considered the standard biography.

ELIOT, T. S. "Shelley and Keats," *The Use of Criticism and the Use of Poetry.* Cambridge: Harvard University Press, 1933.

ELTON, OLIVER. *A Survey of English Literature, 1780-1830.* Vol. II. New York: Macmillan, 1920. Contains a superb chapter on Shelley.

GINGERICH, SOLOMON F. *Essays in the Romantic Poets.* New York: Macmillan, 1924. A sound interpretation.

GRABO, CARL. *The Magic Plant: The Growth of Shelley's Thought.* Chapel Hill: University of North Carolina Press, 1936. This is a sound and useful study, with emphasis on Shelley's Platonism.

HOGG, THOMAS JEFFERSON. *The Life of Percy Bysshe Shelley.* 2 vols. London: Edward Moxon, 1858. Valuable for Shelley's early life. It should be read in HUMBERT WOLFE's edition, (London: J. M. Dent and Sons, 1933), in which Hogg's grossest errors are corrected.

HUGHES, ARTHUR MONTAGUE D'URBAN. *The Theology of Shelley.* London: Oxford University Press, 1939. Suggestive, but incomplete

———. *The Nascent Mind of Shelley.* London: Oxford University Press, 1947. Unsympathetic. Emphasizes Shelley's immature thought.

HUNT, JAMES HENRY LEIGH. *Autobiography.* London: Oxford University Press, 1928. Excellent. A sympathetic interpretation by a close friend.

INGPEN, ROGER. *Shelley in England.* Boston and New York: Houghton Mifflin, 1917. Indispensable for the student.

KURTZ, BENJAMIN P. *The Pursuit of Death.* London: Oxford University Press, 1933.

MacCARTHY, DENIS F. *Shelley's Early Life.* London: Hotten, 1872. Excellent.

MacDONALD, DANIEL J. *The Radicalism of Shelley and Its Source.* Ph.D. thesis, Catholic University, Washington, D.C., 1912.

MAUROIS, ANDRE. *Ariel, or The Life of Shelley.* Translated by ELLA D'ARCY. New York: Appleton, 1924. A biography with popular appeal.

MEDWIN, THOMAS. *The Life of Percy Bysshe Shelley.* H. BUXTON FORMAN (ed.). London: Oxford University Press, 1913. Useful contemporary biography with the errors of the original corrected.

MORE, PAUL ELMER. "Shelley," *Shelburne Essays: Seventh Series.* Boston: Houghton Mifflin, 1910. Shelley in the light of neo-humanist philosophy.

MOUSEL, SISTER M. EUNICE. "Falsetto in Shelley," *Studies in Philology,* XXXIII (Oct., 1936), 587-609. A useful study.

NOTOPOULOS, JAMES A. *The Platonism of Shelley.* Durham: Duke University Press, 1949. This is a valuable study of Shelley—particularly Part Three on Translations.

———. "The Dating of Shelley's Prose," *PMLA* LVIII (June, 1943), 477-498. Suggestive.

PEACOCK, THOMAS LOVE. *Memoirs of Shelley.* London: R. Bentley and Sons, 1875. A valuable contemporary view.

PECK, WALTER E. *Shelley, His Life and Works.* 2 vols. Boston: Houghton Mifflin, 1927. Contains important new material.

READ, HERBERT. *In Defence of Shelley and Other Essays.* London: Heinemann, 1936. Unsympathetic.

RICHTER, HELENE. *Percy Bysshe Shelley.* Weimar: E. Felber, 1898. Excellent.

SALT, HENRY S. *Percy Bysshe Shelley: Poet and Pioneer.* London: Reeves, 1896. An excellent and readable interpretation.

SANTAYANA, GEORGE. "Shelley," *Winds of Doctrine.* New York: Scribner, 1913. Essay on Shelley's idealism.

SHARP, WILLIAM. *Life of Shelley.* Great Writers Series. London: Scott, 1887. Excellent, brief biography.

SMITH, ROBERT M., ET AL. *The Shelley Legend.* New York: Charles Scribner's Sons, 1945. Charges the Shelley family, particularly Mary, with having intentionally concealed the facts of the poet's life.

STEPHEN, SIR LESLIE. "Godwin and Shelley," *Hours in a Library.* Vol. III. London: Smith, Elder and Co., 1899. A brilliantly written essay in the Matthew Arnold tradition.

STOVALL, FLOYD H. *Desire and Restraint in Shelley*. Durham: Duke University Press, 1931. A useful, suggestive study; the author concludes that Shelley compromised his ideals.

STRONG, ARCHIBALD T. *Three Studies in Shelley*. London: Oxford University Press, 1921. A suggestive study.

SYMONDS, JOHN ADDINGTON. *Shelley*. English Men of Letters Series. Revised edition. New York: Macmillan, 1925. An admirable and understanding biography.

THOMPSON, FRANCIS. "Shelley," *Collected Works*. New York: Scribner, 1913. A much overrated essay.

TODHUNTER, JOHN A. *A Study of Shelley*. London: Kegan Paul, 1880. Excellent for the beginner.

TRELAWNY, EDWARD JOHN. *Recollections of the Last Days of Shelley and Byron*. London: Edward Moxon, 1858. Useful. It should be read in the HUMBERT WOLFE edition (London: J. M. Dent and Sons, 1933).

WEAVER, BENNETT. "Pre-Promethean Thought in the Prose of Shelley," *Philosophical Quarterly*, XXVII (July, 1948), 193-208.

———. *Toward the Understanding of Shelley*. Ann Arbor: University of Michigan Press, 1932. Shelley, the prophet.

WHITE, NEWMAN IVEY. *Shelley*. 2 vols. New York: Knopf, 1940. The definitive biography of Shelley.

———. *Portrait of Shelley*. New York: Knopf, 1945. A shortened form of the two-volume life, with some rewriting and the correction of several minor errors.

———. *The Unextinguished Hearth*. Durham: Duke University Press, 1938. A republication of all the reviews of Shelley published during the poet's lifetime.

WINSTANLEY, LILLIAN. "Platonism in Shelley," *Essays and Studies by Members of the English Association*, IV (1913), 72-100. A suggestive, but inconclusive study.

WYLIE, LAURA JOHNSON. "Shelley's Democracy," *Social Studies in English Literature*. Boston: Houghton Mifflin, 1916. Good.

YEATS, WILLIAM BUTLER. "The Philosophy of Shelley," *Ideas of Good and Evil*. New York: Macmillan, 1903. Sympathetic and suggestive.

INDEX

INDEX